animation

Recent Titles in
American Popular Culture
Series Editor: *M. Thomas Inge*

Film: A Reference Guide
Robert A. Armour

Women's Gothic and Romantic Fiction
Kay Mussell

animation
A REFERENCE GUIDE

Thomas W. Hoffer

American Popular Culture

GREENWOOD PRESS
WESTPORT, CONNECTICUT • LONDON, ENGLAND

086207

Library of Congress Cataloging in Publication Data

Hoffer, Thomas W
    Animation, a reference guide.

    (American popular culture ISSN 0193-6859)
    Bibliography: p.
    Includes index.
    1. Animation (Cinematography) 2. Animation
(Cinematography)—Bibliography. I. Title.
II. Series.
TR897.5.H63   778.5'2347   81-67
ISBN 0-313-21095-0 (lib. bdg.)

Library of Congress Catalog Card Number: 81-67
ISBN: 0-313-21095-0   MY 18'82
ISSN: 0193-6859

First published in 1981

Greenwood Press
A division of Congressional Information Service, Inc.
88 Post Road West, Westport, Connecticut 06881

Printed in the United States of America

10 9 8 7 6 5 4 3 2 1

To my parents
Martin Herbert Hoffer
and
Margaret Plum Hoffer
Toledo, Iowa

Contents

Tables

Acknowledgments

A number of individuals have helped this book become a reality. I give my grateful thanks to:

Anne Page Mosby, Gayle Camarda, Delia Tam, Kathie Watters, and Phyllis Holzenberg, the helpful Strozier Library assistants at Florida State University in Interlibrary Loan for borrowing in my behalf an abnormally large number of books and periodicals;

Richard Nelson, Lane Roth, Mel Kiser, Reg Hartt, Anne Erickson, Sam Grogg, Julian Smith, Ron Sigler, James Gelwicks, Mrs. Elmer Littig, Herb Davis, Jay Wilkinson, Charles Sawyer, and Mike Ogden for supplying copies of books, articles, brochures, or advice;

Mitchell Shapiro, for his supervisory work on the indexing project of the trade journals at Florida State University, and the hundreds of film students who also participated, eventually making possible Appendix 6;

Ted Clevenger, Jr., Dean, College of Communication, Florida State University, for general support of this project and the indexing project in the trade journals, partial support for my attendance at the American Film Institute (AFI) Documentation Conference, occasional copies of *Backstage*, and the important intangibles;

Archivists and Librarians Eileen Bowser and Charles Silver (Museum of Modern Art), Andre Malkin (Theater Arts, University of California, Los Angeles), Anne Schlosser (American Film Institute, West), Bob Knutson (University of Southern California), David Smith (Walt Disney Archives), Ruth L. Stumm (Bell Laboratories), and Stanley Yates (American Archives of the Factual Film) for answering numerous inquiries or allowing access to the archives;

Captain and Mrs. Howard J. Kerr (United States Navy), Mr. and Mrs. Robert J. Miller, and Dr. and Mrs. David J. LeRoy for their hospitality during several research trips to New York, Los Angeles, and Houston;

Howard Beckerman, Anthony Slide, John Canemaker, Murray Glass, Sydney Vaughn, John Halas, and Mark Mayerson for comment, audiotapes, citations, and advice;

Dr. Raymond Fielding, for searching for theses and dissertations through his film bibliography before publication by the University Film Association;

Gus Liapis, Simulation Systems of Evans and Sutherland Computer Corporation, for technical reports, and Richard Weinberg, Lockheed;

Len Hollmann, for contributing Appendix 5;

Fernando Lavel (Twentieth Century-Fox Television), Arnold J. Friedman (Cinema Shares International Distribution Corporation), Jack McLaughlin, Helen Killeen, and Stephen L. Elsky (United Artists), Lee Cannon (United Productions of America), Sarah Baisley (Hanna-Barbera Productions), John Peaslee (Cartoon-a-torials, *Newsweek*), Ms. Marion Wood (*Millimeter*), and Charles Tolep (VIACOM Enterprises);

Mr. Robert Lee Miller, Secretary and legal counsel to Walter Lantz Productions, Inc., for permission to publish Table II in this guide; Craig Hoffer, my nephew, and Drew Crossman, a young filmmaker, whose eager help in the summer of 1981 relieved me of a lot of other work which enabled me to finish this book;

M. Thomas Inge, series editor, Marilyn Brownstein, acquisitions editor, Janet Brown, copy editor, and Louise Hatem, production editor, Greenwood Press;

and Diana Bourdon, who typed the manuscript and survived.

animation

CHAPTER I

Introduction

Most of the films made so far are examples not of creative use of motion picture devices and techniques, but of their use as recording instruments only. There are extremely few motion pictures that may be cited as instances of creative use of the medium, and from these only fragments and short passages may be compared to the best achievements in the other arts.[1]

SLAVKO VORKAPICH

The raw material of motion picture animation is movement. Plastic form is necessary only because we cannot perceive movement without forms. . . . The "how" of movement is the real aim of animation.[2]

ALEXANDRE ALEXEIEFF

If it is the live-action film's job to present physical reality, animated film is concerned with metaphysical reality—not how things look, but what they mean.[3]

JOHN HALAS and JOY BATCHELOR

Animated motion pictures of the kind known to mass audiences in the United States from the early 1920s to the 1950s were literally created frame by frame. Of course, all motion pictures are photographed by this method, usually twenty-four frames taken in one second, processed and projected on a screen at the same rate, fused into the appearance of motion in our mind's eye. All of this happens so rapidly we pay little heed to the technology involved or the psychology and physiology of our mechanisms. However, many of the animated films considered in this reference guide, while created frame by frame with a camera, are first drawn by an artist or a group of artists. But there are other animated films which are created by single-frame exposures of objects, models, miniatures, or photographs, manipulating the objects, photographs, or the camera itself between each single exposure. Still other forms of animation completely eliminate the camera and create movement by drawing directly on the film, perhaps across several frames in a fell swoop. The unusual patterns of line and geometry come to life when the film is projected, sometimes with a sound track created in similar fashion—a sound track created by hand drawing, which is a synthetic sound. In 1980 electronic technology enables animators to create sound with multiple synthesizers and computer circuits.

The newer technologies, seemingly impersonal and too complex, have produced yet another form of the animated film. The human element, put into a machine in the form of mathematical equivalents of a given scene, is still present. Yet the memory of such a machine recalls the instructions for creating the key frames far better than human technology and at costs far lower per unit time. Given this technology, there is also conflict among artists and consumers concerning the value of machine-created images. However, both humanly drawn frames or computer-generated images are created or photographed a frame at a time. They consist of the basic, manipulatable elements such as mass, line, perspective, tone, and color.

The common technical element which brings together all of these types of animation is the replay of the images through a film projector, with individual frames interrupted by a shutter. When moved through the projector at a fast rate, the separate images seem fused together into a continuum. The same phenomenon, which physiologists and medical experts still do not understand fully, occurs when the images are projected into a television camera or on our retinas.

There are various kinds of animations that have evolved in film and television since the beginning of filmmaking. These include the cel drawings (celluloid overlays) of Winsor McCay, Raoul Barré, and John Bray; the stop-action tricks of Emile Cohl, Georges Méliès, or Edwin S. Porter; the silhouette cutouts of Lotte Reiniger; the object and puppet animation of Willis O'Brien or George Pal; the animated photographs and drawings of Bob Godfrey or Terry Gilliam; or the drawings on film and soundtracks by Len Lye and Norman McLaren; and the computer generated images orchestrated by John Whitney, Lillian Schwartz, or space-shuttle trainees using interactive computer animation systems.

Animation is far more than drawing, of course. Definitions of "animation" that limit the subject to either photography shot a frame at a time or to movements created frame by frame do not have sufficient breadth to accommodate all of the rich, varied forms noted above. Those examples originate in diverse ways but they share one common element: the manipulation imposed between the frames, whether drawn, photographed individually, or generated by a machine. Norman McLaren, of the National Film Board of Canada, defined the process in this manner:

Animation is not the art of *drawings* that move, but the art of *movements that are drawn*. What happens between each frame is more important than what exists on each frame. Animation is therefore the art of manipulating the invisible interstices that lie between frames. The interstices are the bones, flesh and blood of the movie, what is on each frame, merely the clothing.[4]

For purposes of organizing the literature, this guide defines four basic classes: cel-animation, object-animation, drawing-on-film, and computer animation.

Cel-animation is one of two types that first reached mass audiences as the moving picture evolved in the United States after 1895. This type was manifested in the art of Winsor McCay (Gertie the Dinosaur; Little Nemo), Otto Messmer (Felix the Cat), Walt Disney (Mickey Mouse and others), Max and Dave Fleischer (Koko the Clown; Betty Boop), Tex Avery (Porky Pig, Bugs Bunny), Bob Clampett (Bugs Bunny), Chuck Jones (The Roadrunner) and hundreds of others who created their films frame by frame by drawing them individually for the camera through the use of celluloid overlays (cels). The works of those animators resulted in more than movement of simple drawings: they created characters, told stories, used and exploited stereotypes, and caricatured life and personalities.

Developing a deeper tradition in Europe but increasingly featured in American theater and television, the types of object-animation are also diverse. There are the pinscreen films of Alexandre Alexeieff and Claire Parker; the puppet films of George Pal and Jiři Trnka; clay animated films of Will Vinton; monstrous miniature films of Willis O'Brien and Ray Harryhausen; cutout films of Lotte Reiniger, Sid Marcus, Jan Lenica, Zofia Oraczewska, Larry Jordan; pixilated films of Bernard Longpre and Andre Leduc; kinestasis animation by Charles Braverman and Dan McLaughlin; stills-in-motion films of Al Stahl and many television documentary filmmakers; and the abstractions of Oskar Fischinger, Viking Eggeling, Hans Richter, and Mary Ellen Bute. The abstractionists incorporate many technologies and techniques into their experimental works along with objects. While the examples given above involve manipulation of objects, cutouts, photographs, or puppets, these animators also frequently manipulate the camera by bringing it closer into the objects or by changing the size of the image. Another manipulation, closely related to stop-action or stop-motion photography, involves editing. For example, the kinestasis films of Dan McLaughlin or Charles Braverman incorporate this manipulation. But the early films in Europe and America are full of crude animation, accomplished by stopping the camera and manipulating the staged action, such as the "tricks" of Georges Méliès or Edwin S. Porter, described in the chronology in Appendix 1 and in "The Historic Outline," Chapter 2.

The drawing-on-film technique or cameraless animation is another kind of abstraction which defines its own class because these films by Norman McLaren, Robert Swarthe, Len Lye, and others eliminated the camera in the production process.

The fourth class of animation considered in this reference guide involves the application of the computer either as a supplement to the traditional cel or object-animation process or for generating images directly which are eventually transferred to film or video tape. There is also manifested in this class an application of animation technology and technique in support of photographic special effects, as in the use of rotoscope mattes. In this fourth category of machine-generated images we would also place the transitional or mixed technologies. Digital television, through new character generators and microprocessors, is a new basis for bring abstract forms and titles to local television stations and limited advertising budgets. The electronic technology has animated, through stop-action, the swirl of clouds in weathercasts, or the rotation of clouds around Jupiter.

Since synthesizers and other devices also alter the reality-catching capacity of the TV camera by frames and can manipulate the intervals between frames, it would seem appropriate to place the "video art" animations in the electronic abstractions.

Thus, we have four major classes defined in this guide for the purpose of organizing a historic outline and the literature of this interdisciplinary but interdependent branch of film and television. One major theme in this book is to demonstrate that what appeared to be a distinctly separate branch of film (innovated well before films were invented) is in fact an interdependent relationship of animation with the technology, art, and form of contemporary film and television. Animation is distinct in some respects, but it is far more interdependent in many other respects. In seeking to outline the connections, this guide is divided into six chapters and seven appendixes, all identified in the Contents. Before leaping to reference materials, the reader may want to browse through Chapter 2, "The Historic Outline," which is based on the chronology in Appendix 1 and on other sources. Chapter 3 contains a reference section followed by a discussion of the major literature in each of the four classes defined in the guide. Chapter 4 is a review of literature about the classes of animation as defined in this book, including a reference list to the personalities involved in animation. Chapter 5 contains references for creating animation, and Chapter 6 ties up some theoretical and historical points, quotes predictions, and provides some speculation and opinion. The appendixes contain more detail on research centers, film sources about animation, animated films in Super 8mm, annotated reports from the trade journals and popular press, and comment about periodicals of animation interest.

NOTES

1. Slavko Vorkapich, "Toward True Cinema," *Film Culture*, no. 19 (March 1959), pp. 10-17; and Richard Dyer MacCann, ed., *Film: A Montage of Theories* (New York: E. P. Dutton, 1966), p. 172.

2. Alexandre Alexeieff, "Reflections on Motion Picture Animation," in Robert Russett and Cecile Starr, eds., *Experimental Animation* (New York: Van Nostrand Reinhold, 1972), p. 93.

3. John Halas and Joy Batchelor, "European Cartoon: A Survey of the Animated Film," *Penguin Film Review*, no. 8 (January 1949): 9.

4. Quoted in John Halas, ed., *Computer Animation* (New York: Hastings House, 1974), p. 97 [McLaren's italics].

CHAPTER 2

The Historic Outline

INVENTIONS AND TRICKS, 1895-1915

We're all lineal descendants of Georges Méliès. . . . He was the first to know what cinema was for—not because he invented the trick film, but because he instinctively knew what the main esthetic of the film is.[1]

HANS RICHTER

The condition of film history can become reasonably healthy when it is recognized how unimportant a "first" is in itself. The vital question is the degree to which any departure from routine film making affected the medium.[2]

JAMES CARD

Depending upon whether you define animation as movement or photography, the story could start with successive drawings of animals on cave walls that originated thousands of years ago or with early attempts around 1900 to fuse the moving-picture camera and single drawings to create the illusion of movement.

The animated drawing was a reality decades before the innovation of the motion picture but the animated film did not evolve until the invention of the film camera and projector. C. W. Ceram in his *Archaeology of the Cinema* documents the detailed prehistory of the cinema, outlining three distinct periods of development. There were many experimenters, scientists, and photographers working on a way to photograph objects in motion and project them in motion. In the first period (1824-1833), drawings were animated in parlor toys and other gadgets such as John Aryton's Thaumatrope (1825, Paris) or the Phenakistiscope (1832). But the invention and innovation of still photography by Louis Jacques Mandé Daguerre (after 1838), based on the work of Joseph Nicéphore Niepce, stimulated more investigation into photographic processes, eventually branching out into a second period involving the animation of still photographs (1853-1861). Drawn lantern slides were replaced with photographs by ingenious experimenters such as Coleman Sellers in Philadelphia who built equipment to show several photos in rapid succession. Eadweard Muybridge, Ottomar Anschutz, Jules Marey, and many others, often isolated from news of each other, sought to photograph objects in motion and project the pictures to recreate the movement. With the development of roll film by Hannibal Goodwin and the marketing of roll film cameras by George Eastman, the third period of development began and thousands of households in America created their own "snapshot" portraits and candids by 1890. Using similar film, Thomas Edison Laboratories, through the work of W. Laurie Dickson, developed a film camera as did others in France and Great Britain. In 1896 the first public showing of motion picture films projected upon a screen was held in New York with a projector marketed by Edison but developed by Thomas Armat and C. Francis Jenkins. William Friese-Greene in Great Britain, and Louis and Auguste Lumière in France also developed similar devices, underscoring the fact that the invention of motion pictures cannot be traced back to any single individual nor single line of events. The next few years in the film industry would belong to the inventors as there remained more technical problems to be solved. In the meantime, the experimenters, such as Frenchman Georges Méliès, photographed staged narratives, incorporating tricks and pictorial fantasies. In a short film four years before the new century, Méliès performed his first "substitution trick" in *The Vanishing Lady*. He stopped the camera and removed the lady and resumed photographing. When the film was projected, she merely "popped off" the set, establishing one of the earliest examples of stop-motion photography. This technique was used in hundreds of films and became the photographic basis for object animation in films as recent as *The Empire Strikes Back*.

Animation in the beginning of this period consisted of trick shots by stop-motion, fades, or dissolves, with manipulations made to the photographed action and actors. In 1900 J. Stuart Blackton in Edison's *The Enchanted Drawing* drew a face of a fat man who smiled off-and-on again with the animation created by stop-action technique. In the United States, Edison employee Edwin S. Porter incorporated numerous stop-action tricks in his short films as described in the Chronology (Appendix 1). In 1902 Oscar B. Depue demonstrated the basis for pixilation animation as his ship toured Norway. He exposed his films one frame at a time while his camera was positioned on the bow. When projected at a faster rate to eliminate the flicker, the ship appeared to race through the water at high speed. Similar to the accidental discovery of fades and dissolves by Georges Méliès, was that of Spanish filmmaker Segundo de Chomón while exposing titles one day in 1902. Flies had landed on the title material and were photographed in various positions while the film was exposed one frame at a time. Upon projection, the flies were seen jumping all over the title material. Once learned, filmmakers around the cinema world copied such tricks in their films but other manipulations were also made to the moving image at the Edison plant as early as 1903. In *The Great Train Robbery*, Porter incorporated two matte shots by double exposure. He covered parts of the scene with light-absorbing black velvet and shot the action of the train interior. Then the film was rewound and the train interior was matted out; the previously photographed black velvet (which did not expose an image because it was black) was framed on a passing landscape, and the camera started again. When processed and printed, the composite scene showed the train interior and robbery and an open doorway with passing landscape. When looking at this print today, one can see the faulty registration in the camera as the passing landscape scene vibrates against the train interior when the two join at the matte line. Technical refinements, such as the insertion of registration pins in the camera mechanism, would reduce this problem considerably. Out of these crude examples would eventually come optical printers and traveling matte systems which would enable filmmakers to create various composite shots of actors against all kinds of background plates, such as those who were pursued by monsters in *Jason and the Argonauts* (1963) or rotoscoped mattes in *Star Wars* (1977).

Norman Dawn is credited with an early use of the "glass shot," a term which has survived to the present day, although the technology involved is typically based on static mattes or masks. Dawn combined a painted image on glass, placed in front of the camera, that was designed to merge with some portion of the background which was also in the same shot. While the technology was crude, it is interesting to note that many early filmmakers were using such tricks to destroy the reality-capturing capacity that the film camera easily afforded at such an early period, even before the narrative film was fully developed.

In 1906 J. Stuart Blackton and Albert E. Smith created a cel-animated film called *Humorous Phases of Funny Faces*, the same year that Winsor McCay took to the vaudeville stage to draw cartoons in his "Seven Ages of Man" act. One year later, Segundo de Chomón began making stop-motion animated films. Vitagraph released *The Haunted Hotel* in the United States and France, which contained a sequence using object, stop-motion animation. By 1908 Emile Cohl finished *Fantasmagorie,* an animated film released by Gaumont. About 700 drawings were used in the short film, each photographed twice according to scholar Donald Crafton. In the same year, cameraman Billy Bitzer animated a clay sculpture in *The Sculptor's Nightmare.* By April 1911, Winsor McCay finished his first cel-animation film entitled *Winsor McCay Makes His Cartoons Move; or, Little Nemo,* released by Vitagraph. McCay's animation cels were made of rice paper, not celluloid. Upon each cel he drew the entire image and all of the action, including the background or stationary portions, doing the same for each successive cel. His work was fully animated, which meant that for the sixteen frames in every foot of 35mm film, sixteen different drawings were photographed. For McCay, a cartoonist employed by the William R. Hearst organization (1911), such painstaking and time-consuming work was an art form. But McCay also capitalized on his animation by incorporating *Gertie the Dinosaur* into his vaudeville act.

The animation literature has continued to report numerous dates of McCay's first animated films, ranging from 1906 to 1914. One citation found for this study, contained in the annotated trade journal reports, appears to answer part of the question. The 4 April 1912 issue of *Motography* quotes McCay, indicating that he was contemplating his famous dinosaur, Gertie, but had not yet completed the film:

> What interests me the most, however, is the possibilities of serious and educational work with this method of producing motion pictures [animation]. I have already had a conference with the American Historical Society looking to the presentation of pictures showing the great monsters that used to inhabit the earth. There are skeletons of them on exhibition and I *expect* to draw pictures of these animals as they appeared in real life thousands of years ago.[3]

McCay's first animation was the *Little Nemo* film, described above and reported in *Moving Picture World* on 15 April 1911.[4] The second film, *How a Mosquito Operates*, was reported in *Variety* on 22 July 1911.[5] *Gertie the Dinosaur* was copyrighted in 1914, but McCay could have used the material before the copyright was registered. While "firsts" for cel-animation are not so important, these dates, and those given in the chronology, clearly indicate that a number of animators were expanding animation from stop-motion to the cel medium. In McCay's work, however, there is, by far, a clear distinction in style unmatched by his contemporaries or succeeding generations.

The period 1912-1915 was clearly an important transition period for the American film industry. The Motion Picture Patents Company was disintegrating and its power in mandating one- and two-reel films and its antifeature stand were failing in the face of independents' use of features and the promotion of the star system. The nickelodeon was being replaced by the "movie palace" in the large metropolitan areas, seating far more than the paltry one hundred or so patrons typical of those small five-and-dime theaters. The audiences for films also changed, adding to the low-income and blue-collar Americans who had digested films for ten years. As theaters moved to better locations, and feature films introduced known or publicized stars, higher-income groups increased their attendance.

Moreover, audiences were developing a habit of going to the movies as the programs changed. Such regularity was conditioned upon a production system which divided the labor to the degree that several films could be manufactured in a short time, given to distributors for release to theaters during an appropriate publicity campaign, with continued hype through the newspapers and newly formed fan magazines.

The chief content staples were the two-reeler comedies and action-adventure films. Features enabled directors and writers to explore more complex stories and characters, some adapted from the stage or the novel. In these circumstances, the animated film needed a new production procedure if it were to have any chance for regular exposure to the increasing mass audience. Such mass-production orientations had already been incorporated into the making of short films and features, especially films that exploited a continuing series character and star.[6] Winsor McCay's individual technique in using full animation was clearly out of step with the demands for film products on a regular basis and the emerging mass market. For obvious reasons of efficiency, but more for the presold nature of the content already widely syndicated by newspapers coast to coast, most of the early series animated cartoons were derived from their comic strips. McCay had made one cartoon based on his successful *Little Nemo* strip, but he never exploited the strip with a cartoon series. In 1913 a George McManus strip, *The Newlyweds*, was turned into a cartoon series, animated by Emile Cohl. Weeks later, Essanay released *Dreamy Dud* and *Joe Boko*, originated by Wallace Carlson. Sydney Smith's *Old Doc Yak* was soon released by Selig. John R. Bray released his own series satirizing Theodore Roosevelt and his African safaris using the character "Colonel Heeza Liar."

Bray and Raoul Barré had been working on a systematic method of producing animated cartoons faster without having to redraw everything in each frame, as did McCay. Barré divided up the labor in cartoon production, assigning various tasks to his staff, spending much of his time supervising their work. This model was refined and carried forward by Walt Disney in the early 1930s, supplemented with training sessions, pencil tests, storyboards, script conferences, and other devices to produce a single animated style. But, in 1914, technology and economics conditioned a much simpler yet consistent approach in the Barré studio. Barré's "slash system" enhanced his division of labor by eliminating the expensive effort involved in redrawing everything in each frame, including the stationary portions of the action, as done by Winsor McCay in his animation up to about 1915. In Barré's slash system only the moving portions of an action would be drawn, with the stationary portions put on another cel. Barré also devised a uniform system of peg registration so the holes placed on each drawing would be perfectly registered with successive drawings, eliminating the annoying "jiggle" over the stationary part of the drawn image. His New York studio, organized in 1913, had great significance in the training of a new generation of animators, including Albert Hurter and Richard Huemer who would later animate for Disney. One year later, John Bray formed an animation studio in New York City and with Earl Hurd pooled their patents, which enabled mass production of cartoons on a sound economic basis.

Bray's claims about thinking up the idea of animated cartoons as early as 1909 have been sharply challenged by Donald Crafton.[7] But Bray's technical contributions are no less diminished. He originated the concept of "inbetweening," with the animator drawing the extreme positions of movement and assistants drawing the movement between those extremes. In devising a previewing process, Bray claimed a patent on the process of flipping successive sheets to check animation. Earl Hurd met Bray in 1915, telling him about his process of using transparent glassine sheets. The moving parts were drawn on these sheets and placed in sequence over the background during each single-frame exposure by the camera. This process, along with Bray's achievements, revolutionized animation production well beyond 1915. Numerous refinements were continually devised, but the basic technology was available for such mass production to which the live-action American film industry was clearly geared. Max Fleischer's rotoscope process, in which live-action footage was traced onto cels, and Bill Nolan's moving background system were two of many improvements made later on.

There were no similar mass-production solutions for stop-motion techniques applied to objects. Willis O'Brien produced such a short, *The Dinosaur and the Missing Link* (1914), taking two months for the production. In the area of special photographic effects, which would eventually incorporate animation techniques, Norman Dawn had found a way to eliminate the time-consuming glass painting process and created steadier composite images by single-frame photography of the matte shot.

ANIMATION SHARES AUDIENCES WITH NEW FORMS AND CHARACTERS, 1916-1927

> Whenever a new technology appears, there is a tendency at first to use and perceive it as an imitation of something more familiar—as with photography first seen as realistic painting, films first used for visually recorded stage drama and recording first deployed to document live music. But soon enough the new medium establishes its own validity and people start judging it on its own terms.[8]
>
> JOHN ROCKWELL

Animation need not be the corollary of a subject matter, for it begins with
the very birth of an art work, pervades even the barest geometrical scheme.[9]
                                                                                    JEAN CHARLOT

With shortcuts and labor-saving devices brought to the cel-animation
production process, there were also compromises. Gone were the fully
animated, fluid movements typical in the Winsor McCay animations; they
were replaced with simple backgrounds and staid characters moving in
limited fashion, often with jerks, cycles, and lots of holds. Instead of
having every frame in sixteen animated in each 35mm foot of film, animation on "2's" was typical, meaning that two exposures were made for
each piece of artwork.[10] This amounts to eight or fewer different action
cels for each 35mm foot, resulting in far more limited animation, but more
cheaply and rapidly produced. But these technologies fashioned a more
streamlined production process, enabling more cartoon releases to reach
theater screens and perhaps gain an audience. By 1915 major producers and
distributors released a variety of cel-animated cartoons featuring characters
mostly based on syndicated comic strips. Probably the best-known newspaper cartoonist, Rube Goldberg, signed a $50,000 contract plus a per-
centage deal with Pathe for a cartoon production. Bud Fisher's *Mutt and
Jeff* cartoons were produced by several studios from about 1919 to 1928,
but the series had a relatively long life. Walter Lantz went to work in the
new William R. Hearst International Film Service which produced cartoon
versions of Hearst syndicated comic strips including *The Katzenjammer
Kids*, *Happy Hooligan*, *Jerry on the Job* and *Krazy Kat*. Otto Messmer
was employed by Pat Sullivan who had opened a small studio making
animated films including a Charlie Chaplin series. But Messmer's chief
work was on Sullivan's *Felix the Cat* series, a cartoon character critically
acclaimed as the first to express individuality and personality in the mid-
1920s. Max and Dave Fleischer had a brief association with the John R.
Bray Studio producing a series of *Koko the Clown* before the war when
both went into the Army and became involved in filmmaking for military
training. By 1921 their Koko was revived in the *Out of the Inkwell* series.
Bray also employed Paul Terry who animated the *Farmer Al Falfa* series.

During this period, 1916-1926, new forms and techniques evolved, some
conditioned by new or improved technology. Max Fleischer patented his
rotoscope process which projected live-action film (one frame at a time)
onto a drafting board so an animator could trace the movement. With
refinements, this device is still used today as an aid in creating matte-
process special effects and in the animated films of Ralph Bakshi and many
others in television advertising.

Sid Marcus designed *Animated Hair* cartoons using cutouts and Tony
Sarg animated prehistoric animals in silhouette cutouts. C. Allan Gilbert

and John R. Bray produced *Silhouette Fantasies* for Paramount for a time. The *Paramount Pictographs* consisted of educational subjects in a magazine format and were usually followed with a Bray animation. In fact, many newsreels after 1914 included a cartoon, some of which editorialized or interpreted a news event or satirized a personality. In Italy, Segundo de Chomón and Giovanni Pastrone combined live-action and animated puppets in a film, *The War and the Dream of Momi* (1916). Willis O'Brien, assisted by Marcel Delgado, completed his work in object animation in *The Lost World* (1925), a story of explorers finding prehistoric animals in South America.

Among other technical developments, Bud Fisher and Louis Glackens discovered that painting the underside of the cels permitted the ink outlines of the figure to remain visible and provided a clean line buffer for the painters. Bill Nolan put a moving track underneath the cel plate, enabling the separately drawn background to be moved and creating the illusion that the camera was panning.

Sometime in the 1920s, the process of animation production was refined. The model chart illustrated each character in different poses and was the final guide for several animators working on a single film, so all would draw the character alike. In the Fleischer organization and others, inbetweeners were used to fill in the action between extremes drawn by the animator. The division of labor was increased to the point that beginners would start out opaquing cels, then inking cels (based on the animators' and inbetweeners' tracings), moving to inbetweening, and finally reaching the animator position. Background and layout artists became specialized; storymen were formed into separate departments.

Animation and special photographic effects techniques had joined together in this period with examples of live-action combined with animated characters. The use of masks or mattes would become a reliable method for accomplishing this. In 1918 F. D. Williams patented his traveling matte system which became an industry standard for years. By the 1920s, optical printers greatly enhanced special photographic effects such as freeze frames, reversing action, zoom simulations, wipes, and other manipulations. John Bray was among many who experimented with color, apparently producing a color cartoon in 1919, but high costs cut short further work. Oskar Fischinger invented an animation system involving successive slicings from a prepared wax block, which, when filmed, would produce a time-lapse cross section of the images formed in the wax. While this presented implications for art, the procedure was depicted in the critically acclaimed *National Geographic* series, "Mysteries of the Mind." There, instead of wax, a human brain from a cadaver was sliced and animated using time-lapse photography enabling scientists to closely study the internal structure of the least understood organ in the human body. But Fischinger's idea and machine became the bridge to a newer technology involving computer animation. Slices of tissue were mounted on thousands of slides, and their outlines were carefully drawn on cels (a form of rotoscoping), which were inputted into a computer. When recalled and assigned particular colors and shadings, scientists for the first time could literally jockey inside the outer wall to study the human brain from a most unusual viewpoint.

In sum, new forms of animation were finding audiences although many films failed to attract much interest. Initially in 1914 there was widespread interest, probably because many cartoons drew from their comic-strip appeal. The newspaper-syndicated cartoonists themselves had become celebrities with their highly publicized salaries. But, for those versions that were only limited animations and pale comparisons to their strips, audience and exhibitor interest fell off. Even the Disney animations in the mid-1920s, such as the combined live-action *Alice* series, were not standouts either in terms of style or character.

The formation of the film unit at the Henry Ford Motor Company in 1916, the first industrial film unit in the United States, signaled expansion in the application of film to public relations and instruction. Simple animation techniques were incorporated in some of Ford's training films but most production went into theatrical release including a weekly newsreel which occasionally included animation. About this time, John R. Bray sensed a market for animated training films and a specialized service catering to industrial accounts was started and continues to this day. World War I created a large need for training films, and many animators planned such films even after hostilities ended. Newspaper accounts cited in Appendix 6 and published reports in the animation literature contradict each other in describing the role of the Fleischers in creating a feature film explaining the Einstein theory of relativity. Despite this, by 1923, at least two versions of the Fleischer film were released, demonstrating the continued importance of animation in education. Given this setting, but enhanced with even less expensive technology, the educational applications would become a very important element in the entire range of the animated film.

Walt Disney began his animation career in 1920 with a job at the Kansas City Film Ad Company. His training was largely through trial and error, relying upon the Carl Lutz primer in animation and Eadweard Muybridge's photo studies of animal and human movement. A short time later, Disney's Kansas City business ended in failure and he persuaded his brother and associates to go to California for a fresh start. Walt Disney Productions was founded in Los Angeles in 1923. Many animators such as Hugh Harman, Rudolf Ising, Carmen Maxwell, Lorey Tague, and Ub Iwerks were Disney associates at one time or another. The first core of trained animators who eventually spread out their talents into an expanding industry appeared to have their beginnings in the John R. Bray, Raoul Barré, and Hearst International Film Service studios. In 1927 changes in the studio system and the new vertical monopoly made access to screens difficult for outsiders, especially for independent producers of short films. Disney eventually succeeded and through his organizational genius, his operation became one of the second plateaus for another generation of trained animators and other specialists.

In Europe, painters Viking Eggeling, Georges Braque, and Francis Picabia experimented with abstract animation while their commercial counterparts in America such as Pat Sullivan and Bud Fisher created work for the mass marketplace. Hans Richter soon joined with Viking Eggeling in making films that explored rhythm in painting. Oskar Fischinger experimented with silhouettes, wax, and abstract patterns created by multiple exposures. In Berlin, the Dadaists created photomontage using the photograph as a ready-made image, combining it with other materials from magazines and newspapers. The provocative dismembering of reality would eventually amalgamate into animated collage and kinestasis such as Frank Mouris's *Frank Film* (1973). Indeed, while the American film had refined techniques for silent storytelling or narrative, others abroad were exploring the film medium for more intensive and deeper exploitations of reality.

Walter Ruttman premiered his first abstract film, *Opus 1*, in Frankfurt in 1921. Three years later, French experimentalist Fernand Léger finished *Ballet mécanique* which incorporated abstract animation, some accomplished by editing. Two practitioners and theorists pushed the medium farther in their work with editing. Blaise Cendrar, in editing *La Roue* (1922), created a train collision using rapid intercutting that is, in the words of Standish Lawder, "too fast for the eye to comprehend," with the screen exploding "in a torrential cascade of images."[11] Four years later the Russian, Sergei Eisenstein, edited together three separate shots of static, stone-sculptured lions; when rapidly intercut, the result was an animated lion on the move in ideological behalf of the Soviet Revolution. In *October (Ten Days That Shook the World)* (1927), Eisenstein intercut single frames of a machine gun with another shot of a Soviet soldier in a startling short sequence that exploited the intervals between the frames and audience perception of the pictures. Along with constructive editing, the live-action Soviet filmmakers were dismembering reality as the animated film had done up to this time. In a curious circumstance, Disney would later make animation "lifelike" by modeling his animation from nature while other live-action filmmakers such as Slavko Vorkapich destroyed reality by exploiting montage and editing. The line of influence from the photomontage experimenters, montage and constructive-editing techniques, and the abstract filmmakers is not easily drawn, but manifestations of their visual style are evident in many of today's television commercials, film and TV program titles, and short films.

Perhaps some small influence of the "still-in-motion" technique exploited in film and television documentary can be traced to the photomontage movement, at least in the use of photographs animated by movement of pictures and camera movements over pictures. The use of storyboard, ably illustrated in Disney's "Baby Weems" sequence in *The Reluctant Dragon* (1941), would clearly demonstrate how still-drawings created narrative, especially when designed with a sound track integrated with the pictures.

The technology in this period that stands as a milestone was the animation's exploitation of sound. While Disney did not produce the first sound cartoon, he did eventually reap the rewards for the first aural innovation in the animation medium, but at considerable risk and cost. J. Douglas Gomery described the conditions leading up to the sound innovation during 1926-1929.[12] The major competitors of Warner Brothers were taking a long technical and economic look at several technologies already available in 1926, initially concluding that a hasty decision might jeopardize investment of an estimated thirty million dollars needed to convert to sound. The industry leadership was also extremely sensitive to the years of previous research and failure of sound systems, among them De Forest, who had made a series of short films including an animated cartoon by the Fleischers. At mid-decade, the major producers could afford to wait since their profits were growing, following on the heels of considerable expansion costs in the acquisition of theaters. Warner Brothers and Fox released a large number of short sound films in 1926, using the Vitaphone system, and the public's appetite was perceived to be hungry for more. While the Fox Corporation concentrated on newsfilms and actualities (with little editing or camera manipulation), Warner Brothers released *Don Juan* (1926), a film with a synchronized music score and sound effects, which received critical praise. In October 1927, *The Jazz Singer*, the first synchronized dialogue film, was released to receptive crowds. But the major producers in the industry still had not agreed on a standard system and did not do so until the following spring (1928). Most of the theaters were wired for sound after May 1928 when licensing contracts for use of the Western Electric patents were signed. Disney had followed these developments and by November 1928 found a receptive audience to his first synchronized animation, *Steamboat Willie*.

EXPLOITATION OF SOUND AND COLOR: THE GOLDEN AGE, 1928-1947

There is every reason to believe that undeveloped, and even unborn, arts, requiring very complex tools, may one day equal or exceed the old arts in expressiveness.[13]

RALPH POTTER

Meanwhile, the moral of U.P.A.'s achievement seems to be that no medium is ever truly exhausted, and least of all when it appears to be; and that what is universally regarded as a limitation may be turned by the perceptive artist into an advantage.[14]

JOHN CULSHAW

The so-called golden age of American animation found its beginnings in the exploitation of sound and color. From this grew a large number of producer organizations in search of characters duplicating Disney's success with Mickey Mouse and his fully animated personality style. Disney would continue to outdistance the competition during this period, at least in terms of mass appeal. There were differences over matters of style and out of that rebellion came the United Productions of America (UPA), beginning a major transition in cel-animation style. During this time, animation's role expanded into propaganda and instruction on a major scale. Experimentation in new forms by inventors and independent filmmakers continued with some small influences from and collisions with the theatrical establishment. Object-animated films using puppets and models reached new audiences but these were never as influential as an animated form until their incorporation into television advertising and programming and theatrical special effects years later. Technology also helped establish new styles or maintain existing ones, as in the case of live-action combined with animation in color. Infuences from abroad were minimal due to the war, but this would change after 1948. The economics of production, by 1947, forced some producers to cut back or stop animated short-subject production, signaling the beginning of the end of the animated theatrical cartoon, at least for a decade. The most important regulatory development in this period was the 1948 consent decree which began the breakup of the major film producers' hold on distribution and exhibition. Then, the implications were not so clear, but the result was increasing access to American screens by independents and foreign films, and, some still argue, at the expense of the American animated short.

There is no question that the Disney Studio was the most important in terms of personality or character animation, organization, technical achievement, merchandising, and exploitation of color and sound. John Canemaker, in his brief history of animation, concluded that Disney's

most important accomplishment was to develop personality animation to its highest degree. To do this, Disney drove his artists to create a new style of animation. The elements of this style are fine draftsmanship, a caricatured impression of reality, and a flexibility of form and kinetic energy unique in the history of art.[15]

Disney innovated the use of the storyboard in his organization, allowing his animators to plan entire films more efficiently. He reinvested money and effort in building a cadre of trained personnel who, according to some, were later exploited by him. Disney did not promote himself or his organization as a great contribution to American culture. He insisted on the best quality work and maximized every opportunity to strengthen the organization by maintaining every conceivable control over his product at a time when other producer organizations were struggling against double features that tended to push cartoons out of theaters.

Following the success of *Flowers and Trees* (1932), the first three-strip technicolor sound cartoon, and the popular *Three Little Pigs* (1933), which was promoted in other media with the hit tune "Who's Afraid of the Big Bad Wolf" (itself an appeal against the depression), Disney resisted the general industry practice of following a winner with a duplicate offering, a practice still followed in today's phonograph, radio, television, and film industries. His shrewd deal with Technicolor, insuring exclusive use of the new process for two years, undoubtedly nourished new exhibitor and distributor interest in the animated film and seemed to be quite consistent with the high ideals of competitive bidding in the marketplace. Of course, Disney's competitors did not think so.

The Disney organization also wrung every ounce of profit from merchandising activity and carried it to new heights, later emulated by the Fleischer brothers and others. Winsor McCay, however, was the master of such economic designs in the American cartoon. Such symbiotic activity was critically important for keeping Disney credit active for more investment, particularly for a feature length production in the form of *Snow White and the Seven Dwarfs* (1937). While it was not the first animated feature, *Snow White* was the most economically and artistically successful for many years. In that picture and an earlier short subject, *The Old Mill* (1937), Disney innovated the multi-plane techniques that provided a greater sense of depth.

Today, in retrospect, most animators acknowledge Walt Disney's organizational and business skills, along with those of his brother Roy, as creating renewed interest in cel-animation. Recognizing that individual animators could no longer start and complete whole cartoons on their own and yet maintain economically profitable enterprises, Disney acquired and managed his talent toward larger goals, although relationships among all were not always cordial. Checkpoints in the animation process were designed to help maintain quality and extend animation to new frontiers. These included the conference technique, key drawings, pencil tests, the Leica reel, and stereophonic sound. Initially, in the early 1940s, a film entitled *Fantasia* did badly at the box office but since has withstood the test of time, demonstrating that many of Disney's films now achieve new leases on life with new generations, enhanced with a weekly television program plugging Disney amusement parks and upcoming theatrical features. Few producer organizations or animators could lay claim to such longevity, but the secret was not attributed exclusively to art in animation but in marketing as well.

World War II eclipsed commercial cartoon animation, but other studios released animated cartoons as well, including the Fleischers through Paramount, Warner Brothers, Metro-Goldwyn-Mayer, Twentieth Century-Fox, and Walter Lantz through Universal and Columbia. The Fleischer Studios animated *Betty Boop* (1930), *Popeye* (1933) and *Superman* (1941). Dave Fleischer directed the second American cel-animated feature, *Gulliver's Travels* (1939), completed after the Fleischer Studios moved to Miami, Florida. In 1941 the Fleischer Studios were closed by Paramount and were replaced by Famous Studios which continued animating *Superman*, followed by *Casper the Friendly Ghost* (1946), *Herman and Katnip* (1948), and *Little Audrey* (1949).

Paul Terry's Studio, eventually releasing through Twentieth Century-Fox, animated *Gandy Goose* (1938), *Dinky Duck* (1939), *Mighty Mouse* (1943), and *Heckle and Jeckle* (1946). Terry released over twelve hundred cartoons in the life of his studio but never engaged in feature production. Following *Andy Panda* (1939), Walter Lantz animated *Woody Woodpecker* (1940), originally voiced by his wife, Grace. Columbia's animation unit manufactured *Krazy Kat* (1930), *Scrappy* (1931), *Barney Google* in the mid-1930s, and *The Fox and the Crow* by 1941.

Following labor troubles at the Disney Studio in 1941, a number of artists left and set up United Productions of America (UPA). Their more limited animated style was in considerable contrast to Disney's, with flat, two-dimensional characters and far more abstraction in character and background, as in *Mr. Magoo* (1949) and *Gerald McBoing Boing* (1951), a clever little fellow who spoke in sound effects. While feature production with *Magoo* in *A Thousand and One Arabian Nights* (1959) was not successful in America, UPA later released their longer animations for television, such as *Mr. Magoo's Christmas Carol* (1962), the first hour-long, animated television special, which had a more receptive audience. Like the Disney Studio, UPA had also spawned another generation of animators and directors such as John Hubley, Peter Burness, Bill Littlejohn, Bill Melendez, Jules Engel, and many others, who would continue to express their individuality in animation in their own or associated organizations, mostly catering to the hungry demands of television programming and advertising. For advertising in particular the more abstract style of UPA would find a cordial welcome as well as adaptation for reasons of economy and clarity.

As more animators attempted to tackle feature production, a new word came into the vocabulary: *Disneyfication*, which included the exploitation of a strong story and personality, plus the realistic style Disney cultivated through constant training of his animation cadre and reinvestment in the physical plant. Metro-Goldwyn-Mayer characters came later than those of other studios, but probably the most well known were Tom and Jerry (1939). Warner Brothers began with Bosko (1930), Porky Pig (1935), and later introduced Bugs Bunny and Elmer Fudd (1940), Tweetie Pie (1944), Sylvester (1945), and the clever Roadrunner and the Coyote (1948), conceived by Chuck Jones.

The Disney characters were fewer in number compared to those of most studios but included Mickey Mouse (1928), Goofy (1932), Pluto (1930), Donald Duck (1934), and Chip and Dale (1943). After 1937, Disney's major animation efforts involved feature cartoons, but the company always had animated shorts in production until 1955. *Snow White* (1937) was an immediate box office success. Others followed, including *Pinocchio* (1940), *Fantasia* (1940), *The Reluctant Dragon* (1941), *Dumbo* (1941), *Bambi* (1942)—some live-action, some combinations of animation and live-action, and some all-animation pictures. Despite the highly criticized but profitable animation style and Disneyfication, Walt Disney's organization helped make the difference between his survival and the failure of others in feature animation. Of course, his merchandising, television, and new amusement parks also contributed toward reducing the large debt always held by the Disney organization until the 1960s. With such a stable of characters and personalities, this was indeed a golden era in American animation.

In object-animation, models and puppets still appealed to American audiences. David O. Selznick was executive producer of Willis O'Brien's *King Kong* (1933) which represented a considerable improvement over *The Lost World* (1925). With sound and special optical effects, including transparency projection, mattes, miniatures, and miniature screen projection, the public was shocked back to prehistoric times—perhaps just as effectively as special effects, mattes, and animated manipulations would thrust them forward into the fantasies of *Star Wars* three decades later. But in *King Kong* the vision was anchored against the background of the familiar—New York City. Few had seen Ptushko's *The New Gulliver* (1935), the first Russian puppet-animated film to use sound. George Pal entered the United States and by 1940 released his *Puppetoons* through Paramount, with a young Ray Harryhausen assisting. Eventually, puppet animation vanished from American screens entirely except for a few brief glimpses such as the caricature of film stars in the prologue to Metro-Goldwyn-Mayer's *The Ziegfeld Follies* (1946). In 1947, however, Jiří Trnka was critically acclaimed as one establishing new standards for the puppet film. In America, puppets took to television because such programs with hand marionettes or other devices were cheaply produced, and characters could be easily created without the complicated and expensive synchronizing procedures used in filmmaking. Thus, *Howdy Doody* and *Kukla, Fran and Ollie* found homes, first on large metropolitan stations and then on the networks by 1948. This revival was the last for a long time, however, and they too would vanish from national visibility under the clever orchestration of sound, puppet, and character patterned after the foibles of humans would become too irresistible in the 1970s. *The Muppets* would also shed themselves of stop-action filming and find a world audience outside of the animated form.

In the late 1930s, propaganda films and other persuasive forms were abundant, including a release using limited "pull-through" animation with a poster-style art. *Invasion of Norway* (1939) was not widely distributed but could easily have set the stage for a style transition to the more massive scale of propaganda and instruction in World War II. Disney produced a number of instructional films for the Defense Department and several propaganda shorts including *The New Spirit* (1943) which promoted a timely payment of income taxes. The studio also contributed to the trend in "mapping" allied and enemy progress over those filmed charts which always seemed to be oozing black and white ink, white representing the allies and the black octopus representing the villainous Nazis or Japanese. In the 1950s, the black was changed to red ink. Probably the propaganda peak for the war years was Disney's marvelous *Der Fuehrer's Face* (1942), which proliferated as a song over radio and on the phonograph, satirizing Hitler and the Nazi movement. An overlooked UPA film, *Hell Bent for Election* (1944), is another propaganda piece which at that time made the chief antagonist (a Republican) appear Hitleresque.

This period, 1928-1947, also involved some experimentation in the new sound medium, which was married to the cartoon at first in a very literal way. The music became the leader for all the action, down to the precise beat of each note. It was as if movies returned to the static state of the first decade in the century, when few dared to manipulate camera angle, image size, or editing. Thus, many cartoons, including early Disney, were merely illustrated radio programs or phonograph records, with little imaginative use of sound in asynchronism or counterpoint to the visible action—except that in some cases the cartoons provided greater dimensionality in characterization through the use of different voices. Fortunately, Disney, the Fleischers, and others eventually outgrew the restraints of this technology and turned it around, integrating the sound with the picture instead of having the sound determine the picture.

Audiences were conditioned by radio, so much so that a fake newscast, opening a broadcast on a late October 1938 night, momentarily startled at least one-fifth of a nation into thinking that the Martians had landed in New Jersey. There were no pictures in radio, of course, except those stimulated by aural means in the heads of thousands of listeners. However, there had been imaginative uses of sound in live-action film earlier, such as Rouben Mamoulian's *Dr. Jekyll and Mr. Hyde* (1931) or Rene Clair's *Le Million* (1931). But, radio provided another model for sound film because through sound effects, music, and dialogue, well-timed to the action, the sound track could take over the narrative function or develop another narrative action in the same or different time frame. The best example of this marriage occurred when Orson Welles brought his Mercury Theater ensemble to Hollywood and made *Citizen Kane* (1941). Such exploitations were rare in the animated film at this time. By the late 1930s, Mel Blanc and others had given animated characters their distinct voices and by so doing added considerable dimension to the characters. Most of these voices were anchored in circumstances familiar to the audience. But UPA's Gerald McBoing Boing was a character who uttered sound effects and these may have been misunderstood by an unconditioned or unreceptive TV audience in the 1950s.

King Kong (1933), *The Invisible Man* (1933), and the ghostly story of George and Marion Kirby *(Topper,* 1937) were the memorable illusions created by special photographic effects, mattes, and stop-action in the 1930s. Paul Terry developed an aerial image-projection system enabling cel-animations to be photographed one frame at a time with live-action film. Disney demonstrated live-action combined with animation in full color using a different system, but Metro-Goldwyn-Mayer's *Anchors Aweigh* (1944) is the best-remembered sequence, featuring Gene Kelly dancing with an animated mouse, Jerry of the Tom and Jerry duo. John Oxberry opened a small business in New York and would eventually establish new standards for animation photography in time for television. But the two important technical innovations critical to the period were the application of sound and color to the animated form.

Among the experimentalists Oskar Fischinger, Len Lye, Mary Ellen Bute, Norman McLaren, and John Whitney incorporated animation in their work. Fischinger produced *Composition in Blue* (1935), synchronized to music which may have inspired his later work on *Fantasia* (1940) for Disney. He completed *Optical Poem* (1937) in paper cutouts for Metro-Goldwyn-Mayer, which was released as a short subject, but some of his work was apparently too abstract for Disney. In 1935 Len Lye drew images on film in *Colour Box*, a British government film demonstrating the advantages of parcel post. About the same time Norman McLaren had also experimented with this form and, by the early 1940s, had established the animation department in the Canadian Film Board. In 1947 his film *Fiddle De Dee* won an American Academy Award, but the work of this and other filmmakers was still seldom seen on theater screens.

With the closing of George Pal's puppet-animation business and Columbia's decision to abandon cel-animation, early signals for discontinuing animated shorts were apparent. A combination of factors led to the downfall of the animated short in the United States and the seeds for this change were rooted, in part, in the difficulty producers had in getting commitments from Technicolor and the uncertain status of new color processes such as Polacolor and Cinecolor. Unionization brought higher labor costs into the production process after 1946.

During the organizing of labor in radio broadcasting and the remainder of the film industry in the late 1930s, turmoil broke out, first at the Fleischer Studio and then at Walt Disney Productions. These events were probably more the catalyst than the cause of the break with Disney-style, manifested by the withdrawal of key employees from the Disney studio. The general animation literature contains differing views on the conflict with possibly some resolution contained in the official records of proceedings, now housed in Washington, D.C., held by the federal mediators. Appendix 2 contains more information on leads to these sources.

During the period before television raided the nighttime audiences of radio and theatrical films, the 1948 consent decree provided an important jolt to the film business. This decree required that the studios divest themselves of their theaters either through sale or by dissolution of certain discriminatory and anticompetitive booking practices, admission price fixing, and certain run-and-clearance practices.

TRANSFORMATION IN ANIMATION: CHANGING FORMS, TELEVISION, AND FOREIGN INFLUENCES, 1947-1963

> It is significant that television commercial producers have been the first client and willing user of motion graphics. It has become a joke how innovative achievement in television commercials is embarrassingly more conspicuous than program innovation.[16]
>
> JOHN WHITNEY

> The "factory" reputation came about because we employed different methods of production. We never belittle our competitors, but a competitor who makes only five cartoons a year and calls us a factory is forgetting how many people we give work to.[17]
>
> JOE BARBERA

The impact of the consent decree was to separate producers and exhibitors from their theaters, either by modifying their ownership or, in most cases, by affecting the agreements that bound them together into an oligopolistic configuration. With guaranteed access to theater screens, the major producers could afford to produce a variety of products, even high-cost animation and other shorts, and include these films in packages on a regular basis. Certainly, exhibitors often preferred animated series with particular characters, but just as often they had to take the less popular films as well. These changes in the industry structure did not occur over-night. RKO and Paramount signed the decree right away (1948); Loew's, Warner Brothers, and Twentieth Century-Fox, by 1957, had entered into similar agreements with the U.S. government. Slowly, the smaller dis-tributors such as Columbia, Universal, and United Artists were able to book a larger share of the markets. The removal of block-booking prac-tices opened the window for more independent films and foreign pictures on United States screens. While these events cannot be assigned as a major cause for the demise of the animated short, they certainly affected invest-ment perceptions about potential markets for such films and consequent funding decisions based on them and other factors, especially the growth of television.

In this period, 1947-1963, there were important transitions in broad-casting as well as in the film industry. National interconnection linking up some major television markets was a reality by October 1951, but the industry had certainly not penetrated every household or even one-third of them. But the growth in set penetration was rapid while the film industry adapted to the perceived threat. At first, film studios refused to sell the remainder of their libraries to television, but a trickle soon led to a Niagara and by 1960 television was devouring both the mundane and classic animated films stripped in local programs and network shows.

The UPA style—abstract, two-dimensional (flat), but embellished with personality (through voice characterization and sound effects)—brought new economies to the video medium. There were individual styles in the UPA lineup, unlike the consistent Disneyfication present in the strongest competition. And, for a time, the Magoo and McBoing Boing characters achieved a considerable public following. Coupled with more European and Canadian films becoming available in the United States, the animated cartoon began to release itself from the security blanket of the formula: "star" characters, series, and stories peppered with sight gags. New, individual styles were represented by *The Unicorn in the Garden* (1953), *My Twelve Fathers* from Czechoslovakia (1958), *The Commisar Comes Home* (1959) from Yugoslavia, and *Romance of Transportation* (1952) from the Canadian Film Board.

By the mid-1950s, Saul Bass had become the forerunner of a new trend in animated film titles, adding distinctive stylistic qualities to features.

Moreover, these abstractions, with the UPA style, spread to television advertising. While the lines of influence cannot always be clearly drawn, there was probably some contributing influence to this transition by the availability of more foreign animation in America, particularly New York. In 1958 Zagreb animations were exhibited internationally for the first time. Three years later, an American Academy Award went to a Zagreb animated film.

Probably the most significant change in the experimental or avant-garde community was the expansion of their films to more specialized audiences. That meant more festivals and exhibitions, such as Annecy, and the establishment of improved avenues for distribution, such as the Creative Film Society. While some in the avant-garde condemned the commercial establishment and others issued "decrees" about conditions in the U.S. film industry, audiences were still cut off from the independent film, partly because the full impact of the consent decree had yet to be felt, but mostly because many experimentalists had little interest in reaching mass audiences. The public was still hypnotized by the black-and-white electronic tube which had replaced radio as a piece of furniture in the living room. After 1950 network television initially provided the public with "radio with pictures" in the form of numerous, transplanted radio programs. Just as the silent film had undergone transitions in content and form, radio and television affected each other, especially in those aural programs that appealed to listeners who imagined their own pictures based on the sound. Literal interpretations of these programs, such as "Inner Sanctum," or "Suspense," vanished by the mid-1960s. Until the 1960s, little new in visual terms was presented to the American public over the networks except the narrative forms they had been conditioned by since the beginning of the sound film. Even television textbooks cautioned about "crossing the screen line" and using close-ups "too tightly," without, incidentally, giving one shred of empirical evidence that any confusion would result. Similar to hundreds of earlier movies, editing was more by the numbers than by any sort of creative juxtaposition of time and space, all of this affected by some sort of secretive conservatism inherited from unknown sources or "oracles."

The bold manipulators of form were, as in the 1930s, the magazine layout artists (perhaps influenced by the photomontage Dadaists) and the advertisers. Young and Rubicam and UPA created "Bert and Harry," two animated showmen who promoted Piel's beer in 1955. Two years later, another milestone commercial appeared on "Wagon Train," plugging Ford cars. The commercial used a series of still pictures intercut with a man pantomiming various automobile riding positions, with the scenes synchronized to a sound track. This was a most limited form of animation (simply the "quick-cut" commercial using still photos) but a kind of animation nevertheless. Well-known characters were also introduced, including Magoo plugging General Electric light bulbs. Gradually, a trend in limited-animation commercials took hold, largely conditioned by economics, but it also included collage, "paper sculpture," and still photography combined with cel-animation. Partly to avoid the costs of full animation, editorial devices such as quick-cutting or flash-cutting were also incorporated.

Gerald McBoing Boing was translated into a TV version in 1956. Although short-lived, it stands as one of the earliest animated series for television. "Mighty Mouse Playhouse," at first consisting of reedited theatricals, had begun one season earlier and eventually lasted for twelve seasons. Disney's anthology, occasionally featuring reedited theatrical animations and some original material, began in 1954. Hanna-Barbera formed their own studio, catering to television advertising and programming, and became the largest supplier of animated programming to the networks. By exploiting the limited animation form, they reduced the costs of programming, making these forms attractive for network purchase or syndicated packaging. Other syndicators leaped into the expanding local markets as stations noted growing audiences for children's programs. Up to the 1960s, national TV programmers and advertisers were counting audiences in a very "mass" sense. That is to say, national rating services were keeping tabs on households and estimates of television viewing audiences, and TV networks and stations sold these audiences to advertisers at a certain cost per 1,000 viewers. Advertisers bought entire programs fully sponsored and were more concerned, naturally, about the audience viewership of their program than an entire lineup of programs. The best time to acquire the largest audience was designated prime time, loosely defined as between 7:00 and 11:00 P.M. in any time zone, with considerably smaller audiences available at other times. In the mid-1950s, advertisers were interested in total households and audiences in the cost-per-one-thousand headcount. Slowly TV programmers and advertisers looked more closely at those audiences and began separating them by age groups and sex, common demographic categories now used widely in the industry. Realizing that some audiences could justify premium rates per thousand, network programmers concluded that certain other program types might appeal to only selected portions of the mass audience, yet deliver the "right audience" for the advertiser's commercial messages. Out of this milieu rose ABC-TV's concept of "counterprogramming" and the first prime-time animation for adults, "The Flintstones" (1960-1966). Another factor encouraged this change: the quiz and payola scandals, described below. For the time being, in the mid-1950s, most of the network programs aimed at children were in a live-action format, due to the high expense of the animated product. With the adaptation of limited-animation techniques, and other outside factors, a sharp increase in television animation occurred by the mid-1960s.[18]

Dimensional or object-animation found new life on theater screens, partly because of the audience's renewed interest in science fiction and partly because of the theaters' attempt to lure children and adult TV watchers. A young Ray Harryhausen worked with Willis O'Brien on *Mighty Joe Young* (1949) but surpised the most astute investors by filming the black-and-white *Beast from 20,000 Fathoms* (1953) for a cheap $200,000 and making a considerable profit in competition with three-dimension, wide-screen, and other scoped- and full-color processes. *Hansel and Gretel*, produced by Michael Myerberg, claimed by many to be the most ambitious puppet-animated film ever made, escaped many audiences, who attended instead the monster and science-fiction films typical of this era, including George Pal's *Destination Moon* (1950) and *War of the Worlds* (1953), which incorporated complex mechanical and optical special effects along with animated miniatures.

Slowly incubating were other forms of stop-motion photo animation. The French film *1848* was seen as influential by some in animating still-photographs, exploited further by the Canadian Film Board in the documentary *City of Gold* (1957), recreating the days of Dawson City and the Klondike gold rush by using 300 recovered glass plates. On American television, through the NBC-TV "Project Twenty" series, this form would reach larger audiences, barely familiar with the still-in-motion techniques but receptive to the historic detail delivered by the camera, enlivened by sound effects and recreated dialogue—all tied together by the traditional, omniscient narrator. We had all become accustomed to old photographs gathering dust in hallways and on walls, but rarely had we heard them "talk." In "Project Twenty," animation brought them to new audiences.

Sound and animation helped revive these stills. In a related area, electronic music makers such as Louis and Bebe Barron were exploring other creative dimensions in Metro-Goldwyn-Mayer's *Forbidden Planet* (1956), which introduced a generation of "talking" robots. Jan Lenica explored sound as a counterpoint to image, advocated long ago by Soviet filmmakers Eisenstein, Pudovkin, and Alexandrov (1928). Sound-track manipulations such as high speed playback, with animated characters singing or speaking at high pitch, had been done in the theatrical cartoons of the 1940s, but such tricks were applied more widely to television characters. For several TV seasons, animals in "Mr. Ed" and "The People's Choice" were given voices in a quasi-animated state reminiscent of Paramount's movie shorts, *Speaking of Animals* (1940s), but the TV versions had a longer life.

In 1950, computer-generated images were displayed on a cathode-ray tube foretelling a new age in computer graphics and animation two decades hence. Unlike the experimentation by early animators using stop-action tricks and drawn cels, electronic animation required large budgets, technical expertise, and corporate settings.

As in the previous periods, newer technologies were exploited in film such as John Fulton's multiple mattes and animation in the remake of *The Ten Commandments* (1956). The Oxberry animation stands established new standards for a growing TV commercial industry and made the animated form more widely available to television through the establishment of small production houses in New York, Los Angeles, and elsewhere. At Disney, a three-head optical printer was developed and with the improved technology of the sodium-light-traveling matte process made possible the dazzling *Mary Poppins* (1964). Ub Iwerks developed for Disney a xerography process which eliminated the inking process in cel-animation production.

A new medium, videotape, was invented and fully implemented by 1963 with some progress having been made on manipulating the recorded image by slowing it down to single frames. Earlier, in late 1962, a number of videotape animation processes had been developed and hawked to the trade, especially advertising agencies. Mixed with this video technology were the seeds for digital television and the strong implication it would have for animation and special effects in the 1980s.

Disney was still the dominant studio in theatrical animation but the studio was also changing with the times. Disney's move into live-action that was combined with animation features after World War II turned out to be a steady transition to the all live-action features of 1950. A series of two-reel "true-life" adventures also was profitable. Re-releases of *Fantasia* eventually paid off the investment costs, to the surprise of some Disney marketing men. Television probably saved the Disney enterprises altogether in the crucial 1950s by permitting unbridled promotion of Disneyland, a new amusement park in Anaheim, California. ABC-TV agreed to finance the new park and pay for Disney's program by recycling old cartoons and using some original entries. As in the case of "Davy Crockett," some programs had enormously successful commercial lives of their own. Out to capture a hold on the nation's child audience in late afternoon periods, ABC-TV and Disney launched "The Mickey Mouse Club" in 1955, introducing another generation to the Disney name and characters. While animation had become the foundation for the Disney enterprises, the amusement parks by 1980, including the Florida entry, accounted for nearly 60 percent of operating income. Disney was the first of the major studios to carefully track the economics of short-animated-film production, curtailing Mickey Mouse cartoons in 1953. With this, the studio lost a valuable training opportunity for new animators, but special shorts and two-reelers continued. Metro-Goldwyn-Mayer closed their cartoon department in

1957, but Joe Barbera and Bill Hanna opened their own studio shortly thereafter and turned to satisfying the appetite of television for cheap, animated programs. That same year, Paramount stopped Popeye production and sold its entire shorts backlog to television amid some hysterical cries in the film industry. Finally, the home of Bugs Bunny, Elmer Fudd, the Roadrunner and the rest at Warner Brothers was closed in the early 1960s, but a resurrection on television was just in the wings.

In addition to the effects of the consent decree of 1948, a number of other regulatory developments had some influence on animated film and television. In the early 1950s, the issue of violence in films and television was brought to the public through the Kefauver committee hearings. Dr. Fredric Wertham published *Seduction of the Innocent*, a general indictment against comic books for allegedly contributing to delinquency and personality defects. The quiz and payola scandals in 1959, however, rocked the television industry most severely and provided an impetus for legislation to prevent deceptive advertising and programming. For a time, TV advertisers dropped abstract animation and used "reality" appeals typical of live-action. But the most far-reaching impact of the scandals was the removal of the advertising agency and advertiser from complete control of programming decisions. With rising programming costs, many advertisers were probably happy to rid themselves of such an investment anyway, passing this task to the networks. Coupled with a review of audiences by demographics as well as by household count, the networks were now concerned with the entire schedule and how one audience would "flow" into following programs, or what kinds of audiences, usually defined by age and sex, were attracted to a single program and to the competing programs. ABC-TV was the first to adopt new strategies, one being the counter-programming concept which resulted in "The Flintstones," the first animated program for adults appearing in prime time. In this transition, there was a flurry of self-regulation by the broadcasting and advertising industries but this had little influence over time. Now, the animation industry had two clients, the advertising agencies and the television networks. As program packagers, animation producers would form the third leg in the program production triangle.

EXPANSION IN ANIMATION: ENTERTAINMENT, INSTRUCTION,
AND PERSUASION WITH NEW FORMS CONDITIONED BY ELECTRONICS,
1964 TO THE PRESENT

> If the Industrial Revolution could be described by the words specialization and fragmentation, the information revolution can be described by integration. In this new age, the inter-relatedness of things is man's major interest.[19]
>
> EVARD WILLIAM WADSWORTH

Here a spacecraft was sending back pictures, broken down into numbers for transmission and then reconstructed on their arrival on Earth. Television stations were invited to use the pictures as rapidly as they appeared on the screens of the Jet Propulsion Laboratory . . . but few stations bothered to carry them. It was as if Renaissance television networks passed up their chance to carry live pictures from the Santa Maria in 1492.[20]

WILLIAM K. HARTMAN

By the mid-1960s, television was the dominant national advertising medium in America and had become the chief distributor of animated films. Network ratings demonstrated that audiences important to advertisers were attracted to Saturday morning time periods. Color television also spurred advertiser interest to the point that networks became locked in a three-way race for Saturday audiences by 1967.

Even though Japan claimed to be the world center for television animation, a large number of American-made limited-animation programs and characters, some derived from successful comic strips, made their appearance on the networks. The 1966/67 TV season marked the largest increase in animated programs for children, with 80 percent in that form. Network control over programming tightened to the point that some animation packagers complained that the networks specified everything in the program menu. Whether this was because of some sensitivity to the charges of advertising abuses and too much violence is unknown, but by 1978, Arbitron, one of the television rating services, reported that seven of the top ten children's programs were animated.

There were some interesting variations in animated television programming during this period, including the use of animation to depict the fears and fantasies of John Monroe (played by William Windom) who was cast into a James Thurber-like environment with a hassling wife. This short-run series was "My World and Welcome to It" (1969/70). The earliest live-action combined with animation in a TV series was Hanna-Barbera's "New Adventures of Huckleberry Finn" (1968) probably stimulated by Disney's successful theatrical *Mary Poppins* (1964). In American television, puppets shed their animated technologies for videotaped "live-action" forms. "The Muppets" garnered a world audience by 1979 and were seen in 106 countries by 235 million persons, with the lead character, Kermit the Frog, labeled by *Time Magazine* as the "Mickey Mouse of the 1970s." Their creator, Jim Henson, was unable to convince the U.S. networks that the characters would appeal to all audiences when the series first started. In syndication, Henson demonstrated that the network decision makers were, once again, incorrect in their perceptions of audience preferences. Other unpredictable characters became cult figures. Claiming the idea from Popeye cartoons, Walter Williams submitted a short film for a new NBC program to be telecast live on Saturday night, and "Mr. Bill," as a puppet character with practically no animation at all except through flash-cuts, was born. In Williams's words, Mr. Bill was a "cartoon for today."[21]

Animated theatrical shorts were practically moribund except for Metro-Goldwyn-Mayer's *The Dot and the Line*, and Warner's *The Pink Panther* series animated by DePatie-Freleng. At Disney, the results of a talent hunt began to replenish the ranks of retired and dead animators. Ward Kimball broke Disney cel traditions with a Disney short, *It's Tough To Be a Bird* (1969), using cutout collage sequences.

Norelco's fourteen-year-old Christmas animation, with some updating, seemed to symbolize the stability of full- and limited-animation advertising in the production marketplace by the end of the 1970s. Animation expanded into other areas of persuasion, beginning with the 1964 WDSU-TV editorial cartoons from New Orleans. Years later, Hal Seeger began *Cartoon-A-Torials* distributed by *Post-Newsweek*. Each week, syndicated newspaper cartoons were selected for animation with music and sound effects added. Many of these were incorporated into local TV newscasts, reviving the tradition of using editorial cartoons in newsreels which dated from as early as 1914. Perpetual Motion Pictures, New York, animated "Mr. Hipp" within "NBC's Weekend," but the series was short-lived.

Expo '67 at Montreal became a watershed for film and multimedia techniques with a world showcase of mixed media, including animation. Indeed, mixing media was a distinct characteristic for animation toward the end of the 1970s. Typically, the "mix" had begun with the drawing of cels and their storage on videotape. This expansion would later require satellites, telemetry digital storage modes, and computers.

Science-fiction television programs continued the thread of theatrical films of the same genre as those of the 1950s, with "Voyage to the Bottom of the Sea" (1964) and "Star Trek" (1966-69) ushering in a new era of animation techniques in support of special photographic effects. Kubrick's *2001: A Space Odyssey* (1968) used front projection techniques and a flashy "star-gate" sequence that had a large influence on television commercials, proliferating slit-scan, starbursts, and other visual embellishments made for corporate logos and product names. There seemed to be far more emphasis on form than content, as later films such as *Star Wars* (1977), *The Black Hole* (1979), and *Star Trek: The Motion Picture* (1979) demonstrated. Rod Steiger later typed this resurgence of special effects as "humanized cartoons."[22] And, perhaps taking a cue from the models presented at Expo '67, the producers mixed more of their media. *Star Wars* and others included computer-animation, rotoscoped mattes, stop-action or dimensional animation, computer-directed cameras, synthesized sound effects, miniatures, and, of course, live-action. Like *2001*, this picture had a profound impact on other media and on television advertising in particular, but it should be noted that the animator and special-effects artists who conceived and executed the designs in *Star Wars* were principally from the television-commercial business—not the Hollywood special-effects establishment. Disasters continued in the traditional, earth-bound cycle of catastrophe films such as *Earthquake* (1976) which utilized miniatures, rotoscoped mattes, and Sensurround sound.

New technologies such as the Magicam computer-assisted camera system enabled a man to walk in miniature among giant electronic tubes and components for an IBM commercial without any detectable matte lines. Similar technology helped Disney devise a computer-assisted camera system to replicate camera moves over miniatures for original and matte photography in *The Black Hole*. In the earlier part of this period, Oxberry and other animation stands used computer assistance to eliminate the time-consuming calculations for moves of artwork and camera.

Television began to acquire a graphic look in station logos, advertising, network signatures, and main titles. News had long been accustomed to using watercolor drawings or pencil sketches for judicial trials where TV cameras were routinely excluded. Such graphics then began appearing over the shoulders of anchor-persons and reporters, usually symbolizing or stylizing the event with some logo or object. In many cases, and on local newscasts in particular, this became an overused and simplistic characterization of the story. There was enormous emphasis on making even the live portion of the news "interesting." With the introduction of character generators that had larger memory capacities, newscasts and documentaries returned (to a degree) to the written word, with lines of text often shown, as in the case of a direct quotation. By 1980 these generators provided a variety of lettering fonts and other graphic elements such as "colorizing" and tabular outlines. Some systems could perform limited animation.

The experimentalists moved into video and achieved limited national access to audiences but only over public television. The Rockefeller Foundation funded in San Francisco a National Center for Experiments in Television. Scott Bartlett, in his film *Offon*, incorporated animation concepts with "videographic potentials of electronics." But, unlike filmmakers, video artists had considerably higher equipment costs. For the filmmakers, distribution centers were expanded but audiences for their work did not proliferate, some say, because of the premium experimentalists put on their product.

Object and cutout animation had a better foothold in television than previously, although "Land of the Lost" (1974-78), an NBC-TV Saturday morning program combining dimensional animation with live-action, lasted only four seasons. The zany British import, animated by Terry Gilliam, "Monty Python's Flying Circus," never seemed to wear out with some audiences. In the realm of the theatrical film, Harryhausen's *Jason and the Argonauts* is still seen as his best work, although a number of other films were produced later. *Closed Mondays* (1973) and *Frank Film* (1973) clearly demonstrated that the animated short film in America had not reached any dead end.

The probes into deep space represented the best example of media-mix. Using similar technology, Voyager provided pictures of Jupiter, and Pioneer flew by Saturn. The pictures were broken down into their components and sent back to earth where they were stored digitally and played back in color in time-lapse fashion. The January 1980 issue of *National Geographic* contained the traditional "thumb pages" with successive pictures of Jupiter in the ear of the page depicting a moving cloud cover. Animation is also applied to medical diagnosis using the new computer axial tomography, or CAT scan system. X-ray pictures of specific slices of the human anatomy are stored and, when replayed in color and sequence, an animated sequence is created through that portion of the body.

Computer-assisted animation and the generation of computer-animated images were the most significant technical breakthroughs in the period of 1964 to the present. Scientists at Bell Laboratories made the first computer-animated films in 1963. Many others developed and exploited theory, hardware, and software to evolve computer graphics, first used in the auto and aircraft industries as an aid to design. The theory and applications from numerical control in engineering had direct implications for computer-assisted animation. Experimental filmmakers such as Stan Vanderbeek and John Whitney connected with programmers and the new technology. By the late 1960s, Computer Image in Denver offered limited animation for commercials through its Scanimate system. Others such as Animac, Caesar, Video Cel, and Antics followed, helping to animate TV show titles and cartoons for "Sesame Street" (1969-). Commercial maker Bob Abel developed a neonlike, streaking logo for Whirlpool, opening up a line of adaptations called the "candy-apple–neon technique." The NASA space-shuttle training program purchased an interactive system that generated three-dimensional, shaded images in full color, simulating window views from the shuttle in real time. The American public already had a taste for interactive electronically generated images with the widespread proliferation of home video games which occurred about 1977.

Animation contributed substantially to the new form of children's instructional television, represented by "Sesame Street" (1969-). While this kept a number of animators employed, the program also enabled them to maintain their individual styles while engaging in a unique production experience in working out a program for children with a research component instead of guesswork.

Along with *2001: A Space Odyssey*, another cel-and-collage animated film also had considerable influence on the graphic quality of television and advertising. Al Brodaux, Heinz Edelman, George Dunning, and Fred

Wolf led the team to create *Yellow Submarine*, made for only $1 million—an unusually stylized leap from Disney animation to a fantastic, optical, and surrealistic world of graphics and animated characters. In other theatrical animation, adult audiences had new forms in the *X*-rated cartoon by Ralph Bakshi. Human genitals were openly revealed; sex was explicit. The press played up the transition very heavily, and some asserted that more publicity came to Bakshi than to all other theatrical cartoons, from Winsor McCay to the present. While that may have been an exaggeration, *Fritz the Cat* (1973) was the only non-Disney animated feature released in this period to show a profit. In the more traditional cel-animated form, International Telephone and Telegraph Company financed an animated feature intended to bring the animation industry back to New York. *Raggedy Ann and Andy* premiered in December 1976 but failed to recoup its costs, perhaps spelling doom for the traditional Disney-type film.

Advertising directed toward children had been an issue before the Federal Trade Commission (FTC) since 1960. In 1978 the FTC staff recommended that the commission ban all advertising in children's programs. The industry responded with pressures on the commission through Congress and in the press, claiming that children's programs would disappear without commercial support. A few years earlier, the Federal Communications Commission (FCC) had adopted guidelines designed to increase educational and informational television programs for preschoolers and school-age children and to decrease advertising in those programs. Shortly after the FTC staff recommendation, the FCC staff determined that the FCC guidelines had not been followed at all by the industry. Given the congressional limitations imposed upon the FTC by the spring of 1980, and a not very vigorous declaration for improvement by the FCC, the outcome of these regulatory issues remained in doubt, until after the 1980 elections, when the proposals were abandoned.

But the audiences for animation were still expanding. The biggest potential for specialized audiences likely to consume instruction, experimental films, photographic abstractions, and entertainment was in the growing videodisc and videotape cassette markets. The survival and growth of the animation industry in the late 1950s was attributed to the transition to mass television. Conditions have clearly changed, where animation interests still survive in advertising and mass programming, yet new adaptations have been made in instructional, scientific, editorial, and entertainment forms, incorporating a mixture of media. The immediate past journey into these specializations seems to justify further exploration into new channels where those specialized audiences are likely to grow.

NOTES

The citations to volumes, issue numbers, pages, and columns for trade journals follow the format given in Appendix 6. In note 4 below, for example, 8:16:900:1 refers the reader to volume 8, issue 16, page 900, and column 1.

1. Quoted in Herman G. Weinberg, "30 Years of Experimental Cinema Film," *Films in Review* 2 (December 1951): pp. 25-27.

2. James Card, "Problems of Film History," *Film Quarterly* 4:3 (Spring 1950), p. 287.

3. "Making Motion Pictures by Pencil," *Motography* 7:4 (4 April 1912): 162 [Hoffer's italics].

4. "Winsor McCay," *Moving Picture World* 8:16: 900:1 (22 April 1911).

5. "Film of 6,000 Sketches," *Variety* 23:7:5:3 (22 July 1911). Additional citations are contained in Appendix 6.

6. G. M. "Bronco Billy" Anderson had already, by 1913, developed a mass-production system which best exploited a series character yet enabled rapid production and distribution of new products on a regular basis. See Lane Roth and Tom W. Hoffer, "G. M. 'Bronco Billy' Anderson: The Screen Cowboy Hero Who Meant Business," *Journal of the University Film Association* 30:1 (Winter 1978): 5-13.

7. Donald Clayton Crafton, "Emile Cohn and the Origins of the Animated Film" (Ph.D. diss., Yale University, 1977).

8. John Rockwell, "Electronic Music Takes a New Turn," *New York Times*, 6 April 1980, p. D21.

9. Jean Charlot, *Art from the Mayans to Disney* (New York: Sheed and Ward, 1939), p. 247.

10. Howard Beckerman has closely studied several animated films from the early days to the late 1960s regarding the number of animated frames across different animators. See Howard Beckerman, "1's, 2's, 3's and By God Even 4's," *Filmmakers Monthly* (June 1979): 45-46.

11. Standish D. Lawder, *The Cubist Cinema* (New York: New York University Press, 1975), p. 91.

12. J. Douglas Gomery, "The 'Warner-Vitaphone Peril': The American Film Industry Reacts to the Innovation of Sound," *Journal of the University Film Association* 28:1 (Winter 1976): 11-19.

13. Ralph Potter, "Abstract Films," *Films in Review* 5:2 (February 1954): 88-89.

14. John Culshaw, "The Virtues of Flatness," *Fortnightly Review*, 174 (October 1953): 249.

15. John Canemaker, *The Animated Raggedy Ann and Andy* (New York: Bobbs-Merrill, 1977), p. 54.

16. John Whitney, "Excerpts of a Talk Given At California Institute of Technology— 3/21/68," *Film Culture*, no. 53-54-55 (Spring 1972): 76.

17. Quoted in John Culhane, "The Men Behind Dastardly and Muttley," *New York Times Magazine*, 23 November 1969, p. 109.

18. Joseph Turow, "Program Trends in Network Children's Television 1948-1978," in U.S., Federal Communications Commission, *Television Programming for Children: A Report of the Children's Television Task Force* (Washington, D.C.: FCC, 1979), 5 (supplemental papers).

19. Evard William Wadsworth, "A Study of the Computer as an Aesthetic Visual Generator" (Master's thesis, University of Southern California, 1969), p. 42.

20. William K. Hartman, "Moons of the Outer Solar System Become Real, Although Weird, Places," *Smithsonian* 10:10 (January 1980): 36.

21. Beverly Beyette, " 'Saturday Night's Mr. Bill. America's New Crush—Mash, Squish, Hit." *Los Angeles Times*, 5 March 1980, p. V1.

22. "Rod Steiger Battles With Depression, Wins," *Tallahassee Democrat*, 14 December 1979, p. 4c.

BIBLIOGRAPHY

Canemaker, John. *The Animated Raggedy Ann & Andy*. New York: Bobbs-Merrill, 1977.

Ceram, C. W. [Kurt W. Marek]. *Archaeology of the Cinema*. New York: Harcourt, Brace and World, 1965.

Crafton, Donald Clayton, "Emile Cohl and the Origins of the Animated Film." Vols. 1 and 2. Ph.D. dissertation, Yale University, 1977.

Eisenstein, Sergei. *Film Form: Essays in Film Theory*. Translated by Jay Leyda. New York: Meridian Books, 1957.

_____. *The Film Sense*. Translated by Jay Leyda. New York: Meridian Books, 1957.

Lawder, Standish D. *The Cubist Cinema*. New York: New York University Press, 1975.

Lutz, E. G. *Animated Cartoons: How They Are Made, Their Origin and Development*. New York: Charles Scribner's Sons, 1920.

Muybridge, Eadweard. *Human and Animal Locomotion*. 3 vols. New York: Dover, 1979. (Originally published in 1887.)

Niver, Kemp R. *The First Twenty Years: A Segment of Film History*. Los Angeles: Locare Research Group, 1968.

Pudovkin, V. I. *Film Technique and Film Acting*. Translated and edited by Ivor Montagu. New York: Grove Press, 1960.

CHAPTER *3*

Gateway to the Animation Literature: References and the General Literature

This chapter is divided into two major sections. The first describes numerous references and finding aids which function as important gateways to either specific topics or to the general literature, each crossing several disciplines. The second section brings together important books, scholarly studies, periodical articles, and other materials embracing several types of animation or generalizing on related matters, such as history, political and social aspects of animation, criticism, and others.

But first we must turn our attention to the gateway.

REFERENCES

Readers interested in animation will discover that a number of very useful reference aids have been devised in the last decade to make library research easier. Other than this book and some bibliographic articles, there are no such aids devoted exclusively to animation, but the general film literature has systematically encompassed this topic.

This section divides reference works into four major sections: encyclopedias, dictionaries, and annuals; treatises; bibliographic aids and reference aids; and indexes of existing literature. Given the four major types of animation considered in this guide, and the subclassifications discussed earlier, the reader should be cautioned that using one simple term, *animation*, is no guarantee for complete access to the literature. Indeed, the gateway to the four major areas of cel, object, cameraless, and computer animation will require several different terms. There are some general principles that provide consistent results when using certain types of encyclopedias, treatises, and indexes in particular. So much depends upon the content of the literature being searched. The word *animation* is still used in the traditional film literature finding-aids and indexes, of course. And, with regard to computer animation, the term is still applicable to that literature, much of it very technical in nature. But *computer graphics*, as a distinct but related area, is a term that will yield beneficial data on technical problems in computer animation. Because digital television technology also embraces animation as described earlier, and literally connects with other technology, there is an animation-related technical and television literature, but not accessed with the term *animation*. One must use the term *digital television* and *special effects*. Even in the broadly defined film literature, the term *animation* may be too limiting. For example, a number of abstract, avant-garde, or experimental filmmakers used animation techniques. Typically, these works are not included under the animation subdivision in the film literature. In many cases, accessing the literature with the name of the animator or filmmaker will produce the citations. But in some indexes cross-referencing is kept at a minimum, as in the MacCann *New Film Index*. In this particular reference, MacCann and Perry clearly outline how to use their guide, recognizing the different systems that exist for classifying material. There are some, however, who cannot understand such instructions or insist that all knowledge is susceptible of being defined into discrete categories. While this sounds absurd, there are classifiers who still want to impose a system of "standards" upon a dynamic technology that is continuing to redefine itself, breach old links, and forge new interdependencies. Some have removed their blinders and are able to look farther, beyond the edges of defined categories, to find additional literature in the animation area. MacCann and Perry, among others, designed their works with the thinking researcher in mind, not the mindless surveyors who want all direct categories and all relevant cross-references handed to them on a platter.

Some of these problems of accessing different types of animation are solved nicely in one of the best organized indexes to appear in recent years. This is the *Film Literature Index*, compiled by Vincent Aceto and others, which contains cross-references and a number of key words. One should keep in mind that each index deals with considerably different subject matter, even animation. This becomes important, as the subject begins to expand and evolve into additional subcategories, as animation clearly has in the last forty years. For example, the MacCann index embraces a thirty-year period; the *Film Literature Index* embraces a more limited period of four years. There will be few major shifts in categories in one year; over several years, there will be many changes. There is much that is already available, but the potential user must understand the classification system and be flexible enough to think about possible connections among categories. In the case of animation, the existence of these data bases presents some irony, especially to those who want to develop skills in this technology. While the trades discuss these technologies only from their economic and persuasive standpoints, the nuts-and-bolts technologies are described in technical, professional journals that are not included in the same indexing systems.

ENCYCLOPEDIAS, DICTIONARIES, AND ANNUALS

Reference volumes designed to provide answers to brief questions include Leslie Halliwell's *The Filmgoer's Companion*, Roger Manvell and Lewis Jacobs's *The International Encyclopedia of Film*, Liz-Anne Bawden's *The Oxford Companion to Film*, and Ephraim Katz's *The Film Encylcopedia*. The Halliwell work has the most entries, in excess of ten thousand. Manvell's effort has fewer entries but lists an additional 6,500 film titles plus a bibliography, omitted from the Halliwell edition. Bawden's work contains entries on specific films and personalities, production company histories, discussion of genres, theorists, and critics, descriptions of techniques, and a few specialized items. The Katz work is the most recent, published in 1979.

The Raymond Spottiswoode edited work, *The Focal Encyclopedia of Film and Television Techniques*, is an excellent starting point in learning the animation process. This work clearly contemplated the bridge between film and television and the need for a reference book which explored connections between the two media. While the encyclopedia provides clear explanations of the cel-animation process, the sections on computer applications are clearly outdated. The University Film Association Monograph Number 2, compiled by John Mercer, contains a long *Glossary of Film Terms* that supplements the *Focal Encyclopedia* and has particular applications for special-effects terms such as *mattes*, *bipack*, *Clarke process*, *rotoscope* and many others, all clearly explained.

Translations of Georges Sadoul's works, *Dictionary of Filmmakers* and *Dictionary of Films*, available in paperback, contain fewer listings of films and filmmakers compared to John M. Smith and Tim Cawkwell's *World Encyclopedia of Film*, but the Sadoul books are considerably cheaper. Two additional dictionaries on filmmakers and film personalities are Peter Graham's *Dictionary of the Cinema* and David Thomson's *Biographical Dictionary of Film*. Access to animation topics is by name or film title, and while the name "Walt Disney" is common to all four dictionaries, many of the experimentalists are also included.

Peter Cowie's annual *International Film Guide* published by A. S. Barnes is still the best way to keep updated on film generally, with a number of pages devoted to animation on the world scene. Annual editions contain information on festivals, short films, animation, sponsored films, schools, archives magazines, books, and a cinema directory.

While the initial release of the *American Film Institute Catalog of Motion*

Pictures: Feature Films, 1921-1930 (two volumes) did not contain much data on animated features, because there were very few at the time, future releases will provide details on animation titles, credits, synopses, various indexes, and supplementary information. The second set released in this series was the *American Film Institute Catalog of Motion Pictures: Feature Films 1961-1970* (two volumes). Additional volumes will focus exclusively on short films including animated subjects from 1911 to 1980.

Two encyclopedic volumes on the comic strip contain a number of references to film animation. Stephen Becker's *Comic Art in America* is a history of the comics with a number of references to artists who animated films. The volume is indexed and access is by name. Maurice Horn's *World Encyclopedia of Comics* contains hundreds of short essays on strips, artists, animators, and strip characters. While incomplete, many essays describe artists or characters in animated films. Both books deal only with the comic strips, and incidentally with the traditional cel-animations. There is yet to be published an encyclopedia on animation exclusively, but Anthony Reveaux's reference guide to animated film credits is expected soon. Reveaux, aided with a small grant from the Academy of Motion Pictures Arts and Sciences, has undertaken an ambitious project of identifying every animated film, by title and artists, released to theaters around the world, 1895-1975. Just out in 1981, Jeff Lenburg's *Encyclopedia of Animated Cartoon Series, 1909-1979* lists many individual titles in the series of silent, theatrical, and television animations.

Ronald M. Schulz at Southern Illinois University completed a lengthy list of American studio cartoons as a master's thesis in August 1979. Based upon the Library of Congress copyright volumes and a number of publicly available filmographies, he has brought together for the first time a list of about 6,500 theatrical studio cartoons for the period 1900 to 1970. This list, limited to the drawn cartoon and the George Pal Puppetoons, also contains credit data in the form of director or animator role, cartoon character involved (if any) or series name, copyright year, studio of manufacture, release data, and information of historical interest. In alphabetical order by title, the list is 372 pages long. One distinction claimed in the Schulz work is that the list of Disney films and director credits is the most complete anywhere outside of the Disney Archives in Burbank. The title list published in *Film Dope*, Number 12 (June 1977), apparently checked by Disney Archivist David Smith, is also an extensive listing of shorts and features by the year of release. The *Film Dope* resource also contains additional categories such as animated sequences in features, compilations, films made for the U.S. armed forces, sponsored films, live-action films, and brief biographies of key animation directors. While one may seem ungrateful at the result of the Schulz compilation, there are some additional points that should be mentioned. In its present form, as a master's thesis, the access is extremely limited, since there is only one circulating copy. Moreover, other sources were not consulted, leaving the list incomplete even in the defined area. While the author states the limitations of the list, there is no indication that the extensive film listings in *Moving Picture World*, for example, were consulted to make up for the huge omissions in the copyrighted lists published by the Library of Congress. This, of course, would impose an unbearable task for a master's thesis, which raises another question about the suitability of this project for a thesis in the first place. While one could justify a more extensive and accurate computerized list as a dissertation, with alternative classifications, some analysis of this body of work is clearly required. The dissertation format, along with the analysis, would be more widely available if commercial publishers were not interested. If publication is contemplated, considerably more effort would seem appropriate to make the Schulz work competitive with Anthony Reveau's proposed project embracing world animation credits. The degree of correlation with Jeff Lenburg's *Encyclopedia of Animated Cartoon Series, 1909-1979* is unknown. Since the Schulz work, Scarecrow Press has published the Will Friedwald and Jerry Beck work, *The Warner Brothers Cartoons*, comprised of a brief outline of the studio, a list of characters and their descriptions, and what is claimed to be a complete list of every Warner cartoon in order of release beginning in 1929 and ending in 1969. Each entry contains a synopsis of the storyline and credits.

Walt Disney: A Guide to References and Resources by Lynn Gartley and Elizabeth Leebron, contains a list of Disney features released through 1966, a brief biographical overview of Disney's life and work, and a more valuable annotated list of several hundred references about the Disney work. The short films, which made up the bulk of Disney's earlier films, are omitted in this guide, but this additional data is available from Leonard Maltin's *The Disney Films*, from Film Dope, No. 12 (June 1977), and from the Ronald M. Schulz thesis described above.

Two encyclopedic volumes which bring together a large sampling of international animated film and television artists and illustrations of their work are compiled by Walter Herdeg. The first volume, *Film and TV Graphics* (1967), was edited by Herdeg with the text written by the prolific John Halas with separate chapters devoted to the visual revolution; entertainment, sponsored, advertising, and experimental films; and titling and preproduction design. The next volume was published a decade later (1976), updating the same subjects, providing a useful world overview of the animated film in the 1960s and mid-1970s.

Two annuals that are probably the most authoritative and reliable are the *International Motion Picture Almanac* (1929-) and the *Film Daily Year-*

book of Motion Pictures (1919-   ). The *International Motion Picture Almanac* was previously titled *Motion Picture Almanac* and *Motion Picture and Television Almanac*. Arno Press has revived earlier volumes of the oldest set, in hard cover or microfilm editions.

Newcomers to puppet animation, one among several types of stop-action or stop-motion animation, will find A. R. Philpott's *Dictionary of Puppetry* of considerable value. There are, for example, essays on silhouettes to provide perspective to the Lotte Reiniger silhouette films. Stop-motion or puppet animators such as Jiři Trnka are also described.

The United States Library of Congress publishes a book catalogue of copyrighted films, including animation, entitled *Library of Congress Catalogue: Films and Other Materials for Projection*, issued quarterly and in annual cumulation. The card division of the library issues a semiannual *Catalogue of Copyright Entries: Motion Pictures and Filmstrips* with additional volumes bringing together copyrighted films from 1894 to 1969. These volumes were regularly consulted in constructing the list of Super 8mm films now available to collectors and others, presented in Appendix 5 of this volume.

Television has become the important outlet for animation since the early 1960s, including advertising, series, and special programming. While there has been some critical writing on those offerings, outside of the general condemnation of limited animation a few in the industry espouse, there are now a number of encyclopedias and annuals which bring together basic information about animated and live-action programs. With regard to the medium overall, Les Brown's *The New York Times Encyclopedia of Television* provides an important overview of the industry, a praiseworthy effort because of Brown's expertise and the knowledgeable consultants employed in the work. Steven H. Scheuer's *The Television Annual: 1978-1979* is the first annual in what appears to become several. The first edition claims to cover the most significant aspects of American broadcast TV while dividing the programming year from June to May instead of September to August. The essays are undocumented and the Top 50 Specials selected by unknown editors with unknown criteria are useless. But the separate listings of specials and made-for-TV movies are positive contributions to this slick paperback. Three directories to television programming supplement the Scheuer annual and their scope is considerably beyond one year. Tim Brooks and Earle Marsh have written a chatty but reliable listing titled *The Complete Directory to Prime Time Network TV Shows: 1946 to Present (1978)*. The essays are undocumented yet they are not written in the pop culture or fan style, and this fact further elevates the guide as a major research tool. Vincent Terrace has updated his *Complete Encyclopedia of Television Programs, 1947-1979*, which is considerably broader in scope than the Brooks-Marsh volume. Terrace attempts to embrace all network programming, daytime and nighttime. In two volumes, the price tag is a hefty one (over $25 at last glance), but this is the only complete listing of television programming, and the work does contain a very large number of animation references. However, the most authoritative and best organized annual for daytime and nighttime TV is the Nina David *TV Season* compilations issued for the last four TV seasons, beginning with 1974-75. Animated and other programs on the networks are systematically identified and presented in an attractive alphabetical format including made-for-TV movies, with brief synopses of specials, movies, and series programs. Unfortunately, Oryx Press does not plan any future annual editions of this important resource. There is a large amount of animated programming in TV syndication but very few reliable guides to this material. *Series, Serials and Packages* published annually by the Broadcast Information Bureau contains extensive listings of programming and syndicators, but in a survey conducted for this guide, several letters were returned indicating incorrect addresses, or nonexistent programming. Still, this guide has considerable value when supplemented with trade journal annual editions. For the most updated lists of current syndicators one should consult the issues of *Television-Radio Age* and *Broadcasting*, industry trade journals, for the spring convention announcements of the National Association of Television Program Executives convention held each year. (See Appendix 7 for information on periodicals.)

TREATISES

There are a handful of works in animation which merit special citation because of their systematic attempts in surveying particular types of animation defined in this guide or because they remain the seminal works for a particular category in that field. Certainly Bruno Edera's *Full Length Animated Feature Films* published in 1976 heads this list. Following a section on definitions and aesthetics, Edera surveys the global activity, citing the animation pioneers in the United States, Europe, and South America. His essays also include the rise of animated features in the Middle East, Asia, Australia, and Europe concluding with informed speculation on the new directions for the field. At the end, there is a complete list of animated features and an extensive bibliography.

The John Halas and Roger Manvell *Art in Movement*, published in 1975, surveys contemporary animation at the time, but also connects the more traditional animated forms with the experimental film and includes an essay on new techniques with an emphasis on special effects, live-action and animation, backlighting, multiscreen, multi-image, skip framing, freeze framing, spinning rotation, ripple dissolves, and computer films. Unfortunately, the authors fail to indicate full documentation in their histories, especially the dates of various events.

In stop-motion animation L. Bruce Holman's *Puppet Animation in the Cinema: History and Technique* remains the only book in this field. Most of the book deals with technique, but the history section, filmography, and exposition of "Eight Leading Puppet Animators" is a valuable addition. The introductory chapter on definitions and limitations is somewhat painfully drawn to omit the works of Jim Danforth, Willis O'Brien, Lotte Reiniger, or Ray Harryhausen, among others. In Holman's view, an animated puppet film is one "made by using free-standing, articulated puppets made of wood, plastic, or other materials."[1] The definitional focus comes down to whether the puppets were intended to be viewed as puppets, a rather odd way of making distinctions. There is really little basis for complaint; only a recognition that this book exists and the survey is exhaustive, given the definitions. With regard to other forms of stop-action, James Robert Parrish and Michael R. Pitts have most recently published *The Great Science Fiction Pictures*. The older but still valuable *Reference Guide to Fantastic Films: Science Fiction, Fantasy and Horror* by Walt Lee and Bill Warren also includes expositions on the stop-action animators such as O'Brien and Harryhausen.

Kemp R. Niver's *The First Twenty Years: A Segment of Film History* selectively covers the evolution of the American film based on his work in recovering the paper print collection of the Library of Congress and transferring those films to new acetate stock. A number of early films using stop-action or trick effects are described in detail along with illustrations.

Three additional books deserve special mention as treatises in the experimental or avant-garde film, although not all have uniformly earned high critical praise. Marilyn Singer, as editor of *A History of the American Avant-Garde Cinema*, compiled a useful history and exposition of the American movement, designed to complement the Whitney Museum circulating films on this subject. A more exhaustive introduction to this subject is Sheldon Renan's *An Introduction to the American Underground Film*. In terms of drawing connections, Standish D. Lawder's *The Cubist Cinema* is the definitive work that includes experimental animation history but also extends itself beyond film to the derivative sources in cubism.

BIBLIOGRAPHIES AND REFERENCE AIDS

In the early 1970s, a large number of reference guides in film study were published which contained sections about animation and the experimental film. The latest was *The Film Book Bibliography, 1940-1975* by Jack C. Ellis. Eileen Sheahan's *Moving Pictures: An Annotated Guide to Selected Film Literature with Suggestions for the Study of Film*, published in 1978, updates several of the earlier guides. Sheahan's is well organized and the annotations are informed. There are some small, irritating mistakes such as the implication that *Variety* is completely indexed in the *Music Index*; it is not. The earlier film guides include Peter Bukalski's *Film Research: A Critical Bibliography with Annotations and Essays*, George Rehrauer's *Cinema Booklist* (with supplements) and Frank Manchel's *Film Study: A Resource Guide*. Others are listed in the bibliography at the end of this chapter.

The University Film Association published two of the best-annotated introductions to film research. These were the definitive guides by Richard C. Vincent, "An Introduction to Film Bibliographies," and "A Bibliography of Film Reference Resources." In 1977 the American Film Institute (AFI) published a fact file on animation which contained a long list of citations, information on training programs, and a periodical directory. A number of additional guides are also available from the AFI such as "Film/ Television: A Research Guide" and "Children and Film/Television." All of these and others are available from the American Film Institute, JFK Center for the Performing Arts, Washington, D.C. 20566.

Among the few periodical bibliographies on animation are those by John Canemaker, James Monaco, and Susan Schenker. Canemaker, a prolific author in cel-animation history, provides introductory recommendations in a "Selected Bibliography on Animation" published in *Sightlines*, Winter 1978-1979. A number of specialized bibliographies in related subjects also appear from time to time in this journal. The Monaco-Schenker brochure, *Books about Film: A Bibliographical Checklist*, has been updated three times and is available from New York Zoetrope, 31 East Twelfth Street, New York, New York 10003.

Mass Communication and Performing Arts interests are fortunate to have two reliable reporting services that serve to keep the fields fully informed amid the flood of media literature, including animation and experimental film. Christopher Sterling's *Mass Media Booknotes*, released monthly, covers mass communication, journalism, some aspects of the performing arts, and film. In 1981 the publication was available from the Department of Radio-Television-Film, School of Communication and Theater, Temple University, Philadelphia, Pennsylvania 19122. Ralph N. Schoolcraft published an *Annotated Bibliography of New Publications in the Performing Arts* quarterly. For a subscription, write Drama Workshop, 150 West 52nd Street, New York, New York 10019.

In addition to these reporting services on books and monographs, two other services attempt to keep up with the flow of periodical material in film and television, including animation subtopics. For behaviorists, Thomas F. Gordon's *Communication Abstracts: An International Information Service* is indispensable. The outlook of this publication is similar to Gordon and Verna's *Mass Communication Effects and Processes:*

A Comprehensive Bibliography, 1950-1975, discussed in detail in the Indexes section of this chapter. Anyone following developments in the continuing controversy over children's television programming and advertising, some of which includes the animated form, would need to consult Gordon's work. The second periodical-updating service is published by the compilers of the *Film Literature Index*. This service is called *Film Literature Current* and consists of tables of contents from over one hundred film periodicals. As these become available *Film Literature Current* republishes the tables of contents each month. This service is available from: Filmdex, Inc., Box 22447, *Suny-A*, 1400 Washington Avenue, Albany, New York 12222. *Communication Abstracts* is available from *Sage*, 275 South Beverly Drive, Beverly Hills, California 90212.

Retrospective bibliographies in specialized areas related to animation have been published irregularly. Those studying the role of animation and other manipulations in television instruction would find the Children's Television Workshop (CTW) literature a useful beginning. The *CTW Research Bibliography* has compiled several research papers on "Sesame Street" and "The Electric Company" since their inception in 1968. The completed studies are available through the ERIC Document Reproduction Service, Post Office Box 190, Arlington, Virginia 22210.

The computer graphic and animation fields have enjoyed a proliferation of hundreds of technical and technique articles within the last decade. Retrospective bibliographies include R. H. Anderson's *A Selective Bibliography of Computer Graphics* (Rand Memorandum P-4629, April 1971), available from the Rand Corporation, 1700 Main Street, Santa Monica, California 90406. Leslie Mezei published another dealing with "Computer Art: A Bibliography," in the late 1960s. Another dated but still useful introduction is "Computer Graphics: An Introductory Bibliography" by Mary Vance, in the Vance Bibliographies (series), Post Office Box 229, Monticello, Illinois 61856.

A considerable amount of the computer animation and graphic technical literature is accessible through systematically organized data bases and data-base brokers such as Lockheed. These are discussed in James W. Brown's *Educational Media Yearbook 1978* in the chapter on "Data Base Resources for Library/Educational Institutions" by Martha West and Dennis E. Read. Available data bases are described along with the role of the data-base brokers through which access can be accomplished for various fees. The three principal data-base brokers are Lockheed Information Systems, System Development Corporation, and the Bibliographic Retrieval System. Lockheed and System are the largest and oldest; Bibliographic is the youngest and smallest. The fees include searching, telecommunications, and off-line printing of the bibliographies. Fees will vary depending upon the data bases utilized with off-line printing charges usually based on a cost per citation. Very few research libraries are able to search these data bases directly, but the brokers can accommodate direct requests by mail. Users do not just request "animation" as a subject and expect the machine to quickly reprint all the appropriate citations. At this point, potential searchers do need to know the protocol of each data base (or obtain advice) in order to tap all possible citations in a given subject area. For good reason, there is not a single protocol that applies to every data base, just as one finds that subject categories for various indexes will differ, some very sharply. This, of course, is a function of the type and content of journals, books, and other documents cited in the data base.

Potential users should write to the data-base brokers for a complete listing of their data bases and fees. These are: Bibliographic Retrieval System, 1462 Erie Boulevard, Schenectady, New York 12305; Lockheed Information Systems, Code 5020/201, 3251 Hanover Street, Palo Alto, California 94304; System Development Corporation, Search Service, 2500 Colorado Avenue, Santa Monica, California 90406. A review of the West-Read chapter in Brown's *Educational Media Yearbook 1978* is also recommended.

INDEXES

Two important ongoing indexes are critically important to animation scholars and buffs desiring to keep up with new periodical material published in trade journals, critical magazines, and the popular press. Surveying the international scene is the *International Index to Film Periodicals*, an annual publication by the International Federation of Film since 1972. About eighty of the film serials are regularly indexed and annotated by film archivists around the world. A card catalogue service released weekly and totaling about 9,000 citations each year is also available. *The Film Literature Index* embraces over three hundred film periodicals. This index, compiled by Vincent J. Aceto, Jane Graves, and Fred Silva, is issued in quarterly and annual cumulations. With over one thousand subject headings, the alphabetical subject-author index is among the most comprehensive finding aids for contemporary data and by far better and more comprehensive than the *International Index to Film Periodicals*. So far only four annual cumulations are available, which precludes serious historical work.

Five additional indexes help overcome the history void left by the *Film Literature Index*. *The New Film Index* by Richard Dyer MacCann and Edward S. Perry; *Retrospective Index to Film Periodicals, 1930-1971* by Linda Batty; *The Critical Index, 1946-1973*, edited by John C. Gerlach and Linda Gerlach; *The Film Index: A Bibliography*, Volume 1: *The Film as Art* (silent era); and *Motion Picture Directors: A Bibliography of Magazine and Periodical Articles, 1900-1972* by Mel Schuster provide a huge number of animation and experimental film citations published in a wide range of film and general publications. Most of these titles, except Schuster's, are reviewed in three articles cited in the bibliography of this chapter: Abigail Nelson's "Guide to Indexes of Periodical Literature on Film," Marshall Deutelbaum's "A Guide to Recent Indexes to Film Literature," and the Donald E. Staples and Donald Walker article, "The Reference Shelf. Film Literature Indexes Reviewed."

Mel Schuster's *Motion Picture Directors: A Bibliography of Magazine and Periodical Articles, 1900-1972* contains numerous citations of many animators including Alexandre Alexeieff, Tex Avery, Saul Bass, Joy Batchelor, Jordan Belson, Robert Breer, Mary Ellen Bute, Bob Clampett, Gene Deitch, Walt Disney, Bob Godfrey, John Halas, John and Faith Hubley, Ub Iwerks, Chuck Jones, Yoji Kuri, Jan Lenica, Norman McLaren, George Pal, Ernest Pintoff, Lotte Reiniger, Hans Richter, Frank Tashlin, Jiři Trnka, and Stan Vanderbeek. Schuster searched 340 periodicals and other sources and arranged his citations alphabetically. While the above list certainly does not exhaust published animators, his efforts will help anyone get started. He also provides a list of directors on whom no material has been published. His bibliography also embraces several fanzines such as *Cinefantastique*, *Famous Monsters of Filmland*, and *Photon* which are not normally indexed in the standard locators.

The *Cumulated Dramatic Index, 1909-1949* is a cumulation of forty-one annuals of the *Dramatic Index* covering critical, historical, and biographical articles in American and British journals. Users should note that access to the material is by animator name, film title, and perhaps character name, and the subjects "animated cartoons" and "moving pictures." There appears to be little cross-referencing.

Kemp Niver's *Motion Pictures from the Library of Congress Paper Print Collection, 1894-1912* is a critically important guide to 3,000 early motion pictures deposited in the Library of Congress in the form of paper prints. After 1948 the prints were rephotographed onto 16mm negative film, resulting in the recovery of projectable records of this early period. Cartoons and other animations are separated by category and each film listed is accompanied with a detailed synopsis and provides producer, director, distributor, and length data.

Other standard indexes can lead one into more animation literature, usually accessed with the terms *moving picture, motion pictures,* or *cartoons*. These include the *New York Times Index* (1951-), *British Humanities Index* (1915-), *Arts and Humanities Citation Index* (1978-), *Public Affairs Information Service Bulletin* (1915-), *Art Index* (1929-), *Readers Guide to Periodical Literature* (1890-), *Catholic Periodical Index* (1930-), and the *Business Periodicals Index* (1960-).

There is now an index for *TV Guide*, the important chronicle of the programming side of American television: *TV Guide Twenty-Five Year Index*. The scope of coverage is from the first issue 3 April 1953 through 31 December 1977, 520 pages long, with the index embracing the feature articles of the journal, not the program listings. Hundreds of categories include programs that were developed as features in the magazine, cartoon programs, animated characters, authors, and many others. The microfilms for each year are also available, or as a twenty-six year package.

A great deal of material about the business and regulatory side of animation is contained in the trade journals *Broadcasting* (1931-), *Variety* (1905-), *Moving Picture World* (1907-1927), and *Motography* (1909-1918) at various times during their runs (see Appendix 7). *Topicator* (1965-) has selectively indexed *Variety* and *Broadcasting* material as it related to animation in television and advertising since the mid-1960s. *Moving Picture World* printed generalized indexes for each volume but these are nearly useless for animation subjects unless one is very familiar with company names or cartoonists whose work was animated. *Motography* also contains numerous reports about early animation, but these are inaccessible unless one has the time for a page-by-page review. For the first time, over four hundred citations from these trades and other serials, including the *New York Times*, are provided in Appendix 6 of this reference guide, "Selected and Annotated Trade Journals and Popular Press Reports in Animation, 1906-1979." The annotated citations have their own index by subject, personality, and film titles.

Systematic scholarly studies about animation and experimental subjects are contained in Raymond Fielding's updated *A Bibliography of Theses and Dissertations on the Subject of Film: 1916-1979*, published by the University Film Association as Monograph No. 3. This is an indispensable aid for any serious study of animation, experimental film, or film theory. Fielding's earlier reports were contained in separate issues of the *Journal of the University Film Association*. Of the 2,129 entries, twenty-eight were classified as animation theses or dissertations. However, as with any index, readers should take careful note of related categories such as "science fiction, fantasy and horror films," "film and television/video," and "special effects in films." While some studies in computer graphics and computer animation are reported in the Fielding compilation, a number are missing. Frequently, when theses and dissertations are titled, with key words selected by their authors, the terms *film* or *computer animation* or *computer graphics* are not always mentioned. Then again, the last two labels are not defined by the authors as having film implications. So these studies, typically originated in engineering departments in American universities, are not accumulated in the Fielding or other reports. When using *Dissertation Abstracts* in search of these technical studies, searchers should note that computer applications in animation are typically found in engineering categories. If using the *Dialogue* data base from Lockheed Information Systems, the same protocol would apply. *Dissertation Abstracts* can be criticized on this point because this classification system is not always abundantly clear, but trial-and-error searching should minimize crucial omissions. Because animation and graphic art found a new distribution outlet on television, the John Kittross *Bibliography of Theses and Dissertations in Broadcasting: 1920-1973* is of some limited use. But the technical subjects of digital television and related animated titles and special effects are not found in this guide. Those access words mentioned above can also be applied to *Dissertation Abstracts* or *Dialogue* data base.

In the experimental film realm which also involves animation, Thomas Brandon annotated all the articles which appeared in the short-lived *Experimental Cinema* (1930-1933) in an article in the *Journal of the University Film Association*, entitled, "The Advance Guard of a New Motion Picture Art: Experimental Cinema, 1930-1933." Concentrating on two filmmakers, one an experimentalist (Richter), Herman Weinberg compiled *An Index to the Creative Work of Robert J. Flaherty and Hans Richter*, published as a supplement in the *Sight and Sound* series by the British Film Institute. Georges Sadoul published a similar list of Georges Méliès's work one year later, 1947.

Another specialized resource with a behavioral orientation containing citations about media effects, processes, and socialization is *Mass Communication Effects and Processes* by Thomas F. Gordon and Mary Ellen Verna. Here users will find the studies dealing with the effects of televised (or filmed) violence or advertising upon children and others. The literature review is well organized under five main categories with several subtopics, all clearly described in a preliminary note.

Television News Index and Abstracts, published monthly by the Vanderbilt Television News Archive, contains outlines and abstracts for each of the nightly network television newscasts. Vanderbilt also offers a service of compiling rental videotapes of selections made from its videotape collection if users want to study the use of graphics, video art, digital special effects, or computer animation in TV news. In this case, the Vanderbilt archive has existed from 1968 to the present, so it is slightly older than the newer electronic technologies. Additional information on this archive and others is contained in Appendix 2, "Major Research Centers."

In 1980, the Archives of American Art announced the long awaited *Arts in America: A Bibliography*, comprised of 24,000 annotated entries from the literature of the visual and performing arts, including film. The index claims to be the most comprehensive list of persons, places, institutions, societies, exhibition catalogues and related materials, media, techniques, styles, events, and objects.

Animation has a body of critical literature, but this is often buried in book-length anthologies by critics, some theoretical tomes, and numerous periodicals and newspapers. The collection of reviews from one of the country's reliable newspapers is contained in the *New York Times Film Reviews* (1913-1976, with supplements) published by Arno Press. The reprinted reviews are arranged chronologically, but there is an index for film titles, production companies, and names. Stephen E. Bowles has published *Index to Critical Film Reviews in British and American Film Periodicals*, with an extensive collection of citations from thirty-two film magazines (1932-1971). In three volumes, one and two concentrate on the film reviews and the third volume contains reviews of books about film. Three additional finding aids published in the last five years have opened the gates to critical literature more than ever before. Gordon Samples wrote *How to Locate Reviews of Plays and Films: A Bibliography of Criticism from the Beginnings to the Present*, published by Scarecrow in 1976. Richard Heinzkill provided yet another unusual but valuable access tool in his *Film Criticism: An Index to Critics' Anthologies*, which quickly identifies anything and everything James Agee, Raymond Durgnat, Penelope Gilliatt, Pauline Kael, Graham Green, Stanley Kauffman, John Simon, and thirty-three other authors have written on animation or other subjects. Film titles are also listed.

Finally, the *Newsbank Review of the Arts* is comprised of four sections with the "Film and Television" section listing directors, media celebrities, film and television program titles, and subjects. *Newsbank* selects local news stories, reviews, and other materials from 120 newspapers published in all states. The articles are reproduced in their entirety on microfiche and released monthly along with an index. Monthly indexes are cumulated quarterly and annually. For animation, the *Newsbank* system brings together criticism and reviews of animated films and television programs in one place and is reasonably up-to-date but some major newspapers such as the *New York Times*, *Christian Science Monitor*, and *Los Angeles Times* are omitted from the collection.

One index to film awards in the United States was available by the end of the 1970s: Richard Shale's *Academy Awards: An Ungar Reference Index*. This authoritative listing begins with the inception of the Academy of Motion Picture Arts and Sciences in 1927. Shale's opening chapter provides a fascinating history of the awards but most of the book is devoted to the films, filmmakers, and titles earning the Oscars in the numerous categories, including animation and special effects.

THE GENERAL LITERATURE

Six subdivisions comprise this organization of the general literature to animation. These are (1) General History, (2) Animation in Television, (3) Political and Social Aspects of Animation, (4) Audiences for Animation,

(5) Criticism and (6) Theory. As in the preceding section, a bibliography of citations is presented by topic and in alphabetical order at the end of this chapter. There are also related topics in this guide which should be checked. Two other lists include the essays on individual animators and the four individual classes of animation established for this guide; both are contained in Chapter 4.

GENERAL HISTORY

Three book-length treatments outline early attempts to animate drawings and photographs in the prehistory of the motion picture. C. W. Ceram's *Archaelogy of the Cinema* is cited most often and begins with the early attempts to animate drawings, mostly in games and toys. But, Olive Cook's *Movement in Two Dimensions* focuses on related areas, such as the panorama shows and Oriental puppet influences in the early motion picture, with more detail on the attempts to animate lantern slides. Helmut and Alison Gernsheim's work *L. J. M. Daguerre* focuses on the invention of photography along with descriptions of early attempts to create the illusion of reality through the diorama. Two additional books explain the contributions of Eadweard Muybridge. Keven MacDonnell's *Eadweard Muybridge: The Man Who Invented the Moving Picture* is a more orderly exposition of his contributions, but, for those learning to animate human and animal forms, the models presented in Muybridge's *Human and Animal Locomotion* are still relevant today.

Practically every history of the American or world film has given short shrift to animation, collapsing this rich and related history into a few pages at most. Some books at least recognize the form, as in Thomas W. Bohn and Richard L. Stromgren's *Light and Shadows: A History of Motion Pictures*, or the more worldwide view in Jack C. Ellis's *A History of Film*. The Ellis volume includes a fuller description of European influences, especially those stemming from the French and German experimental groups in the 1920s. The earlier Lewis Jacobs history, *The Rise of the American Film*, contained a short hymn to Mr. Disney and omits all others. William K. Everson's *American Silent Film* also devotes only four to five pages to the subject, but these emphasize the often overlooked silent era.

Leonard Maltin's *Of Mice and Magic: A History of American Animated Cartoons* devotes an entire chapter to silent cartoons. Moreover, his book remains the only history which attempts to embrace the whole evolution of American theatrical animation from the silent period up through the 1960s. Maltin has organized his work by studio or producer organization, including the major producers such as Disney, the Fleischers, United Productions of America, Warner Brothers, and, for the first time, detailed accounts of the personalities, procedures, and products of the minor studios. Paul Terry, Walter Lantz, Van Beuren, MGM, Paramount's Famous Studios, Ub Iwerks, and Columbia's Screen Gems are those included in the minor list, based on original interviews, quotations from previously published (but not referenced) materials, and other descriptions of what Maltin and others considered "important" animation examples by each producer. The organization of the book works well, to a point, and one does grasp some sense of continuity despite the fact that the small cadre of animators which developed and innovated story, technique, and technical devices in this industry were often split apart, constantly on the move, and into and out of various producer organizations. To organize this tome by animator would endlessly confuse the reader.

The most disappointing aspect of this work is the lack of documentation except for casual and incomplete references to names of the other interviewers or the published and unpublished data. There is no bibliography in the 1980 version, which becomes a cardinal sin in a book calling itself a history. As history, Maltin does fill in the presumably factual story, but none of the chapters attempts to bring the producer organization into any other context. The concluding chapter, "The Rest of the Story," does little to draw the entire work together for some assessment, interpretation, or concluding set of arguments. While some changes are identified in the conclusion, other factors contributing to high costs of production and competition for audiences are omitted, although these matters affected the demise of the theatrical cartoon in the United States. The early 1970s is a good place to conclude the history, but not without some assessment of American animation and a fuller picture of the American animated film in related contexts, such as the film industry. The author is occasionally given to oversimplification or exaggeration in spots. From his description of Charles Mintz (p. 206), ". . . when he stole Disney's staff and starring character . . . " one gets an incomplete and inaccurate picture. "One might say that Gertie [the Dinosaur, animated by Winsor McCay, described on p. 5] launched an entire industry . . ." is a statement of some exaggeration that potentially misleads the reader. Whether sound sent "shock waves" through the film industry depends upon the point of view at the time (p. 127).

Despite the documentation problem, *Of Mice and Magic: A History of American Animated Cartoons* is still a useful description. The citations to the landmark cartoons, together with the filmography of each studio given at the end of the volume, provide useful perspectives for the scholar or teacher requiring informed opinion for renting or purchasing representative examples. These sections also provide a strong complement to Appendix 5 of this reference guide, which lists over 1000 Super 8mm silent and sound cartoons now available for sale.

Other general histories include Mike Barrier's long planned *History of American Cartoons* to be published by Oxford University Press, which was, in 1980, still being completed. Ralph Stephenson's *The Animated Film* has some historical aspects but is mainly a dated world survey of animation and distinctly favors British and European offerings. Thelma Schenkel's 1977 dissertation contains a lengthy and very useful review of European and Russian animation literature including Robert Benayon's study of Walt Disney and Gianni Rondolino's world animation history with some attention to individual artists. The Schenkel dissertation is available in microfilm or hard xerox copy from University Microfilms. Schenkel's study also emphasizes the work of John and Faith Hubley and Jan Lenica and contains historical perspectives. However, Donald Clayton Crafton's study, "Emile Cohl and the Origins of the Animated Film," is more to the historical mark, with a more definitive and well-documented historical framework in the silent period.

While animation in the teens and early 1920s is superficially treated, Kalton C. Lahue's *World of Laughter: The Motion Picture Comedy Short, 1910-1930* contains some references to the form. The more definitive work which carefully documents early, trick, animated forms is Kemp R. Niver's *The First Twenty Years*, based on his work recovering the paper positives in the Library of Congress. Anthony Slide's *The Big V: A History of the Vitagraph Company* contains the most authoritative descriptions of J. Stuart Blackton's early work in filmmaking and animation. Slide's *Aspects of American Film History Prior to 1920* also contains a useful chapter describing early film magazines and trade journals reviewed by one who has read and sifted the contents of a large number of these issues in several books. An overview of film technology, and the often-quoted Earl Theisen piece on animation history which contains some inaccuracies, are reprinted in Raymond Fielding's *A Technological History of Motion Pictures and Television*. This book also republishes several pieces about early special effects, laboratory practices, and color technology, originally published in the *Journal of the Society of Motion Picture and Television Engineers*. This journal, along with many other periodicals of animation interest, is described in Appendix 7.

Danny and Gerald Peary have put together a useful anthology about American animation published by E. P. Dutton in 1980. *The American Animated Cartoon: A Critical Anthology* has six major divisions with selections on early history, Walt Disney, Warner Brothers, cartoon characters, other studios, and opinion about "cartoons today." There is a rich but buried literature in this area of film, and the Peary volume has helped locate and preserve it for students, buffs, and practitioners. However, the inclusion of Walt Disney's testimony before the House Committee on Un-American Activities is trivial, apparently reprinted to demonstrate that even animation is touched with politics—which has been known all along. The author's omission of Disney's followup retraction about the League of Women Voters leaves a distorted impression. (See Appendix 6, item 288 for an appropriate citation to balance this problem.) Further, the authors are incorrect about having the "only interview with Robert McKimson," as another is contained in a master's thesis by Roger Bullis described in Chapter 4 under "personalities." Despite these problems, this anthology redeems itself on the strength of the contributors.

Some interesting historical perspectives in animation at midpoint in World War II were published in an obscure but important document entitled *Writers' Congress*, which was a report of a 1943 conference sponsored by the Hollywood Writer's Mobilization and the University of California. The conference presented papers by practitioners in film, radio, and other media and their perceptions about their work in the war effort. Reports by Sergeant John Hubley, Karl Van Leuven, Phil Eastman, and Sergeant Franklin Thomas are published. Another document based on lectures given to students in the Harvard Business School in the late 1920s by film industry leaders contains important perspectives for the short subject by Earle W. Hammons, which have distinct implications for the animated film in that period. The work was edited by Joseph P. Kennedy and titled *The Story of the Films*.

Several books describing the technique of animation also contain brief history sections but the most perceptive and interdisciplinary work is contained in Roy Madsen's *Animated Film: Concepts, Methods, Uses*. The carefully researched Thomas Cripps study of blacks in film, *Slow Fade to Black: The Negro in American Film, 1900-1942*, contains an important review of animated stereotypes of the 1920s and 1930s, along with observations on Cab Calloway's singing in the Fleischer animations of *Betty Boop*.

Donald Heraldson's *Creators of Life: A History of Animation* is titled a history, but according to his own published report in *Film Collector's World*, and a close reading, it was his publisher who put that title on the book. Heraldson's work is distinctly a book about technique, not a history, and should be read for that kind of experience. While the history sections are informative in a general sense, there are too many errors or contradictions, along with undocumented interviews, which make this book, as history, only marginally reliable.

Other works which have documented historical material on animation include Tino Balio's *The American Film Industry*, a reader which contains very useful perspectives on film history in which animation was clearly influenced. Terry Ramsaye's *A Million and One Nights: A History of the Motion Picture* is an important anecdotal and personal history but unreliable, without corroboration from other sources. Animation is neglected in this book, but, in fairness, this form of film in American silent films did not have much visibility during the period. There are, however, mentions of newspaper cartoonists some of whom had their strips animated. Typical of the sketchy treatment given the silent animated cartoon, Kalton C. Lahue's *Motion Picture Pioneer: The Selig Polyscope Company*, one of the few company histories, barely mentions Sidney Smith's animation efforts, which were among the earliest based on a comic strip. David L. Lewis's *The Public Image of Henry Ford: An American Folk Hero and His Company*, upon first glance, appears to be limited to a review of the Ford public relations story. But the book opens new leads to the Ford film unit, the first established by a corporation in America. Some animation was included in Ford newsreels released free to theaters. The Maurice Bardeche and Robert Brasillach text, *The History of Motion Pictures*, is of only marginal use for animation, but Arthur Knight's revised *The Liveliest Art: A Panoramic History of the Movies* provides the overview of the films themselves, telling the reader in the preface that animation is left out of his book because, in his rationale, animation has developed independently and merits a separate book on the subject. With regard to this independence, he is incorrect. Animation in the 1930s and 1940s developed more fully because the studio system could afford this investment in shorts. Disney led the way, and others were eager to, and did, emulate this experiment. When the studio system was broken up by the consent decrees, the demise of the short-subject animated cartoon soon followed. While there were multiple forces acting upon these subjects, it is abundantly clear that the studio system helped sustain the animated film in America through the 1930s and 1940s. Thus, these situations were not independent but interdependent.

The Technique of Film Music by Roger Manvell and John Huntley contains a valuable, although incomplete, history of music in the American and British film but is still a useful starting point in exploring the use of sound with animated images. The appendixes contain a select bibliography, Gerald Pratley's criticism of film music, and a chronology.

Since the early animated cartoon spun out of the comic strip, a number of comic strip histories also contain chapters and sections about animation. Stephen Becker's *Comic Art in America* clearly describes the evolution of that print form and personalities, but the narrative also mentions the numerous and complex interdependencies early animated cartoons obtained with their print counterparts and their original artists. Pierre Couperie's *History of the Comic Strip* attempts to integrate the strips in societal and media contexts with a useful chapter on audiences for the comics and another on narrative technique. John Geipel's *The Cartoon: A Short History of Graphic Comedy and Satire* has one chapter on animated cartoons but contains some small inaccuracies. The larger perspective for these amusements is also provided in Foster Rhea Dulles's *A History of Recreation: America Learns to Play*.

William Murrell emphasizes the contributions of William R. Hearst in promoting the comic strip and several of the early cartoonists whose strips were converted into animated films. His *A History of American Graphic Humor* embraces the period 1865 to 1938. Martin Sheridan's *Comics and Their Creators*, originally published in 1942, is more a gossipy collection of anecdotes about many of the early strip artists, their cartoons and animations.

A number of periodical articles have appeared since the earliest silent days of animation, but only a few are discussed here, with the remainder indicated in the bibliography at the end of the chapter. Vlada Petric's essay, which organizes various approaches to film history, is an important starting point for anyone undertaking this task. In animation, Jules Schwerin's 1949 piece in *Theater Arts* is a good review of animation's prehistory, embracing the traditional cave drawings, Mediterranean sculptural arts, and the Oriental influences. But, the Joseph Anderson and Barbara Fisher destruction of the historic basis of the "persistence of vision" theory gives us all reason for pause, and clearly indicates the need for returning to original sources to check "facts" that mushroom into misleading generalizations. Conrad Smith's "Early History of Animation" fills a void in the development of the early silent cartoon along with Isadore Klein's recollections about Winsor McCay in *Cartoonist Profiles* (no. 34) in which McCay's relationship with the Hearst organization is clarified. "Of Mice, Wabbits, Ducks and Men" by Mike Barrier is among the few analytical pieces on animation style among several characters and studios. The articles by Andre Martin, Roger Manvell, and Leonard Maltin form a nicely dovetailed chronology of sound animation through World War II. Arthur Knight's "Engaging the Eye-Minded" draws connections between the live-action film and experimental animated films instead of considering them separate, independent entities. The postwar period is outlined by John Hubley, John Halas, David Bowman, and Mark Trost up through 1979. The educator, Arthur Edwin Krows, published a long-running series of detailed articles in *Educational Screen* from mid-1936 through the early 1940s, discussing the development of the educational, nontheatrical film. Upon subsequent checking with an independent indexing project in the trade journals and other sources, a number of assertions by Krows find more contradiction than corroboration in the animation literature. His long series was ostensibly based upon trade journal reports collected over twenty years, when the movies were young, and it does provide at least the broad brushstrokes in an area of film history still neglected.

ANIMATION IN TELEVISION

Lincoln Diamont's *Television's Classic Commercials: The Golden Years, 1948-1958* provides a brief history of commercials, including the animated winners. Three dissertations by Anthony M. Maltese, Robert Lee Bailey, and Robert Hammel Stewart provide authoritative and reliable data on, respectively, the evolution of children's TV programming, prime-time specials, and network television program types up to 1953. Animated programs were discussed in all three works and others are identified in John Kittross's *Bibliography of Theses and Dissertations in Broadcasting: 1920-1973*. Chapter three in William Melody's *Children's TV: The Economics of Exploitation*, while containing an inherent bias as suggested by the title, is still a useful history on this controversial topic. With regard to programming, the periodical articles by John C. Waugh, Stan Crock, Alexis Greene, and Tom Shales provide important perspectives on the development of animated programs aimed at children. In the arena of animated commercial messages, the landmark is probably John Halas's "Cartoon Films in Commerce." Several citations about specific product "case studies," assertions and arguments on behalf of animation in TV sports, and perceptions of current trends are included in the bibliography for this section. Brief histories of varying quality include the pieces by Arthur Ross, Harry Wayne McMahan, Jeffrey Altshuler, DeWitt O'Kieffe, and Alice C. Wolf. *Millimeter* published Wolf's seven-part "History of American Television Commercials, 1947-1977," which started out strong but ended quite diluted and rambling.

POLITICAL AND SOCIAL ASPECTS OF ANIMATION

I. C. Jarvie in his 1970 survey of the literature, *Movies and Society*, views film as a social phenomenon, ". . . one social institution among many" (p. xiv). While he has little to say about animation except for Walt Disney (and that is brief), his book is a good framework for understanding the industry and the audience. The bibliography, which comprises slightly over one-third of the book, is worth the price alone at used book costs. But the value of this work is not for animation exclusively but for its social and critical orientations and its thorough review of literature from 1914 to about 1968.

Another synthesized work which concentrates on the legal and political dimensions of the American film is the dissertation by Garth S. Jowett which has been published as *Film: The Democratic Art*. Except for some irritating minor errors, and a euphoric and constant reference to the "best" of various cited works, Jowett's academic study is a useful review of "Media Power and Social Control: The Motion Picture in America, 1894-1936." With respect to the numerous mini-hymns Jowett sings to various references, one must be refuted here: that is his bald assertion that the "best" available history of the animated cartoon is Ralph Stephenson's *The Animated Film* (discussed in the "General History" section above). For one thing, it is not a history. For another, as animation history, the book is most inadequate. Jonathan Price's *The Best Thing on TV— Commercials* is a bouncy salute to commercials, explaining their production and characteristics, along with a historical thread woven into the outline of the book. In some ways, his book presents another critical orientation for commercials if one classifies them by danger elements, violence, sex, overdirection, extravagance, and regulation.

Journal articles on the political and social aspects of animation encompass a large range of subjects, from propaganda applications, censorship and religious implications, to political satire. Robert Yung's "Animation's Role: Projection of Ideas, Logic, Abstractions" in *Public Relations Journal* is one of the few detailed arguments in behalf of using animated films for promoting abstract ideas. A number of citations given in the bibliography to this chapter describe the recent political barriers the American cartoons have encountered overseas, providing an important counterpoint to the often-held assertion that animation crosses political frontiers without any hassles from indigenous governments. Bill Paul's piece, "Donald Duck Faces a Morals Charge in Western Europe," is a typical example. Other pieces have more ominous political overtones such as Dave Wagner's "interview" with Donald Duck. Stephen Jay Gould's research in "This View of Life: Mickey Mouse Meets Konrad Lorenz" changes the mouse by a metamorphosis to a more juvenile character, enhancing his appeal among adults. Other articles seem appropriate for listing in the bibliography for this section because they deal with the system in which animation is produced or influenced, such as the Francis Arnold essay, "Out of This World," a rare review of science fiction which the animated form has often exploited. A number of recent reports about animation in news and public affairs television and the rise of their graphic quality are also listed.

AUDIENCES FOR ANIMATION

This subdivision of the general literature brings together some key research sources, the important essays and reports on educational applications in animation, aspects of the children and television issues, and scientific applications.

First, anyone researching educational applications in the media generally, and animation in particular, should include certain benchmark references and finding aids which will provide guideposts to this very large body of literature. The research sources by Charles F. Hoban, Jr.; J. Christopher Reid and Donald W. MacLennan; Godwin C. Chu and Wilbur Schramm; and George Comstock and Marilyn Fisher should not be overlooked. Recent reports by the staffs of the Federal Trade Commission and Federal Communications Commission use empirical studies as a base for their regulatory recommendations and have an advantage in providing reasonably up-to-date information in a dynamic field. Other works such as Leo A. Handel's *Hollywood Looks at Its Audience* are more historical from this point in time but, like Jarvie's *Movies and Society* (discussed in the preceding section), provide the framework for problem analysis. The two theses by William B. Stutler and Kenneth Bauer Frye are examples of early academic research into the impact of animated advertising. The necessary updates can be found by consulting the John Kittross *A Bibliography of Theses and Dissertations in Broadcasting: 1920-1973*, and *Journalism Abstracts*, published annually by the Association for Education in Journalism (AEJ), 431 Murphy Hall, University of Minnesota, Minneapolis, Minnesota 55455. This guide lists doctoral and masters theses at some sixty AEJ member institutions in the United States.

Publications of the Educational Resources Information Center (ERIC), 4833 Rugby Avenue, Suite 303, Bethesda, Maryland 20014, are available in most research libraries at major universities. ERIC systematically gathers reports of media applications in education and publishes cumulative catalogues indexing those reports, along with a document reproduction service.

More directly to the subject of animation and cultural influences is Michael R. Real's *Mass-Mediated Culture*. The author organized the interdisciplinary approaches to mass culture with specific case studies describing the dynamics and categories of that culture. Chapter 2 describes the "Disney Universe" based on a questionnaire from about two hundred respondents who spent considerable time in Disneyland. While Real's case studies suggested some kind of Armageddon in media-culture, he overlooked the implications of specialized media which serve to fragment mass-communication audiences. Still more to the point, Richard Schickel's *The Disney Version* exhaustively reviewed one view about Disney's influence in the mass culture of America.

A selection of assorted trade journal and other periodical articles is included in the bibliography to illustrate the general scope and type of material typically published. Among the more interesting perspectives are those of Ray Bradbury and Chuck Jones concerning the role of fantasy in film in an interview published by Mary Harrington Hall. On a practical but commercial side, one would find "What's Wrong With Children's Commercials?" by Shel Feldman and Abraham Wolf a typical analytical piece by researchers that might be of some value to animators. The independent or experimental film is less direct in its influence on the film and television media and its own audiences. Indeed, some of these filmmakers espouse contempt for mass audiences entirely; others seek some audience if only to pay for their increasing costs in the marketplace. Scott

MacDonald's article, "Independent Film: Where's the Audience?" is one of the few pieces that attempt to identify the barriers to acceptance. I would add also that the extremely high print costs these filmmakers put on their films work to their distinct disadvantage, since institutional acquisitions and personal prints are also severely affected by limited budgets. The most outrageous price escalations in Super 8mm (1980) have occurred in the offerings of some selected experimental or independently produced films distributed by Pyramid, where costs are simply gouging the public and private purses.

In educational applications, Lewis Herman's book *Educational Films: Writing, Directing and Producing for Classroom, Television and Industry* is useful because it gives a practical perspective. Kathryn Smoot Caldwell's dissertation, "Guidelines and Principles for the Utilization of Animation in Instructional Films and Videotapes," should be carefully consulted before research is conducted in the animated medium. Two other dissertations by Judith Elaine Garrett and Dennis T. Aronson are of lesser value but contain adequate reviews of literature. Periodical literature in the educational applications of animation is typically historical, such as Walt Disney's reminiscences of techniques used in educational films during World War II. William D. Schmidt has distilled some findings from his dissertation in "Analyzing the Design of Outstanding Instructional Films," to see to what degree research results and producer opinions have affected the final product.

The most carefully researched and designed instructional films and television programs have been based on the various techniques used in numerous episodes of "Sesame Street" on public television. Some of the dissertations, books, and contract studies referring to animation are cited in the bibliography under the "audiences for animation" category. Recent periodicals have published criticism of the techniques along with some historical analyses on the form of the program.

The issue of children's television is multidimensional, involving potential regulation, program design, violence and subsequent aggression and whether advertising has some negative impact on children. Most of the literature has dealt with the two major issues of the last three decades: aggression and advertising. Among the dissertations is that of Naomi Slutzky Goldstein which claims to be the first (1957) dealing with the aggression issue and cartoons. While the results of this study were not significant, it does give an adequate literature review up to 1956. But the flood of studies in this subject occurred after 1956 and continued through the 1970s. Some television networks also sponsored research and the CBS studies are but one example. The Marianne P. and Charles Winick book and the earlier work by Grant Noble are restatements or reconceptualizations of the overall problems but only offer modest opinions concerning the impact of animated forms on children. The Douglas Cater and Stephen Strickland report describes the "fate" of the surgeon general's report on television violence and the child.

John Murray's *Television and Youth: 25 Years of Research and Controversy* is a very recent literature review embracing thirteen specialized bibliographies and an overview of the topic, including the effects process, violence issues, advertising, socialization of television, public policy matters, and role portrayals. The bibliographies begin with the violence issue, socialization functions of television, and advertising, and extend to audience viewing patterns, public policy questions, and private actions. A master index ties this important tool together. Write: Boys Town Center for the Study of Youth Development, Boys Town, Nebraska 68010.

A recent review and critical synthesis of theory and research in the learning process involving television is contained in the *Human Communication Research* article by Tannis Macbeth Williams, "How and What Do Children Learn From Television?" From an animation vantage point, children are strongly attracted to action, scene and character changes, unusual voices, optical effects such as dissolves, fades, and reverse actions, and special visual effects. However, Williams concludes that American television, given its current content overall, has not performed a positive role in children's learning. This conclusion is discussed in the context of learning theory and dozens of scientific studies, fully referenced in the extensive bibliography of the article.

Content analyses, such as the F. Earle Barcus studies and the thesis by Birna R. Smith are important contributions because they document reliably what was actually telecast. A more detailed exposition of this history, however, is contained in the October 1979 Federal Communications Commission task force report on *Television Programming for Children* (five volumes).

Two major document sets created from the research by the National Commission on the Causes and Prevention of Violence and the U.S. Surgeon General's Report on *Television and Social Behavior* (listed in the bibliography under United States) contain valuable empirical studies and content analyses of American television and its hypothesized effects. The Robert Baker and Sandra Ball staff report is the summary for the commission. The hearings by the Senate Subcommittee on Communications contain the explanation and report of George Gerbner's violence profile and Alan Pearce's report on the economics of children's television programming by the networks.

John Culshaw's "Violence and the Cartoon" is an interesting piece because of its early publication in 1951 (before the issue gained wide currency) and his view that violence in this animated form was governed by a moral code also present in the cartoon, with some distinctions made among cartoons. Other citations in the bibliography involve content analyses, "popular culture," and summaries of current issues.

Animation techniques in support of scientific research and training have been incorporated into various films since about 1915. But in recent years, stop-motion photography, digital transmission from outer space, and digital memory systems tied to computers have brought new applications of the animated form in support of science. Many of these applications are widely available now, such as the stop-motion weather photographs taken from synchronous satellites, regularly seen on local TV weather shows. The 1980 flybys of Jupiter and Saturn used complex data transmission and picture reconstruction techniques, including a return to the old-fashioned thumb books in the January 1980 issue of *National Geographic*. There, in the corner of several pages, are reproduced time-lapse shots of the Jupiter cloud cover, easily animated with the flip of the pages. The article by William Rempel about navigational training aboard ship is another typical application, using interactive, computer-generated pictures projected on large television screens in full color and shaded to look three dimensional. Probably the most complex and medically significant application involves the second generation of x-ray scanners as described in the Lawrence Ingrassia and Charles W. Stevens material. There, finely focused x-rays radiate a target, forming images on a TV-like camera, building up "slices" of the anatomy into a composite picture of the body's interior.

CRITICISM

There is a distinct difference between criticism and theory in the literature of film. J. Dudley Andrew, in the introduction to *The Major Film Theories*, provides an informed and succinct basis for the distinction between criticism and theory and, by so doing, a definition for each. Many will recognize that scientific traditions influence these bases and definitions. Andrew is certainly not the first to articulate them but, in the context of film theory, he is among the few who clearly see the difference between criticism and theory. Film theory is simply a systematic understanding of a general phenomenon and, in Andrew's view, that phenomenon is the capability of cinema itself—operating or governing both the filmmaking process and the audience. I would add that this general understanding, developed systematically, aims to explain the phenomenon to such a degree that prediction is possible or testable. Criticism, on the other hand, relies to some degree on theory, but is simply an *evaluation* of examples of the phenomenon. Out of this exercise, a critic might help consumers "appreciate" individual films or one process without fully explaining film capabilities. Here, Andrew reminds us, criticism is not systematic. It can be random or casual. Indeed, as the citations to this section indicate, criticism of animation has covered a very broad range, from the fanzine, hobbyhorse opinions of favored animators and directors to the classic question, "Is animation art?" In between, the literature contains numerous chapters in books and articles that evaluate previously anonymous artists and their roles in the animation process. Various "schools" and persuasions are present, adding a rich dimension to the criticism of film generally but very little to animation in comparison. There is a school of criticism that persists in defining animation or film for us, by telling us anew what we saw, and attempting to provide some grand scheme about "what it all means." These are the content-analyzers of the latent material who usually manifest a symbol system of their own to emblazon the grand design of meaning, often mistakenly and erroneously labeled as "theory," unchecked and unsystematically determined.

The first written work which contemplated the film seriously was Vachel Lindsay's *The Art of the Moving Picture*, first published in 1915. Most of the critical writing about animation began in the early 1930s with a good portion dealing with artistic questions and Walt Disney. Some chapters in books, such as Jean Charlot's *Art from the Mayans to Disney*, took a long, historic view. Others, such as Ralph M. Pearson's *Experiencing American Pictures*, simply condemned Disney because of his interpretations of reality as represented in fully animated characters. For Pearson, "art" in animation or comics was based on manipulation, selection, isolation, and distortion which would ideally symbolize universal themes. Parker Tyler's chapter on Snow White in *The Hollywood Hallucination* followed with a similar argument. Disney's *Snow White and the Seven Dwarfs* (1937) was met with positive reviews overall, but considerable critical comment came later concerning the scary depiction of the witch. *Fantasia* (1940) brought forth the massive but mixed response to Disney's first attempt in mixing "high culture" with "low brow," in the words of one critic. Until the 1960s, most criticism consisted of reviews of animated films with some attention given the major transition away from "Disneyfication" manifested in the UPA product and foreign influences. Since many of these writings also discuss technique and history, readers should check other appropriate sections of this reference guide for those citations.

Ernest Callenback wrote *Our Modern Art: The Movies* in 1955, with two chapters devoted to the animated and experimental film in America. Manny Farber's *Negative Space: Manny Farber on the Movies* pays some attention to Warner Brothers cartoons in "Short and Happy, 1943." *Film: The Creative Eye* by David Sohn emphasizes the filmmaker and the creative process by analyzing the films of Saul Bass, Dan McLaughlin, Charles

Braverman, David Adams, and others. Gerald Mast and Marshall Cohen's *Film Theory and Criticism: Introductory Readings* contains Joe Adamson's "Suspended Animation," which beats to death *Charlotte's Web* with the club of traditional animation history in America, mainly that of Warner Brothers cartoons (Porky Pig, Bugs Bunny, the Roadrunner) and their creators, as well as the Disney works. The point is that the classic animations struck responsive chords with their audiences and dealt "with forces deeper within us than we sometimes care to admit."[2] The "externalization of internal life" in the Adamson universe[3] is also manifested in the films of Ray Harryhausen, Norman McLaren, Winsor McCay, Alexandre Alexeieff, and Karel Zeman, among others.

Gilbert Seldes's first review of Disney's work is republished in the Lewis Jacobs reader, *Introduction to the Art of the Movies*. In 1969, Jacobs put together another anthology entitled *The Emergence of Film Art*, dividing criticism in terms of silent film, the sound and color film, and the creative present. In each category, he included important essays involving animated film by Len Lye, William Kozlenko, Aline Saarinen, Harold Benson, Raymond Gid, and Jonas Mekas. The subjects critically examined include color, Walt Disney, animation as an art form, drawing in film, film titles by Saul Bass, and the experimental film in America. Michael Gould's *Surrealism and the Cinema* also includes a review of Disney's *Bambi* and *Fantasia* and the traditional arguments involving the mixing of two abstract media, animation and music. His comparisons of Disney and the Fleischers' Betty Boop is one of the better critiques of characters and technique. Critic Harry Alan Potamkin, who died in the early 1930s, had his writings brought together by Lewis Jacobs in *The Compound Cinema: The Film Writings of Harry Alan Potamkin*, in which Potamkin concluded that the Disney works were lacking too much in ideas. *Mastering the Film and Other Essays* contains the collected works of Charles Thomas Samuels which include critical discussions of animated forms and the experimental film.

While the anthologies of authors indicated above bring together some animation criticism, there are still other writings that remain buried in periodicals. The criticism section of this chapter's bibliography is one attempt to identify the forgotten pieces.

Criticism by the artist-practitioners is occasionally to be found in specialized film and art journals. Increasingly, although of limited distribution and irregular publication, the journals called fanzines contain a great deal of critical comment on technique, films, and filmmakers. These journals include *Cinefantastique, Funnyworld,* and *Animania* (formerly *Mindrot*) and are described in more detail in Appendix 7. While these criticisms are normally published in film reviews, letters to the editor often contain critical comment, as indicated in the three examples by Shamus Culhane, Reg Hartt, and Michael Sporn (listed under "Letters" in the bibliography).

THEORY

Theories about the capabilities of the film developed from two approaches in French cinema, according to Roy Armes, writing in his theoretical work, *Film and Reality: An Historical Survey*. Georges Méliès, before the turn of the century, was known for his "artificially arranged scenes," including the use of tricks. But Louis Lumière and his brother used the camera to record reality. From this, audiences have become conditioned to mixtures of realism and fantasy, including animation. In Armes's view, the film has evolved into three aesthetic perspectives: the ability to record and reproduce reality; the ability to imitate reality; and the ability to explore meanings of photographed objects or the inner reality beneath the surface. These three perspectives involve sign systems, comprising an index, an icon, or a symbol—concepts borrowed from Peter Wollen and his *Signs and Meaning in the Cinema*. The Armes work is an historical approach to explain the capacity of film "to cope with the contradictory demands of reality, fiction and modernist ideals."[4] Included in the last category, we would find the experimentalists, with the animators somewhere between fiction and the abstract film or those films relying upon symbols. About the time *Film and Reality* was published, Calvin Pryluck had defended his doctoral dissertation at the University of Iowa, entitled "Source of Meaning in Motion Pictures and Television," which has been since published by Arno Press in its film dissertation series. Both Pryluck and Armes have similar orientations concerning sign systems and the film experience, but Pryluck develops his theory more fully along empirical lines by first establishing the domain of film which, in his view and that of others, has not been appropriately defined. Thus, these works and that of J. Dudley Andrew, referenced earlier, serve as a summation of literature reviews of film theory but are not substitutes therefor, of course. Each contains comprehensive bibliographies of the major theoretical works.

Robert T. Eberwein developed a guide to film theory writings entitled *A Viewer's Guide to Film Theory and Criticism*, providing a gateway to the ideas of some twenty critics and theorists.

With respect to the history of the animated form in American film and the chronology in Appendix 1, there is a clearly defined audience acceptance of newer forms in film and television, affected by previous epochs of experimentation and innovation. For example, in terms of technique, the close-up around 1909 was not met with universal acceptance. In fact, Pryluck cited one irate critic who complained about the cutting off of characters at their waists and shoulders. There are other such critical commentaries on the evolving form still buried in the trade journals and related literature. But American audiences, once reared on the narrative form and storytelling editorial techniques, bristled when jump-cuts were introduced experimentally and later appeared in numerous films by the mid-1960s. Younger audiences, not as long conditioned to the film narrative, seemed to relish these changes and accepted them almost immediately.

The quest for certainty (to avoid live-TV goofs) and economic considerations sharply expanded the use of film in television advertising in the early 1950s, and as time got more expensive to buy for long, sixty-second messages, the costs further influenced the form of those messages. Shorter, twenty- and thirty-second messages used stylized images, stills-in-motion, and stereotyped ideas and themes to put across several bits of information, usually anchoring them in emotional appeals. The abbreviated and graphic manner in which the messages were made, some using animated forms, was transplanted to television titles, news, and public affairs programs by the 1970s. Because editing requires an understanding of intervals between frames in a micro-sense (one shot placed against another), and in a macro-sense (sequences into films), the formerly "realist" perspective associated with the traditional Lumière methods (early documentary) has been drastically altered to manipulations approaching the Méliès "artificially arranged scenes," along with synthesized and asynchronous sound tracks. In some film sequences, the sound track has taken over the narrative while the images project abstractions. The traditional forms of animation have expanded far beyond the use of drawings and cels, and include rotoscope mattes used to build up composite images, computer-generated images for cartoons or documentaries, and other special effects. The narrative film developed in America is not out of date, but its form had been altered. Changes in form seem to have occurred faster than in earlier periods in the history of film and television, probably because the internal, conservative, decision-systems in the film industry, at least, no longer had the same monopoly. The infection of following a winner and clinging to the status quo, absent from an independent Disney organization and many others, is still a disease that could potentially consume the television industry. On the horizon are new channels in the form of pay cable, home computers, and cassette and disc programs which, if developed, will fragment the television industry perhaps to the state that network radio now exhibits. Financially, there is a lot at stake.

If the past is any guide, the assessments about film and TV capabilities being underutilized are correct. What is more interesting are the few glimpses available in the image versions of popular music released on videodisc. If these examples are reliable signs, the form of such content is moving farther away from realism into the realm of the fantastic.

NOTES

1. L. Bruce Holman, *Puppet Animation in the Cinema: History and Technique* (New York: A. S. Barnes, 1975), p. 12.

2. Joe Adamson, "Suspended Animation," in *Film Theory and Criticism: Introductory Readings*, edited by Gerald Mast and Marshall Cohen (New York: Oxford University Press, 1974), p. 615.

3. Ibid.

4. Roy Armes, *Film and Reality: An Historical Survey* (Middlesex, England: Penguin Books, 1974), p. 13.

BIBLIOGRAPHY

REFERENCES

Aceto, Vincent J.; Graves, Jane; and Silva, Fred. *Film Literature Index.* Albany, N.Y.: Filmdex, 1975.

American Film Institute. *The American Film Institute Catalog of Motion Pictures Produced in the United States: Feature Films, 1921-1930.* 2 vols. New York: R. R. Bowker, 1971.

_____. *The American Film Institute Catalog of Motion Pictures Produced in the United States: Feature Films, 1961-1970.* 2 vols. New York: R. R. Bowker, 1976.

_____. *Factfile: Animation.* Washington, D.C.: American Film Institute, 1977.

Anderson, R. H. *A Selective Bibliography of Computer Graphics.* Santa Monica, Calif.: Rand Memorandum P-4629, April 1971.

Archives of American Art. *Arts in America: A Bibliography.* 4 vols. Edited by Bernard Karpel. Washington, D.C.: Smithsonian Institution and Archives of American Art, 1980.

Art Index. New York: H. W. Wilson, 1929.

Arts and Humanities Citation Index. Philadelphia: Institute for Scientific Information, 1977-.

Batty, Linda. *Retrospective Index to Film Periodicals, 1930-71.* New York: R. R. Bowker, 1975.

Bawden, Liz-Anne, ed. *The Oxford Companion to Film.* New York: Oxford University Press, 1976.

Becker, Stephen. *Comic Art in America.* New York: Simon and Schuster, 1959.

Bowles, Stephen E. *An Approach to Film Study, A Selected Booklist.* New York: Revisionist Press, 1974.

_____. *Index to Critical Film Reviews in British and American Film Periodicals.* New York: Burt Franklin, 1974-75.

Brandon, Thomas. "The Advance Guard of A New Motion Picture Art: Experimental Cinema, 1930-1933." *Journal of the University Film Association* 30:1 (Winter 1978): 27-35.

British Humanities Index. London: Library Association, published annually.

Broadcast Information Bureau. *Series, Serials and Packages: A TV Film/Tape Source Book.* New York: Broadcasting Information Bureau, published annually.

Brooks, Tim, and Marsh, Earle. *The Complete Directory to Prime Time Network TV Shows: 1946 to Present (1978).* New York: Ballentine Books, 1979.

Brown, James W. *Educational Media Yearbook 1978.* New York: R. R. Bowker, 1978.

Brown, Les. *The New York Times Encyclopedia of Television.* New York: New York Times Book Co., 1979.

Bukalski, Peter J. *Film Research: A Critical Bibliography with Annotations and Essays.* Boston: G. K. Hall, 1972.

Business Periodicals Index. New York: H. W. Wilson, published annually.

Canemaker, John. "Selected Bibliography of Animation." *Sightlines* 12:2 (Winter 1978-1979): 14-16.

Catholic Periodical Index. Haverford, Pa.: Catholic Library Association, 1930-.

Chicorel, Marietta. *Chicorel Index to Film Literature.* New York: Chicorel Library Publishing Corp., 1975.

Children's Television Workshop, Research Division. *CTW Research Bibliography.* New York: CTW, n.d.

Communication Abstracts: An International Information Service. Edited by Thomas F. Gordon. Los Angeles: *Sage,* 1978-.

Cowie, Peter. *International Film Guide* (1966 to date). New York: A. S. Barnes, and Co., 1966-.

Cumulated Dramatic Index, 1909-1949. Boston: G. K. Hall, 1965.

David, Nina, comp. *TV Season, 74-75; TV Season, 75-76; TV Season, 76-77.* Phoenix, Ariz.: Oryz Press, published annually, 1976-.

Deutelbaum, Marshall. "A Guide to Recent Indexes to Film Literature." *Image* 19:1 (March 1976): 26-27.

Dialogue. Palo Alto: Lockheed, 1978.

Dissertation Abstracts International. Michigan: University Microfilms, published annually.

Dyment, Alan R. *The Literature of Film: A Bibliographic Guide to the Film as Art and Entertainment,* 1936-1970. London: White Lion Publisher, 1975.

Edera, Bruno. *Full Length Animated Feature Films.* New York: Visual Communication Books, Hastings House, 1976.

Ellis, Jack C. *The Film Book Bibliography 1940-1975.* Metuchen, N.J.: Scarecrow Press, 1979.

Fielding, Raymond. *A Bibliography of Theses and Dissertations on the Subject of Film: 1916-1979.* Monograph no. 3. Houston, Tex.: University Film Association, 1979.

Film Daily Yearbook of Motion Pictures. New York: Film Daily, 1919-.

Film Index: A Bibliography. The Film as Art. Vol. 1. New York: Arno Press, 1970.

Film Literature Current. Albany, N.Y.: Filmdex, Part II, Inc., published monthly.

Friedwald, Will, and Beck, Jerry. *The Warner Brothers Cartoons.* Metuchen, N.J.: Scarecrow Press, Inc., 1981.

Gartley, Lynn, and Leebron, Elizabeth. *Walt Disney: A Guide to References and Resources.* Boston: G. K. Hall, 1979.

Gerlach, John C., and Gerlach, Linda. *The Critical Index: A Bibliography of Articles on Film in English, 1946-1973, Arranged by Name and Topic.* New York: Teachers College, Columbia University, 1974.

Gordon, Thomas F. *Communication Abstracts: An International Information Service.* Los Angeles: *Sage,* published quarterly with annual cumulations, 1979-.

_____, and Verna, Mary Ellen. *Mass Communication Effects and Processes: A Comprehensive Bibliography, 1950-1975.* Beverly Hills, Calif.: Sage, 1978.

Gottesman, Ronald, and Geduld, Harry. *Guidebook to Film: An Eleven-in-One Reference.* New York: Holt, Rinehart and Winston, 1972.

Graham, Peter. *Dictionary of the Cinema.* New York: EFLA, 1968.

Halas, John, and Manvell, Roger. *Art in Movement.* New York: Hastings House, 1975.

Halliwell, Leslie. *The Filmgoer's Companion.* 7th ed. New York: Charles Scribner's Sons, 1979.

Heinzkill, Richard. *Film Criticism: An Index to Critics' Anthologies.* Metuchen, N.J.: Scarecrow Press, 1975.

Herdeg, Walter. *Film and TV Graphics 2.* Switzerland: Graphis Press, 1976.

———, ed. *Film and TV Graphics. An International Survey of Film and Television Graphics.* Switzerland: Graphis Press, 1967.

Holman, L. Bruce. *Puppet Animation in the Cinema: History and Technique.* New York: A. S. Barnes and Co., 1975.

Horn, Maurice. *The World Encyclopedia of Comics.* New York: Chelsea House, 1976.

International Federation of Film Archives. *International Index to Film Periodicals.* New York: St. Martin's Press, 1972-.

International Motion Picture Almanac. New York: Quigley Publishing, 1929-.

Jenks, William. *The Celluloid Literature: Film in the Humanities.* New York: Glenco Press, Macmillan, 1971.

Katz, Ephraim. *The Film Encyclopedia.* New York: Lippincott and Crowell, 1979.

Lawder, Standish D. *The Cubist Cinema.* New York: New York University Press, 1975.

Lee, Walt, and Warren, Bill, eds. *Reference Guide to Fantastic Films: Science Fiction, Fantasy and Horror.* Los Angeles: Chelsea-Lee Books, 1973.

Lenburg, Jeff. *The Encyclopedia of Animated Cartoon Series: 1909-1979.* New York: Arlington House, 1981.

MacCann, Richard Dyer, and Perry, Edward S. *The New Film Index: A Bibliography of Magazine Articles in English, 1930-1970.* New York: E. P. Dutton, 1975.

Maltin, Leonard. *The Disney Films.* New York: Crown Publishers, 1978.

Manchel, Frank. *Film Study: A Resource Guide.* Cranbury, N.J.: Associated University Presses, 1973.

Manvell, Roger, ed. *The International Encyclopedia of Film.* New York: Crown Publishers, 1972.

Manvell, Roger; Jacobs, Lewis; et al. *The International Encyclopedia of Film.* New York: Crown Publishers; London: Joseph, 1972.

Mercer, John, comp. *Glossary of Film Terms.* Philadelphia: University Film Association, Monograph no. 2, Summer 1978.

Mezei, Leslie. "Computer Art: A Bibliography." *Computer Studies in the Humanities and Verbal Behavior.* 1:1 (January 1968): 48-50.

Monaco, James, and Schenker, Susan. *Books about Film: A Bibliographical Checklist.* 3d ed. New York: New York Zoetrope, 1976.

Nelson, Abigail. "Guide to Indexes of Periodical Literature on Film." *University Film Study Newsletter* 6 (October 1975): 3.

New York Times. *New York Times Film Reviews (1913-1976)* with supplements. New York: Arno Press, 1978.

New York Times Index. New York: New York Times Co., published annually.

Newsbank Review of the Arts. Stamford, Connecticut, 1978-.

Niver, Kemp R. *The First Twenty Years: A Segment of Film History.* Los Angeles: Artisan Press, 1968.

_____. *Motion Pictures from the Library of Congress Paper Print Collection, 1894-1912*. Berkeley: University of California Press, 1967.

Parish, James Robert, and Pitts, Michael R. *The Great Science Fiction Pictures*. Metuchen, N.J.: Scarecrow Press, 1977.

"Parlez-vous Television Programming?" *Broadcasting* 16 (April 1979): 32.

Philpott, Alexis, R. *Dictionary of Puppetry*. Boston: Play's, 1969.

Public Affairs Information Service Bulletin. New York: Public Affairs Information Service, published annually.

Readers Guide to Periodical Literature. New York: H. W. Wilson, published annually.

Rehrauer, George. *Cinema Booklist. Supplement One. Supplement Two*. Metuchen, N.J.: Scarecrow Press, 1972, 1974, 1977.

Renan, Sheldon. *An Introduction to the American Underground Film*. New York: E. P. Dutton, 1967.

Sadoul, Georges. *Dictionary of Filmmakers*. Translated and updated by Peter Morris. Berkeley: University of California Press, 1972.

_____. *Dictionary of Films*. Translated and updated by Peter Morris. Berkeley: University of California Press, 1972.

_____. *Georges Méliès*. Sight and Sound Index Series. Supplement no. 11. London: British Film Institute, 1947.

Samples, Gordon. *How to Locate Reviews of Plays and Films: A Bibliography of Criticism from the Beginnings to the Present*. Metuchen. N.J.: Scarecrow Press, 1976.

Scheuer, Steven H., ed. *The Television Annual: 1978-79*. New York: Macmillan 1979.

Schoolcraft, Ralph N., ed. *Annotated Bibliography of New Publications in the Performing Arts*. New York: Drama Workshop, published quarterly.

Schulz, Ronald M. *A Filmography of American Studio Cartoons: Cartoon Shorts Made from 1900-1970*. Master's thesis, Southern Illinois University, 1979.

Schuster, Mel. *Motion Picture Directors: A Bibliography of Magazine and Periodical Articles, 1900-1972*. Metuchen, N.J.: Scarecrow Press, 1973.

Shale, Richard, comp. *Academy Awards: An Ungar Reference Index*. New York: Frederick Ungar Publishing Co., 1978.

Sheahan, Eileen. *Moving Pictures: An Annotated Guide to Selected Film Literature with Suggestions for the Study of Film*. New York: A. S. Barnes and Co., 1978.

Singer, Marilyn, ed. *A History of the American Avant-garde Cinema*. New York: American Federation of the Arts, 1975.

Smith, John M., and Cawkwell, Tim, eds. *The World Encyclopedia of Film*. New York: World Publishing Co., 1972.

Spottiswoode, Raymond. *The Focal Encyclopedia of Film and Television Techniques*. New York: Hastings House, 1969.

Staples, Donald E., and Walker, Donald. "The Reference Shelf. Film Literature Indexes Reviewed." *Sightlines* 8:4 (Summer 1975): 25-30.

Sterling, Christopher, ed. *Mass Media Booknotes*. Philadelphia: Department of Radio-Television Film, Temple University, published monthly.

Television News Index and Abstracts. Nashville, Tenn.: Vanderbilt Television News Archive, 1968-.

Terrace, Vincent. *The Complete Encyclopedia of Television Programs, 1947-1979.* 2 vols. Rev. ed. New York: A. S. Barnes and Co., 1976.

Thomson, David. *A Biographic Dictionary of Film.* New York: William Morrow, 1976.

Topicator. Denver, Colo.: Thompson Bureau, published annually.

TV Guide Twenty-Five Year Index. Radnor, Pa.: TV Guide, 1978.

U.S., Library of Congress. *Audiovisual Materials.* Library of Congress: Washington, D.C., 1979. Published quinquennially with cumulations annually. This continues the U.S. Library of Congress *Films and Other Materials For Projection* series, given below.

_____. *Author Catalogue, 1948-1952.* Films. Vol. 24. Washington, D.C.: Library of Congress, 1953.

_____. *Library of Congress Catalogue: Films and Other Materials for Projection.* Washington, D.C.: Library of Congress, 1973-75.

_____. *Library of Congress: Motion Pictures and Filmstrips—A Cumulative List of Works Represented by LC Printed Cards.* Washington, D.C.: Government Printing Office, 1953-1972.

_____. *Motion Pictures 1894-1959.* 4 vols. Washington, D.C.: Library of Congress, 1951-60.

_____. *National Union Catalogue, 1953-1957.* Motion Pictures and Film Strips. Vol. 28. Ann Arbor, Mich.: J. W. Edwards, 1958.

_____. *National Union Catalogue: 1963-1967.* Motion Pictures and Film Strips. 2 vols. Ann Arbor, Mich.: J. W. Edwards, 1969.

Vance, Mary. *Computer Graphics: An Introductory Bibliography.* Monticello, Ill.: Vance Bibliographies, n.d.

Vincent, Richard C. "A Bibliography of Film Reference Resources." *Journal of the University Film Association* 29:3 (Summer 1977): 43-56.

_____. "An Introduction to Film Bibliographies." *Journal of the University Film Association* 28:3 (Summer 1976): 39-43.

Weinberg, Herman. *An Index to the Creative Work of Robert J. Flaherty and Hans Richter.* Sight and Sound Index Series. Supplement no. 6. London: British Film Institute, 1946.

Willis, Donald C. *Horror and Science Fiction Films: A Checklist.* Metuchen, N.J.: Scarecrow Press, 1972.

GENERAL HISTORY

Anderson, Joseph, and Fisher, Barbara. "The Myth of Persistence of Vision." *Journal of the University Film Association* 30:4 (Fall 1978): 3-8.

"Animated Cartoons in the Making." *Scientific American* 115 (14 October 1916): 354.

"Animated Drawings in the Moving Pictures." *Scientific American* 114 (8 January 1916): 57.

Baker, Stephen. "An Art Director's Viewpoint. Walt Disney Era Ends; Animation Comes of Age." *Advertising Age*, 27 January 1969, p. 54.

Balio, Tino. *The American Film Industry*. Madison: University of Wisconsin Press, 1976.

Bardeche, Maurice, and Brasillach, Robert. *The History of Motion Pictures*. New York: W. W. Norton and the Museum of Modern Art, 1938.

Barkin, Don. "The Beauty and the Short: It May Be Returning to Your Local Theater." *Washington Post*, 29 June 1978, p. B1.

Barrier, Mike. "Of Mice, Wabbits, Ducks and Men: The Hollywood Cartoon." In *AFI Report* 5:2 (Summer 1974): 18-26.

Beaupre, Lee. "U.S. Cartoons, 1906 to 1973; Lewis Selznick's Scoffing Quip; New Trend to Adult (Sexy) Fare." *Variety*, 9 January 1973, p. 76.

Becker, Stephen. *Comic Art in America*. New York: Simon and Schuster, 1959.

Beckerman, Howard. "A Sly History of Style in the Animated Film." *Filmmakers Newsletter* 10:1 (November 1976): 63-64.

Benayoun, Robert. *Le Dessin Anima Aprés Walt Disney*. Paris: Jean-Jacques Pauvert, 1961.

Bohn, Thomas W., and Stromgren, Richard L. *Light and Shadows: A History of Motion Pictures*. 2d ed. Sherman Oaks, Calif.: Alfred Publishing, 1978.

Bowman, David. "Scenarios for the Revolution in Pepperland." *Journal of Popular Film* 1:3 (Summer 1972): 173-84.

Cahaney, Roger (vice-president of Association Films). "The Sponsored Film 1919-1979—Those 20 Vital Years Before the 40." *Business and Home TV Screen*, February 1979, pp. 27-28.

Canemaker, John. "Animation History and Shamus Culhane." *Filmmakers Newsletter* 7:8 (June 1974): 23-27.

_____. "Behind the Scenes With Raggedy Ann and Andy." *Millimeter* 4:2 (February 1976): 36-40.

_____. "Disney Without Walt." *Print* 32:6 (November-December 1978): 35-43.

_____. "Pioneers of American Animation: J. Stuart Blackton, Winsor McCay, J. R. Bray, Otto Messmer, Disney." *Variety*, 7 January 1975, p. 38.

Cantor, Norman F., and Werthman, Michael S., eds. *The History of Popular Culture*. New York: Macmillan, 1968.

Ceram, C. W. [Kurt W. Marek]. *Archaeology of the Cinema*. New York: Harcourt, Brace and World, 1965.

Cook, Olive. *Movement in Two Dimensions*. London: Hutchinson, 1963.

Couperie, Pierre, et al. *A History of the Comic Strip*. New York: Crown, 1968.

Cripps, Thomas. *Slow Fade to Black: The Negro in American Film, 1900-1942*. New York: Oxford University Press, 1977.

Deutelbaum, Marshall. *"Image" on the Art and Evolution of the Film*. New York: Dover; Rochester, N.Y., International Museum of Photography, 1979.

Dulles, Foster Rhea. *A History of Recreation: America Learns to Play*. New York: Appleton-Century-Crofts, 1965.

Ellis, Jack C. *A History of Film*. Englewood Cliffs, N.J.: Prentice-Hall, 1979.

Everson, William K. *American Silent Film*. New York: Oxford University Press, 1978.

Fielding, Raymond. *A Technological History of Motion Pictures and Television*. Berkeley: University of California Press, 1967.

Geduld, Harry M. *The Birth of the Talkies*. Bloomington, Ind.: Indiana University Press, 1975.

Geipel, John. *The Cartoon: A Short History of Graphic Comedy and Satire*. London: David and Charles, 1972.

Gernsheim, Helmut, and Gernsheim, Alison. *L. J. M. Daguerre: The History of the Diorama and the Daguerreotype*. New York: Dover, 1968.

Halas, John. "The Animated Film." *Art and Industry*, July 1947, pp. 2-7.

_____. "Animation, Its Scope Today." *Animafilm* (ASIFA quarterly), no. 1 (October-December 1978): 29-32.

Heraldson, Donald. *Creators of Life: A History of Animation*. New York: Drake Publishers, 1975.

Hollywood Writers' Mobilization and the University of California. *Writer's Congress*. Berkeley: University of California Press, 1944.

Hubley, John. "The Decentralization of the Animation Industry." *Telefilm* (March-April 1958): 14-15.

Jacobs, Lewis. *Introduction to the Art of the Movies*. New York: Noonday Press, 1960.

_____. *The Rise of the American Film: A Critical History*. New York: Harcourt, Brace and Co., 1939.

Karr, Kathleen. "Early Animation: The Movement Begins." In *Impressions from the American Film Institute Archives*. Washington, D.C.: Acropolis Books, 1972.

Kausler, Mark. "Tom and Jerry: The Aesthetics of Violence." *Film Fan Monthly*, no. 89 (November 1968): 15-18.

Kennedy, Joseph P. *The Story of the Films*. New York: A. W. Shaw Co., 1927.

Klein, Isadore. "The Fabulous Winsor McCay." *Cartoonist Profiles*, no. 34 (n.d.): 49-51.

Knight, Arthur. "Engaging the Eye-Minded." *Saturday Review*, 28 December 1968, p. 17.

_____. *The Liveliest Art: A Panoramic History of the Movies*. Rev. ed. New York: New American Library, 1979.

Krows, Arthur Edwin. "Motion Pictures Not For Theaters." *Educational Screen*, September 1938, pp. 211-15.

_____. "Motion Pictures Not For Theaters." *Educational Screen*, October 1938, pp. 249-53.

_____. "Motion Pictures—Not For Theaters." *Educational Screen*, September 1939, pp. 242-45.

_____. "A Quarter-Century of Non-Theatrical Films." *Educational Screen*, June 1936, pp. 169-73.

Lahue, Kalton C. *World of Laughter: The Motion Picture Comedy Short, 1910-1930*. Norman, Okla.: University of Oklahoma, 1966.

_____, ed. *Motion Picture Pioneer: The Selig Polyscope Company*. New York: A. S. Barnes and Co., 1973.

Lewis, David L. *The Public Image of Henry Ford: An American Folk Hero and His Company*. Detroit: Wayne State University Press, 1976.

MacDonnell, Kevin. *Eadweard Muybridge: The Man Who Invented the Moving Picture*. Boston: Little, Brown and Co., 1972.

Madsen, Roy. *Animated Film: Concepts, Methods, Uses.* New York: Interland Publishing Co., 1969.

Maltin, Leonard. "An Animation Scrapbook." *Print* 28:2 (March-April 1974): 38-50.

_____. *Of Mice and Magic: A History of American Animated Cartoons.* New York: McGraw-Hill, 1980.

Manvell, Roger. "Giving Life to the Fantastic: A History of the Cartoon Film." *Films and Filming* 3 (November 1956): 7-9.

_____, and Huntley, John. *The Technique of Film Music.* New York: Focal Press, 1957.

Marsa, Linda. "Animation Moves to An Important Line." *Los Angeles Times* (calendar), 9 September 1979, p. 31.

Martin, Andre. "Animated Cinema. The Way Forward." *Sight and Sound* 28:1 (Winter 1958-59): 80-85.

Moreland, Pamela. "Demographic Research—Its Job Is Drawing Customers." *Los Angeles Times*, 24 February 1980, p. VI 3.

"Movies. Behind the Scenes. Mousetrap." *Newsweek*, 7 July 1958, p. 72.

Murrell, William. *A History of American Graphic Humor (1865-1938).* New York: Cooper Square Publishers, 1967.

Muybridge, Eadweard. *Human and Animal Locomotion.* 3 vols. 1887. Reprint. New York: Dover, 1979.

Niver, Kemp R. *The First Twenty Years.* Los Angeles: Artisan Press, 1968.

O'Sullivan, Judith. *The Art of the Comic Strip.* College Park, Md.: University of Maryland, 1971.

Peary, Danny, and Peary, Gerald, eds. *The American Animated Cartoon: A Critical Anthology.* New York: E. P. Dutton, 1980.

Petric, Vlada. "Approaches to the History of Film." *Film Library Quarterly* 6:2 (Spring 1973): 7-12.

Polt, Harriet. "The Death of Mickey Mouse." *Film Comment* 2:3 (Summer 1964): 34-39.

Pratley, Gerald. "The Cartoon's Decay." *Films in Review* 2:9 (November 1951): pp. 34-36.

Ramsaye, Terry. *A Million and One Nights: A History of the Motion Picture.* New York: Simon and Schuster, 1926.

Rondolino, Gianni. *Storia del cinema d'animazione.* Turin: Giulio Einaudi, 1974.

Schenkel, Thelma. "Exploring the Cinema of Figurative Animation With Special Consideration of the Work of John and Faith Hubley and Jan Lenica." Ph.D. dissertation, New York University, 1977.

Schwerin, Jules. "Galloping Mirror of Nature." *Theater Arts* 33:9 (October 1949): 34-37.

Sheridan, Martin. *Comics and Their Creators.* Boston: Hale, 1942.

Slide, Anthony. *Aspects of American Film History Prior to 1920.* Metuchen, N.J.: Scarecrow Press, 1977.

_____. *The Big V: A History of the Vitagraph Company.* Metuchen, N.J.: Scarecrow Press, 1976.

Smith, Conrad. "The Early History of Animation: Saturday Morning TV Discovers 1915." *Journal of the University Film Association* 29:3 (Summer 1977): 23-30.

The Spanish Cinema. Madrid: Diplomatic Information Office, 1949, pp. 18-19.

Spehr, Paul C. *The Movies Begin: Making Movies in New Jersey 1887-1920*. New Jersey: Newark Museum, 1979.

Stephenson, Ralph. *The Animated Film*. New York: A. S. Barnes and Co., 1973.

Theisen, Earl. "The History of the Animated Cartoon." *Journal of the Society of Motion Picture Engineers* 21 (September 1933): 239-49.

Tibbetts, John. "Of Mouse and Man." *American Classic Screen* 2:5 (May-June 1978): 9-10.

Trost, Mark; Higa, Lori; and Lindner, James. "Commercial Animation Update 1980: Complex Spots Require Time—Animators Speak Up for More of It." *Millimeter* 8:2 (Feburary 1980): 36-50.

Waldron, Gloria. *The Information Film*. New York: Columbia University Press, 1949.

ANIMATION IN TELEVISION

Altshuler, Jeffrey. "Robert Abel: Video Surrealist." *Print* 29:6 (November 1975): 34-41.

Bailey, Robert Lee. "An Examination Of Prime Time Network Television Special Programs 1948 to 1966." Ph.D. dissertation, University of Wisconsin, 1967.

"Cartoons Endure for UAA: Stations Rush to Renew at Same Rates." *Broadcasting*, 10 August 1959, p. 74.

"The Case For Animated TV Spots: An Expert Argues That Cartoons Can Sell Things Live Actors Can't." *Broadcasting*, 15 August 1960, pp. 38-39.

Crock, Stan. "A Long View, or TV For Kids Is and Isn't What It Used to Be." *Wall Street Journal*, 24 October 1978, p. 1.

"DDB's Newest Technique In Commercials." *Television Magazine* 22:4 (April 1965): 44-45.

Diamant, Lincoln. *Television's Classic Commercials: The Golden Years, 1948-1958*. New York: Hastings House, 1971.

Gould, Stephen Jay. "This View of Life: Mickey Mouse Meets Konrad Lorenz." *Natural History* 88:5 (May 1979): 30-36.

Greene, Alexis. "For Children, A Few Nuggets Amid the Cartoons." *New York Times*, 2 September 1979, p. D 25.

Halas, John. "Cartoon Films In Commerce." *Art and Industry* 29:173 (November 1940): 170-76.

Hall, James. "Cartoon Spots In Retrospect." *Backstage*, 1 September 1978, p. 19.

"Ingredients of a Top-Selling Television Commercial." *Television Magazine* 17:4 (April 1960): 52.

Kittross, John M., comp. *A Bibliography of Theses and Dissertations in Broadcasting, 1920-1973*. Washington, D.C.: Broadcasting Education Association, 1978.

Kriegsman, Alan M. "The Faddish Realism of TV Commercials." *Washington Post*, 29 April 1979, p. H 3.

Kroeger, Albert R. "How Honest Can You Get?" *Television Magazine* 19:5 (May 1962): 51.

McMahan, Harry Wayne. "The Television Commercial." *Television Magazine* 14:5 (May 1957): 59.

Maltese, Anthony M. "A Descriptive Study of Children's Programming on Major American Television Networks from 1950 through 1964." Ph.D. dissertation, Ohio University, 1967.

"Marketing. East Meets West in Cartoon Venture." *Business Week*, 11 May 1963, p. 105.

Melody, William. *Children's TV: The Economics of Exploitation*. New Haven: Yale University Press, 1973.

O'Kieffe, DeWitt. "Realism—New Trend in Commercials." *Television Magazine* 13:9 (September 1956): p. 49.

"Puppet Characters Open New Possibilities For Animation." *Sponsor* 17:9 (4 March 1963): 34-50.

" 'Reduce the Gamble' Is Now The Watchword." *Television Magazine* 13:7 (July 1956): p. 72.

Ross, Arthur. "The Animated Commercial: A Retrospective View From the Late 1940s To Present." *Millimeter* 5:2 (February 1977): 12.

Sanderson, Lucinda Ann, and Tawney, Michael J. "Ross Bagdasarian Remembered." *Mindrot*, no. 12 (1 November 1978): 21-27.

Shales, Tom. "Television and The Animation Gap." *Washington Post*, 18 November 1979, p. 3 TV review.

Stewart, Robert Hammel. "The Development Of Network Television Program Types To January 1953." Ph.D. dissertation, Ohio State University, 1954.

"Stone Age Hero's Smash Hit. TV's First Cartoon For Grownups Stars The Suburban Flintstones." *Life* 49:21 (21 November 1960).

Sutton, Howard. "How To Be Visible In The Clutter. TV Animation Isn't Just Cartoons." *Advertising Age*, 31 January 1972, p. 51.

Trost, Mark, and Lindner, James. "Commercial Animation Update 1980: Complex Spots Require Time—Animators Speak Up for More Of It." *Millimeter* 8:2 (February 1980): 36.

Waugh, John C. "Cartoons Squiggle Their Way to Video; Home-Screen Animation Keeps Arts Doodling." *Christian Science Monitor*, 18 October 1960, p. 7.

Weiner, Jack B. "To Market To Market With Toys and TV." *Television Magazine* 18:11 (November 1961): 46.

White, Hooper. "A Leading Animator Makes an Old Technique Look New." *Advertising Age*, 18 July 1977, pp. 50-51.

_____. "Return of the Cartoon: Early TV Technique Shows New Animation." *Advertising Age*, 20 November 1978, p. 45.

Wolf, Alice C. "The History of American Television Commercials, 1947-1977: Part I." *Millimeter* 5:4 (April 1977): 22.

_____. "The History of American Television Commercials, 1947-1977: Part II." *Millimeter* 5:5 (May 1977): 42.

_____. "History of TV Commercials, Part III: Breaking Into the Station Break, Chapter 2." *Millimeter* 5:7 (July-August 1977): 38.

_____. "History of TV Commercials, Part IV: Chicago Enters Commercialdom." *Millimeter* 5:8 (September 1977): 46.

_____. "History of TV Commercials, Part V: California Shares The Spot Light." *Millimeter* 5:9 (October 1977): 56.

_____. "History of TV Commercials, Part VI: The Psychology of Copywriting." *Millimeter* 5:11 (December 1977): 52.

_____. "History of Television Commercials, Part VII: The Rave New World of Color." *Millimeter* 6:4 (April 1978): 80-81.

Woolery, George W. "The Television Commercial Everybody Is Talking About . . . and How It Was Produced." *American Cinematographer* 40:6 (June 1959): 348.

Yoshihara, Nancy. "A Word From the Sponsor. Hamm's Bear Out of Hibernation." *Los Angeles Times*, 12 February 1980, p. IV 5.

POLITICAL AND SOCIAL ASPECTS OF ANIMATION

"Animated Cartoons: TV Is Keeping Them Alive." *Christian Science Monitor*, 7 August 1974, p. 3 c.

"Animated Cartoons With Editorial Zip Set for TV Screens: Washington Post Unit To Sell Humor From Newspapers To Commercial Stations." *Wall Street Journal*, 17 February 1978, p. 14.

Arnold, Francis. "Out Of This World." *Films and Filming* 9:9 (June 1963): 14-18.

Balkin, Richard. "Mae Questel's Betty Boop: America's First Sexpot." *Afterdark*, October 1977, pp. 69-73.

Beckerman, Howard. "Jimmy Picker Goes to the Movies." *Filmmakers Newsletter* 11:11 (September 1978): 55-56.

_____. "Mr. Hip Goes To Television." *Filmmakers Newsletter* 11:9 (June 1978): 52.

Benson, Robert J. "Artists In The Courtroom." *Print* 31:5 (September-October 1977): 80-84.

Bilowit, William. "In Production: Seeger's Cartoon-A-Torial." *Millimeter* 7:7 (July 1979): 107.

Birnbaum, Jeff. "Even Disney Movies Checked for Smut By Maryland Censors." *Wall Street Journal*, 22 August 1977, p. 1.

"Comic Strips On the TV News." *Washington Post*, 13 May 1977, p. D 1.

Dart, John. "Religion Goes to the Movies." *Los Angeles Times* (calendar), 25 November 1979, p. 4.

"Graphics Set Mood." *Television/Radio Age*, 24 October 1978, pp. 80-81.

Hentoff, Nat. "Spider-Man, Hitler, and Me." *Village Voice*, 13 May 1978, p. 30.

Jarvie, I. C. *Movies and Society*. New York: Basic Books, 1970.

Jowett, Garth S. "Media Power and Social Control: The Motion Picture in America, 1894-1936." Ph.D. dissertation, University of Pennsylvania, 1972.

_____. *Film: The Democratic Art*. Boston: Little, Brown and Company, 1976.

Lardner, Maurice Rapf, Jr.; Hubley, John; and Eastman, Phil. " 'Brotherhood of Man': A Script." *Hollywood Quarterly* 1:4 (July 1946): 353-59.

Levy, Barry. "Star Wars: An Inspiration to Television Advertisers." *American Cinemeditor* 28:1-2 (Spring-Summer 1978): 6-7. (Reprinted from *Backstage*).

Maltin, Leonard. "TV Animation: The Decline and Pratfall of a Popular Art."
Film Comment 11:1 (January-February 1975): 76-81.

Margulies, Lee. "Syndicated TV: Something For All." *Los Angeles Times*, 10
March 1978, p. IV 20.

"Mickey Mouse—Censored." *Living Age* 339:4371 (December 1930): 429.

"Mother Goose Goes To Hollywood." *Mindrot*, no. 12 (1 November 1978): 34.

Munsey, Cecil. *Disneyana*. New York: Hawthorn Books, 1974.

Murphy, William Thomas. "The Method of Why We Fight." *Journal of Popular
Film* 1:3 (Summer 1972): 185-96.

O'Malley, Becky. "Mickey Say, Mickey Do." *New Times* 11:8 (16 October 1978):
40-49.

Paul, Bill. "Donald Duck Faces A Morals Charge In Western Europe." *Wall Street
Journal*, 10 February 1978, p. 1.

Price, Jonathan. *The Best Thing on TV—Commercials*. New York: Penguin Books,
1978.

Rosenthal, Edmond M. " 'Star Wars' Creates Effects Boom in Animated Commercials." *Television/Radio Age* 25:14 (13 February 1978): 38.

"Saludos Seversky." *Newsweek*, 19 July 1943, pp. 86-87.

Schneider, Cy. "The Licensed Characters: Today's Hot Salesmen." *Advertising
Age*, 30 April 1979, pp. 59-60.

"Seriocomics: Donald Duck, Meet Karl Marx." *Time*, 2 April 1979, p. 87.

Speier, Hans. "Magic Geography." *Social Research* 8:3 (Fall 1941): 310-29.

Wagner, Dave. "Donald Duck: An Interview." *Radical America* 7:1 (1973): 1-19.

Yung, Robert. "Animation's Role: Projection Of Ideas, Logic, Abstractions."
Public Relations Journal 18:12 (December 1961): 40.

AUDIENCES FOR ANIMATION

Ahl, Frances Norene. "Disney Techniques in Educational Films." *Social Studies*
35:8 (December 1944): 344-46.

"Animation." *Stage* 12 (January 1935): 35.

Arlen, Michael. "The Air. Kidvid." *New Yorker*, 4 November 1974, p. 136.

Aronson, Dennis T. "Formulation and Trial Use of Guidelines for Designing and
Developing Instructional Motion Pictures." Ph.D. dissertation, Florida State
University, 1977.

Baker, Robert, and Ball, Sandra. *Mass Media and Violence*. Staff Report to the
National Commission on the Causes and Prevention of Violence. Vol. 9.
Washington, D.C.: Government Printing Office, 1969.

Barcus, F. Earle, and Wolkin, Rachel. *Children's Television: An Analysis of
Programming and Advertising*. New York: Praeger, 1977.

Berelson, Bernard, and Steiner, Gary A. *Human Behavior: An Inventory of Scientific Findings*. New York: Harcourt, Brace and World, 1964.

Bernstein, Lewis Jay. "Design Attributes of *Sesame Street* and the Visual Attention
of Preschool Children." Ph.D. dissertation, Columbia University, 1978.

Bogart, Leo. *The Age of Television*. 3d ed. New York: Frederick Ungar Publishing
Co., 1972.

Caldwell, Kathryn Smoot. "Guidelines and Principles For the Utilization of Animation in Instruction Films and Videotapes." Ph.D. dissertation, University of Southern California, 1973.

Cater, Douglas, and Strickland, Stephen. *TV Violence and the Child: The Evolution and Fate of the Surgeon General's Report*. New York: Russell Sage Foundation, 1975.

CBS Television. Office of Social Research. CBS Economics and Research. *Communicating with Children Through Television*. New York: CBS Television, 1977.

Christopher, Maurine. "Syndie Favorites Stay That Way." *Advertising Age*, 13 August 1979, p. 80.

Chu, Godwin C., and Schramm, Wilbur. *Learning from Television: What the Research Says*. Washington, D.C.: National Association of Educational Broadcasters, 1967.

Clancy, Kevin J., and Ostlund, Lyman E. "Commercial Effectiveness Measures." *Journal of Advertising Research* 16:1 (February 1976): 29-34.

Comstock, George. *Television and Human Behavior: The Key Studies*. Santa Monica, Calif.: Rand Corporation, 1975. (Rand R-1747-CF)

Comstock, George; Chaffee, Steven; Katzman, Natan; McCombs, Maxwell; and Roberts, Donald. *Television and Human Behavior*. New York: Columbia University Press, 1978.

Comstock, George, and Fisher, Marilyn. *Television and Human Behavior: A Guide to the Pertinent Scientific Literature*. Santa Monica, Calif.: Rand Corporation, 1975. (Rand R-1746-CF)

Comstock, George, and Lindsey, George. *Television and Human Behavior: The Research Horizon, Future and Present*. Santa Monica, Calif.: Rand Corporation, 1975. (Rand R-1748-CF)

Connell, David D., and Palmer, Edward L. "Children's Television Workshop: Not For Children Only." *AFI Report* 5:1 (Spring 1974): 14-24.

Cook, Thomas D., et al. *'Sesame Street' Revisited*. New York: Russell Sage Foundation, 1975.

Cowen, Robert C. "Weather Satellites: A 20-Year Success Story." *Christian Science Monitor*, 23 June 1980, p. 14.

Culshaw, John. "Violence and The Cartoon." *Fortnightly*, December 1951, pp. 830-35.

Disney, Walt. "Mickey As Professor." *Public Opinion Quarterly* 9:2 (Summer 1945): pp. 119-25.

Fadiman, Clifton. "The Classroom's Ubiquitous Rival: Pop Culture." *New York Times*, 13 June 1979, p. A 25.

Feldman, Shel, and Wolf, Abraham. "What's Wrong With Children's Commercials?" *Journal of Advertising Research* 14:1 (February 1974): 39-43.

Frye, Kenneth Bauer. "A Study of Opinions of Animated Advertising In Television." Master's thesis, American University, 1956.

Garrett, Judith Elaine. "Instructional Media Research: A Review of the Literature, Recommended Framework for Future Research, and a Test of the Contribution to Instructional Effectiveness of Two Steps in a Design Model." Ph.D. dissertation, Florida State University, 1972.

Gibson, James Jerome, ed. *Motion Picture Testing and Research*. Washington, D.C.: Government Printing Office, 1947.

Goldstein, Naomi Slutzky. "The Effect of Animated Cartoons on Hostility in Children." Ph.D. dissertation, New York University, 1957.

Gore, Rick. "What Voyager Saw: Jupiter's Dazzling Realm." *National Geographic* 157:1 (January 1980): 2-29.

Hall, Mary Harrington. "The Fantasy Makers: A Conversation With Ray Bradbury and Chuck Jones." *Psychology Today* 1:11 (April 1968): 28.

Hanauer, Joan. "11th TV Season. 'Sesame Street': Mixed Emotions." *Los Angeles Times*, 27 November 1979, p. V 13.

Handel, Leo A. *Hollywood Looks at Its Audience*. Urbana: University of Illinois Press, 1950.

Hartmann, William K. "Moons of the Outer Solar System Become Real, Although Weird, Places." *Smithsonian* 10:10 (January 1980): 36-47.

Herman, Lewis. *Educational Films: Writing, Directing, and Producing for Classroom, Television and Industry*. New York: Crown, 1965.

Hoban, Charles F., Jr., and van Ormer, Edward B. *Instructional Film Research, 1918-1950*. Technical Report No. SDC 269-7-19. Port Washington, Long Island: U.S. Naval Training Devices Center, 1950.

Holt, John. "Big Bird, Meet Dick and Jane." *Atlantic Magazine* 227:5 (May 1971): p. 72.

Ingrassia, Lawrence, and Stevens, Charles W. "New Mayo Clinic X-Ray Scanner Promises To Add to Medical Knowledge—and Costs." *Wall Street Journal*, 7 March 1980, p. 24.

Journalism Abstracts. Minneapolis: Association for Education in Journalism, published annually, 1962-.

Kendig, Frank. "CTW's '3-2-1 Contact' Aims At Sparking An Interest in Science." *New York Times*, 13 January 1980, p. D 27.

Kernan, Michael. "The Sesame Decade: Smithsonian Status For Big Bird and Pals." *Washington Post*, 1 June 1979, p. C 1.

Lesser, Gerald S. *Children and Television: Lessons from Sesame Street*. New York: Vintage Books, 1974.

"A Look At Programs For Young Children." *Nielsen Newscast*, no. 2 (1979).

Lorch, Elizabeth Pugzles, and Anderson, Daniel R. "Paying Attention to Sesame Street." Mimeographed. Contract Research for Children's Television Workshop. July 1978.

MacDonald, Scott. "Independent Film: Where's the Audience?" *Afterimage* 5:9 (March 1978): 6-7.

"Marketing. TV's Saturday Gold Mine." *Business Week* (2 August 1969): 96-98.

May, Mark A., and Lumsdaine, Arthur A. *Learning from Films*. New Haven: Yale University Press, 1958.

Melody, William. *Children's Television: The Economics of Exploitation*. New Haven: Yale University Press, 1978.

Murray, John. *Television and Youth: 25 Years of Research and Controversy*. Boys Town, Nebraska: Boys Town Center for Study of Youth Development, December 1980.

Network Project. *Down Sesame Street*. New York: Columbia University, 1973.

Niven, Hal. "Children's Shows Sell Family Products." *Television Magazine* 13:4 (April 1956): 54.

Noble, Grant. *Children in Front of the Small Screen*. Beverly Hills, Calif.: *Sage*, 1975.

Palmer, Charles. "Cartoon in the Classroom." *Hollywood Quarterly* 3:1 (Fall 1947): 26-38.

Real, Michael R. *Mass-Mediated Culture*. Englewood Cliffs, N.J.: Prentice-Hall, 1977.

Reid, J. Christopher, and MacLennan, Donald W., eds. *Research in Instructional Television and Film*. Washington, D.C.: Government Printing Office, 1967.

Rempel, William. "Ship Simulators Pose Real-Life Navigational Problems. Mariners Face Dangers of Sea While Safe Ashore." *Los Angeles Times*, 26 December 1979, p. I 26.

Research on the Effects of Television Advertising on Children. Washington, D.C.: National Science Foundation, 1977.

Robertson, Thomas S.; Rossiter, John R.; and Gleason, Terry C. *Televised Medicine: Advertising and Children*. New York: Praeger, 1979.

Ross, Lee Barkley. "The Effect of Aggressive Cartoons on the Group Play of Children." Ph.D. dissertation, Miami University, 1972.

Rowley, Susan Linda. "Film Cartoon Violence and Children's Aggressive Behavior." Ph.D. dissertation, Boston University, 1971.

Rubinstein, Elia. "Television and the Young Viewer." *American Scientist* 66 (November-December 1978): 685-93.

Rust, Langbourne. "Sesame Street Characters: Children's Attention Patterns." 2 vols. Mimeographed. Contract Research for Children's Television Workshop, 1979.

_____, and Watkins, Thomas W. "Children's Commercials: Creative Development." *Journal of Advertising Research* 15:5 (October 1975): 21-26.

Salisbury, David F. "3-D Films: Computer Art Takes Off In Space." *Christian Science Monitor*, 20 July 1976, p. 6.

Sanders, James Taggart. "A Developmental Study of Preferences for Television Cartoons." Ph.D. dissertation, Ohio State University, 1969.

Schickel, Richard. *The Disney Version: The Life, Times, Art and Commerce of Walt Disney*. New York: Simon and Schuster, 1968.

Schmidt, William D. "Analyzing the Design of Outstanding Instructional Films." *Sightlines* 10:1 (Fall 1976): 6-8.

Schramm, Wilbur; Lyle, Jack; and Parker, Edwin B. *Television in the Lives of Our Children*. Stanford: Stanford University Press, 1961.

" 'Sesame Street' Isn't On Easy Street, Says Creator." *Los Angeles Times*, 31 July 1979, p. V 12.

Shaffer, Richard A. "The Big Picture. Computers, Linked to TV-Like Screens, Are Drawing Graphs, Blueprints, Maps." *Wall Street Journal*, 5 March 1980, p. 48.

Shelby, Maurice, Jr. "Children's Programming Trends on Network Television." *Journal of Broadcasting* 8:2 (Summer 1964): 247-55.

Shepard, Albert. "Studies in Commercial Effectiveness: Hamm's Beer." *Television Magazine* 14:6 (June 1957): 55.

Smith, Birna R. "Content Analysis of Selected Television Network Cartoon Programs." Master's thesis, Ohio University, 1968.

Soderblom, Laurence A. "The Galilean Moons of Jupiter." *Scientific American* 242:1 (January 1980): 88-101.

Steiner, Gary A. *The People Look at Television: A Study of Attitudes*. New York: Alfred A. Knopf, 1963.

Stutler, William B. "The Techniques, Costs, and Selling Abilities of the Animated Television Commercial." Master's thesis, Michigan State University, 1961.

"TV Advertising to Children: Chronology of A Controversy." *Marketing and Media Decisions* 14:5 (May 1979): 59.

U.S., Department of Health, Education, and Welfare. *Research in Instructional Television and Film*. Edited by Christopher Reid and Donald W. MacLennan. Washington, D.C.: Government Printing Office, 1967.

U.S., Department of Health, Education, and Welfare. *Television and Growing Up: The Impact of Televised Violence*. Washington, D.C.: Government Printing Office, 1972.

U.S., Department of Health, Education, and Welfare. *Television and Social Behavior*. Media Content and Control, edited by George A. Comstock and Eli A. Rubinstein, vol. 1. Washington, D.C.: Government Printing Office, 1972.

U.S., Department of Health, Education, and Welfare. *Television and Social Behavior*. Television and Social Learning, edited by John P. Murray, Eli A. Rubinstein, and George A. Comstock, vol. 2. Washington, D.C.: Government Printing Office, 1972.

U.S., Department of Health, Education, and Welfare. *Television and Social Behavior*. Television and Adolescent Aggressiveness, edited by George A. Comstock and Eli A. Rubinstein, vol. 3. Washington, D.C.: Government Printing Office, 1972.

U.S., Department of Health, Education, and Welfare. *Television and Social Behavior*. Television in Day-to-Day Life: Patterns of Use, edited by Eli A. Rubinstein, George A. Comstock, and John P. Murray, vol. 4. Washington, D.C.: Government Printing Office, 1972.

U.S., Department of Health, Education, and Welfare. *Television and Social Behavior*. Television's Effects: Further Explorations, edited by George A. Comstock, Eli A. Rubinstein, and John P. Murray, vol. 5. Washington, D.C.: Government Printing Office, 1972.

U.S., Federal Communications Commission. *Television Programming for Children: A Report of the Children's Task Force*. 5 vols. Washington, D.C.: FCC, 1979.

U.S., Federal Trade Commission. *Staff Report on Television Advertising to Children*. Washington, D.C.: FTC, 1978.

U.S., Congress, Subcommittee on Communications. *Surgeon General's Report by the Scientific Advisory Committee on Television and Social Behavior*. Appendix A. 92d Cong., 2d sess. Washington, D.C.: Government Printing Office, 1972.

Williams, Tannis Macbeth. "How and What Do Children Learn From Television?" *Human Communication Research* 7:2 (Winter 1981): 180-92.

Winick, Marianne Pezzella, and Winick, Charles. *The Television Experience: What Children See.* Beverly Hills, Calif.: *Sage*, 1979.

CRITICISM

Arnheim, Rudolf. "From Flickers to Fischinger." *Saturday Review*, 18 February 1950, p. 34.

Callenbach, Ernest. *Our Modern Art: The Movies.* Chicago: Center for the Study of Liberal Education Studies, 1955.

"The Cartoon Colour-Film." *Close Up* 10 (1933): 86-87.

Cavalcanti, Alberto. "Comedies and Cartoons," in Charles Davy, ed., *Footnotes to the Film.* 1938. Reprint. New York: Arno Press, 1970.

Charlot, Jean. *Art from the Mayans to Disney.* New York: Sheed and Ward, 1939.

_____. "But Is It Art? A Disney Disquisition." *American Scholar* 8:3 (July 1939): 260-70.

Culshaw, John. "The Virtues of Flatness." *Fortnightly Review* 174 (October 1953): 248-52.

"The Experimental Film." *Film Comment (Vision)* 1:1 (Spring 1962): pp. 3-4.

Farber, Manny. *Negative Space: Manny Farber on the Movies.* New York: Praeger, 1971.

_____. "Saccharine Symphony." *New Republic*, 29 June 1942, p. 893.

_____. "Short and Happy." *New Republic*, 20 September 1943, p. 394.

Gould, Michael. *Surrealism and the Cinema.* New York: A. S. Barnes and Co., 1976.

Haggin, B. H. "Music." *Nation* 152:1 (11 January 1941): 53-54.

Halas, John. "Not For Fun!" *Films and Filming* 3 (November 1956): 6.

Hodgens, Richard. "A Brief, Tragical History of the Science Fiction Film." *Film Quarterly* 13:2 (Winter 1959): 30-39.

Hubley, John. "Beyond Pigs and Bunnies: The New Animator's Art." *American Scholar* 44:2 (Spring 1975): 213-23.

Hughes, Robert. "Disney: Mousebrow to Highbrow." *Time*, 15 October 1973, pp. 88-91.

Hurwitz, Leo T. "Mice and Things: Notes on Pierre Roy and Walt Disney." *Creative Art* 8 (May 1931): 359-63.

Jacobs, Lewis. *The Emergence of Film Art.* New York: Hopkinson and Blake, 1969.

_____. *Introduction to the Art of the Movies.* New York: Noonday Press, 1960.

_____, comp. *The Compound Cinema: The Film Writings of Harry Alan Potamkin.* New York: Teachers College Press, 1977.

La Farge, Christopher. "Walt Disney and The Art Form." *Theater Arts* 25:9 (September 1941): 673-80.

Letter of Shamus Culhane to Mike Barrier. *Funnyworld*, no. 2 (Summer 1979): 2-5.

Letter of Reg Hartt to David Murtz. *Mindrot*, no. 14 (20 May 1979): 10-11.

Letter of Michael Sporn to Mike Barrier. *Funnyworld*, no. 21 (Fall 1979): 2.

Lindsay, Vachel. *The Art of the Moving Picture.* Reprint. New York: Liveright, 1970.

MacGowan, Kenneth. "Make Mine Disney." *Hollywood Quarterly* 1:4 (July 1946): 376-77.

Marlow, David. "Working for Mickey Mouse." *New York* 6:32 (6 August 1973): 43-46.

Martarella, Frank David. "Animated Cinema. Cartoons, as a Separate Art Form, Should Not Imitate Live Action Films." *America* 120:9 (1 March 1969): 271-73.

Mast, Gerald, and Cohen, Marshall. *Film Theory and Criticism: Introductory Readings*. New York: Oxford University Press, 1974.

Missinne, Jeff. "The Catbird Seat." *Mindrot*, no. 15 (20 August 1979): 6-7.

Morrow, James. "In Defense of Disney." *Media and Methods* 14:8 (April 1978).

Nash, Paul. "The Colour Film," in Charles Davy, ed., *Footnotes to the Film*. 1938. Reprint. New York: Arno Press, 1970.

Pearson, Ralph M. *Experiencing American Pictures*. New York: Harper and Brothers, 1943.

Pichel, Irving. "Stills in Motion." *Film Quarterly* 5:1 (Fall 1950): 8-13.

Quinn, Thomas, and Hanks, Cheryl, eds. *Coming to Our Senses: The Significance of the Arts for American Education*. New York: McGraw-Hill, 1977.

Rieder, Howard Edward. "The Development Of The Satire Of Mr. Magoo." Master's thesis, University of Southern California, 1961.

Samuels, Charles Thomas. *Mastering The Film and Other Essays*. Edited by Lawrence Graver. Knoxville, Tenn.: University of Tennessee Press, 1977.

Schickel, Richard. "Brining Forth The Mouse." *American Heritage* 19:3 (April 1968): 24.

_____. "The Films: No Longer Jung at Heart." *Time*, 30 July 1973, p. 65.

Seldes, Gilbert. "The Krazy Kat That Walks By Himself," in Gilbert Seldes, ed., *The Seven Lively Arts*. New York: Sagamore Press, 1957.

Sohn, David. *Film: The Creative Eye*. New York: George A. Pflaum, 1970.

Talbot, Daniel. *Film: An Anthology*. New York: Simon and Schuster, 1959.

Tsuchiya, Haruki. "The Philosophy of Computer Art." *Computers and Automation* 18:10 (September 1969): 18.

Tyler, Parker. *The Hollywood Hallucination*. New York: Creative Age Press, 1944.

Wanger, Walter. "Mickey Icarus, 1943. Fusing Ideas With the Art of the Animated Cartoon." *Saturday Review* 26:36 (4 September 1943): 18-19.

White, Kenneth. "Film Chronicle: Animated Cartoons," in *Hound and Horn: Essays on Cinema*. New York: Arno Press, 1972.

Williams, Sheldon. "The Arts: Animation." *Contemporary Review* 211 (August 1967): 98-104.

THEORY

Andrew, J. Dudley. *The Major Film Theories: An Introduction*. New York: Oxford University Press, 1976.

Armes, Roy. *Film and Reality: An Historical Survey*. Baltimore: Penguin Books, 1974.

Carter, Huntly. *The New Spirit in the Cinema*. 1930. Reprint. New York: Arno Press, 1970.

Culkin, John M. "Understanding Media Means Understanding Me." *Sightlines* 6:4 (March-April 1973): 4-5.

Davy, Charles. *Footnotes to the Film*. London: Readers' Union, 1938.

Dick, Barnard F. *Anatomy of Film*. New York: St. Martin's Press, 1978.

Eberwein, Robert T. *A Viewer's Guide to Film Theory and Criticism*. Metuchen, N.J.: Scarecrow Press, 1979.

Hubley, John, and Schwartz, Zachary. "Animation Learns a New Language." *Hollywood Quarterly* 1:4 (July 1946): 360-63.

Pryluck, Calvin. "Sources of Meaning In Motion Pictures and Television." Ph.D. dissertation, University of Iowa, 1973.

_____. U.S., Department of Health, Education, and Welfare. *Structure and Function in Education Cinema*. Washington, D.C.: Government Printing Office, 1969.

Vorkapich, Slavko. "Toward True Cinema." *American Cinematographer* 54:7 (July 1973): 884.

Wollen, Peter. *Signs and Meaning in the Cinema*. London: Seeker and Warburg, 1969.

CHAPTER 4

Classes of Animation and Personalities

Art is never conscious. Things that have lived were seldom planned that way. If you follow that line, you're on the wrong track. We don't even let the word "art" be used around the studio. If anyone begins to get arty, we knock them down. What we strive for is entertainment.[1]

WALT DISNEY

Even the cartoon film is today on a very low artistic level. It is a mass product of factory proportions, and this, of course, cuts down the creative purity of a work of art. No sensible creative artist could create a sensible work of art if a staff of co-workers of all kinds each had his or her say in the final creation.[2]

OSKAR FISCHINGER

The quotations from Disney and Fischinger reflect differing views about two goals in filmmaking; generating audiences and self-expression. At the same time, their statements establish limits for the continuum of types of animated film. Traditional cel-animation and some object-animation evolved primarily as a part of the mass media, subject to the whims of changing tastes, part of which the mass media also stimulated. Drawing-on-film and computer-animation have richer traditions in self-expression. This chapter examines the four classes of animation defined in Chapter 1 and the usually anonymous personalities who have created those animations.

CLASSES OF ANIMATION

Historically, cel-animated films in the United States evolved through producer organizations, later called studios. These films typically featured characters in a continuing series of episodes. Characters and studios thus form the major topics for discussion of the cel type of animation. Object-animation includes stop-action photography of models, as well as cutouts, silhouette figures, stills-in-motion, and other abstractions. In the drawing-on-film techniques, the camera is typically discarded, resulting in an abstract form, along with mixtures of live-action and animation, as in titles. The discussion which follows of the younger, computer forms of animation is concerned with theory and practice in a general sense.

I will admit that these types and their subdivisions are not perfect fits in the overall framework of animation. But in terms of technology, the classes described do have a logical progression which takes into account old and new forms. For example, cel- and object-animations used photography, with a gradual transition toward cameraless animation and, later, computer-generated imaging. In terms of abstraction, the continuum is without limits. It started with cel-animation, extended farther into abstraction, as indicated by the works of Hans Richter, Viking Eggeling, and others, but also reflected an emphasis on realism, as in the works of Disney and others. Our continuum further extends as we come to computer forms that manifest either highly realistic, three-dimensional representations of reality (a "created reality") or highly abstract works.

The materials cited in the first part of this chapter emphasize the general aspects of each category of animation. Users of the guide are urged to check the second part, "Personalities in Animation," for more specific material about the creators and their techniques.

CEL-ANIMATION

Studios. Four studios have been widely publicized over the years, although many more have existed. The organization most written about was, not surprisingly, Walt Disney's. One of the earliest books that attempted a serious review of his art and organization was *The Art of Walt Disney* by Robert D. Feild, with an emphasis on the process of animation through a studio system. However, the definitive book about Disney, his animators, and the organization is Bob Thomas's more recent *Walt Disney: An American Original*. Thomas drew from interviews with Disney and others, interoffice memoranda, shorthand minutes of studio meetings, and Disney correspondence, revealing for the first time a more accurate picture of the Disney story. While quoting from these documents, sometimes at great length, Thomas has provided a more accurate version of events than interviews permit, although personal interviews, as a research tool, certainly fulfill other functions. His earlier book, *The Art of Animation*, was aimed at a young-adult audience with easy-reading narration, a glossary, and excellent illustrations of the animation process at Disney Studios. A more official, family-oriented biography was provided by Disney's daughter, Diane, and Pete Martin, in a book published in 1956, a decade before Mr. Disney's death, *The Story of Walt Disney*. In considerable contrast, Richard Schickel's *The Disney Version* attempts to cut through the so-called

Disney myths and present an objective overview of cartoon content and organization in American culture. Schickel surveyed most of the enormous periodical material on Disney with several of these references included in the bibliography. Readers who want another view might read Al Kigore's "The Disney Assault," and Leonard Maltin's "More on the Disney Version," published in *Film Fan Monthly*. Other recent books reviewing the Disney experience include *The Art of Walt Disney* by Christopher Finch, and *Walt: Backstage Adventures with Walt Disney*, a personal recollection of the studio by Charles Shows. Finch's work was originally published in a 458-page deluxe edition in 1973 but two years later a shorter 160-page version was published. The shorter version is still lavishly illustrated with Disney characters and ephemera. One large chapter on Disney's operation distilling several references cited in this chapter is contained in Roy Pickard's *The Hollywood Studios* which also has a detailed chronology. Another overview of the studio was published in *You Must Remember This*, edited by Walter Wagner, in his "Ward Kimball: The Wonderful World of Walt Disney."

There have been a few academic studies about Disney, but from the standpoint of the studio, Richard Allen Shale's dissertation, "Donald Duck Joins Up: The Walt Disney Studio During World War II" is the most relevant here. Shale has reliably canvassed the publically available literature including some government documents. With the assistance of David Smith, archivist at the Disney Archives, Shale was able to exploit that resource, interview several Disney personnel including Ward Kimball, Frank Thomas, Lou Debney, and Harry Tytle among others and compile extensive lists of Disney's wartime products. His work is one of the few systematic studies of an animation organization. The study suffers from having to summarize and outline the films analyzed, but Shale weaves the comments of Kimball and others, including various critics, into the narrative. For example, the "Panchito footage" in the *Three Caballeros*, the main responsibility of Ward Kimball, is one of the most overlooked plateaus in Disney abstraction (which Shale describes as a Rorschach test). When Donald Duck gets caught up in the sound track, the vibrations burst into a rhythmic pattern, orchestrated with the music, with such precision that it might be mistaken for a computer-generated sequence. The visual "jumps" (while the Panchito character holds the final note of the bouncy "Three Caballeros" song) were revolutionary for the time and yet have a timely relevance to today's forms. Shale's study explains the reaction of the sequence director to Kimball's assertive freedom and Walt Disney's personal approval " . . . that nothing be changed."[3] Portions of his study have been published in *Funnyworld* and other limited-circulation magazines identified in the thesis.

Several meritorious periodical articles have analyzed and reported the business aspects of the Disney organization and these are identified under this heading in the bibliography.

With respect to a specific list of Disney output, two sources are useful starting points. Leonard Maltin's *The Disney Films* gives an encyclopedic coverage. Issue number 12 of *Film Dope*, published in England, has what claims to be a complete filmography of Disney products from the early days through the live-action films of the 1950s. The remainder of the citations in the Disney category embraces historical, critical, or technical matters from the beginning to the present.

Only a few periodical articles about the cartoon unit at Metro-Goldwyn-Mayer have been published in recent years, and the most authoritative are by authors Mark Mayerson, Mark Kausler, and Mike Barrier. Joe Adamson once complained that film historians usually discarded any reference to cartoons while cleaning out the desk in preparation for writing film history. In the same instance, writers of studio biographies, such as Bosley Crowther, Arthur Marx, and Alvin H. Marill are no exception to Adamson's observation. None of them mentions the animation unit at Metro-Goldwyn-Mayer nor any of the animators while chronicling the history of this studio and the major movers and shakers.

The Warner Brothers cartoon unit should be the subject of at least one new book in the near future. Mike Barrier was scheduled to author one, apparently with a heavy emphasis on animation art. Three academic studies on the Warner Brothers cartoons were completed in the last decade. Roger Bullis conducted a thematic study of Warner's films during the post-World War II period using the resources of the Mass Communication History Center, Wisconsin Center for Film and Theater Research, at the University of Wisconsin, Madison, where about one-fourth of the Warner's cartoon films are available for research. The center is described in more detail in Appendix 2. Darryl J. Fox focused on Warner cartoons directed by Tex Avery and Bob Clampett in a similar study at Stevens Point, Wisconsin. Marilyn Hempstead's master's thesis, in a loosely organized study, described character images based on the graphic direction of the human form. The more informed periodical pieces published in fanzines and limited circulation journals such as the now defunct *Velvet Light Trap* include those by Elizabeth Dalton, Mitchell S. Cohen, and an anonymous "The New Bugs Bunny Feature" in *Mindrot*. John Canemaker, Joe Adamson, and Greg Ford have contributed to other national periodicals. Researchers should also consult the personality section of this chapter, including the names Chuck Jones, Frank Tashlin, Bob Clampett, Tex Avery, and other Warner animators.

There have been large numbers of articles published on the United

Productions of America (UPA), frequently cast as the rebels against Disney's fully animated style. The periodical articles cited in the bibliography embrace several reports, many evaluative, on the UPA forms and history. Additional relevant materials which concentrate on characters, such as Mr. Magoo or Gerald McBoing Boing, are included in the following section.

Characters. One oversized and illustrated volume still in print and providing brief historical notes on the principal animated cel characters from 1915 to 1950 is *The Great Movie Cartoon Parade* by John Halas and David Rider. Joe Adamson's "Cartoon Constellation," a foldout in the American Film Institute Report Volume 5, no. 2 (Summer 1974), identifies the principal characters animated from the late 1920s to 1950. John Culhane wrote *Retrospectives of Popular Cartoon Characters*, which accompanied a film festival in California in the early 1970s. A copy was located in the University of Southern California Doheny Library containing his notes on selected cartoons of Popeye, the Pink Panther, Tom and Jerry, Mr. Magoo, Woody Woodpecker, and Bugs Bunny, along with biographical material on some of the artists who developed the characters. Much of Culhane's material about Joseph Barbera, Stephen Bosustow, Fritz Freleng, David DePatie, William Hanna, Chuck Jones, and Walter Lantz was based on company press releases, general literature, and personal interviews.

The Disney characters are also prominently represented in the character literature. Two books feature *Mickey Mouse: Fifty Happy Years* and *Donald Duck*, by David Bain and Bruce Harris, and Marcia Blitz, respectively. The Donald Duck biography describes the history of the character, is lavishly illustrated, and describes the transformations through the years. Both book emphasize the picture and drawing formats, with a number of film-frame layouts presented in storyboard fashion in the Bain-Harris book, written in commemoration of the fiftieth anniversary of Mickey Mouse. Interestingly, in this "official birthday book," Richard Schickel's scathing critique of the Disney role in American culture is included in the bibliography.

Howard Edward Rieder's master's thesis, available from the University of Southern California, carefully outlines "The Development of the Satire of Mr. Magoo" including a history of the character, filmography of theatrical films, and an extensive bibliography. Rieder published a section of his study in *Cinema Journal* in 1969, "Memories of Mr. Magoo." A few other published analyses of UPA characters are also indicated in the bibliography.

Warner Brothers characters have been studied in a few master's theses, listed under the studio rubric below, and in a number of periodical articles listed in the bibliography. The Fleischers have not been completely forgotten, particularly with the Bud Sagendorf recap of *Popeye: The First Fifty Years*, but this work emphasizes the comic strip more than the Fleischer animations. *Animania* (formerly *Mindrot*), a fanzine published in Minneapolis since 1976, has included several filmographies of various characters including the Superman character and some of the Betty Boop animations. Leslie Carbarga's book *The Fleischer Story*, cited in the personality section of this chapter, contains the most complete listing of Fleischer films. Other characters are listed in the bibliography.

OBJECT ANIMATION

> Yet stills have become a new rage in TV. It now appears that a new frontier exists in the ability of TV to present stills and capitalize on their virtues. Many agencies, producers and advertisers have found that for a number of purposes it has worked best to disregard TV's ability to represent actual life, to set aside all the rules and techniques that contribute to this and take a fresh look at what would be expressed through film or tape.[4]
>
> RICHARD A. LEHMAN

> And the future? The experimental film will have as definite and recognized a place in the future as the documentary film has today.[5]
>
> HANS RICHTER

Television has given new life to object-animation represented in the early, dimensional, animated films of Willis O'Brien or George Pal, in cutouts by Bob Godfrey or Frank Mouris, in the silhouettes of Tony Sarge or Lotte Reiniger, in stills-in-motion techniques in various TV and film documentaries, and in a cornucopia of abstractions by Oskar Fischinger, Hans Richter, or Walter Ruttman.

Miniatures. The most traditional application of object-animation was in the use of miniatures and models, typically found in science fiction films. John Baxter's *Science Fiction in the Cinema* devotes some attention to the masters of what some call dimensional animation, Willis O'Brien and Ray Harryhausen. *Millimeter* and *Cinefantastique* have published histories of this form including Mark Wolf's "Stop Frame: The History and Technique of Fantasy Film Animation." Jeff Rovin's books *From the Land Beyond Beyond: The Making of Movie Monsters You've Known and Loved* and *Movie Special Effects* are recent histories partially based on interviews with Harryhausen and others. While Rovin's explanations are often clearly expressed, there are occasional lapses into generality. These sections read like a 1930s *Popular Science* explanation when filmmakers were not anxious to reveal their trade secrets. With regard to his historical treatments, one has the impression that Rovin draws too often from *Popular Science* and *Popular Mechanics*.

The first study to seriously survey the science fiction film was Douglas Menville's 1959 master's thesis, since published in book form by Arno Press. As mentioned in Chapter 2, the landmark study in puppet animation is L. Bruce Holman's *Puppet Animation in the Cinema* based upon his 1971 Syracuse University dissertation. The latter study contains all the extensive documentation which is omitted in the book version. Holman's study is both a history and a how-to guide. Steven Wilson's master's thesis, completed at the University of Southern California in February 1977, reviews in detail the use of animated puppets in live-action films, and includes interviews with Jim Danforth, Miles Pike, and David Allen. A number of techniques are identified and discussed. His thorough review of the literature includes a close scrutiny of *American Cinematographer* and the thirty-three films using the combined live-action and animated technique. *Closeup*, a small but well-printed limited-circulation fanzine, has featured several retrospective pieces on puppet animators. (Appendix 7 has more information on this irregular publication.) While puppet or dimensional animation is still seen on television by mass audiences, the form has extended itself into live-action abstractions such as "Mr. Bill" on "Saturday Night Live" and "The Muppets," along with stop-motion work mixed with other media, as in *Star Wars* or *The Empire Strikes Back*.

Cutouts. Very little has been published on cutout animation per se, but the program notes by Ian Birnie for the Museum of Modern Art's Department of Film 1978 Retrospective form a good historical treatment, divided into the pioneers, formalists, and expressionists. The pioneers included Sid Marcus, Bryant Fryer, Emanuele Luzzati and Giulio Gianini, Jiři Trnka, Norman McLaren, Evelyn Lambart, Lotte Reiniger, Noburo Ofuji, and the Fleischer brothers, Max and Dave. The formalists, in Birnie's scheme, included French filmmaker Jean-Francois Laguionie, George Dunning, Michael Snow, Miroslaw Kijowicz, Réné Jodoin, Harry Smith, Larry Jordan, Stan Vanderbeek, Robert Breer, and Oskar Fischinger. According to Birnie, the animated expressionists demonstrate psychological pressures and private obsessions, with a form drawn from the movement in Germany during and after World War I. Filmmakers in this classification include Jan Lenica, Berthold Bartosch, Zofia Oraczewska, Frank Mouris, and Victor Faccinto. Terry Gilliam's *Animations of Mortality* is a recent fantasy collage, in book form, that will take the reader behind the scenes of animation into a wacky world. If you have a sense of humor, your eyes will not be very dry by the fifth page or so, and you may not be able to finish the book in one sitting because of giggling interruptions. Gilliam is the "aging animator" of *Monty Python and the Holy Grail* and the creator of the film *Jabberwocky*.

Silhouettes. Silhouette technology is explained in the Norman Laliberte and Alex Mogelon book *Silhouettes, Shadows and Cutouts: History and Modern Use* without any particular application to film. The Lotte Reiniger autobiography published by B. T. Batsford in 1970 is probably the best exposition of technique in this filmmaking. An earlier history by Frederick A. Talbot, *Moving Pictures: How They Are Made and Worked*, has a chapter on early silhouette techniques and other tricks.

Photo. The still-in-motion technique used in film and television documentaries since the late 1940s derived some influence from cutout collages and photomontages of many earlier decades. The chief influences in photomontage and the techniques used to dismember reality and reconstruct new interpretations based on photography are described in Dawn Ades's *Photomontage*. Two master's theses, by Mac Owen Shaffer and Pierre Norman Sands, trace the later development of still-photography animation. The Sands study, completed at the University of Southern California in 1957, describes one specialization of this form, the filmagraph or slide-film printed on film stock with a soundtrack. Shaffer's 1963 study takes a longer view of the still-in-motion technique by identifying the early attempts to animate photos, the military's training adaptations during World War II, and the European influences on the form, concluding with NBC's "Project Twenty" series and applications in television advertising. Phillip Joseph Lane's dissertation concentrates on the "Project Twenty" series. Several periodical citations are included in the bibliography for this segment, including the most recent technological media-mix with the form, the use of computer-assisted animation stands that animate slides, and other art work as described by Elinor Stecker in *Filmmakers Newsletter*.

Experimental. At once we come to the problem of finding a term upon which most would agree but which also correctly describes an individually creative branch of filmmaking—films usually conceived and made by one person and considered a personal statement of that filmmaker. Some of these cinematic personal statements incorporate animation. But a satisfactory label to describe them and their creators has not been determined in the literature. Such films have been called "underground," "experimental," "avant-garde," "abstractions," or "the new American cinema." There is more agreement, however, on the derivations of these works, springing out of the pictorial fantasies of Georges Méliès and the independent film movement in Europe between 1921 and 1930, called the avant-garde. The chief characteristics of these films were that they were non-representational and noncommercial. One of the earliest theorists and filmmakers was Hans Richter who has written his views of such work in *Dada: Art and Anti-Art*. William S. Rubin, Malcolm Le Grice, and Standish

Lawder have more broadly described the films in the art context of the times. For example, Lawder's *The Cubist Cinema* emphasizes the interconnection between film and modern art while documenting the key filmmakers and their work. The influences on the work of Fernand Léger and *Ballet Mecanique*, which incorporated animation techniques, are discussed with a photo-shot analysis. In America one of the earliest anthologies to treat the experimental film seriously was Roger Manvell's 1949 *Experiment in the Film*, reprinted by Arno Press in 1970. Another Arno reprint, Frank Stauffacher's *Art in Cinema*, contains the program notes and biographical sketches for films shown at the San Francisco Museum of Art (1947). *Film Quarterly* published Lewis Jacobs's two-article history of experimental film in 1947-1948, in which he found German expressionism an important influence on the early form. In the United States, Jacobs concluded, the experimental movement had always been small, viewed by only a few, with widely scattered filmmakers. Mary Bute, Ted Nemeth, and Oskar Fischinger were among the few active in America in the 1930s. But following World War II, film appreciation programs and cinema societies, using the new 16mm formats, expanded the audiences for the experimental film. The forms of film varied considerably, from the early works of Maya Deren and Kenneth Anger to abstractions and animations of Oskar Fischinger and John Whitney. Others, such as Slavko Vorkapich, dealt with reality more objectively. Sheldon Renan's 1967 survey of the American "underground" film is among the best organized biographical surveys of major artists. Gregory Battcock's *The New American Cinema* is an anthology of theory, criticism, and filmmakers, and it complements the Renan book. P. Adams Sitney has written or edited four additional works in recent years including reprints from the scarce *Film Culture* issues of the 1950s and a list of independent film awards from 1959-1968. *Visionary Film: The American Avant-Garde* (1974) was his second book, followed by *The Essential Cinema: Essays on Films in the Collection of Anthology Film Archives* (1975). The latter contains an extensive bibliography compiled by Caroline S. Angell on books and articles organized by name and title in the files of Anthology Film Archives, a critically important resource for the abstract film. Appendix 2 contains more information on the Anthology Film Archives. In 1978 Sitney published a reader on the avant-garde film containing writings by several filmmakers who incorporate animation technology in their work. *Essential Cinema* also outlines the derivations of the independent American cinema including an identification of the filmmakers and descriptions of their techniques. A more abbreviated history, edited by Marilyn Singer, *A History of the American Avant-Garde Cinema*, is designed to accompany the Whitney Museum of American Art film program, which is an extensive, circulating program of experimental films.

For criticism, readers have Parker Tyler's *Underground Film: A Critical History* and the collection of Jonas Mekas's *Village Voice* columns entitled *Movie Journal: The Rise of a New American Cinema, 1959-1971*.

Contemporary experimenters in abstractions and animation have exploited new tools such as computers, some since the early 1960s. Robert Russett and Cecile Starr put together an informative anthology about the major independent experimentalists beginning with Leopold Survage, Walter Ruttmann, Viking Eggeling, Hans Richter, Oskar Fischinger, and Len Lye. Several writings by the animators themselves are included in this well-illustrated and important volume embracing European, Canadian, and American artists. Gene Youngblood's *Expanded Cinema* surveys the film in a more general universe but includes the new animated forms such as computer-generated images and mixed media. A number of experimentalists such as Jordan Belson and the Whitneys are emphasized. Moreover, this volume expands into the television medium and holography, perhaps a bit prematurely, but consistent with the book's title. Some selected, but very useful, periodical materials are also appended to the bibliography for this section.

DRAWING-ON-FILM

> The main difference between immobile painting and cinematic drawing lies in the fact that the element of time which is artificial to the former becomes one of the essentials of the latter. In this sense animated drawing partakes of the qualities of music, poetry and the dance. It must be appreciated not only in terms of simultaneous proportion, as in painting, but also in successive tempos that have a beginning and an end.[6]
>
> JEAN CHARLOT

Cameraless Animation. Drawing-on-film was, in the era before computer-generated images, the most abstract form of animation and was probably the first to combine with other techniques if the early works of Len Lye are any indication. David Curtis and Malcolm Le Grice have described these early works by Lye and others cited in the section about experimental film. Sheldon Renan, in his inventory volume, *An Introduction to the American Underground Film*, concluded that the influence of Lye and McLaren extended to the American experimental forms. Oskar Fischinger was another important animator influencing the postwar American film. In *Abstract Film and Beyond*, Le Grice describes how Lye's drawing-on-film technique later combined with color printing and developing techniques to produce graphic, nonrepresentational shapes. While Lye is probably the first to draw images on film, McLaren was probably the first to draw sound tracks and create his own sound without the technology of sound cording. What separates these films from all other experimental animation is the removal of the camera and the sound recorder from the production process, truly manifesting a completely drawn work from the ground up. This animated form is also relatively inexpensive and is within the reach of most amateur budgets. Two articles by Bert Anderson and Michael Witsch that discuss variations in the technique are cited in the bibliography.

Titles. Another related abstraction but with far more definition has been the increase in animated titles in feature films and other graphic techniques used in television advertising. Saul Bass is most often associated with film-titling animation but Bob Abel, Al Stahl, and Buzz Potamkin are among the video counterparts using computers, stills-in-motion, or traditional cel techniques. The periodical materials by Thomas Barry, Everett Aison, and Irwin Rothman provide some historical perspective for the graphic qualities applied to features and commercials.

COMPUTER ANIMATION AND TV GRAPHICS

To many of the older Hollywood producers and production designers, images generated by computers look spiritless compared to animation done by hand. But the generation that has grown up with television seems to have less difficulty accepting this kind of graphics.[7]

JOHN CULHANE

We all have to get to know one another these days, cross all kinds of barriers, now that it is imperative for us to mix our media.[8]

JAMES BROUGHTON

By the mid-1970s, economic conditions suddenly grew worse. Movie and television audiences lost their taste for realism, since they figured they were getting more realism than they could handle looking at grocery prices. They were ready again for illusion.[9]

JIM SEALE

Computer-animation literature encompasses a large range of theory and practice. The two major areas in this burgeoning technology are computer-generated animation and computer-assisted or computer-controlled animation. In computer-generated animation, the machine generates images on a screen or directly on film. Computer-assisted animation uses a programmed machine to control an animation camera and the positioning of artwork. Unlike the early cel-animators, computer-generated animation requires substantial investment in hardware seldom available outside a few large industrial concerns, such as IBM, Bell Telephone, or Boeing (Seattle), and major university research centers, such as Ohio State University or the

University of Utah. Computer-generated animation of crude dimensions was first completed in the early 1960s. Up to that time, computer graphics had evolved in industry to aid in research and design. This later expanded as a tool into scientific and medical research with widespread application in the mass media only in the last five to seven years.

There are three basic methods of generating images by computer. The raster-scan method uses the machine to change the intensity, color, and brightness of a scanning beam as it moves across the face of a cathode-ray tube, constructing an image in a manner similar to a TV set. Line- or vector-generation, a second method, uses the program and machine to create lines, perhaps resulting in sticklike cartoon characters or engineering drawings. Dot-generation is the third and most expensive method but is by far more elegant in appearance. The program and computer generate animated images a dot at a time, requiring that each image be mathematically defined in order to position all the dots that make up the image, each having a defined intensity, color, and position.

Computer-generated animation and graphics are unique in contrast to the traditional cel forms. Depending upon the program, one has an extremely large range of image manipulation including rotation, twisting, multiplication, flyovers, changing points of view, or turning around the image. By adding a mathematical model or modeled outcomes to a phenomenon, such as piloting a ship through the water, the computer can generate new animation to correspond to the planned outcomes when a steering mechanism is turned by a trainee. This is an interaction of the machine with the human who triggers new animation depending upon what controls are activated and how. Boeing Aircraft Corporation developed such training devices using computer graphics, less sophisticated at first, by the mid-1960s. The Evans-Sutherland Corporation delivered an interactive system to the Houston Space Center, now used to train space shuttle pilots. Two color-TV receivers correspond to front and rear views from inside the space ship and present shaded, three-dimensional views in full color of the ship's exterior. The rear view shows an opening cargo hold and a boom for loading or unloading. The front view, when the author and David LeRoy "flew" the joystick in November 1978, had animated the Skylab satellite, which later fell to earth. (At that time there was a modest expectation that perhaps the space shuttle might be able to maneuver the satellite into a safe splashdown area.) Many owners of TV games that hook into home television sets are actually using programmed computer-graphics in crude forms. These interactive technologies work in similar fashion to the more sophisticated computer-driven training systems such as those designed by Evans and Sutherland.

Before getting too euphoric about computer-generated images, there are still substantial problems to be overcome. Image quality still suffers in comparison to traditional photographic media. Image quality can be enhanced as storage capacity in the computer memory is increased, but this can add to the cost. Others complain that in the display of computer-animated images, resolution, color, or brightness values are not always reliably displayed. Costs are still high for hardware, but with the new computer-chip generations even the home computers such as the Apple now have simple computer-graphic displays and games.

Computer-assisted or computer-controlled animation, on the other hand, is now widely available and clearly introduces distinct improvements and economic efficiencies into the traditional animation processes. The computer controls the photography of the artwork or positions the artwork which is eventually photographed and animated. The filmmaker, using simple instructions, can control the camera, artwork, and sequencing of actions for both or separately, with complete accuracy and repeatability. To perform a simple camera move into a visual, photographed one frame at a time, requires several calculations if done conventionally. One key instructional word, given a computer program on this move, would activate the program and the machine would execute the move accurately, eliminating the time required to calculate the move by hand. The repeatability advantage can enhance an animator's design to incorporate more complex manipulations of the artwork and camera. More experimentation can take place because the animator can always return to the earlier actions and repeat or modify the manipulations.

The literature on computer animation and television graphics has grown enormously in the last two decades. It can be organized into three fairly distinct subgroups. The first subgroup contains the "traditional" film and broadcast literature, typically emphasizing biographical, business, or mildly critical views of the so-called underground film and video. The second subgroup attempts to bridge art and the machine and involves the humanistic side of machine-generated art. Many of these writings evolved from the nonanimated aspects of computer graphics, in which programs generated drawn output of various designs. The third subgroup, which looms with far greater importance now that home computers are becoming available, is the technical and technique literature that embraces both theory and application. Most of the basic histories and critical volumes cited earlier in experimental film contain chapters outlining the work of such computer animators as Ken Knowlton, Lillian Schwartz, Jordan Belson, Stan Vanderbeek, and John Whitney. These books and periodical materials are generally descriptive and rarely critical. Similar to treatments of the filmmakers of live-action films, a great deal of space is given to descriptions of the films themselves. Such books include those by Gregory Battock, Malcolm Le

Grice, and Gene Youngblood. The best of this lot is *Experimental Animation: An Illustrated Anthology*, by Robert Russett and Cecile Starr, which contains a meaningful set of photographs, something unusual for many film texts which merely reproduce publicity pictures. Russett and Starr have carefully selected strips of film and actual frame enlargements to better illustrate this abstract phenomenon. The nearly three hundred illustrations are well balanced with an informed text, interviews, and reprinted articles. Several periodicals and trade journals regularly report on industrial applications of computer-animation and generalized technical developments. Hooper White's "Computer Rising Star in Art of Animation," from *Advertising Age* or the anonymous "Two New Devices Debut in CBS's Coverage of the Super Bowl," from *Broadcasting* magazine, are typical examples. *Print* and *Television/Radio Age*, *Filmmakers Newsletter*, and *Millimeter* are other trades that also report these developments in generalized fashion, but none would provide a satisfactory basis for keeping up with the technical aspects of the technology. However, the journals do provide the reader timely information about the state of the art in a field that is quite dynamic.

The bridge between art and machine is represented in the dated overview, *The Computer in Art*, by Jasia Reichardt. The illustrations include the work of Charles Csuri, Lillian Schwartz, Michael Nolls, and F. W. Siden, with explanations of the computer processes which produced the work. *Cybernetic Serendipity: The Computer and the Arts*, an earlier book by Reichardt, is a catalogue which accompanied an early computer art exhibition. The best work of this type is Herbert W. Franke's *Computer Graphics: Computer Art* because of the theoretical view coupled with the applications of the hardware and software. The historical section is more extensive than the others, and the book also has a list of individual biographies plus an extensive bibliography. Theses, such as Evard Wadsworth's "A Study of the Computer As An Aesthetic Visual Generator" (University of Southern California), appeared in 1969 and dealt with technical problems in computer-animation or graphics. This thesis is somewhat unusual in that the author is among the earliest to raise questions of artistic application.

The technical literature is complex, with some works using the familiar jargon of the professional filmmakers and others incorporating the highly technical terms, concepts, and notations of the mathematician and computer specialist. A large amount of these materials report on problems and tentative solutions, new computer languages, or new hardware and software, as the citations in the bibliography to this chapter indicate. In the decades of the 1960s and 1970s, computer-graphics was developing into a more distinctive discipline within the field of computer science. One sign of these developments was the emergence of specialized books and professional journals which, in part, correlated and reported the expanding knowledge about the specialty. The key journals of vital interest to new or traditional computer-graphic filmmakers are described in more detail among the entries in Appendix 7. Some citations to these important publications are listed in this chapter's bibliography, such as Michele Kaplan and Donald P. Greenberg's "Parallel Processing Techniques For Hidden Surface Removal," in *Computer Graphics* or Edwin E. Catmul's "New Frontiers in Computer Animation," a more generalized piece for *American Cinematographer* readers. In the late 1960s, annual conferences were staged in various parts of the United States which brought specialists together on a variety of computer-graphic topics. Reports of many of these conferences were subsequently published and formed another basis for this burgeoning literature. The Don Secrest and Jurg Nievergelt edited work, *Emerging Concepts in Computer Graphics*, published in 1968, is one example, among many. Up to 1973 there was not even a textbook in computer graphics where beginners could cope with fundamental problems. In 1979 William Newman and Robert F. Sproull released their second edition of *Principles of Interactive Computer Graphics* which is critically acclaimed by many as the definitive text. Other useful training materials are discussed in Chapter 5.

While now out of print, *Computer Animation*, edited by John Halas and published in 1974 by Hastings House, was the earliest anthology on this subject. While dated, this book still serves as a good introduction to theory and practice. Halas's introduction is a lucid opening to a new technology with a new vocabulary but without any traditions.

Keeping up with the continuing stream of technical papers can be a problem of some magnitude since although many film and television journals usually report generalized developments the very specialized journals, such as *Computer Graphics* and *Image Processing* or *Computers and Graphics*, are expensive and not widely available. However, this scientific material and some of the professional film literature is thoroughly indexed and accessible through the finding aids discussed in Chapter 3.

As industrial and educational television systems expanded into nonbroadcast applications and the costs for systems decreased, more experimentation by amateurs and "video artists" was possible. Jonathan Price has discussed this evolution, the rise of video art, and has identified video artists largely unknown outside of the experimental centers such as WNET (New York). Some experimenters have incorporated synthesizers, feedback systems, and animation of TV images in their work, which are reported in a fanzine called *Radical Software*.

Digital TV. Closely linked to the computer and television is a new technology that has already had considerable public visibility but little recognition. Digital video-processing and storage systems have given scientists and the public the longest look ever experienced of the solar system when cameras flew by the planets Saturn and Jupiter and sent back pictures in color. The new digital systems do not generate electronic images but more efficiently store and transmit them, thus enabling multiple generations or copies without introducing the normal distortions common to analog systems. Harold E. Ennes's *Digitals in Broadcasting* is a good text on theory and application. The *Journal of Motion Picture and Television Engineers* (SMPTE) regularly reports on digital- and computer-animation technologies. David A. Howell's "A Primer on Digital Television," published in the journal (July 1975), is another starting point for understanding this technology. The SMPTE has published two symposium books, titled *Digital Television 1* and *2*, consisting of technical papers on theory and practice. The broadcasting trades, such as *Broadcasting*, *Television/Radio Age*, *Advertising Age*, and *Broadcast Management Engineering*, continue to report generalized information about the new technology, as indicated by the recent citations in the bibliography to this chapter.

Special Effects. The creative destruction of reality in today's theatrical films and television is clearly manifested in the late 1970s science fiction films and television advertising. But there was little that was new in the special effects used in *Star Wars*, *The Black Hole*, and similar films, although the methods of executing the effects were distinct improvements. The computer applications were among the new approaches, but this electronic technology still has little influence on dimensional or miniature animation. Rotoscoped mattes, composite matte shots, video effects (in *Superman*), and slitscan were among the devices used to build the fantasies, while demonstrating the value of mixing media. The public was dazzled and developed a new appreciation for created reality and a thirst for information on how it was accomplished. While the professional trade journals dutifully published generalized reports (not always revealing all of the trade secrets) books about the "*Making of . . .* " *2001, Star Trek, The Movie,* and others appeared in bookstores and paperback racks. For the professional, Raymond Fielding's *The Technique of Special Effects Cinematography* is indispensable for clear explanations of numerous special effects and supporting animation technology but it is becoming dated in electronic applications. Historically, John Brosnan's *Movie Magic: The Story of Special Effects in the Cinema* identifies more fully than most articles and few books, the personalities responsible for landmark and notable camera, laboratory, or staged effects. *American Cinematographer* has featured a large number of review articles explaining some aspects of special-effects technology in recent films. Some pieces in *Millimeter* identify several of the anonymous craftsmen in the major markets. Robert Rivlin's "Special

Effects: How They Entered Our System and Where They're Headed,'' and Peter McAlevy's "Special Effects and Titling—Magic Through Technology,'' are the most important recent reviews.

PERSONALITIES IN ANIMATION

Recent animation literature has also emphasized the artists who have, for decades, avoided the public visibility experienced by their live-action counterparts. This anonymity has not always occurred by choice, but the nostalgia wave cutting through American culture in the last two decades has provided some thrust in identifying the animators, background artists, and directors who have given animation life and form. In many cases, these materials are not so much about the *auteurs* as about their work and techniques. The list is selective and excludes film reviews and materials cited in Chapter 3 and Appendix 6.

General

Canemaker, John. "Redefining Animation." *Print* 3:2 (April 1979): 60-71. Discussion of Will Vinton, Caroline Leaf, and Dennis Pies and their recent films.

"Closeup." *Millimeter* 7:2 (February 1979): 76-81. Profiles of Ray da Silva, Mike Jones, Alan Miller, Bill Railey, and Richard Williams.

Goldrich, Robert. "TV Crowd Seen." *Backstage*, 1 September 1978, p. 11.

Huemer, Dick. "Huemeresque. Thumbnail Sketches." *Funnyworld*, no. 21 (Fall 1979): 38-43. Excerpts from Huemer's interview with Joe Adamson recorded in 1968. Norm Ferguson, Earl Hurd, Albert Hurter, Ham Luske, Fred Moore, and Perce Pearce are described.

Alexeieff, Alexandre

Alexeieff, Alexandre. "Making 'Pictures At An Exhibition.' " *Journal of the Society of Film and Television Arts* (Great Britain), Winter 1974-1975, pp. 19-20.

Starr, Cecile. "Films Without Actors. The Art of Animation." *Popular Photography* 57:3 (July-December 1968): 152. Exposition of work by Czech puppet-filmmaker Jiří Trnka and Russian-born animator Alexandre Alexeieff.

Allen, David

Mandell, Paul. "Producing 'The Primevals' Or Whatever Happened to Raiders of the Stone Ring." *Cinefantastique* 8:1 (Spring 1979): 4-11. Progress report on a dinosaur movie animated by Allen.

_____. "Laser Blast: Stop-Motion Animator David Allen Talks About His New Science Fiction Film and the Problems of Doing Model Animation Special Effects on a Modest Budget." *Cinefantastique* 6:4/7:1 (Spring 1978): 4-7.

Avery, Tex

Adamson, Joe. "Tex Avery and the Pleasures of the Flesh." *Funnyworld*, no. 15 (n.d.): 20-23.

_____. *Tex Avery: King of Cartoons.* New York: Popular Press, 1975.

Barrier, Mike. "Tex Avery: The Warner Years." *Funnyworld,* no. 15 (n.d.): 18-19.

Canemaker, John. "Animation: The Hollywood Cartoon." *Filmmakers Newsletter* 7:6 (April 1974): 32-35.

Jones, Chuck. "Confessions of a Cel Washer." *Take One* 6:10 (4 August 1978): 43.

Rosenbaum, Jonathan. "Dream Masters II: Tex Avery." *Film Comment* 11:1 (January-February 1975): 70-73.

Babbitt, Art

Canemaker, John. "Art Babbitt: The Animator As Firebrand." *Millimeter* 3:9 (September 1975): 8.

Williams, Richard. "Goofy and Babbitt." *Sight and Sound* 43:2 (Spring 1974): 94-95.

Bagdasarian, Ross

Sanderson, Lucinda Ann, and Tawney, Michael J. "Ross Bagdasarian Remembered." *Mindrot,* no. 12 (1 November 1978): 21-27.

Bakshi, Ralph

Alpert, Hollis. "The Manic World of Ralph Bakshi." *Saturday Review: World,* 9 March 1974, p. 40.

Barrier, Mike. "The Filming of 'Fritz The Cat.' " (Part 1) *Funnyworld* no. 14 (n.d.): 4.

_____. "The Filming of 'Fritz The Cat.' " (Part 2) *Funnyworld* no. 15 (n.d.): 26.

_____. "Ralph Bakshi: The Cartoon Grows Up." *Print* 28:2 (April 1974): 51.

Beckerman, Howard. "Fritz The Cat: See Fritz Run." *Filmmakers Newsletter* 5:12 (October 1972): 27-31.

_____. "Heavy Traffic Is Heavy, Heavy." *Filmmakers Newsletter,* October 1973, p. 44.

Beigel, Jerry. "Ralph Bakshi: Animation As A Director's Tool." *Action,* March-April 1976, pp. 20-25.

Beke, Gyorgy. "Ralph Baskhi: MOMA Will Never Be The Same." *Millimeter* 3:4 (April 1975): 18-19.

Bilowit, William. "Producing The Lord of The Rings." *Millimeter* 6:10 (n.d.): 8-20.

"Bombshell in Disneyland." *Newsweek,* 27 August 1973, p. 87. Bakshi Productions and *Heavy Traffic* described.

Bruce, Scott. "Bakshi On Lord Of The Rings." *Cinefantastique* 8:1 (n.d.): 34.

Champlin, Chuck, Jr. "Animator Army Advances on the Tolkien Trilogy." *Los Angeles Times,* 24 August 1978, p. VI 1.

Counts, Kyle B. "Wizards . . . The Jump from Art of Hackery Is Blinding," *Cinefantastique* 5:4 (Spring 1977): 19.

Dreyfuss, Joel. "Bakshi's 'Coonskin': Wondering What All The Fuss Is About." *Washington Post,* 17 September 1975, p. B 1.

Eyman, Scott. "The Young Turk: Junk-Culture-Junkie Takes on a Hobbit." *Take One* 6:12 (November 1978): 34-41.

Gottschalk, Earl C. J. "Move Over, Mickey—Sex, Drugs, Violence Come to Cartoonery." *Wall Street Journal*, 13 September 1971, p. 1.

Gottschalk, Earl, Jr. "What If They Showed Cartoons and No Kids Could Come?" *Los Angeles Times (West Magazine)*, 12 December 1971, pp. 42-43.

Kaplan, Alan. "Lord of the Rings Rotoscoping May Not Be the Answer." *Mindrot*, no. 14 (20 May 1979): 13-14.

Meyers, Richard. "Ralph Bakshi on the Making of The Lord of the Rings." *Starlog* 2:10 (December 1977): 57.

Olshan, Mike. "Animation Grows Up. An Interview With Ralph Bakshi." *Millimeter* 2:9 (September 1974): 28-47.

Spicer, Bill, and Zuber, Bernard. "Ralph Bakshi and The Wizards." *Fanfare*, no. 1 (Spring 1977): 9-14. Lists a number of key personnel on the Bakshi films.

Sterritt, David. "Hobbits, Hobbits Everywhere." *Christian Science Monitor*, 4 January 1979, pp. 12-13.

Stewart, Jon. "Fritz The Cat." *Ramparts* 10:9 (March 1972): 43-48. Story of the production of the film and a review of the storyline.

Zito, Stephen. "Bakshi Among The Hobbits." *American Film* 3:10 (September 1978): 58-63.

Barks, Carl

Barrier, Mike. "Screenwriter for a Duck. Carl Barks at the Disney Studio." *Funnyworld*, no. 21 (Fall 1979): 9-14.

Barré, Raoul

Martin, Andre. "In Search of Raoul Barré." Festival catalog. Ottawa: International Animated Film Festival, 1976.

Bartosch, Berthold

Starr, Cecile. "Berthold Bartosch—Animation Pioneer." *Millimeter* 5:4 (April 1977): 28.

Bass, Saul

Aison, Everett. "Saul Bass: The Designer As Filmmaker." *Print* 23:1 (January-February 1969): 90. Review of Bass's work and an interview about his approach to his work.

Bach, Robert O. "Hall of Famers Typify Best of Art Direction." *Advertising Age*, 2 April 1979, pp. 57-58. About art direction in advertising; some examples include titling by Saul Bass.

Bodger, Lowell A. "Modern Approach To Film Titling." *American Cinematographer* 41:8 (August 1960): 476-478. Work of Saul Bass explained with photos and written examples from *St. Joan*, *Around the World in 80 Days*, *Anatomy of a Murder*, *Man with the Golden Arm*.

Kane, Bruce, and Reisner, Joel. "A Conversation With Saul Bass." *Cinema* 4:3 (Fall 1968): 31-34.

"Movies. Man With A Golden Arm." *Time*, 16 March 1962, p. 46.

"Saul Bass." *Print* 11:6 (May-June 1968): 17-37.

Belson, Jordan

Eliscu, Lita. "Jordan Belson Makes Movies." *Show* 1:1 (January 1970): 57.

Polt, Harriet. "Outside the Frame. Vortex." *Film Quarterly* 14:3 (Spring 1961): 35. Detailed review of Jordan Belson's *Vortex*, which ran at the Morrison Planetarium in San Francisco from 1957 to 1960. While Belson considered this an experiment, the program consisted of nonobjective images which moved and changed, expanded and contracted, with color and monochrome effects, along with planetarium devices. Other Belson film work is described.

Blackton, J. Stuart

Slide, Anthony. *The Big V: A History of the Vitagraph Company.* Metuchen, N.J.: Scarecrow Press, 1976.

Smith, Albert E., and Koury, Phil A. *Two Reels and a Crank.* Garden City, N.Y.: Doubleday, 1952.

Blechman, R. O.

"R. O. Blechman." *Print* 28:2 (April 1974): 65.

Tyler, Ralph. "R. O. Blechman Puts His Sly Mark on Christmas." *New York Times,* 17 December 1978, p. D41. Reviews public TV's *Simple Gifts.*

Borowczyk, Walerian

Claren, Carlos. "Artist as Pornographer." *Film Comment* 12:1 (January-February 1976): 44-47. Interview with Borowczyk, who moved from animations to live-action films.

Durgnat, Raymond. "Borowczyk and The Cartoon Renaissance." *Film Comment* 12:1 (January-February 1976): 37-44. Detailed description of Borowczyk's films *Renaissance, The House, Game of Angels.*

Strick, Philip. "The Theatre of Walerian Borowczyk." *Sight and Sound* 38:4 (Autumn 1969): 166-71.

Bosustow, Steve

"Boing!" *Time,* 5 February 1951, p. 78.

Bozzetto, Bruno

Arnold, Gary. "A Misguided 'Allegro.' " *Washington Post,* 16 November 1977, p. B 10.

Daruskzka, David. "Bozetto." *Zoetrope,* no. 4 (August 1979).

Korkis, Jim. "Bruno Bozzetto." *Mindrot,* no. 14 (20 May 1979): 4. Quotations from Bozzetto about state of animation and his work.

"Neo-Fantasia (Allegro Non Troppo)." *Time,* 3 October 1977, p. 100.

Braverman, Chuck

Braverman, Charles. "The World of Kinestasis," in David A. Sohn, ed., *Good Looking: Film Studies, Short Films and Filmmaking.* Philadelphia: North American Publishing Co., 1976.

Bray, John R.

Bray, J. R. "How the Comics Caper." *Photoplay*, January 1917, pp. 67-70. Discusses how his animations are manufactured.

Canemaker, John. "J. R. Bray." *ASIFA 1975 Yearbook*. Los Angeles: ASIFA, 1975.

_____. "Profiles of A Living Animation Legend: John R. Bray." *Filmmakers Newsletter* (January 1975): 28-31.

Harding, Allan. "They All Thought Him Crazy, But They Don't Think So Now." *American Magazine* 99 (January 1925): 30.

Winchester, Tarleton. "Amazing Silhouette Pictures Produced by Noted Artists." *Miami Herald*, 23 January 1916, p. 18. C. Allan Gilber, J. R. Bray and others are described using this process.

_____. "Col. Heeza Liar: To 'Star' With Mary Pickford at NE Studio." *Miami Herald*, 21 December 1915, p. 12. Bray has a staff of six cartoonists, twenty assistant artists, and four cameramen in his description of the process of making animations.

Breer, Robert

Fischer, Lucy. "Independent Film: Talking With Robert Breer." *University Film Study Center Newsletter* 7:1 (October 1976): 5-7.

Mekas, Jonas. "An Interview With Robert Breer Conducted by Jonas Mekas and P. Adams Sitney on May 31, 1977—In New York City." *Film Culture*, nos. 56-57 (Spring 1973): 39-72.

Moore, Sandy. *Robert Breer*. Film in the Cities Monograph. Minneapolis: Walker Art Center. n.d.

"Robert Breer." *AFI Report* 5:2 (Summer 1974): 33-35.

Bute, Mary Ellen

Bute, Mary Ellen. "Abstronics: An Experimental Filmmaker Photographs the Esthetics of the Oscillograph." *Film in Review* 5:6 (June-July 1954): 263-66. She discusses recent work with abstractions and electronics in film *Abstronic* made from the face of an oscilloscope with assistance of Ted Nemeth and Dr. Ralph Potter of Bell Telephone Labs.

"Letters and Art. Expanding Cinema's Synchromy 2." *Literary Digest* 122:6 (8 August 1936): 20-21. Theodore J. Nemeth and Mary Ellen Bute discuss their second film which premiered at Radio City Music Hall, New York: *Synchromy 2*.

"Mary Ellen Bute." *AFI Report* 5:2 (Summer 1974): 40-41.

Clampett, Robert

Barrier, Mike, and Gray, Milton. "Bob Clampett: An Interview With A Master Cartoon Maker and Puppeteer." *Funnyworld*, no. 12 (n.d.): 13-37.

Canemaker, John. "Animation Journal." *Millimeter* 3:7-8 (July-August 1975): 64-65. Comments about Bob Clampett's appearance on "Camera Three" program reviewing Warner Brothers animation.

Clampett, Bob. "Beany and Cecil, Animated Cartoon Show, 1961-1962." *Mindrot*, no. 13 (1 November 1978): 31-34.

Etcheverry, Paul, and Kausler, Mark, comps. "The Films of Bob Clampett." *Mindrot*, no. 13 (1 November 1978): 26-30.

Glut, Don. "What's Up Frankenstein?" *Monsters of the Movies* 1:3 (October 1974): 4-25.

Mindrot, no. 13 (1 November 1978). Issue devoted to Bob Clampett.

"Oldtimer Clampett Regains His Beany." *Variety*, 23 February 1977, p. 31.

Onosko, Tim (transcriber). "Bob Clampett: Cartoonist." *Velvet Light Trap*, no. 15 (Fall 1975): 38-41.

Clark, Les

"Les Clark, Animator of Mickey Mouse, Snow White." (Obituary). *Los Angeles Times*, 17 September 1979, p. I 18.

Cohl, Emile

Crafton, Donald Clayton. "Emile Cohl And The Origins Of The Animated Film." Ph.D. dissertation, Yale University, December 1977.

Collins, Vincent

Reveaux, Anthony. "Reviews. Euphoria." *Film Quarterly* 29:3 (Spring 1976): 40-43. Discussion of a film by Vincent Collins which describes the production process and the film in detail.

Cuba, Larry

Hutchinson, David. "The Digital Brush: An Interview with Star Wars Animator Larry Cuba." *Starlog*, no. 12 (March 1978): 50-53.

Culhane, Shamus

Canemaker, John. "Animation History and Shamus Culhane." *Filmmakers Newsletter* 7:8 (June 1974): 23-28.

Danforth, Jim

Clarke, Frederick S. "Whatever Happened to Jim Danforth's *Timegate*?" *Cinefantastique* 8:4 (n.d.): 8-11.

Scapperotti, Dan. "The Aftermath." *Cinefantastique* 9:1 (1979): p. 5. Another article about low-budget science fiction with temperamental production chiefs and few Indians.

da Silva, Ray

"Closeups: Ray da Silva." *Millimeter* 7:2 (February 1979): 76.

Davenport, Tom

Gaffney, Maureen. "An Interview with Tom Davenport." *Film Library Quarterly* 9:3 (1976): 16-24.

David, Tisa

"Close-up." (Tisa David). *Millimeter* 3:4 (April 1975): 46.

Natwick, Grim. "Tissa." *Cartoonist Profiles*, no. 33 (March 1977): 14-17.

Davis, Marc
See Hench, John.

Deitch, Gene
"Just Call Him Howdy Dude-y, Pardner." *Collier's* 134 (23 July 1954): 64-65.
Gene Deitch directs a cutout animation film using the Howdy Doody
character for the home movie market.

DePatie-Freleng: David DePatie; Isadore ("Fritz") Freleng
Beck, Jerry. "Cartoon Review." *Mindrot*, no. 11 (24 July 1978): 6-8. List of
DePatie-Freleng theatrical cartoons released by United Artists.
_____. "Cartoon Review." *Mindrot*, no. 12 (1 November 1978): 10. Continues list
of theatrical *Pink Panther* shorts released by United Artists.
Care, Ross. "The Pink Panther Strikes Again." *Cinefantastique* 6:1 (Summer 1977):
20.
"Cartoons: Put A Panther In Your Tank." *Time*, 1 October 1965, p. 90.
Henderson, Scott. "Life In A Pink Panther Factory." *American Cinematographer*
159:7 (July 1978): 670.
Missinne, Jeff. "The Catbird Seat." *Mindrot*, no. 11 (24 July 1978): 5.
Shales, Tom. "Clouseau Encounters for the Fifth Time." *Washington Post*, 19 July
1978, p. E1.

Disney, Walt
See: Studios: Disney and appropriate text in this chapter. See also animators and
directors by name in this list.
Capra, Frank. *The Name Above the Title*. New York: Macmillan, 1971. Capra
describes his meetings with Walt Disney and the beginning of the Disney
sound film *Steamboat Willie*.
Culhane, John. "The Last of the 'Nine Old Men.'" *American Film* 2:8 (June 1977):
10-16.
Disney, Walt. "How I Cartooned 'Alice'; Its Logical Nonsense Needed a Logical
Sequence." *Films in Review* 2:5 (May 1951): 7-11.
Hollister, Paul. "Genius At Work. Walt Disney." *Atlantic Monthly* 166 (Decem-
ber 1940): 689-701.
Jacobs, Lewis. *The Rise of the American Film*. New York: Harcourt, Brace, and
Co., 1939.
Kausler, Mark. "The Changing of the Guard." *Funnyworld*, no. 19 (Summer 1978):
49-51. About the "last hurrah" of the "nine old men" and the new Disney
animators.
Kimball, Ward. "The Wonderful World of Walt Disney." In Walter Wagner, ed.,
You Must Remember This. New York: G. P. Putnam's Sons, 1975.
Klein, I. "When Walt Disney Took Another Giant Step." *Cartoonist Profiles*,
no. 33 (March 1977): 72-75.
Kurland, Gerald. *Walt Disney: Master of Animation*. Charlotteville, N.Y.: Sam Har
Press, 1971.

"Last of Disney's 'Nine Old Men' In Quip Re Auditors, Lawyers." *Variety*, 30 November 1977, p. 26. Data on *The Small One*; also covers transition of Disney animation to the 1980s.

Smith, David R. "Up To Date In Kansas City: But Walt Disney Had Not Yet Gone As Far As He Could Go." *Funnyworld*, no. 19 (Fall 1978): 22-34.

Dunning, George

Grove-Baxter, Grange. "Snow White Meets the Blue Meanies." *Film*, no. 54 (Spring 1969): 23-31.

Millar, Gavin. "Yellow Submarine." *Sight and Sound* 37:4 (August 1968): 204-5.

Eggeling, Viking

"The International Theatre Exposition, New York." *The Little Review*, Winter 1926, p. 78. Stages 8, 9, 11, 12 from Part 1 and the whole of Part 2 of *Horizontal-Vertical Orchestra*, an experimental animated film by Viking Eggeling.

O'Konor, Louise. "The Film Experiments of Viking Eggeling." *Cinema Studies* 2:2 (June 1966): 26-31.

_____. *Viking Eggeling 1880-1925: Artist and Film-Maker, Life and Work*. Translated by Catherine G. Sundstrom and Anne Bibby. Stockholm: Tryckeri AB Bjorkmans Eftertadare, 1971. An attempt to restore the outlines of Eggeling's life work based on materials in public archives, private records, museums, and libraries in Europe and the United States.

Fedder, Tobe T.

"Tobe T. Fedder." *Millimeter* 3:4 (April 1975): 47.

Fischinger, Oskar

Canemaker, John. "Elfriede! On The Road With Mrs. Oskar Fischinger." *Funnyworld*, no. 18 (Summer 1978): 4-14.

Janiak, Larry, and Daruszka, Dave. "Oskar Fischinger: An Interview With Elfriede Fischinger." *Zoetrope*, no. 3 (March 1979): 4-5.

Long Beach Museum of Art. *Bildmusic: Art of Oskar Fischinger*. Long Beach, Calif.: Museum of Art, 1972.

Moritz, William. "The Films of Oskar Fischinger." *Film Culture*, nos. 58, 59, 60 (1974): 37-188. The principal and authoritative monograph on Fischinger based on surviving papers, art, films, and other memorabilia.

_____. "The Importance of Being Fischinger." Quebec: International Animated Film Festival, 1976.

"Pioneer Of Animation: Oskar Fischinger." *Ohio Media* 1:4 (February 1978): 1-6. Interview with Elfriede Fischinger. Copy in Museum of Modern Art, Film Department, New York, N.Y.

Sheratsky, Rodney E. "Oskar Fischinger's Absolute Films." *Film Library Quarterly* 6:2 (Spring 1973): 14-19.

Fitzgerald, Wayne

"Wayne Fitzgerald Designs Important First Impressions." *Executives Financial Newsletter* (Eastman Kodak) 4:9 (n.d.). Title designer Fizgerald is a designer responsible for the quick-cut snapshots at the start of *Bonnie and Clyde*.

Fleischer, Max and David

"Boo To You." *American Magazine*, February 1940. Two-picture story of Pinto Colvig, animator and cartoonist at the Fleischer studios, Miami, seen posing in front of mirrors and drawing board.

Carbarga, Leslie. *The Fleischer Story in the Golden Age of Animation*. New York: Nostalgia Press, 1976.

_____. "The Untold Fleischer Story." Mimeographed, distributed by author, n.d.

"Cinema. Gulliver's Travels." *Time*, 1 January 1940, p. 29. Fleischer, with 678 artists in Miami studio, turning out 665,280 drawings, using up to 16 tons of paper, 49,000 pencils, and 27,600 aspirin tablets, releases second cel-animated feature in America.

Dobbs, Michael. "Reviews. Betty Boop's Biographers." *Funnyworld*, no. 21 (Fall 1979): 44-48. This review is a preliminary hype for an allegedly definitive work on the Fleischers by the reviewer!

Etcheverry, Paul. "The Max Fleischer Color Classics." *Mindrot*, 28 February 1980, pp. 8-12. He laments on low level of public visibility for the *Color Classics*, one of the Fleischers' major series.

"A Giant Comes To Town." *Good Housekeeping*, January 1938, p. 38. Feature piece obviously designed to promote the Fleischers' *Gulliver's Travels*. Article describes the production of the film in Miami and the new air-conditioned Fleischer studio where about 600 persons worked on the feature. Bill Turner is head of the script department; discusses aspects of the film plot. Edith Vernick, only woman animator on the staff, comments on characters. Seymour Kneitel discusses discovery of Gulliver model. Details about sound characterization are also discussed.

"Gulliver in Technicolor: 214-Year-Old Classic Converted Into Diverting Film Cartoon." *Newsweek*, 1 January 1940, pp. 30-32.

Hoberman, J. "Out of the Inkwell." *Village Voice*, 24 March 1980, p. 50. Author sees an influence of the Fleischers on animators Sally Cruikshank, R. Crumb, and Kim Deitch.

Hoffman, Eric. "A Nostalgic Visit With Superman, The Animated Kryptonian." *Fantastic Films* 1:2 (June 1978): 45-47.

Huemer, Dick. "Huermeresque: A New Column." *Funnyworld*, no. 18 (Summer 1978): 15-16.

_____. "Huemeresque: A Column." *Funnyworld*, no. 19 (Fall 1978): 35-36.

Kneitel, Ruth F. "Out of the Inkwell." *World of Comic Art* 1:2 (Fall 1966): 41-46. Kneitel is the daughter of Max Fleischer and widow of the late Seymour Kneitel.

Langer, Mark. "Max and Dave Fleischer." *Film Comment* 11:1 (January-February 1975): 48-56.

Maltin, Leonard. "Betty Boop Is Back." *Film Fan Monthly*, no. 130 (April 1972): 3-5.

"Popeye Boycott." *Time*, 20 September 1937, pp. 32-33. Review of Fleischer New York studio labor problems, starting in May 1937.

Press Release. "Dave Fleischer Biography." Fleischer Studios, Miami. In the museum of Modern Art, Film Department, New York, N.Y., n.d.

Press Release. "Max Fleischer Autobiography." Fleischer Studios, Miami. In the Museum of Modern Art, Film Department, New York, N.Y., n.d.

Press Release. "Thirty Years of Continued Progress Marks Growth of Animated Cartoons." Fleischer Studios, Miami. In the Museum of Modern Art, Film Department, New York, N.Y., n.d.

"Real Scenery for *Popeye*. Midget Sets Give Depth to New Movie Cartoons." *Popular Science Monthly* 129 (November 1936): 16-17. Describes the Max Fleischer process of enhancing depth in cel-animation. As in most *Popular Science* and *Popular Mechanics* publications, the exact specifications are kept vague.

Wright, Milton. "Inventors Who Have Achieved Commercial Success." *Scientific American* 136 (April 1927): 249.

Freleng, Isadore ("Fritz")

Jones, Chuck. "Fritz Freleng and How I Grew." *Millimeter* 4:11 (November 1976): 20.

Fulton, John

Mandell, Paul R. "Anything You Can Do . . . John Can Do Better." *Photon*, no. 25 (1974): 30-35. Special effects work of John P. Fulton discussed with an associate, David "Stan" Horsley. Fulton is responsible for special photographic effects in *The Invisible Man*, parting of the Red Sea in *The Ten Commandments* (1956), matte paintings of Tara in *Gone With the Wind* and *Mighty Joe Young*.

Garbutt, Bernard

Lovoos, Janice. "Bernard Garbutt: The Day of the Horse." *American Artist* 41:414 (January 1977): p. 57-61. Review of life and work of a former Disney layout artist and animator. Illustrations shown.

Gardiner, Bob

Fellman, Doug. "Twenty Nights In Clay." *American Cinematographer* 59:4 (April 1978): 392. About Bob Gardiner and Will Vinton and their project *Closed Mondays*.

Hood, George. "Dialogue With a Plasticine Sculptimator." *American Cinematographer* 59:4 (April 1978): 394-99. About Bob Gardiner and cinematographer Doug Fellman.

Gifford, Lew
See also Kim, Paul.
Hawley, Tom. "Lew Gifford on Animation." *Making Films in New York* (December-January 1975-1976), pp. 36-38.

Gillette, Burton
Farel, Frank. "The Rainbow Man." *Blackhawk Film Digest* (September 1979 Supplement), p. 6. Brief overview of career in 1916. Animated *Mutt and Jeff* in the 1920s. Later a Disney employee.

Godfrey, Bob
Rider, David. "Godfrey Goes It Alone." *Films and Filming* 11:4 (January 1965): 42.
_____. "Roobarb and Thunderclump." *Films and Filming* 21:5 (April 1975): 54.

Goldman, Frank
Kirkpatrick, Diane. "Animation Gold: Pioneer Animator, Frank Goldman, Part 2." *Cinegram* 3:1 (Summer 1978): 30-31. Worked with J. R. Bray and Max Fleischer.

Gottfredson, Floyd
Gottfredson, Floyd. "Floyd Gottfredson: A Mini-Autobiography." *Cartoonews*, no. 14. (n.d.). Disney animator.

Griffin, George
Canemaker, John. "George Griffin. Making Art, Frame by Frame." *Funnyworld*, no. 20 (Summer 1979): 42-47. Description of his work with a decided thrust on the personal film. Distributor listed as Serious Business Company. Relates some of his experiences on *Fritz The Cat*.

Grooms, Red
DeNeve, Rose. "Red Grooms: The Artist As Animator." *Print* 24:5 (September-October 1970): 59-65.

Halas-Batchelor: John Halas; Joy Batchelor
"Animation News." *Film Series 2*, no. 11/12 (February-March 1974), unpaged.
Cote, Guy. "Animal Farm." *Film*, no. 4 (March 1955): 17-18.
"Halas and Batchelor: Profile of A Partnership." *Film*, no. 4 (March 1955): 15-16.
Halas, John, and Batchelor, Joy. "Producing 'Animal Farm.'" *British Film Academy Quarterly*, no. 17 (October 1952): 2-4.
Manvell, Roger. *Art and Animation: The Story of Halas & Batchelor Animation Studio*. New York: Hastings House, forthcoming.
"Time-Saving Device for Animated Cartoons." *Broadcasting*, 19 December 1960, p. 76. New series of animation for TV. Uses some shortcuts.

Hanna-Barbera: Bill Hanna; Joe Barbera

Beck, Jerry, letter to David Murtz (undated). *Mindrot*, no. 12 (1 November 1978): 8. Lists Jack Hannah animations done for Walter Lantz.

"Delayed Start of Productions From AIP/Hanna-Barbera Pact." *Variety*, 10 May 1978, p. 6.

"Hanna-Barbera's Kidvid Umbrella: A Sat A.M. Concept." *Variety*, 26 April 1978, p. 54.

Korkis, Jim. "Jack Hannah Filmography." *Mindrot*, no. 11 (24 July 1978): 28-31.

_____. "Jack Hannah Interview." *Mindrot*, no. 11 (24 July 1978): 16-27.

" 'Popeye' Coming to CBS." *Variety*, 14 December 1977, p. 44.

Stimson, Thomas E., Jr. "TV Hit From A Cartoon Factory." *Popular Mechanics* 114:3 (September 1960): 120-26.

"They Paint A Million Cats." *Films and Filming* 3 (November 1956): 10-11. About Hanna-Barbera work at MGM, outlining the Oscared *Tom and Jerry*.

"Yabba-Dabba-Doo." *AV Communications* 12:9 (September 1978): 12.

Harman-Ising: Hugh Harman; Rudolf Ising

Barrier, Mike. "The Careers of Hugh Harman and Rudolf Ising." *Millimeter* 4:2 (February 1976): 46-50.

Hall, Ron. "Hugh Harman and Rudolph Ising at MGM." *Mindrot*, no. 3 (16 August 1976): unpaged.

"U.S. Japan Cartoon Co-Production Set by Toei With Harman-Ising." *Variety*. (Undated, unpaged, clip from New York Public Library).

West, Julian. "MGM Cartoons of Hugh Harman and Rudolph Ising (Happy Harmonies)." *Mindrot*, no. 3 (16 August 1976): unpaged.

Harryhausen, Ray

Carducci, Mark. "Ray Harryhausen: An Interview with the Master of Stop-Motion Animation." *Millimeter* 3:4 (April 1975): 20-21.

Harryhausen, Ray. *Film Fantasy Scrapbook*. 2d ed. New York: A. S. Barnes and Co., 1974. Together with the Goldner-Turner book, *Making of King Kong*, the Harryhausen work constitutes the bulk of the best literature on puppet or model animation.

Jackson, Frank. "Sinbad and the Eye of the Tiger." *Cinefantastique* 6:2 (Fall 1977): 26-27.

Meyers, Richard. "Ray Harryhausen: 'I'm Intrigued with the Art of Motion . . . ' " *Starlog* 2:10 (December 1977): 52-56.

Mitchell, Steve. "Ray Harryhausen Discusses 'Sinbad and the Eye of the Tiger.' " *Filmmakers Newsletter* 10:11 (September 1977): 20-24.

"Ray Harryhausen: The Man for Monsters." *Film Series 2*, no. 7 (October 1973): 10-11.

Scapperotti, Dan. "The Golden Voyage of Sinbad: One of the Better Fantasy Films in Recent Years but Not Harryhausen's Definitive Work." *Cinefantastique* 3:2 (Spring 1974): 44-45.

_____. "Sinbad and the Eye of the Tiger: Ray Harryhausen Interview." *Cinefantastique* 6:2 (Fall 1977): 6-16.

_____, and Bartholomew, David. "The Golden Voyage of Sinbad." *Cinefantastique* 3:2 (Spring 1974): 4.

Stein, Elliott. "The Thirteen Voyages of Ray Harryhausen." *Film Comment* 13:6 (November-December 1977): 24-28.

Uman, Joel. "The Monstrous World of Ray Harryhausen." *Take One* 4:8 (November-December 1973): 22-23. Sketch of Harryhausen's animation work, beginning with George Pal.

Wolf, Mark. "Sinbad and the Eye of the Tiger: The Special Visual Effects." *Cinefantastique* 6:2 (Fall 1977): 40-47.

Hayward, Stan

Crick, Philip. "The Freelance Vision of Stan Hayward." *Film*, no. 42 (Winter 1964): 10-13.

Hench, John

Eisen, A. "Two Disney Artists." *Crimmer's: The Harvard Journal of Pictorial Fiction*, Winter 1975, pp. 35-44. Interviews with John Hench and Marc Davis.

Henson, Tex

"Disney Films' Animator Recalls That Golden Age, Now Is Home in Texas." *Houston Chronicle*, 12 September 1979, Section 3, p. 11. At 55, Tex Henson left California and eventually arrived in Houston, doing free-lance work and teaching. He recalls the "golden era" of Disney animation.

Hoedeman, Co

Reingoldas, Elena. "The Sand Castle: Sandscrit Spoken Here." *Media and Methods* 15:1 (September 1978): 99.

Schupp, Patrick. "Co Hoedeman." National Film Board of Canada. Excerpted and translated from *Sequences*, quarterly published in French, Office des Communications Sociales, Montreal, Quebec, n.d.

_____. "Who's Who in Filmmaking: Co Hoedeman." *Sightlines* 3:12 (Spring 1979): 29-33. An interview with the maker of *Sand Castle*.

Horvath, Ferdinand Huszti

Cochran, Russ. *Graphic Gallery* no. 8. West Plains, Missouri. This is a catalogue of the work of Disney concept and story artist, Ferdinand Huszti Horvath, who worked for Disney from 1933 to the late 1930s.

Hubley, John and Faith

Archibald, Lewis. "Animation Comes Of Age: John Hubley." *Film Library Quarterly* 3:2 (Spring 1970): 5-10.

Beckerman, Howard. "In Memoriam: John Hubley." *Filmmakers Newsletter* 10:8 (May 1977): 59.

Ford, John. "Animation: A Creative Challenge—John and Faith Hubley." Kansas City, Mo.: Kansas City Art Institute, 1974.

Hubley, John; Hubley, Faith; and Trudeau, Gary. *A Doonesbury Special: A Director's Notebook*. Mission, Kans.: Sheed, Andrews, and McMeel, 1978.

Irwin, Ben. "John and Faith Hubley." *ASIFA 1975 Yearbook*. Los Angeles: ASIFA, 1975.

Korty, John. "Of Stars and Men." *Film Quarterly* 15:4 (Summer 1962): 45-48. *Of Stars and Men* is the first animated feature of John and Faith Hubley.

Schenkel, Thelma. "Exploring the Cinema of Figurative Animation: With Special Consideration of the Work of John and Faith Hubley and Jan Lenica." Ph.D. dissertation, New York University, 1977.

Huemer, Dick

Adamson, Joe. "Joe Adamson Talks With Richard Huemer." *AFI Report* 5:2 (Summer 1974): 10-17.

Adamson, Joe. "With Disney On Olympus." *Funnyworld*, no. 17 (Fall 1977): 27-45.

_____. "Working For the Fleischers." *Funnyworld*, no. 16 (n.d.): 23-29.

Huemer, Dick. "Huemeresque: A Column by Dick Huemer. The Bilking of Bunny." *Funnyworld*, no. 20 (Summer 1979): 23-26.

Hurter, Albert

Hurter, Albert. *He Drew as He Pleased*. New York: Simon and Schuster, 1948. Sketch book of Hurter with a brief biography.

Iwerks, Ub

Arnold, H. B. "Hollywood Column." *Zoetrope*, no. 4 (August 1979). Max Morgan recalls Ub Iwerks who built and designed many of Disney's effects.

Kausler, Mark. "Ub Iwerks And the Animated Film." *Film Fan Monthly*, no. 79 (January 1968): 17-19.

Lenburg, Jeff. "Ub Iwerks, Part One." *Blackhawk Film Digest*, March 1979, pp. 76-78.

_____. "Ub Iwerks, Part Two." *Blackhawk Film Digest*, April 1979, p. 76.

Mayerson, Mark. "Ub Iwerks." *Film Collector's World*, no. 14 (1 May 1977): 31.

Smith, David R. "Ub Iwerks, 1901-1971: A Quiet Man Who Left a Deep Mark On Animation." *Funnyworld*, no. 14 (n.d.): 33.

"Ub Iwerks." *Mindrot*, no. 3 (16 August 1976): unpaged.

"Ub Iwerks Restored." *Variety* (5 April 1978): 7.

Jackson, Wilfred

Letter of Wilfred Jackson. "From Wilfred Jackson." *Funnyworld*, no. 19 (Fall 1978): 4-5.

Jones, Chuck

Adamson, Joe. "Cartoonographies." *Film Comment* 11:1 (January-February 1975): 38. Cartoon lists of Chuck Jones and Tex Avery.

Albano, Robert. "Cartoon Showcase." *Mindrot*, no. 11 (24 July 1978): 13-15.

Barrier, Mike. "An Interview with Chuck Jones." *Funnyworld*, no. 13 (n.d.): 5-19.

_____. "Jones: 'Night Watchman.' " *Funnyworld*, no. 13 (n.d.): 36-37.

Canemaker, John. "The Hollywood Cartoon." *Filmmakers Newsletter* 7:6 (April 1974): 32.

Cocks, Jay. "Show Business. The World Jones Made." *Time*, 17 December 1973, pp. 77-78. Brief recap of Jones's career.

"Corrections and Reactions—Letters to *Funnyworld*. Chuck Jones (with Mike Barrier reply)." *Funnyworld*, no. 14 (n.d.): 45.

Ford, Greg, and Thompson, Richard. "Chuck Jones." *Film Comment* 11:1 (January-February 1975): 21-38.

Jones, Chuck. "Diary of a Mad Cel-Washer." *Film Comment* 12:3 (May-June 1976): 40-41.

Korkis, Jim. "Chuck Jones." *Mindrot*, no. 14 (20 May 1979): 5. Discusses major failings of Saturday A.M. animated TV programs, noting Jones's activities.

Millar, Jeff. "The Biggest Laugh." *Houston Chronicle*, 15 April 1979, p. 22.

Shales, Tom. "Looney Tuneup. Chuck Jones, Live." *Washington Post*, 25 February 1980, p. B1. Finally, Jones reveals the coyote and catches the "Roadrunner" in a May 1980 CBS-TV special. Those whom Jones "influenced" are identified.

Thompson, Maggie. "Pogo, Pogoing . . . " *Funnyworld*, no. 12 (n.d.): 39-40.

Thompson, Richard. "Duck Amuck." *Film Comment* 11:1 (January-February 1975): 39-43.

_____. "Meep Meep!" *Film Comment* 12:3 (May-June 1976): 37-43.

Ward, Alex. "Chuck Jones, Animated Man." *Washington Post*, 27 October 1974, p. G1.

Warga, Wayne. "Chuck Jones—Director Behind the Animated Stars." *Los Angeles Times* (Calendar), 27 August 1978, p. 29.

"The World Jones Made." *Time*, 17 December 1973, pp. 77-78.

Jones, Mike

"Closeups: Mike Jones." *Millimeter* 7:2 (February 1979): p. 76.

Kim, Paul

"Kim and Gifford." *Print* 28:2 (April 1974): unpaged.

Kimball, Ward

Care, Ross. "Ward Kimball: Animated Versatility." *Millimeter* 4:7-8 (July-August 1976): 18.

Lanken, Dane. "The Old Master: Being Disney's 'Artistic Conscience' Was No Mickey Mouse Job." *Take One* 6:12 (November 1978): 38-40.

Wagner, Walter. "Ward Kimball: The Wonderful World of Walt Disney." In Walter Wagner, ed., *You Must Remember This*. New York: G. P. Putnam's Sons, 1975, pp. 264-82.

Kimmelman, Phil

"Closeup: Phil Kimmelman." *Millimeter* 4:2 (February 1976): 44.

"Phil Kimmelman." *Print* 28:2 (April 1974): unpaged.

Klein, Isadore

"The I. Klein Story." *IATSE Official Bulletin*, Autumn 1967, unpaged.

Klein, I. "A Vision of Katzenjammers." *Funnyworld*, no. 14 (n.d.): 29-31.

_____. "When Walt Disney Took Another Giant Step!" *Cartoonist Profiles*, no. 33 (March 1977): 72-75.

Knight, Eric

Culbert, David. " 'A Quick, Delightful Gink' Eric Knight at the Walt Disney Studio." *Funnyworld*, no. 19 (Fall 1978): 13-17.

Knowlton, Kenneth C.

Knowlton, Kenneth. "Computer Made Films." *Filmmakers Newsletter* 4:4 (December 1970): 13-23. From a lecture by Dr. Knowlton in New York City, March 1968. Knowlton has collaborated with Lillian Schwartz and Stan Vanderbeek in production of computer films. Discusses his language BEFLIX and the paradigm of questions required for computer-animation technique.

_____. *Computer-Produced Movies*. Bell Telephone Laboratories Monograph, no. 5112. Murray Hill, N.J.: Bell Laboratories, n.d.

_____. "Computer-Produced Movies." *Science*, 26 November 1965, pp. 1116-20. Discusses BEFLIX computer language, simulation plans, drafting functions of the computer, and description of the technology.

_____. *A Computer Technique For Producing Animated Movies*. Bell Telephone Laboratories Monograph, no. 4815. Murray Hill, N.J.: Bell Laboratories, n.d.

Kurtz, Bob

"Bob Kurtz." *Millimeter* 4:2 (February 1976): 45.

Lamb, Derek

"Derek Lamb." *AFI Report* 5:2 (Summer 1974): 42-44.

Lantz, Walter

Black, Hilda. "Future of Commercial Cartoons." *International Photographer*, February 1946, pp. 5-7. Reviews Walter Lantz's predictions of a rosy future for commercial cartoons or sponsored films. Descriptions of the Lantz-sponsored films, made during World War II and thereafter, are also given.

"Filmex Hails Lantz." *Variety*, 10 May 1978, p. 40.

Irwin, Michael. "Walter Lantz Is the Only Pioneer Still Producing Cartoon Shorts for Theatres." *Films in Review* 22:4 (April 1971): 211-16. Quote from Lantz about the high cost of theatrical cartoon production and length of time for recouping investment costs.

McFadden, Irwin S. "Hahahahaha!" *Flashback* 1:3 (September 1972): 32-33.

Mertens, Ellene. "TV Crowd Seen." *Backstage*, 12 May 1978, p. 22.

Rider, David. "Don't Shoot The Woodpecker." *Films and Filming* 11:10 (July 1965): 37.

Laughlin, Kathleen

Anderson, Phil. "Who's Who in Filmmaking: Kathleen Laughlin." *Sightlines* 10:3 (Spring 1977): 21-23. With quotes, Laughlin describes many of her films as audience-oriented rather than as exercises for herself, typically using a mix of animation, matting, live-action, and other devices.

Leaf, Caroline

Blumer, Ronald H. "Caroline Leaf. Smiles in the Sand." *Cinema Canada*, October 1976, pp. 21-23. Profile of Leaf and a description of her approach to the animation medium, including her reluctance to use opticals or special effects, and a shyness about cutting (editing).

Lenica, Jan

Rosner, Charles. "Lenica." *Graphis* 16:87 (January-February 1960): 20-31.

Schenkel, Thelma. "Exploring the Cinema of Figurative Animation: With Special Consideration of the Work of John and Faith Hubley and Jan Lenica." Ph.D. dissertation, New York University, 1977.

Steiner, Henri. "Jan Lenica." *Graphis* 21:119 (1965): 240-49.

von Borresholm, Boris. "Ubu Roi." *Graphis* 32: 183-188 (1976-1977): 28-33. Jan Lenica's animated film, a 50-minute production, is referred to as "graphic works set in motion," not "cartoons."

Love, Harry

Love, Harry. "Animation Nostalgia." *Cartoonist Profiles*, no. 34 (June 1977): 62-63.

Lye, Len

Rider, David. "The Happiness Acid." *Films and Filming* 15:8 (May 1969): 72-73.

McAdow, Ron

Film Library Quarterly Staff. "An Interview with Animator Ron McAdow." *Film Library Quarterly* 9:3 (1976): 34-36.

McCay, Winsor

Canemaker, John. "The Birth of Animation: Reminiscing with John A. Fitzsimmons, Assistant to Winsor McCay." *Millimeter* 3:4 (April 1975): 14.

———. "Winsor McCay." *Film Comment* 11:1 (January-February 1975): 44-47.

Carlson, Oliver. *Brisbane: A Candid Biography*. New York: Stackpole Sons, 1937. Contains references to McCay and his work with Brisbane.

Fell, John. "Mr. Griffith, Meet Winsor McCay." *Journal of the University Film Association* 23:3 (1971): 74-87.

Hearn, Michael Patrick. "The Animated Art of Winsor McCay." *American Artist* 39:394 (May 1975): 28.

Hoffer, Thomas W. "From Comic Strips to Animation: Some Perspective on Winsor McCay." *Journal of the University Film Association* 28:2 (Spring 1976): 23-32.

Hubbard, Freeman H. "Movie-Cartooning Secrets." *St. Nicholas Magazine* 56 (March 1929): 385.

Inge, M. Thomas. "Little Nemo." *Crimmer's: The Journal of the Narrative Arts*, no. 3 (Spring 1976): 44-49. (Formerly the *Harvard Journal of Pictorial Fiction*.)

Klein, I. "The Fabulous Winsor McCay." *Cartoonist Profiles*, no. 34 (June 1977): 49-51.

McCay, Winsor. *Winsor McCay's Dream Days: An Original Compilation, 1904-1914*. Westport, Conn.: Hyperion Press, 1977.

O'Sullivan, Judith. "In Search of Winsor McCay." *AFI Report* 5:2 (Summer 1974): 3-9.

———. *Winsor McCay (1869?-1934): Aspects of American Art Nouveau*. Lecture delivered at the Smithsonian Institution, National Collection of Fine Arts, Washington, D.C., 12 July 1973. Smithsonian Archives.

Phister, Montgomery. "People of the Stage." *Cincinnati Commercial Tribune*, 28 November 1909. Report on McCay and the musical play *Little Nemo*.

Smith, Conrad. "The Early History of Animation: Saturday Morning TV Discovers 1915." *Journal of the University Film Association* 29:3 (Summer 1977): 23-30.

"Two Fantastic Draftsmen: Winsor McCay and Herbert Crowley." *Arts Magazine*, April 1966, p. 54.

McDermott, Gerald

McDermott, Gerald. "Anansi The Spider." *Sightlines* 2:6 (July-August 1969): 6-9. McDermott's film is described along with the story behind its production, the first film in the African folklore series.

McKimson, Robert

Bullis, Roger Alan. "A Thematic Study of the Post-War Warner Brothers Animated Films." Master's thesis, University of Wisconsin, 1971. Contains an interview with Robert McKimson conducted by the author in April 1970.

McLaren, Norman

Anderson, Bert. "The Filmmaker Speaks: An Interview With Norman McLaren." *Film Library Quarterly* 3:2 (Spring 1970): 13-17.

Benson, Harold. "Movies Without A Camera." *American Cinematographer* 36:1 (January 1955): 34. Norman McLaren's work described.

Collins, Maynard. *Norman McLaren*. Ottawa, Ont.: Canadian Film Institute, 1976.

Cote, Guy L. "Living With 'Neighbors'—An Interview with Norman McLaren." In *Film Book 2: Films of War and Peace*, edited by Robert Hughes. New York: Grove Press, 1962.

Glover, Guy. "Norman McLaren." *ASIFA 1975 Yearbook*. Los Angeles: ASIFA, 1975.

Jackson, Fiona Winifred. "An Analysis of the Films of Norman McLaren." Master's thesis, University of North Carolina, 1971. Outlines McLaren's career (1932-1970), his philosophy of filmmaking, and also contains a detailed analysis of his films in addition to a filmography, personal interview, and bibliography.

Jordan, William E. "Norman McLaren: His Career and Techniques." *Film Quarterly* 8:1 (1953-1954): 1-14.

McWilliams, Don. "The Career of Norman McLaren." *Cinema Canada*, no. 9 (August-September 1973): 43-49.

Norman McLaren. Montreal: Cinematheque Canadienne, 1965. Booklet listing tributes to Norman McLaren and a listing of his films up to 1965.

Pratley, Gerald. "The Latest 3-Dimensional Films." *Films in Review* 3:4 (April 1954): 171-74. Description of two Norman McLaren stereoscopic films, *Now Is the Time* and *Around Is Around*, the latter accompanied by synchronized stereophonic 4-track sound.

Ropchan. "The Career of Norman McLaren." *Cinema Canada*, August-September 1973, pp. 43-49.

Rosenthal, Alan. "Norman McLaren on Pas de deux." *Journal of the University Film Association* 22:1 (1970): 8-15.

Maltese, Michael

Adamson, Joe. "Well, for Heaven's Sake! Grown Men!" *Film Comment* 11:1 (January-February 1975): 18-20.

Melendez, Bill

See also Schulz, Charles.

Korkis, Jim. "The Lion, The Witch, The Wardrobe and Bill Melendez." *Mindrot*, no. 14 (20 May 1979): 4.

Messmer, Otto

Canemaker, John. "Otto Messmer and Felix the Cat." *Millimeter* 4:9 (September 1976): 32.

Fox, Julian. "Felix Remembered." *Films and Filming* 21:2 (November 1974): 44-51.

Mayerson, Mark. "What's Up Doc?" *Film Collectors World*, no. 2 (October 1976). Column devoted to Felix.

Miller, Alan

"Closeups: Alan Miller." *Millimeter* 7:2 (February 1979): 77.

Miller, Ian

Spicer, Bill, and Zuber, Bernard. "Ralph Bakshi and the Wizards." *Fanfare*, no. 1 (Spring 1977): 9-15.

Mintz, Charles

Klein, I. "Cartooning Down Broadway." *Film Comment* 11:1 (January-February, 1975): 62-63. Charles Mintz Screen Gems studio mentioned.

Love, Harry. "Animation Nostalgia." *Cartoonist Profiles*, no. 34 (June 1977): 62-63.

"Off The Record." *Fortune*, May 1936, p. 26.

Mogubgub, Fred
"Fred Mogubgub." *Print* 28:2 (April 1974): unpaged.

Mouris, Frank
Beckerman, Howard. "Frank Film." *Filmmakers Newsletter* 7:4 (February 1974): 44-45.

Eastman Kodak. *Short Film Showcase Provides Exposure For Quality Independent Productions*. Kodak Professional Forum. Rochester: Eastman Kodak, n.d. Comments from Frank and Caroline Mouris on their independently distributed short films and their favorable reception among theater audiences. Other animated shorts mentioned in this piece about the potential for the short subject in the 1980s.

"Frank Mouris." *AFI Report* 5:2 (Summer 1974): 36-37.

Grant, Lee. "It's L. A. For Makers of 'Making It.' " *Los Angeles Times*, 11 February 1980, p. VI 6. Profile on Frank and Caroline Mouris in Los Angeles.

Kerbel, Michael. "Frank's Films." *Film Comment* 11:5 (September-October 1975): 54-58. Detailed description of *Frank Film* made by Frank Mouris and brief biography of his filming work.

Murakami, Teru
Crick, Philip. "Notes on Jimmy Murakami." *Film*, no. 43 (Autumn 1965): 34-37.

Rider, David. "No Holds Barred." *Filmmakers Newsletter* 12:6 (March 1966): 50.

Natwick, Grim
Canemaker, John. "Grim Natwick." *Film Comment* 11:1 (January-February 1975): 57-61.

Culhane, Shamus. "Grim Natwick." *ASIFA 1975 Yearbook*. Los Angeles: ASIFA, 1975.

Natwick, Grim. "A Whimsey Night in London." *Cartoonist Profiles*, no. 34 (June 1977): 24-27.

Niblock, Phil
Nelson, Abigail. "Who's Who In Filmmaking: Phil Niblock." *Sightlines* 7:3 (1973-1974): 21-23.

Noll, A. Michael
Noll, A. Michael. "Animation in a Four Dimensional Space." *Filmmakers Newsletter* 4:5 (March 1971): 29-32. General descriptions of the software components in the use of digital computer.

―――. *Computer Generated Three-Dimensional Movies*. Bell Telephone Laboratories Monograph, no. 5077. Murray Hill, N.J.: Bell Laboratories, 1965.

―――. *The Digital Computer As A Creative Medium*. Bell Telephone Laboratories Monograph. Murray Hill, N.J.: Bell Laboratories, 1967.

Noyes, Eliot, Jr.
Film Library Quarterly Staff. "Interview with Eli Noyes." *Film Library Quarterly* 9:2 (1976): 7-14.

"Interviews With . . . " (Eliot Noyes, Jr.). *AFI Report* 5:2 (Summer 1974): 38-39.

Trojan, Judith. "Who's Who In Filmmaking: Eliot Noyes, Jr." *Sightlines* 8:1 (Fall 1974): 13-15. Maker of *Clay* while a senior at Harvard.

O'Brien, Willis

"The 8th Wonder of the World." *Closeup*, no. 3, n.d.

Behlmer, Rudy, ed. *Memo From: David O. Selznick*. New York: Avon Books, 1973. Memoranda dealing with *King Kong*, RKO Radio Pictures, and Willis O'Brien.

Danforth, Jim. "The 25,000,000 Understanding." *Cinefantastique* 5:4 (Spring 1977): 24-25.

Dunn, Linwood G. "Creating Film Magic for the Original 'King Kong.' " *American Cinematographer* 58:1 (January 1977): 64-65.

Goldner, Orville, and Turner, George E. *The Making of King Kong*. New York: A. S. Barnes and Co., 1975. Discusses the major *King Kong* film (1933) but also explains techniques used in the earlier Willis O'Brien stop-motion project, *Lost World* (1925), and the later *Son of Kong* (1933).

_____. "The Making of the Original 'King Kong.' " *American Cinematographer* 58:1 (January 1977): 60.

Kelley, Bill. "King Kong." *Cinefantastique* 5:4 (Spring 1977): 20-21.

Marshek, Archie. "King Kong . . . 1933, With Kong in Telluride Memories of Kong." *American Cinemeditor* 26:4 (Winter 1976-1977): 8.

Wellman, Harold. " 'King Kong'—Then and Now." *American Cinematographer* 58:1 (January 1977): 66-67.

Opper, Frederick

Opper, Frederick Burr. *Happy Hooligan: A Complete Compilation: 1904-1905*. Westport, Conn.: Hyperion Press, 1977.

Pal, George

"Cinema. Jasper and the Watermelons." *Time*, 9 March 1942, pp. 82-83.

Hickman, Gail Morgan. *The Films of George Pal*. New York: A. S. Barnes and Co., 1977.

Johnson, Dennis S. "The Five Faces of George Pal." *Cinefantastique* 1:4 (Fall 1971): 10-27.

"Puppet Movies." *Popular Science Monthly* (April 1941): 83-84. General overview of the methods used by George Pal in producing *Puppetoons*.

Rubin, Steve. "War of the Worlds." *Cinefantastique* 5:4 (Spring 1977): 4.

Zarmati, Elio. "George Pal: Producing Special Effects Features Without Special Budgets." *Millimeter* 6:2 (February 1978): 59-63.

Pegler, Don

Sinnott, Tom. "The Animated Commercial; A Conversation with Don Pegler." *Zoetrope*, no. 3 (March 1979): 11.

Picker, James

Rivlin, Michael A. "In Production. 'Arnold.' " *Millimeter* 8:2 (February 1980): 129.

About clay animator Jimmy Picker and "Arnold," a character with a weight problem in a series of spots in the campaign against obesity.

Pintoff, Ernest

Beckerman, Howard. "Whatever Happened to Ernest Pintoff?" *Filmmakers Newsletter*, January 1974, pp. 40-41.

Selby, Stuart A. "Ernest Pintoff, Fireman." *Film Comment* 2:3 (Summer 1964): 4-9.

Pitt, Susan

Canemaker, John. "Susan Pitt. Moving, Changing and Animating." *Funnyworld*, no. 21 (Fall 1979): 15-19.

Potamkin, Buzz

"Buzz Potamkin." *Backstage*, 1 September 1978, p. 43.

"Closeup. Buzz Potamkin." *Millimeter* 6:2 (February 1978): 86.

Railey, Bill

"Closeup: Bill Railey." *Millimeter* 7:2 (February 1979): 79.

Rankin-Bass: Arthur Rankin; Jules Bass

"The Puppet Films: Part II—Rankin/Bass Productions." *Closeup*, no. 3, n.d., unpaged.

Reiniger, Lotte

Gelder, Paul. "Lotte Reiniger, Figures In Silhouette." *Film* 59 (Summer 1970): 9-10.

Reiniger, Lotte. "The Adventures of Prince Achmed or What May Happen to Somebody Trying to Make a Full Length Cartoon in 1926." *Silent Pictures*, no. 8 (Autumn 1970): 2-4.

Reiniger, Lotte. "Scissors Make Films." *Sight and Sound* 5 (Spring 1936): 13-14.

Reiniger, Lotte. *Shadow Puppets, Shadow Theatres and Shadow Films*. 1970. Reprint. Boston: Plays, 1975.

"She Made First Cartoon Feature: Lotte Reiniger Now Works In London." *Films and Filming* 2:3 (December 1955): 24.

Weaver, Randolph T. "Prince Achmed and Other Animated Silhouettes." *Theater Arts* 50:6 (June 1931): 505-8.

Reynaud, Emile

Orna, Bernard. "Cartoons Before Films." *Films and Filming* 1:3 (December 1954): 12.

Richter, Hans

Richter, Hans. "Easel—Scroll—Film." *Magazine of Art* 45:2 (February 1952): 78-86. Richter describes his early work and relationship with Viking Eggeling and the evolution he experienced from cubism through scroll painting to film.

Starr, Cecile. "Hans Richter's Experimental Work: From the Abstract to the Concrete." *Film Library Quarterly* 1:1 (1974): 13-16.

Young, Vernon. "Films. The Fantasies of Hans Richter." *Art Digest* 29:1 (1 October 1954): 19.

_____. "Painter and Cinematographer." *Arts* 33:10 (September 1959): 48-55.

Rimmer, David

Nordstrom, Kristina. "The Films of David Rimmer." *Film Library Quarterly* 5:3 (Summer 1972): 28.

Roccos, Stelios

"Who's Who in Filmmaking. Stelios Roccos." *Sightlines* 1:2 (November-December 1967): 4-5. Describes background and his work in instructional films, highlighting the *Rediscovery: Art Media* series.

Rose, Kathy

Hoekzema, Loren; Fleishman, Michael; and Klinger, Barbara. "Evolution of a Style: An Interview With Kathy Rose." *Wide Angle* 2:3 (1978): 60-66.

Schulz, Charles

Champlin, Chuck, Jr. "A Happy Collaboration. Working for More Than Peanuts." *Los Angeles Times*, 21 June 1980, p. II 8.

"Charlie Brown's New Pal." *Newsweek*, 29 July 1968, pp. 68-69. Franklin is his name and he is black.

Hulse, Jerry. "Good Grief! Snoopy's Come Home." *Washington Post*, 10 September 1978, p. H1.

LePelley, Guernsey. "You've Come A Long Way Charlie Brown." *Christian Science Monitor*, 3 October 1975, pp. 16-17. On the occasion of the twenty-fifth birthday of the Charles Schulz strip, "Peanuts."

"Mendelson on Screen, Tube; 16th Year; See $8-Mil Investment." *Variety*, 29 March 1978, p. 4.

Mitchell, Henry. "Any Day. Charles Schulz's Cartoon Complex." *Washington Post*, 24 October 1979, p. B1.

Robinson, Jeffrey. "The Beagle Has Landed." *Christian Science Monitor*, 20 July 1977, p. 20. Discussion with Charles Schulz about the popularity of "Peanuts." Background of the strip and Schulz are given, along with generalized descriptions of the merchandising activities.

Schulz, Charles. "Communications and The Cartoonist." In *Sourcebook on Corporate Image and Corporate Advocacy Advertising*. Washington, D.C.: Government Printing Office, 1978.

_____. "What Do You Do With A Dog That Doesn't Talk?" *TV Guide* 28:8 (23 February 1980): 22-26. Typical hype article in anticipation of a "new" "Peanuts" program telecast on 25 February 1980, giving background and Schulz's ideas about the character.

Sharpsteen, Ben

Smith, David R. "Ben Sharpsteen . . . 33 Years With Disney." *Millimeter* 3:4 (April 1975): 38.

Sheehan, Gordon
Arnold, Harry, and Daruszka, Dave. "Interview with Gordon Sheehan." *Zoetrope* no. 3 (March 1979): 9. Sheehan worked with the Fleischers and on early TV animation.

Simon, Jim
"Jim Simon." *Millimeter* 3:4 (April 1975): 46-47.
Simmons, Judy D. "Cartoons As Commerce." *Black Enterprise* 7:10 (May 1977): 39-43. About James A. Simon, founder of Wantu Animation, Los Angeles, California.

Smith, Harry
Carroll, Noel. "Mind, Medium and Metaphor in Harry Smith's Heaven and Earth Magic." *Film Quarterly* 31:2 (Winter 1977-1978): 37-44.

Smith, Myron P.
Smith, Myron P. "A Computer You Could Easily Learn To Love." *American Cinematographer* 51:4 (April 1970): 320-22. Smith, the director of Photography of Computer Image Corporation, describes his early work with Lee Harrison (1967), founder of Computer Image, and early computer animation in the Animac system.

Smith, Sidney
Galewitz, Herb, and Winslow, Don, eds. *Sidney Smith's The Gumps*. Chicago: Chicago Tribune, 1974.

Starevitch, Ladislas
Ford, Charles. "Ladislas Starevitch: The Pioneer with Puppets on Film Has Persevered Despite War and Revolution." *Films in Review* 9:4 (April 1958): 190.
Potamkin, Harry. "Ladislas Starevitch and His Doll Films." *Theater Guild Magazine* 7:3 (December 1929): unpaged.

Tashlin, Frank
Johnston, Claire, and Willemen, Paul, eds. *Frank Tashlin*. Edinburgh: Edinburgh Film Festival in association with Screen: Great Britain, 1973.

Taylor, Richard
"Animation Limited." *Film*, no. 57 (Winter 1969-1970): 16-17.

Taylor, Robert
"The Nine Lives of Fritz the Cat." *Films and Filming* 20:10 (July 1974): unpaged.

Terry, Paul
Krohn, Lewis J. "Paul Terry and His Terry-toons." *Classic Images*, no. 64 (July 1979): 52.
Missinne, Jeff. "Aesop's Fables Cartoons." *World of Yesterday*, no. 8 (October

1976): 5-10. Among the earliest series of cartoon animations, Paul Terry's *Aesop's Fables* began about 1923. Six years later, when Terry left to form Terrytoons, Amedee J. Van Beuren, the distributor, continued production with John Foster as director. By 1930 Van Beuren had produced an animated series of *Amos 'n Andy*. By 1934 *Aesop's Fables* was discontinued. Van Beuren hired Burton Gillette to reorganize; John Foster returned to the Terry fold. Terry revived the *Aesop* series in the 1940s in color.

Thomas, Frank

Canemaker, John. "Sincerely Yours, Frank Thomas." *Millimeter* 3:1 (January 1975): 16.

Trnka, Jiři

See also Alexeieff, Alexandre.
Orna, Bernard. "Trnka's Little Men." *Films and Filming* 3 (November 1956): 12.

Trudeau, Gary

Trudeau, Gary. "The Rolling Stone Interview: Jimmy Thudpucker." *Rolling Stone*, 9 February 1978, pp. 40-43.

Tytla, Vladimir William

Canemaker, John. "Vladimir William Tytla. (1904-1968), Animation's Michelangelo." *Cinefantastique* 5:3 (n.d.): 9-18.

Van Beuren, A. J. (Amedee J.)

Klein, I. "Cartooning Down Broadway." *Film Comment* 11:1 (January-February 1975): 62-63.

Vanderbeek, Stan

Christgau, Robert. "Vanderbeek: Master of Animation." *Popular Photography* 57:3 (September 1965): 106-11. Describes his second major contribution, "drawing right on the board." Gives examples in *Mankinda* and *Days and Nights in Black and White*.
Vanderbeek, Stan. "Movie . . . Disposable Art—Synthetic Media—and Artificial Intelligence." *Take One* 2:3 (January-February 1969): 14-16.
————. "New Talent—The Computer." *Art in America* 58:1 (January-February, 1970): 86. According to Vanderbeek, "The image revolution that movies represented has now been overhauled by the television evolution, and is approaching the next visual stage—to computer graphics to computer controls of environment to a new cybernetic 'movie art.' " He discusses his view of this evolution from 1900.

Vasulka, Woody

Hagen, Charles. "An Interview with Woody Vasulka." *Afterimages* 6:1-2 (Summer 1978): 20. A rambling account of Vasulka's reaction to interfacing with computer technology, not as a specialist but as an artist. The final section has some useful theoretical observations on where computer-generated images may take the culture and its members.

Vinton, Will

" 'Martin The Cobbler' in 3-Dimation." *Millimeter* 5:7 (July-August 1977): 84.

Verheiden, Mark. "The Making of Closed Mondays." *Cinefantastique* 4:3 (Fall 1975): 40-45.

White, Charles

"Charles White, III." *Print* 28:2 (April 1974), pp. 7-8.

Whitney, John

Brick, Richard. "John Whitney Interview." *Film Culture*, nos. 53-55 (Spring 1972): 39-82.

"John Whitney. 2." *Film Comment* 6:3 (Fall 1970): 34-38. Interview with Whitney recorded at the 1969 Flaherty Film Seminar in Lakeville, Connecticut.

Lamont, Austin. "An Interview with John Whitney." *Film Comment* 6:3 (Fall 1970): 28-33. Whitney relates more of his early background as experimental filmmaker with his brother. Also describes homemade 8mm optical printer, their 16mm optical printer, and his work with IBM.

Whitney, John. "Animation. Mechanisms." *American Cinematographer* 52:1 (January 1971): 26-31. Whitney explains some of the computer graphic technology he has devised for his films since the 1940s, indicating the films involved.

_____. "Excerpts of Talk Given at California Institute of Technology—3/21/68." *Film Culture*, nos. 53-54-55 (Spring 1972): 73-78.

_____. "Notes on 'Matrix.' " *Film Culture*, nos. 53-54-55 (Spring 1972): 79-80. Includes bibliography and filmography.

_____. "Notes on 'Permutations.' " *Film Culture*, nos. 53-54-55 (Spring 1972): 78-79.

Willis, Eli. "Abstract Film Explorations." *Theater Arts* 31:2 (February 1947): 52-53. Brief essay about John and James Whitney, describing their computer animations.

Williams, Richard

Beckerman, Howard. "A Visit With Richard Williams in London." *Filmmakers Newsletter* (May 1973): 51.

"Cartoons and Commercials." *Sight and Sound*, no. 2 (Spring 1963): 67.

"Closeups: Richard Williams." *Millimeter* 7:2 (February 1979): 80.

Crick, Philip. "The Need To Draw 80,000 Bug-Eyed Men." *Film*, no. 40 (Summer 1964): 16-20.

Culhane, Shamus. Letter (to Mike Barrier). *Funnyworld*, no. 20 (Summer 1979): 2. Disputes Richard Williams's version of what happened to *Raggedy Ann and Andy* film.

Gray, Milt, "Richard Williams, Reaching." *Funnyworld*, no. 19 (Fall 1978): 7-12.

Maltin, Leonard. "Advancing Backward, With Animation." *Print* 30:2 (March-April 1977): 70.

"Richard Williams Studio: In A Class By Itself." *Backstage*, 1 September 1978, p. 20.

Rider, David. "Four's Company." *Films and Filming* 10:1 (October 1963): 35.

Williams, Richard. "Animation and the Little Island." *Sight and Sound* 27 (August 1958): 309-11.

Letter (to Mike Barrier). *Funnyworld*, no. 20 (Summer 1979): 2. Discusses his upcoming feature *Thief and the Cobbler*.

Wilson, John

"Shinbone Alley." *American Cinematographer* 51:8 (August 1970): 763. Produced by John Wilson for Fine Arts Films Inc., Hollywood. Wilson was a former employee of Disney before forming his own company, Fine Arts.

Zander, Jack

"Jack Zander." *Print* 28:2 (April 1974): unpaged.

NOTES

1. "Disney Cinesymphony," *Time*, 18 November 1940, p. 55.

2. Oskar Fischinger, "My Statements Are My Work," in Frank Stauffacher, ed, *Art in Cinema* (San Francisco: Museum of Art, 1947), p. 39.

3. Richard A. Shale, "Donald Duck Joins Up: The Walt Disney Studio During World War II" (Ph.D. diss., University of Michigan, 1976), p. 227.

4. Richard A. Lehman, "New Vogue In Old Stills," *Television Magazine* 20:1 (January 1963): 48.

5. Quoted in Herman G. Weinberg, "30 Years of Experimental Film," *Films in Review 2* (December 1951): 25.

6. Jean Charlot, "But Is It Art? A Disney Disquisition," *American Scholar* 8:3 (July 1939): 265.

7. John Culhane, " 'The Black Hole' Casts the Computer As Movie-Maker," *New York Times*, 16 December 1979, p. D19.

8. James Broughton, "The Necessity of Living Poetically In An Electronic Age," *Film Culture*, no. 61 (1975-1976): 20.

9. Jim Seale, "Special Effects: California," *Millimeter*, September 1979, p. 78.

BIBLIOGRAPHY

CEL-ANIMATION

Studios: Disney

Balio, Tino. *United Artists: The Company Built by the Stars*. Madison: University of Wisconsin Press, 1976. Sections discuss Disney's distribution deal with United Artists, based on United Artists records at the Wisconsin Center for Film and Theater Research (see Appendix 2).

Barrier, Mike. "Building a Better Mouse: Fifty Years of Disney Animation." *Funnyworld*, no. 20 (Summer 1979): 6-22.

"The Big Bad Wolf." *Fortune*, November 1934, pp. 88-95; 142.

Boone, Andrew R. "When Mickey Mouse Speaks." *Scientific American* 148 (March 1933): 146-47.

Bower, Anthony. "Films. Snow White and the 1,200 Dwarfs." *Nation* 152:19 (10 May 1941): 565. Review of organized labor in the Disney studio.

"But Is It Art?" *Business Week*, 10 February 1945, p. 72. Overview of Disney enterprises from about 1938 to 1945 with emphasis on stock transactions and other business aspects.

Canemaker, John. "A Visit to the Walt Disney Studio." *Filmmakers Newsletter*, January 1974, pp. 32-34.

_____. "Disney Design 1928-1979: How The Disney Studio Changed The Look of the Animated Cartoon." *Millimeter* 7:2 (February 1979): 102.

Carstairs, John Paddy. *Movie Merry-Go-Round*. Newnes: London, 1937.

Chapman, Cynthia; Dolan, Kent M.; Sullivan, Kevin J.; and Thompson, Neil F. "The Relationship of Marketing Strategies Used by Walt Disney Productions to the Evolving Family Audience." Master's thesis, University of California, Los Angeles, 1977. An informative and detailed report drawing upon Disney archive data discussing the Disney film audiences over time.

"Cinema. Mouse & Man." *Time*, 27 December 1937, pp. 19-21. Recap of Disney enterprises up through the late 1930s.

Coordinator of Inter-American Affairs. *History of the Office of the Coordinator of Inter-American Affairs: Historical Reports on War Administration*. Washington, D.C.: Government Printing Office, 1947.

Culbert, David H. "Walt Disney's Private Snafu: The Use of Humor in World War II Army Film." In Jack Salzman, ed., *Prospects: An Annual Journal of American Cultural Studies* 1 (December 1975): 80-96.

"Disney After Walt Is A Family Affair." *Time*, 30 July 1973, pp. 64-66. Reviews the growth of the business, especially of the most profitable amusement (theme) parks.

Disney, Diane, and Martin, Pete. *The Story of Walt Disney*. New York: Henry Holt, 1956.

Disney, Walt. "Growing Pains." *Society of Motion Picture Engineers* 36 (January 1941): 30-40.

"The Disney Way With The Dollar." *Forbes*, 15 March 1977, pp. 79-80. EPCOT, Disney's "dream community of tomorrow," scheduled to open in Florida in 1982.

"Entertainment: Disney Without Walt." *Newsweek*, 20 October 1969, p. 90. Recap of Disney activities since Walt Disney's death (1966) to mid-1969.

Feild, Robert D. *The Art of Walt Disney*. London, Glasgow: Collins, 1944.

Finch, Christopher. *The Art of Walt Disney: From Mickey Mouse to the Magic Kingdom*. Concise ed. New York: Harry N. Abrams, 1975.

Garity, W. E., and Ledeen, J. L. "The New Walt Disney Studio." *Journal of the Society of Motion Picture Engineers* 36 (January 1941): 3-29.

Goldrich, Bob. "Ideas On Trial. Disney Exodus and the State of Animation." *Backstage* (supp.), 21 December 1979, pp. 25-31. Interview by Goldrich with Don Bluth, James Stewart, Mel Griffin, Rich Irvine on the state of animation and the reasons behind the exodus of animators from Disney enterprises in early winter 1979.

Gottschalk, Earl C., Jr. "Disney Is Dealt Blow By the Resignations of 11 Animators to Start Production Firm." *Wall Street Journal*, 19 September 1979, p. 6.

————. "Less Mickey Mouse: Disney to Shift Target of Some Parks, Movies To Teen-Agers, Adults; Planned Facilty At Orlando To Display Technology; A 'Snow White' Parody. 'Baby Bust' Spurs the Switch." *Wall Street Journal*, 26 January 1979, p. 1.

Hammond, David. "Giving A Personality to An Animated Dragon." *American Cinematographer* 58:10 (October 1977): 1032-33. About Ken Anderson and the animation team working on *Pete's Dragon*.

Hollie, Pamela G. "Animators' Loss Shakes Disney." *New York Times*, 10 October 1979, p. D14. Led by Don Bluth, thirteen animators resigned to establish their own company.

Houseman, Jerry P. "A Study of Selected Walt Disney Screenplays and Films and Stereotyping of the Role of the Female." Ph.D. dissertation, University of the Pacific, 1973.

Kalmus, H. T. "Technicolor Adventures in Cinemaland." *Journal of the Society of Motion Picture Engineers* 31 (December 1938). An account of technicolor's history from the point of view of business relationships with the film industry and the practical applications to the industry. Kalmus mused over whether Disney's later success with *Flowers and Trees* did more for technicolor or technicolor did more for Disney.

Kaye, Jeffrey. "Disney Disenchantment: Animators Draw Away." *Washington Post*, 1 November 1979, p. L7.

King, Margaret. "The Disney Sensibility." Master's thesis, Bowling Green State University, 1972.

King, T. W. "The Image in Motion." *Crimmer's: The Harvard Journal of Pictorial Fiction*, Winter 1975, pp. 11-18.

McDonald, John. "Now The Bankers Come To Disney." *Fortune* 73:5 (May 1966): 138. One of the best financial articles about the Disney operation, summing up the history of Disney, with insights into key changes in organization and policies over the years.

MacGowan, Kenneth. "Make Mine Disney: A Review." *Hollywood Quarterly* 1:4 (July 1946): 376-77.

Maltin, Leonard. *The Disney Films*. New York: Bonanza, 1973.

"Names & Faces. Disney's Live-action Profits." *Business Week*, 24 July 1965, pp.

78-82. Traces financial aspect of Walt Disney Productions to current day, with late high earnings at $7 million in 1964—a first.

Pickard, Roy. *The Hollywood Studios*. London: Frederick Muller, 1978. Pickard writes about nine major studios operating in Hollywood, including Disney, and follows each narrative section with a detailed chronology.

"Profiles: The Quack and Disney." *New Yorker*, 29 December 1975, pp. 33-41.

Real, Michael R. *Mass-Mediated Culture*. Englewood Cliffs, N.J.: Prentice-Hall, 1977. Has a chapter on the "Disney Universe."

Roos, Robert de. "The Magic Worlds of Walt Disney." *National Geographic* 124:2 (August 1963): 159-207. "Mickey Mouse Explains The Art To Mr. G. O. Graphic," outlining the process of Disney animation. The main article is about the evolution of the Disney work and post-World War II expansion into other activities such as TV and theme parks.

Sammon, Paul. "The Black Hole." *Cinefantastique* 9:1 (1979): 6.

Schickel, Richard. *The Disney Version: The Life, Times, Art and Commerce of Walt Disney*. New York: Simon and Schuster, 1968.

Shale, Richard Allen. "Donald Duck Joins Up: The Walt Disney Studio During World War II." Ph.D. dissertation, University of Michigan, 1976.

Shows, Charles. *Walt: Backstage Adventures with Walt Disney*. LaJolla, Calif.: Communication Creativity, 1979. Former producer, writer, and director Charles Shows worked for Disney over a ten-year period.

Smith, David R. "Disney Before Burbank: The Kingswell and Hyperion Studios." *Funnyworld*, no. 20 (Summer 1979): 32-38.

_____. "The Sorcerer's Apprentice: Birthplace of Fantasia." *Millimeter* 4:2 (February 1976): 18.

Stravinsky, Igor, and Craft, Robert. *Expositions and Developments*. New York: Doubleday, 1962. Has composer's version of events and "quarrel" with Disney.

Thomas, Bob. *The Art of Animation*. New York: Simon and Schuster, 1958.

_____. *Walt Disney: An American Original*. New York: Simon and Schuster, 1976.

Tusher, Will. "Disney Relies on Magic Formula—Recycling Cinema." *Hollywood Reporter*, 22 October 1971.

Wagner, Walter. "Ward Kimball; The Wonderful World of Walt Disney." In Walter Wagner, ed., *You Must Remember This*. New York: G. P. Putnam's Sons, 1975, pp. 264-82.

"Walt Disney Presents." *Film Dope* 12 (June 1977): 2-28. Probably the most complete list of Disney films, together with brief biographies of some Disney animators and directors.

"Walt Disney Sets 1982 Opening Date of Tomorrow World," *Wall Street Journal*, 3 October 1978, p. 1.

Whitefield, Debra. "Profits, Parks and Products Boom But Disney Strives to Bolster Movie Image." *Los Angeles Times*, 5 February 1980, p. IV 1. Overview about the Disney attempt to broaden the appeal of their films to older audiences.

_____. "The Wonderful World of Disney May Be Changed." *Los Angeles Times*, 14 February 1980, p. IV 1. What is now the longest running American weekly prime-time series TV program in history, "World" is considering changing the format in the face of declining ratings against the CBS "Sixty Minutes."

"Yes, Virginia, There Is A Walt Disney." *Forbes* 113:4 (15 February 1974): 30-31. Recap of Wall Street thinking about Disney Enterprises as investment.

Studios: Metro-Goldwyn-Mayer

Barrier, Mike. "The Careers of Hugh Harmon and Rudolf Ising." *Millimeter* 4:2 (February 1956): 46-50.

Crowther, Bosley. *The Lion's Share: The Story of an Entertainment Empire*. New York: E. P. Dutton, 1957. Does not have any reference to animation or Fred Quimby.

"Inside TV: MGM Revives Tom and Jerry." *Los Angeles Times*, 3 June 1977, p. IV 26.

Kausler, Mark. "MGM Cartoon List." *Mindrot*, no. 11 (24 July 1978): 36-40.

_____. "Tom and Jerry." In Leonard Maltin, ed., *The Movie Factory*. New York: Popular Library, 1969.

Kiesling, Barrett. "They Paint A Million Cats." *Films and Filming* 3:2 (November 1956): 10-11.

Marill, Alvin H. *Samuel Goldwyn Presents*. New York: A. S. Barnes and Co., 1976.

Marx, Arthur. *Goldwyn: A Biography of the Man Behind the Myth*. New York: Ballantine Books, 1976.

Mayerson, Mark. "The Lion Began With A Frog." *Velvet Light Trap Review of Cinema*, no. 18 (Spring 1978): 39-45.

Studios: UPA

Armitage, Peter. "The Business of Things Moving: Animation." *Film*, no. 45 (Spring 1966): 24-29.

Beckerman, Howard. "Abe Liss Never Hired Me." *Filmmakers Newsletter*, June 1976, pp. 57-58.

_____. "What Ever Happened to Ernest Pintoff?" *Filmmakers Newsletter*, January 1974, p. 40.

"Boing." *Time*, 5 February 1971, p. 78.

Borshell, Allan. "The Animated Film." *Film*, no. 4 (March 1955): 12.

Crowther, Bosley. "McBoing Boing, Magoo and Bosustow." *New York Times Magazine*, 21 December 1952, p. VI 14.

"80 New UPA Cartoonists Swell Magoo Factory; Studio's 7 Cameramen." *Variety* (Unidentified clip in New York Public Library files).

Fisher, David. "U.P.A. In England." *Sight and Sound* 26:1 (Summer 1956): p. 45.

Knight, Arthur. "Films. UPA, Magoo and McBoing-Boing." *Art Digest*, 1 February 1952, p. 22. Recounts the beginnings of UPA listing major films and personalities in the organization. Titles are identified and described.

Korkis, Jim. "Harlequin." *Mindrot*, 28 February 1980, pp. 4-5. History of the UPA studios, beginning with the Industrial Films and Poster Service.

Langsner, Jules. "UPA." *Arts and Architecture* 71:12 (December 1954): unpaged.

Orna, Bernard. "Cartoon and Puppet." *Films and Filming* 1:7 (April 1955): 29.

Sagar, Isobel C. "The UPA Cartoons." *Films in Review* 2:9 (November 1951): 36-37.

Seldes, Gilbert. "SR Goes To The Movies: Delight in Seven Minutes." *Saturday Review*, 31 May 1952, p. 27.

Stocker, Joseph. "Magnificent Magoo." *American Mercury* 86:411 (April 1958): 129-33.

Sullivan, Catherine. "United Productions of America: The Modern Look in Animated Cartoons." *American Artist* 9:19 (November 1955): 34. Characters, history, and "success-awards" earned by UPA shorts are identified. Unit method of UPA described.

Turner, G. Alan. "New Horizons In Animated Cartooning." *Design* 55:3 (January-February 1954): 128-29.

"United Productions of America: The Modern Look in Animated Cartoons." *American Artists* 19:9 (November 1955): 34.

Studios: Warner Brothers

Adamson, Joe. "Well, for Heaven's Sake! Grown Men!" *Film Comment* 11:1 (January-February 1975): 18-20.

Bullis, Roger Alan. "A Thematic Study of the Post-War Warner Brothers Animated Films." Master's thesis, University of Wisconsin, 1971.

Canemaker, John. "The Hollywood Cartoon." *Filmmakers Newsletter* 7:6 (April 1974): 32.

Champlin, Chuck. "Warner Bros. Sequel. 'Duck Dodgers' Flies Again." *Los Angeles Times*, 3 September 1979, p. IV 11. Warner Brothers commissions a sequel to the 1953 Daffy Duck cartoon; animators involved included Mike Maltese, Chuck Jones, and Maurice Noble.

Cohen, Mitchell S. "Looney Tunes and Merrie Melodies." *Velvet Light Trap*, no. 15 (Fall 1975): 33-37.

Dalton, Elizabeth. "Bugs and Daffy Go To War." *Velvet Light Trap*, no. 4 (Spring 1972): 44.

Ford, Greg. "Warner Brothers." *Film Comment*, 11:1 (January-February 1975): 10.

Fox, Darryl J. "A Thematic Analysis of Selected Warner Brothers Animated Films Directed by Tex Avery and Bob Clampett." Master's thesis, University of Wisconsin, 1976.

Hempstead, Marilyn Zahl. "Characters Images In Animated Cartoon Produced At Warner Brothers Studio From 1933 To 1945 As Determined By the Graphic Depiction Of The Human Form." Master's thesis, University of Wisconsin, 1976.

Maltin, Leonard. "The Warner Bros. Cartoons." *Film Fan Monthly*, July-August 1973, unpaged.

"The New Bugs Bunny Feature!" *Mindrot*, no. 14 (20 May 1979): 9. Lists cartoons and new animations for 1979 Warner Brothers release currently in distribution.

Rider, David. "Deadly Blow." *Films and Filming* 12:8 (May 1966): 59.

"Warner Brothers." *Fortune* 116 (December 1937): 110. Interesting profile on the Warner Brothers and studio life in the mid-1930s. Several details given about the studio structure and budgeting clearly indicate that Warner management was tight, with as low an overhead as possible.

Warner, Jack. *My First Hundred Years in Hollywood*. New York: Random House,

1965. Not one reference to cartoons, animated films, Leon Schlesinger, any animators, or characters, except Bugs Bunny.

Characters

Adamson, Joe. "Cartoon Constellation." *AFI Report* 5:2 (Summer 1974).

Albano, Robert. "Cartoon Showcase: Minnie the Moocher." *Mindrot*, no. 12 (1 November 1978): 28-30.

Bain, David, and Harris, Bruce. *Mickey Mouse: Fifty Happy Years*. New York: Crown Publishers, 1977. Picture-book format with filmography and bibliography of Mickey Mouse character.

Beckerman, Howard. "Animation Kit: Cartoon Characters Move People." *Filmmakers Newsletter*, April 1972, p. 32.

_____. "Animation Kit: Mickey Mouse Under the Microscope." *Filmmakers Monthly*, July 1979, pp. 48-49. Using an article by Stephen Jay Gould, Beckerman traces the evolution of Mickey Mouse character.

_____. "Animation Kit: Some Call It 'Popeye Sweet.' " *Filmmakers Monthly*, October 1979, pp. 46-47. Nostalgic return to Famous Studios headquarters in New York City in 1942, with a present-day perspective of animation in the Big Apple.

_____. "Animation Kit: The Superman Story."*Filmmakers Newsletter*, February 1976, pp. 54-55.

_____. "Fritz the Cat: See Fritz Run." *Filmmakers Newsletter*, October 1972, pp. 27-31. Also contains inset: Cat Contributions to Animation History.

Benayoun, Robert. "Animation: The Phoenix and the Roadrunner." *Film Quarterly* 17:3 (Spring 1964): 17-25.

Blitz, Marcia. *Donald Duck*. New York: Harmony Books, 1979. History of the character from the beginning. Lots of color plates illustrating the character, films, merchandise, and posters. Book outlines in some detail the animators working on Donald Duck cartoons, the process of animation in general, Donald Duck in World War II, books and comic strips featuring Donald Duck, the character during the "TV years," and international reaction. Filmography and bibliography included.

Bragdon, Claude. "Mickey Mouse and What He Means." *Scribner's Magazine* 96: 1 (July 1934): 40-43.

Cawley, John, Jr. "Disney Out-Foxed. The Tale of Reynard at the Disney Studio." *American Classic Screen* 3:6 (July-August 1979): 41-43. Documented study of a "crook-fox" character that was considered despite the contradictions in the "Disney image."

Corliss, Richard. "More Disneyfied Mice—What Would Walt Have Said?" *New Times*, 8 May 1977, pp. 66-67.

Culhane, John. "Retrospectives of Popular Cartoon Characters." Mimeographed. University of Southern California: Doheny Library, n.d.

Fair, Steven, and Fair, Cherie. "Mickey's First Fifty." *Christian Science Monitor*, 13 November 1978, p. 19.

Friedwald, Will Timbes. "Of Mighty Mouse and Men." *Mindrot*, 28 February 1980, pp. 18-33. Detailed description of most of the Mighty Mouse character cartoons produced by Paul Terry, 1943-1955 when Terry sold out to CBS. Titles, animators, directors, and other credits given.

Gould, Stephen Jay. "This View of Life: Mickey Mouse Meets Konrad Lorenz." *Natural History* 88:5 (May 1979): 30-36. As Mickey's chronological age increases to fifty, the author concludes he is progressively more juvenile in appearance which appeals more to his audience. K. Lorenz argues that features of juvenility trigger human mechanisms for affection and nurturance in adults.

Grossberger, Lewis. "Popeye Tells All." *TV Guide* 27:50 (15 December 1979): 17-18. Brief historical treatment of the comic character with some emphasis on Robin Williams and a new film role.

Halas, John, and Rider, David. *The Great Movie Cartoon Parade.* New York: Crown, Bounty Books, 1976.

Hine, Al. "McBoing-Boing and Magoo." *Holiday* 9:6 (June 1951): 6.

Jones, Chuck. "The Roadrunner and Other Characters." *Cinema Journal* 8:2 (Spring 1969): 10-16.

Kausler, Mark. "Tom and Jerry." *Film Comment* 11:1 (January-February 1975), pp. 74-75.

Kinney, Jack. "Bambi and the Goof." *Funnyworld.* No. 21 (Fall 1979), pp. 28-33.

La Roche, Catherine De. "Mad About Cats." *Films and Filming* 1:8 (May 1955), p. 6.

McLellan, Joseph. "The Mouse on the Hill: Mickey and the Whole Disney Menagerie." *Washington Post*, 21 November 1978, p. B1.

Mann, Arthur. "Mickey Mouse's Financial Career." *Harper's Magazine*, May 1934, pp. 714-21. Details the financial relationships Disney entered into with Powers, Columbia Pictures, and others in the formative years of the Walt Disney Productions. The alleged "facts" are at variance with Schickel and Thomas versions.

"Mickey At 50 A Spry Mouse." *Variety*, 7 December 1977, p. 36.

Missinne, Jeff. "Krazy Kat." *Mindrot*, no. 15 (20 August 1979): 18-21. Calls the Kat cartoons archetypical of the animation style of the 1930s, "absurd surrealism rivaling that of Fleischer."

Orna, Bernard. "Magoo Has A Sennett Touch." *Films and Filming* 2:5 (February 1956): 29.

Rieder, Howard Edward. "The Development Of The Satire Of Mr. Magoo." Master's thesis, University of Southern California, 1961.

————. "Memories of Mr. Magoo." *Cinema Journal* 8:2 (Spring 1969): 17-24.

"Roadrunner Cartoons." *Mindrot*, no. 3 (16 August 1976).

Rosenberg, Milton J. "Mr. Magoo As Public Dream." *Quarterly of Film, Radio and Television* 11:4 (Summer 1957): 337-42.

Sagendorf, Bud. *Popeye: The First Fifty Years.* New York: Workman Publishing, 1979. Light treatment of the Popeye evolution, along with other characters in the Elzie Crisler Segar strip, later continued by Bud Sagendorf and others.

Shales, Tom. "Mouse of the Hour: Whistlestop Tour for Middle-Aged Mickey." *Washington Post*, 15 November 1978, p. D 1.

Sherwood, Lydia E. "The Eternal Road-Company: A Biography, More Free-Hand Than Literal, of the Unsinkable Walt Disney Troupe." *Vogue*, 15 June 1937, p. 40.

"Superman Cartoons." *Mindrot*, no. 3 (16 August 1976): unpaged.

"Walt Disney and Mickey Mouse." *Sight and Sound* 4:14 (Summer 1935): 64-65.

"Walt Disney's Scrooge McDuck and Money." *Mindrot*, no. 3 (16 August 1976): unpaged.

"Watch 'Em Move: A Short Biography of Krazy Kat and Some of His Goofy Friends." *Photoplay* 38:4 (September 1930): 71.

Young, Charles M. "Oryctolagus Cuniculus—a.k.a. Bugs Bunny." *Village Voice*, 29 December 1975, p. 126.

OBJECT-ANIMATION

Miniatures

Asherman, Allan. "Animation and Stop-Motion in Features: A Retrospective." *Millimeter* 2:3-4 (March-April 1974): 16-19.

Baxter, John. *Science Fiction in the Cinema*. New York: A. S. Barnes and Co., 1970. Includes section on special effects by Haskin and Harryhausen.

Beckerman, Howard. "Animation Kit: Puppets In Wonderland." *Filmmakers Newsletter*, November 1975, p. 36.

Gorney, Sondra. "The Puppet and the Moppet." *Hollywood Quarterly* 1:4 (July 1946): 371-75.

Holman, Lloyd Bruce. "The History and Technique of Puppet Animation in Cinema." Ph.D. dissertation, Syracuse University, 1971. This dissertation brings together a history of puppet animation largely ignored even by writers about animation in the popular and scholarly press. Holman canvassed the trade press, visited puppet animators, surveyed catalogues, and searched archives in London, Amsterdam, Prague, Montreal, Washington, and New York, along with viewing puppet animation films. Excludes stop-action works of O'Brien, Harryhausen, Danforth, and Pal.

Mankofsky, Isidore. "Through The Rainbow With Lens and Camera." *American Cinematographer* 60:7 (July 1979): 668. The director of photography on *The Muppet Movie* discusses his approach in using the Muppets on location. Used a through-the-lens video system to ensure muppet "animators" were out-of-frame.

Martin, Judith " 'Muppets': A Ragbag of Idolatry." *Washington Post* (Weekend), 6 July 1979, p. 23. About the movies and the phenomenon.

Menville, Douglas. *A Historical and Critical Survey of the Science-Fiction Film*. New York: Arno Press, 1974.

"Motion Picture Comedies in Clay." *Scientific American* 115 (16 December 1916): 553.

Moulton, Robert H. "Tyland in the Films: Where Dolls, as Movie Actors, Rival Living Stars." *Scientific American* 117 (29 December 1917): 496.

Prestone, David, and Mandell, Paul. "The Puppet Films: Animator—Lou Bunin." *Closeup*, no. 2 (n.d.): 4-12.

_____. "The Puppet Films: Animator—Richard Catizone." *Closeup*, no. 2 (n.d.): 43-45.

_____. "The Puppet Films: Animator—Kermite Love." *Closeup*, no. 2 (n.d.): 24-31.

_____. "The Puppet Films: Animator—Don Sahlin." *Closeup*, no. 2 (n.d.): 14-23.

_____. "The Puppet Films: Animator—Teddy Shepard." *Closeup*, no. 2 (n.d.): 32-35.

_____. "The Puppet Films: Interview with Animator Lee Howard." *Closeup*, no. 2 (n.d.): 12-13.

_____. "The Puppet Films: Scenic Designer—Evalds Dajevskis." *Closeup*, no. 2 (n.d.): 36-42.

Rovin, Jeff. *From the Land Beyond Beyond: The Making of the Movie Monsters You've Known and Loved*. New York: Berkley Publishing, 1977.

_____. *Movie Special Effects*. New York: A. S. Barnes and Co., 1977.

Warren, Bill. "Model Animation? What's a Dat?" *Cinefantastique* 5:3 (n.d.): 34-35.

Warren, Neil. "3-D Animation. Plasticine and Puppet People." *Cinema Canada*, August 1976, pp. 38-39. Plasticine is a substance which is very bendable into a variety of shapes. Article features Canadian filmmakers who have recently made films in the three-dimensional medium using puppets made out of plasticine materials.

Westheimer, Joseph. "Optical Magic for 'The Muppet Movie.' " *American Cinematographer* 60:7 (July 1979): 706. Explains normal optical effects and new variations. Rotoscoping was done for some shots.

Wilkie, Bernard. *Creating Special Effects for TV and Films*. New York: Hastings House, Publishers, 1977.

Wilson, Steven Seth. "Puppet Action Combined With Live Action in Feature Films." Master's thesis, University of Southern California, 1977. Review of sparse literature and several interviews with special effects animation practitioners including Jim Danforth, Miles Pike, David Allen. Discusses replacement and displacement stop-action/model animation devices; "mid-air" animation; how live-action work is combined with puppet animation and offers some advice concerning judging such animation. Has comprehensive bibliography.

Wolf, Mark. "Stop Frame: The History and Technique of Fantasy Film Animation." *Cinefantastique* 1:2 (Winter 1971): 6-21.

_____. "Stop Frame: The History and Technique of Fantasy Film Animation." *Cinefantastique* 2:1 (Spring 1972): 9.

Cutouts

Birnie, Ian. "A Retrospective of Cut-out Animation." (Program at the Museum of Modern Art, Department of Film, New York, N.Y., 13 March 1978).

_____. "Cut-Out Animation: Formalists." (Program at the Museum of Modern Art, Film Department, New York, N.Y., 17-18 March 1978).

_____. "Cut-Out Animation: Pioneers." (Program at the Museum of Modern Art,

Film Department, New York, N.Y., 18-19 March 1978).

Cushman, George W. "Animated Movies With Paper Cutouts." *American Cine-matographer* 34:12 (December 1953): 600.

Gilliam, Terry. *Animations of Mortality*. New York: Metheun, 1978.

Puspurica, Nik. "Cut-Out Animation." *Filmmakers Newsletter* 6:12 (October 1973): 46-47.

Silhouettes

Laliberte, Norman, and Mogelon, Alex. *Silhouettes, Shadows and Cutouts: History and Modern Use*. New York: Reinhold Books, 1968. Traces the history of silhouettes from the seventeenth through the nineteenth centuries, with a separate chapter on the Asian shadow play.

Mitchell, M. "The Silhouette Films of Bryant Fryer." *Motion* 5:3 (1976): 16-19. Canadian Fryer's background is described, beginning with his work with Tony Sarg (puppet filmmaker) in New York City, his later advertising films, and independent work. Early films described.

Reiniger, Lotte. *Shadow Puppets, Shadow Theatres and Shadow Films*. 1970. Reprint. Boston: Plays, 1975.

Sarg, Tony. "Movies on Strings." *Photoplay* 21 (December 1921): 36.

Talbot, Frederick A. *Moving Pictures: How They Are Made and Worked*. 1912. Reprint. New York: Arno Press, 1970.

Photo

Ades, Dawn. *Photomontage*. New York: Pantheon, 1976.

Boyars, Albert. " 'Visual Squeeze'—New Technique For Commercials." *American Cinematographer* 40:2 (February 1959): 118.

Kalman, Gabor. "The Making of Documentary Filmstrips Exploring a New Audio-Visual Form." *American Cinematographer* 58:4 (April 1977): 374.

Lane, Phillip Joseph, Jr. "NBC-TV's Project XX: An Analysis of the Art of The Still-In-Motion Film In Television." Ph.D. dissertation, Northwestern University, 1969.

Lehman, Ricard A. "New Vogue In Old Stills." *Television Magazine* 20:1 (January 1963): 48. Summary of 1962 "flash cut," "squeeze frame" techniques which flowered that year, with several commercials cited. Film techniques now applied to stills giving them animation, but enabling strong design patterns to be visible in commercial messages. This led to the "quick-cut" spot. Saul Bass work is also cited.

Manilla, James. "Camera Animation: Baby Weems Grows Up." *Industrial Photography* 27:3 (March 1978): 25.

"Photograms." *Print* 11:5 (March-April 1958): 46. With illustrations, Lawrence Gussin of Gussin-Radin Studios explains applications of the photographic technique which is created by placing objects on photographic paper, and creating "profiles." These can be combined in other graphics and transposed to TV ads.

Sands, Pierre Norman. "The Filmagraph: Its Development and Applications." Master's thesis, University of Southern California, 1957.

Shaffer, Mac Owen. "The Development of Still-Photography Animation." Master's thesis, Ohio State University, 1963.

Sobieszek, Robert A. "New Acquisitions. A Note on Early Photomontage Images." *Image* 15:4 (December 1972): 19-23. Composite and montage photographs are works that rearrange space, while photomontage in film, kinestasis, or collage used the same photo, or cutout, or multiples over time.

Stecker, Elinor. "Animation. Slides That Move." *Filmmakers Newsletter*, December 1973, p. 40. Description of Al Stahl's "Fotomation" techniques of animating slides.

Wilke, David A. "Still Pictures Into Motion Pictures." *College Arts Journal* 7 (Autumn-Summer, 1947-48). Early piece discussing animation of photographs including a proposal that live television use animation of paintings. Also described generally is a patented microphoto motion picture camera capable of panning and tilting over a photograph or two-dimensional surface.

Experimental

American Federation of Arts. *New American Filmmakers: Selections from the Whitney Museum of American Art Film Program*. New York: American Federation of Arts, n.d.

Battcock, Gregory. *The New American Cinema*. New York: E. P. Dutton, 1967.

Cameron, Ian. "Spare A Thought For The Entertainers." *Film Quarterly* 15:2 (Winter 1961-62): 62-64. Cameron attacks the view of the experimentalists, some of whom espouse the view that the presentation of entertainment or commerce is the antithesis of art. Indeed, mass entertainment and art can be mutually beneficial he says.

Curtis, David. *Experimental Cinema*. New York: Universe Books, 1971. A very useful work in outlining the derivations of independent American film and removing the mystique and jargon from the experimental movement. Good identification and discussion of filmmakers and their techniques, with some perspective.

Early, Steven C. *An Introduction to American Movies*. New York: Mentor, New American Library, 1978.

Giannetti, Louis D. *Understanding Movies*. Englewood Cliffs, N.J.: Prentice-Hall, 1976.

Jacobs, Lewis. "Experimental Cinema In America." *Film Quarterly* 3:2 (Winter 1947-48): 111-25. Among the earliest attempts to bring the history of American experimental films together.

_____. Ibid., 3:3 (Spring 1948): 278-92.

Knight, Arthur. "Ideas On Film. Eyewitnessing the World of the 16mm Motion Picture." *Saturday Review*, 27 May 1950, pp. 38-40. General survey of several abstract filmmakers. "What comes out of all this are pictures that can be felt rather than understood," tied together with a continuity of mood rather than formal storyline.

Lawder, Standish D. *The Cubist Cinema*. New York: New York University Press, 1975.

Le Grice, Malcolm. *Abstract Film and Beyond*. London: Cassell and Collier Macmillan, 1977.

Manvell, Roger, ed. *Experiment in the Film*. London: 1949. Reprint. New York: Arno Press, 1970. One of the earliest anthology volumes which treated the experimental film seriously. Contains Lewis Jacobs's history essays originally published in *Film Quarterly*.

Mekas, Jonas. *Movie Journal: The Rise of A New American Cinema, 1959-1971*. New York: Macmillan Co., 1972.

Potter, Ralph. "Abstract Films." *Films in Review* 5:2 (February 1954): 82-89. Somewhat off-the-track commentary on topic-specific matter in abstract film, this piece attempts a hopeful assessment of the state of abstract film in the early 1950s.

Renan, Sheldon. *An Introduction to the American Underground Film*. New York: E. P. Dutton, 1967.

Richter, Hans. "The Avant-garde Film Seen From Within." *Film Quarterly* 4:1 (Fall 1949): 34-41.

_____. *Dada: Art and Anti-Art*. New York: McGraw-Hill, 1965. Although Richter claims a painstaking sifting of documentary evidence, very little of this is directly cited in his work. He does offer conflicting points of view and admits problems of resolution in factual matters when discrepancies occur. However, this is essentially Richter's recollection and viewpoint of Dada from about 1914 to 1924. A small section is given over to his collaboration with Viking Eggeling in filmmaking, circa 1920-1924.

Rubin, William S. *Dada and Surrealist Art*. New York: Harry N. Abrams, 1968. Reissue of a 1948 work which reviews the roots of Dada art and the transition to surrealism in Europe. The work of Marcel Duchamp, Max Ernst, and others is discussed in the links made to experimental animated films of Richter, Eggeling, and others.

Russett, Robert, and Starr, Cecile. *Experimental Animation: An Illustrated Anthology*. New York: Van Nostrand Reinhold Company, 1976.

Singer, Marilyn, ed. *A History of the American Avant-Garde Cinema*. New York: American Federation of the Arts, 1975.

Sitney, P. Adams. *The Essential Cinema: Essays on Films in the Collection of Anthology Film Archives*. New York: New York University Press, 1975.

_____. *Film Culture Reader*. New York: Praeger, 1970.

_____. *Visionary Film: The American Avant-Garde*. New York: Oxford University Press, 1974.

_____, ed. *The Avant-Garde Film: A Reader of Theory and Criticism*. New York: New York University Press, 1978.

Stauffacher, Frank, ed. *Art in Cinema*. 1947. Reprint. New York: Arno Press, (Arno Series of Contemporary Art No. 21) Catalogue and anthology of biographies and articles on experimental filmmaking.

Tyler, Parker. *Underground Film: A Critical History*. New York: Grove Press, 1969.

Weinberg, Herman G. "A Forward Glance At The Abstract Film." *Design* 42:6 (February 1941): 24.

_____. "30 Years of Experimental Film." *Films in Review* 2 (December 1951): 22-27.

Youngblood, Gene. *Expanded Cinema: The Audio-Visual Extension of Man*. New York: E. P. Dutton, 1970.

DRAWING-ON-FILM

Cameraless Animation

Anderson, Bert. "Cameraless Animation: How It Can Turn Kids On." *Film Quarterly* 6:1 (Winter 1972-73): 27-30.

Witsch, Michael. "A Primer on Cameraless Filmmaking." *Media and Methods* 12:5 (January 1976): 38. Describes various types of drawing on film including some adaptations of techniques by Stan Vanderbeek.

Titles

Aison, Everett. "The Current Scene: Film Titles." *Print* 19:4 (July-August 1965): 26-30.

Barry, Thomas. "The Current Scene: TV On-Screen Graphics." *Print* 19:4 (July-August 1965): 31-35. The 1964-65 TV season seems to mark the change in network and TV station logos, from complicated and busy visuals to greater design simplicity and animation. Barry reviews what some large metropolitan stations and the three TV networks have done in this TV season.

Rothman, Irwin. "The Current Scene: TV Promotion/Advertising." *Print* 19:4 (July-August 1965): 36-41. About the creative advertising departments of the three networks metromedia. NBC and CBS have a "corporate look"; ABC less so—quality varies between programs promoted. Discusses the rise of creative design in company logos, "images," and creative development.

COMPUTER ANIMATION AND TV GRAPHICS

Altshuler, Jeffrey. "Computer Animation: Promising Still." *Print* 28:2 (March-April 1974): 58-64. Overview of the state of the art in 1973-74.

Barry, Thomas. "The Current Scene: TV-On-Screen Graphics." *Print* 19:4 (July-August 1965): 31-33.

Battcock, Gregory, ed. *The New American Cinema*. New York: E. P. Dutton, 1967.

Catmull, Edwin E. "New Frontiers in Computer Animation." *American Cinematographer* 60:10 (October 1979): 1000. New York Institute of Technology has been developing the Computer-Aided Animation System (CAAS). Three-dimension images and visual effects provided with digital techniques. CAAS process explained and computer software packages described.

"Commercials Production, Spring '78: Computer Animation Continues To Make Strides in Both Technology and Advertiser Acceptance." *Television/Radio Age* 25:21 (22 May 1978): 28.

Davis, Hatfield. "Computer Animation." *Filmmakers Newsletter* 4:4 (December 1970): 24-26. One of the most lucid explanations of computer technology as applied to filmmaking. Distinctions between digital and analogue systems; hybrid systems used in early commercial TV animation.

Faiman, M., and Nievergelt, J., eds. *Pertinent Concepts in Computer Graphics: Proceedings of the Second University of Illinois Conference on Computer*

Graphics. Urbana: University of Illinois Press, 1969. Twenty-two scientific papers on various aspects of computer graphics, many of which have direct bearing on computer animation techniques.

Franke, Herbert W. *Computer Graphics, Computer Art*. London: Phaidon Press, 1971.

Gage, Theodore. "Special Effects: Birth of New Commercial Realities." *Advertising Age* (23 July 1979): S-2. Reviews various commercials using animation and special effects. Use of mattes (electronic and film) and rotoscoping, with examples given.

Gruenberger, Fred. *Computer Graphics: Utility, Production, Art*. Washington, D.C.: Thompson Book Co., 1967. Selected papers from the Graphics Symposium sponsored by Informatics, Inc., and UCLA. Papers provide data on background, tools of computer graphics (as of 1965) and applications including motion picture animation and use of digital computer in "animating" Tiros cloud-cover pictures.

Hackathorn, Ronald J. "Anima II: A 3-D Color Animation System." *Computer Graphics* 11:2 (Summer 1977): 54-64.

Halas, John. *Computer Animation*. New York: Hastings House, 1974.

Hanson, Wallace. "Computers, The World's Fastest Animators." *Popular Photography*, December 1968, p. 156. Nontechnical summary of the state of the art including history.

Hill, Ray. "SynthaVision: How A Computer Produces Movies At Your Command." *Popular Science Monthly*, November 1973, p. 5. Color of each TV dot can be controlled. Objects are simulated by mathematical formula, reproduced on cathode-ray tube.

Kallis, Stephen A., Jr. "Motion Animation By Computer." *Computers and Automation* 18:12 (November 1969): 30-34. Summary article describing in general terms the state of the art in using computers as supplements to an animation stand, in either on-line or off-line modes.

Kaplan, Michael, and Greenberg, Donald P. "Parallel Processing Techniques For Hidden Surface Removal." *Computer Graphics* 13:2 (August 1979): 300.

Kitching, Alan. "Computer Animation With Antics." *Journal of the Film and Television Arts* (Great Britain), Winter 1974-75, pp. 33-39.

Klein, Stanley. "Computers That Draw Pictures. Some Even Work in Color." *New York Times*, 6 July 1980, p. F1. Detailed review of the state of computer graphics in industry and animation.

Krampen, Marin, and Seitz, Peter, eds. *Design and Planning 2*. New York: Hastings House, 1967.

Le Grice, Malcolm. *Abstract Film and Beyond*. Cambridge, Mass.: MIT Press, 1977.

McCauley, Carole Spearin. *Computers and Creativity*. New York: Praeger, 1974. A general and non-technical introduction to computers and creative works such as graphics, choreography, music, poetry, and animation by the earlier artists including an early interview with computer animators Ken Knowlton and Lillian Schwartz. A brief history of computers, a glossary, and a reference list are also given in this book by lay author McCauley.

Max, Nelson L., and Clifford, William H., Jr. "Computer Animation of the Sphere Eversion." *Computer Graphics* 9:1 (Spring 1975): 32-39.

Moffat, Anne Simon. "Computers Become A Major Design Tool." *New York Times*, 4 December 1979, p. C1.

Newman, William M., and Sproull, Robert F. *Principles of Interactive Computer, Graphics*. 2d ed. New York: McGraw-Hill, 1979.

Parslow, R. D.; Prowse, R. W.; and Green, R. Elliot. *Computer Graphics: Techniques and Applications*. New York: Plenum Press, 1969. A compilation of key papers presented at a July 1968 International Computer Graphics Symposium held at Brunel University, Uxbridge, England. The book presents an overview of the technology (1967-68), applications in science and industry including some case studies, material for specialists, and an outline of computer hardware currently available.

Reichardt, Jasia. *The Computer in Art*. New York: Van Nostrand Reinhold, 1971.

_____. *Cybernetic Serendipity: The Computer and the Arts*. New York: Praeger, 1969.

Rhodes, Bill. "Creating Computer Images." *Broadcast Engineering* 20:10 (October 1978): 74-78.

Russett, Robert, and Starr, Cecile. *Experimental Animation: An Illustrated Anthology*. New York: Van Nostrand Reinhold, 1976.

Secrest, Don, and Nievergelt, Jurg, eds. *Emerging Concepts in Computer Graphics*. New York: W. A. Benjamin, 1968. A compilation of papers presented at the November 1967 Illinois conference in Computer Graphics. Papers cluster around three major topics: hardware, software and applications, current to 1967 or so.

Smiley, Logan. "TV Film/Tape: Computer Animation." *Print* 24:3 (May-June 1970): 78.

"10 Years of Interactive Graphics." *Computer Aided Design* 10 (September 1978): 287-88. Reviews high expectations for computer graphics in 1968 with low but steady level of activity in the United Kingdom. High labor costs are seen as a major barrier to full development of computer automated-display systems along with the economic recession in the 1970s and changes in hardware and associated costs.

"Two New Devices Debut In CBS's Coverage of the Super Bowl." *Broadcasting*, 16 January 1978, p. 60.

Wadsworth, Evard William. "A Study of the Computer as an Aesthetic Visual Generator." Master's thesis, University of Southern California, 1969.

White, Hooper. "Computer Rising Star in Art of Animation: Adds New Dimension." *Advertising Age*, 25 December 1978, p. 17.

Youngblood, Gene. *Expanded Cinema*. New York: E. P. Dutton, 1970.

Digital TV

"ADDA's Stills Recall Saturn Fly-By For World Television." *Backstage* (Supplement), 21 December 1979, p. 12. Brief report on the contractors and their digital TV processing system enabling scientists and the general public to have their longest "look" across space in man's history.

Alexander, George. "Science's Latest Close-Up View of Jupiter: Both Clear and Cloudy." *Los Angeles Times*, 15 July 1979, p. I 3. About the digital technology in getting pictures relayed back to earth.

"Digital Video Recording Still Far From Market, But Said to Promise Outstanding Quality." *Television/Radio Age* (International), April 1979, p. A73.

Ennes, Harold E. *Digitials in Broadcasting*. Indianapolis, Howard Sams and Co., 1977.

Gallese, Liz Roman. "Electronic Switch: A Digital Wave Begins To Sweep Industries; New Products Emerge." *Wall Street Journal*, 25 May 1979, p. 1. Review of the new technology from an investment standpoint.

Holm, Wilton R. "The New Electronic Composite Photography and New Image Modification System (ECP & M)." *American Cinematographer* 56:4 (April 1975): 424. Claiming to do much more than merely replacing traditional matte processes, this process asserts "it can modify the image of persons and objects within a scene 'using electronics.' "

Howell, David A. "A Primer on Digital Television," *Journal of the Society of Motion Picture and Television Engineers*, July 1975, p. 539.

Myers, Allan J. "A Digital Video Information Storage and Retrieval System." *Computer Graphics* 10:2 (Summer 1976): 45-50.

Price, Jonathan. *Video Visions: A Medium Discovers Itself*. New York: New American Library, 1977.

"Special Report: Digital Technology in Broadcasting Begins To Look Like A System." *Broadcast Management Engineering* 15:2 (February 1979): 41-84.

"The State of Digital Video." *Educational and Instructional Television* (March 1979): 73-75.

White, Hooper. "The Art of TV Commercial Production. Computer Previews Film Shoot." *Advertising Age*, 24 March 1980, pp. 51-52. Using the Evans and Sutherland (E-S) Picture System II Vector Display, Bob Abel is able to preview his animated film before the final photography. White explains the E-S process.

Special Effects

Agel, Jerome, ed. *The Making of Kubrick's 2001*. New York: New American Library, 1970. Reader consisting of reviews, interviews, reprinted interviews, short paragraphs, and lots of photographs about the film. Sections describe the photographic special effects and animated portions of the film.

Anderson, Howard A. "Out-Of-This-World Special Effects for 'Star Trek.' " *American Cinematographer* 48:10 (October 1967): 714-17. Westheimer Company and Anderson, separate special effect firms, contracted to do work on "Star Trek." These are described by representatives from both houses.

Brosnan, John. *Movie Magic: The Story of Special Effects in the Cinema*. New York: St. Martin's Press, 1976.

Canemaker, John. "Star Wars Special Effects." *Millimeter* 5:7 (July-August 1977): p. 46.

"Designing a Deep Space World For 'The Black Hole.' " *American Cinemato-*

grapher 61:1 (January 1980): 28. Interview with Peter Ellenshaw about his background and work on the most recent film.

Fielding, Raymond. *The Technique of Special Effects Cinematography*. 3d ed., rev. New York: Hastings House, 1979.

"Front Projection for 2001: A Space Odyssey." *American Cinematographer* 49:6 (June 1968): 420-22. General description of one of the earliest, dramatically effective uses of front projection, as contained in the *Dawn of Man* sequence.

Gentleman, Wally. "Animated Reflections." *Cinema Canada*, August 1978, pp. 28-29. Describes a front projection system for self-matting animated cartoon (cel) characters.

Gerani, Gary. *Fantastic Television*. New York: Harmony Books, 1977.

Lightman, Herb A. "Filming 2001: A Space Odyssey." *American Cinematographer* 49:6 (June 1968): 412-13.

———. "The Very Special Effects For *Star Trek* The Motion Picture." *American Cinematographer* 61:2 (February 1980): 144-45. Interview with John Dykstra on the special effects in *Star Trek*.

McAlvey, Peter. "Special Effects and Titling—Magic Through Technology." *Millimeter* 7:9 (September 1979): 28. Updating overview of computer graphics and animation.

Meyers, Richard. "Producing Science Fiction for Television." *Millimeter* 8:2 (February 1980): 96-101.

Pelton, Dale. " 'Death of the Red Planet' Filmed in Laser Images." *American Cinematographer* 54:7 (July 1973): 842-43. Pelton writes of his "introduction" to laser light-shows for a new film based on Dr. Elsa Garmire's work at the California Institute of Technology. Wet-gate printing is used to reposition images, add color, vary speeds, insert fades and dissolves, add solarization and strobe effects, and otherwise animate the film.

"Photographing 'The Black Hole.' " *American Cinematographer* 61:1 (January 1980): 32-36. Interview with Director of Photography Frank Phillips. He describes outline of the production and problems such as completing original photography before special effects were completed, creating potential blending problems. Lasers were animated; sodium light screen versus blue screen discussed.

Reiss, David S. "The Making of 'Star Trek—The Motion Picture,' An Interview with D. P. Richard H. Kline, ASC." *Film and Video Monthly* 13:3 (January 1980): 15-21. A generalized discussion about some aspects of the film, including special effects, with the chief cinematographer.

Rivlin, Robert. "Special Effects: How They Entered Our System and Where They're Headed." *Millimeter* 5:8 (September 1977): 14.

Trumbull, Douglas. "Creating Special Effects for 2001: A Space Odyssey." *American Cinematographer* 49:6 (June 1968): 416-19.

Whitlock, Albert. "Special Photographic Effects." *American Cinematographer* 55:11 (November 1974): 1330-31. Whitlock describes his work on *Earthquake*, including the use of rotoscoped mattes and the tedious cel by cel inking of individual frames in mattes used for superimposing shots of people moving "across" a given painting (glass shot, so-called).

CHAPTER 5

Creating Animation

Everybody says Walt wasn't a businessman. . . . He was a HELL of a businessman.[1]

E. CARDON WALKER

What emerged from Hollywood's first encounter with the New American Cinema was the suspicion that its advocates are less film makers than anti-film makers, rebels without either cause or purpose. Technically, they may be accused of sheer incompetence, while thematically they seem to be leading the way to a blind alley of self-indulgence and self-satisfaction from which there is no escape.[2]

ARTHUR KNIGHT

People forget that animation is a one-generation business. . . . Many of the people who worked on "Fantasia" are still around. To survive [animation] has to modernize.[3]

FRED CALVERT

Turning to literature describing the process and procedures for creating animation, this chapter is divided into two major areas: (1) the animation production literature, and (2) publications about the business of animation.

PRODUCTION LITERATURE

Historically, the E. G. Lutz volume, *Animated Cartoons: How They Are Made, Their Origin and Development*, is probably the most notable book explaining the cel production process at a time when cartoons were finding their audiences. This was one resource, Bob Thomas tells us, that Walt Disney used in learning how to animate. An earlier work, published in 1915, and now available in an Arno reprint, also embraced animation in stop-action forms. David Sherill Hulfish published *Motion-Picture Work; A General Treatise on Picture Taking, Picture Making, Photo-Plays and*

Theater Management and Operation. Chapters in *How Motion Pictures Are Made* by Homer Croy and *Behind the Motion Picture Screen* by Austin C. Lescarboura have generalized descriptions about animation production, with little detail on personalities or characters. For the mid-to-late 1920s, C. W. Taylor's chapter, "Animating Hand-Made Pictures: As in Early Experiments, the Cast Is Sometimes Manufactured," contained in *Masters and Masterpieces of the Screen*, reflects the state of the art. The trade journals and fan magazines also published several more generalized versions of the production process. Popular Bud Fisher, creator of Mutt and Jeff, told *Photoplay* readers, "Here's How!—Says Bud," in a production description of his animated characters. The Bray studios were described in "Drawing Animated Cartoons for the Movies," in an October 1924 *Popular Mechanics*. Dana Parker's "Making Comic Cartoons Move . . . " and Hi Sibley's "Those Aggravatin' Animations," are the most detailed overviews for the 1920s. In the 1940s, Nat Falk's *How to Make Animated Cartoons: The History and Technique* was evenly divided between history, technique, and a review of the major studios including Disney, Fleischers, Paul Terry's Terrytoons, Metro-Goldwyn-Mayer, Walter Lantz Productions, Leon Schlesinger Productions (Warner Brothers), and Screen Gems. There were certainly not the large number of "how-to-animate" books before this time because comparatively few organizations were engaged in animation production for theatrical distribution. Without television or widespread innovation of the sixteen-millimeter technology, the market for advertising industrial or training films was considerably limited. For the small business, cel-animation was an expensive proposition from the standpoint of staff or equipment. Thus, animation texts were typically limited to generalized explanations of how the theatrical cartoons were produced, with great emphasis in the literature going to Disney.

Embodying more contemporary cel techniques and technology, Roger Manvell's *The Animated Film* and Eli Levitan's *Animation Art in the Commercial Film* provide overviews for feature and short cel-animated films in the 1950s. But the most illustrated and detailed explanation of the feature process is the Bob Thomas volume, *Walt Disney: The Art of Animation—The Story of the Disney Studio Contribution to a New Art. American Cinematographer*, the professional journal of cinematography, published a nine-part series beginning in July 1958. Authors Carl Fallberg and Vern Palen began with the role of the story man and moved through the production process. Other role players and procedures, given separate monthly treatment, included the animation director, layout artists, animator problems, the in-betweener, handling dialogue, photography, inking, painting (a process revised by the technology of xerography), television commercial production, and limited animation. Each monthly issue is listed in the bibliography to this chapter.

There are numerous volumes currently available that review and describe the cel-animation processes for the interested beginner or professional who wants a reliable text. With regard to the single cel frame, but having distinct implications for shots eventually formed into sequences, two volumes are especially useful for both beginners and professionals. Donald W. Graham's *Composing Pictures* is an extensive analysis of compositional elements in single frames with a concluding chapter on some aspects of animation. Graham taught animation techniques at the Disney studios for several years, described in the Bob Thomas book, *Walt Disney: An American Original*. *The Cinema As a Graphic Art*, by Russian cinematographer Vladimir Nilsen, is more concerned with the structure of the filmed image as it is intercut with other shots. The meticulously planned *Brazen Horseman* storyboard is a classic still used in film production courses.

In the beginning there is a script and probably a storyboard for an animated film. John Halas compiled *Visual Scripting* to provide examples of how such preproduction materials can be prepared. This is the first lesson, and oftentimes a hard one for beginners to master. The book is a distinct appreciation of what previsualization can do for a completed film. Halas asked several filmmakers to contribute to his volume, so an array of examples for different types of films is presented, including advice on format, collaboration, painting and the film, tension charts, typography and combinations of live-action with animation, budgeting, storyboarding, and a perspective for the experimentalist. Beginning with the theoretical and practical implications of visual "grammar" by Sergei Eisenstein, the illustrated volume provides examples and production anecdotes from TV commercials, European films, the production design of John Wilson's *Shinbone Alley*, and examples of visual continuity in the films of Saul Bass and Norman McLaren. Stan Hayward has written an inexpensive guide, *Scriptwriting for Animation*, with brief explanations of storyboard, timing problems, formats, abstraction, barnstorming for ideas, stereotypes, humor, defining concepts, design techniques, the production process, rotoscoping, and experimenting. This complements Zoran Perisic's detailed but clearly illustrated handbook on *The Animation Stand*, ideal for the beginner. There are simplified explanations of the stand, tracking and field sizes, the required camera mechanism, optical effects, movements, various rotations, the pantograph table, floating peg bar, zoom techniques, motorized and automated tables, lighting, exposure, aerial image work, dope sheets, timing, strobing problems, shadow-board effects, rotoscoping, mattes, animated figures in live-action, and special effects such as slit-scan.

The volume with the most detailed overview of animation as a process together with explanations about cel, object (or dimensional) silhouette and flat-figure, stills-in-motion, drawing-on-film, pin screen, and computer techniques is *The Technique of Film Animation* by John Halas and Roger

Manvell. With a heavier historical emphasis that most other how-to books, Halas and Manvell carefully identify factors influencing animation, including physical laws, aesthetic principles, values, color, and external influences such as advertisers, the sponsor, or the public. The work concludes with interviews with Gene Deitch, Joy Batchelor, Stephen Bosustow, Geoffrey Sumner, John Hubley, Adrian Woolery, and Philip Stapp responding to questions about the future of the animated form. Another useful volume surveying several types of animated film but concentrating on the technology of cel-animation in an instructional sense is Roy Madsen's *Animated Film: Concepts, Methods, Uses*. A well-illustrated book, including clear examples of storyboard technique, exposure sheets, sound recording and bar sheets, and various manipulations on the animation stand, Madsen begins with a brief historical outline, then moves to concepts which are supplemented with a glossary at the back of the book. A more detailed volume about the photography phases is Zoran Perisic's *The Focal Guide To Shooting Animation*. His paperback mentioned above, *The Animation Stand*, provides a simplified breakdown of the stand and better illustrated explanations for various techniques, such as calculating moves, fairings, and field size changes.

Brian G. D. Salt's *Basic Animation Stand Techniques* and *Movements in Animation* (two volumes) are intended for the artist and technician. Although Salt claims *Basic Animation Stand Techniques* to be an "elementary work," potential users will quickly learn that a mathematical approach can improve results and increase production efficiency. Because calculations are necessary to produce satisfactory animations Salt has included the basic math techniques in chapters about linear movements and fairings, exponential movements, rotations, and circular pans. In his *Movements in Animation* the mechanics of movement are carefully described and mathematically derived. The reason for including these derivations is because most animation stands have counters or dials that require calculations to set on the counters. Salt's first volume discusses the applications of these coordinates to the animation stand and the subject of fairings, which involves the speeding up and slowing at the beginning and end of a movement to "soften" the transition from and to a stationary (static) hold. While the first volume of *Movements* deals with normal mechanics, there are other types of motion explained such as exponential movements, movements along curves, and methods of moving along curves whose equation is not known. Volume 2 is a collection of mathematical tables which should provide solutions to most movement problems. There are eighteen tables of fairings of various lengths and seven of middle fairings which are used when the speed of a movement is changed in the course of a shot. Other tables provide data on trigonometrical ratios, squares, square roots, reciprocals, and falls under gravity as well as logarithms, antilogarithms, field proportions, and exposures for different field sizes. Salt has also published *Programmes for Animation: A Handbook for Animation Technicians*. The programs in this book are suitable for programmable calculators or computers; each book segment has its own explanation. Sections of the book are devoted to the use of the calculator, field widths, and zoom-counter readings; field charts and coordinate systems; linear movements and fairings; zooms using several pieces of artwork; movements along a curve; and many other programs. This is a technical work dovetailing with the introductory volume, *Basic Animation Stand Techniques*, and it is of special relevance to computer-assisted animation. The *Handbook* and *Movements in Animation* are for technicians and artists already intimately familiar with the animation stand. Except for *Basic Animation Stand Techniques*, the technical volumes are also very expensive, over $200 for all three.

There are, of course, other suitable guides for the filmmaker on a budget and Ray da Silva's *The World of Animation* is the most recent paperback. Sold as Eastman Kodak Publication No. 35, and available in most photography stores, this lavishly illustrated guide outlines animation types and mechanics and gives an overview of the cel-animation process. A glossary and a light treatment of animation studios are also included. But the most useful section in this inexpensive guide is a complete set of plans for a home-built animation stand. Kit Laybourne's *The Animation Book* is considerably expanded in scope and detail by comparison. A larger number of animation types are explained including traditional cel, painting-on-film techniques, time-lapse and pixilation, kinestasis, collage, sand and painting-on-glass, clay and puppet animation, rotoscoping, pinscreen, pastel, optical techniques, and computer applications. Segments on production planning, and tools (cameras, stands, registration devices, lighting, editing tables, art supplies, and film stocks), conclude the work. In addition to the comprehensive, but not complex, survey of animation types, Laybourne has also included a valuable chapter on books, periodicals, and publications, a portion of which includes books on topics related to animation. Addresses and current prices are given for various fanzines and professional publications. An organizational list is also included, giving current data for the American Film Institute, unions in animation, the International Association of Animated Filmmakers (ASIFA) and others. Another chapter lists films about animation, distributors, screening centers, and festivals. There is a separate list of films illustrating or using various techniques in animation which would be especially useful for animation instructors.

Robert P. Heath has put together *Animation in Twelve Hard Lessons* catering specifically to those working in the cel medium. Organized along the lines of a quasi programmed instruction, each lesson has written and art work assignments. The only separate needs, in order to use the book, are to obtain an animation disc (addresses furnished) and build a simple light box. This is a "hands-on" book, requiring active participation if the student is to get anything out of Heath's advice. He has provided dozens of useful models, drawings, and examples. The first three lessons are about the in-betweening process. The next three deal with the assistant animator, starting out with the cleanup of an animator's rough drawing, one of the tasks of the assistant animator. Later, exposure sheets are laid out along with animator roughs showing the connection between the two to a piece of dialogue. Lesson 7 introduces pans with simpler calculations given compared to those of Brian Salt. Later lessons feature the animation stand, tricks of the trade (limited animation, slash techniques, faking the action), animation actions (waving objects, character "takes," hand actions, mouth actions), and technical animation, such as that used in instructional films depicting a technical subject. A glossary is also provided. The value of Heath's approach is to "walk through" the student from the first drawings to more ambitious sequences, correlating the drawing with the critical notations on the exposure sheets. Preston Blair's *How To Animate Film Cartoons*, an updated version of his 1949 book, *Advanced Animation*, is considered by some to be the best guide on animating drawings.

Howard Beckerman has been writing an animation column for *Film and Video Monthly: Filmmakers*, formerly known as *Filmmakers Newsletter*, for several years. Some selected columns have been put into the bibliography of this chapter under "The Business of Animation" section because they provide another important perspective on the process and instruction.

With the current emphasis on more inexpensive formats and the introduction of Super 8mm cameras with electric motors and single-frame exposure there have been a few books and chapters of books devoted to Super 8mm animation. Bebe Ferrell McClain's *Super 8 Filmmaking From Scratch* is one such example. John Halas and Bob Privett published a popular volume, *How to Cartoon for Amateur Films*, as did Anthony Kinsey. One volume coordinated with five TV programs telecast in Great Britain on this subject is Bob Godfrey and Anna Jackson's *Do-It-Yourself Film Animation Book*. Copyright and contractual restrictions have kept the television programs out of the United States, but the thin volume is available. It is packed with instructional data, including Terry Gilliam on cutout and dimensional animation and Richard Williams on the traditional cel medium.

There is no question that the Super 8mm format is an excellent way for inexperienced filmmakers to learn how to communicate through the motion picture medium. However, occasionally Super 8mm investors put themselves into a hypnotic trance, mesmerized with apparent low costs when considering the original raw stock and not worrying about labor costs and quality. Super 8mm has gone through some development of what would be considered professional-level equipment especially in editing and other postproduction gear. But for some forms of animation, such as painting-or drawing-on-film, the medium is clearly most inadequate. Other problems arise when, for example, ambitious amateurs want to gain a larger release requiring prints from their originals. For films having double-system sound tracks, there are devices to edit them in synchronism, but there are very few laboratories that can edge-number the track with the picture workprint. Indeed, Super 8mm originals do not carry latent image edge-numbers, making the conforming of the original film with the workprint a negative cutter's nightmare. After all that is done, the user is left with a substandard release print, full of grain, usually with undersaturated color, and a lot less choice in printing genealogies, film stocks, and opticals. One solution would be to take the Super 8mm original and, before projection, blow up the film to a 16mm original, strike a workprint and go through the post-production in that medium, and release in 16mm. Parenthetically, this seems a waste of quality and time given current technologies, lab practices, and printing stocks. One should not overlook the current and limited technical side in Super 8mm photography. Super 8mm equipment rarely has the critical registration pin system which is needed for serious work, particularly if the release versions will be projected on theater screens or if matte work is contemplated. (Mattes, as a practical matter, require 35mm formats.) Variable shutters and interchangeable lenses are also important elements left off of many Super 8mm cameras costing less than $1,200. Many film equipment manufacturers still consider the narrow gauge an amateur format since they have not provided for manual F-stop provisions on their automated exposure systems, especially for cameras selling for under $1,200. For dimensional animation, this is an extremely inhibiting factor, shortchanging dimensional filmmakers of their needed depth-of-field. Given the large amount of time required to photograph even limited animation, it makes more sense to use the larger format for better quality. On the other hand, with the original animation photography in video, 35mm or 16mm, Super 8mm still serves as an excellent release medium in certain forms of exhibition, particularly film-to-video in industrial applications or for small group projection. The Super 8mm projection systems, particularly the Elmo systems, have excellent picture and sound reproduction capabilities. While Super 8mm is a good release medium for specialized uses, serious and original work in this medium for the process and large audience release will result in poor quality, an exercise in poor judgment and wasted effort.

America Cinematographer, Filmmakers Newsletter, and other professional trades have published perceptive pieces on new animation technologies and techniques. Leon S. Rhodes, in 1966, discussed the creative potential for animation cameramen. John Hoke, in a much earlier issue, described the use of a zoom lens on an animation stand for those faced with low budgets. Leon S. Rhodes and Lowell Bodger have published on various facets in limited animation. An interesting piece by Vern Palen describes Paul Terry's aerial image-animation setup especially relevant for the low budget, live-action, and cel-animation combinations in the late 1950s that still have relevance for many filmmakers. George Griffin's advice on the xerography system indicates that this may not be the complete panacea for cost problems of the inking process in some situations. The finding aids discussed in Chapter 2 can locate on occasional gem in the animation literature, such as a report by Jaan Pill about Frank Thomas and Ollie Johnston discussing Disney guidelines for the audience and the animated form.

A great deal of the animation literature about the use of sound is either biographical or retrospective in terms of the procedures used after 1928.

Theoretical implications are outlined in two important periodical articles by Joe Adamson and Chuck Jones. Adamson, in the defunct *Take One*, traces the evolution of early sound cartoons concluding, in part, that the aural medium added to animation was a major thrust in developing the cartoon film, in contradiction to the live-action film at least, after sound was introduced. Some attention is given to the use of asynchronous sound, a major point in the arguments of Russian theorists and filmmakers S. M. Eisenstein, V. I. Pudovkin, and G. V. Alexandrov (see Appendix 1, "Chronology," 1928). Jones, on the other hand, laments the retarded state of sound cartoons in 1946, "more concerned with exact synchronization or 'Mickey Mousing' than with the originality of their contribution or the variety of their arrangement."[4] Citing examples from *Fantasia* and the Warner Brothers-Fritz Freleng short, *Rhapsody in Rivets*, Jones discusses the "perfect wedding of music and graphics which occurs when the visual and auditory impacts are simultaneous and almost equal."[5]

A number of books are available on sound production as this relates to the motion picture and broadcasting, including the volumes and "packages" published by Hastings House. Recording dialogue, sound effects, and music follow general practices outlined in standard texts such as Robert S. Oringel's *Audio Control Handbook for Radio and TV Broadcasting* or Milton Lustig's *Music Editing for Motion Pictures*. There are no known books exclusively devoted to sound for animated films. One should remember that technical requirements for high fidelity, stereo sound recording are similar for all forms of audio and video media, but in sound for animation a number of important procedural differences exist. For example, dialogue for most cel-animated films is recorded in the preproduction stage, not during photography as is the practice with live-action filming. During the 1930s, when sound was still relatively new, studios varied in this procedure; some recording dialogue, effects, and music to coincide with a projected print. An interesting article by Disney Sound Director C. O.

Slyfield described the postwar sound recording process from the time of *Steamboat Willie* to 1946. Several segments of the Roger Manvell and John Huntley book, *The Technique of Film Music*, describe previous techniques in the early sound films of Disney, Anthony Gross, Hector Hoppin, Berthold Bartosch, and others. Some music transcripts for cartoons demonstrate the scoring process. Generalized articles, such as "The Making of a Sound Fable" in *Popular Mechanics*, are typical periodical material, similar to articles about cartooning in the 1930s and 1940s. Disney's Fantasound was the subject of several popular press and specialized journals, including articles by Hermine Rich Isaacs, Edward H. Plumb, William E. Garity and Watson Jones. Roy Prendergast's *A Neglected Art* devotes some attention to music in animated films and to the work of Scott Bradley.

Most of the literature about sound in animated films has concentrated on the personalities voicing the cartoon characters. Mike Barrier's *Funnyworld*, No. 18 (Post Office Box 1633, New York, New York 10001), is almost entirely devoted to sound in the animated cartoons, featuring essays and fragments of interviews, with Clarence Nash (Donald Duck), Jim Macdonald (Mickey Mouse), Bill Bletcher (Disney characters), Mel Blanc (numerous characters), June Foray (numerous characters), Jack Mercer (Popeye), Jerry Hausner (numerous characters), and Daws Butler (Captain Crunch, among others). Short essays about sound characterizations for the Warner Brothers, Disney, MGM, Columbia, and UPA, Walter Lantz, Fleischer, and Paramount cartoons are also included. An article by Ross Care discusses the composers for the Disney shorts. One chapter in Bernard Rosenberg's *The Real Tinsel* is about voice animator Billy Bletcher who did the wolf voice in Disney's *Three Little Pigs* (1933). A more extensive exposition on Mel Blanc, with the usual trappings of a fanzine piece, is contained in Walt Mitchell's "Mel Blanc's World of Fantasy," a 48-page review of Blanc's career and a list of Mel Blanc recordings, all published in *World of Yesterday*, No. 19. (Published by Ron Downey, 13759—60th Street, North, Clearwater, Florida 33520.) Tony Hiss and David McClelland wrote an interesting study of Clarence Nash, the voice of Donald Duck. Drawing upon interviews with Nash and Disney directors Jack Hanah, Frank Thomas, and Jack Cutting, the authors discussed procedures for using sound in early Disney films along with the Nash role in voicing the Duck. Several anecdotes about Nash's career are also included. Howard Rieder's master's thesis on UPA's Magoo character contains information about Jim Backus's role in voicing the Magoo character and the use of music in the Magoo animations made for theaters.

With regard to music in animation, much of the critical literature, accessible by using the finding aids discussed in Chapter 3, comes to focus on Disney's *Fantasia* and the controversial outcome of the Leopold Stokowski-Mickey Mouse (Walt Disney) partnership. Chapter 10 in a Stokowski biography by Abram Chasins provides one interpretation of the relationship; Bob Thomas in *Walt Disney, An American Original*, provides another but much briefer view. Ross Care contributed an informative article to *Sight and Sound* in early 1977 entitled, "Cinesymphony: Music and Animation at the Disney Studio, 1928-1942," complementing his material about the Disney composers published in *Funnyworld's* special issue on sound. The earlier piece discussed the innovation of the bar sheet at Disney by Wilfred Jackson and gave interview-recollections by Jackson on how sound was added to the first synchronized cartoon by Disney. A number of interesting insights are also presented in his interview with Carl Stalling, Disney's first music director. Mike Barrier in *Funnyworld* also interviewed Stalling.

Several experimenters have used various techniques in creating their own sound tracks by simply drawing them. Len Lye, Max Fleischer, and Norman McLaren were among those who designed procedures or painted on soundtracks, or mixed various sound designs together to synthesize or animate sound. McLaren is the only one who wrote in detail about how he synthesized sound in several of his animations. Leon Becker's "Synthetic Sound and the Abstract Image" describes in detail the experiments of the Whitney brothers around 1943. While this particular aspect of the sound in animation literature is fragmented and thin, the subject is far from dead. Given new forms of electronic music and synthesization, articles such as "Movies from Music: Visualizing Musical Compositions," by J. B. Mitroo and others, are not unusual in the computer and music literature.

One additional point should be made. As the visual side of the motion picture has turned to new forms of destroying reality and creating new fantasies, the use of the sound track, in many instances, is also now used to create and maintain the old continuity or narrative. While this is nothing new in terms of technique (flowing out of several editorial devices such as using sound over a cut), the mixing of components resulting in new sounds attributed to unfamiliar objects (such as Wookies—*Star Wars*, *Empire Strikes Back*—or space explosions) adds new dimensions to the photographed or drawn image, sometimes to the point that the narrative is really in the sound track. To see how far the sound and other technologies brought audiences in such fantasies, compare *Barbarella* (1968) with *Star Wars* (1977). Until readers become aware of the story of sound recording in *Star Wars* under the supervision of Ben Burt, they will be surprised to learn of the emphasis placed on advanced audio-recording technology and postsynchronized dialogue, created after many of the live-action scenes were photographed. The view that younger audiences, conditioned by high fidelity and Dolby noise-reduction systems, bring high expectations for sound to new films may partially explain the new emphasis on sound tracks. But, most likely, the burgeoning technology of sound recording and mixing, along with the emerging digital audio systems, is paving the way to more efficiently and automatically exploited sound for films. Moreover, there are a number of music-studio craftsmen moving into the film-mixing world, according to Michael Rivlin writing in "Motion Picture Sound Re-recording and Mixing: Dawn of a Digital Decade."

Together with sound effects and the symphonic musical score, a continuum is established and easily maintained, with the subtle nuances and mood changes indicated more by sound track than the action. Walter Murch's work on *Apocalypse Now* is typical of the kind of synthesis obtained in contemporary sound tracks, utilizing new combinations of technology. Zoetrope, Francis Cappola's postproduction facilities in San Francisco, represent the current state of the art, particularly in sound-mixing. What is likely to wrinkle the brows of traditional film mixers is the introduction of sprocketless media, tied-in synchronism to the picture with the Society of Motion Picture and Television Engineers' (SMPTE) time code.

There is one more ingredient in the media-mix for today's motion picture that requires animation support and embellishes the newly created reality. Special photographic effects, together with dimensional animation (puppet), have been carefully orchestrated in some films to elevate the fantasies to new heights. Special photographic effects include rear-screen projection, front projection, stop-motion animation, static or traveling mattes, or cel-animation techniques used in conjunction with mattes or combined with models or live-action. The definitive work which explains the technology and techniques is Raymond Fielding's *The Technique of Special Effects Cinematography*. Bernard Wilkie's *Creating Special Effects for TV and Films* is an abbreviated guide giving helpful tips on how to accomplish some mechanical and photographic effects. The most recent popularized overview of the current emphasis on such photographic effects is Richard Schickel's special-effects survey published in the *New York Times Magazine*, 18 May 1980.

These techniques are contributors to the destruction-of-reality syndrome so characteristic of the television and film media since their inception. Reaction to these changes is clearly reflected in Arthur Knight's criticism quoted at the beginning of this chapter, along with the business emphasis made by E. Cardon Walker, a longtime employee of the Disney organization. To survive, as the Fred Calvert quote suggests, modernizing forms of animation and other techniques such as sound recording must anchor themselves with audiences that can readily accept new forms and not become so innotative that those audiences become disoriented. The reality-capturing ability of the camera and microphone is modified by editing, special effects, and synthesized sound, but the resulting creations are still anchored to a form the audience can comprehend. The form with the deepest tradition for audiences is the narrative, and in the 1980s, directors and editors anchor their narrative in the sound track, intercut with seemingly discontinuous images. For example, audiences are not aware of the large amount of looping dialogue put into *Star Wars*, thinking that all the dialogue that was recorded on the set was the same used in the film. On the contrary, much was added later, in postproduction, sometimes using different voices to accompany the speaking of a given character. The voice of David Prowse, playing Darth Vadar, was considerably different from that of James Earl Jones, which was eventually used. Combined, the soundtrack (Jones) and picture (Prowse) created a character that did not exist in either aural or visual reality.

The improved image and sound technologies are only part of the explanation for the creation of what borders on the fantastic. The intervals between those images and sounds (tied together into shots and then sequences, or building upon a narrative) are the key toward understanding the capacity of the film and television media. Manipulating these intervals, and consequently timing (which is the duration of a screen action), exploits the chief element for which audiences are conditioned, and that is the narrative form. The improved technologies, especially the animated forms used in support of special effects, have brought filmmakers and audiences to a new peak in the destruction of reality, but the manipulation of images and sound tracks through editing has been exploited for decades. Filmmakers following a documentary tradition, beginning with the Lumière brothers and moving forward into the era of television news and public affairs programming, have even incorporated such manipulations while exploiting the narrative form. There are many examples of this art, but most sequences from *Victory At Sea*, a revered compilation documentary, easily illustrate such manipulations of storytelling, sound effects, and a highly dramatic, perhaps romantic, musical score.

Narrative forms incorporating the stills-in-motion animated techniques are the basis for recreating historical subjects and personalities. Animators using those approaches require the basic still material from which to shape and exploit their film idea. Several guides now exist that lead producers to libraries, archives, and commercial sources, identify holdings by subject, and provide cost, copyright, and access information. With regard to one of the largest public archives, the Special Collections of Prints and Photographs in the Library of Congress, Paul Vanderbilt's *Guide* is indispensable. Each of over eight hundred collections is alphabetically listed and accompanied with an annotated description-and-quantity data, followed with a detailed description of each collection. Ann Novotny has edited *Picture Sources 3*, listing over eleven hundred sources of photographs from government, industry, and associations, divided into fifteen subject-chapters. Detailed subject, numerical, alphabetical, and geographic indexes are also included. Fred W. McDarrah edited *Stock Photo and Assignment Source Book: Where to Find Photographs Instantly*. Hillary Evans and others compiled an earlier source book entitled *The Picture Researcher's Handbook: An International Guide to Picture Sources—and How to Use Them*. The Linda Mehr union catalogue for manuscript and special collections in the Western United States is another important source for stills. This is described in Chapter 3 and Appendix 2.

The use of still photographs edited to a sound track, reflected in the work of Dan McLaughlin and Charles Braverman, can be done on a modest budget, without a high investment in expensive equipment or a large number of cels. Such films are made by a kinestatis technique. Dan McLaughlin's film that first brought the technique to the public was *God Is Dog Spelled Backwards*, a three-and-one-half minute view of 3000 years of art history edited to Beethoven's Fifth Symphony. Charles Braverman made *American Time Capsule* for the "Smothers Brothers Comedy Hour" (1968) edited to a sound track of a Sandy Nelson drum solo. Braverman has described one approach to kinestasis film in a chapter in David A. Sohn's *Good Looking: Film Studies, Short Films and Filmmaking*.

Unlike traditional cel-animation, or any of the other forms discussed in this guide, there are no computer-animation handbooks that present an easy recipe to generate computer images. Aside from the technical requirements, the hardware is often inaccessible except for the resources of university research centers, large corporations, or computer-animation firms. There is some irony in the fact that this growing technology has high visibility in the professional journals and trades, yet there are comparatively few locations in the world where one can obtain systematic training in specific techniques. Part of this problem is compounded by the dynamics of the technology itself; there is always a new generation of hardware around the corner. While this situation presently appears restrictive, there are considerable indications that the hardware packages will increasingly become available to schools, industry, and private individuals as the costs are more affordable. Indeed, some home computers already have capabilities of generating programmed graphics. Moreover, with home units, it is entirely possible to access several data banks for a fee and the use of your telephone. With the foregoing in mind, a few textbooks and other materials are listed below.

William M. Newman and Robert F. Sproull have published the second edition of their landmark text in computer graphics entitled *Principles of Interactive Computer Graphics*, claimed by many to be the first complete text in computer graphics which covers display devices, files, interactive modes, three-dimensional graphics, and graphics systems. One of the pioneers in computer graphics, Sylvan H. Chasen, applies basic geometric principles and demonstrates their implications for curve fitting and data presentation in his 1978 book, *Geometric Principles and Procedures for Computer Graphic Applications*. This work is aimed at users and systems programmers, moves into mathematical formulation to match known or desired data constraints, and concludes with three-dimensional geometry. Another text, also for system programmers and designers, is *Interactive Computer Graphics: Data Structures, Algorithms, Languages*, by Wolfgang K. Giloi, a teacher and researcher who has taught these techniques at the University of Minnesota and Berlin. Another work cited frequently in the literature, but not seen for this report, is *Digital Picture Processing* by Azriel Rosenfeld and Avinash C. Kak.

Readers are cautioned that many of the books and other materials cited in Chapter 4, under the rubric of computer animation, may have some training relevance to persons already familiar with theory and data processing by machine. Thus, *Computer Animation*, edited by John Halas, may also function as a training manual, to a degree, as well as research reports published in the technical journals.

Trade and professional associations in the early American film and later broadcasting industries, performed several important functions for their membership, including the diffusing of information about the new technologies. While these associations were also formed for political, social, and economic reasons, their publications also include an enormous amount of material about the technical aspects of any new medium. In some ways, this information served an instructional purpose, and for researchers the materials were mandatory to avoid reinventing the wheel. They also permitted more rapid research and development. The Association for Computing Machinery, a professional association founded in 1947 and since splintered into several special-interest groups including computer graphics, has served similar purposes over the years. The special interest group in computer graphics is coded SIGGRAPH, which publishes a quarterly journal, *Computer Graphics*. One issue each year is comprised of papers from an annual conference. Membership information for the association and SIGGRAPH can be obtained from the Association for Computing Machinery, 1133 Avenue of the Americas, New York, New York 10036. A publication list which includes several computer graphic reports is also available. The association has also prepared the *ACM Guide to Computing Literature* (formerly *Bibliography and Subject Index of Current Computing Literature*) which is an important annual guide to this specialized literature, including computer graphics and animation.

Other trade journals, such as *Millimeter*, often contain generalized reports of new applications in computer-animation or a survey of the field. A series of three articles by Jim Lindner began in June 1980, reviewed the technology for controlling animation stands, and then covered analogue and digital systems. Similar reports are typically found in *Television/Radio Age, Backstage*, and *Broadcast Management-Engineering*.

In dealing with references for creating animation, it seems appropriate to identify guides which may point the way to more formal education in animation. Three publications describe university programs, generalized curricula, student enrollments, and other information. Ernest D. Rose authored *World Film and Television Study Resources: A Reference Guide to Major Training Centers and Archives* available through the University Film Association, Department of Photography-Cinema, Southern Illinois University, Carbondale, Illinois 62901. The American Film Institute has published *The AFI Guide to College Courses In Film and Television*, available from Peterson's Guides, Book Order Department, Post Office Box 2123, Princeton, New Jersey 08540. A separate listing of schools offering course work in animation is included, along with other categorized data such as schools by areas of curricular emphasis, screenwriting, teacher training, and foreign curricula. The most recent report, subsidized by Eastman Kodak, was prepared by C. William Horrell, *A Survey of Motion Picture Still Photography and Graphic Arts Instruction*, free of charge from Eastman Kodak. Write: Motion Picture and Audiovisual Markets Division, Rochester, New York 14650, and ask for publication T-17. Several summary statistics indicating the large number of semester hours offered at the undergraduate and graduate levels, student enrollments (which are growing enormously), degrees earned, and other information are given in this useful booklet. While the code scheme for computer graphics and animation is ambiguous, a close reading of each entry for various institutions, arranged by state, will identify the animation courses and the number of credit hours possible. While the summary statistics report a low number of courses in computers and graphic communications, a spot check under some institutions known to conduct computer animation research did not indicate any course work offered at the University of Minnesota, Ohio State University, or the Massachusetts Institute of Technology, for example. This raises some suspicions about the survey, perhaps indicating that the search was restricted to the traditional speech, radio, television, and film departments. Course work in computer-animation and graphics is more likely to be offered in engineering, mathematics, or computer-science departments. Potential students should use these dated lists to isolate the likely schools and then write to the administrators directly, raising questions and requesting a detailed listing of course offerings or a catalogue. Study carefully the facilities descriptions, as some schools tend to overinflate their physical-plant resources by making more out of facilities jointly managed, for example, and not exclusively controlled by a single department.

For teachers of animation, the published advice of John Canemaker and Howard Beckerman may be relevant. Certainly instructors will find announcements of new films about filmmaking in *Film Library Quarterly* and *Sightlines* and new book announcements and reviews in the *Journal of the University Film Association* important. Appendix 4 contains additional information for locating films and videotapes about animation for instructional or home use.

THE BUSINESS OF ANIMATION

For advertising, instructional, and perhaps employment purposes, it is helpful to know who is creating animation and in what specialties they practice. Howard Beckerman's list, published in mid-1980, entitled "Animation Special: What's Everybody Doing . . . " is one of the best lists around. Large and small houses from every coast and throughout the midlands are represented with addresses and telephone numbers. Five years earlier, Mr. Beckerman published an animation and filmmakers map of Manhattan, which still might have some relevance. One trade journal of the commercials industry, *Backstage*, annually publishes an animation issue, usually in September, containing numerous stories and advertisements for animation production houses. *Backstage* also publishes an annual *TV Film/ Tape Directory* of industry references, advertising agencies, and service and equipment companies. Comparable lists are available periodically in *Advertising Age* and *Television/Radio Age*. In animation, *Millimeter* has frequently published extensive reviews of numerous production houses and anecdotal reports about internal philosophies and animation orientations. The materials cited in the bibliography by Patricia Alexander, Richard Meyers, and William Bilowit are typical examples.

In Howard Beckerman's view, "if you're trying to make it in animation, the small individually owned studio is the way to go."[6] His two articles in earlier issues of *Filmmakers Newsletter* provide perspective for that view. The report given in "More House-Owned Studios Seen" seems to temper animation activity, but one must remember that this industry is subject to some sharp, cyclic forces from time to time.

There are very few published reports on the actual economics of specific animation productions and commercials. For programming, the social, economic, and sometimes political forces affecting the production process are clearly established in the Muriel G. Cantor study, *The Hollywood TV Producer: His Work and His Audience*, based on confidential interviews among various television producers. In animated programming, Cantor interviewed twenty producers and four writers of children's programs and fifty-nine producers of dramatic programs. Cantor contributed to Volume 1 of the Technical Reports to the Surgeon General's Scientific Advisory Committee on Television and Social Behavior, cited in Chapter 4. In both reports, the production process for animated programs for the early 1970s was described, with network "norms" (approval behavior in content matters) varying from year to year as the networks' perceptions of the audience varied along with the social climate. John Canemaker's piece on "The Business of Successful Animated Feature" discusses the factors affecting features on 1977 and reports only generalized money returns on some pictures. Canemaker considers the year unique because of so many independently produced films in distribution, including one foreign film, Bruno Bozzetto's *Allegro non troppo*. The background on Ralph Bakshi's films is particularly interesting. Howard Beckerman's "How Much Does a Cartoon Cost?" has an artful breakdown along with the usual high statistics.

For equipment and supplies, the trades such as *Millimeter*, *Backstage*, occasionally *Variety*, *American Cinematographer*, and others listed in Appendix 7 are the best sources for updating information, with the word-of-mouth channels serving as primary sources among the relatively close-knit animation community.

After creation, the independently produced animation film may seek a distribution channel either for theaters, television, or specialized audiences. Sponsored films and commercials already have their distribution channels established long before completion, often before production. Again, the newcomer may turn to sage Howard Beckerman, the prolific columnist in *Filmmakers Monthly*, for his advice in "Animation Kit: Distributing Animated Films." Steve Feltes, Charles Silver, and Robert Pike provide useful perspectives on days past and producers who overprice their work. There is no substitute for direct personal contact, however. The addresses contained in Appendix 4 would be one place to start.

Several organizations are involved in animated film production as producer associations, unions, or professional craft guilds. Many of these organizations produce a highly specialized literature intended only for their membership and a select number of repositories. While much of this material is not intended to be of literary value but is rather intended to further the ends of the organization, there are exceptions, as in the case of the ASIFA publications. Beginning with producers, the Association of Independent Commercial Producers (AICP) has served in the past to consolidate guidelines attempting to govern business relationships between members and advertising agencies. For example, the article "AICP Takes Aim At Agency 'Abuses' With New Guidelines," in *Television/Radio Age*, or the Patrick Collins piece, illustrate typical functions. There are several associations similar to AICP which espouse policies, set guidelines, or otherwise have an impact on business and professional standards in the communications industries in the United States. The *Aspen Handbook on the Media* (current edition) is a selective guide to research, organizations, and publications in the communication field, and contains dozens of profiles, addresses, and descriptions of producer and practitioner organizations. Included in their list are data for: the Advertising Research Foundation, American Association of Advertising Agencies, Broadcast Education Association, Children's Television Workshop, Public Broadcasting Service, Association for Educational Communications and Technology, and dozens of others.

The National Cartoonist Society (NCS) was organized in 1946 and is comprised of about 500 members from magazine, syndicated features, advertising, illustration, comic book, animation and many other fields of the professional cartoon. The *Cartoonist* is the society journal. NCS establishes and continues close relations with other associations such as the Advertising Council, Magazine Publishers Association, and newspaper interests. Prospective members should write: NCS, Membership Chairman, 19 West 44th Street, Room 309, New York, New York 10036.

The International Animated Film Society (ASIFA) was organized in 1960 and has grown to over 1,000 members in thirty-three countries. The stated purpose of the international organization is to advance all aspects of animated films worldwide, including animation in all forms. Regular bulletins are published by ASIFA in three languages and distributed from Europe. Several books have been published by Focal Press (London and New York) and Hastings House (New York). The association maintains an archive in Berlin with plans for circulation in 35mm and video cassette. A quarterly magazine, *Animafilm*, is published by the international arm of ASIFA, further explained in Appendix 7. The international organization supports or organizes international film festivals in animation held annually in either Annecy, France; Zagreb, Yugoslavia; or Ottawa, Canada.

There are four regional chapters of ASIFA in the United States and one in Canada. These addresses are as follows:

ASIFA/EAST. Room 1018, 25 West 43rd Street, New York, New York 10036.

ASIFA/CENTRAL. 7549 North Oakley, Chicago, Illinois 60645.

ASIFA/HOLLYWOOD. 1258 North Highland Avenue, Suite 102, Hollywood, California 90038.

ASIFA/SAN FRANCISCO. Post Office Box 14516, San Francisco, California 94114.

ASIFA/CANADA. C. P. 341, Succ. Post. St. Laurent, Quebec, H4L 4V6.

Each of these regional organizations sponsors programs unique to the area of its membership, including the sponsoring of various animated-film festivals, various screenings, and awards convocations. ASIFA/HOLLY-WOOD has an annual animation award dinner, where an Annie, "cousin to Oscar, Emmy, Grammy, and Tony," is awarded to individuals who have dedicated their lives and talents to animation. Along with all ASIFA chapters, they also participate in the International Tournée of Animation (ITA). ASIFA/HOLLYWOOD assisted in the selection of films for an unusual archive established by the Professional, Technical, and Clerical Employees' Union, Local 986, described below.

The two major unions for animation activities on the West Coast are the Motion Picture Screen Cartoonists, Local 839 (IATSE-AFL-CIO), 12441 Ventura Boulevard, Studio City, California 91604, and the Professional, Technical and Clerical Employees' Union, Local 986, 15300 Ventura Boulevard, Suite 401, Sherman Oaks, California 91403. *Pegboard* is the newsletter of Local 839. The Professional, Technical and Clerical Employees' Union (Local 986) has organized an animated film study collection consisting of numerous examples of the animated art in various forms from the beginning of motion pictures to recent years. The complete list is provided in Appendix 2, Research Collections, West, and the UCLA Film and Television Archive. In the New York area, the Motion Picture Screen Cartoonists, Local 841 (IATSE-AFL-CIO), 25 West 43rd Street, New York, New York 10036 is the principal organizer. *Top Cel* is the union newsletter for the membership.

NOTES

1. Quoted in "The Disney Way With The Dolar," *Forbes* (15 March 1977): 80.

2. Arthur Knight, "SR Goes To The Movies. New American Cinema?", *Saturday Review*, 2 November 1963, p. 41.

3. Quoted in Jim Harwood, "Animation Biz At Crossroads. Ascendancy of Live-Action Makes Sharp Inroads on Cartoonery Work," *Variety*, 30 April 1975, p. 278.

4. Chuck Jones, "Music and the Animated Cartoon," *Hollywood Quarterly* 1:4 (July 1946): 365.

5. Ibid.

6. Howard Beckerman, "Animation Special: What's Everybody Doing . . . ," *Filmmakers Newsletter*, July 1980, p. 24.

BIBLIOGRAPHY

AMERICAN CINEMATOGRAPHER SERIES ON PRODUCTION

Fallberg, Carl. "Animated Film Techniques." *American Cinematographer* 39:7 (July 1958): 434. Describes the role of the story man and other related personnel.

_____. "Animated Film Techniques. Part 2: Production Preparation." *American Cinematographer* 39:8 (August 1958): 488. Animation director determines tempo and pacing of picture, staging and performances of characters, and coordinates all production activities.

_____. "Animated Film Techniques. Part 3." *American Cinematographer* 39:9 (September 1958): 558. About the layout man who plans the staging and setting; the analogy in live-action is the art director.

_____. "Animated Film Techniques. Part 4: The Animator's Problems." *American Cinematographer* 39:10 (October 1958): 626. Dialogue scenes differ from those with straight action. Straight action may require personality mime, or fast action, for example. Coherence of style is necessary in order to maintain continuity throughout the film, given the asembly-line style of animation.

_____. "Animated Film Techniques. Part 5." *American Cinematographer* 39:12 (December 1958): 694. Usually there are four cels; the cel on bottom, next to the background, is first level. Fourth level is on top. Most action can be successfully handled in a procedure knwon as "2s"—that is, exposing each drawing on two frames of film. Gives example from *Bambi* in the use of "2s and 1s."

"Animated Film Techniques. Part 6. *American Cinematographer* 40:1 (January 1959): 38. Function of the in-betweener is discussed with illustrations from *Bambi.*

"Animated Film Techniques. Part 7." *American Cinematographer* 40:2 (February 1959): 114. About dialogue and effects animation.

"Animated Film Techniques. Part 8." *American Cinematographer* 40:3 (March 1959): 170. Final stages of production, inking, and painting are described. Photography, music, and sound effects production conclude the article.

Palen, Vern. "Animated Film Techniques. Part 9." *American Cinematographer* 40:5 (May 1959): 298. Animation in TV and commercial film production. Here movements are confined to principal characters and action; backgrounds simplified for TV, if any given at all.

PRODUCTION LITERATURE

Adamson, Joe. "Crabquacks." *Take One* 6:2 (January 1978): 18-22.

American Film Institute. *The AFI Guide to College Courses in Film and Television.* Washington, D.C.: AFI, 1978.

Andrews, Stanley. "The Inside Story of In-Betweens." *Popular Photography* 55:5 (November 1964): 172.

Association for Computing Machinery. *The ACM Guide to Computing Literature.* New York: ACM, published annually.

Barrier, Mike. "An Interview With Carl Stalling." *Funnyworld*, no. 13 (n.d.): 13-27.

Becker, Leon. "Synthetic Sound and the Abstract Image." *Film Quarterly* 1:1 (October 1945): 95-96. Describes in some detail the process used by the Whitney brothers to make synthetic sound tracks.

Beckerman, Howard. "Animation Kit: Saturday Under the Lights." *Filmmakers Newsletter*, June 1972, pp. 32-33.

_____. "Animation Kit: The Pan." *Filmmakers Newsletter*, November 1972, p. 48.

_____. "Animation Kit: Creating Motion." *Filmmakers Newsletter*, December 1972, p. 35.

_____. "Animation Kit: The Cel." *Filmmakers Newsletter*, February 1973, p. 40.

_____. "Animation Kit: Problems, Problems, Problems." *Filmmakers Newsletter*, June 1973, p. 44.

_____. "Animation Kit: Shadows, Anyone?" *Filmmakers Newsletter*, May 1974, pp. 46-47.

_____. "Animation Kit: The Little Details." *Filmmakers Newsletter*, December 1974, p. 42.

_____. "Animation Kit: Keep on Trucking." *Filmmakers Newsletter*, January 1975, pp. 46-47.

_____. "Animation Kit: The Walk." *Filmmakers Newsletter*, March 1975, p. 36.

_____. "Animation Kit: The Pencil Test." *Filmmakers Newsletter*, May 1975, p. 57.

_____. "Animation Kit: Teaching Animation." *Filmmakers Newsletter*, June 1975, p. 34.

_____. "Animation Kit: Wantu Means 'Beautiful.' " *Filmmakers Newsletter*, January 1976: 34-35.

_____. "Animation Kit: Animating Characters That Interact." *Filmmakers Newsletter*, September 1976, p. 60.

_____. "Animation Kit: The Animated Insert." *Filmmakers Newsletter*, February 1977, p. 57.

_____. "Animation Kit: Animating Hands." *Filmmakers Newsletter*, April 1977, p. 54.

_____. "The Animator as Performing Artist." *American Cartoonist*, 17 April 1978, unpaged.

_____. "Animation Kit: 1's, 2's, 3's and By God Even 4's." *Filmmakers Monthly*, June 1979. Excellent article about the variety of exposures used per drawn cel in various films.

Blair, Preston. *Animation: Learn How to Draw Animated Cartoons*. Laguna Beach, Calif.: Foster Publishers, 1949.

Block, Alex Ben. "Oxberry: Animation's Family Name." *Filmmakers Newsletter*, October 1972, p. 24.

Bodger, Lowell. "Production Advantages In Limited Animation." *American Cinematographer* 42:6 (June 1961): 358.

_____. "Animation Cycles." *Filmmakers Newsletter*, February 1972, p. 46.

Boone, Andrew R. "A Famous Fairy Tale Is Brought To The Screen As The Pioneer Feature-Length Cartoon In Color." *Popular Science Monthly*, January 1938, p. 50. *Snow White* estimated 362,919 frames exposed; 1,500,000 pen-and-ink drawings and watercolor paintings. Article describes multiplane camera.

――――. "Movie Cartoons In Color." *Scientific American* 156:1 (January 1937): 16-17.

Burks, J. E. "A Third-Dimensional Effect in Animated Cartoons." *Society of Motion Picture Engineers Journal* 28:1 (January 1937): 39-42.

Canemaker, John. "Reflections on Teaching Animation." *Millimeter* 4:2 (February 1976): 30-34.

Care, Ross, "Cinesymphony: Music and Animation at the Disney Studio, 1928-1942." *Sight and Sound* 46:2 (Spring 1977): 40-44. With Mildred Jackson describing the process of using music in the Disney *Silly Symphonies* and gag-cartoons, the author reviews the evolution of sound at Disney.

――――. "Symphonists for the Sillies: The Composers for Disney's Shorts." *Funnyworld*, no. 18 (Summer 1978): 38-48.

Chasen, Sylvan H. *Geometric Principles and Procedures for Computer Graphic Applications*. Englewood Cliffs, N.J.: Prentice-Hall, 1978.

Chasins, Abram. *Leopold Stokowski: A Profile*. New York: Hawthorn Books, 1979.

"Cheaper Cartoons." *Business Week*, 4 May 1957, pp. 192-93. Illustrated Films, Hollywood, has developed the Artiscope which is a mechanical drawing machine transforming live-action human figures into animated characters. Similar to the rotoscope process, but using special film which provides an outline of the live-action person, the Artiscope "fills in" the drawing five times faster than a human could trace.

Comorau, Gary. "John Oxberry: The Man behind the Machine." *Millimeter* 3:4 (April 1975): 26-27.

Croy, Homer. *How Motion Pictures Are Made*. New York: Harper and Brothers, 1918.

Darino, Edward. "Animation With A Xerox 6500 Copier." *Industrial Photography* 26:3 (March 1977): 34-35. Independent animator Darino discusses use of the Xerox 6500 color copies for animation. Films using the procedures are described.

da Silva, Ray. *The World of Animation*. Rochester, N.Y.: Eastman Kodak Company, 1979.

Daugherty, Frank. "How Donald Comes Out of the Paint Pots." *Christian Science Monitor (Magazine)*, 14 December 1940, p. 6. Disney organization has developed some 2,000 paints so far, all catalogued by number. The work of the paint department is described.

――――. "Mickey Mouse Comes Of Age." *Christian Science Monitor (Magazine)*, 2 February 1938, p. 8. Discusses problems of animating human figures on the screen, as in *Snow White*. Importance of the multiplane camera indicated with an example described from *The Old Mill*.

Dixon, Dougal. "The Technique of Glass Paintings." *Cinemagic*, no. 7 (Summer 1976): 24-26.

Dougherty, Walter S. "AV Production: Making It Move." *Audio-Visual Communications* 13:5 (May 1979): 36. Creation of simple animation for audio-visual work.

"Drawing Animated Cartoons for the Movies." *Popular Mechanics* 42 (October 1924): 611-14. Using illustrations from the Bray studios, the article describes the process of animation in general terms.

"Dumbo At The Circus." *Modern Plastics* 19:1 (September 1941): 31-37. Riddled with some errors of animation "landmarks," this piece explains the role of plastic in the cel system used by the Fleischers, Paul Terry, and Disney, among others.

Eastman Kodak. *Basic Titling and Animation for Motion Pictures.* (Data Book S-21). Rochester, N.Y.: Eastman Kodak, 1972.

————. "Movies and Slides Without A Camera." (Brochure S-47). Rochester, N.Y.: Eastman Kodak, n.d. Useful brochure describing needed materials, procedures, sound, magnetic recording, splicing, and other techniques for making films and slides by drawing on the film or soundtrack.

Evans, Hilary; Evans, Mary; and Nelki, Andra. *The Picture Researcher's Handbook: An International Guide to Picture Sources—And How To Use Them.* New York: Charles Scribner's Sons, 1974.

Falk, Nat. *How to Make Animated Cartoons: The History and Technique.* New York: Foundation Books, 1942.

Fielding, Raymond. *The Technique of Special Effects Cinematography.* 3d ed. New York: Focal Press, 1972.

Fisher, Bud. "Here's How!—Says Bud." *Photoplay* 18 (July 1920): 58.

Funnyworld, no. 18 (Summer 1978): 17-53. Several essays and fragments of interviews about sound in the animated cartoon are published in this issue.

Garity, William E., and Jones, Watson. "Experiences in Road-Showing Walt Disney's Fantasia." *Society of Motion Picture Engineers Journal* 39 (July 1942): 6-15.

————, and McFadden, W. C. "The Multiplane Camera Crane for Animation Photography." *Society of Motion Picture Engineers Journal* 31:2 (August 1938): 144-56.

Giloi, Wolfgang K. *Interactive Computer Graphics: Data Structures, Algorithms, Languages.* Englewood Cliffs, N.J.: Prentice-Hall, 1978.

Godfrey, Bob, and Jackson, Anna. *The Do-It-Yourself Film Animation Book.* London: Amplion Press, 1974.

Gordon, Jay E. *Motion-Picture Production for Industry.* New York: Macmillan 1961.

Graham, Donald W. *Composing Pictures.* New York: Van Nostrand Reinhold, 1970.

Griffin, George. "Xerox and Animation." *Filmmakers Newsletter*, October 1972, pp. 52-53.

Halas, John, ed. *Computer Animation.* New York: Hastings House, 1974.

————. *Visual Scripting.* New York: Hastings House, 1976.

————, and Privett, Bob. *How to Cartoon for Amateur Films.* 3d ed. New York: Focal Press, 1958.

————, and Manvell, Roger. *The Technique of Film Animation.* 4th ed. London: Focal Press, 1976.

Halferty, Guy. "Famous But Unknown. Bugs Bunny and Donald Duck Accept Adoration While Alter Egos Remain Anonymous." *Christian Science Monitor*

(Magazine), 9 August 1947, p. 6. About the voices of these characters, Mel Blanc and Clarence Nash. Blanc's background goes back to Joe Penner radio program, Judy Canova Show, Jack Benny, et al. Nash has done effects, such as the whistle in Rinso White commercial.

Hayward, Stan. *Scriptwriting for Animation*. New York: Hastings House, 1977.

Heath, Robert P. *Animation in Twelve Hard Lessons*. New York: Robert Heath Productions, 1972.

Hill, Derek. "Homemade Animation Stand." *American Cinematographer* 40:4 (April 1959): 238.

Hiss, Tony, and McClelland, David. "Profile. The Quack and Disney." *New Yorker*, 25 December 1975, pp. 33-42. About Clarence Nash, voice of Donald Duck, on the occasion of Nash's seventy-first birthday. Drawing upon interviews with Nash, Jack Hanah, Frank Thomas, Jack Cutting (headed foreign division for Disney until retirement October 1974). Piece discusses early procedures for adding sound to cartoons; Nash's career with Disney including several anecdotes.

Hoke, John. "Zoom Effects in Animation." *American Cinematographer* 38:2 (February 1957): 88.

Holman, L. Bruce. "Building A Rotoscope, Part 2." *Filmmakers Newsletter*, March 1977, p. 47.

_____. "Building Cine Stuff: A Somewhat Easier Way of Producing Animation Cels." *Filmmakers Newsletter*, September 1972, p. 50.

Horrell, C. William. *A Survey of Motion Picture Still Photography and Graphic Arts Instruction*. Rochester, N.Y.: Eastman Kodak, 1979.

Hulfish, David Sherill. *Motion-Picture Work. A General Treatise on Picture Taking, Picture Making, Photo-Plays and Theater Management and Operation*. 1915. Reprint. New York: Arno Press, 1970.

Isaacs, Hermine Rich. "New Horizons: Fantasia and Fantasound." *Theater Arts* 25:1 (January 1941): 55-61.

Jones, Chuck. "Music and the Animated Cartoon." *Hollywood Quarterly* 1:4 (July 1946): 364-70.

Kinsey, Anthony. *Animated Film Making*. New York: Viking Press, 1970.

_____. *How to Make Animated Movies*. New York: Viking Press, 1970.

Laybourne, Kit. *The Animation Book*. New York: Crown, 1979.

Lescarboura, Austin C. *Behind the Motion Picture Screen*. 2d ed. New York: Scientific American Publishing Co., 1921.

Levitan, Eli L. *Animation Art in the Commercial Film*. New York: Reinhold Publishing, 1960.

Lindner, Jim. "Computer Animation Part I: The Animation Stand and Computer Control." *Millimeter* 8:7 (July 1980): 124-26.

_____. "Computer Animation Part II: Analog Animation and Television." *Millimeter* 8:8 (August 1980): 144.

_____. "Computer Animation Part III: Digital Animation and Television." *Millimeter* 8:9 (September 1980): 128-37.

Lustig, Milton. *Music Editing for Motion Pictures*. New York: Hastings House, 1980.

Lutz, E. G. *Animated Cartoons: How They Are Made, Their Origin and Develop-

ment. New York: Charles Scribner's Sons, 1920.

McClain, Bebe Ferrell. *Super 8 Filmmaking from Scratch.* Englewood Cliffs, N.J.: Prentice-Hall, 1978.

McClenahan, Cheryl. "Animation Skyrockets with Technological Advances." *Backstage,* 1 September 1978, p. 51.

McCormick, Lynde. "Do You Know What Wookies Sound Like?" *Christian Science Monitor,* 17 June 1980, p. B 6.

McDarrah, Fred W., ed. *Stock Photo and Assignment Source Book: Where to Find Photographs Instantly.* New York: R. R. Bowker, 1977.

McLaren, Norman. "Notes On Animated Sound." *Quarterly of Film, Radio and Television* 7:3 (Spring 1953): 223-29.

Madsen, Roy. *Animated Film: Concepts, Methods, Uses.* New York: Interland Publishing, 1969.

"The Making of a Sound Fable." *Popular Mechanics Magazine,* September 1930, pp. 353-55.

Manvell, Roger. *The Animated Film.* London: Sylvan Press, 1954. Features pictures from film *Animal Farm* by Halas and Batchelor.

_____, and Huntley, John. *The Technique of Film Music.* London: Focal Press, 1957.

"Mickey Mouse in Symphony: Disney and Stokowski Combine Talents in Film 'Fantasia.'" *Newsweek,* 25 November 1940.

Mitchell, Walt. "Mel Blanc's World of Fantasy." *World Of Yesterday,* no. 19. (n.d.).

Mitroo, J. B.; Herman, Nancy; and Badler, Norman I. "Movies from Music: Visualizing Musical Compositions." *Computer Graphics* 13:2 (August 1979): 218-25.

Newman, William M., and Sproull, Robert F. *Principles of Interactive Computer Graphics.* New York: McGraw-Hill, 1979.

Nilsen, Vladimir. *The Cinema as a Graphic Art.* London: Newnes, 1936.

Novotny, Ann, ed. *Picture Sources 3: Collections of Prints and Photographs in the U.S. and Canada.* New York: Special Libraries Association, 1975.

Oringel, Robert S. *Audio Control Handbook for Radio and TV Broadcasting.* New York: Hastings House, 1972.

Palen, Vern W. "Aerial Image and Animation." *American Cinematographer* 40:7 (July 1959): 430.

_____. "Integrated Design of Animated Film Equipment." *Journal of the Society of Motion Picture and Television Engineers* 66:4 (April 1957): 197-204.

Parker, Dana. "Making Comic Cartoons Move: A Peep into the Busy Studio of One Famous Animator of Humorous Drawings." *Theater Magazine,* January 1928, p. 32.

Peck, A. P. "What Makes 'Fantasia' Click." *Scientific American* 164:1 (January 1941): 28-30.

Perisic, Zoran. *The Animation Stand.* New York: Hastings House, 1976.

_____. *The Focal Guide to Shooting Animation.* New York: Focal Press, 1978.

Pill, Jaan. "Disney Animation." *Cinema Canada,* August 1978, pp. 25-27.

Plumb, Edward H. "The Future of Fantasound." *Society of Motion Picture Engineers Journal* 39 (July 1942): 16-21.

Prendergast, Roy M. *A Neglected Art*. New York: New York University Press, 1976.

Reardon, Craig. "Creating Realistic Miniature Sets." *Cinemagic*, no. 10 (Summer 1977): 22-26.

Rhodes, Leon S. "The Creative Potential of the Animation Cameraman." *American Cinematographer* 47:1 (January 1966): 40-43.

_____. "One-cel Complex Animation." *American Cinematographer* 41:9 (September 1960): 540. Using a strobe principle, Rhodes explains a method of producing complex animation using a single cel, enhancing flexibility in cycle animation.

Rieder, Howard Edward. "The Development of The Satire of Mr. Magoo." Master's thesis, University of Southern California, 1961.

Rivlin, Michael. "Motion Picture Sound Re-recording and Mixing: Dawn of a Digital Decade." *Millimeter*, May 1980, pp. 106.

Rose, Ernest D. *World Film and Television Study Resources: A Reference Guide to Major Training Centers and Archives*. Bonn: Friedrich-Ebert-Stiftung, 1974.

Rosenberg, Bernard, and Silverstein, Harry. *The Real Tinsel*. New York: Macmillan, 1970.

Rosenfeld, Azriel, and Kak, Avinash C. *Digital Picture Processing*. New York: Academic Press, 1976.

Salt, Brian G. D. *Basic Animation Stand Techniques*. Oxford: Pergamon Press, 1977.

_____. *Movements in Animation*. 2 vols. Fairview Park, N.Y.: Pergamon Press, 1976.

_____. *Programmes for Animation: A Handbook for Animation Techniques*. Fairview Park, N.Y.: Pergamon Press, 1978.

Schickel, Richard. "A Conjuror of Catastrophes and Castles." *New York Times Magazine*, 18 May 1980, p. 44. About Albert Whitlock, special-effects artist at Universal's Special Visual Effects Department.

_____. "The New Technology of Hollywood's Special Effects. Far Beyond Reality." *New York Times Magazine*, 18 May 1980, pp. 40-44.

Schreger, Charles. "Film Clips. Sounds of 'Apocalypse.' " *Los Angeles Times*, 27 August 1979, p. IV 9.

Sibley, Hi. "Those Aggravatin' Animations." *Motion Picture Magazine* 13:4 (May 1917): 44-50.

Slyfield, C. O. "Sound in Animated Motion Pictures." *International Sound Technician* 1:5 (July 1953): 2-5.

Sohn, David A., ed. *Good Looking: Film Studies, Short Films and Filmmaking*. Philadelphia: North American Publishing Co., 1976.

Solomon, Charles. " '101 Dalmatians'—A Disney Milestone." *Los Angeles Times*, 19 June 1979, p. V 10. Brief piece on use of xerography in this film and a review of the film.

"Stahl: Spots From Slides." *Television/Radio Age*, 14 August 1978, p. 58.

Taylor, C. W. "Animating Hand-Made Pictures: As in Early Experiments, the Cast Is Sometimes Manufactured." In *Masters and Masterpieces of the Screen*, edited by C. W. Taylor. New York: P. F. Collier and Son Co., 1927.

Thomas, Bob. *Walt Disney: An American Original*. New York: Simon and Schuster, 1976.

Thomas, Bob. *Walt Disney: The Art of Animation—The Story of the Disney Studio Contribution to a New Art*. New York: Golden Press, 1958.

Trojanski, John, and Rickwood, Louis. *Making It Move*. Dayton, Ohio: Pflaum/ Standard, 1973.

Tucker, Tommy N. "Animation Kit. Product Report. PES Image Expander." *Filmmakers Monthly*, September 1979, pp. 43-46.

UNESCO. *Film Animation: A Simplified Approach*. (U238). UNESCO, 1976.

Vanderbilt, Paul., comp. *Guide to the Special Collections Of Prints and Photographs in the Library of Congress*. Washington, D.C.: Reference Department, Library of Congress, 1955.

Wadler, Joyce. "Hi Dear, Aunt Blubell's Here! Mae Questel, Former Vaudevillian, the Original 'Betty Boop' and Still the Voice of Olive Oyl." *Washington Post*, 20 February 1978, p. D 1.

Wilkie, Bernard. *Creating Special Effects for TV and Films*. New York: Hastings House, 1977.

Wright, Milton. "Inventors Who Have Achieved Commercial Success: The Fourth Interview of This Series Is With the Inventor Who Has Perfected the Production of Animated Cartoons." *Scientific Animation* 136 (April 1927): 249.

THE BUSINESS OF ANIMATION

"AICP Takes Aim At Agency 'Abuses' With New Guidelines." *Television/Radio Age*, 21 November 1977, pp. 24-25.

Alexander, Patricia. "Animation House: West Coast." *Millimeter* 6:2 (February 1978): 42.

American Film Institute. *The AFI Guide to College Courses In Film and Television*. Washington, D.C.: AFI, 1978.

"Animation A Cost Middle Ground." *Television/Radio Age* 25:12 (16 January 1978): 42.

Artel, Linda, and Wengraf, Susan E. "Selection, Publicity, Evaluation: Programming Children's Film." *Film Library Quarterly* 7:3/4 (1974): 50-60.

Aspen Handbook on the Media. Edited by William L. Rivers, Wallace Thompson and Michael J. Nyhan. New York: Praeger, 1977.

Beckerman, Howard. "Animation Kit: Distributing Animated Films." *Filmmakers Monthly*, April 1980, pp. 49-50.

_____. "Animation Special: What's Everybody Doing . . . " *Filmmakers Monthly*, July 1980, pp. 24-31.

_____. "The Animators and Filmmakers Map of Manhattan." *Filmmakers Newsletter* 8:2 (October 1975): 31-36.

_____. "How Much Does A Cartoon Cost?" *Filmmakers Newsletter*, January 1977, p. 50.

_____. "The Small Studio, Part 1." *Filmmakers Newsletter*, June 1974, p. 40.

_____. "The Small Studio. Part 2." *Filmmakers Newsletter*, October 1974, p. 36.

Bilowit, William. "Animation Houses: East Coast." *Millimeter* 6:2 (February 1978): unpaged.

"Broadcast Production List Gives Variety of Choices." *Advertising Age*, 23 July 1979, p. S6.

Canemaker, John. "The Business of Successful Animated Features." *Millimeter* 6:2 (February 1978): 14.

Cantor, Muriel G. *The Hollywood TV Producer: His Work and His Audience.* New York: Basic Books, 1971.

Collins, Patrick. "AICP: Settles Cost Questions, Gripes." *Advertising Age*, 23 July 1979, p. S27.

"Commercials Production, Fall, '77. AICP Takes Aim At Agency 'Abuses' With New Guidelines." *Television/Radio Age*, 21 November 1977, pp. 24-25.

"Corporate Communications Centers, Guide 3." *Audio-Visual Communication*, February 1978, pp. 19-35.

Feltes, Steve. "Non-Theatrical Distribution." *Filmmakers Newsletter* 4:9-10 (Summer 1971): 32-35.

Meyers, Richard. "What's New At Commercial Animation Houses, Part I." *Millimeter* 7:2 (February 1979): 26-28.

"More House-Owned Studios Seen." *Television/Radio Age* 25:16 (13 March 1978): 36.

Pike, Robert. "The Growth of Independent Filmmaking." *Filmmakers Newsletter* 4:9-10 (Summer 1971): 26-31.

Silver, Charles. "For a Fair Distribution of the Film Wealth." *Film Comment* 6:3 (Fall 1970).

TV Film/Tape Directory, 1979 Edition. New York: Backstage Publications, 1979.

CHAPTER 6

New Directions

The stories may change, but the art will not. Hand craftsmanship will never be replaced in the production of true animation, and the artist will never become obsolete.[1]

MARK ZANDER

The question of whether or not we need video records may be totally irrelevant because young musicians, who grew up with television as a basic part of their lives, are inevitably going to use video as a creative tool. In fact, because they grew up with television, some of them seem to instinctively know what works.[2]

STEVE FOX

And instead, contrary to every worried expectation on the part of those, including myself, who saw in the computer the end of the art of animation, it is precisely technological animation that is opening new unlimited vistas, of fantasy and humour to cybernetic artists.[3]

GIANNI RONDOLINO

But I think there are tough times ahead for animators who have grown rusty at doing nothing but sparkles and bobbing heads which move with their mouths. I can see a lot of scurrying around to re-learn the old tricks.[4]

HOWARD BECKERMAN

What is past can be observed; it can be praised or damned or ignored. The future can only by awaited.[5]

STEPHEN BECKER

To some degree, many of the articles and books digested in the process of constructing this reference guide have reflected an uncertain, confident, or neutral view about the future of animation, as the quotations given above suggest. What value, then, is there in reviewing the predictions of a few sages about the future of this form of abstract film? Well, such futurism might signal some goals for a younger generation contemplating new careers. On the other hand, since these insights are frequently based on a clear understanding of the present and an informed view of the past, the predictions may also point toward possible changes for all filmmakers in this dynamic environment. Even for the audience, a view of the future can potentially provide a checklist for assessing new directions in tastes. Very little of the literature has exhausted ideas about the prospects of animation, although there have been many soothsayers along the way.

Howard Beckerman and John Halas have been among the most prolific writers about animation, although most of the crystal-ball predicting can be found in Halas's writings. Mr. Beckerman has provided a retrospective for the 1970s and perhaps a preview of the 1980s. In recounting the history since *Yellow Submarine* (1968), a landmark many acknowledge as a crucial turning point in style and content, Beckerman predicts an increase in animated television production, serious work on Super 8mm, more mixing of traditional animation with computer-generated images, flatter styles in full animation (due to increasing costs), and continued anonymity for most animators. John Halas was among the earliest to predict the ascendency of the computer in the animation process, indicating that machine-assisted or machine-produced images would alter the form and content of animated films. Halas and others, by the early 1960s, realized that animation had become an international business and art form, not restricted to the United States nor captured by the lingering history of the Disney Studio.

Writers cited in the Bibliography to this chapter also mentioned the expansion of animation's role beyond entertainment forms. Animation techniques are now essential for persuasion and public relations, for instruction in schools and industry, for interpretations as used in kinestasis and collage, for documentaries using stills-in-motion techniques, and for individual expression as reflected in the experimental film that exploits design and movement for its own sake. Animation techniques have been mixed with special photographic effects and computer technologies to create eye-filling fantasies of which some 1980 audiences cannot seem to get enough. A great deal of this emphasis on effects seems to come at the expense of the story, but some audiences are still attracted to new forms of characters based on robot hardware and sound-effects dialogue. In these films, the sound track has taken over the narrative and much of the effort in playing the character.

New technologies are introduced both for economic and aesthetic reasons, but in the commercial marketplace the economic conditions vitally influence the entrance of new techniques and hardware. While traditional cel-animation is far from being discarded, there are important mixtures of the traditional techniques with the machine, as in the example of computer-driven animation stands. Indeed, not foreseen in many of the writings was the mixture of media in many of today's films. Live-action films that incorporate animated titles and science-fiction dramas using animation in special effects are two developments that were rarely discussed a decade earlier. There would appear to be an important implication from this mixture of science and art, and that is the question of training future filmmakers to be able to fully exploit the capabilities of the computer.

Long ago, many have written, animation was recognized to be more than drawing. To develop a sense of timing, an understanding of the manipulatable qualities of frames in quick succession, and the intervals between those frames, required a medium in which to practice and develop such timing, among other skills. But today's new technologies are more expensive and require not only a mastery of the traditional elements but, in addition, a competence in some new science. Since simply reading about this technology will not guarantee proficiency, where can such skills and knowledge be learned and applied efficiently? Perhaps the proliferation of the home computer will, as a by-product, generate a solution. Most who write about these concerns have an optimist view that the new technologies, such as computer-generated images, will create new animated forms.

There would seem to be an invisible ceiling on development if new channels are not established. Since the late teens to the 1950s channels were opened, were then constrained and, later, were almost clogged because of certain business practices that caused a high degree of economic concentration in the film industries and their available technologies. After 1950, television established new channels but only to become another force itself in the shaping of form and content of the animated program for children, largely due to internal business decisions based on the needs and perceptions of the mass audiences as interpreted by the networks.

New channels now loom on the horizon such as pay television, and home video-cassettes and discs, but current pay services still do not offer the predicted cornucopia of content for specialized audiences. If greater individuality is the key to greater growth in the animated film, as Richard Arnall argues, perhaps the model for innovating such forms for various publics would be in the phonograph industry instead of the film and television industries. For the last decade there has been a clear emphasis on removing the anonymity from the personalities who have labored on this art form, followed with a renewed appreciation of their work. This may set the stage for the new model. There are already distinct signs that the phonograph industry is using home video-discs to exploit both the music personalities and *video graffiti*, a mixture of synthesized video-images and computer-generated patterns, usually synchronized with the music. The traditional channel for animated forms, the theatrical screen, seems to create too many psychological and economic hang-ups among those in distribution and exhibition. Steve Lawson, in "Shorts Are Films, Too," described a successful U.S.-government-sponsored program which finally got shorts booked into theaters but at considerable personal time and expense. This approach seems to imply continued government subsidy and continued bottlenecks among distributors and exhibitors.

Whether audiences will easily accept new styles and forms remains to be seen. We knew little about changing styles in the so-called Golden Age, or why Disneyfication was a formula that worked. Certainly much more ought to be researched since audience acceptance affects the maintenance of the medium, whether it is used for political propaganda, for the marketing of consumer products, or for the ambiguous "entertainment." The artistic factors are important for their own sake. But such art still communicates ideas in some fashion. More research should help us understand the economic and organizational conditions under which animation is produced and the political, psychological, and social environments within which these films are consumed by mass or specialized audiences.

NOTES

1. Mark Zander, "The Disneyesque Look Prevails," *Backstage*, 1 September 1978, p. 1.

2. Steve Fox, "Twenty-Twenty," ABC Television, 6 April 1980.

3. Gianni Rondolino, *International Animated Film Society (ASIFA) Yearbook*, 1975, unpaged.

4. Howard Beckerman, "Slow X-Dissolve to the 80's," *Filmmakers Monthly*, February 1980, p. 47.

5. Stephen Becker, *Comic Art in America* (New York: Simon and Schuster, 1959), p. 377.

BIBLIOGRAPHY

Arnall, Richard. "The Future of Animation." *Film*, no. 52 (August 1968): 39-42.

Beckerman, Howard. "Slow X-Dissolve To The 80's." *Filmmakers Monthly*, February 1980, pp. 45-47.

Halas, John. "Animation Tomorrow." *Journal of the Society of Film and Television*, Winter 1974-1975, pp. 1-2.

_____. "Tomorrow's Animation: Its Technique and Its Content Will Be Revolutionized." *Films in Review* 20:5 (May 1969): 293-96.

Lawson, Steve. "Shorts Are Films, Too." *American Film* 4:2 (November 1978): 48-50.

Siegel, Morton H. "The Shape of Things To Come." *Audiovisual Communications* 12:9 (September 1978): 16.

Chronology of Animation

The reader will find a variety of animated forms presented in this chronology, but there is a distinct focus: the movement of the use of film from a simple attempt to record reality to a reconstruction of reality—a form typical of the visual media around the world in the late 1970s. The chronology also attempts to establish, for the first time, an orderly list of what happened, when, and by whom, with some indication of the relationships involved.

The chronology is not intended to be a definitive chronicle. Undoubtedly there are many events over whose omission buffs and scholars will exclaim. In the annotations there may be a mistake by a year or two—corrections are invited. Trade journal annotations in Appendix 6 and comments concerning other sources given in Appendix 7 have served as guides for this appendix. The text in this guide is based on other, nonlisted sources that shaped the content and determined the weight given to various events contained in the chronology. One theme in this reference guide has been paramount from the outset: the clear, unequivocal conclusion that animation in most forms is headed into the computer age. From the history, it is also clear that the recording of reality, the function of the early camera, is being increasingly discarded for the manufacture of a recreated or constructed reality. One kind of "created reality" is the fantastic film embellished with animated effects.

Photographs lie, even without animated qualities, as was demonstrated decades ago when photographers began constructing montages in static pictures. Any chronology needs to take us beyond techniques similar to those used in drawings on cave walls where blurred legs indicated moving animals. We must focus more on mechanisms that contributed to the deceptions that were made possible by technique and technology. This does not mean that the chronology ignores the "golden age" of cel-animation or the Warner Brothers cartoons, for example. These have their place. But, the issues about the animated form, as given above, continue to evolve.

70 B.C.

Lucretius in *De Rerum Natura* described an apparatus that projected hand-drawn moving images on a screen.

A.D. **900**

While the origins of the Chinese shadow show are obscure, some date the use of silhouetted objects in the eleventh century. The shadow show used brightly painted paper-thin figures which glowed through a screen or glass.

1500s

In Europe, flipbooks, consisting of small pages of sometimes lewd drawings, became available. When the pages were thumbed or riffled together, the drawings were animated.

1553

Leonardo da Vinci published *Magica Naturalis* in which he described the camera obscura.

1660s

The shadow show migrated from China throughout Asia. The plays featured shadow puppets, eventually becoming formatted with each character singing short songs, giving monologues, and acting in scenes.

1800s

Traveling magic-lantern showmen in Europe exhibited painted slides, some in panoramic dimensions.

1825

In a scientific paper, Peter Mark Roget articulated what was later called the "persistence of vision" theory. According to this theory, humans can perceive pictures that appear to move and animators can create and control movement in inanimate objects.

1830

Jean Charles Langlois exhibited the panorama *The Battle of Navarin*, which combined natural objects and painting. The illusion, a view of the battle from a ship's deck, was recreated with parts of the ship's interior merged with a gigantic painting of the battle background. Later Langlois used photographic transparencies in combination with natural objects.

1831

Professor Joseph Antoine Plateau fabricated his Phenakistoscope which consisted of two discs mounted on an axle. When the inside disc, which had separate pictures of an object, was rotated the object appeared to move.

1837

L. J. M. Daguerre completed his photographic process with the development of a method to permanently fix the images.

1853

Austrian military officer Baron Franz von Uchatius, using several Phenakistoscopes, projected images which appeared to move.

1857

O. G. Rejlander, in Great Britain, printed a photograph, *The Two Ways of Life*, built up with thirty negatives, each superimposed or printed on top of each other. Joseph Bamforth and his son Edwin were later known for using similar techniques to enhance the poetic, fantastic, or surrealistic dimensions of their narratives composed from projected lantern slides.

1860

Hand-painted and hand-drawn lantern slides were replaced by photographic scenes, as the magic lantern changed its role. Often used to supplement panorama and other exhibitions, the magic lantern itself was manipulated by inventors and exhibitors in an effort to animate the slides. The content of this medium expanded to encompass scenes from popular fiction, comics, news items, and educational subjects.

1861

Coleman Sellers, Philadelphia, patented a Kinematoscope, a viewing device consisting of a series of photographs mounted on a wheel and rotated in front of a viewer. When the wheel was rotated the illusion of movement was created.

C. Jabez Hughes, in *Photographic News*, defended composite photography. He stated: "If a picture cannot be produced by one negative, let him [the photographer] have two or ten; but let it be clearly understood, that these are only means to the end, and that the picture when finished must stand or fall entirely by the effects produced, not by the means employed."

1870

Triple lanterns, enabling dissolves among photographic slides, to ease transitions from slide to slide and to create the illusion of movement were commercially sold and widely available.

Philadelphian Henry R. Heyl mounted wet-plate lantern slides of a dancing couple on a disc and revolved it in the light of a projection lantern.

1875

Casper W. Briggs, Philadelphia, marketed a device using the intermittent mechanism and shutter similar to that employed in the modern motion picture projector. He photographed a series of drawings on the edge of a mica disc which was turned in front of the projector lens.

1877

Frenchman Emile Reynaud invented his projecting Praxinoscope, a device which projected animated pictures by using a strip of hand-painted images mounted inside a revolving drum and reflected by mirrors.

1879

Eadweard Muybridge began his motion studies using wet plates and dozens of cameras arranged along a track.

1880

Eadweard Muybridge successfully projected pictures in rapid succession upon a screen at a private exhibition. The moving pictures were "instantaneous photographs of animals in motion" projected by an illuminated Zoetrope device. Between 1883 and 1887 Muybridge worked at the University of Pennsylvania. His work was finally published in 1888.

1885

The Reverend Hannibal Goodwin invented the transparent celluloid flexible film which enabled successive images to be recorded on one long strip.

1886

Louis Aime Augustin Le Prince applied for a U.S. patent for a moving picture camera which would expose successive images and also project the finished film. Between 1887 and 1890 he refined his apparatus to a single-lens camera and in 1890 he publicly demonstrated projected films on a screen in Paris. In September 1890 Le Prince left for Paris and mysteriously disappeared.

1888

Dr. E. J. Marey, in studies of motion analysis similar to Muybridge's, used a roll of film which was intermittently fed past the aperture of his camera.

1889

Thomas Edison and his assistants began work on a motion picture machine later called the Kinetoscope. In Great Britain, Friese-Greene exhibited a moving picture camera in 1890 and by 1895 was developing a projector. The Lumière brothers in France were also engaged in the dual project, finally arriving in America in 1897 to promote the camera and projector.

1890

Essential elements for the comic strip were in place in the American print industries: continuing characters, narrative sequencing, dialogue, and artists drawing for magazines. These included Frederick Burr Opper and Richard Outcault.

1892

Using hand-painted figures on celluloid bands, Emile Reynaud projected drawings which appeared to move on a large screen in a process called Theatre Optique.

1893

With the installation of color printing at the *New York World*, Joseph Pulitzer engaged William Randolph Hearst's *New York Journal* in a long, highly competitive struggle for Sunday and daily circulation. Comic strips in color, along with sensationalist reporting (later characterized as "yellow journalism") were the key ingredients of the circulation wars.

1895

Herman Castler patented the Mutoscope viewing system consisting of a large drum upon which was mounted a thousand or more picture cards. As the crank was turned, each card was flipped by a viewing glass for each observer.

1896

According to a story often retold, Georges Méliès "discovered" the making of a dissolve in camera when he repaired a camera jam and backed up his film a few frames. Upon projection, one scene simultaneously faded out while the next scene faded in, creating the effect. In a few short years, Méliès exploited other trick effects by incorporating stop-motion, fast and slow motion, and split screen into his fantasy films. As a "Lightning Cartoonist" he drew film caricatures of various personalities, accelerating the drawings by undercranking the camera. Later, Méliès incorporated stop-action technique in *Le Livre magique* (1900) in which an artist-magician transforms drawings into "living persons." In the *Vanishing Lady*, Georges Méliès performed his first substitution trick, an application of stop-action technique.

In 1896 the first public projection of moving pictures in the United States occurred in New York City using a projector marketed by Thomas Edison but developed by Thomas Armat and C. Francis Jenkins.

1897

Vitagraph used stop-motion in *A Visit to the Spiritualist* and a more fully animated stop-motion film, *Humpty Dumpty Circus*, which used small figures with movable joints.

1898

Albert E. Smith and J. Stuart Blackton photographed a trick film on the rooftop of the Morse Building, New York City, accidentally and intermittently photographing steam clouds from a generator as they drifted into the set area. Upon projection, both discovered the steam jumping about the screen.

The Edison Company copyrighted a short stop-motion film entitled *The Cavalier's Dream* featuring a room full of changing characters, food, and decorations while a man slept.

1900

In *The Bombardment of Taku Forts by the Allied Fleets*, Edison filmmakers staged a miniature Taku Harbor, China, before their cameras and photographed a faked newsreel, producing one of the earliest uses of miniature special effects in American films.

J. Stuart Blackton, in *The Enchanted Drawing*, appeared in his "Lightning Cartoonist" vaudeville act, showing him quickly drawing a face of a fat man, adding a cigar, wine, and a glass, as "the drawing smiles," using stop-motion. Donald Crafton concluded that Blackton learned the technique from Georges Méliès.

1901

Edwin S. Porter, an Edison photographer, completed *The Martyred Presidents*, a short film honoring the memory of Garfield, Lincoln, and McKinley. In the film, Porter used a matte shot, a form of double exposure, by fashioning cutouts in such a way as to make the three faces of the fallen presidents appear on a tombstone monument. This was among hundreds of films made by Porter in which he gradually incorporated special effects as part of the narrative and not for the sake of the "tricks" per se, as was common at that time.

1902

Georges Méliès released *A Trip to the Moon*, comprised of his usual stop-motion camera tricks, dissolves, and a miniature set. Known as pictorial fantasies, the Méliès films were the earliest to be distributed worldwide. As the form of the cinema changed, the Méliès films still retained their staged, uncinematic appearance yet had charming theatrical qualities.

Edwin S. Porter completed *Fun in a Bakery Shop* for Edison. Running just under one minute, a baker is shown sculpting loaves of clay into faces belonging to famous people. Porter stopped the camera at regular intervals as the sculpture progressed, resulting in an early American attempt at stop-motion animation. Porter also used live-action combined with a previously photographed action made possible by an optical printer made at the Edison studio. The double exposure and matte shots in *Uncle Josh at the Moving Picture Show* show a live-action Josh near a moving picture screen in a theater, and a matte image taken from earlier Edison films.

Elsewhere, Oscar B. Depue, partner of Burton Holmes, took single-frame exposures at long intervals to speed up the action as seen from the bow of a ship during a tour of Norway, resulting in a pixilation.

In Europe filmmaker Segundo de Chomón accidentally photographed some flies in stop-action as he completed titles for Ferdinand Zecca. Upon processing, Chomón saw the flies "jumping" over the titles.

1903

Life of an American Fireman, completed by Edwin S. Porter, marked an early attempt to tell a story in a sequence of pictures in which the story relied on actions unfolding through a series of shots. This film was followed by the more commercially successful *The Great Train Robbery* which also used similar narrative development and matte shots.

1904

Theodore Roosevelt approved of the manufacturing of a "Teddy Bear" by Ideal Toy Company, making the toy one of the earliest known licensing arrangements involving a personality or character. Newspapers, radio, motion pictures, and television would later become the influential forces for creating and sustaining these licensed properties. Through three quarters of this century, Mickey Mouse became the best-known of all the merchandised and licensed personalities.

By 1904 the Cooper-Hewitt step printer and printing process were developed, enabling special effects to be made in postproduction rather than in camera.

1905

Spanish filmmaker-animator Segundo de Chomón incorporated a stop-action, object-animation technique in his film *El Hotel electrico*. Scholar Donald Crafton questioned the early date in light of later French and U.S. release dates, amid the presence of similar films by Méliès, Edison, and Blackton.

Norman Dawn combined painted images with a photographic one while taking pictures of Los Angeles buildings. He called this special effect *glass shots*, a term which has survived to the present day. By 1907 Dawn used the technique in a motion picture, *Missions of California.* Stop-motion photography was used by Edwin S. Porter for the titles of *How Jones Lost His Roll.*

1906

J. Stuart Blackton and Albert E. Smith, cofounders of Vitagraph, released an animated film, *Humorous Phases of Funny Faces,* consisting of a man rolling his eyes, blowing his nose, and a dog jumping through a hoop. British professional magician Walter R. Booth completed *The Hand of the Artist,* utilizing a stop-action technique in which a sketch made by a hand "comes to life."

Winsor McCay presented his vaudeville cartoon act, *Seven Ages of Man* using a novelty of colored chalk and musical accompaniment, reminiscent of the "Lightning Sketch" vaudeville acts of Georges Méliès (in France), J. Stuart Blackton, and Albert E. Smith.

1907

Chiefly influenced by Picasso and Braque, and perhaps Cézanne, the new art of cubism did not represent objects as they directly appeared. Instead, cubists would paint the whole structure of a given object, combining several views of the object more or less superimposed. Early adherents to the new form included Fernand Léger, who later produced the abstract film of animated objects, *Le Ballet mécanique.*

Vitagraph offered *L'Hotel hante: fantasmagore epouvantable* for sale in France, released in the United States as *The Haunted Hotel,* directed by J. Stuart Blackton. The film contained a sequence using stop-action, object-animation.

1908

Stop-motion photography by Billy Bitzer was used to animate sculpture in *The Sculptor's Nightmare* which showed the statues of famous political figures smoking a cigar or laughing. Emile Cohl's *Fantasmagorie* was completed and exhibited in France.

British film trade journal, *Kinematograph and Lantern Weekly* published an article explaining the technique of blackboard animation.

1909

The Motion Picture Patents Company (MPPC) was formed in the United States, a consortium of patent holders for cameras and projection equipment. While the trust did establish stability for a young industry, the unit price of film was based on a per foot cost to exhibitors. By 1914 the hold of the MPPC would be broken and out of its ashes would arise a new concentration to be fully operational by 1925, known as the studio system.

Emile Cohl's *Clair de lune espagnol,* combining live actors and animated figures in the same frame, was released by Gaumont in 1909.

1910

Cutout animation film by Emile Cohl entitled *En route* was released in the United States.

1911

Winsor McCay and Walter Arthur produced a cel-animated film, *Winsor McCay Makes His Cartoons Move*, that was released through Vitagraph. McCay's early technique involved rice-paper cels upon which were fully drawn each successive image, including the stationary and moving portions.

In 1911 John R. Bray, son of a Methodist minister and cartoonist on the Detroit *News*, joined Earl Hurd and Max Fleischer working on the *Brooklyn Eagle* art department.

1912

International News Service was formed by William Randolph Hearst to distribute news to member newspapers, followed by King Features Syndicate in 1914. The syndicates were important in circulating comic strips on a regular basis, thereby enlarging the potential audiences for successful characters and artists, soon followed by animated cartoons featuring many of these characters.

In 1912 Bruno Corra published his paper, "Abstract Cinema-Chromatic Music," describing the work of Corra and Arnaldo Ginna, handmade on clear celluloid. Winsor McCay completed his second animation, *The Story of a Mosquito* but stipulated that the film could not be shown in those cities where he appeared on the vaudeville stage.

Princess Nicotine, released by Vitagraph, was filmed with mirrors, camera masks, and complicated trick setups. A man, sitting in his chair, placed a smoking pipe on the table to his left. As the smoke rose, a fairy princess appeared, surprising the man. When he blinked, she disappeared. Gaumont's *Little Milliner's Dream*, made one year earlier, used similar techniques.

1913

John R. Bray produced *The Artist's Dream—The Dachshund and the Sausage* using his new cel-animation process. According to Mark Langer, the process put the stationary cartoon elements on a translucent sheet which was placed over each drawing of the moving elements. A variation of the multicel system would eventually become the standard for the industry, would eliminate the need to redraw the static parts of each frame and would promote the mass production of animated films.

Raoul Barré organized a systematic method of producing animated cartoons in an assembly-line fashion and John R. Bray developed a similar method one year later. In 1913 Eclair, in the United States, released the first animated cartoon based upon a comic strip: *The Newlyweds* from the strip by George McManus. According to Donald Crafton, Emile Cohl was not credited in the advertising for the animation; McManus was.

Essanay released *Dreamy Dud* and *Joe Boko*, originated by Wallace A. Carlson. Sydney Smith (cartoonist of the *Chicago Tribune*) animated a comic strip, *Old Doc Yak*. Released by Selig one year later, the second film in the series used a new cel process.

1914

Norman Dawn used his improved matte-shot technique in *Story of the Andes*. Given the technical limitations of the camera pulldown claw, Dawn developed a new technique eliminating the time-consuming image painting on glass and provided far better control over matte shots. To reduce wiggle or weave during the photography of the matte image, he finished off a composite shot by single-frame photography.

Fire at Eclair laboratories in Fort Lee, New Jersey, destroyed prints and negatives including most of Emile Cohl's animations. Willis O'Brien produced a short stop-action film, *The Dinosaur and the Missing Link*, over a two-month period in San Francisco.

Rube Goldberg arranged to draw animations for Vitagraph based on his comic strips. Wallace A. Carlson, cartoonist for the *Chicago Interocean* animated World Series winners. In 1915 Essanay became the distributor of Carlson's *Dreamy Dud* series.

John R. Bray released the first of a series of cartoons exploiting a continuing character, similar to the comic strips, *Colonel Heeza Liar*. With the technical innovations in production developed by Earl Hurd and Raoul Barré, and Bray, the Bray Studios demonstrated the mass production of cartoons and their economic viability. The patents on technical improvements in animation were registered, including "in-betweening," previewing animated cels, and a printed background system.

1915

Earl Hurd, in June, registered a patent for a cel process and later became a partner with John Bray to form the Bray-Hurd Process Company. International Film Service began producing animated films based on the Hearst newspaper comic strips, including "Krazy Kat," "Jerry on the Job," and "The Katzenjammer Kids," supervised by Gregory LaCava.

In March, John R. Bray began a regular series of animated cartoons released as part of the Pathe News. Thomas Edison followed with the release of Raoul Barré's *Grouch Chaser* series. These incorporated cels and holds, beginning the reel with live-action and including three to four animated sequences. Barré used a division of labor to produce the films. Essanay contracted with Wallace A. Carlson for cartoons.

Max and Dave Fleischer completed their first film using the rotoscope, which projected a film of a live figure, frame by frame, to be traced onto a separate cel. The film was about a new character, "Koko the Clown."

Encouraged by state producer Winthrop Ames, Tony Sarg began a series of shorts called *Tony Sarg's Almanac* which featured prehistoric, silhouetted characters animated by stop-action techniques. Sarg was assisted by Herbert M. Dawley. Sid Marcus designed *Animated Hair Cartoons* using cutouts.

1916

Raoul Barré formed a partnership with Charles Bowers to animate films, obtaining the rights to Bud Fisher's *Mutt and Jeff*. By 1919 Barré abandoned animation except to assist Pat Sullivan and Otto Messmer in the mid-1920s on a temporary basis. About 1916 Pat Sullivan animated a series of cartoons featuring a Charlie Chaplin character.

R. L. Goldberg's *The Boob Weekly*, a burlesque cartoon on the news weeklies, brought the press screening room in the Pathe exchange, New York City, to boisterous laughter.

Frank Moser established the animation department for International News Service in New York which animated *Krazy Kat, Bringing up Father, Jerry on the Job, Happy Hooligan,* and *Little Jimmy,* current comic strips in Hearst newspapers. George Herriman, Leon Searl, and Frank Moser introduced comic-strip characters to animated films: *Krazy Kat Bugologist* and *Krazy Kat and Ignatz Mouse.*

The Hearst-Vitagraph newsreel, with cartoon, was released in January. By mid-year, Hearst proclaimed his International Film Service to be a modern extension of the publishing business for publicity purposes. Cartoons based on strips in his newspapers were released through the service and when Gregory LaCava joined the film organization several technical improvements were added to the process. C. Allan Gilbert and John R. Bray combined to produce *Silhouette Fantasies* for Paramount.

About 1916 animation created for the commercial American marketplace obtained specialization, technology, and divisions of labor. Formerly, individual animators such as Winsor McCay, could perform all tasks, but the apparent demand for more animated films necessitated larger staffs and complex organization to produce a larger volume. Bill Nolan innovated a panning background consisting of a moving track underneath animation cels, enabling filmmakers to create the illusion that figures were moving against the background or a camera was panning a scenic vista.

In early 1916 *Paramount Pictographs* became a split-reel, with one half consisting of animated cartoons produced by John Bray and the remainder educational subjects. Paramount continued to release these for only about one year. Bray then released the item through Goldwyn Pictures Corporation, known as the *Goldwyn Bray Pictograph,* lasting to about mid-1920. Animators working with Bray in this period included: C. T. Anderson, Wallace Carlson, Max Fleischer, W. L. Glackens, Milt Gross, Pat Sullivan, and Paul Terry.

In Italy, cinematographer Segundo de Chomón and director Giovanni Pastrone combined live-action and animated puppets in a film *La Guerra e il sogno di Moni (The War and the Dream of Momi).*

In the United States, the Henry Ford Motor Company established the first industrial film unit, beginning with public relations films, including a weekly newsreel which included animation.

Walter Lantz went to work for Gregory LaCava in the new William R. Hearst cartoon studio, but World War I removed all animators from that studio except Lantz and LaCava.

1917

In Europe, painters Viking Eggeling, Georges Braque, and Francis Picabia experimented with abstract animations while their American counterparts, such as Pat Sullivan, Frederick Burr Opper, and Bud Fisher created cartoons for a commercial marketplace.

Henry Ford film production unit produced an instructional film using an animated sequence to explain the Bessemer steel process. As instructional film demand increased, John R. Bray established a technical department in his New York studios. Other filmmakers established industrial-educational units in Pittsburgh, Chicago, and Cleveland, incorporating animation into their sponsored works.

1918

Frances Lyle Goldman, originally from Saint Louis, became a specialist for Bray in scientific animation. Goldman is credited with the moving representation of the human larynx for the *Pictograph* demonstrating how human speech was made. Later J. F. Leventhal joined John R. Bray. With W. J. Nirgenau, using Bray's patents, Leventhal was chiefly responsible for *The Science of Life* series, about communicable diseases and personal hygiene. Major Herbert W. Dawley completed a one-reel subject using three-dimensional models of prehistoric animals, entitled *The Ghost of Slumber Mountain*.

In Europe, Hans Richter and Swedish painter Viking Eggeling began their working relationship which explored rhythm in painting. Richter's first adaptation to film was *Rhythm* (or *Rhythmus 21*) completed in 1921. Eggeling's best-remembered scroll work was exhibited in 1922, entitled *The Diagonal Symphony*.

In special photographic effects, F. D. Williams received a patent for his traveling mask (matte) system. In this process the action is photographed against a black background, yielding a negative that is transparent except for the action print of the negative. The action negative and first mask are then printed on raw stock.

In 1918 Winsor McCay released *Sinking of the Lusitania*, a propaganda cartoon of unusual length for the time, requiring 25,000 drawings and twenty-two months of work. Max Fleischer animated *The Tantalizing Fly* while working at the Bray Studio. This became one of the first *Out of the Inkwell* productions, featuring a character, "Koko," entering and exiting an inkwell on the animator's desk.

1919

Painter Marcel Gromaire published a series of articles in *La crapouillot* which called for a union between modern painting and film.

According to Arthur Edwin Krows, the movement in American visual education gained emphasis through formation of professional educator organizations geared to film and visual education in the use of classroom films.

A character that would later become known as *Felix the Cat*, the earliest animated personality in film, first appeared in a short film supervised by Otto Messmer. Pat Sullivan would later take the credit for the "Felix" character as films featuring the famous cat were distributed around the world by the mid-1920s.

1920

Berlin Dadaists describe their works which incorporated photographs as "photomontage," using the photograph as a ready-made image, combining it with other materials from media such as magazines and newspapers to form a destruction of reality. In film, this would eventually amalgamate to collage, kinestasis, and new narrative forms, sometimes at the expense of story.

In the United States, Walt Disney began employment with the Kansas City Film Ad Company, learning the fundamentals of animation by studying the Carl Lutz primer, Eadweard Muybridge's photo studies of animal and human movement, and by doing trial-and-error work for his employer.

By the 1920s, there was the introduction of optical printing equipment, which greatly enhanced the use of photographic special effects using traveling mattes and other devices. Optical printers allow for reverse action, freeze-frames, wipes, slit-frames, and zoom simulations.

Sometime in the 1920s, the model chart was introduced into the animation manufacturing process. This chart, which frequently illustrated the model of all characters in different poses, became the final guide for the numerous animators working on a single film, so they would all draw the characters alike.

Oskar Fischinger engaged in his first experiments in film silhouettes, wax, and abstract patterns created with multiple exposures.

By September, Major-General P. C. Harris, Adjutant General of the United States Army, announced the awarding of contracts to produce a series of vocational training films to help rehabilitate returning veterans. John R. Bray was awarded the contract for *The Elements of the Automobile.*

1921

Walter Ruttmann's first abstract animation was shown publicly in Berlin, entitled *Lichtspiel Opus 1*, presented in color with live music. Al Paganelli opened a small animation studio in New York City and, by 1974, he was still going.

Sometime in 1921 or thereafter, Oskar Fischinger invented an animation system based on successively slicing thin layers from a prepared wax block. This seems similar to the use of slices of objects for models in cel- and computer-animation in medical subjects innovated in the 1970s.

French poet and filmmaker Blaise Cendrar, in editing *La roue*, created a train collision with rapid flash cuts. The alternating images or film montage were next seen in the cinema with Eisenstein's *Potemkin* (1925). *La roue* was directed by Abel Gance.

1922

In Germany, Walter Ruttmann's first of a series of films, *Opera* (*Opus 1, 2,* and so forth), was exhibited in Berlin. Stop-action, hand colored, and the dynamic display of dots in the first film won him immediate recognition.

In the United States, Walter Lantz produced and directed his first cartoon series, entitled *Colonal Heeza Liar.*

Walt Disney incorporated a new Kansas City film animation business called Laugh-O-Gram Films. He persuaded Ub Iwerks to join him in the new venture. Hugh Harman, Rudolf Ising, Carmen Maxwell, Lorey Tague, and Otto Walliman were the other animators in the Disney enterprise but within two years the business was bankrupt.

1923

The Fleischers released a four-reel educational film with animated sequences entitled *Einstein Theory of Relativity.*

Alexander Victor, founder and owner of Victor Animatograph Company of Davenport, Iowa, marketed a 16mm film projector and camera and Eastman Kodak formed extensive libraries of film in the 16mm format. Eastman marketed black-and-white 16mm stock, thereby expanding the film medium to experimentalists and amateurs. Sound stocks were available in 1933 and color in 1934.

Sometime in the 1920s, the animation process was streamlined in the Max

Fleischer organization. Inbetweeners were introduced, who filled in the action drawings between extremes drawn by the key animator. Newcomers to animation were initiated in a step process before being called animators. Beginners would become opaquers, then inkers, then graduate to inbetweening, thence becoming assistant animators and finally achieving animator, thereby establishing a division of labor.

There was a public showing of Man Ray's *Retour à raison*, using the rayogram technique created by laying objects over raw stock and exposing it temporarily to light. The images created, without camera, cut across the separately framed lines so that, when projected, objects were not easily recognized. Lee De Forest presented a demonstration of his sound-on-film optical process, Phonofilm, in New York.

Walt Disney Productions was founded in Los Angeles, California. In the same year, Disney completed the first reel of a revived *Alice* cartoon series distributed by Margaret Winkler, New York, eventually reaching theaters on the East Coast by March 1924.

Beginning in 1923, Walter Ruttmann assisted Lotte Reiniger by designing cloud and special effects for her feature-length cut-out silhouette animation, *The Adventures of Prince Achmed*.

1924

Ballet mécanique by Fernand Léger used abstract animation and stop-motion editing techniques. In New York, working with Lee De Forest, the Fleischer brothers produced the first sound-on-film cartoon, *Oh Mabel*. Viking Eggeling completed his experimental stop-motion animation *Diagonal Symphony*, which was shown in November. Soviet propaganda cartoons began to appear: *Incident in Tokyo* (1924) and *China in Flames* (1925).

1925

Following the release of *Rhythmus 25*, Hans Richter received commissions for additional work in Germany, creating *Film Study* (1926) and an introduction to the UFA film *Die dame mit der maske* (*The Lady with the Mask*). His work in the 1930s consisted of documentaries, essays, and commercials. The First International Avant-Garde Film Exposition was held in Berlin featuring the work of Rene Clair, Fernand Léger, Hans Richter, and Viking Eggeling, bolstering the morale of the German experimental film community.

Assisted by Marcel Delgado, Willis O'Brien completed *The Lost World*, a story of explorers who happened upon a South American plateau where prehistoric animals still roamed.

1926

In *Battleship Potemkin*, directed by Sergei Eisenstein and photographed by Edward Tisse, the editing together of three static shots of a marble lion effectively demonstrated that editing could also animate static objects as in the individually drawn frame or stop-action photography. Given this editorial organization, a narrative film could be made from still photographs.

Lotte Reiniger and her husband Karl Koch, at the UFA Studios in Germany, completed *Prince Achmed*, a 65-minute, silhouette animated film. In Europe, cine clubs, film societies, and other groups were founded, demonstrating that there was a small but growing audience for new films and perhaps the rejection of the commercial film largely based on the novel or "canned theater."

In the United States, with the signing of the basic studio agreement by nine studios and five unions, the West Coast film industry became unionized. While the event seemed to bring a hiatus in the industry-labor tensions, the next twenty years would involve additional strife with the nonrepresented groups such as actors, animators, and directors desiring standardized agreements.

1927

Hans Richter's *Film Study* was released, incorporating tricks, animations, and printing techniques. Frank Goldman, Chicago, filed for patents on a three-peg system, with one round, center peg flanked by two elongated pegs. Goldman received the patent two years later, and the system eventually replaced the two round-peg system.

Walt Disney Studio began production of a series of cartoons based on "Oswald the Rabbit." During the production of this series, Disney developed the pencil test, which was simply the photographing of pencil drawings to determine the correctness of the animation, before proceeding to other stages in the production process.

The founding of the Academy of Motion Picture Arts and Sciences occurred in May. While the Academy Awards are the most publicized activity, the academy also developed active programs in technical, publications, and educational areas.

In October, Warner Brothers premiered *The Jazz Singer*, a lip-synchronized film. While the picture had no artistic merit, *The Jazz Singer* was nevertheless the first sound film in which synchronized sound was meaningfully integrated with the action, not just as an accompaniment to the action.

1928

Walter Lantz became head of Universal's animation department, producing *Oswald the Rabbit* cartoons, twenty-six per year for the next ten years.

In the Soviet Union, Sergei Eisenstein, V. I. Pudovkin, and G. V. Alexandrove published in the Leningrad magazine *Zhizn iskusstva* (5 August) their historic statement regarding the new sound technology. They expressed a concern that sound would be used merely to record reality. They advocated that sound used asynchronously would develop new potentials in montage. American live-action and cartoon films did manifest the former technique, in using sound literally or realistically. For example, many cartoons were animated to the beat of the music and depicted various animated musical figures in the 1930s. With the growth of synthesized sound techniques, including speeding up or slowing down of tracks, or other technical improvisations imposed upon "realistic" recordings, animated sound cartoons explored, asynchronously, more abstract ideas. The works of Oskar Fischinger in the 1930s, and Disney's *The Old Mill* are examples of these changes.

In November, Disney's third *Mickey Mouse* cartoon, *Steamboat Willie*, premiered in New York City, demonstrating the first synchronized-dialogue cartoon. Largely as a result of the premiere, enthusiastic trade press, and public response, Disney was able to find a distributor for his films.

1929

Swiss animator Rudolf Pfenninger experimented with synthesized sound tracks. Paramount released the first Fleischer sound cartoon, beginning a fifteen-year association. Berthold Bartosch, in Paris, built an animation bench which was, according to David Curtis, the first multiplane camera.

Disney released the first *Silly Symphony, Skeleton Dance*, which used sound effects and music synchronized to the animated design. The experience gained with this series enabled the Disney organization to evolve an altered style of action with sound. Dialogue and effects became closely and interdependently tied to the music, laying the groundwork for a more figurative use of sound.

Terrytoons was organized by Paul Terry. The Museum of Modern Art, New York City, was established. Eventually, with the film department founded in the mid-1930s, the museum would become an important leader in the acquisition and preservation of animated and other films for future generations to view and study.

1930

This year marked the beginning of the demise of the European avant-garde film movement largely due to European politics and economic reasons. In Italy, abstract artists were ridiculed by the government and in France major studios were closed.

In the United States the cost of production for a *Mickey Mouse* cartoon by the Disney Studios averaged $5,500. In February, Walt Disney Studios contracted with George Gorgfeldt Company, New York, to merchandise the Minnie and Mickey Mouse characters, beginning an expanding and financially important source of revenue for Disney by the 1940s and later. Ub Iwerks left Walt Disney and established his own production unit, releasing a series, *Flip the Frog*, through MGM.

By May, the first of Hugh Harman-Rudolf Ising cartoons for Leon Schlesinger premiered in New York, titled *Sinkin' in the Bathtub*, the beginning of the *Looney Tunes* series. Like Disney's early *Silly Symphony* series, the animations were essentially illustrated musical radio programs with a literal use of the visual medium. But, with *Flowers and Trees, The Band Concert*, and *The Old Mill*, the Disney style was far more flexible.

In 1930, Eastman Kodak introduced 8-millimeter films for the home market. Leon Schlesinger contracted to furnish animated films to Warner Brothers. Hugh Harman and Rudy Ising were among the original animators in the Warner Brothers cartoon unit. With Grim Natwick, the Fleischer brothers introduced a new screen character, Betty Boop, in a *Talkartoon, Dizzy Dishes*.

Universal Pictures released *The King of Jazz*, a technicolor feature with animated cartoon sequence by Walter Lantz and Bill Nolan, featuring a caricature of Paul Whiteman.

1931

Oskar Fischinger experimented with drawing sound tracks on film. In June, synthetic sound and drawings were exhibited in Berlin. Max Fleischer received a patent on a process for creating synthetic sounds on film. The first major exhibition of photomontage art was held in Berlin. On that occasion, Raoul Hausmann recalled that to that time, photomontage had not been used successfully either for political propaganda or for advertising. But, in terms of technique, photomontage developed by the Dadaists demonstrated a creative use of photography that their contemporaries did not have the courage to exploit. *Photographic Amusements* for the 1931 annual issue contained an essay by Harry Potamkin illustrating Moholoy-Nagy and others experimenting in photomontage.

In the United States, Mickey Mouse appeared in comic-strip form.

1932

Mary Ellen Bute and Leon Thermin demonstrated *The Perimeters of Light and Sound and Their Possible Synchronization,''* an early use of electronics for drawing. Limited funds and Thermin's departure and later death stopped continued work.

Dr. Herbert T. Kalmus, inventor of the technicolor three-color system, demonstrated his system for Walt Disney. Disney incorporated the process in to *Flowers and Trees*, a *Silly Symphony*, and negotiated an exclusive contract with Kalmus.

Fleischer Studios translated the Popeye character, created by Elzie Crisler Segar, to the screen. The song signature, popularized through film and radio, enhanced the character as well as the spinach industry.

Oskar Fischinger's *Experiments in Hand-Drawn Sound* (1931) was first shown. In late 1932, Don Graham began formal art instruction at the Disney Studios as part of Walt Disney's training plan. The high degree of emphasis on training would pay off to increase the pool of animators available for more ambitious projects.

Oskar Fischinger produced *Composition in Blue* synchronized to the music of Nicolai's Overture to *Merry Wives of Windsor*. The film consisted of three-dimensional forms moving in synchronism with the music. Some asserted that this film inspired Fischinger's work on *Fantasia* and the "Toccata and Fugue" sequence.

1933

Norman McLaren, using a 300-foot length of film he stripped of its emulsion, painted on it abstractions with color dyes with the help of Stewart McAllistar.

In Europe, using live-action and puppet animation, Ladislas Starevich released *The Mascot*, the story of a puppy hero experiencing an amazing adventure of traffic and danger. Hailed now as a masterpiece, the film used animated paper, straw, dishes, and puppets.

In the area of special effects, a demented scientist, played by Claude Rains, successfully made himself invisible, with the help of special-effects cinematographer John P. Fulton, working on *The Invisible Man*.

In 1933, Disney Studios released the thirty-sixth *Silly Symphony* cartoon entitled *The Three Little Pigs*. With a catchy and very popular song, "Who's Afraid of the Big Bad Wolf," and a new emphasis on personality animation, the cartoon became an unexpected hit. Perhaps more significant than the cartoon was the demonstration of the symbiotic power of radio and film to popularize the song throughout the country. Disney's licensed by-products featuring various characters and books also worked into similar, mutually beneficial media relationships. Walt Disney Productions won the Academy of Motion Picture Arts and Sciences Oscar for *Flowers and Trees*, the first three-strip technicolor cartoon.

Max Fleischer was licensed to make Popeye a cartoon character with the first cartoon appearing in this year. Many argued that *Snow White*, a Betty Boop cartoon with Cab Calloway's music, was the best of the Boop animations with Koko the Clown. The Boop character contained numerous merchandising opportunities for the Fleischers as Mickey Mouse had for Disney. Max Fleischer filed for a patent on his three-dimensional setback, later used in the *Popeye* cartoons. The device enhanced the depth in a moving background.

Using a sixteen-inch-high model of an ape, Willis O'Brien completed stop-action animation in *King Kong*. The picture, however, also used other special and optical effects including transparency projection, glass mattes, miniatures, and slow motion.

1934

The creation of Donald Duck was not as important as the impact of the character on the Disney enterprises' fortunes in the marketplace during the depression, the war years and the postwar period.

Hugh Harman and Rudolf Ising joined Metro-Goldwyn-Mayer to continue their animation work. Leon Schlesinger formed his own unit with former employees of Harman and Ising. At MGM, the new series of cartoons similar to the Warner *Merry Melodies* was called *Happy Harmonies*.

Also in 1934, Len Lye produced abstract color films in Gasparcolor, a process perfected in Germany. Alexandre Alexeieff completed his first film animation, an "illustration" of Mussorgsky's *Night on Bald Mountain*. Alexeieff and Clair Parker used a board covered with thousands of pins, which could be raised or lowered, with the light and shade created by the height of the pins. Each change was made on the pinscreen and then photographed one frame at a time. The variations this technique allowed were illustrated in Orson Welles's version of *The Trial* (1962).

French animators Hector Hoppin and Anthony Gross demonstrated that limited animation could be humorously expressive in *Joie de vivre*. It was later used by Disney in *Toot, Whistle, Plunk and Boom* and exploited by UPA.

Berthold Bartosch produced a 30-minute cutout animated film, *L'idee*, based on a book of woodcuts by Frans Masereel, with an electronic music score for an electronic instrument (called the *Ondes Martenot*) composed by Arthur Honegger.

In the United States at the Bijou Theater, New York City, an exclusive exhibition of animated films began. Six months later, under new ownership, the theater's survival was attributed to baby-sitting functions (for busy mothers downtown shopping), birthday parties, and the appeal to children of various characters.

1935

This was the first season on the NBC radio network for "Popeye the Sailor Man," broadcast three times weekly in a fifteen-minute program at 7:15 P.M. The program lasted one season.

In pioneering animation by painting or drawing on film, Len Lye completed *Colour Box*, a British Government propaganda film demonstrating the advantages of parcel-post rates. Norman McLaren made his first animated film, *Camera Makes Whoopee*. In Germany, Oskar Fischinger completed *Komposition in blau* (*Composition in Blue*) using the pixilation technique, with animation of three-dimensional cubes and columns.

In Hollywood "Tex" Avery joined the Warner Brothers cartoon unit, eventually developing an abstract style that would have characters interrupting their madcap antics to comment to the audience or using wild insertions of other devices that destroy cartoon narratives in a funny manner.

In the same year, Russian puppet artist and filmmaker Aleksandr Lukich Ptushko, using live actors and puppets, concluded his production, *The New Gulliver*, the first Russian feature fantasy film to use sound.

1936

Len Lye completed *Rainbow Dance*, using a three-strip color process, allowing him to introduce control over the color of real or abstract objects. By 1939, in *Swinging the Lambeth Walk*, Lye employed color mattes and an optical printer in his animated abstractions. In the same year, Norman McLaren and Helen Biggar produced an antiwar film using animation, object photography, animated maps, puppets, and live-action.

Paramount Studios began a color cartoon series entitled *Color Rhapsodies*. Oskar Fischinger arrived in the United States to accept a contract with Paramount Pictures. A color film, *Allegretto*, was produced by Fischinger for a feature, *The Big Broadcast of 1937*, but a disagreement ensued because Fischinger did not want Paramount to use his film in a black-and-white feature.

By June, Don Lee Broadcasting System performed the first public demonstration of cathode-ray TV in the United States with daily telecasts using a system developed by Harry Lubcke.

1937

Metro-Goldwyn-Mayer established their own animation unit under former exhibition and distribution employee Fred Quimby. Carmen Maxwell became production manager; Bill Hanna and Bob Allen were directors. Jack Zander came from the East Coast with Joe Barbera.

Following the upholding of the constitutionality of the Wagner Act which, in part, provided for the formation of the National Labor Relations Board, 100 workers at the New York Fleischer Studio announced their affiliation with a new union and complained about Max Fleischer's reluctance to negotiate with them. A strike occurred in May.

Disney's *Silly Symphony, The Old Mill*, was a demonstration of the new multiplane camera developed by a team headed by William Garrity. In terms of sound, the short marked a departure from simple rhythm numbers of singing characters typical of many sound cartoons of the 1930s.

With the release of the Hindenburg destruction films edited for the home market, Eugene Castle marketed home versions of educational and news subjects at prices from $1.75 to $22.50 (16mm sound versions). Castle distributed free films to schools, producing various subjects for industrial sponsors, guaranteeing them two million circulation. Such developments, while small, demonstrated the expansion of markets for the animated film.

From Hollywood, the "Mickey Mouse Theater of the Air," heard over the NBC radio network, was a short-lived audio version that never obtained a satisfactory radio audience, gaining only an average 8.4 rating.

Mel Blanc began a prolific career of voicing animated characters with his first assignment for director Frank Tashlin. With experience gained in radio, Blanc furnished voice characterizations for Bugs Bunny, Elmer Fudd, Porky Pig, and numerous other characters. Hal Roach produced *Topper* which incorporated animated split screen, animated traveling mattes, stop-action animation, and subtractive matting for telling the ghostly story of George and Marion Kirby. Norman McLaren made his first drawing on film, *Love on the Wing*, an ad for airmail.

By May, the national labor organizations began formal efforts to organize employees in the radio broadcasting industry. In the same month, one hundred Fleischer employees (New York) affiliated themselves with the Artists and Designers Union and went on strike, complaining that Fleischer refused to negotiate. The strike was settled in October 1937. At year's end, Disney's first animated feature *Snow White and the Seven Dwarfs* premiered in Hollywood.

1938

The Mercury Theater of the Air presented H. G. Wells's *The War of the Worlds*, which simulated a newscast and incorporated fictional elements as the story unfolded. Conditioned by "eyewitness" newscasting so prevalent on network radio and polished dramatic techniques, many radio listeners panicked or called police stations, newspapers, and radio stations, believing that there was a Martian invasion of the planet.

The Fleischer Studio moved from New York City to Miami. An opinion poll indicated that the Popeye character was the most popular cartoon character in the United States.

Caravel Pictures, a subsidiary of Business Training Corporation (formed about 1917), New York City, engaged in production of industrial films to distribute to theaters, previewed a Bristol-Meyers Ipana toothpaste cartoon *Boy Meets Dog*, the first of a series of sponsored shorts in animation.

Oskar Fischinger, under MGM contract, completed *Optical Poem* released as a theatrical short subject.

In April, the Wheeler-Lea Act gave the Federal Trade Commission new powers to curtail false and misleading advertising.

1939

The second cel-animated color feature of United States origin premiered in Miami Beach, Florida. *Gulliver's Travels* was produced by the Miami Fleischer Studio.

George Pal emigrated to the United States and thereafter moved to Los Angeles, where he was signed by Paramount to produce a series of dimensional animation shorts. Harry Smith began hand painting, etching, or batiking on film stock while John Whitney experimented in 8mm in France. In Canada, Norman McLaren produced *Allegro*, a two-minute color, 35mm film, with hand-drawn images and sound track.

Paul Terry patented an aerial image projector, using a stop-motion camera on a stand and a hand-driven projector under the table top. A live-action scene was projected into a reflecting prism that reflected the image into two condensing lenses. Animation cels were placed on top, lighted and photographed, incorporating background image.

Paul Fennel, Cartoon Films Limited, Beverly Hills, produced a limited-animation film, *Invasion of Norway*, using a poster-style art. This was a ten-minute propaganda film with a "pull-through" animation technique, but, moreover, demonstrating that economy and expression could be fulfilled using limited animation.

Leopold Stokowski began work with Walt Disney Studios on a loosely defined scenario that would eventually result in an animated feature blending classical musical themes with animated images, to be titled *Fantasia*. Also at Disney, Oskar Fischinger made designs for Bach's "Toccata and Fugue" but terminated his agreement when his designs were altered by committee decision-making. He requested that his name be withheld from the credits.

This year, and throughout the war years, the comic strip clearly reflected the international conflicts with Germany and Japan. The strips included *Joe Palooka, Terry and the Pirates, Jungle Jim, Dick Tracy*, and *Charlie Chan*. After hostilities were openly declared, animated cartoons reflected wartime events and attitudes, but to a more limited degree.

On 3 May 1939, at 8:00 P.M., W2XBS, New York City, began regular TV broadcasting, featuring Richard Rodgers, a Lowell Thomas news commentary, and a Donald Duck cartoon.

1940

Advertising in the pages of *Saturday Evening Post, Life, Collier's*, and *Mademoiselle* clearly reflected new uses of still photographs combined with line drawings, collage techniques, distorted perspective, and other devices that the public appeared to readily accept. Yet the theatrical animated film in America did not reflect or adapt these changes for many years.

The National Film Board of Canada was founded by John Grierson. Metro-Goldwyn-Mayer released the first *Tom and Jerry* (as cat and mouse characters) cartoon. The series was animated for seventeen years by Joe Barbera and Bill Hanna. George Pal opened his studio in Los Angeles, producing a new series of animated puppet cartoons, *Puppetoons* and *Madcap Models* assisted by twenty-year-old Ray Harryhausen.

By January, Walt Disney operations had moved to their new Burbank studios, with production work on *Bambi* and *Pinocchio* begun. With the release of *The Reluctant Dragon*, the Disney Studio opened some doors to the general public about the mysteries of producing animated films, although some evolutions depicted in the film were misleading. However, the *Baby Weems* storyboard sequence remained a classic, clearly demonstrating the effectiveness of limited animation yet maintaining economy of scale.

By May, the Screen Cartoonists Guild picketed the Disney Studios, stepping up tension between Walt Disney and his staff that would continue into the 1940s and have considerable impact on the organization. A strike eventually occurred. In Great Britain, John Halas and Joy Batchelor formed a cartoon production company.

1941

In the United States, John and James Whitney began their *Variations* series of film animations including the composition and recording of synthetic sound tracks.

The United States Army Pictorial Service expanded into a major production unit for design and manufacture of training films for the war effort. Multiple uses of animation were incorporated into technical training films, continued by most service agencies from the war to the present time.

In October, with the release of *Dumbo*, the Disney Studio demonstrated than an animated feature could be produced on a low budget in a reasonable time. On the heels of losses from *Fantasia* and *Pinocchio, Dumbo* earned a profit.

In November, Disney's *Fantasia* opened with Fantasound, a new four-track optical stereophonic system, in New York. The film, a synthesis of eight musical compositions, generated mixed reviews and initially failed to make back the investment. On re-releases *Fantasia* found more receptive audiences. By December the Fleischer Studio, Miami, completed their second animated feature, *Mr. Bug Goes to Town*.

1942

Walt Disney Studios hastily prepared a propaganda short for the United States Treasury Department featuring Donald Duck in *The New Spirit*, which promoted timely payment of income taxes. Over one thousand prints were seen by sixty million theater patrons.

The Woody Woodpecker character, animated by Walter Lantz Productions, became a regular cartoon series. Paul Terry released the first *Mighty Mouse* cartoon, an amalgamation of Mickey Mouse and Superman. The series continued until Paul Terry sold his studio to CBS in 1955.

Famous Studios replaced the Fleischer Studio as makers of *Superman* and *Popeye* cartoons. The Fleischer unit was dissolved. In April Dave Fleischer was appointed head of the Columbia Pictures animation unit while Max Fleischer joined the Jam Handy organization in Detroit, Michigan.

By September, Short Subject Department heads from major studios complained to the War Activities Committee that *Victory* and government shorts were crowding out regular shorts made to show a profit. Frank Capra previewed the first film in a series of seven for General George Marshall, entitled *Prelude to War*, the first in the *Why We Fight* series shown to United States and Allied armed forces. *Prelude* and the six others utilized Disney animation and captured war film to explain United States policies to our fighting men.

1943

Metro-Goldwyn-Mayer characters Tom and Jerry in *Yankee Doodle Mouse* won an Academy Award. William Hanna and Joseph Barbera, the team who did the animation, would go on to win six more Oscars, equalling Disney's *Silly Symphonies*. In Canada, Norman McLaren established the animation film department at the Canadian National Film Board.

Oliver Wallace, former theater organist, composed a catchy theme which formed the basis for Disney's Academy Award-winning short with Donald Duck, *Der Fuehrer's Face*. The song proliferated throughout America and the world, satirizing Hitler and the Nazi movement. Leon Schlesinger Studio released the first color *Looney Tune, Daffy's Southern Exposure*.

1944

Hell Bent for Election, directed by Chuck Jones, was the first film of the Industrial Film and Poster Service, which consisted of principals who later became the nucleus of the United Productions of America (UPA). Commissioned by the United Auto Workers-CIO for the Franklin Roosevelt presidential campaign in 1944, the film was produced by Steve Bosustow.

James and John Whitney completed five abstract film exercises. Their work was awarded first prize at the first experimental film competition in Belgium in 1944. The release of *Anchors Aweigh*, a Metro-Goldwyn-Mayer technicolor musical, featured a later-acclaimed, live-action Gene Kelly dancing with an animated mouse.

The first digital computer, Mark I, was created.

1945

Disney released *The Three Caballeros* using live-action combined with animation for the first time since his *Alice in Cartoonland* films made in the 1920s. Ub Iwerks returned to Walt Disney Studios. With assistance from Eustace Lycett and others, he designed the industry's first two-head printer.

In Czechoslovakia, Jiři Trnka made his first cartoon, *Grandpa Plants Beetroot*.

United Productions of America was incorporated with Stephen Bosustow as principal owner. In 1946 UPA completed a race-relations film, *The Brotherhood of Man*, for UAW-CIO which brought the fledgling studio to national attention. Later, John Hubley asserted that *McGoo* and *Gerald McBoing Boing* cartoons could be produced for $25,000 each compared to the $35,000 cost at Metro-Goldwyn-Mayer and Warner Brothers, due principally to less detail in the figures, simpler backgrounds, and a limited form of animation.

1946

In January, Famous Studios and Terrytoons were the only major film-animating organizations in the East.

With the release of *The Bureau of Aeronautics Industrial Planning Program* filmagraph, a filmstrip printed on 16mm film with optical sound track, the United States Navy began an eventual phaseout of conventional filmstrips for training. The filmagraph embodied the economic efficiencies of the filmstrip while taking advantage of greater reliability in projection. Using still pictures, the filmagraph was a forerunner of the increased animation of stills. Created by pans, tilts, opticals, and stop-action, it later appeared on American television in advertising and historical recreations such as NBC's "Project Twenty" series.

John Oxberry opened a small business in New Rochelle, New York, manufacturing animation stands, which would eventually become the industry standard. In later years, he developed an inexpensive stand, thereby opening up animation to experimenters, schools, and amateurs.

With the release of *Song of the South*, a combined live-action and animated film, the Disney Studio began the transition to the live-action feature as the costs of animated shorts and features continued to climb.

1947

The Association for Computing Machinery (ACM) was founded to be a scientific, technical, and educational society for professionals in the information-processing field, including a division devoted to computer-graphics and animation. Through this organization and its publications, similar to the Society of Motion Picture and Television Engineers in the first decades of this century, the ACM served professional and educational needs in computer-animation.

Oskar Fischinger completed his *Motion Painting #1*, synchronized to Bach's "Brandenburg Concerto #3," using a new technique of oil on plexiglass. In Canada, Norman McLaren won an Academy Award for *Fiddle De Dee*, an abstract film made without a camera. *The Czech Year* gained international recognition for Jiři Trnka, puppet animator, and his fellow workers. According to many critics, Trnka's work established new standards for the puppet film.

In special photographic effects, Jean Kudar disclosed the sodium-lamp method in traveling mattes for color films. It was later improved by others, adopted by Rank Laboratories, Great Britain, and used by Disney enterprises for combining animation with live-action in such films as *Mary Poppins*.

On the growing NBC television network, boy puppet Howdy Doody was the forerunner of a puppet revival in American film and television media aimed at children. By 1954 he was the idol of a daily audience of fifteen million children and was the highest-rated daytime program. The relatively inexpensive format spawned hundreds of imitators at local TV stations who also served as cartoon jockeys, introducing cartoons and kibitzing with local children transported to the TV station. About the same time, Burr Tillstrom and Fran Allison presented the antics of the Kuklapolitans over WBKB-TV, Chicago. In 1948 the program was seen on a Midwest TV network and by November the NBC-TV network picked up the show for five years. In September 1954 "Kukla, Fran and Ollie" moved to ABC-TV before going off the air. Other versions were revived temporarily on NBC and the Public Broadcasting System.

In the experimental animated film, Jordan Belson, influenced by Hans Richter and Oskar Fischinger, completed a first film, *Transmutations*, animated from painted scrolls, each scroll divided into frames and photographed in succession.

By the fall of 1947, Amos and Marcia Vogel held their first program of 16mm films, destined to become *Cinema 16 Showcase*, at the Provincetown Playhouse, Greenwich Village.

Leonard L. Levinson began his film company, Impossible Pictures, which attempted to cut animation costs by substituting camera action for animation. This cut the number of drawings for a one-reel cartoon from about 15,000 to a surprising 350, according to Levinson and his partner David Flexer. By early 1948 only one reel in a projected series of twelve cartoon travelogues had been produced.

Production economics forced George Pal to abandon dimensional animation and his *Puppetoon* series. An animated squirrel, later acclaimed in *The Great Rupert* (1949), was the signal for Pal's move into other animation subjects. Within two years, he was planning his first science fiction film, *Destination Moon* (1950).

1948

Columbia Pictures ceased their own animation production and continued distribution of UPA cartoons.

The United States Supreme Court in the Paramount case, in upholding an earlier district court decision, declared block-booking, admission price-fixing, certain runs and clearance practices, and discriminatory distribution arrangements favoring affiliated exhibition circuits to be in restraint of trade and therefore prohibited.

Mike Maltese and Chuck Jones created *The Roadrunner* which turned into a cartoon series with little or no dialogue. It was intended as a parody on chase films. By December, the Disney Studios released *Seal Island*, a two-reel live-action documentary that won an Academy Award the next year. The first entry in the true-to-life adventure series made good profits, running as a second feature.

1949

The French film *1848* was one of the first art films imported into the United States that used animation techniques on still pictures and influenced the form in subsequent American films and TV programs.

Willis O'Brien and a crew of several stop-motion animators and modelers had been at work at least two years before the release of *Mighty Joe Young*. Among that group was a young Ray Harryhausen, whose first sequence was the basement scene with the drunks taunting the huge Joe.

By July, in the context of changing audience tastes and the release of "issue films" such as *Gentleman's Agreement* and *Best Years of Our Lives*, Disney reported that the re-release of *Fantasia* was doing surprising business. Since then, audiences have been exposed to an upsurge in serious music in long-play recordings and over the radio, probably enhancing the acceptance of Disney's animated interpretations.

Mr. Magoo appeared in a UPA cartoon, *Ragtime Bear*, as a supporting character. His popularity from this film encouraged Steve Bosustow to make more Magoo films.

Later in 1949, RKO and Paramount entered into consent decrees thereby divesting themselves of their theaters. Loew's Warner Brothers and Twentieth Century-Fox, by 1957, entered into similar agreements.

With regard to a new crisis in the film industry, 2.3 percent of the United States homes were equipped with a television receiver (940,000 homes).

1950

Robert Flaherty arranged for the release of Curt Oertel's *The Titan* in the United States. While this film was old, it was based on limited animation through editing and selective photographic treatment of static art, and was praised by critics in the United States.

At the Massachusetts Institute of Technology, a Whirlwind I computer was used to generate simple pictures using a cathode-ray tube as an output device. *Destination Moon*, the George Pal epic in technicolor, opened in New York City, beginning a revival of space exploration or science fiction films employing special effects.

Funds frozen in Great Britain after the war affected Walt Disney's decision to make his first live-action feature, *Treasure Island*, there. Charles Schulz created "Peanuts," following in a general way the intellectual format of Walt Kelley's characters but using young children who think and act like adults.

Oskar Fischinger invented the Lumigraph, a device for creating special lighting effects. Ben F. Laposky, using an analog computer, generated images electronically based on the superimposition of electric oscillations of varying time functions. Laposky termed these images electronic abstractions.

1951

Alexandre Alexeieff, in his advertising films, used a new technique, *Pendules composés*, in which lighted tracers were recorded on a single frame, forming a kind of solid object. *Sève de la terre* (1955 advertisement) was typical of his work.

Two versions of *Alice in Wonderland* were released. One used the animated puppets of Louis Bunin with a live actress playing Alice. Disney's version was fully animated. The release of the two films followed months of litigation started by Disney with the Bunin version experiencing continuing difficulties in obtaining suitable release prints. Finally, in 1975, the Bunin version was revived.

The UPA cartoon *Gerald McBoing Boing* won an Academy Award as best short-subject cartoon.

Willard Van Dyke completed *The Photographer*, showing Edward Weston at work and film using motion-images of Weston's photographs.

By fall, live network TV interconnection was demonstrated, carrying President Truman's speech at a San Francisco conference officially ending the war with Japan. Regular interconnection soon ushered in larger, national audiences of greater interest to advertisers.

1952

The 1,000th cartoon was released by Terrytoons. The Museum of Modern Art, New York City, sponsored a retrospective showing. The Hungarian, Peter Foldes, made his first film, *Animated Genesis*, with funds from the British Film Institute.

Senator Estes Kefauver, chairman of the United States Senate Subcommittee on Juvenile Delinquency, questioned the necessity of violence in TV programs.

1953

Bing Crosby Enterprises demonstrated an improved video tape-recording system. By May, Walt Disney's *Melody*, the first three-dimensional cartoon, was released and was followed by Walter Lantz's Woody Woodpecker in *Hypnotic Hick*.

Typical of many, Shamus Culhane, former Disney and Fleischer animator, opened animation studios in New York, catering to the TV business. By 1958 six animation houses in New York were bankrupt, due in part to rising costs including union demands.

Fredric Wertham published *Seduction of the Innocent* which claimed that comic books contributed to juvenile delinquency and personality defects in children.

Ray Bradbury's screenplay, serialized in the *Saturday Evening Post*, was turned into *The Beast from 20,000 Fathoms*. In this film, Ray Harryhausen used a front-projection technique combining animated models with live-action backgrounds. The film, made for a paltry $200,000, proved to be a surprising money-maker against three-dimension and Cinemascope competition.

Paramount released George Pal's *War of the Worlds*, incorporating ambitious mechanical and optical special effects, along with miniatures, on a scale seldom seen by theater audiences. Animation was used in support of optical special effects, as in the use of over 4,000 cels for matte process photography supervised by Gordon Jennings, his last film before his death.

In mid-year, Warner Brothers announced the temporary shutdown of the animation unit but a skeleton staff was kept on in the summer. Disney Studios stopped production of Mickey Mouse cartoons. With this drop in production, the studio lost a valuable training opportunity for young animators.

John Fulton began special effects work on *The Ten Commandments*. Using animation, numerous mattes, matching location shots, and complicated staging in several opticals, Fulton's greatest achievement was probably manifested in the sequence featuring the parting of the Red Sea.

By the end of 1953, the Federal Communications Commission approved the RCA compatible-color TV standards for the United States.

1954

The bear for Hamm's Beer first appeared in TV commercials, becoming one of the most recognized commercial pluggers in United States television. (Withdrawn from the market since the late 1960s, Olympia Brewing Company, the new owner, reintroduced the character in Hamm's advertising in 1978.)

The first British feature-length cartoon was released. Three years in the making, *Animal Farm* was produced by Halas and Batchelor.

With their first film released in America, *Godzilla*, the Japanese studio, Toho, began a string of science-fiction films that bore a pale resemblance to the dimensional animation of Ray Harryhausen, George Pal, and Jim Danforth.

Hansel and Gretel, produced by Michael Myerberg, was claimed by many to be the most ambitious puppet-animation film ever made. The models and techniques used in *Hansel and Gretel* were also incorporated in TV commercials for Green Giant and Hazel Bishop lipstick.

In October, ABC-TV presented a Walt Disney anthology, in what would become the longest running prime-time series by 1980. With a switch to the NBC network in 1961, the Disney program circulated various forms to its youth audiences, including Westerns, action-adventures, documentaries, promotions for the California and Florida theme parks, and frugally released animations for which the Disney name was initially famous.

At year's end, 55.7 percent of United States homes were equipped with a TV receiver (26 million homes).

1955

Young and Rubicam and UPA Productions created *Bert and Harry*, two animated showmen promoting Piel's Beer, who clearly demonstrated the strong appeal animation could bring to advertised products.

John Oxberry marketed his animation stand to the film industry. This would become one of the industry standards for quality and reliability and would help expand animation production to more producers. He also devised an aerial-image optical-printer providing a simpler method of mixing live-action cinematography with animation.

John and Faith Hubley formed Storyboard, a New York film production company. While their early work involved television commercials, the Hubleys also established new trends in animation. Funded by the Guggenheim Museum, *Adventures of an ** was completed in 1956, the first of many award-winning films on world problems and childen's needs that would thrust the Hubleys into international prominence.

Terrytoons was purchased by CBS Films.

Making a lasting impression on filmmakers and perhaps audiences, the titles to Otto Preminger's *Man with the Golden Arm* were animated by Saul Bass. This began an era in film and television in which title graphics manifested imaginative but symbolic motifs related to the film.

Reflecting a reorientation in Disney revenues, Disneyland in Anaheim, California, opened to the public. With Disneyworld in the 1960s, the amusement parks would eventually account for 71 percent of Disney's revenue in 1979 and 59 percent of operating income. One year following Disney's entrance into prime-time television programming, the first major studio to do so, *The Mickey Mouse Club* premiered on the ABC-TV network. While a great deal of new material originated in this series, several Disney characters including Mickey Mouse were recycled through the program, thus familiarizing another generation with the Disney name and quality.

Beginning in the fall of 1955, the situation comedy *The People's Choice* lasted three seasons on NBC and featured Cleo, a pet basset hound, who was shown in closeup at appropriate points, "voicing" some commentary on the situations. The device demonstrated how sound used asynchronously, compounded by the incongruity of a dog "talking" in live-action, could be very funny. By this time, audiences were also familiar with such manipulations in some cartoons.

1956

With the establishment of an animation unit in Zagreb Films, Yugoslavia's first organized production of cartoon films has continued to the present.

MGM released *Forbidden Planet*, a science-fiction spectacular embellished with electronic music by Louis and Bebe Barron; animation by Joshua Meador. Derived from the theories of Norbert Weiner (feedback and cybernetics), the Barrons' electronic experiments formed the basis for the electronic tonalities used in the film. Using animated special effects, *Forbidden Planet* generated critical praise, something unusual for a science-fiction film. The character Robby the Robot reappeared in *Lost in Space*, a short-lived TV program in the 1960s, and had more than a casual resemblance to the robots in *Star Wars*.

Speculating that educated persons may have a greater affinity for abstract thinking, Kenneth B. Frye, in a master's research project at American University found that a preference for animated advertising increased as the educational level rose among the groups he studied. Except for persons fifty-five or older, preferences based on age did not vary much; most preferred animated commercials compared to live-action.

A remake of Cecil B. DeMille's 1920 epic *The Ten Commandments* featured the parting of the Red Sea sequence, orchestrated by special-effects expert John Fulton. M. Klein and D. Bolitho presented the earliest computer-generated music, with their composition "Push Button Bertha." At the University of Illinois, Lejaren A. Hiller and Leonard Isaacson premiered "Illiac-Suite" the same year. Two years later, Isaacson and Hiller founded an experimental music studio, training Robert Baker, Herbert Brun, and John Myhill, now known as computer composers.

Mighty Mouse began on CBS television for the longest network run of an animated program, twelve years.

A three-headed printer was developed at Disney Studios, apparently the first in the industry. This enabled putting background in the back head, mattes in the front head and the foreground optic in the side head.

A sodium-light traveling-matte process was developed by the J. Arthur Rank organization and was first used in *Plain Sailing*. The process, which eliminated the matte-line effect, was later used by Disney in *Mary Poppins* (1964) combining live-action with animation.

With national TV coverage reaching a large portion of United States audiences, national advertising strategies focused on the cost-per-thousand of viewers, with prime time defined as 7 P.M. to 11 P.M. each night, with the peak between 8 P.M. and 9 P.M. Demographics were not widely sought by rating services nor used by TV advertisers until the mid-1960s. In the mid-1950s, with the attention given to prime time, advertisers were not interested in specialized children's programs.

1957

The National Film Board of Canada released *City of Gold*, a twenty-two-minute documentary about Dawson City and the Klondike gold rush. Based upon some 300 recovered glass plates, the Canadian filmmakers applied animation techniques to the pictures.

Fantasia was re-released again and paid off the investment costs which were originally $2.3 million in 1940. Metro-Goldwyn-Mayer closed their animation unit and employees Joe Barbera and Bill Hanna opened their own studio.

Hanna-Barbera, Hollywood, California, was formed. In ten years, they produced a total of eighteen TV cartoon series and employed a staff of 450 persons. The organization is credited by *Variety* with introducing the limited animation form, reducing the number of animated cels, and thereby reducing the costs for animated programming. Their first animated TV series premiered on NBC-TV, the prelude to dozens of animated TV series in the following twenty years.

Paramount stopped production of the Popeye series and sold its shorts backlog, including 234 Popeye cartoons to a television distributor.

A Rotoscope-like device called the Artiscope, using special film, claimed a substantial speedup in the manufacture of animated images based on live-action photography.

A filmmaker-controlled distribution service to a potential nine thousand colleges and film societies was established by Bob Pike and others in Los Angeles. But interest in experimental film in the United States was at low tide.

FORTRAN (formula translator), the computer language enabling engineer-designers to directly express their computations to the input of a computer in algebraic terms, was developed. The language, devised by J. W. Bachus and associates at IBM, led the way to several higher-level languages, enabling designers to exploit the graphic capability of the computer.

Columbia requested UPA to accelerate their rate of Magoo productions. Jan Lenica collaborated with Walerian Borowczyk in two films, *Once upon a Time* and *Love Requited*. Lenica would go on to develop his collage technique, his use of sound as a counterpoint to the image (the opposite of synchronization), and his satirical themes.

1958

Mathematician Stephen Smale, at the University of Chicago, demonstrated that it was possible to turn the surface of a sphere inside out. These calculations led to experimentation with computers to visualize such a deformation, similar to the opening graphics in the public TV program, "Washington Week in Review." Meanwhile, the production costs of a seven-minute, fully animated theatrical animation-short rose to about $70,000. While double-feature bills speeded up the demise of the animated short, the high cost of production coupled with a four-to-five-year time for a return on the original investment, were primary reasons for the disestablishment of animated shorts by Warners, Disney, and Metro-Goldwyn-Mayer.

Dick Brown's *Clutch Cargo* release was followed with similar animated programs for television, such as *Space Angel* and *Captain Fathom*. Using a horizontal multiplane animation stand, real-time pans on static backgrounds, point-of-view shots, reactions, over-the-shoulder shots and other devices, he reduced the amount of animation in a series and consequently the cost.

Off-network runs of children's programs and old theatrical cartoons became increasingly available to local stations as a part of syndicated film packages. Low costs for film and afternoon audiences attracted local sponsorship, creating a new syndication market for cheaply produced children's programs. Hanna-Barbera was the earliest to revamp their production to lower costs, and in this year sold their first TV series to Kellogg, which syndicated the program for local stations.

Zagreb animated films were exhibited internationally at film festivals for the first time.

The *Vortex Concerts* were presented at the Brussels World's Fair by Jordan Belson and Henry Jacobs. *Concerts* were developed in San Francisco between 1957 and 1960 and involved the use of a planetarium dome as a screen, with special films and light sources synchronized with music and effects through a directionalized (stereo) 40-speaker system. Curtis concluded that the Belson-Jacobs work contributed to the wide interest in light-show type abstractions in future "expos."

On *Wagon Train*, a commercial called "Backseat Blues" for Ford was telecast. A series of still pictures had shown a man pantomiming various riding positions in a car with the scenes synchronized to a sound track. Produced by Storyboards, this may have been the first quick-cut commercial for TV, another form of limited animation.

1959

Examples of analog graphics from cathode-ray oscillosopes were exhibited by Herbert W. Franke and others in Germany, Austria, Switzerland, and Great Britain.

NBC's "Project Twenty" staff produced their first still-and-motion film, *Meet Mr. Lincoln*, a thirty-minute film telecast over that network. Producer Don Hyatt and others had reviewed *The City of Gold* and other films, gradually concluding that the limited-animation technique could be employed for dramatic as well as informational emphasis. In conventional cel-animation, with the help of Ub Iwerks, Disney adapted the Xerox process to animation. Pencil drawings were transferred directly to cels, eliminating the inkers (usually women). Moreover, the Xerox process made possible changes in size or position of original animated cels.

Charles Schulz's characters Charlie Brown and Lucy took form in limited animation. Animator and film producer Joe Oriolo acquired rights to the Felix the Cat character and produced nearly 300 cartoons for TV distribution. *Rocky and His Friends*, featuring a flying squirrel and a moose called Bullwinkle, began on the ABC-TV network, demonstrating that limited animation was no particular drawback to creative programming.

General Electric and the advertising agency BBDO incorporated "Near-Sighted Magoo" into GE bulb commercials. The cartoon character lasted through a fifth season (1964-1965) with 10,000 Magoo spots in 200 markets plus network participation.

A New York grand jury's inquiry into TV quiz programs concluded with Charles Van Doren admitting complicity in rigging "Twenty One," an NBC-TV quiz program. Coupled with new broadcast controversies involving payoffs to disc jockeys for playing potential hit records (payola), the attorney general of the United States asked for new legislation to eliminate false advertising and deceptive program practices. The FCC ordered a general inquiry into TV program and advertising practices.

UPA ended its contract with Columbia Pictures and began to make five-minute Mr. Magoo series for TV. Another series, Dick Tracy, was also started. UPA released *1001 Arabian Nights*, receiving negative reviews.

1960

This decade began a trend toward more limited animation in commercials because of economic reasons. But experimentation in abstractions, collage, paper sculpture, and combinations of photos with cel-animation continued until a movement emphasizing realism took hold in commercials in the late 1960s.

The quiz scandals brought governmental and public attention to the network TV-program procurement process, eventually resulting in greater network control over offerings, rather than control by advertisers. Beginning with ABC, networks, concerned with the entire schedule, occasionally designed schedules to counterprogram against known competition. This change in programming strategy brought about the entrance of *The Flintstones* into prime time.

William A. Fetter and Walter Bernhardt, at the Boeing Company, Seattle, reconceptualized a plan for perspective drawing that, when translated into mathematics and put into computer language, produced a computerized perspective drawing. Shortly thereafter, the term *computer-graphics* was coined at Boeing.

The Federal Trade Commission complained that commercials of Lever Brothers, Standard Brands, and Colgate-Palmolive among others were phony, beginning a long-term controversy in broadcasting advertising. "Recreation" was out, through animation or other means; "reality" was "in" for commercials.

The International Animated Film Society (Association Internationale du Film D'Animation) (ASIFA) was formed and chartered in the United Nations with chapters in New York, Los Angeles and other world-production centers.

In advertising, a definite trend toward more limited animation, quick cutting, semiabstracts, paper sculpture, photo-animation combinations, and a more graphic quality occurred, partly as a reaction to the high cost of traditional, full animation, but each technique emphasized photography as a basis for the animation.

Tiros I, the first weather-satellite system, was launched to transmit TV pictures from space back to earth. New generations of satellites provided weather data and photographic reports that were used as stop-action animation in local TV newscasts by the mid-1970s. Audiences accepted stop-action animation as a source of information, not as fantasy or "tricks" as it had previously been regarded over the past sixty years.

At the invitation of Lewis Allen and Jonas Mekas, several filmmakers met in New York City and formed the New American Cinema Group.

The 1960 TV premiere of *The Flintstones*, a Stone Age family with situations resembling twentieth-century suburban life was the earliest animated TV series aimed at adults in prime time, running to early September 1966 and still having a syndicated life through the 1970s. The 1960-1961 TV season featured more TV series having animated opening titles for the show signature such as *Twilight Zone, Small World* (Bass), *Peter Gunn*, and *Mr. Lucky*.

By year's end, 87.1 percent of all United States homes had a TV receiver (46 million households); seven-tenths of one percent were equipped to receive color television.

By August, the International Festival of Animated Films held at Annecy in France emphasized experiment and discovery.

Ub Iwerks was awarded the Herbert T. Kalmus Gold Medal by the Society of Motion Picture and Television Engineers for his contributions to motion picture technology. Mr. Iwerks included among his technical achievements the development of Xerography in animation, multiplane photography, the double-headed optical printer, anamorphic lens and photo systems for 8-perforation color negatives, three-camera cinerama, and sodium traveling-matte improvements.

1961

Disney released *101 Dalmatians*, their first film to use xerography which enabled the animator's drawings to be xeroxed directly to acetate cels instead of being traced by hand. Moreover, this feature caricatured living characters that were not rotoscoped. Critics' reactions were mixed; some indicated that xerox substitution of the inking process gave animation a more graphic look.

Robert Breer's *Blazes*, one hundred basic images changing positions over several thousand frames, forced the eye to choose what it wanted to see. What Breer discovered was the simple phenomenon of interchanging two different images, one after another, creating a superimposed effect. This was demonstrated in the mid-1920s with Eisenstein's *Ten Days That Shook the World* (*October*).

The American Academy Award was awarded to D. Vukotic, a Zagreb animator, for his film *The Substitute*, the first time the award in animation was won by a European. Hanna-Barbera character Yogi Bear spun out of *Huckleberry Hound* to become the star of his own TV animated series.

By July, in response to complaints about TV ads for children's toys, the National

Association of Broadcasters Code Review Board adopted a series of guidelines designed to prevent misleading ad appeals to kids. While lacking any legal enforcement, the code attempted to address the problem of glamorizing toys and animating them in situations that bordered on misrepresentation.

The debated question of TV violence and the FCC's Newton Minow's prodding of the network programmers had some influence on improving the quality of children's programs such as *Discovery*, but these were short-lived.

By October, continuing for five TV seasons, *Mr. Ed* appeared. This was a live-action fantasy involving a talking horse and an architect, Wilbur Post, played by Alan Young. The device of the talking animal and the fantasy were adapted from the *People's Choice* and other live-action and animated films. While there was no actual animation involved in *Mr. Ed*, the sound track and the editing built the illusion that the horse was an "animated talker."

At the same time, *Walt Disney's Wonderful World of Color* premiered on the NBC television network, moving from the ABC schedules of the previous six seasons. By the beginning of the 1979-1980 TV season, the program was in its twenty-fifth year on television.

The Alvin Show featuring three chipmunks began a season on NBC-TV. While American cartoons had used speeded-up voice and music tracks, songwriter Ron Bagdasarian used the technique he developed in phonograph records for the chipmunk characters. He separately voiced each character and played back the tracks at higher speeds. The abstraction in sound was lost on TV audiences; the program went into syndication after one season.

ABC-TV technicians developed playback of videotape in slow motion. *Catalogue* by John Whitney demonstrated a full range of techniques Whitney used with an analog computer. William A. Fetter, credited with originating the term *computer graphics* created a series of graphic works for Boeing, intended to develop an efficient design for a cockpit in a military aircraft.

1962

The costs of TV commercials rose markedly with producers blaming unions and advertising agency bidding practices.

Lou Scheimer and Norman Prescott established Filmation Associates in Hollywood, California, becoming one of the most prolific animation producers for network TV by the early 1970s. In the 1962-1963 TV season, up to twelve quarter-hours of animated programming were featured on the three TV networks, the highest number for the period 1949 to 1973.

"Flash-cut," "squeeze-frame" or "quick-cut" commercials obtained wide use by TV advertisers by the end of 1962. Agency producers moved away from using live-TV-action techniques to film, but incorporated strong design and selection. This led to the "quick-cut" commercial, divided into several scenes, but each carefully composed.

1963

The first half-hour animated TV program produced in Japan and released in the United States was titled *Astro Boy* (*Tetsuwan*).

The first computer-animated film was made at Bell Telephone Laboratories by E. E. Zajac and colleagues. The animation simulated the motion and autorotation of a communication satellite.

L. G. Roberts published his solution to the hidden-line problem in computer-graphics. The Massachusetts Institute of Technology technical report appeared to be the first solution to this problem, making possible better illusions of depth, with shading, in computer-generated scenes. Research by J. E. Warnock and G. S. Watkins at the University of Utah and elsewhere, would add improvements to the process of eliminating the hidden lines and hidden surfaces in half-tone pictures on interactive systems by 1969.

The periodical *Computers and Automation* announced the first competition for computer-graphic works with the selection based on aesthetic criteria, not technical. The Disney organization developed Audio Animatronics. Employing the computer technology, "live" Disney characters such as Donald Duck, could be programmed to participate in live-action shows. In a *Business Week* article, Arthur Rankin, president of Video Crafts, New York, outlined problems involving cultural differences in his imported animated productions from Japan.

Photographer Ben Rose built up multiple images, creating a stroboscopic effect without using strobes. He also developed a "guillotine" technique for creating a ripple effect in an image. A tiny horizontal slit allowed only a portion of the image to be recorded per unit time, as it was lowered or raised over the subject.

First classes for children began at the Yellow Ball Workshop, Lexington, Massachusetts. Through the years, the films produced there by children and adults have won numerous awards and high enthusiasm from audiences viewing them, clearly demonstrating that there is considerable life in individually produced animated films that are not subjected to conditions of the marketplace or the business orientation of the film industry.

Warner Brothers closed its cartoon film unit. Bob Godfrey's *Do It Yourself Cartoon Kit* won first prize at Oberhausen. The New York Filmmaker's Cooperative was established by Jonas Mekas, editor of *Film Culture*, as an informal voice of the New American Cinema. The co-op's link with a theater, the newsletter, and *Film Culture* made possible faster recognition of filmmakers.

Ivan Sutherland, at the Massachusetts Institute of Technology, developed a computer-design system dubbed "Sketchpad." The artist can develop a drawing in real time by simply drawing on the face of a cathode-ray tube. By year's end, Ampex, manufacturer of audio and video recording equipment, announced the development of a stop-frame animation technique. Aniforms announced development of a continuous-movement animation process invented by Morey Bunin, TV puppeteer.

Following *Mysterious Island* (1961), Ray Harryhausen created the magic of Greek mythology in *Jason and the Argonauts*. The most memorable and difficult sequence of his career probably remained the dramatic and skillfully executed sword fight Jason and his companions had against seven skeletons.

Metro-Goldwyn-Mayer established the Animation/Visual Arts Division, six years after closing down the animation unit (1957). *The Dot and the Line* was a notable theatrical produced by this division.

1964

Fred Barzyk, producer-director at WGBH, Boston, a public-TV station of long-standing reputaiton, produced *Jazz Images*. The five short videotapes were among the earliest examples of using TV for nonrepresentational images.

The Pink Panther originally appeared in the title of a Peter Sellers movie, and was later launched into a new series of theatrical cartoons animated by DePatie-Freleng. While Warner Brothers closed down their animation unit in 1962, in two years they contracted with DePatie-Freleng for the Pink Panther series.

WDSU-TV, New Orleans, began regularly scheduled daily editorial cartoons on TV. The opening of *Mary Poppins* in Hollywood, California, was followed with highly positive critical praise. The year's TV season began with the TV networks and many large metropolitan stations dumping their complex station-logos for better-designed, shorter, simpler, and animated identifications.

Beginning a four-year run on ABC-TV, *Voyage to the Bottom of the Sea* was the earliest TV series to embrace war and CIA-type themes, science-fiction forms, and general gadgetry, featuring a flying submarine and fantastic creatures, among other examples. The era of special effects was beginning to take hold on the tube. The Magoo theatrical character of UPA began a half-hour weekly nighttime series on NBC-TV as *Famous Adventures of Mr. Magoo*.

1965

A number of exhibitions increased public awareness of the aesthetic aspects of data processing. Frieder Nake, George Nees, and A. Michael Noll organized the first exhibition of computer-graphics using digital devices. The Howard Wise Gallery in New York exhibited digital graphics. Others followed in Michigan, Nevada, Utah, and New Hampshire over the next fifteen months. Kenneth Knowlton, Bell Labs, published his studies on computer-produced movies using BELFLIX (Bell-Flicks) language and the technology developed at Bell Laboratories, Murray Hill, New Jersey.

By the mid-1960s, computer-graphics had been introduced into the automobile and aircraft industries for use in design. The chief disadvantages of these systems were their complexity, expense, and demand for experts to write complicated application programs.

According to Chuck Jones, producers of TV cartoons could make a six-minute animation with limited animation for about $10,000 compared to about $35,000 for full animation. According to the Society of Film and Television Arts, Japan became the world's largest center for animation production.

Later in the year, Bill Melendez animated *A Charlie Brown Christmas*. The program won an Emmy and has played in most Christmas seasons since the premiere.

Network ratings demonstrated that cheaply produced programs generated more homogeneous audiences (defined demographically). National advertisers were attracted to Saturday morning and late afternoon time periods. Color television spurred these interests because more children were attracted to color. By 1967, the networks were in a three-way race for Saturday morning audiences. Color also increased the demand for more program production.

Highband videotape recorders capable of producing up to third-generation copies without degradation became available. This technology is compatible with electronic editing devices which were not widely available until 1965.

1966

In San Francisco, Canyon Cinema Co-op was founded opening up more channels for animated and experimental film. Stan Vanderbeek completed *Computer Art*. He also planned a satellite-connected Movie Drome, using giant dome screens similar to the *Vortex Concerts* of the late 1950s.

Fordham Film Study Project (New York City) received the first grant-in-film from the National Endowment for the Arts, signaling the importance of developing children as critical consumers of film and TV, to help them learn filmmaking.

Using a Xerox process, Marvel Comics announced five new syndicated-TV cartoon series featuring *Captain America, Ironman, The Incredible Hulk, Sub-Mariner*, and *The Mighty Thor*. The technique merely reduced the comics to a cel with speech balloons eliminated. Sound effects and dialogue were used on the sound track in these limited-animation series.

Widespread interest was found in popular and optical art with an attendant rise in the popularity of experimental films. The Creative Film Society, for the first time since 1957, became self-supporting in six months. The 1966-1967 TV season marked the largest gain in animated children's TV programming over all previous seasons with 81 percent of the programs being animated. Two seasons earlier, 47 percent of children's programs were animated.

September marked the beginning of a three-year NBC-TV run of *Star Trek*, and the adventures of the crew of Starship Enterprise 200 years in the future. However, stories and situations often had contemporary relevance quite distinct from earlier science-fiction programs such as *Captain Video* or *Space Patrol*. In an unusual pattern, developing from a growing cult of *Trek* fans, the series spun-off into an animated program telecast on Saturday mornings and, by 1979, into a theatrical feature.

Bell engineers screened five computer-generated animated films at a symposium in Murray Hill, New Jersey. The films consisted of simple line drawings and complex patterns in black and white.

At the Massachusetts Institute of Technology, Ron Baecker devised the Genesys system which interpreted a series of light pen movements either as a shape or the patch that the shape should follow. A similar system was created by the National Research Council of Canada, which performed all the inbetweening based on key drawings sketched on the computer's display screen.

1967

Expo '67, Montreal, which began at midyear, publicized multiple-media, multiple-screens, and strong design, and showcased animated films.

The Rockefeller Foundation funded the National Center for Experiments in Television in San Francisco. Two years later, the Corporation for Public Broadcasting and the National Endowment for the Arts provided additional funds for the electronic medium which required a far higher investment than the traditional film.

What's Happening, Mr. Silver, a thirty-show series over Boston's public TV station experimented with non-narrative images which blossomed into a TV collage. Scott Bartlett, in his film *Offon*, incorporated animation concepts with videographic potentials of electronics. ABC News in *Mission Mind Control* used segments of the film to illustrate the hallucinations of patients on acid drugs.

President Lyndon Johnson, by executive order, established the National Commission on Civil Disorders.

1968

John Whitney's *Permutations*, made with a digital computer, was supplemented with editing, rephotography, and color printing on an optical printer.

Stanley Kubrick's *2001: A Space Odyssey* was the first major film to utilize front-projection techniques in special effects. The chief advantage of the technique was to present a much brighter background image compared to traditional rear projection, which was increasingly being replaced. John Brosnan concluded that several special-effects technicians developed the technique independently, perhaps as early as 1942. The film, however, had a large influence on television commercials, proliferating slit-scan, starbursts, and other visual embellishments to corporate logos and product names. *2001* revealed the assimilation of experimental techniques forged by Jordan Belson and James and John Whitney.

Al Brodaux (producer), Heinz Edelman (graphic designer), George Dunning (director), Fred Wolf (head animator) and many others completed *Yellow Submarine*, an unusual leap from Disney animation to a fantastic, op, and surrealistic world of stylized graphics and animated characters with Beatles' music.

Barbarella, starring Jane Fonda, was a science-fiction comic strip probably inspired by the current interest in Pop Art. The film eventually became the bridge between the ambitious science-fiction film (such as *2001, Forbidden Planet, When Worlds Collide*), and the fantasy and visual razzle-dazzle of *Star Wars*. The audience acceptance of the last fairy tale was complete because *Star Wars* convincingly destroyed the reality of the cinema and reconstructed a funny and eye-appealing but simple story, that inspired thousands of theatergoers. Jordan Belson was credited for special effects in *Journey to the Far Side of the Sun*.

The new TV season for children's shows reflected a downtrend in violence and other programs considered by pressure groups to be offensive. Each network developed an image for Saturday; CBS aimed for comedy, NBC for adventure and action, and ABC for adventure and youth appeal. The change was attributed to public opinion, revitalization for the sake of advertising interests, and probably a desire to achieve higher quality.

Network control over children's programming was dominant due to their continuing concern with audience flow and the selling of participations to national advertisers, who bought "package minutes" spread around various children's programs. The network power lay in selling the audiences to advertisers and in buying programs from package producers. In buying programs, the networks specified the final menu by word and deed.

Hanna-Barbera's *New Adventures of Huckleberry Finn*, while lasting only one season, was among the earliest TV series using live-action combined with animation. The biggest influence for this series and technique was probably the highly successful Disney film, *Mary Poppins* (1964).

1969

The Medium Is The Medium was telecast to a national audience through the Public Broadcasting Laboratory financing. Nam June Paik, Allan Kaprow, and Otto Piene contributed their video art to this first-time telecast.

My World and Welcome To It, starring William Windom as John Monroe, was a short-lived series on NBC, revived for a summer on CBS. Monroe was a cartoonist-writer with an imagination that put him into a James Thurber-like, animated home environment with a wife about to hassle him. Animation was used to depict his fantasies and fears.

Breaking cel traditions, Disney animator Ward Kimball included cutout collage sequences in the Disney short, *It's Tough to be a Bird.*

Computer Image, Denver, demonstrated their SCANIMATE computer-animation in New York City. The system worked with original art transferred to the computer's cathode-ray tube by a TV camera. Images could be zoomed, enlarged, reduced, revolved, twisted, squeezed, or turned inside out. The ANIMAC system generated its images internally and enabled sound modulation for lip synchronization. SCANIMATE and ANIMAC produced title sequences for *Get Smart* and *The Ed Sullivan Show.*

According to Ronald M. Baecker, demonstrative or interactive computer-animation systems by this time were rigid with poor image quality which lacked a choice of tone, color, or texture. Animators could draw images and movements with a fixed set of drawing commands, but they could not compute images and movements directly.

Fantasia was re-released again, and in New York City did high box office business, surprising Disney promoters.

On 10 November the first *Sesame Street* program was telecast using animation to teach recognition of simple numbers, simple counting, and recitation of the alphabet. Later, the series taught affective skills designed to help preschoolers make the transition from home to classroom.

1970

In the 1970s, television news increasingly focused on formal investigations and trials. Because many of the legal proceedings were closed to TV cameras, the graphic artist returned to TV news, sketching with considerable speed the court-room scenes. The resulting artwork was edited into a continuity with single shots and moving camera treatment. About the same time, local TV newscasts features an increasing amount of graphic art, some stylized, to illustrate news stories.

The partially animated *Frito Bandito* commercial was discontinued following complaints from Mexican-Americans. Walt Disney Archives was founded to preserve and collect historical materials about the Disney Studio.

In computer-animation, an era of experimentation and cross-adaptation began as specialized journals reported results of experiments in interactive systems, and professional trades extolled the virtues of favored systems.

In 1970, 95.2 percent of all United States homes were equipped with a TV receiver, or nearly 70 million households; of those, 39.2 percent had a color set.

1971

CAESAR (Computer Animated Episodes Single Axis Rotation), a system developed by Lee Harrison, III, Computer Image Corporation, enabled animators to produce short sequences and review them immediately on a color TV monitor. When satisfied, the animator could dump the finished sequence in a digital computer memory-system and move on to the next sequence. The *Learn to Count* series on *Sesame Street* (1971) was animated with this system.

Disney Studios began a talent development program seeking to replenish the ranks of dead or retired animators.

The De Joux animation process was modified to enable local stations to produce their own limited animation with low costs. Using twin 70mm rolls of film, artists could review work quickly by projecting the finished work through a polarized-lens system, with lap dissolves merging images.

The Surgeon General's Scientific Advisory Committee on Television and Social Behavior was formed, a United States government reaction to public concern over violence in TV programs and the television industry's reluctance to change their programming.

Walt Disney World opened in Orlando, Florida.

Cinetron developed a computer-assisted animation stand based on work by Charles Vaughn and Gene Nottingham. Previously, stand operators had to make long calculations and operate various handles and switches in animating each frame of film. With the Cinetron system, a computer made the complex calculations and sent instructions to motors which drove the table and camera.

1972

With grants from the Rockefeller Foundation and the New York State Council on the Arts, an experimental TV center was established at WNET, New York City.

With the publication of the independently researched aspects of United States media content and control, as part of the Surgeon General's Scientific Advisory Committee on TV and Social Behaviour, Professor George Gerbner (Annenberg) reported that animated children's programming, already the most violent program form on TV in 1967, was by 1969 increasing the lead in the amount of violence on TV.

The first of fifty 3 ½-minute films produced for the Office of Child Development in the Department of Health, Education and Welfare appeared on CBS's "Captain Kangaroo," marking the first time a federally funded project was broadcast over a commercial TV network. The films, which utilized animation and live-action, dealt with nutrition, care of the body, and aspects of emotional states common to children. These were aimed at the three-to-six-year-old audience of the Captain.

Image Transformation entered into contracts with National Aeronautics and Space Administration to process Apollo 16 lunar and trans-earth transmissions. In December, they processed the live Apollo 17 video transmissions.

Computer tomography scanners were introduced into medical diagnosis, forerunners of the Dynamic Spatial Reconstructor (DSR) in use at the Mayo Clinic in 1980. Computer tomography uses a finely focused x-ray which radiates a target area. The images are fed into a computer capable of "slicing" the target into parts. The machinery costs between $100 thousand to $800 thousand; DSRs, which incorporated motion, could go as high as $3 million.

Television commercial maker Bob Abel developed a neonlike, streaking logo for Whirlpool, thus opening up a line of adaptations by other filmmakers later called the "candy-apple-neon technique."

Fritz the Cat, an X-rated cartoon feature directed by Ralph Bakshi, attracted media and public attention to the animated form. Human genitals were revealed openly; sex action was explicit. *Fritz the Cat* was not only aimed at adult audiences, but was among the few non-Disney animated features to show a profit. *Flesh Gordon* became a sex fantasy and satire incorporating animated special effects.

New York animator Al Stahl offered a "Fotomation" service to advertisers, creating limited animation from slides. Using a uniquely equipped, computer-controlled Oxberry animation stand, the Fotomation process could pan, tilt, and zoom on small transparencies in 16mm or 35mm formats. The process extended the earlier work performed in NBC's *Project Twenty* series and other film documentaries using still-photos as their basic material.

1973

A nationwide study of the arts and cultural activities was conducted by Lou Harris and Associates. Of those aged sixteen or older 49 percent attended cultural activities, more than those attending sporting events. Thirty-four percent used libraries, took adult education courses, or attended lectures. Eighty-nine percent thought art appreciation courses should be taught in school.

Funding was made available for a Young People's Film Festival for Public Television at the Center for Understanding Media headed by John Culkin. In the next year, over 100 public TV stations were involved and more than 5,000 films submitted for judging.

In *Frank Film* by Frank Mouris over 10,000 images cut from catalogues and magazines were combined into collages and won an Academy Award, 1974.

Evans and Sutherland Computer Corporation, Salt Lake City, delivered to Case Western Reserve University a continuous-tone image-generating perspective system. The first textbook in computer graphics was published by McGraw-Hill, *Principles of Interactive Computer Graphics*, written by William M. Newman and Robert F. Sproull.

Parade Magazine reported results of a study about children's TV, indicating that *Sesame Street* was watched by more children than any other child TV program. Most parents wanted no commercials. The most frequent complaint about children's TV was too much violence. While the study had some methodological shortcomings, the heavy vote in behalf of public television programs strongly pointed the way for change.

1974

The trade journal *Variety* reported that free-lance animators in New York typically earned $475 per week. Most of the fifteen animation houses in the city had small staffs, bolstering their manpower with free-lance talent driven by sharp deadlines.

The Federal Communications Commission adopted guidelines designed to increase the amount of educational and informational TV programs for preschool and school-age children and to decrease the amount of advertising therein.

Land of the Lost, an NBC-TV Saturday morning program, began its four-season network life. The program was one of the very few to incorporate dimensional animation with live-action on a regular basis.

The zany *Monty Python's Flying Circus*, a thirty-minute weekly comedy show, was syndicated to public television stations. Animated by Terry Gilliam, the program consisted of skits, sight-gags, and a variety of animated forms.

The Muppets of Sesame Street won an Emmy this year and again in 1976 for "Outstanding Achievement in the Field of Children's Programming." Despite this and the sale of children's records, United States TV networks refused to accept owner Jim Henson's arguments that the Muppets would appeal to everyone. Henson took his program ideas to London and produced *The Muppet Show* for syndication to a world market.

1975

Of all United States households, 97.9 percent had a TV receiver, or 68.5 million homes; of these 70.8 percent had a color set.

Digital graphics systems were introduced on American television beginning with words stored in memory and instantly retrieved for superimposition on a TV picture. Within five years, various systems would expand storage capacity and provide a variety of lettering fonts along with logos and other graphic elements such as "colorizing" and tabular outlines. Some systems offered a retrieval capability that produced limited animation.

Evans and Sutherland Computer Corporation installed a computer-image generation system for the United States Maritime Administration for research and training. Using five television projectors, the system displayed animated images of navigation aids, ships, docking areas, lighting configurations with smooth shading, and color.

An animation system was developed at Visual Images, Washington, D.C., that enabled still photographs or other graphic media to be animated more efficiently. An electronic memory system allowed exact and instant repeatability of camera and zoom lens movement. The Syntha Vision computer-animation process was promoted in *Advertising Age* as a cost-saving, flexible system by the president of Computer Visuals, Phillip Mittelman.

CPC Associates, Hollywood, developed a "laser-light" animation technique which opened the "Cher" television program in February. Overexposed negative images were combined with laserlike "explosions" and color filters.

Dolphin Productions, New York, gained a considerable reputation for sophisticated computer-animation in real time. The process brought new life to corporate identities (logos) and Everready Batteries.

Computer Creations, South Bend, Indiana, was formed by Tom Klimek and Richard Brown, using a patented Video-Cel technique. Drawing upon their experience in developing computer simulations for missile systems, the two adapted those computer-graphics to a key-frame system. For example, in a United Airlines spot, the production agency furnished twelve key drawings for a thirty-second spot. Computer Creations' computer completed the remaining 708 inbetween drawings adding color and three dimensions.

Closed Mondays, an object-animated film, was awarded the Academy Award for Best Animated Short. It was created by Will Vinton and Bob Gardiner.

Financed by Sir Lew Grade of the British-owned Independent Television Corporation, *Space: 1999* was syndicated to United States television stations after the three

TV networks turned down the program. Special effects were supervised by Brian Johnson (*2001*). The hourly cost of $275,000 for each episode was among the highest for syndicated programs.

In October, during the premiere season of *Saturday Night Live*, the Mr. Bill character became a regular feature after amateur movie-maker Walter Williams submitted a short film to the program.

1976

An International Telephone and Telegraph Company-financed animated feature, intended to restore the animation industry in New York, entitled *Raggedy Ann and Andy*, premiered in New York, but followed with mixed reviews and losses.

The American Federation of Arts organized the first touring film series concentrating on the American avant-garde. Screenings were staged in museums, film archives, universities, and art centers in the United States and abroad. Perpetual Motion Pictures, New York, animated *Mr. Hipp* sequences for NBC's *Weekend*. The shorts editorialized on a variety of news personalities and public affairs. Universal released *Earthquake*, another in the series of disaster films. Using a variety of stunts, miniatures, shaker platforms, and rotoscoped mattes, craftsmen produced the most ambitious special-effects film in years.

An electronic scene-generator, developed by Evans and Sutherland Corporation, was delivered to the National Aeronautic and Space Administration's Johnson Space Center (Houston) for training prospective pilots in the shuttle program. The system generated animated, three-dimensional (shaded) color images of various objects in space and the shuttle in an out-of-the-window perspective in real time.

1977

The publication of the David Rockefeller report *Coming to Our Senses* (McGraw-Hill) called attention to the need for training critical consumers of the media, in addition to the role of the media in spreading the other arts.

Snow White was still the largest grosser in the United States and Canada at $26.5 million, followed by *Bambi* at $17.8 million. Among the ten most successful animated features, compiled from *Variety* statistics, Disney animated features occupied the remaining eight slots. Ralph Bakshi's *Fritz the Cat* and Lee Mendelson's *A Boy Named Charlie Brown* were on the *Variety* list of films generating revenues above $4 million.

Widespread proliferation of home video games occurred, bringing interactive computer-graphics to the American public. Hollywood Screen Cartoonists Guild officials concluded that 1977 was a good year for employment in the animation industry due to the rise of animated features and the comeback of animated TV series. Walter Lantz celebrated his fifty-sixth year as a film cartoon producer, a record unmatched by any other currently active producer.

Lyon Lamb Video Animation system provided fast and cheap pencil tests using videotape. Drawings were recorded on half-inch tape a frame at a time with up to five levels of drawings possible. Time efficiencies and low costs were the chief advantages along with distinct applications in training as well as production. CPC Associates, Los Angeles, successfully incorporated laser-light techniques into their animation specialties.

Star Wars, which would become the largest grossing film so far, was released.

Comprised of a simple fairy tale with plenty of action, the film dazzled audiences with its humor and array of special effects. For economic reasons, John Dykstra (special photographic effects supervisor), Gary Kurtz (producer), and George Lucas (writer-director) decided to set up a complete in-house system to produce the photographic effects. Stop-motion puppets were animated by Jon Berg and Philip Tippet. Adam Beckett (animation and rotoscope designer) and Frank Van Der Veer were responsible for the laser-light sword sequences. Larry Cuba created some digital computer-animation. Ben Burtt was responsible for sound effects, all original to the film and comprised of an innovative selection and synthesis of numerous natural sounds.

While *Star Wars* has had a profound influence on other media, particularly television advertising, the special-effects creators were mostly derived from the commercial TV production business.

1978

A staff report of the Federal Trade Commission concluded that two petitions had merit in arguing that the majority of TV advertising aimed at kids was deceptive and unfair. Petitions requested that the Federal Trade Commission ban certain advertising during hours when children were a large proportion of the TV audience. Animation was among ten techniques used in children's TV advertising. The report concluded that animation and other techniques "turn on" kids. Action for Children's Television submitted a petition to the Federal Trade Commission requesting an end to candy advertising on children's TV programs.

The jointly developed CBS-Ampex Electronic Palette digital-computer graphics-system was demonstrated on the Super Bowl telecast by artist Leroy Neiman. Alan Kitching, an animation and computer specialist in London, developed Antics, a technique enabling a programmer to enter the coordinates of a drawing into a computer with a light pen and modify its configuration. The system can accommodate up to forty commands and 100 different color picture elements. Animac system married the horizontal multiplane camera with a video system in a TV series, *Space Force*, which used the system. Foote, Cone and Belding/Honig produced four TV commercials emphasizing "Brand Name Logo" for Levi's, using a slightly surrealistic approach resulting from rotoscoping.

Hal Seeger began production of *Cartoon-A-Torials*, limited-animation cartoons on political and social subjects distributed by *Newsweek* broadcasting. Each week, Seeger selected newspaper cartoons and animated them, adding music and sound effects. Many of these animations were eventually incorporated into local TV newscasts, reviving the tradition from 1914 of using cartoons in newsreels.

Disney enterprises had their best year so far with record net income of nearly $61 million. Disney animated features *The Jungle Book* (in re-release) and *The Rescuers* were performing well at the box office, the latter outdrawing *Star Wars* in Paris. The studio also celebrated the fiftieth anniversary of their Mickey Mouse character.

Opening titles to *The Best of Families* by Elinor Bunin Productions illustrated the increasing involvement of graphic designers in the animation medium and the growth of subspecialties. At MAGI-Synthavision, New York, digital and analog computers are used to create combinations of basic geometrical shapes as in the Lee Maxi Filter TV spots.

Illustrating the continuing appeal of graphic design in corporate logos and television commercials, Zeplin Productions, New York, created NBC's "spinning cube" network identification. A Paramount subsidiary, Magicam, developed a system with its own name that enabled a video camera to be moved during a matting shot. The IBM television spot, featuring a man walking among electronic tubes and components, used the Magicam system without any matte lines present.

Several producers began planning live-action features incorporating comic-strip characters such as Flash Gordon, Popeye, Conan the Barbarian, and Tarzan. Ralph Bakshi's *Lord of the Rings* opened by year's end, the first of two features based on J. R. R. Tolkien's epic trilogy. The entire film was shot as live-action, and, with the rotoscope system, turned into an animated version. The rising number of disaster and science-fiction films put heavy demands on matte artists and other special-effects personnel. Matte and optical work was also affected by rising costs for set construction and elaborate miniatures.

The Small One, a Disney featurette, was released at Christmas, partly as a way of providing more experience for the small number of young animators at the Disney Studio.

According to a Neilsen analysis of November 1978 sweeps, *The Muppets Show* was the top syndicated-TV program in the United States. The Muppets were seen by an estimated 235 million persons in 106 countries. One character in the series, Kermit the Frog, was reported by *Time* to be the Mickey Mouse of the 1970s. According to Arbitron, seven of the top-ten children's TV programs were animated.

The Lion, The Witch, and the Wardrobe, produced by the Children's Television Workshop actually involved three animation studios in collaboration: Bill Melendez (London), TVC (London), and Pegbar (Barcelona). Each was contracted by the workshop to do 33.3 percent of the programmed 100 minutes on a $1 million budget overall.

Citing increased production costs and an uncertain regulatory policy on children's TV advertising, the *Mickey Mouse Club* stopped distribution in January 1979.

1979

The animated Norelco TV commercial continued into its fourteenth Christmas season with some updating for their new product line.

Following the development of digital graphics systems, the newer digital effects systems offered video programmers a large range of effects such as picture compression or expansion, wipes, inserts, repositioning, chroma key tracking, automatic masking, and digital frame storage. With such storage, picture noise and generation loss were eliminated, making possible the building up of multiple picture elements into a total composite.

By March, Voyager, a deep-space probe, relayed by telemetry picture data of the planet Jupiter and her largest moons. Earth launched Pioneer, which made a historic fly-by of Saturn, sent back digital TV pictures, and continued to travel outside our known solar system. The Pioneer encounter with Saturn demonstrated the Adda Corporation's electronic still-storage system which received and stored pictures of the fly-by.

The New York Museum of Modern Art honored artist Peter Ellenshaw for his work in a prelude to the release of *The Black Hole*.

In the fiftieth year of Popeye's creation, the British Nutrition Foundation debunked the myth that quickly eating a can of spinach increases one's strength. Actually, iron in vegetables is not easy for the body to assimilate. At least ten times more spinach is required in order to get the same amount of iron found in red meat.

Computer-Aided Animation System (CASS) became operational at the Computer Graphics Laboratory at the New York Institute of Technology. Using several new software packages and technologies, the laboratory was now able to produce three-dimensional animated features.

Dubbed "Shadow Chroma Key" by Home Box Office, an improved electronic-key insertion-process put a superimposed character casting his own shadow against the background plate in such a way that the composite was lifelike. About sixty inserts of Dick Cavett in Home Box Office's "Time Was" series were completed using the process, known by its trade name, Ultra-Mat. The process was also used on ABC's *A Crack in Time*.

Owners of home video-recorders who record over-the-air broadcasts do not violate the copyright law, according to Judge Warren Ferguson's decision following the long litigation between Sony Corporation, Walt Disney, and MCA. The case was appealed.

Encouraged by the economic success of *Watership Down* and *Lord of the Rings*, Hanna-Barbera planned an $8 million animated feature, *Heidi's Song*. Warner Brothers cartoons animated by Chuck Jones were recycled in *The Bugs Bunny/Roadrunner Movie*.

Walt Disney Productions released *The Black Hole*, obtaining their first PG rating and borrowing razzle-dazzle appeal in special effects. The script was a translation of a Jules Verne undersea epic to the edge of a swirling star sieve. Along with *Star Trek, The Motion Picture*, the Disney epic seemed a fitting end to the decade that featured a revival in animation technique, marking a special departure from family films for the Disney organization.

Star Trek, The Motion Picture used the Evans and Sutherland Picture System II Vector Display which takes individual drawings of an object and turns them into an animated, three-dimensional object, shaded and in color. The object can be manipulated with a joystick: rolled, tilted, moved up and down, or turned inside out.

The Motion Picture Screen Cartoonists Local 839 (Hollywood) claimed up to 75 percent of animation work was being exported to other countries where costs were lower. In mid-August more than 800 animators and associated personnel went out on strike, protesting the runaway cartoon production in Taiwan, Korea, and Spain. An "antirunaway" clause was agreed to for inclusion in an industry-wide package for the first time.

Eleven veteran and experienced animators left Walt Disney Studio over a creative dispute, including Don Bluth, director of *Pete's Dragon* and *The Small One*.

The Federal Communications Commission reported that the 1974 guidelines for children's TV programming had not been complied with by United States broadcasters.

Columnist Harry Wayne McMahan, in *Advertising Age*, picked a numbers fight with researchers who put down animated commercials. He asserted that successful campaigns use up to 23 percent animation, relieving audiences of the live-action clutter.

Major Research Centers

INTRODUCTION

Compared to general film collections, the number of archives containing even a fraction of animation material is very small. However, some libraries and museums in the United States do contain animated films and a smaller number collect and preserve papers, memorabilia, and ephemera in that subject.

REFERENCE GUIDES TO ANIMATION ARCHIVES

William C. Young's *American Theatrical Arts: Guide to Manuscripts and Special Collections in the United States and Canada* is a useful but dated list of theater and film collections organized by name and subject area. Careful reading and a letter request to the cited research center are required in most cases since Young's entries do not classify material under comic art or animation. For example, the references to the State Historical Society of Wisconsin Mass Communication History Center do not note any animation subjects, but the center does indeed have a collection of several hundred animated films. These are found in the Warner Brothers and United Artists Collections and are described in more detail in this appendix.

The Margaret Young *Subject Directory of Special Libraries and Information Centers* is a multivolume collection of references to special libraries. Volume 2 ("Education and Information Science Libraries") notes audiovisual collections and volume 4 ("Social Sciences and Humanities Libraries") lists art and theater collections.

For other researchers there are still untapped libraries and archives housing animation films. Olga S. Weber's *North American Film and Video Directory* is a more comprehensive locator of film collections throughout the United States, especially in the public library system. This is supplemented by the new Bowker *Educational Film Locator*, described below. Nineteen animation collections are separately listed in the Weber index, but more can be located with careful reading. The directory is organized by states with references made to cities in alphabetical order. Each listing provides the full name and address of the repository and curator or librarian followed by broad descriptions of the film collections indicating by percentage the scope of animation holdings. The percentage device has little meaning for anyone in search of specific works but ought to signal attention to investigate further. No specific titles are listed in the directory, but overall the *North American Film and Video Directory* is a substantial accomplishment in providing leads to museums and libraries collecting animated films. Some collections are omitted (the State Historical Society of Wisconsin Mass Communication History Center, for example) but the authors had to rely on busy librarians to respond to questionnaires and some did not.

The fourth edition of *Subject Collections* by Lee Ash has numerous leads to film collections, some of which contain materials on animation. The listings are more detailed than the Weber work.

After many years of preparation, the film holdings of the fifty-member Consortium of University Film Centers are brought together in the *Educational Film Locator* published in 1978 by R. R. Bowker. With a subject list (800 headings), and index and annotated entries, about 40,000 films are identified and arranged alphabetically by title. In addition to the annotation, each film has bibliographic, purchasing, and rental information with a unique cross-referencing system enabling users to retrieve titles by alternates, earlier and translated titles, or editions taken from features. A large number of animated films, and films about animation, are available in these collections.

NICEM (National Information Center for Educational Media, available through the University of Southern California, University Park, Los Angeles, California 90007) provides a computer-printed list describing over 14,000 16 mm films, listed alphabetically by title. The subscription service also includes locators for filmstrips, 8mm films, and a variety of other audiovisual media.

One of the critically important guides to reference collections in the United States is *Motion Pictures, Television and Radio: A Union Catalogue of Manuscript and Special Collections in the Western United States.* Edited and compiled by Linda Mehr and envisioned and directed by Anne G. Schlosser, the catalogue is intended to locate research collections currently available for use in established institutions in eleven western states. The descriptions of holdings are current to March 1977. Potential users of various research collections described in this Appendix should also consult the Mehr work for additional information on the holdings of a particular center in film and broadcast subjects.

Other important guides to collections in mid-America, the east or west, are contained in the work edited by Ted Perry, *Performing Arts Resources.* In volume 1 Anne G. Schlosser surveys film and broadcasting research sources in the Los Angeles area; Louis A. Rachow briefly describes major research centers in the New York area; John Kuiper describes the Library of Congress collections and procedures for access; and other chapters are devoted to descriptions of the Wisconsin Center for Theater Research, broadcasting archives, and the American Film Institute film program.

Volume 2 of the *Performing Arts* series has a sketchy yet wordy description of the George Foster Peabody Collection at the University of Georgia. The David Haynes essay on the Helmut Gernsheim Collection at the University of Texas, Austin, is far more definitive and useful. This chapter is a shorter version of his 1969 master's thesis. For nearly twenty years, Gernsheim and his wife sought out early photographs, apparatus, and books to preserve them. Their search paid off as the Gernsheims were eventually able to acquire the oldest extant photograph, the 1826 picture of Nicéphore Niepce's courtyard and thousands of other antique materials. Their collection also contained a large number of early, parlor devices of a nonprojection and projection type, along with cameras and translucent materials intended to create movement on a screen. The Haynes chapter contains an inventory of these items.

Volume 3 in the Performing Arts series contains an update on the holdings of the Cinema Collection at the University of Southern California, referenced in that section of this Appendix.

Available in 1980, Bonnie Rowan's *The Scholars Guide to Washington, D.C., Film and Video Collections*, published by the Smithsonian Institution Press, attempts to describe important manuscript, photographic, audio, and moving image collections of the Washington area which claims to have the most important media archives in the Western Hemisphere.

RESEARCH COLLECTION: GENERAL

Center for Research Libraries
5721 South Cottage Grove Avenue
Chicago, Illinois 60637
312-955-4545

The Center for Research Libraries is operated by member institutions for the purpose of increasing research resources for the entire membership. Organized in 1949, the center is now an international organization with over 165 members and has a collection of more than three million volumes of research matter. Unlike interlibrary loans, the center has no primary local constituency having first priority over the material. Requests for loans are typically handled in a rapid manner. An inventory to the center's holdings is contained in their printed catalogue. With respect to mass communication, the medium of film, and animation in particular, the Center for Research Libraries is an untapped reservoir. For example: the center has retained annual reports of corporations whose stock has sold on the Midwest Stock Exchange since 1935; member institutions may request the center to provide a loan copy of *any* foreign dissertation available; long runs of over 100 newspapers published in the United States are readily available; trade journals such as *Variety* and other specialized journals are retained in the center's archives; a sample collection of magazines and comic books is maintained (the accumulation is not systematic but formed by purchasing a selection of current issues at twice yearly intervals from a Chicago wholesale distributor). Other materials include foreign language newspapers, government documents, and other serials and monographs routinely acquired by the center. Individuals must submit their requests through their member institutions.

A general description of center holdings is contained in *Handbook: The Center for Research Libraries, 1978.* An eight volume catalogue is available at the member institutions.

Bibliography

Adams, William and Schreibman, Fay, eds. *Television Network News: Issues in Content Research.* Washington, D.C.: School of Public and International Affairs, George Washington University, 1978.

Archives of American Art. *Arts in America: A Bibliography*. Edited by Bernard
    Karpel. Washington, D.C.: Smithsonian Institution and Archives of American
    Art, 1980.
Ash, Lee, comp. *Subject Collections*. 4th ed. New York: R. R. Bowker, 1974.
*Aspen Handbook on the Media: 1977-79 Edition; A Selective Guide to Research,
    Organizations and Publications in Communications*. New York: Praeger
    Special Publications, 1977.
Behlmer, Rudy. "A Guide to Researching Hollywood's Past." *Los Angeles Times*,
    8 August 1976, *Calendar*, p. 30.
Bureau, June D. *Nonprint Materials on Communication: An Annotated Directory of
    Select Films, Videotapes, Videocassettes, Simulations and Games*. Metuchen,
    N.J.: Scarecrow Press, 1976.
Center for Research Libraries. *Handbook: The Center for Research Libraries*,
    1978. Chicago, Ill.: Center for Research Libraries, 1978.
Directory of Business Archives in the U.S. Chicago: Society of American Archivists.
    Business Archives Committee. 1980.
Educational Film Library Association. *Film Resource Centers in New York City*.
    New York: Educational Film Library Association, 1976.
*Educational Film Locator of the Consortium of University Film Centers and R. R.
    Bowker Company*. New York: R. R. Bowker, 1978.
Kone, Grace Ann. *8mm Film Directory, 1969-70*. New York: Educational Film
    Library Association, 1969.
Library Trends. 27:1 (Summer 1978). Issue devoted to films in public libraries.
Limbacher, James L. *A Reference Guide to Audiovisual Information*. New York:
    R. R. Bowker, 1972.
Link, Tom. "Saving What We've Seen." *Emmy* 2:1. (Winter 1980): 39. Description
    of major TV archives: Academy of Television Arts and Sciences/UCLA Televi-
    sion Archive; Museum of Broadcasting, New York City, Robert Saudek, direc-
    tor; Library of Congress.
Mehr, Linda, ed. and comp. *Motion Pictures, Television and Radio: A Union
    Catalogue of Manuscript and Special Collections in the Western United States*.
    Boston: G. K. Hall, 1977.
National Information Center for Educational Media. *Index to 16mm Educational
    Films*. 2d ed. New York: R. R. Bowker, 1969.
Perry, Ted, ed. *Performing Arts Resources*. Vols. 1, 2. New York: Drama Book
    Specialists, 1974, 1975. Worth MacDougald and J. E. Fletcher write about the
    uncertain status of the George F. Peabody Collection of film at the University of
    Georgia, promising a long-awaited inventory. Richard Dyer MacCann's essay
    on reference works for film and David Haynes's informative essay on the Gern-
    sheim Collection at the University of Texas, Austin, are worth reading.
————. *Performing Arts Resources*. Vol. 3. New York: Drama Book Specialists,
    1976. Of interest to experimentalists is the Stephen Kovacs's bibliography on
    surrealism in film. For traditional animators, there is an update on the cinema
    collections at the University of Southern California.
Raskin, Judith. "L. A. Photography Collections: Our Best-Kept Secret." *Los
    Angeles Times*, 21 December 1975.
Rowan, Bonnie. *The Scholars Guide to Washington, D.C., Film and Video Collec-
    tions*. Washington, D.C.: Smithsonian Institution, 1980.

Sharples, Win. "Symposium on Film Archives." *Journal of the University Film Association* 29 (Fall 1977): 49-57. General descriptions of holdings in major U.S. film archives.

Turan, Kenneth. "Movie Madness: The Fine Art of Archive Programming." *Washington Post*, 29 May 1977. About the three major archives in the U.S. that continue to offer archival film programs to the public: Museum of Modern Art, Pacific Film Archive (Berkeley) and the American Film Institute, East.

University Film Study Center. *1978 Guide to Film and Video Resources in New England*. Cambridge, Mass.: University Film Study Center, 1978.

Waldron, Gloria. *The Information Film*. New York: Columbia University Press, 1949.

Weber, Olga S. *North American Film and Video Directory: A Guide to Media Collections and Services*. New York: R. R. Bowker, 1976.

Whalon, Marion K. *Performing Arts Research: A Guide to Information Sources*. Detroit: Gale Research, 1976.

Young, Margaret Labash, et al. *Subject Directory of Special Libraries and Information Centers*. Vols. 2 and 4. Detroit: Gale Research, 1975.

Young, William C. *American Theatrical Arts: Guide to Manuscripts and Special Collections in the United States and Canada*. Chicago: American Library Association, 1971.

Zane, Bobi. "Movies To Go: Places Where You Can Rent or Borrow Films to Show at Home for Your Family and Friends." *Los Angeles Times*, 26 June 1979, *Calendar*, p. 2. Convenient listing of various Los Angeles libraries and rental agencies that have animation and other films.

RESEARCH COLLECTIONS: EAST

WASHINGTON, D.C.

Motion Picture, Broadcasting, and Recorded Sound Division
The Library of Congress
Washington, D.C. 20540
202-287-5840

The Library of Congress, the National Archives, and the American Film Institute collections constitute the largest film resources in the United States at the same location.

The *Library of Congress Catalogue: Films and Other Materials for Projection* is a useful guide to titles issued quarterly and in an annual cumulation. The Card Division of the Library of Congress issues a semiannual *Catalogue of Copyright Entries: Motion Pictures and Filmstrips* with additional volumes bringing together copyrighted films from 1894 to 1969. But there is no single list of film holdings in the library except for the card catalogue. The card catalogue lists over 75,000 films individually along with technical information and relevant copyright data. Over 10,000 television programs are also catalogued and housed in this section of the library.

A letter or telephone request can quickly determine if a given title is available for viewing in the library: 8:30 A.M. to 4:30 P.M., Monday through Friday.

The Louise Ernst Collection has several animated films which were a part of the Hearst-Vitagraph News Pictorial series, produced by International Film Service in 1916. Viewing prints are available for many in the following list.

Cooks vs. Chefs: The Phable of Olaf and Louis. 4 min. Animated by Raoul Barré
Feet is Feet: A Phable. 4 min. Animated by Raoul Barré
The Joys Elope. 4 min. Unknown animator
Krazy Kat and Ignatz Mouse Discuss the Letter G. 3 min. Animated by Frank Moser
Krazy Kat and Ignatz Mouse In a Tale That Is Knot. 4 min. Animated by Bert Green
Krazy Kat and Ignatz Mouse in Their One Act Tragedy, The Tale of the Nude Tail. 4 min.
Animated by Leon Searl
Krazy Kat, Bugologist. 5 min. Animated by Frank Moser
Krazy Kat Goes A-Wooing. 3 min. Animated by Leon Searl
Krazy Kat, Invalid. 3 min. Animated by Leon Searl
Krazy Kat to the Rescue. 3 min. Animated by William C. Nolan
Mr. Nobody Holme in He Buys a Jitney. 2 min. Animated by Leon Searl
Never Again! The Story of a Speeder Cop. 3 min. Animated by Raoul Barré
A Newlywed Phable. 2 min. Animated by Raoul Barré
Old Dock Gloom in He Orders Gentle Exercise. 2 min. Animated by Frank Moser
Parcel Post Pete's Nightmare. 3 min. Animated by Frank Moser
The Phable of a Busted Romance. 3 min. Animated by Raoul Barré
The Phable of the Phat Woman. 3 min. Animated by Raoul Barré
'Twas But a Dream. 2 min. Animated by Raoul Barré

Others in the Ernst Collection include:

Bonzo. 12 min. Created by George Ernest Studdy. Released in the U.S. in 1924. New Era
Films, Ltd., England.
Colonel Heeza Liar, Hobo. 3 min. Animated by J. R. Bray.

The Fleming-Moore Collection and Dunston Collection contain these early
animations.

Fleming-Moore:

Kidnapped. 9 min. Van Beuren Corp., 1929. Animated by Paul Terry
A Lad and His Lamp. 8 min. Van Beuren Corp., 1929. Animated by Paul Terry

Dunston:

Untitled from the series *Colonel Heeza Liar.* 5 min. 1923. Bray Productions
Untitled "Farmer Al Falfa" cartoon. 7 min. 192? Animated by Paul Terry
Felix in Chinatown. 11 min. 192? Animated by Otto Messmer (Pat Sullivan)
Goodrich Dirt Sleeps and Spot Goes Romeo-ing. 8 min. 1916. Bray Productions
Iceland. 9 min. 1928. Animated by Paul Terry
The Jail Break. 11 min. 192? Animated by Otto Messmer (Pat Sullivan)
Judge Rummy Goes to a Dance. International Film Service, 192?
Krazy Kat In Love's Labor Lost. 10 min. 1920. International Film Service
Westward Whoa!! 9 min. 1926. Animated by H. C. Fischer

Many major studios are represented in the copyright deposit holdings after 1943
including animated cartoon makers such as Warner Brothers, Metro-Goldwyn-
Mayer and Paramount. About 5,000 shorts and features are in the holdings seized
from the Germans and Japanese during World War II with some containing
propaganda animation.

The earliest materials were received by the library before 1895 but the collection grew as filmmakers deposited positive photographs on paper of their films. The paper prints survived longer than the original nitrate films and up to 1912 were the only legal means of registering a copyright, given the statutes at the time. These prints were rephotographed on motion picture film after 1948, resulting in a revived and projectable collection of the earliest film work available to U.S. audiences for the period 1894 to 1912. Known as the "Paper Print Collection," these 3,000 short films contain numerous examples of trick effects such as stop-action, dissolves, and mattes as the early film struggles to find its form. This paper print collection, 1894-1912, describes the few surviving animated films and, moreover, a number of other films using stop-action and other trick effects. In tandem with Niver's book, *The First Twenty Years: A Segment of Film History*, the paper-print digest is a critically important tool for access to the library's collection.

The library also has a large and growing collection of television programs forming a substantial basis for the American television and radio archives, mandated by the 1976 copyright act.

Bibliography

Jones, Clayton. "Library of Congress: Serious, But Not Solemn." *Christian Science Monitor*, 5 December 1978, p. B12.

Kuiper, John B. "Opportunities for Film Study at the Library of Congress." *Film Library Quarterly* 1:1 (Winter 1967-68): 30-32.

Niver, Kemp R. *The First Twenty Years: A Segment of Film History*. Los Angeles: Artisan Press, 1968. Especially important resource for a review of selected short films in the Library of Congress paper print collection, which were restored by Niver and his staff. A number of films incorporating special or trick effects are illustrated and described.

———. *Motion Pictures from the Library of Congress Paper Print Collection, 1894-1912*. Berkeley: University of California Press, 1967.

"Profile: Library of Congress." *AFI Education News* 2:4. (March-April 1979).

U.S., Library of Congress. *Library of Congress Catalogue: Films and Other Materials for Projection*. Washington, D.C.: Library of Congress, 1973-1975. (with supplements).

U.S., Library of Congress. *Motion Pictures, 1894-1959*. 4 vols. Washington, D.C.: Library of Congress, 1951-1960.

U.S., Library of Congress. *National Union Catalogue, 1953-1957*. Ann Arbor, Mich.: J. W. Edwards, 1958. Vol. 28, *Motion Pictures and Film Strips*.

U.S., Library of Congress. *National Union Catalogue, 1963-1967, Motion Pictures and Film Strips*. 2 vols. Ann Arbor, Mich.: J. W. Edwards, 1969.

The American Film Institute
Kennedy Center for the Performing Arts
Washington, D.C. 20566
202-828-4080

The American Film Institute deposits its holdings, numbering about 14,000 in 1977, in the Library of Congress. The institute was established in June 1967 to preserve the heritage and advance the art of film and television in the United States. Major programs include the location and preservation of films, financial aid to film-makers, the publication of film books, periodicals, and reference works, and the support of basic research in film.

While there is no central listing of all films in the Library of Congress collection, the American Film Institute (AFI) has published the *Catalog of Holdings: The American Film Institute Collection and the United Artists Collection at the Library of Congress*. This is a provisional inventory of the 14,124 films acquisitioned into the American Film Institute Collection and the United Artists Collection at the Library of Congress. Films are listed alphabetically by title, with date, director, producer, and one cast member included for identification purposes. Titles have been coded to define category (feature, short, serial, or trailer), what films have been copied onto acetate from the nitrate originals, and total footage counts. If a film is available to researchers, a reference copy is required. Inquire by letter to the AFI even if the catalogue does not indicate a reference copy exists since printing priorities are sometimes changed.

Animated films accessioned into the AFI collection include examples of the Hearst-Vitagraph *Phables*, early Disney films such as the 1922 *Puss In Boots*, the Herald Film Corporation's animated version of Charlie Chaplin, several *Mutt and Jeff* World War I training films, early 1920s popular song parodies (similar to song slides a decade earlier), and examples of the experimental work of Oskar Fischinger.

The institute also publishes, through its National Education Services Program, a bimonthly newsletter, *AFI Education News*, containing letters, publication announcements, course syllabi in film and television, calendar data, occasional job announcements, and profiles of research centers and archives.

Bibliography

American Film Institute, *Catalog of Holdings: The American Film Institute Collection and the United Artists Collection at the Library of Congress*. Washington, D.C.: American Film Institute, 1978.

Karr, Kathleen. "Early Animation: The Movement Begins." In *Impressions from the American Film Institute Archives*, edited by Kathleen Karr. Washington, D.C.: Acropolis Books, 1972.

Microfilming Corporation of America. *The American Film Institute/Louis B. Mayer Oral History Collection, Part 1*, n.d. Includes list of oral-history interviews conducted under the auspices of AFI.

Archives of American Art
National Collection of Fine Arts
Smithsonian Institution
Washington, D.C. 20560

The Archives of American Art collects various materials about artists including letters, taped interviews, exhibition catalogues, journals, sketchbooks, business papers, photographs, and miscellaneous ephemera now totaling in excess of seven million items. In 1970 the organization became a department of the Smithsonian. While the entire collection is retained in Washington, and open only to scholars and other researchers, the holdings are also available on microfilm in regional centers in Detroit, New York, San Francisco, Boston, and Houston.

In another part of the Smithsonian, the National Collection of Fine Arts has some limited interest in animation as indicated by the deposit of a manuscript by Judith O'Sullivan on Winsor McCay while she was a Fellow there in the early 1970s.

Bibliography

Increase and Diffusion: A Brief Introduction to the Smithsonian Institution, *1975.*

Lewis, Jo Ann. *"Tidbits of Treasure. Notes and Pawn Stubs From the Art Archives." Washington Post*, 9 November 1979, p. F1. Description of the facilities and a general comment about the holdings.

McQuaid, James; Tait, David; and Lewis, Steven. "Oral History Material on Photography," *Image* 18:2 (June 1975): 1-12. A list of collections of oral history materials dealing with photography. Archives of American Art has a few materials.

Stall, Bill. "Wide Purpose: Smithsonian: U.S. Attic and Much More." *Los Angeles Times*, 28 January 1980, p. I1. Detailed profile of this scientific research organization, one of the most popular tourist attractions in the United States.

Motion Picture and Sound Recording Branch
Audiovisual Archives Division
General Services Administration
National Archives and Records Service
Washington, D.C. 20408

The National Archives hold United States government-produced films in a collection exceeding forty million feet. All photographic and paper holdings in the National Archives are organized under more than four hundred record groups representing several hundred past and present United States government agencies.

The Motion Picture and Sound Recording Branch of the Audiovisual Archives holds over 105,000 reels of film dating from 1894 to the present, including newsreels, documentaries, training films, and outtakes to those productions. An additional number of audio and video recordings or speeches, press conferences, network TV news broadcasts, and other programs date from 1900 to the present. The card catalogue and lists of selected films and reference papers are the key finding aids for using this collection. With prior arrangements, groups may view motion pictures in the National Archives theater. While the film holdings are not available for loan, government films currently in circulation may be rented or purchased from the National Audiovisual Center, Washington, D.C. 20409.

The branch also maintains and makes available for research video copies of the nightly network TV newscasts. Additional data on these and other collections are contained in the article by Fay C. Schreibman cited in the Bibliography for this section.

An inquiry for this section produced leads to three record groups (RG) on *Private Snafu* cartoons (RG 111) and Walt Disney films such as *New Spirit* and *Der Fuehrer's Face* (RG 56 and 306). Reservations are required for use of viewing machines and prints of animated subjects are available at moderate costs. Occasionally, preliminary inventories are available for public distribution, but often researchers will have to await their arrival at the National Archives in order to use in-house inventories.

A critically important introduction to the archives holdings and organizational scheme is contained in *Guide to the National Archives of the United States*. For example, perusal of this guide produced leads to records of the Office of Inter-American Affairs (RG 229) and paper and film materials involving this agency, which contracted with Walt Disney Productions and others to produce animated and live-action training and propaganda films during World War II. The records of the Committee on Fair Employment Practices (RG 228) and the National Labor Relations Board decisions have developed leads to papers dealing with the Walt Disney Production labor strife which occurred in the early 1940s. The guide lists each record group and provides an administrative history of the agency or agencies involved, with major divisions indicated for the entire record group along with a chronology and amount estimate by linear feet. Often, a preliminary inventory exists and copies may be available by mail. Potential users would benefit by requesting "Select List of Publications of the National Archives and Records Service." This free guide gives the available preliminary inventories and costs, along with inventory lists and other information about the presidential libraries, the National Audiovisual Center, and the office of the National Archives.

In 1963 the Ford Motor Company presented to the National Archives 1.5 million feet of historical motion picture film along with money to transfer aging nitrate stock to safety film and to compile a guide to the collection. In Record Group 200, the Ford collection is one of the few corporate collections ever established involving the use of film for public relations, advertising, documentary, and instructional purposes. It began in 1914 with the *Ford Animated Weekly*, a newsreel distributed free to theaters. Mayfield Bray's *Guide to the Ford Film Collection in the National Archives* identifies some animated films such as the *Liberty Loan* other patriotic cartoons and gives examples of newsreel animations such as the *Pathe News* lampooning of Ford's "Jitney Submarine."

Bibliography

Bauer, K. Jack, comp. "Special Lists. Number 14. List of World War I Signal Corps Films." Washington, D.C.: National Archives and Records Service, 1957.

Bray, Mayfield. *Guide to the Ford Film Collection in the National Archives.* Washington, D.C.: National Archives, 1970. Of some limited use in locating a few pieces of animation in this collection from the first industrial film unit in the United States. *Liberty Loan* and patriotic cartoons, comedy cartoons, a Bray cartoon (*The Lunch Detective*) and a newsreel cartoon (*Pathe News*) lampooning Ford's "Jitney Submarine" are in the collection.

_____ and Murphy, William T. "Audiovisual Records in the National Archives." Washington, D.C.: National Archives, 1971.

_____. "Audiovisual Records in the National Archives Relating to World War II." Mimeographed. Washington, D.C.: National Archives, 1972.

_____. "Motion Pictures in the Audiovisual Archives Division of the National Archives, 1972.

Murphy, William T. "Film at The National Archives: A Reference Article." *Film and History* 2:3 (1972): 7-13.

National Archives and Records Service. "Audiovisual Archives Division." (Brochure.) Explains the audiovisual division within the National Archives and Records Service.

———. *Guide to the National Archives of the United States.* Washington, D.C.: Government Printing Office, 1974.

Schreibman, Fay C. "Television News Archives: A Guide to Major Collections." In William Adams, et al., eds., *Television Network News: Issues in Content Research.* Washington, D.C.: School of Public and International Affairs, 1978.

PRINCETON, N.J.

Curator
William Seymour Theater Collection
Princeton University Library
Princeton, New Jersey 08540

The Princeton University library, in 1979, received the business records of the Warner Brothers Corporation, including scanty information dealing with the animation unit. At that time computer-generated inventories made by the Warner organization were just becoming available. The Warner Brothers records are divided between Princeton University and the Cinema Collection at the University of Southern California.

Not much is known about the scope or content of the Warner Brothers business records acquired by Princeton University. Apparently, the New York offices donated business materials to Princeton and creative materials such as scripts, animation art, and production memoranda went to the University of Southern California. Each university repository was furnished a computerized inventory which had a subject list and locator. The extent of the Princeton collection is unknown, but materials at the University of Southern California have been described in the dimensions of 3,000 or more boxes. Warner's research library, used for various authentication purposes in set design, script development, and historical recreations, was donated to the Burbank Public Library several years ago. Researchers will have to communicate directly with the respective curators at Princeton and the University of Southern California for further information.

NEW YORK CITY

Film Department
Museum of Modern Art
11 West 53rd Street
New York, New York 10019
212-956-4212

The Film Department of the Museum of Modern Art has retained about 250 animated films of which less than half are from the silent period. There are also special materials such as scripts, sketches, production information, and business papers as in the Paul Terry, Isadore Klein, or Hans Richter collections. Documentation also includes several hundred scripts and dialogue continuities, reference volumes, a seven-year collection of *Vitagraph Bulletins* (1909-1916), Edison Company scripts, and Cinema 16 program notes indexed and donated by Amos Vogel. For years, the department's best-known collections were the papers of D. W. Griffith, the Merritt Crawford archives, and about 8,000 films acquired for artistic and film-history value.

As in many other film research centers, there are also still-photo collections and voluminous clip files some of which involve animation subjects. Film Study Center facilities are available for conducting research upon advance notice.

The Museum of Modern Art has carried on an extensive publication program including the *Bulletin*. Back-runs of this important record of articles and catalogues are now available from Arno Press together with a new index by Cornelia Corson. This particular feature should be used for the early issues of the *Bulletin* since the *Art Index* did not systematically report all citations.

Unlike many archives, the Film Department has made about 10 percent of its film collection available outside its walls in the form of circulating programs available at nominal rates. Many animations and experimental films using animation and computer-graphics are available in the circulating program. Catalogues are available upon request.

Bibliography

Perry, Ted, et al. "The Museum of Modern Art Department of Film." *Quarterly Review of Film Studies* 4:1 (Winter 1979): 103-6. Description of the facility and holdings as of 1978.

"Profile: Museum of Modern Art." *AFI Education News* 2:5 (May-June 1979).

Van Dyke, Willard. "The Museum of Modern Art Film Department: From Archive to Study Center." *Sightlines* 7:3 (1973-1974): 4-6.

_____. "The Role of the Museum of Modern Art in Motion Pictures." *Film Library Quarterly* 1:1 (Winter 1967-1968): 36-38.

Anthology Film Archives
80 Wooster Street
New York, New York 10012

The experimental and avant-garde film and video media are preserved in New York's Anthology Film Archives established in 1970. The archives has the most complete collection of American independent cinema anywhere, exceeding 1,000 titles. Among the special features of this program are the repertory screenings of many of the films in the collection. Screenings for special groups in the afternoons can be arranged for a nominal fee. Apart from the repertory collection, there are about 750 films, 200 videotapes, and nearly 700 audiotapes of lectures and interviews available for research.

A research library, consisting of several hundred reference volumes, unpublished notes and writings on American avant-garde film, and a detailed card catalog cross-referencing subjects of periodicals and books in the library is open to researchers by appointment.

Anthology Film Archives publishes *Film Culture*, an important film journal in the art of American film, as funds permit, and usually on a quarterly basis. P. Adams Sitney's *The Essential Cinema* is the best guide to the archive collections, history, and activities. His volume contains essays about films in the collection and an extensive bibliography of books and articles on films in the collection along with a distributor list.

Bibliography

"Anthology Film Archives." *Filmmakers Newsletter* 4:4 (February 1971): 12-18. Description of the facilities and philosophy of Anthology Film Archives. "As a polemical group the selection committee of Anthology Film Archives has affirmed consistently that the art of cinema surfaces primarily when it divests itself of commercial norms" (p. 12).

Melton, Hollis, ed. "A Guide to Independent Film and Video." *Film Culture*, no. 62 (1976). In a special issue published by Anthology Film Archives, Melton organizes information of vital use to independent filmmakers, including animators. The guide embraces video as well as film concerns and, while now dated, is still a useful compilation of valuable information on film study, distribution, exhibition concerns, and funding.

"Profile: Anthology Film Archives." *AFI Education News* 2:1 (September-October 1978).

Sitney, P. Adams, ed. *Essential Cinema: Essays on the Films in the Collection of Anthology Film Archives.* Vol. 1. New York: Anthology Film Archives and New York University Press, 1975.

Curator, Theater Collection
New York Public Library at Lincoln Center
111 Amsterdam Avenue
New York, New York 10023
212-799-2200

The New York Public Library houses a large collection of materials in American theater of which a small part is comprised of animation subjects. Holdings include press books, posters, and clipping files. The George Kleine and Robinson Locke collections contain hundreds of papers related to early American film and personalities. Since 1928 the library has collected press books from the major film companies and over one million stills.

The catalogue of the Theater and Drama Collection provides an alphabetical listing by person and subject. The category "Cinema: Animated Cartoons" lists materials on characters, artists, plot synopses of early animations, photographs, periodical articles, and catalogues.

Bibliography

Mitgan, Herbert. "Library Cataloguing 10 Million Cards." *New York Times*, 1 January 1980, p. 11.

New York Public Library. *Catalog of the Theater and Drama Collections.* Part 2: Theater Collection: Books on the Theater. 9 vols. Boston: G. K. Hall, 1967.
_____. *Catalog of the Theater and Drama Collections.* Part 3: Nonbook Collection. Boston: G. K. Hall, 1976.

New York Public Library. "The Theater Collection." (Brochure.)

Television Information Office
National Association of Broadcasters
745 Fifth Avenue
New York, New York 10022
212-759-6800

Established in 1959 as a public relations and information arm of the television industry in the United States, the Television Information Office (TIO) provides a continuing information service to broadcast and related industries, government agencies, the press, educators, librarians, and the general public. The most visible information service has probably been the Roper national surveys underwritten by TIO, which assess public attitudes toward television and other mass media. Other publications have included bibliographies, statistical studies, and teachers' guides. The library has the most direct relevance for animation. About 200 periodicals are received regularly and all volumes published in fields related to broadcasting are collected. Moreover, the library maintains a large clipping file containing more than 100,000 items.

American Federation of the Arts Film Program
41 East 65th Street
New York, New York 10021
212-988-7700

The American Federation of the Arts is a nonprofit cultural service organization which assembles and circulates film programs and art exhibitions throughout the United States. Package and individual films, many including new forms of animation by young artists, are available through the federation project which operates in tandem with the Whitney Museum of American Art Film Department, New York. In animation, the package of *Unreal Time* consists of thirty-three works by independent animators such as Will Vinton, Bob Gardiner, Carmon D'Avino, Kathleen Laughlin, Buffy Holton, John H. Whitney, Frank and Caroline Mouris, Mary Beams, Jules Engel, George Griffin, and Robert Breer. *New American Filmmakers* is a cooperative distribution plan operated through the Whitney Museum and provides 240 films, including dozens of offerings by Adam K. Beckett, Scott Bartlett, Jordan Belson, Tom Dewitt, George Dunnin, Victor Faccinto, Oskar Fischinger, Larry Jordan, Susan Pitt Kraning, Caroline Leaf, Robert Mitchell, Dale Case, Eliot Noyes, Jr., Lillian Schwartz, Robert Russett, Pat O'Neill, Steve Segal, Harry Smith, and James A. Whitney. Another package, *A History of the American Avant-Garde Cinema*, consists of thirty-eight films by twenty-eight artists who produced their works in the period 1943 to 1972.

The creation of these circulating programs came from the Whitney Museum's exhibition of independent film in New York City in the early 1970s. The exhibitions were designed to present the work of independent filmmakers in programs running for at least one week with several showings each day. The New American Filmmakers Series, as the program is called, became another important outlet for avantgarde, narrative, documentary, and animation films in New York City. Unlike Anthology Film Archives, Film Forum, and other exhibitions, the film programs circulate at the Whitney Museum to libraries, museums, and academic institutions around the world.

Bibliography

Aronson, Steven. "The American Federation of Arts Film Service." *Sightlines* 17:3 (1973-1974): 19-20.
Gross, Linda. " 'Encounter' with Experimental Cinema." *Los Angeles Times*, 2 October 1979, p. V12.

New York Historical Society
170 Central Park West
New York, New York 10024

The New York Historical Society specializes in American history with over 600,000 volumes, many about New York. At the time Max Fleischer's animation studio operated in New York, monthly copies of his in-house mimeographed newspaper, the *Animated News*, were deposited with the society. The accumulated run embraces the period December 1934 through April 1937 with only a few issues missing. By 1939 Dave and Max Fleischer had moved their studio to Miami, Florida. The *Animated News* is described in detail in Appendix 7 and is available on microfilm from the society.

Museum of Broadcasting
1 East 53rd Street
New York, New York 10022
212-752-4690

The Museum of Broadcasting is dedicated to the study and preservation of radio and television programming by accumulating, cataloging, cross-referencing, and transferring to videotape about 1,200 broadcast programs each year. Opened in 1976, the museum experienced the pressure of over 100,000 visitors by mid-1980 who were eager to select radio or TV programs for viewing at one of sixty consoles or to attend special video screenings in the new 63-seat theater. Many of the television programs are selected from the first five years of network broadcasting, beginning in 1948.

A subject guide organizes the 2,800 radio and television programs available in early 1979. Animation subjects include the 50-year retrospective on Walt Disney, the Dr. Seuss animated films on "Omnibus," the two "Star Trek" programs, "The Making of Star Wars," several editions of "Monty Python's Flying Circus," and selections from the Apollo 11 TV coverage that utilized animation.

Bibliography

"A Booming Business in Yesterday." *Broadcasting* 29 (January 1979): 57.

Museum of Broadcasting. *Subject Guide to the Radio and Television Collection of the Museum of Broadcasting.* 2d ed. New York: Museum of Broadcasting, 1979.

Shepard, Richard F. "Tune in Soon for Best of Yesteryear." *New York Times,* 22 July 1979, p. 33.

Sloan, Gwen. "The Museum of Broadcasting." *Sightlines* 11:2 (Winter 1977-1978): 13-14.

Smith, Cecil. "Saudek Is Capturing History of TV, Radio." *Los Angeles Times,* 3 April 1980, p. VII.

NEW YORK STATE

Museum of Cartoon Art
Comly Avenue
Port Chester, New York 10573
914-939-0234

Established in 1974, the Museum of Cartoon Art is a collector of original cartoon artwork but also provides film programs in a small theater upon request or reservation. The public foundation grew out of a need to collect and display an American art form largely ignored by other museums. Memberships and book lists are available to interested persons. Their film holdings include works of John Bray, Winsor McCay, Pat Sullivan, Paul Terry, Walt Disney, Ub Iwerks, Max and Dave Fleischer, Tex Avery, Chuck Jones, Fritz Freleng, and Bob Clampett. An antipollution film animated by Walt Kelly and his wife Selby entitled *We Have Met the Enemy and He Is Us* and a selection of animated TV commercials are included in the film list.

Bibliography

Swan, Christopher. "What Ever Happened to Dick Tracy." *Christian Science Monitor*, 19 June 1979, p. B6.

Senior Librarian
New York State Library
Manuscripts and Special Collections Division
Albany, New York 12234

In all, there are some seventy thousand scripts of all films reviewed by the defunct New York State Board of Censors in this repository. When the board operated, they used scripts to help evaluate films proposed for exhibition in the state. When abolished, board files went to the New York State Library, including the scripts which are filed by title. The collection spans 1915 to 1964. While the files are open for research, the senior librarian has advised that photocopies cannot be made without written permission (addressed to the library) from the copyright owner of the particular film. Potential users should submit a list of prospective titles, including shorts, to the library at least two weeks prior to a visit. An inventory is currently being established.

Director
International Museum of Photography
Eastman House
900 East Avenue
Rochester, New York 14607
716-271-3361

The International Museum of Photography at the George Eastman House is among the earliest formed and privately endowed archives in the United States. Public exhibitions are a regular part of their research and acquisition activities. *Image*, a journal on the history of technology and art in photography and film, is published quarterly by the museum. Memberships to the museum are are also available. These provide discounts on photographic books, free lectures and museum admissions, and access to the museum archives. The film collection numbers about 5,500 titles with a distinct emphasis on silent films from various countries and American silent and sound films. Animation is a very small part of the Eastman collection.

Bibliography

Card, James. "The Historical Motion-Picture Collections at George Eastman House." In R. E. Fielding, ed., *A Technological History of Motion Pictures and Television.* Berkeley: University of California Press, 1967, pp. 105-8. Describes the reasons and historical background for the George Eastman House, Rochester, New York.

Littell, Alan. " 'Photo City,' N.Y. Puts Its Art and Technology on Display." *New York Times*, 30 March 1980, p. 3. Discussion of photography attractions in Rochester, New York, including Eastman Kodak and the International Museum of Photography.

Manuscripts Librarian
George Arents Research Library
Syracuse University
Syracuse, New York 13210

At Syracuse University in the George Arents Research Library are two important collections related to animation. Arthur Brisbane, employed by William Randolph Hearst for thirty-nine years, has some of his personal papers there, including numerous scrapbooks of various works, along with the cartoons by Winsor McCay, a close associate from 1913-1934. While the register in the library does not reveal any correspondence with or about McCay, a close search has resulted in at least two letters about this cartoonist and filmmaker.

The Arents Research Library is also the repository for the papers and work of Isadore Klein. There are some restrictions on use of the collection, but the materials span the period 1926 through 1947, including cartoon and political illustrations. Klein worked on the animated versions of *Mutt and Jeff, Krazy Kat* and other films, including work for Hal Segler Productions and Screen Gems.

RESEARCH COLLECTIONS: MID-AMERICA

Vanderbilt Television News Archive
Joint University Libraries
Nashville, Tennessee 37203
615-322-2927

As the amount of animation in news coverage has increased since 1970, the Vanderbilt archive is another important contemporary resource for traditional cel and computer-generated images in support of public affairs programming. Numerous examples using these and other techniques are telecast daily, including satellite stop-action photography, the continuing story of interplanetary space exploration, explanations of complex processes such as nuclear reactors, and computerized axial tomography showing new views of the human body and other objects.

Since 1968 Vanderbilt University has been video recording the evening newscasts of the three major commercial television networks. The entire collection has been indexed and annotated. Since January 1972 the indexes and annotations have been published each month and are now available on an annual subscripton basis with microfilms of back files available. Each monthly index contains listings of personalities and categories cross-referenced to a complete abstract of each telecast. The abstracts provide additional information about the news story, keyed to beginning and ending times.

The indexes are designed to be used in tandem with the actual video recordings, which now carry identifications on the video portions of the tapes at ten-second intervals. The videotapes may be borrowed from the archive or may be compiled from several broadcasts if, for example, one wanted to study how the interplanetary exploration story had been told in animation over a period of time. Audio-only tapes are also available. Information about charges for all services is available from the archive.

A regional center for the Vanderbilt archive is located at George Washington University Library, Audiovisual Department, 2130 H Street, N.W., Washington, D.C. 20052.

Bibliography

"Profile: Vanderbilt Television News Archive." *AFI Education Newsletter* 2:3 (January-February 1979).

Schreibman, Fay C. "Television News Archives: A Guide to Major Collections." In William Adams, et al. eds., *Television Network News: Issues in Content Research*. Washington, D.C.: School of Public and International Affairs, 1978. William C. Adams opens the volume with a bibliographic essay on network news research. Lawrence W. Lichty and George A. Bailey reflect upon various problems and issues in "reading the wind" or content analyzing images.

Trotsky, Judith. "The Networks Try to Keep History on the Shelf." *Wall Street Journal*, 7 March 1980, p. 17. Discusses the news archive operations of the three TV networks and the massive task of preserving and cataloguing the enormous annual collection of outtakes and final TV news reports.

Archivist
Mass Communication History Center
Wisconsin Center for Film and Theater Research
State Historical Society of Wisconsin
816 State Street
Madison, Wisconsin 53706
608-262-9706

The major research collection of films and print materials in animation between the East and West coasts is housed in the State Historical Society of Wisconsin. While no films circulate, researchers can have a visual feast on about 500 animated subjects from the Warner Brothers and United Artists collections, including characters such as Daffy Duck, Bugs Bunny, Porky Pig, Elmer Fudd, and Popeye. Inventories listing release dates, call numbers, titles, and special classifications such as war, minorities in cartoons, and gangster themes are available at the center or, for a nominal fee, through the mail. As part of the several thousand features, television print, and short-subject collections, the center has a good selection of early work of Tex Avery, Bob Clampett, Robert McKimson, Chuck Jones, Fritz Freleng, Paul

Smith, Ben Hardaway, Cal Dalton, Frank Tashlin, Jack King, Ben Clopton, Sandy Walker, and Ub Iwerks. Of the some 1,200 cartoons produced for Warner Brothers released from 1929 to 1962, the center has 300 titles including a large sample of *Looney Tunes* and the *Merrie Melodies* series. The Paramount holdings include 200 Popeye titles form 1933 to 1957.

Additional materials in the broadcasting, film, and theater holdings include scripts, continuities, press books and photographs, some of which pertain to the animated films. The corporate papers of United Artists from 1919 to 1951, which formed the basis of Tino Balio's *United Artists: The Company Built by the Stars*, contain materials about Walt Disney's distribution relationships with the company in the early 1930s. As a part of the United Artists collection, records and dialogues related to the Warner Brothers films and shorts are also open for research.

A feature film list, catalogue to the collections in the state historical society, and other information on access are available through the archivist.

Curator
American Archives of the Factual Film
Iowa State University Library
Ames, Iowa 50011
515-294-6672

A few hundred miles to the west of Madison is a growing collection of documentary, instructional, and animated film called the American Archives of the Factual Film (AAFF). Established at the library of Iowa State University, the AAFF had its beginning in the gift of Ott Coelln, a founder of the Industrial Audio-Visual Association and, for thirty or more years, editor and publisher of *Business Screen*. The goals of the archive are to gather, process, index, and publicize all aspects of the factual film. By January 1980, the film collection had grown to over 2,200 titles with contributions from Exxon Company, Byron Friend, Pioneer Hi-Bred International, Encyclopaedia Britannica, American Telephone and Telegraph, American Airlines, and many other companies and individuals with active careers in the nontheatrical film world. A computer index is still under development, and plans include a more definitive content analysis of the wide variety of subjects already represented in the collection, including techniques used, such as animation and special effects. The earliest film containing animation in the collection appears to be *Peevish Pete the Pipe Peddler*, made in the mid-1920s for the American Cast Iron Pipe Company (Birmingham). The film is actually live-action combined with animated sequences.

AAFF is also eager to review potential donations in the form of films and papers documenting the evolution of the nontheatrical film.

RESEARCH COLLECTIONS: WEST

The major archives and libraries for animation study on the West Coast include the Theater Arts and Film-Television Collections at the University of California (Los Angeles), the Charles K. Feldman Library at the American Film Institute Center for Advanced Studies, the Walt Disney Archives, the Margaret Herrick Library at the Academy of Motion Picture Arts and Sciences, and the cinema collection at the University of Southern California.

Theater Arts Library
405 Hilgard Avenue
University of California
Los Angeles, California 90024
213-825-4880

Curator
UCLA Film and Television Archive
Department of Theater Arts
University of California
Los Angeles, California 90024
213-825-4142

The Theater Arts Library and Film Archives, UCLA, have long been known by film scholars as among the most significant collections of papers, scripts, and films described in *Motion Pictures: A Catalogue of Books, Periodicals, Screenplays and Production Stills* which reports on materials collected through March 1976. For animation graphics, a continuity outline for the Disney short on Paul Bunyan continuities and shooting scripts from the period 1937-1939. A book of MGM animation graphics, a continuity outline for the Disney short on Paul Bunyon (1957), and some UPA (Magoo) TV scripts by True Boardman are also in the collection.

The most recent addition in animation to the Theater Arts Library has been the Walter Lantz collection consisting of drawings, scripts, clippings, layouts, and music scores. The preliminary inventory lists fifty-one archive boxes consisting of TV commercials and sponsored film continuities, story sketches (many of which are xeroxed), numerous original sketches, stills, and negatives.

Also at UCLA, in the Department of Special Collections, University Research Library, are some oral history transcripts by animators including Tex Avery, Dave Fleischer, Fritz Freleng, and Richard Heumer. The research library also has a small collection of animated pictures based on early parlor toys common to the Zoetrope and Phantascope devices. These are described in more detail in the Linda Mehr guide, *Motion Pictures, Television and Radio*, cited at the beginning of this appendix.

The UCLA film and Television Archives is an entity distinct from the Theater Arts Library. The archives are a part of the Department of Theater Arts. About 17,000 film and TV titles are stored on campus. In the last four years, the exact number and titles of animation and other film and TV holdings have been in an uncertain status due to the absence of an updated catalogue of holdings, often promised in various published newspaper and journal articles, but not available upon specific inquiry.

Trade reports in the last two years indicate that some Hanna-Barbera cartoons were donated along with 3,000 TV commercials. George Pal's personal 35mm nitrate collection of animation of unknown scope and content was stored in this archive for several years, but with his recent death (April 1980) there has not been a formal resolution concerning the final deposit of his work. Correspondence and telephone calls directed to the UCLA Film Archives on these questions remain unanswered.

Bibliography

"ATAS/UCLA Library Collects 13,000 Titles." *Backstage*, 25 August 1978.

Malkin, Audree, ed. *Motion Pictures: A Catalog of Books, Periodicals, Screenplays, Television Scripts and Production Stills.* 2d rev. ed. Boston: G. K. Hall, 1976.

Margulies, Lee. "Preserving Video Images for Posterity." *Los Angeles Times*, 25 August 1978, p. IV 1.

"Old TV Shows Don't Die, They Go To UCLA." *Variety,* 19 March 1978.

Tuchman, Mitch. "Douglas Edwards: Guardian of the Avant-Garde Film." *Los Angeles Times*, 2 October 1979, p. V 112. Review of UCLA exhibition program under superivision of Douglas Edwards.

Ward, Alex. "Where the Best of TV Is Being Preserved." *New York Times*, 11 March 1979, p. D 33.

Professional, Technical and Clerical Employees
Union Local 986
Education and Training Trust Fund
15300 Ventura Boulevard, Suite 401
Sherman Oaks, California 91403

The Animated Film Study Collection is directly administered by the Professional, Technical, and Clerical Employees Union Local 986. The collection is made up of more than one hundred examples of animation from around the world. The list, as of mid-1979, included the titles shown in Table 1.

Table 1 ANIMATED FILM STUDY COLLECTION

TITLE	ANIMATOR	FORMAT
"A"	Jan Lenica	16mm
Ab Ovo	Ante Zaninovic	35mm
Acceleration	Pavel Prochazka	16mm
Ad Aspera Ed Astra	. . .	35mm
African Daze (*The Lion Hunt*)	. . .	16mm
Apel	Ryszard Czekata	16mm
Après le silence	Les Goldman	16mm
Bajka	Ryszard Kuziemski	35mm
Between Lips and Glass	Dragutin Vunak	35mm
Billiards	Paul Campani	35mm
The Box	Fred Wolf	16mm
The Boxes	Pavoa Stalter	35mm
The Boy and the Moon	Jannik Hastrup	35mm
Breath	Jimmy Murakami	16mm
Cages	. . .	35mm
Canon	Norman McLaren	16mm
The Cat Concerto	William Hanna and Joe Barbera	16mm
Cat Meets Mouse	Manny Davis	16mm
The Charge of the Light Brigade	Richard Williams	16mm
Claude	Dan McLaughlin	16mm

Table 1 (continued)

TITLE	ANIMATOR	FORMAT
Cognosco Ergo Sum	Marcel Jankovics	35mm
Commercials from Storyboard Plus	Various animators	16mm
Configuration	Reber Laszlo	35mm
Contre-pied	Manuel Otero	16mm
Corticella	. . .	35mm
Crazy World	Yoji Kuri	16mm
Creators and Creations	Jozsef Nepp	35mm
The Critic	Ernest Pintoff	16mm
Crunch Crunch	Carlos Marchiori	16mm
Dialogue	Boris Kolar	35mm
The Diamond	Paul Grimault	35mm
Dr. Gibaud	Paul Campani	35mm
Dr. Vogelbird	Jiri Brdecka	16mm
Donald's Tire Trouble	Dick Lundy	16mm
The Dot and the Line	Chuck Jones and Maurice Noble	16mm
Dreams on Wings	Marcell Jankovich	16mm
Duo	Norman McLaren	35mm
Eggs	John Hubley	16mm
Elverskud	Jannik Hastrup	35mm
Ember and Globus	Macskassy Varnai	35mm
Ember es meg egy ember	Szoboszloy Pete	35mm
Fantasy City	Tatsuo Shimamura	16mm
Felix in Fairyland	Otto Messmer	16mm
Fiddle-De-Dee	Norman McLaren	16mm
Figlarna nutka	L. Lorek	35mm
Gerald McBoing Boing	Robert Cannon	16mm
A Gonsolat	Kouagnai Gyorgy	35mm
The Great Toy Robbery	Jeffrey Hale	16mm
The Great Walled City of Xan, Terra Incognita	Hal Barwood	16mm
Grizzly Golfer	John Hubley	35mm
Gulliver's Travels	Dave Fleischer	16mm
Hangman	Paul Julian and Les Goldman	16mm
Happy End	. . .	35mm
The Hoffnung Symphony Orchestra	Harold Whitaker	16mm
The Hole	John Hubley	35mm
Human Folly	C. Iscrulescu	35mm
I'm Cold	Tex Avery	16mm
Impressio	Seppo Suo-Antilla	16mm
The Insects	Jimmy Murakami	16mm

Table 1 (continued)

TITLE	ANIMATOR	FORMAT
Is It Always Right to be Right	Lee Mishkin	16mm
Joe and Petunia	Nicholas Spargo	35mm
Kidnapped	Paul Terry	16mm
K-9000 A Space Oddity	Robert Mitchell and Robert Swarthe	16mm
Keep Cool	Barrie Nelson	16mm
Kouzelnik	Pavel Hobl and T. Renc	35mm
Krazy Kat & #1	Leon Searl	16mm
Krazy Kat & Ignatz Mouse Discuss the Letter G	Frank Moser	16mm
Krazy Kat & Ignatz Mouse: He Made Me Love Him	. . .	16mm
Labyrinth	Jan Lenica	16mm
The Letter	D. Szczechura	35mm
The Little Island	Richard Williams	16mm
The Little Orphan	William Hanna and Joe Barbera	16mm
Love Me, Love Me, Love Me	Richard Wiliams	16mm
Madeline	Robert Cannon	16mm
Mama's New Hat	Milt Gross	16mm
Man Alive—Part One	William T. Hurtz	16mm
Man's Pest Friend	Seymour Kneitel and George Hill	16mm
Miss Kemeko	Yoji Kuri	16mm
The Mitten	R. Kachanov	35mm
Moonbird	John Hubley	16mm
Mouse Trouble	William Hanna and Joe Barbera	16mm
Nursery Crimes	Al Geiss	16mm
Of Men and Demons	John Hubley and Faith Hubley	16mm
The Old Man and the Flower	Ernest Pintoff	35mm
Op Hop	. . .	35mm
Paladina	Emanuele Luzzati	16mm
Pas de deux	Norman McLaren	16mm
Peace on Earth	Hugh Harman	16mm
Pin Feathers	Walter Lantz and Bill Nolan	16mm
The Playful Pest	Paul Sommer	16mm
Plenty Below Zero	Bob Wikersham	16mm
Portraits	Mirostaw Kyowicz	35mm
The Prayer	R. Guozdanovic	35mm

Table 1 (continued)

TITLE	ANIMATOR	FORMAT
Puss Gets the Boot	William Hanna and Joe Barbera	16mm
The Question	John Halas	16mm
Quiet Please	William Hanna and Joe Barbera	16mm
The Reclining Act	Zlatko Pavlinic	35mm
Recuerdos de madrid	Dean Spille	. . .
Red and Black	Witold Giersz	. . .
Rhapsody	Robert Bruce Rogers	. . .
Rooty Toot Toot	John Hubley	35mm
Rope Trick	Bob Godfrey	16mm
Round Trip in Modern Art	Robert Bruce Rogers	16mm
The Saints	Bent Barford	16mm
A Scout with the Gout	Bill Tytla	16mm
A Self-made Mongrel	. . .	16mm
A Sense of Responsibility	. . .	35mm
The Shooting of Dan Magoo	Tex Avery	16mm
Sirene	Raoul Servais	16mm
Sisyphus	Aleksandar Marks and Vladimir Jutrisa	16mm
A Struggle	. . .	35mm
Summertime	Ub Iwerks	16mm
Super Lulu	Bill Tytla	16mm
Syncopated Sioux	. . .	16mm
The Tell-tale Heart	Ted Parmelee	35mm
The Thieving Magpie	Emanuele Luzzati and Giulio Gianini	16mm
Time of Vampires	. . .	16mm
Tow Low	. . .	16mm
The Tuba	Ante Zaninovic	35mm
Two Grilled Fish	Yoji Kuri	16mm
The Two Mouseketeers	William Hanna and Joe Barbera	16mm
The Unicorn in the Garden	Wiliam T. Hurtz	16mm
The Violinist	Ernest Pintoff	35mm
Walking	Ryan Larkin	16mm
What a Life	Ub Iwerks	16mm
What's Buzzin' Buzzard	Tex Avery	16mm
When Magoo Flew	Pete Burness	16mm
Why Do You Smile, Mona Lisa?	Jiri Brdecka	. . .
Why Not	Marija Miletic	16mm

Table 1 (continued)

TITLE	ANIMATOR	FORMAT
Windy Day	John Hubley and Faith Hubley	16mm
Winsor McCay	Winsor McCay	16mm
Yankee Doodle Mouse	William Hanna and Joe Barbera	16mm
Yellow Submarine	George Dunning	35mm
Zoopman	Bob Kurtz	16mm

As of mid-1979, the collection was stored in the UCLA Film and TV Archives. Inquiries should be addressed to the Union Local 986 for access to the collection.

Bibliography

Thompson, Richard. "Study Collection for Animated Students." *Magazine* 1:1 (January-February 1976): 3. About the ASIFA study collection.

Department of Special Collections
Doheny Library
University of Southern California
University Park
Los Angeles, California 90007
213-741-6058

The University of Southern California's Library and Special Collections houses thousands of cinema books and over one hundred manuscript collections. The materials are generally described in *Primary Cinema Resources* by Christopher D. Wheaton and Richard B. Jewell. They have also updated their report in *Performing Arts Resources, Volume 3* by listing taped interviews with film professionals, collected at USC since 1961, and by describing in more detail additional collections in the cinema holdings. Interviews of interest to animation researchers are those with Al Brodax (*Yellow Submarine*), Les Goldman, William Hansard (front projection), and Chuck Jones and Steve Krantz (*Fritz the Cat*). An MGM collection includes cartoon outlines, scripts, pencil sketches, and some musical scores. The Warner Brothers collection is in two parts. One is the massive amount of animation art and other materials accumulated on the West Coast over three decades. As described above, the surviving papers from the New York offices have been given to Princeton University. A common inventory, created by the donor, indicated only fragmentary information by names; mostly there are contracts in folders identified as "Bob Clampett," "Leon Schlesinger," or "Bob McKimson." There is some surviving animation art (cels) and backgrounds and dialogue transcripts. In the second part of the Warner Brothers collection are the papers of Jack Warner, now closed at the request of the family.

Motion picture and television-clip files are maintained in the cinema holdings of Special Collections broken down by name, production, and subject files. The production matter involves reviews and other data about specific films or programs. These vertical files contain a rich variety of animation material which would be difficult to locate anywhere else. However, similarly organized collections also exist in the Theater Arts Library at UCLA and the Margaret Herrick Library at the Academy of Motion Picture Arts and Sciences, and there was little duplication in the animation subjects searched during a 1978 visit.

Bibliography

Knutson, Robert. "USC Cinema Library Spans Years." *Magazine* 1:3 (May-June 1976): 1.
Wheaton, Christopher D. and Jewell, Richard B. *Primary Cinema Resources: An Index to Screenplays, Interviews and Special Collections at the University of Southern California*. Boston: G. K. Hall, 1975.

Archivist
Walt Disney Archives
500 South Buena Vista Street
Burbank, California 91521
213-845-3141

While the number of archives in American corporate environments has increased in the last three decades, the collections at the Walt Disney Archives remain unique. Organized in 1970, the archive was established to collect and preserve historical materials relating to all the Disney enterprises. Primary files deal with Disney, amusement parks, merchandising, publicity and promotion matter, publications of Disney enterprises and tape and disc recordings. Researchers will find most of the Disney correspondence from 1930 until his death in 1966, with a few files from the Laugh-O-Gram Studio in Kansas City in 1922. Access to many recent legal and business files is restricted. There is a small but growing collection of files on animation history generally with some correspondence from early animators. Other artists' and directors' files represented in the collection include Carl Barks, James Algar, Burton Gillett, David Hand, and Ben Sharpsteen. Long-range plans include building a study collection of Disney animation but at present videotaped versions of the *New Mickey Mouse Club* are available for use on the premises. The archives has actively sought and preserved dozens of pre-Mickey Mouse cartoons and these are retained in the Film Library at the Disney Studio. The book collections include virtually all Disney books published in the United States and a representative collection of foreign versions. Over 1,300 recordings published by the Disney Music Company are available. A complete collection of Disney comic books beginning in 1932, including a comprehensive collection of foreign editions, is stored in the archives. The photographic collection in the Still Camera Department numbers 500,000 with hundreds of still books on each Disney production and 8,000 additional pictures of Walt Disney. The art work extends from 1927 to the present and consists of hundreds of thousands of story sketches, cels, backgrounds, and pencil drawings. Motion picture promotional materials consisting of posters, press clippings, press releases, and press books are extensive.

Disney Productions has subscribed to a press-clipping service since 1924, and the resulting accumulation defies quantification. Screenplays and TV scripts are available for all productions, including identifications of all animators working in each sequence of a given film. The tape-recording collection consists of interviews with present and former Disney employees and includes the following interviews: Jim Algar, Bob Allen, Ken Anderson, Julie Andrews, Alfonso Arau, Art Babbitt, Buddy Baker, Welton Becket, Ruth Disney Beecher, Dale Beer, Ted Berman, Ken Berry, Don Bluth, Ray Bradbury, Ray Brewer, Roger Broggie, Jack Bruner, George Bruns, Jack Buckley, Michele Carey, Les Clark, Ron Clements, Larry Clemons, Eric Cleworth, Jim Coleman, Bob Cook, Mary Costa, Bill Cottrell, Jack Cutting, Hank Dains, Marc Davis, Martin Davis, Virginia Davis, Lou Debney, Al Dempster, Earl Disney, Edna Disney, Elias and Floru Disney, Lillian Disney, Roy O. Disney, Walt Disney, Agneta Eckemyr, Gabe Essoe, Joe Fowler, Andy Gaskill, Harper Goff, Floyd Gottfredson, Don Griffith, David Gwillim, Jack Hannah, David Hartman, Helen Hayes, John Hench, Dick Heumer, Winston Hibler, Bill Hoelscher, Dick Irvine, Ub Iwerks, Wilfred Jackson, Robert Jani, O. B. Johnston, Ollie Johnston, Dick Jones, Milt Kahl, N. Paul Kennworthy, Jr., Katherine Kerwin, Ward Kimball, Jack Kloepper, Angela Lansbury, Eric Larson, Rick Lenz, Gunther Lessing, Arnold Lindberg, Jack Lindquist, B. Llewellyn, Barbara Luddy, Sharon Disney Lund, Ham Luske, Eustace Lycett, Bob McCrea, Jim MacDonald, Vera Miles, Diane Disney Miller, Ron Miller, Elma Milotte, Nadine Missakian, Bob Moore, Paul Murry, Clarence Nash, Carl Nater, Grim Natwick, Cliff Nordberg, Richard A. Nunis, Ken O'Connor, Jack Olsen, Anthony G. O'Rourke, Dean Penlick, Walt Peregoy, Ken Peterson, Walt Pfeiffer, John Pomery, Dolly and Owen Pope, Stephanie Powers, Harrison A. Price, Frank Reilly, Woolie Reitherman, Wathel Rogers, Herb Ryman, Hank Schloss, Joe Sears, Dick Sebast, Ben Sharpsteen, Donald Sinden, Dave Smith, Paul Smith, Art Stevens, Robert Stevenson, Bill Sullivan, Frank Tashlin, Donn Tatus, Don Taylor, Herb Taylor, Frank Thomas, Ruthie Tompson, Grace Turner, Harry Tytle, Erwin Verity, Card Walker, Bill Walsh, Stuart Whitman, and Tommie Wilck.

Transcripts for many of these interviews are also available. Many of the Walt Disney recordings consist of anniversary tributes, speeches, press conferences, and radio programs including the shortlived "Mickey Mouse Theater of the Air," (1938). A separate listing identifies interviewers and their interviewees.

A growing videotape collection includes the fiftieth anniversary program, *The Art of Oskar Fischinger* and two parts of *Boys From Termite Terrace*, these three being from "Camera Three" as identified in Appendix 4.

While the vertical files are organized along general categories, archivist David Smith and his staff are able to retrieve materials that are normally not covered in general or specialized serial indexes. Two examples illustrate this point: Fleming, R. C. "The Saga of Michael Rodent," *Compressed Air Magazine* (July 1934); "Wiring the 'A' Frame at Walt Disney World," *Electrical Contractor* 37 (June 1972).

Public libraries in Anaheim, California, and Orlando, Florida, also collect Disney material such as books, press releases, operating manuals, newsletters, posters, press books, handbills, and other ephemera.

Bibliography

"Profile—Walt Disney Archives." *AFI Newsletter* 2:2 (November-December 1978).
Smith, David R. "Comics and Cels: The Walt Disney Archives." *California Historical Society Quarterly*, Fall 1977, pp. 270-74.
_____. "It All Started With a Mouse—The Walt Disney Archives." *California Librarian* 34 (January 1972): 23-28.
_____. "Walt Disney Productions Celebrates Its 50th Anniversary." *Manuscripts* 25 (Fall 1973): 254-60.
"Walt Disney Archives." Burbank, California: Walt Disney, 1978. (Brochure.)

Head Librarian
Margaret Herrick Library
Academy of Motion Picture Arts and Sciences
8949 Wilshire Boulevard
Beverly Hills, California 90212
213-278-4313

The Margaret Herrick Library has served the Academy of Motion Picture Arts and Sciences and the public since 1927.

Extensive still photo, script, production file, finding aids, and special collections identify the Herrick library as one unique among the film research archives. With respect to animation, the magazine index is an important finding aid not available anywhere else. Citations from the library's almost complete, hard-copy run of *Photoplay* form the core of the index, supplemented with International Federation of Film Archives card citations, and indexing of other periodicals by film titles, subjects, and personalities. Trade publications form another important foundation in the research collection, beginning with the 1906 issue of *Views and Film Index*, and include runs of *Variety, Moving Picture World, Motion Picture News, New York Dramatic* (after 1915), *Mirror*, and *Billboard*. A number of company journals are also available including *Essany, Kalem, Vitagraph, Edison, Universal* and *Eclair* as well as several professional and popular British periodicals. Many of the major studios or former employees have donated stills, scripts, and other materials. These are listed in the Linda Mehr guide, *Motion Pictures, Television and Radio*, described at the beginning of this appendix. Production files exist for more than 40,000 American and foreign films, each containing photos, clippings, press books, credit lists, and reviews. There is an indexing system for keeping track of title changes and announcements pertaining to the purchase of literary properties. Another set of general files embraces numerous categories such as the film industry in foreign countries, independent producers, guilds, unions, and associations.

Among the ninety items in the Sol Lesser collection of historical film apparatus is the Praxinoscope theater of M. Emile Reynaud who exhibited animations to Paris audiences as early as 1892. Lesser also collected the Muybridge animal locomotion machine and Georges Demeny's Phonoscope in addition to numerous other pieces of early equipment.

Of special interest to animation scholars and others identifying different versions of films are the unusual Technicolor continuity sheets. The library acquired

Technicolor's accumulation of over twenty years' worth of continuities. For each film using the Technicolor three-strip process, and for each version of the film, a continuity sheet listing scene, frame and footage counts, and the total footage would be prepared for the complex printing process. Table 2 illustrates one such sheet for the second continuity of a Walter Lantz cartoon entitled *Banquet Busters*, prepared on 20 October 1954.

Table 2 TECHNICOLOR CONTINUITY SHEET

BANQUET BUSTERS
Prod. No. 6004
Produced By WALTER LANTZ PRODUCTIONS
Released By UNIVERSAL INTERNATIONAL FILMS INCORPORATED

REEL 1   SECOND CUTTING   10-20-54

Beginning footage/frame	Ending footage/frame	Shot total in feet/frames	Shot number	Description of shot
		8-0	1	Head Leader
000	4-6	5-11	2	Academy Leader
4-7	11-15	7-9	3	Academy Leader
12-0	22-14	10-15	4	Title Woody Woodpecker-diss to
22-15	29-15	7-1	5	Title A Walter Lantz-diss to
30-0	40-14	10-15	6	Title Direction Dick Lundy-diss to
40-15	49-10	8-12	7	MT Banquet Busters FO
49-11	59-8	9-14	8	FI Skyscrapers and building-diss to
59-9	78-10	19-2	9	Thatched roof shop-sign "Music Makers"
78-11	114-7	35-13	10	CU Musical instruments-store-character
114-8	151-11	37-4	11	Character tears sign-Woody in can of beans
151-12	163-11	12-0	12	Newspaper-society page-"Dinner"
163-12	176-10	12-15	13	Woody and pals read paper-exit-wipe
176-11	179-3	2-9	14	LS Road to mansion-Woody and pals
179-4	182-10	3-7	15	Woody rings doorbell
182-11	203-2	20-8	16	Butler opens door-characters whiz by
203-3	206--11	3-9	17	ELS Orchestra
206-12	209-12	3-1	18	Hall-band-characters
209-13	214-15	5-3	19	Character blowing horn
215-0	220-15	6-0	20	Woody playing flute
221-0	226-8	5-9	21	Small character playing bass
226-9	241-3	14-11	22	Butler carries in roast pig
241-4	260-11	19-8	23	Woody smells roast pig
260-12	280-10	19-15	24	Woody gets on butler's head-eats pig/dishes
280-11	321-15	41-5	25	MS Woody running around on table set with/
322-0	326-8	4-9	26	MS Woody on top candle // through air

SOURCE: Technicolor continuity volumes, Margaret Herrick Library. © *Walter Lantz* 1954. Reprinted by permission of Walter Lantz Productions, Inc.

Table 2 (continued)

Beginning footage/ frame	Ending footage/ frame	Shot total in feet/ frames	Shot number	Description of shot
326-9	341-0	14-8	27	MCU Woody eats large piece of cheese
341-1	378-4	37-4	28	CU Woody plays violin-snatches turkey
378-5	392-12	14-8	29	MS Woody on chair pulls turkey and butler //
392-13	408-6	15-10	30	MS Table covered with food-hands
408-7	427-12	19-6	31	CU Butler to MCU-Woody by food covered table
427-13	447-2	19-6	32	MCU Fat woman and cake
447-3	450-2	3-0	33	CU Butler
450-3	460-12	10-10	34	MCU Fat woman throws cake at butler
460-13	464-0	3-4	35	MCU Woody on chair
464-1	469-2	5-2	36	MS Butler throws axe at Woody
469-3	478-2	9-0	37	MS Woody on chair blows bugle
478-3	479-14	1-12	38	MS Butler-bugle flies through room /it
479-15	490-2	10-4	39	MCU Cat sits in front of catsup bottle throws/
490-3	500-2	10-0	40	MCU Butler ducks behind chair-bottle thru air
500-3	505-2	5-0	41	MS Woody on table throws pies
505-3	512-2	7-0	42	CU Pig lights cigar-pig hits face
512-3	513-10	1-8	43	MS Various sized pigs
513-11	525-10	12-0	44	MS Parrot with violin on stool
525-11	527-2	1-8	45	MS Various sized pies
527-3	532-2	5-0	46	MS Pig and others dodging pies
532-3	544-1	11-15	47	MS-CU Butler by phone-answers it-Wipe
544-2	560-10	16-9	48	MCU Group by table-butler in with gun
560-11	572-15	12-5	49	MCU Cat and parrot eating turkey-cat exits
573-0	575-3	2-4	50	CU Butler with gun /Iris out
575-4	590-7	15-4	51	MS-LS Group runs away-gets hit with turkey-/
590-8	596-8	6-1	52	Title-The End
		3-0	53	Clear Leader
		0-8	54	Chart
		7-8	55	Tail Leader
		616-13		TOTAL FOOTAGE

Note: Kindly void First Cutting Continuities dated 12-12-47, Prod. #3645
7118

The continuity sheets are accumulated chronologically and are filed according to the official release date of each film.

As a part of the academy's extension program to the industry and general public, the National Film Information Service stands ready to respond to specific research questions, providing photocopies of reviews or rare articles if appropriate. Other services include advice for film programming, stills duplication, research guides, program notes, touring exhibits, and distribution of a documentary about the Academy of Motion Picture Arts and Sciences. Contact the coordinator at the Academy address given above or by phone (213-278-8990).

Bibliography

Academy of Motion Picture Arts and Sciences. *Annual Index to Motion Picture Credits*. Westport, Conn.: Greenwood Press, 1978-. This reference work is essentially for live-action films. No TV or film credits are included unless the film is exhibited theatrically in the Los Angeles area.

Schreger, Charles. "Film Clips. The Movie Industry Know-It-All." *Los Angeles Times*, 13 August 1979, p. IV6. Description of the Academy of Motion Picture Arts and Sciences "Annual Index to Motion Pictures" series.

_____. "Film Clips. Who's Who—Or Wants To Be." *Los Angeles Times*, 6 June 1979, p. IV14. Describes the Motion Picture Academy of Arts and Sciences Screen Credits series.

Slide, Anthony. "The Academy of Motion Picture Arts and Sciences." *Films in Review* 27:5 (May 1976): 289.

Librarian
Louis B. Mayer Library
American Film Institute
2021 North Western Avenue
Los Angeles, California 90068
213-278-8777

The Charles K. Feldman Library in the American Film Institute Center for Advanced Film Studies (or AFI, West) was established to serve needs of the fellows, faculty and staff of the center. Resources of the library are also available on a noncirculating basis to visiting scholars and all members of the film and television industries.

The Feldman Library has the Max Fleischer collection of patents in animation and motion picture apparatus, 1917-1942. A copy of the Joe Adamson UCLA-AFI Oral History interview with Dave Fleischer, now presumably opened to the public, is also available. Among the some 2,000 film and television scripts in the library's holdings are about fifty MGM animation scripts.

AFI has jointly sponsored with industry, or conducted on its own, a number of conferences since 1967. One which merits the attention of serious scholars and librarians involved in media print and nonprint materials is the annual Film/TV Documentation Workshop held each summer. In a six-day period, participants receive an intensive short course in print and nonprint acquisitions, film publications, reference sources, research materials, cataloguing procedures, radio-TV organizations and in addition take field trips to major archives in the area. Past conferences included visits to Walt Disney Archives, USC Cinema Collection, UCLA Theaters Arts Library, Margaret Herrick Library in the Academy of Motion Picture Arts and Sciences building, UCLA Television Archives, and the RKO Archives. The workshop is directed by Charles K. Feldman Librarian Anne G. Schlosser who is assisted by the AFI staff and a number of faculty from academia and industry. Attendees are advised to bring along an empty, moderately sized, suitcase to bring back the handouts, flyers, and brochures distributed at the workshop.

RKO Radio Pictures Corporate Archives
129 North Vermont Avenue
Los Angeles, California 90004
213-383-5525

The working corporate archives of RKO Radio Pictures have been opened to scholars, but any potential resources for animation are probably limited to paperwork involving Walt Disney Productions and RKO distribution deals.

Art and Music Department
Los Angeles Public Library
630 West Fifth Street
Los Angeles, California 90071
213-626-7555

The Los Angeles Public Library, Art and Music Department, has an extensive list of books on animation subjects and is a subscriber to the Newsbank *Film and Television Arts* service. The library also clips the *Los Angeles Times* and has a subject file.

Industrial Technology Department
Los Angeles County Museum of Natural History
900 Esposition Boulevard
Los Angeles, California 90007
213-746-0410

The museum's technology collection is best known for a large assortment of early film projectors, cameras, and catalogues for such antique-quality equipment. The collection also contains some early Disney equipment and art. There is a Willis O'Brien scrapbook containing stills depicting his stop-motion special effects in a number of 1930s films including *King Kong* (1933). Complete runs of difficult-to-locate professional journals such as the *SMPTE Journal* or *International Photographer*, and directories, patents, and some correspondence from Thomas Edison, Thomas Armat and others are also available. Special arrangements must be made to use these artifacts.

Curator
Pacific Film Archive
University Art Museum
University of California, Berkeley
Berkeley, California 94720
415-642-1437

The Pacific Film Archive at University Art Museum, University of California, Berkeley, is among the three archives in the United States that have regular exhibitions. The other two are the Museum of Modern Art Film Library, New York, N.Y., and the American Film Institute, Washington, D.C. About 1,500 films are booked into the nearly 200-seat theater each year. Some of these come from the 6,000-film collection of the archive which strongly emphasizes Asian films. In animation, about 270 films in the collection represent the work of Oskar Fischinger, Moholy-Nagy, John Whitney, Robert Breer, Lillian Schwartz, Ken Knowlton, Jules Engle, Pat

O'Neill, Jordan Belson, the Fleischers, early Disney, George Dunning, Milos Macourek, I. Norstein, R. Kachanov, Walerian Borowczyk, Yoji Kuri, Bela Ternovszky, Zlatko Grgic, Bruno Bozzetto, Guido Manuli, Michel Mills, Fred Wolf, Hugh Foulds, Robert Mitchell, Dale Case, Kaj Pindal, Mitchell Rose, Jeff Hale, Bill Melendez, and Len Lye.

Scholars with an identified research need are most welcome to use the facilities and resources of the Pacific Film Archive. There is a 1,500-volume library, a small screening room, and 16mm and 35mm flatbed editing tables.

Bibliography

Artel, Linda J. "The Pacific Film Archive Film/Media Center." *Sightlines* 7:3 (1973-1974): 17.

McBride, Stewart. "The Ultimate Movie Theater." *Christian Science Monthly*, 25 March 1980, p. B15.

Schreger, Charles. "Film Clips. It's Movies As Usual At Archives." *Los Angeles Times*, 22 October 1979, p. IV10.

Sources for Collectible Animation Art

REPRODUCTIONS

Adams, Richard. *Watership Down Film Picture Book*. New York: Macmillan, 1975.

The Film Book of the Lord of the Rings. New York: Ballantine Books, 1979.

Griffin, George. *Frames: A Selection of Drawings and Statements by Independent American Animators*. New York: George Griffin, 1979.

The Hobbit. New York: Harry N. Abrams, 1977.

McLaren, Norman. *The Drawings of Norman McLaren*. Montreal: Tundra Books, 1975.

Sumner, Lloyd. *Computer Art and Human Response*. Charlottesville, Va.: Paul B. Victorius, 1968.

Taylor, Deems. *Fantasia*. New York: Simon and Schuster, 1940.

Tolkien, J. R. R. *The Hobbit or There and Back Again*. New York: Ballantine Books, 1978.

Walt Disney's Snow White and the Seven Dwarfs. New York: Viking Press, 1979.

The Watership Down Film Picture Book. New York: Macmillan, 1979.

Wilk, Max. *Yellow Submarine: This Voyage Chartered by Max Wilk*. New York: Signet Books, 1968.

ORIGINAL WORK

While animation studios had been selling their art since the late 1930s, the establishment of formal agencies buying, displaying, and selling these products rarely existed outside of New York or Los Angeles. In the 1970s, coupled with the nostalgia phase in American popular culture, museums and "showcase" organizations having collected such art advertised more widely to a growing collectors' market. A number of these, located away from New York or Los Angeles, offer a wide range of original comic and animation art. Some art is signed and emphasizes main or supporting characters in a strip or cartoon. Animation drawings or cels may be signed; often they are not. Frequently the cels are trimmed and framed. Animation drawings, which form the basis for the cel by tracing, are usually done in pencil on bond paper with peg holes and drawing numbers. Other materials are also frequently traded, collected, or sold: such as, concept drawings, layouts, publicity materials, model sheets, and storyboards.

Museum Graphics, Box 743, Costa Mesa, California 92627, (714) 540-0808, was formed in 1971, based on a hobby in collecting comic and animation art of Jerome K. Muller. He has created a traveling show in animation art entitled *The Moving Image*, containing examples of one hundred works beginning with Winsor McCay's *Gertie the Dinosaur*. Catalogues and cost estimates for the show are available, along with *The Moving Image* presentation upon request. In 1979 Museum Graphics became the agent for Bakshi Productions, Inc., in selling their animation art. An informative brochure on the museum and sales lists are available by writing Mr. Muller.

Gallery Lanzberg, 417 Guaranty Building, Cedar Rapids, Iowa 52401, (319) 363-6136, opened in 1975. The Gallery Lanzberg Catalogue, available at nominal cost, contains biographies of each animator, followed by a current listing of individual offerings, some illustrated. Past offerings include characters from Disney films, Betty Boop, Warner Brothers animated characters, and many others. Prices begin as low as $35 for some items; most are $90 and up. Edith Rudman directed the gallery in 1979.

Russ Cochran, Post Office Box 437, West Plains, Missouri 65775, (417) 256-9400, publishes *Graphic Gallery* and other sales lists on an irregular basis. *Gallery* is an illustrated catalogue of original comic and animation art for sale by Cochran. Issue Number 8 was devoted to Ferdinand Huszti Horvath, who worked as an idea man and model-creator for Walt Disney. At the outbreak of World War II, he joined North American Aviation and later worked in a technical capacity on designs for the Howard Hughes organization. Cochran established Horvath's credentials, using documentary evidence including notes from Horvath's notebooks in the estate papers. Such "finds" as the Horvath materials simply occur by remaining on the *Graphic Gallery* mailing list.

Elvena M. Green operates "One-Of-A-Kind" Cartoon Art, 775 Livingston Place, Decatur, Georgia 30030 and will forward the current brochure listing animation art from such producers as Bakshi Productions, Disney, Hanna-Barbera, Chuck Jones, Walter Lantz, and Bill Melendez. Telephone: (404) 377-3333.

Another way of maintaining contact with the collector and trader circuit is through numerous fanzines and other publications. Bud Plant, Post Office Box 1886, Grass Valley, California 95945, issues catalogues and "quick lists" quarterly. These announce the availability of fanzine or journal back issues, frequently with a brief abstract of contents, and a variety of portfolios, animation and comic art catalogues, ephemera, posters, and books.

Sources of Films and Videotapes about Animation

16MM FILM SOURCES OF ANIMATION SUBJECTS

INTRODUCTION

This Appendix is presented in two major sections, films and videotapes. Within each section are listed appropriate references for updating the lists or for a more specific title search.

REFERENCES TO 16MM FILMS

Canemaker, John. "Informational Films About Animation and Animators." *Millimeter* 6:2 (February 1978): 88. A long list of films plus other vital information concerning future sources of films and videotapes about animators and animation. Some addresses, such as the sources for Canemaker films, have changed and updates are included below.

Educational Film Locator of the Consortium of University Film Centers and R. R. Bowker Company. New York: R. R. Bowker, 1978. The first union list of film titles held by member institutions representing about 200,000 film holdings and a consolidation and standardization of about fifty catalogues. About 37,000 individual films are listed with multiple sources for their availability. For animation interests, this catalogue will lead the users to more titles often considered unavailable simply because of the absence of a list such as this.

Laybourne, Kit. *The Animation Book.* New York: Crown, 1979. Chapter 21 (in Part 4: Resources) contains a list of recommended films about animation, followed by a useful list of films representing different animation techniques such as cameraless animation, object, cutout, silhouette, stop-action (time-lapse), pixilation, kinestasis, collage, glass painting, clay, puppet, line, cel and other techniques. Names of distributors of animation films are at the end of this chapter.

Limbacher, James L. *Feature Films on 8mm and 16mm.* 5th ed. New York: R. R. Bowker, 1977. While limited to features, this is a useful guide to films available for rental or sale. There is a director's index. Check *Sightlines* for quarterly updates; see Appendix 7.

Nicem Index to 16mm Education Films. Los Angeles: National Information Center for Educational Media, University of Southern California, 1977. Four-volume guide to 16mm films listing rental sources for hard-to-find subjects.

"The Reference Shelf." *Sightlines* 7:3 (1973-1974): 2. Contains lists for locating experimental and avant-garde films, reviews of independently produced films, and numerous references for film programmers in search of animation subjects.

Rehrauer, George. *The Short Film.* New York: Macmillan Information, 1975. A compact, useful guide to film selection by the director of audiovisual services at Rutgers University. Given Rehrauer's estimates of nearly 100,000 short films released annually, the task of reviewing a mere 500 recommended films is of some challenge. His survey starts with films that have already been recommended often. His chief resources for the recommended list of 500 were thirty-six books and periodicals and in the opening pages he explains how he utilized these resources. The format of the "top 500" includes the title, release date, producer-distributor, length, hue, suggested audiences, form (animation, films without words), the annotation, and identification of the sources recommending the film. A subject listing, with titles, is included at the end of the volume.

Speer, Rick; Kovacs, Bill; and Ruth, Kovacs, comps. "An International Guide To Computer Animated Films." Mimeographed. Seattle, Washington, 98111: Animation Research, Post Office Box 2651, 1979. This fifty-one-page booklet brings together the small but growing number of computer-animated films available from research institutions, filmmakers, and commercial distributors, using four major divisions. The first is an alphabetical list, by title, with annotations. Filmmakers are then listed with their works, followed by a subject breakdown, and a concluding address list of sources. A number of the films are available free or at nominal rates; others may be purchased.

ANIMATION SUBJECTS ON 16MM

Alexeieff at the Pinboard. English-language version of Alexandre Alexeieff's work involving thousands of pins implanted into a board, giving the illusion of depth and distance, then animated.

8 min., b/w   Cecile Starr

Animated Cartoons: The Toy That Grew Up. Contains demonstrations of early animating devices such as Emile Reynaud's Praxinoscope Theater, W. G. Horner's Zoetrope, and J. A. F. Plateau's device. Develops the prehistory of moving pictures for animation and realism.

17 min., b/w   Indiana University
                                                  Film Images, Radim Films, Inc.

Animation: A Living Art Form. Based on the 1971 animated feature *Shinbone Alley* this film reviews the process of animating a feature, including script to storyboard evolutions, photography, sound recording, editing, and the composite print.

10 min., color   See Educational Film Locator

Animation Goes to School. Describes the Horace Mann project in which high school students produced animated films for teaching and creative art.

15 min., color   Contemporary-McGraw-Hill
                                   Educational Film Locator

Animation Pie. Students create an animated film and the final product is shown. Various techniques are demonstrated such as flip books, pixilation, cel, clay, and object animation.

27 min., color   B. Bloomberg
                                   Educational Film Locator

The Art of Lotte Reiniger. Stills, excerpts from her cutout silhouette films, and live-action descriptions by Lotte Reiniger are used to review her work since 1919. Excerpts are from: *Parapegno, The Adventures of Prince Achmed,* and *The Star of Bethlehem.*

16 min., color   Macmillan Films
                                   Audio Brandon Films

The Artist and the Computer. Computer animation artist Lillian Schwartz demonstrates her computerized animation along with excerpts from nine of her films.

10 min., color   Lilyan Productions

Bass on Titles. Saul Bass explains his approach to developing film titles, corporation logos, and product designs. Some of his earlier film titles are included in the film, such as *Man with the Golden Arm, A Walk on the Wild Side, Around the World in 80 Days,* and *West Side Story.*

32 min., color   Pyramid Films

Behind the Scenes of the Walt Disney Studios. Adapted from Disney's *The Reluctant Dragon* (1941), the process of Disney character animation is shown, including the rarely seen "Baby Weems" storyboard sequence. Overall, many details in the animation procedures are omitted and some errors were permitted to remain in the films, such as the depicted studio session recording sound to picture.

26 min., color   Walt Disney

                                   Twyman Films
                                   Educational Film Locator

Behind the Scenes at the Walt Disney Studio with the Reluctant Dragon. A 72-minute version including Robert Benchley's tour of the 1940 Disney studio and the animated featurette, *The Reluctant Dragon.*

72 min., color   Audio Brandon Films
                                   Educational Film Locator

Biography of the Motion Picture Camera. Continuing from *Animated Cartoons: The Toy That Grew Up,* this film shows the early studies of Etienne-Jules Marey and a recreation of Eadweard Muybridge's experiments. Thomas Edison's Kinetoscope is depicted along with Cinematographe created by the Lumière brothers.

21 min., b/w   Film Images
                                                  Educational Film Locator

Claymation. Documentary on the process of animating in clay with Will Vinton.

17 min., color   Billy Budd Films, Inc.

Click Click—Creating Animated Films in the Classroom. Depicts the steps in making animated films in the classroom including the use of clay, cutouts, and flip books.

13 min., color   USC Film Distribution
                                                  Educational Film Locator

Color Commercials. A selection of Alexandre Alexeieff's advertising films using techniques from cutout animation to object manipulation.

8 min., color   Cecile Starr

Computer Animation. About the role and function of computers with examples of animation from analog and digital hardware. Kinescope.

30 min., color   See Educational Film Locator
                                                  University of California, Berkeley

Computer Generation. CBS-TV "Camera Three" documentary depicting Stan Vanderbeek making computer films at the Massachusetts Institute of Technology and using a video synthesizer at WGBH-TV. Three films included in the program: *Symmetricks, Poemfield No. 8* and *Videospace.*

29 min., color and b/w   Film-makers' Cooperative

Computer Sketchpad. Depicts a new program that enables an individual to communicate with the machine by drawing sketches on an oscilliscope. Examples shown in the use of the machine to develop flow charts; other applications described including animation.

29 min., b/w   See Educational Film Locator

The Creative Person—Richard Williams. Produced by National Educational Television in 1968, the film shows a typical day in the Williams studio. Excerpts from his works *The Little Island* and *Love Me, Love Me, Love Me* are shown.

30 min., b/w   Association Films, Inc.
                                                  NET-Indiana University

Cubism. Explains the development of cubism from Cezanne to the work of Picasso. An important film for the connection of cubism to the experimental film, some of which involve animation.

21 min., color   International Film Bureau

Dada. About the beginnings of this movement in modern art, featuring interviews with Max Ernst, Hans Richter, Marcel Duchamp, and others who also made experimental animated films. Rationale for the movement is discussed.

31 min., b/w   International Film Bureau

Date with Dizzy. Several John Hubley techniques are illustrated in this light satire on the TV commercial.

10 min., b/w	Audio Brandon Films

The Experimental Film. Robert Breer, Norman McLaren, and others discuss their work and the experimental film generally. Excerpts from *Man Out Walking His Dog, Blazes, Blinkety Blink* are shown. The complete *Very Nice, Very Nice* is also included in the program.

28 min., b/w	Creative Film Society
	National Film Board of Canada
	Contemporary — McGraw-Hill

Experiments in Motion Graphics. John Whitney explains the processes used in his motion graphic films.

13 min., color	Pyramid Films
	USC Film Distribution
	Creative Film Society

The Eye Hears, The Ear Sees. Explores the work of Norman McLaren, including excerpts from several films.

59 min., color	International Film Bureau

Fantastic Animation Festival. Fourteen shorts tied into one package with some new and a bit of some old. The list includes these artists and their films: Iam Emes (*French Windows*), Mihai Badica (*Icarus*), Loren Bowie (*A Short History of the Wheel*), Steven Lisberger, Eric Ladd (*Cosmic Cartoon*), Jeff Hale, Derek Lamb (*The Last Cartoon Man*), Paul Driessen (*Cat's Cradle*), Cat Stevens (*Moonshadow*), Bernard Palacios (*Nightbird*), Randy Cartwright (*Room and Board*), Marv Newland (*Bambi Meets Godzilla*), Will Vinton (*Mountain Music*), Jordan Belson (*Light*), Max Fleischer, Dave Fleischer (*Superman vs. the Mechanical Monsters; Award-winning Animated Commercials*), Kathy Rose (*Mirror People*), Robert Swarthe (*Kick Me*), and Bob Gardiner (*Closed Mondays*).

112.5 min., color	Audio Brandon Films

Film "Firsts." In this anthology of the first years of the moving picture industry, some examples of animated films are included.

55 min., b/w	Sterling Educational Films

The Films of Georges Méliès. A 1964 National Educational Television production outlining the career of the French filmmaker noted for his pictorial fantasies and trick films. Using stills, excerpts from his films, and a conversation with his granddaughter, his career from 1897 is described.

60 min., b/w	National Educational Television

First (Motion) Picture Show. About the first exhibition of moving pictures before public audiences. Using stills, newspaper clips, and music of the period, the 4 May 1880 screening of Eadweard Muybridge's experiments at the San Francisco Art

Association is recreated. The reporter-narrator reviews the prehistory of the Thaumatrope, Phenatisticope, Zoetrope, and other devices and theories finally brought to a focus in the Muybridge screening.

26 min., color   UC Extension Media Center

Flicks II. Produced by WTTW-TV, Chicago, for "What's New" (program #270), this film reviews animation from cave drawings through the work of Winsor McCay, Walt Disney, Walter Lantz, and many others.

30 min., b/w   National Educational Television

Frame by Frame. Demonstrates object, cel, and cutout animation techniques in an entertaining manner.

13 min., color   Pyramid Films

Frame by Frame: The Art of Animation. Explores various animation techniques such as cutouts, cel, object, and pixilation.

13 min., color   Pyramid Films
                                              USC Film Distribution

Frank and Ollie: 4 Decades of Disney Animation. Disney animators Frank Thomas and Ollie Johnston provide a limited personal perspective but considerable professional insight into the Disney animation process through *Pinocchio, Cinderella, Snow White and the Seven Dwarfs, Fantasia, Bambi,* and *Lady and the Tramp.*

21 min., color   Walt Disney
                                              Educational Film Locator

From Magic Lantern to Today. A compilation film detailing how animation evolved from primitive toys to the popular forms, with examples given.

28 min., b/w   Em Gee
                                              Educational Film Locator

Handy Dandy Do-It-Yourself Animation Film. Three youngsters are shown making their animated film, using various materials such as clay, finger paints, cutouts, pen and ink.

12 min., color   Educational Film Locator

Hans Richter: Artist and Filmmaker. Before his death in 1976, Hans Richter was interviewed about his work, life, philosophy, and his films. His works included in the film are: *Rhythmus 21* (1921) and excerpts from: *Inflation, Ghosts Before Breakfast, Dreams That Money Can Buy, 8 x 8,* and *Dadascope.*

45.5 min., color   International Film Bureau

A History of American Avant-Garde Cinema. This series consists of seven programs, thirty-eight films by twenty-eight filmmakers. They include the following animators: Harry Smith, Robert Breer, Stan Vanderbeek, Jordan Belson, James Whitney, Standish D. Lawder, and Larry Jordan.

590 min., color and b/w   American Federation of Arts

History of Animation. Survey of Disney animation from early examples, such as *Skeleton Dance* and *Steamboat Willie*, to limited animation and computer technology.

21 min., color and b/w   Walt Disney

History of Aviation. The thrust of this film is an animated view of the airplane. However, there are some segments from the scarce *Victory through Airpower*, a propaganda film produced by Walt Disney in World War II that would interest the animation buff.

18 min., color   Audio Brandon Films
                                  Twyman Films

The History of the Motion Picture. A series of thirty-one films each about 26.5 minutes in length, surveying the history of the American film and foreign influences. One title in the series is *Trends in Early Experimental Film.*

26.5 min., b/w   Sterling

Homage to Eadweard Muybridge. Uses photographs taken by Muybridge in his early experiments in the study of movement, forerunner to the moving picture (animated photographs).

20 min., b/w   USC Film Distribution

How to Make a Movie without a Camera. About several techniques used in making a film without use of a conventional motion picture camera or photographic processing, similar to the work of Len Lye and Norman McLaren.

5 min., color   Educational Film Locator

James Whitney Retrospective. Package of animated films by James Whitney available from Creative Film Society including the following: *Exercises 2, 3* and *4, Yantra, Lapis, Dwija, Wu Ming.*

76 min., color   Creative Film Society

Jiři Trnka. Puppet animator is at work on a diorama for the 1967 Montreal Expo.

11 min., color   Contemporary-McGraw-Hill

A Laser Images Demonstration. Demonstration of laser images using music in combination with kaleidoscopic laser forms.

10 min., color   Creative Film Society

The Light Fantastick. Using actuality footage, interviews, and excerpts from animated films, this documentary explains pinscreen, drawing-on-film, stop-action, pixilation, and shadow puppet animation techniques.

58 min., color   National Film Board of Canada

"The Lost World" Revisited. A condensed version of the 1925 First National Film

concerning the discovery of a prehistoric world in South America. Willis O'Brien produced the stop-motion photography and the miniatures used in the production.

27 min., b/w with soundtrack   Sterling

The Magic Lantern Movie. Examples of slides from the era before motion pictures form the major emphasis of this film yet the important basis of the motion picture is also underscored. The magic lantern's history includes the familiar popular stories, travelogs, and tricks as popular entertainment. Music used is drawn from antique music boxes of the era in which the magic lantern shows were featured.

9 min., color   Serious Business Company
                                       Cecile Starr

The Magic World of Karel Zeman. Discusses and excerpts the work of the late Karel Zeman, Czechoslovakian animator.

16 min., color   Contemporary-McGraw-Hill

Make a Movie without a Camera. Students draw directly on a piece of transparent film in the manner of Norman McLaren and the results are shown.

6 min., color   BFA Educational Media

Milestones for Mickey. A retrospective series emphasizing Walt Disney's character Mickey Mouse. Short films included in this package include: *Plane Crazy* (1928), *Mickey's Service Station* (1935), *The Band Concert* (1935), and the marvelous *Through the Mirror* (1936). The package concludes with the sequence featuring the mouse from *Fantasia* ("The Sorcerer's Apprentice," 1940) and the introduction from the *Mickey Mouse Club* TV series.

41 min., color and b/w   Twyman Films
                                       Walt Disney
                                       Audio Brandon Films

Milestone in Animation. A program of five Walt Disney short animated films informally outlining his animation history through the examples presented. Titles include: *Steamboat Willie* (1928), *The Skeleton Dance* (1929), *Flowers and Trees* (1932), *The Three Little Pigs* (1933), and *The Old Mill* (1937).

40 min., color and b/w   Audio Brandon Films
                                       Walt Disney
                                       Twyman Films

Movie Magic. Using single-frame exposures, or stop-action techniques, this film demonstrates the construction of a battle scene.

14 min., b/w   Sterling

Movies from Computers. Several excerpts from computer-animated films are included along with a presentation of how they are produced.

20 min., b/w   Education Development Center

Moving Picture Boys in the Great War. Blackhawk Films production depicting the changes in the American film during the period 1914 to 1919. Contains several animations used in propaganda along with other live-action film excerpts illustrating the changing content of the film.

52 min., color and b/w   Educational Film Locator

Moving Pictures: The Art of Jan Lenica. Depicts Lenica at work on a short *Landscape* in 1975.

19 min., color   Phoenix Films, Inc.
USC Film Distribution

Otto Messmer and Felix the Cat. Otto Messmer is finally recognized as the creator of the famous *Felix the Cat*. At age 84, Messmer recalls the production of the Pat Sullivan-produced cartoons. Excerpts from five of Messmer's works are included in this film, revealing considerable cinematic influence, unlike most animations of the silent era.

25 min., color   Phoenix Films, Inc.

Pin Point Percussion. Norman McLaren explains synthetic sound in some of his films.

6 min., b/w   International Film Bureau

Pinscreen. Explanation and demonstration of the pinscreen animated technique characteristic of Alexandre Alexeieff's work.

39 min., color   Pyramid Films

Remembering Winsor McCay. Excerpting three of McCay's animations, producer John Canemaker weaves anecdotal recollections of McCay's work in creating *Gertie the Dinosaur, The Sinking of the Lusitania* and a hand-colored version of *Little Nemo* (1911).

20 min., color   Phoenix Films, Inc.

Richter on Film. Early avant-garde filmmaker and dadaist Hans Richter is interviewed along with excerpts shown from *Rhythmus 21* and *Ghosts before Breakfast*.

14 min., color   Cecile Starr

A Short History of Animation. Beginning with Max Skladanowsky's animated slides (circa 1879) this collection of short animated films attempts to highlight work by Emile Cohl, Winsor McCay, Bud Fisher cartoon series, Otto Messmer, Walt Disney, and Lotte Reiniger.

60 min., silent and sound, b/w   Museum of Modern Art

A Talk with Carmen D'Avino. Cecile Starr interviews D'Avino about his animated, painted, pixilated, and abstract styles.

8 min., color   Cecile Starr

Teenagers Create an Animated Film. Depicts a group of junior high school students making an animated movie *Gone with the Antenna*. Idea conception, script writing, storyboards, artwork, photography, and editing stages are shown.

10 min., color   USC Film Distribution

Time-Lapse Photography. John Ott demonstrates the technique of time-lapse photography.

19 min., color   International Film Bureau

Tricks of Our Trade. A primer on Disney animation showing art of exaggeration and personality animation in Disney characters, effects-animation and the multiplane camera with numerous examples from *Snow White and the Seven Dwarfs, Fantasia,* and *Bambi.*

27 min., color   Walt Disney
                                                          Educational Film Locator

Unreal Time. A package of thirty-three short films by independent animation and film graphics artists demonstrating the inventiveness and creativity of independents since 1950. Artists included are: Eliot Noyes, Jr., Will Vinton, Bob Gardiner, John Straiton, Stan Vanderbeek, Carmen D'Avino, Kathleen Laughlin, Buffy Holton, John H. Whitney, Al Jarnow, Larry Jordan, Frank and Caroline Mouris, Victor Faccinto, Derek Lamb, Jon Jost, Mary Beams, J. P. and Lillian Somersaulter, Jules Engel, George Griffin, Robert Breer, Sally Cruikshank, Adam K. Beckett, Steve Segal, Dan McLaughlin, Norman McLaren, Peter Rose, Jordan Belson, Ryan Larkin, Teru Murakami, and Susan Pitt.

219 min., color and b/w   American Federation of the Arts

Window on Canada: An Interview with Norman McLaren. McLaren discusses his work and techniques, showing *La haut sur ces montagnes, c'est l'aviron* and *Boogie Doodle.* The film was released in 1956.

31 min., b/w   International Film Bureau
                                                          Contemporary-McGraw-Hill

VIDEO SOURCES OF ANIMATION SUBJECTS

REFERENCES TO VIDEOTAPES

These sources are important for keeping up-to-date in this fast-changing software industry supporting videotape and videodisc hardware. By 1980 thousands of films and TV programs were already available in various video formats, recycled through the new technology in search of new markets.

Brown, James W., ed. *Educational Media Yearbook (1978).* New York: R. R. Bowker, 1978. Begun in 1973, this is the fifth edition attempting to bring together information about educational media throughout the world. For animation, the sections dealing with print and nonprint resources, and guides to training programs, organizations, and funding sources are useful. The description of the new Consortium of University Film Centers and its directory will lead the researcher to new caches of animated films. Reference tools, media-related periodicals and newsletters, and films and videotapes about media are described in detail. A directory of producers, distributors, and publishers is attached as an appendix.

National Video Clearinghouse. *The Video Programs Index.* Edited by Ken Winslow. Syosset, N.Y.: National Video Clearinghouse, 1980-. Lists subjects, formats, and rental/purchase data from about 350 video program distributors including addresses and telephone numbers.

National Video Clearinghouse. *The Video Source Book.* Syosset, N.Y.: National Video Clearinghouse, 1980-. Commercially produced listing of prerecorded videotape content, including feature films, educational-instructional, and documentary subjects, claiming over 15,000 titles. Producers, casts, ratings, and relevant awards listed. Index is also broken down by subject and title.

Videolog: Programs for General Interest and Entertainment. New York: Esselte Video, 1979. Claiming to list over 4,500 programs and 600 features on videotape, this 1979 guide has a subject index and alphabetical listing of annotated titles. A separate listing of producers and distributors with addresses and telephone numbers is also included. Each entry contains program or series title, producer, distributor, order number, year produced, hue, length, available formats and sales, lease or rental data. Distribution restrictions and availability of foreign-language versions are also indicated. Separate guides for health sciences programming and programs for business and industry are also available.

Winslow, Ken. "Video Program Distribution: Media, Formats, Pricing, Rights." *Educational and Industrial Television* 10:11 (November 1978): 35-65. Discussion of the battle of the formats and speculation on the future of software for videotape and disc. The "Directory of Program Sources" is updated annually by this journal—amply demonstrating that the tidal wave of software for new generations of videotape and disc players is just beginning.

ANIMATION SUBJECTS ON VIDEO

Because the references to videotapes about animation are nearly exhaustive and regularly updated, this section includes only those sources that may be overlooked.

University of the State of New York
State Education Department
Bureau of Mass Communications
Albany, New York 12234

Under a special agreement among the commercial networks, unions, and program producers, certain telecasts are available free to school systems within New York State. The bureau's catalogue explains the procedures to follow. Out-of-state users may also have access to these programs for one year upon payment of a dubbing fee. Programs dealing with animation subjects include the following.

The Art of George Dunning. Key creator of a new wave in animation, manifested in *Yellow Submarine* in the late 1960s, Dunning is seen at work; he describes his approach to this art form.

30 min., color

The Art of Oskar Fischinger.
30 min., color

The Boys from Termite Terrace, Parts 1 and 2. About the Warner Brothers cartoon unit featuring Bob Clampett.

58 min., color

Give Chance A Chance: Portrait of Hans Richter. A "Camera Three" program which interviews Richter and includes examples of his films.

30 min., color

Norman McLaren: Film Artist. McLaren discusses cameraless animation and his own work at the Film Board of Canada. Other techniques described include synthetic sound, stop-motion, and optical overprinting.

30 min., color

Pin Board Technique of Illustration. Alexandre Alexeieff and his wife Claire Parker illustrate the method used in their animations.

30 min., b/w

Stan Vanderbeek: The Computer Generation. His work described with examples.

30 min., color

Animated Motion. A series of five films designed for students who are learning about animation or for those with only an elementary technical knowledge about animation. If used in sequence, the films will provide an overview of the possible outcomes in animating using a disc exercise. The films classify and demonstrate the possibilities of movement including constant, accelerated, decelerated, zero, and irregular. Available singly or as a package.

41.5 min., color   International Film Bureau

Color Abstract Images. Abstract images created by an audio synthesizer plugged into an oscilloscope with electronic sounds to match.

30 min., color   Ernest Gusella

FILM AND VIDEO DISTRIBUTORS

American Federation of the Arts, 41 East 65th Street, New York, New York 10021.

Association Films, Inc., 512 Burlington Avenue, LaGrange, Illinois 60525. (312) 352-3377.

Audio Brandon Films, 34 MacQuestern Parkway South, Mount Vernon, New York 10550. (914) 664-5051. Among the largest and oldest distributors of 16mm film offering *Fantastic Animation Festival*, Disney features and shorts, and the work of Max and Dave Fleischer, Charles Schultz, and UPA. A separate shorts catalogue is available.

B. Bloomberg, 80 Norwood Avenue, Kensington, California 94707.

BFA Educational Media, 211 Michigan Avenue, Santa Monica, California 90404. (213) 829-2901. Distributes some animation from Zagreb.

Billy Budd Films, Inc., 235 East 57th Street, New York, New York 10022. (212) 755-3968.

Budget Films, 4590 Santa Monica Boulevard, Los Angeles, California. (213) 660-0187; (213) 660-0800.

Canyon Cinema Cooperative, 2325 Third Street, Suite 338, San Francisco, California 94107. (415) 626-2255. This is a nonprofit cooperative distribution center for independent filmmakers with no restrictions as to form, content, or length. The known and unknown filmmakers coalesce in these listings often with sketchy descriptions of each film. Many of these films use animation techniques.

CBS/Education and Publishing Group, Columbia Broadcasting System, Inc., 383 Madison Avenue, New York, New York 10017. (212) 688-9100. This agency services requests for CBS programs on film or videotape that are not otherwise distributed by other agencies. If in doubt, write for an updating list which will indicate if films are obtainable from the network or an authorized distributor.

Cecile Starr, 50 West 96th Street, New York, New York 10025. (212) 749-1250. Starr has taken over distribution of several animated films formerly available from Van Nostrand.

Contemporary-McGraw-Hill Films, 1221 Avenue of the Americas, New York, New York 10020. (212) 997-6759.

Creative Film Society, 7237 Canby Avenue, Reseda, California 91335. (213) 881-3887. Formed in 1957, the Creative Film Society began as an informal affiliation of West Coast filmmakers. Their services of rental film expanded to colleges and private organizations using the some 900 films in the library. These include some works of Jordan Belson, Oskar Fischinger, Walt Disney, the Fleischers, John Whitney, Salvador Dali, Dan McLaughlin, Mary Ellen Bute, Hy Hirsh, Ben Van Meter, Len Lye, Pat Sullivan, James Whitney, Emile Cohl, Jana Merglova, Winsor McCay, Hans, Richter, Jiři Trnka, George Pal, Ivan Dryer, Bob Pike, Curtis Opliger, and Arthur Lipsett. Included in the collection is the anonymous left-handed "tribute" to Walt Disney. For years this film was shown to the "in" crowd but CFS obtained rights to distribute the spoof nationally.

CRM/McGraw-Hill Films, Del Mar, California 92014. (714) 453-5000.

Education Development Center, 39 Chapel Street, Newton, Massachusetts 02160. (617) 969-7100. Distributes several computer-animated films explaining physics, mechanics and other science subjects.

Em Gee Film Library, 6924 Canby Avenue, Suite 103, Reseda, California 91335. (213) 981-5506. Undoubtedly the best resource for examples of early animation including the work of Emile Cohl, Winsor McCay, Raoul Barré, J. Stuart Blackton, John Bray Studio, International Film Service (Gregory LaCava, Frank Moser, Leon Searl, Tom E. Powers), Willis O'Brien, Walt Disney, Otto Messmer (Felix the Cat), Ladislas Starevich, Ub Iwerks, Tony Sarg, Paul Terry, Max Fleischer, Walter Lantz, George Pal, Sid Marcus, Stephen Bosustow, Lass Lindberg, Derek Phillips, Nicholas Spargo, Les Drew, Kaj Pindal, Stephen Leacock, Caroline Leaf, Michael Mills, Chuck Menvile, Zlatko Grgic, Richard Roberts, Emanuele Luzzati, Giulio Gianini, Norman McLaren, Maurice Blackburn, Lotte Reiniger, Shel Silverstein, Yoji Kuri, Faith and John Hubley, Viviane Elnacave, Susanne Olivier, Judith Klein, Ante Zaninovic, Jeffrey Hale, Warner Brothers animators, Eliot Noyes, Jr., Bob Cannon, various Zagreb animators, and Alexandre Alexeieff. A number of compilation packages in the history of animation are also available.

Ernest Gusella, 118 Forsyth Street, New York, New York 10002.

Film Classic Exchange, 1926 South Vermont Avenue, Los Angeles, California

90007. Distributes packages of silent and sound films for cinema appreciation classes including special effects.

Film Images, Radim Films, Inc., 1034 Lake Street, Oak Park, Illinois 60301. (312) 386-4826.

Film-Makers' Cooperative, 175 Lexington Avenue, New York, New York 10016. Accepting all films, this cooperative has an enormous list of available titles, many of which use animation either in traditional ways or experimentally. The annotations are often supplied by the filmmakers themselves and just as often contain cryptic references and meanings, making the search for any basis of selection difficult. Outside criteria have no place in listing these offerings, so programmers and others enter this marketplace nude, usually without benefit of published criticism. But there are numerous gems in these archives.

Films Incorporated, 1144 Wilmette Avenue, Wilmette, Illinois 60091. (312) 256-3200.

Good Films, 841 Broadway, New York, New York 10003. (212) 986-7678.

Indiana University, Audiovisual Center, Bloomington, Indiana 47405. National Educational Television videotapes, kinescopes and other program materials approved for national distribution are now handled through the Indiana University Audiovisual Center.

Institutional Cinema, 915 Broadway, New York, New York 10010. (212) 673-3990. Distributes entertainment films, including animation. Several television animated programs, Fleischer's features, cartoon packages, and UPA films are available.

International Film Bureau, Inc., 332 South Michigan Avenue, Chicago, Illinois 60604. (312) 427-4545. Some films of the Canadian National Film Board are available through this agency, and others through additional agencies. Users must obtain the Film Board of Canada listing indicating which channel is operative for a given film.

Kit Parker Films, Carmel Valley, California 93924. (408) 659-3474; (408) 659-4131. Among the more reasonably priced rental agencies, Kit Parker Films has a gigantic catalogue for contemporary and traditional animation including: Fleischer features and shorts, George Pal, Ray Harryhausen features, Van Buren's *Aesops Fables*, Ub Iwerks, Winsor McCay, and Walter Lantz.

Lilyan Productions, 524 Ridge Road, Watchung, New Jersey 07060.

Macmillan Films, 34 MacQuesten Parkway South, Mount Vernon, New York 10550. (914) 664-4277. A large number of European animated subjects are available in addition to several UPA films.

Museum of Modern Art, 11 West 53rd Street, New York, New York 10019. With their circulating film program, the museum's film department has a large range of traditional and experimental animation including early Disney, Len Lye, Robert Breer, John Whitney, and Oskar Fischinger.

National Educational Television, Audiovisual Center, Indiana University, Bloomington, Indiana 47401.

National Film Board of Canada, 16th Floor, 1251 Avenue of the Americas, New York, New York 10020. (212) 586-2400.

National Film and Video Center, 4321 Sykesville Road, Finksburg, Maryland 31048. (301) 795-3000.

New Line Cinema Corporation, 853 Broadway, 16th Floor, New York, New York

10003. (800) 221-5150. Most of their products are offbeat, avant-garde, or imported features catering to college audiences. Some films of Susan Pitts, Kathleen Laughlin, Claudia Weil, Eliot Noyes, Jr., and other contemporary experimentalist animators are in the New Line Collection.

Phoenix Films, Inc., 470 Park Avenue South, New York, New York 10016. (212) 684-5910.

Pyramid Films, Box 1048, Santa Monica, California 90406. (213) 828-7577. Among the largest distributors of short films, the Pyramid collection contains a large amount of contemporary animation. By types and filmmakers these include: kinestasis (Charles Braverman), animated geometric shapes (Alan Slasor), collage (Caroline and Frank Mouris), line animation (Hubley studio), clay (Will Vinton, Bob Gardiner), object (Tadeusz Wilkosz), computer (John Whitney). The works of Michael Whitney, Walerian Borowczyk, Marcel Jankovics, Oskar Fischinger, Ken Rudolph, Sylvia Dees, Jan Lenica, Steve Bosustow, Witold Giersz, Istvan Ventilla, Chuck Menville, Len Janson, Jordan Belson, Ishu Patel, Charles Braverman, John and Faith Hubley, Jimmy Picker, Saul Bass, Dan McLaughlin, and Carlos Marchiori are also available for rental or purchase.

Serious Business Company, 1145 Mandana Boulevard, Oakland, California 94610. (415) 832-5600. This distributor concentrates on contemporary animation with a large number of offerings. Filmmakers include: Jane Aaron, Gil Beach, Mary Beams, Adam Beckett, Robert Breer, Carter Burwell, Jeff Carpenter, Betty Chen, Vincent Collins, Clint Colver, Bruce Conner, Lisa Crafts, Sally Cruikshank, Margaret Bailey Doogan, Robert Dvorak, Ed Emshwiller, Paul Gabicki, Andrea Gomez, George Griffin, Jeffrey Hale, Maxine Haleff, John Haugse, Linda Heller, Al Jarnow, M. Henry Jones, Larry Jordan, Kaina Krumins, Kathleen Laughlin, Phyllis, MacDougals, Sandy Moore, John Nelson, Sara Petty, Dennis Pies, Susan Pitts, Josie Ramstad, Kathy Rose, John Straiton, John Teton, Anita Thacher, Tricepts Productions (Judith Keller, Shula Wallace, and Shirley Joel), Antoine Valma, and Stan Vanderbeek.

Sterling Educational Films, 241 East 34th Street, New York, New York 10016. (212) 593-0198.

Swank Motion Pictures, Inc., 201 South Jefferson Avenue, St. Louis, Missouri 63103. (314) 534-6300. Distributes some Disney features and packages of animated shorts with holiday themes.

Twyman Films, 329 Salem Avenue, Box 605, Dayton, Ohio 45401. (800) 543-9594. In addition to recent features, Twyman offers a moderate array of animation subjects including several Disney features, and works by Steve Bosustow, Norman McLaren, Ryan Larkin, Ernest Pintoff, and Bill Melendez. Individual cartoon titles can be booked out of their Warner Brothers, Walter Lantz, George Pal, UPA, and Columbia (Color Fantasies) collections.

University of California, Extension Media Center, 2223 Fulton Street, Berkeley, California 94720. (414) 642-0460.

University of Southern California, Film Distribution Center, Division of Cinema-Television, University Park, Los Angeles, California 90007.

Walt Disney Educational Media Company, 500 South Buena Vista, Burbank, California 91521.

Animated Films on 8mm
Compiled by Leonard Hollmann

INTRODUCTION

This compilation of over one thousand animated cartoons available for sale in 8mm (Super 8 and Standard 8) is intended as a guide for prospective purchasers and collectors. The list includes puppet cartoons, which are often similar in style to the drawn type, but does not include films with stop-motion animation of the Ray Harryhausen type, used in such movies as the original *King Kong*, and earlier in various shorts.

The films and formats in which they are available are listed here as described in the dealer catalogues. The list includes only titles shown in dealer catalogues, as news releases and advertisements often turn out to be inaccurate or premature. Availability of a particular title or format is sometimes uncertain. Because of the large amount of money that can be tied up in an inventory, some dealers do not stock in depth; they apparently order prints from the lab in small numbers as required. In this situation, slow-selling titles or formats may be quickly discontinued.

After several years, the home movie industry has virtually completed its conversion to Super 8 sound, resulting in the availability of many new titles and new sound versions of older silent cartoons. Silent versions are still frequently offered to attract the buyer on a budget. In any event, prospective buyers will need to obtain catalogues before ordering. The dealers listed below are those which advertise in film fanzines; all will send a catalogue upon request.

Cartoons available from British dealers are listed only when they are not offered for sale in the United States.

A system of classification was imperative for a list this large. Although not a perfect solution, the films have been grouped according to the studio or animator that produced them. At times, problems made a few exceptions necessary. The major argument for this method is that cartoons of any particular studio have tended to

Author's Note: The first draft of this list was finished in late 1978 when the flood of new titles in Super 8mm magnetic sound and color was still continuing. By 1980 dozens of additional titles were added to the Super 8mm color and magnetic sound formats. Most of these have been included in Hollmann's list but every supplier is not indicated in these updates. Many dealers have probably sold off their short black-and-white silent versions but the designations are still maintained in the list.

have an identifiable style. Whenever practical, the output of a studio has been subdivided into smaller units, by a series title or names of characters who appeared in their own series. While some characters remained in their own series, others were intermingled so freely that subdividing was not practical.

For each title available, a code indicates from which dealers and in what formats it may be obtained. The letters are the initials of the dealers, and the numbers represent the formats. A lower case "s" immediately behind a format number indicates a "short" version, which is mounted on a 50-foot reel in contrast to the usual 200-foot reel. Whether or not a cartoon is intact or has been edited is seldom indicated in the catalogues, other than for feature highlights or a reel made up of excerpts.

Films made specifically for television are so designated by the letters "TV" immediately following the date, but only when designated as a TV cartoon in the Library of Congress *Catalogue of Motion Pictures* which lists copyright registration. Background information on the animated films, including dates, has been drawn from the U.S. copyright catalog and reliable published sources. Dealer catalog dates are frequently unreliable and the U.S. copyright catalog is also subject to error. Often, early cartoons were not registered at the time of release, or not registered at all. In other cases, the Super 8mm versions have been retitled and consequently not located in the copyright listings. Thus, the dates for those titles are missing in this list.

The list of dealers and formats follows.

DEALERS

UNITED STATES

BHF	Blackhawk Films, Inc., 1235 West 5th Street, Davenport, Iowa 52808.
BMH	Brenda's Movie House, 6736 Caster Avenue, Philadelphia, Pennsylvania 19149
CBF	Canterbury Films, 15 Canterbury Road, Great Neck, New York 11021
CE	Cinema Eight, Middlesex Avenue, Chester, Connecticut 06412
DMFS	DeMaio Film Service, 20222 Morristown Circle, Huntington Beach, California 92646
EPF	Enterprise Films, Inc., 561 N.E. 79th Street, Miami, Florida 33138
FC	Filmco—Dave Thomas, R.D. 10, Box 421, Greensburg, Pennsylvania 15601
GPS	Glenn Photo Supply, 6924 Canby Avenue, Suite 103, Reseda, California 91335
GSF	Gaines "Sixteen" Films Co., 15207 Stagg Street, Van Nuys, California 91405
HFE	Hollywood Film Exchange, 1534 North Highland Avenue, Hollywood, California 90028
HFRP	Heritage Films/Ra-Cine Products Co., 1687 Perry Avenue, Racine, Wisconsin 53406
IVY	Ivy Film, 165 West 46th Street, New York, New York, 10036
MWFS	Midwest Film Service, Ranchmart South, 3859 West 95th Street, Overland Park, Kansas 66206
NFL	Nostalgia Films, Ltd., Post Office Box 666, Gracie Station, New York, New York 10028

NFP   Niles Film Products, Inc., 1141 Mishawaka Avenue, South Bend, Indiana 46615

RAR   Reels and Reels, 1532 Kennedy Boulevard, Jersey City, New Jersey 07305

RFF   Red Fox Films, Rt. 209, East, Elizabethville, Pennsylvania 17023

RI   Reel Images, 495 Monroe Turnpike, Monroe, Connecticut 06468

SFL   Select Film Library, 115 West 31st Street, New York, New York 10001

TBF   Thunderbird Films, Post Office Box 65157, Los Angeles, California 90065

WDHM   Walt Disney Home Movies, 800 Sonora Avenue, Glendale, California 91201

CANADA

JEF   Jef Films Reg'd., Film House, 10 St. Andrews Road, Baier D'Urfe, Quebec, Canada H9X2T8

GREAT BRITAIN

DFS   Derann Film Services, Film House, 171 Stourbridge Road, Holly Hall, Dudley, West Midlands DYI 2EQ, England

FFL   Fletcher Films, Ltd., Unit 7, Space Waye, Pier Road, North Feltham Trading Estate, Feltham, Middlesex, England

PFDL   Powell Film Distributors, Ltd., 6 Hermitage Parade, High Street, Ascot, Berkshire, England

PMF   PM Films, 39, Windsor End, Beaconsfield, Bucks., HP9 2JN, England

WDPL   Walt Disney Productions, Ltd., 68 Pall Mall, London, SW1Y 5EX, England

FORMATS

- 1 = Super 8, color, magnetic sound
- 2 = Super 8, b&w, magnetic sound
- 3 = Super 8, color, silent
- 4 = Super 8, b&w, silent
- 5 = Standard 8, color, silent
- 6 = Standard 8, b&w, silent

CHARACTER LOCATOR

As an aid to quickly locating cartoons with specific characters there follows an index of characters and series titles showing the studio under which they appear. This index lists only those characters available on 8mm. Not all characters indexed have their own subdivision in the studio listings.

CHARACTER OR SERIES TITLE	STUDIO
Aesop's Fables	Terrytoons (Paul Terry)
	See also Aesop's Fables
Alice in Cartoonland	Walt Disney
Andy Panda	Walter Lantz
Animated Grouch Chaser	see Miscellaneous, Raoul Barré
Astronut	Terrytoons

CHARACTER OR SERIES TITLE	STUDIO
Atom Ant	Hanna-Barbera
Betty Boop	Fleischer Studio
Bobby Bumps	see Miscellaneous, Earl Hurd
Bonzo	see British cartoons
Bubble and Squeak	see British cartoons
Buck Mouse	Walter Lantz
Bugs Bunny	Warner Brothers
Cattanooga Cats	Hanna-Barbera
Chilly Willy	Walter Lantz
Chip N' Dale	Walt Disney
Col. Heeza Liar	see Miscellaneous
Col. Rat & Willie the Worm	see British cartoons
Color Classics	Fleischer Studio
Color Rhapsody	Screen Gems
ComiColor Cartoons	Ub Iwerks
Daffy Duck	Warner Brothers
Dastardly & Muttley	Hanna-Barbera
David Hand Cartoons	see British cartoons
Deputy Dawg	Terrytoons
Dinky Doodle	Walter Lantz
Dinky Duck	Terrytoons
Donald (& Daisy) Duck	Walt Disney
Dreamy Dud	see Miscellaneous, Wallace Carlson
Dynamo Doc	Walter Lantz
Elmer Fudd	Warner Brothers
Farmer Al Falfa	Terrytoons
Felix the Cat	Van Beuren; see also Miscellaneous
The Flintstones	Hanna-Barbera
Flip the Frog	Ub Iwerks
Foghorn Leghorn	Warner Brothers
Fox and Crow	Screen Gems
Gabby	Fleischer Studio
Gandy Goose	Terrytoons
Gerald McBoing Boing	UPA
Gertie the Dinosaur	Winsor McCay
Goofy	Walt Disney
The Great Grape Ape	Hanna-Barbera
Half Pint	Terrytoons
Hashimoto	Terrytoons
Heckle and Jeckle	Terrytoons
Hector Heathcote	Terrytoons
Henery Hawk	Warner Brothers
Hillbilly Bears	Hanna-Barbera
Hot Dog series	Walter Lantz
Huckleberry Hound	Hanna-Barbera

CHARACTER OR SERIES TITLE	STUDIO
Huey, Dewey & Louie (Donald's nephews)	Walt Disney
Inspector Willoughby	Walter Lantz
James Hound	Terrytoons
Jerry on the Job	see Miscellaneous
The Jetsons	Hanna-Barbera
Jolly Frolic	UPA
Koko the Clown	Fleischer Studio
Krazy Kat	Screen Gems; see also Miscellaneous
Laugh-O-Grams	Walt Disney
Little Nemo	Winsor McCay
Little Roquefort & Percy	Terrytoons
Looney Tunes	Warner Brothers
Loopy de Loop	Hanna-Barbera
Luno	Terrytoons
Magic Pen of Mother Goose	Terrytoons
Magilla Gorilla	Hanna-Barbera
Merrie Melodies	Warner Brothers
Mickey (& Minnie) Mouse	Walt Disney
Mightor	Hanna-Barbera
Mighty Heroes	Terrytoons
Mighty Mouse	Terrytoons
Mr. Magoo	UPA
Moby Dick	Hanna-Barbera
Molly Moo-Cow	Van Beuren
Motor Mouse and Autocrat	Hanna-Barbera
Mutt and Jeff	see Miscellaneous
Newman's Laugh-O-Grams	Walt Disney
Oswald the Rabbit (1927-28)	Walt Disney
Out of the Inkwell	Fleischer Studio
Pepito Chickeeto	Walter Lantz
Pete the Pup	Walter Lantz
Peter Potamus	Hanna-Barbera
Pierre Bear	Walter Lantz
Pixie and Dixie	Hanna-Barbera
Pluto (the dog)	Walt Disney
Popeye	Fleischer Studio; Famous Studio
Porky Pig	Warner Brothers
Possible Possum	Terrytoons
Precious Pupp	Hanna-Barbera
Puppetoons	George Pal
Quick Draw McGraw	Hanna-Barbera
Rainbow Parade Cartoons	Van Beuren
Roadrunner	Warner Brothers
Sad Cat	Terrytoons

CHARACTER OR SERIES TITLE	STUDIO
Scooby Doo	Hanna-Barbera
Secret Squirrel	Hanna-Barbera
Silly Sidney the Elephant	Terrytoons
Silly Symphony	Walt Disney
Snagglepuss	Hanna-Barbera
Snuffy Smith & Barney Google	Paramount
Song Car-Tunes	Fleischer Studio
Sourpuss	Terrytoons
Speedy Gonzales	Warner Brothers
Squiddley Diddley	Hanna-Barbera
Superman	Fleischer Studio; Famous Studio
Swing Symphony	Walter Lantz
Sylvester	Warner Brothers
Terry Bears	Terrytoons
The Three Musketeers	Hanna-Barbera
Tom & Jerry (early thirties, Mutt and Jeff-like)	Van Beuren
Tom & Jerry (cat and mouse)	MGM
Top Cat	Hanna-Barbera
Tweety (and Sylvester)	Warner Brothers
Unnatural History series	Walter Lantz
Willie the Walrus	Terrytoons
Willie Whopper	Ub Iwerks
Winsome Witch	Hanna-Barbera
Wombles	BBC TV
Woody Woodpecker	Walter Lantz
Yakky Doodle Duck	Hanna-Barbera
Yogi Bear	Hanna-Barbera
Yosemite Sam	Warner Brothers

STUDIOS

WALT DISNEY

While several dealers have issued early Disney films, cartoons dating from the middle 1930s onward (with the exception of one World War II item) are distributed in their 8mm versions by the home movie division of the Disney organization. The Disney unit has earned an excellent reputation for the high quality of their 8mm prints.

The first four subdivisions below are representative films of Disney's earliest work. *Newman's Laugh-O-Grams* were very short cartoons made for Newman's Theater in Kansas City, Missouri. The *Laugh-O-Grams* were another series Disney made while still in Kansas City. *Alice in Cartoonland* was Disney's first series after he moved to Hollywood, followed by *Oswald the Rabbit.*

Newman's Laugh-O-Grams (1920)

Newman's Laugh-O-Grams (1920) GPS 4, 6

Laugh-O-Grams (1922-23)

Puss in Boots (1922-23) BHF 2, 4; GPS 4, 6

Alice in Cartoonland (1924-26)

Alice Cans the Cannibals (1924) GPS 4, 6
Alice's Egg Plant (1925) GPS 4, 6; NFP 6
Alice on the Farm (1925) BHF 2, 4
Alice the Toreador (1924) GPS 4, 6; NFP 4, 6; TBF 4

Oswald the Rabbit (1927-28)

Great Guns (1927) GPS 2
The Mechanical Cow (1927) GPS 2

The following cartoons are reprints of home movie versions marketed by Hollywood Film Enterprises in the thirties. HFE retitled the cartoons; the original titles are given following the date.
Alice's Orphan (1925, Alice's Ornery Orphan, from the *Alice in Cartoonland* series) NFP 2, 4, 6
Mickey Plays Santa Clause (1932, Mickey's Good Deed) TBF 2, 4
Movie Star Mickey (1933, Mickey's Gala Premiere) HFRP 2, 4; TBF 2, 4
Robinson Crusoe Mickey (1931, The Castaway) TBF 2, 4

Silly Symphonies (1929-39) (Disney prints)

The Three Little Pigs (1933) BHF 3, 4; SFL 3, 4; WDHM 3, 3s, 4. (See compilations)
The Tortoise and the Hare (1935) BHF 3, 4; SFL 3, 4; WDHM 3, 3s, 4
The Ugly Duckling (1939) BHF 3, 4; EPF 4; SFL 3, 4; WDHM 3, 3s, 4

The following cartoons feature the regular Disney characters. The characters in each cartoon, when known, are given following the date; if identified by the title, they are not repeated.
Bell Boy Donald (1942) PMF 3, 3s, 4; WDPL 3, 3s, 4
Boat Builders (1938, Mickey, Donald, Goofy) PMF 3, 3s, 4; WDPL 3, 3s, 4
Bone Trouble (1940, Pluto) EPF 4; SFL 3, 4
Chef Donald (1941) BHF 3, 4; SFL 3, 4; WDHM 3, 3s, 4
Chip N' Dale (1947, Donald) PMF 3, 3s, 4; WDPL 3, 3s, 4
Clock Cleaners (1937, Mickey, Donald, Goofy) BHF 1; SFL 1, 3, 4; WDHM 3, 3s, 4
Clown of the Jungle (1947, Donald) BHF 3; SFL 3, 4; WDHM 3
Don Donald (1937) PMF 3, 3s, 4; WDPL 3, 3s, 4
Donald and Pluto (1936) BHF 3, 4; SFL 3, 4; WDHM 3, 3s, 4
Good Scouts (1938, Donald and nephews) BHF 3; SFL 3, 4; WDHM 3, 3s, 4
Goofy's Glider (1940) BHF 3; SFL 3, 4; WDHM 3, 3s, 4
Hawaiian Holiday (1937, Mickey, Donald, Pluto) SFL 3, 4; WDHM 3, 3s, 4

A Knight for a Day (1946, Mickey, Donald, Goofy) BHF 3; SFL 3, 4; WDHM 3, 3s, 4

The Legend of Coyote Rock (1945, Pluto) BMH 1; DMFS 1; BHF 1; WDPL 1
Lion Around (1950, Donald and nephews) BHF 3; SFL 3, 4; WDHM 3, 3s, 4
Lonesome Ghosts (1937, Mickey, Donald, Goofy) BHF 2; SFL 2; WDHM 2
Mickey's Circus (1936) PMF 3, 3s, 4; WDPL 3, 3s, 4
Mickey's Delayed Date (1947, Minnie, Pluto) BHF 3; SFL 3, 4; WDHM 3, 3s, 4
Mickey's Trailer (1938) BMH 1; DMFS 1; BHF 1; WDPL 1
Minnie's Yoo Hoo (early 1930s, public domain item released by TBF) TBF 2
Moose Hunters (1937, Mickey, Donald, Goofy) BHF 3; SFL 3, 4; WDHM 3
No Sail (1945, Donald, Goofy) PMF 3, 3s, 4; DWDPL 3, 3s, 4
The Olympic Champ (1942, Goofy) BHF 3; SFL 3, 4; WDHM 3
On Ice (1935, Mickey, Donald, Goofy) PMF 3, 3s, 4; WDPL 3, 3s, 4
Pluto's Christmas Tree (1952, Mickey, Chip N' Dale) BHF 3; SFL 3, 4; WDHM 3, 4
Pluto's Fledgling (1948) BHF 3; SFL 3, 4; WDHM 3
The Riveter (1940, Donald) PMF 3, 3s, 4; WDPL 3, 3s, 4
The Simple Things (1953, Mickey, Pluto) PMF 3, 3s, 4; WDPL 3, 3s, 4
Soup's On (1947, Donald and nephews) BHF 1; PMFS 1; BMH 1; WDPL 1
The Spirit of '43 (1943, Donald, World War II patriotic cartoon) BMH 1; HFE 1; MWFS 1; RI 1
Tea for Two Hundred (1948, Donald) BHF 3; SFL 3, 4; WDHM 3, 4
Three for Breakfast (1948, Donald, Chip N' Dale) BHF 3, 4; SFL 3, 4; WDHM 3, 3s, 4

Three Little Pigs (1933) BHF 3; WDHM 3; BMH 3
The Tortoise and The Hare (1935) BHF 3; BMH 3; DMFS 3; WDHM 3
Trailer Horn (1950, Donald, Chip N' Dale) BHF 3; SFL 3, 4; WDHM 3, 3s, 4
Trick or Treat (1952, Donald and nephews) BHF 3, SFL 3, 4; WDHM 3, 3s, 4
The Ugly Duckling (1939) BHF 3; BMH 3; DMFS 3; WDHM 3
Working for Peanuts (1953, Donald, Chip N' Dale) PMF 3, 3s, 4; WDPL 3, 3s, 4

Compilations

Cartoon Classics, Volume 1: The Three Little Pigs (1933), Old King Cole (1933), Grasshopper and the Ants (1934), Three Little Wolves (1936), and The Pied Piper (1933) (400-foot reel) BHF 1; DMFS 1; BMH 1; WDPL 1

Donald Duck: Donald's Golf Game (1938) and Inferior Decorator (1948) (300-foot reel) BHF 3, 4; SFL 3, 4

Goofy: Goofy and Wilbur (1939) and Two Gun Goofy (1952) (300-foot reel) BHF 3, 4; SFL 3, 4

Mickey Mouse: Mr. Mouse Takes A Trip (1940) and Mickey Down Under (1948) (300-foot reel) BHF 3, 4; SFL 3, 4

Cartoon Parade No. 1: Boat Builders, Clown of the Jungle, Moose Hunters. See previous entries for descriptions; these are on a 200-foot reel, abridged to 1/3 length BHF 3, 4; SFL 3, 4; WDHM 3, 4

Cartoon Parade No. 2: Don Donald, Chip N' Dale, Mickey's Garden (1935). Same format as previous entry BHF 3, 4; SFL 3, 4; WDHM 3, 4

Cartoon Parade No. 3: The Brave Little Tailor (1938), Modern Inventions (1937, Donald), Zorro the Imposter (live action). Same format as the others in this series PMF 3, 4; WDPL 3, 4

Donald Duck's Dilemmas: highlights from Donald's Golf Game (1938), Modern Inventions (1937), Donald's Garden (1942), Dude Duck (1951), The Riveter (1940) (400-foot reel) BHF 1; BMH 1; CE 1; DMFS 1; EPF 1; GSF 1; HFE 1; RFF 1; SFL 1; WDHM 1
Donald Duck's Dilemmas, Volume 2: highlights from Test Pilot Donald (1950), Wet Paint, Donald's Camera (1941), The Plastic Inventor (1944), The New Neighbor (1953) BHF 1; BMH 1; DMFS 1; WDHM 1
Goofy's Golden Gags: highlights from Goofy's Glider (1940), Baggage Buster (1941), The Art of Self Defense (1941), Tiger Trouble (1945), A Knight for a Day (1946) (400-foot reel) BHF 1; BMH 1; CE 1; DMFS 1; EPF 1; GSF 1; HFE 1; RFF 1; SFL 1; WDHM 1
Goofy's Golden Gags, Volume 2: highlights from Hold That Pose, Two Gun Goofy (1952), They're Off (1947), Goofy and Wilbur (1939) and Bill Posters (1940) (400-foot reel)   BHF 1; BMH 1; CE 1; DMFS 1; EPF 1; GSF 1; HFE 1; RFF 1; SFL 1; WDHM 1
Mickey's Memorable Moments: highlights from Magician Mickey (1937), The Brave Little Tailor (1938), Mickey's Delayed Date (1947), Mickey and the Seal (1948), The Simple Things (1953) (400-foot reel) BHF 1; BMH 1; CE 1; DMFS 1; EPF 1; GSF 1; HFE 1; RFF 1; SFL 1; WDHM 1
Pluto's Playful Pranks: highlights from Pluto's Fledgling (1948), Pluto's Playmate (1941), Canine Caddy (1941), Pluto's Quintuplets (1937), Bone Trouble (1940) (400-foot reel) BHF 1; CE 1; DMFS 1; GSF 1; RFF 1; WDHM 1

A Walt Disney Christmas: excerpts from holiday cartoons: Donald, Mickey, Pluto, Chip N' Dale (400-foot reel) BMH 1; CE 1; GSF 1; WDHM 1

Mickey Mouse: The First Fifty Years. Excerpts from Steamboat Willie, The Sorcerer's Apprentice (Fantasia), the Mickey Mouse Club, etc. (400-foot reel) BMH 1, CE 1; GSF 1; WDHM 1
Highlights of the Mickey Mouse Club: contains both animated and live-action excerpts from the TV show BHF 2; BMH 2; RFF 2

Highlights from Features and Featurettes

This is a listing of animated films only; live-action excerpts from the features are also available.
Alice in Wonderland (1951): Alice and the White Rabbit BHF 1, 3; BMH 1; DMFS 1; GSF 1; HFE 1; NFP 1; RFF 1; SFL 1, 3, 4; WDHM 1, 3
Alice in Wonderland (1951): The Mad Tea Party BHF 1; BMH 1; DMFS 1; GSF 1; HFE 1; MWFS 1; NFP 1; RFF 1; SFL 1; WDHM 1
The Aristocats (1970): The Aristocats BHF 3, 4; DMFS 3; SFL 3, 4; WDHM 3, 4
Bambi (1942): Bambi and His Friends RFF 1
Bambi (1942): Bambi Falls in Love BHF 1, 3, 4; BMH 1; DMFS 1; EPF 4; GSF 1; HFE 1; MWFS 1; NFP 1; SFL 1, 3, 4; WDHM 1, 3, 3s, 4

Bedknobs and Broomsticks (1971): The Beautiful Briny (live-action and animation) DFS 1; PFDL 1; PMF 1; WDPL 1

Bedknobs and Broomsticks (1971): The Match of the Century BHF 1, 3, 4; BMH 1; DMFS 1; GSF 1; HFE 1; RFF 1; SFL 1, 3, 4; WDHM 1, 3, 4

Cinderella (1950): Cinderella's Fairy Godmother BHF 1, 3, 4; BMH 1; DMFS 1; GSF 1; NFP 1; RFF 1; SFL 1, 3, 4; WDHM 1, 3, 3s, 4

Cinderella (1950): Cinderella's Surprise Dress BHF 1; BMH 1; CE 1; DMFS 1; GSF 1; RFF 1; WDHM 1

Dumbo (1941): Dumbo Makes the Big Top EPF 4

Dumbo (1941): Dumbo, the Flying Elephant BHF 1, 3; BMH 1; DMFS 1; GSF 1; HFE 1; NFP 1; RFF 1; SFL 1, 3, 4; WDHM 1, 3

Fantasia (1940): Dance of the Hours PMF 1

The Jungle Book (1967): I Wan'na Be Like You BHF 1; BMH 1; DMFS 1; GSF 1; HFE 1; NFP 1; RFF 1; SFL 1; WDHM 1

The Jungle Book (1967): Mowgli, The Jungle Boy BHF 1; BMH 1; CE 1; DMFS 1; GSF 1; RFF 1; WDHM 1

Lady and the Tramp (1955): An Evening with Lady and the Tramp BHF 1; BMH 1; CE 1; DMFS 1; GSF 1; RFF 1; WDHM 1

Lady and the Tramp (1955): Muzzle Trouble BHF 1, 3; BMH 1; DMFS 1; GSF 1; HFE 1; RFF 1; SFL 1, 3, 4; WDHM 1, 3

Mary Poppins (1963): Jolly Holiday (live-action and animation) RFF 1

101 Dalmatians (1961): The Dapper Dalmatian BHF 1, 3; BMH 1; DMFS 1; EPF 3; GSF 1; HFE 1; NFP 1; SFL 1, 3, 4; WDHM 1, 3, 4

Peter Pan (1953): Peter Pan Meets Captain Hook BHF 1, 3, 4; BMH 1; DMFS 1; GSF 1; HFE 1; NFP 1; RFF 1; SFL 1, 3, 4; WDHM 1, 3, 4

Pete's Dragon (1977): Pete's Dragon (live-action with animated dragon) BHF 1; BMH 1; DMFS 1; GSF 1; HFE 1; NFP 1; RFF 1; SFL 1; WDHM 1.

Pinocchio (1940): Monstro the Whale BHF 1, 3, 4; BMH 1; DMFS 1; GSF 1; HFE 1; NFP 1; RFF 1; SFL 1, 3, 4; WDHM 1, 3, 3s, 4

Pinocchio (1940): Pinocchio Comes To Life BHF 1; BMH 1; DMFS 1; WDHM 1

The Rescuers (1977): The Rescue BHF 1, 3; BMH 1; CE 1; DMFS 1; GSF 1; HFE 1; RFF 1; WDHM 1, 3

Robin Hood (1973): Robin Hood and Little John BHF 1, 3, 4; BMH 1; DMFS 1; GSF 1; HFE 1; NFP 1; RFF 1; SFL 1, 3, 4; WDHM 1, 3, 4

Robin Hood (1973): Robin Hood Rescues Maid Marian BHF 1; BMH 1; CE 1; DMFS 1; GSF 1; RFF 1; WDHM 1

Saludos Amigos (1943): Donald Duck in the High Andes BHF 1, 3; BMH 1; DMFS 1; GSF 1; HFE 1; MWFS 1; NFP 1; RFF 1; SFL 1, 3, 4; WDHM 1, 3

Sleeping Beauty (1959): Once Upon a Dream BHF 1; BMH 1; CE 1; DMFS 1; GSF 1; RFF 1; WDHM 1

Sleeping Beauty (1959): The Prince and the Dragon BHF 1, 3, 4; BMH 1; DMFS 1; GSF 1; HFE 1; NFP 1; RFF 1; SFL 1, 3, 4; WDHM 1, 3, 4

The Small One (1978): DMFS 1; BHF 1; BMH 1

Snow White and the Seven Dwarfs (1937): The Dwarfs' Dilemma BHF 1, 3, 4; BMH 1; DMFS 1; GSF 1; HFE 1; NFP 1; RFF 1; SFL 1, 3, 4; WDHM 1, 3, 3s, 4

Snow White and the Seven Dwarfs (1937): Whistle While You Work DFS 1, PMF 1; WDPL 1

Song of the South (1946): Brer Rabbit and the Tar Baby BHF 1; BMH 1; DMFS 1; GSF 1; HFE 1; NFP 1; RFF 1; SFL 1; WDHM 1, 3

The Sword in the Stone (1963): Duel of the Wizards BHF 1, 3; BMH 1; DMFS 1; GSF 1; NFP 1; RFF 1; SFL 1, 3, 4; WDHM 1, 3

The Three Caballeros (1945): The Three Caballeros BHF 1; BMH 1; DMFS 1; GSF 1; HFE 1; NFP 1; RFF 1; SFL 1; WDHM 1

Winnie the Poor and the Honey Tree (1966): BHF 3, 4; EPF 3, 4; SFL 3, 4; WDHM 3, 4

Winnie the Pooh and and Tigger Too (1974): BHF 1; BMH 1; DMFS 1; GSF 1; HFE 1; NFP 1; RFF 1; SFL 1, 3, 4; WDHM 1, 3

FAMOUS STUDIO

Famous Studio, the cartoon unit of Paramount Pictures, was a reorganization of the former Fleischer Studio. Among other cartoons, Famous produced a *Noveltoon* and a *Screen Song* series during the forties and fifties.

Popeye (see Fleischer Studio for the earlier Popeye cartoons)

Cookin' With Gags (1954) GSF 1
Hill-Billing and Cooing (1955) GSF 1
House Tricks (1945) GSF 1
Let's Stalk Spinach (1951) GSF 1
Out to Punch (1956) GSF 1
She-Sick Sailors (1945) BMH 1; NFP 1, 2
Toreadorable (1953) GSF 1

The following Popeye cartoons are unidentified as to which studio animated them (Famous or Fleischer), because they could not be located in the Library of Congress, *Catalogue of Motion Pictures* (1921-1939; 1940-1949; 1950-1959; 1960-1969). Some of these have apparently been retitled; others appear to be TV cartoons.

Ace of Space JEF 1; PMF 1
The Astro-Nut JEF 1; PMF 1
Autographically Yours JEF 1
Battery Up JEF 1
The Big Sneeze JEF 1
Billionaire JEF 1; PMF 1
The Bird Watcher JEF 1
Bullfighter Bully JEF 1; PMF 1
The Champ DMFS 4s
Circus Man DMFS 4s
Crystal Ball Brawl JEF 1
The Cure JEF 1
Deep Sea Diver DMFS 4
Fancy Skater DMFS 4
Fleas a Crowd JEF 1
Flim Flam Fireman DMFS 4s
The Glad Gladiator JEF 1; PMF 1
The Green Dancing Shoes JEF 1

Hits and Missiles JEF 1
Hoppy Jalopy JEF 1; PMF 1
House Wrecker DMFS 4s
Indian Fighter DMFS 4
Intellectual Interlude JEF 1
Invisible Popeye JEF 1; PMF 1
Knife Juggler DMFS 4
The Magic Hat JEF 1; PMF 1
A Mite of Trouble JEF 1
My Fair Olive JEF 1
A Pal for Olive Oyl JEF 1
Pest of the Pecos JEF 1
Pop Goes the Whistle JEF 1
Popeye and Buddy Brutus JEF 1
Popeye and the Dragon JEF 1; PMF 1
Popeye and the Herring Snatcher JEF 1
Popeye and the Phantom JEF 1; PMF 1
Popeye in the Woods JEF 1
Popeye the Lifeguard JEF 1; PMF 1
Popeye's Car Wash JEF 1; PMF 1
Popeye's Folly JEF 1
Popeye's Pet Store JEF 1; PMF 1
Popeye's Picnic JEF 1
Potent Lotion JEF 1
Robot Popeye JEF 1
Skeleton Schooner DMFS 4s
Ski Jump Chump JEF 1
Spare Dat Tree JEF 1; PMF 1
Spoil Sport JEF 1
Suddenly It's Spring (1944) RI 1
Train Buster DMFS 4s
The Trojan Horse JEF 1
Which is Witch JEF 1; PMF 1
Who's Kiddin' Zoo? JEF 1
Wimpy's Lunch Wagon JEF 1

Superman (see Fleischer Studio for the earlier Superman cartoons)

Destruction, Inc. (1942) NFP 2; RFF 2

The Eleventh Hour (1942) TBF 2

The Japoteurs (1942) BMH 1; DMFS 1, 2; EPF 1, 2; NFP 1, 2; RFF 1, 2; RI 1; SFL 1; TBF 1, 2

Jungle Drums (1943) BMH 1; DMFS 1, 2; EPF 1, 2; NFP 1, 2; RFF 1, 2; RI 1; SFL 1

The Mechanical Monsters (1941) BMH 1; DMFS 1, 2; GSF 1; HFE 1; NFP 1, 2; RFF 1, 2; RI 1; SFL 1; TBF 2

Secret Agent (1944) NFP 2; RFF 2; TBF 2

FLEISCHER STUDIO

Max and Dave Fleischer began making animated cartoons in 1915, using the rotoscope which they had developed. An early *Out of the Inkwell* series featured Ko-Ko the Clown. Other series in the 1920s were *Song Car-Tunes, Inkwell Imps, Screen Songs*, and, in 1929, *Talkartoons*. The Fleischer Studio was assocaited with Paramount from 1927 until the early 1940s when the brothers departed.

Early Fleischer Cartoons

Bubbles (1922, with Ko-Ko the Clown) GPS 4

The Clown's Little Brother (1918, with Ko-Ko) GPS 4; RI 4

Darwin's Theory of Evolution (1923, five-reel feature with animated sequences) GPS 3, 4

Einstein's Theory of Relativity (1923, two-reel condensation of the feature, comprising most of the animated footage) GPS 4

Finding His Voice (1929, explains how sound is put on film) GPS 2

In My Merry Oldsmobile (Screen Song) BHF 2

In the Good Old Summertime (ca. 1924-25, a *Song Car-Tune*) BHF 2, 4

Ko-Ko the Kop (1927) GPS 4

Modeling (1920, from the *Out of the Inkwell* series, with Ko-Ko the Clown) GPS 4, 6

The Ouija Board (1920, with Ko-Ko) GPS 4; RI 4

Perpetual Motion (1918, with Ko-Ko) GPS 4; RI 4

Surprise (1921, from the *Out of the Inkwell* series, with Ko-Ko the Clown) HFRP 4

The Tantalizing Fly (1917, from the *Out of the Inkwell* series, with Ko-Ko) GPS 4; EPS 2

Betty Boop

Baby Be Good (1935) MWFS 2; NFP 2; SFL 2

Be Human (1936) TBF 2

Betty and Henry (1936, this is the comic strip Henry) MWFS 2; NFP 2; SFL 2

Betty and the Little King (1936) NFP 2; SFL 2

Betty Boop for President (1932) BMH 1; GSF 1; IVY 1; RFF 1; RI 1; TBF 1

Betty Boop's Life Guard (1934) TBF 2

Betty Boop's Museum (1932) HFRP 2, 4; TBF 2

Betty Boop's Penthouse (1933) BMH 1; GSF 1; IVY 1; MWFS 1; RFF 1; RI 1; TBF 1

Betty Boop's Rise to Fame (1934) BMH 1; IVY 1; RFF 1; RI 1; TBF 1; DMFS 1

Betty in Blunderland (1934) HFE 2, 4; NFP 2; SFL 2; TBF 2

Boop-Oop-A-Doop (1932) TBF 2

Crazy Town (1932) TBF 2

Ding Dong Doggie (1937) TBF 2

Dizzy Red Riding Hood (1931) HFRP 2, 4; TBF 2

Ha! Ha! Ha! (1934, with Ko-Ko) BMH 1; IVY 1; RFF 1; RI 1; TBF 1; DMFS 1

Happy You and Merry Me (1936) TBF 2

Hot Air Salesman (1937) TBF 2

I'll Be Glad When You're Dead You Rascal You (1932, with Bimbo and Koko) BHF 1; BMH 1; IVY 1; MWFS 1; RFF 1; RI 1; TBF 1

Jack and the Beanstalk (1931) HFRP 2, 4

Keep in Style (1934) TBF 2, 4

A Little Soap and Water (1935) RI 1

Minnie the Moocher (1932, with Bimbo) BHF 1; BMH 1; IVY 1; RFF 1; RI 1; TBF 1

Mother Goose Land (1933) HFRP 2, 4; TBF 2

Musical Mountaineers (1939) GPS 2

My Friend the Monkey (1939) TBF 2

No! No! A Thousand Times No!! (1935) TBF 2

The Old Man of the Mountain (1933) BHF 1; BMH 1; IVY 1; RFF 1; RI 1; TBF 1

Parade of the Wooden Soldiers (1933) TBF 2, 4

Poor Cinderella (1934) NFP 2; SFL 2; TBF 2

Rise to Fame DMFS 1

Snow White (1933) BHF 1; BMH 1; IVY 1; MWFS 1; RFF 1; RI 1; TBF 1; DMFS 1

S.O.S. (Swim or Sink) (1932, with Bimbo and Ko-Ko) HFRP 2, 4; TBF 2

Yip Yip Yippy (1939) CBF 2; FC 2

Color Classics

The Cobweb Hotel (1936) BMH 2; CBF 2; FC 2; MWFS 2

The Kids in the Shoe (1935) CBF 1; FC 1; TBF 2, 4

Small Fry (1939) BMH 1; CBF 1; FC 1; RI 1; TBF 1, 2, 4

The Song of the Birds (1935) HFE 1

Gabby

King for a Day (1940) BMH 1; CBF 1; FC 1; MWFS 1; TBF 1

Popeye (see Famous Studio for the later Popeye cartoons)

Aladdin and his Wonderful Lamp (1939) BMH 1; DMFS 1; NFP 1, 2; RFF 1, 2; SFL 1

Customers Wanted (1939) MWFS 2; NFP 2; RFF 2

Eugene the Jeep (1938) NFP 2; RFF 2

I-Ski Love-Ski You-Ski (1936) NFP 2; RFF 2

Let's Singalong with Popeye (1934) GPS 2

Poopdeck Pappy (1940) NFP 2; RFF 2

Popeye the Sailor meets Ali Baba's Forty Thieves (1937) BMH 1; DMFS 1, 2; NFP 1, 2; RFF 1, 2; SFL 1; TBF 1, 2

Popeye the Sailor meets Sinbad the Sailor (1936) BMH 1; DMFS 1; NFP 1, 2; RFF 1, 2; SFL 1; TBF 1, 2

Superman (see Famous Studio for the later Superman cartoons)

Arctic Giant (1942) NFP 2; RFF 2

Billion Dollar Ltd. (1942) TBF 2

The Bulleteers (1942) BMH 1; DMFS 1, 2; EPF 1, 2; NFP 1, 2; RFF 1, 2; RI 1; SFL 1; TBF 2

The Electric Earthquake (1942) NFP 2; RFF 2; TBF 2

Magnetic Telescope (1942) RFF 1; TBF 2

The Mummy Strikes (1943) BMH 1; DMFS 1, 2; EPF 1, 2; NFP 1, 2; RFF 1, 2; RI 1; SFL 1

Superman (1941) BMH 1; DMFS 1, 2; EPF 1, 2; NFP 1, 2; RFF 1, 2; RI 1; SFL 1

Terror on the Midway (1942) BMH 1; RFF 1

The Volcano (1942) NFP 2; RFF 2; TBF 2

Full-Length Animated Features

Gulliver's Travels (1939) BHF 1; BMH 1; DMFS 1; EPF 1, 2; HFE 1; IVY 1; NFP 1, 2; RFF 1; TBF 1, 2

Mr. Bug Goes to Town (1941, often listed as "Hoppity Goes to Town") BHF 1; BMH 1; EPF 1, 2; FC 1; IVY 1; NFP 1, 2; RFF 1; RI 1

Highlights from Animated Features

Gulliver's Travels (1939) DMFS 4, 4s

HANNA-BARBERA PRODUCTIONS

Organized by Bill Hanna and Joe Barbera (formerly with the MGM cartoon unit) in the late 1950s for the production of television cartoons, the studio has also produced some theatrical cartoons and several animated features.

The Cattanooga Cats

The Cattanooga Cats DFS 1; PMF 1

Dastardly and Muttley

Barnstormers DFS 1, 4; JEF 1; PMF 1, 4

Cuckoo Patrol DFS 1; JEF 1; PMF 1

Follow That Feather DFS 1, 4, 4s; JEF 1; PMF 1, 4, 4s

Home Sweet Homing Pigeon DFS 1; JEF 1; PMF 1

Movies are Badder than Ever DFS 1; JEF 1; PMF 1

Operation Anvil DFS 1, 4, 4s; JEF 1; PMF 1, 4, 4s

Pest Pilot DFS 1, 4; JEF 1; PMF 1, 4

The Flintstones

Ann Margrock Presents FC 1; SFL 1

Baby Barney FC 1

Barney the Invisible (1962, TV) FC 1; SFL 1

The Bedrock Hillbillies FC 1; SFL 1, 3

Big League Freddie BMH 1; FC 1

The Big Move FC 1

The Birthday Party BMH 1; FC 1

Boss for a Day FC 1
The Bowling Ballet (1962, TV) BMH 1; FC 1
Cave Scout Jamboree FC 1
Circus Business BMH 1; FC 1
Curtain Call at Bedrock FC 1
Daddy's Little Beauty FC 1; SFL 1
Dino Disappears FC 1; SFL 1
Flashgun Freddie FC 1
Flintstone and the Lion BMH 1; FC 1; SFL 1
The Flintstone Canaries BMH 1; FC 1; SFL 1
The Flintstone Flyer BHF 1; FC 1; SFL 1
Foxy Grandma FC 1; SFL 1
Fred El Terrifico FC 1; SFL 1
Fred Goes Ape FC 1; SFL 1
Fred Meets Hercurock FC 1; SFL 1
Fred's Flying Lesson SFL 3
Fred's Island FC 1; SFL 1
Fred's Monkeyshines FC 1; SFL 1
The Great Gazoo BMH 1; FC 1; GSF 1; SFL 1
Groom Gloom FC 1; SFL 1
The Gruesomes FC 1; SFL 1, 3
The Hero FC 1
Hot Lips Hanigan FC 1; SFL 1
The House that Fred Built BMH 1; FC 1; SFL 1
Indianrockopolis 500 SFL 3
Ladies Day FC 1
Little Bamm Bamm BMH 1; FC 1; SFL 1
The Masquerade Party (copyright catalog has "The Masquerade *Ball*," 1961) FC 1
The Monster from the Tar Pits BHF 1; FC 1; GSF 1; SFL 1
No Biz Like Shoe Biz FC 1; SFL 1, 3
Nothing But the Tooth FC 1
The Return of Stoney Curtis FC 1
Rip Van Flintstone FC 1
Seeing Doubles FC 1
Shinrock-A-Go-Go FC 1
Son of Rockzilla FC 1; GSF 1; SFL 1
Surfin' Fred BHF 1; FC 1
Ten Little Flintstones BMH 1; FC 1
The Twitch (1962, TV) BMH 1; FC 1; SFL 1
Two Men on a Dinosaur BMH 1; FC 1

The Great Grape Ape

First Grape in Space PMF 1
The Grape is Born PMF 1
The Invisible Ape PMF 1
Public Grape No. 1 PMF 1

Huckleberry Hound

Huckleberry Hound Meets Wee Willie (1958, TV) FC 1; SFL 1
Lion Hearted Huck (1958, TV) FC 1; SFL 1
Rustler-Hustler Huck (1958, TV) FC 1; SFL 1
Sir Huckleberry Hound (1958, TV) BHF 1; FC 1; SFL 1
Tricky Trapper (1958, TV) FC 1; SFL 1

The Jetsons

Astro's Top Secret (1962) FC 1
A Date with Jet Screamer (1962, TV) FC 1; SFL 1
Elroy's TV Show (1962, TV) FC 1; SFL 1
The Flying Suit (1962, TV) FC 1; SFL 1
G. I. Jetson (1963, TV) FC 1
Jane's Driving Lesson (1963, TV) BMH 1; FC 1
Jetson's Night Out (1962, TV) FC 1; SFL 1
Millionaire Astro (1962) FC 1
Private Property (1963) FC 1
Rosey the Robot (1962, TV) FC 1; SFL 1
Test Pilot (1962, TV) SFL 3
Visit from Grandpa (1962, TV) SFL 3

Loopy de Loop

Pork Chop Phooey (1963) FC 1; SFL 1
Zoo is Company (1961) FC 1; SFL 1

Magilla Gorilla

Makin' it with Magilla FC 1; SFL 1

Mightor

Mightor and the Giant Insects JEF 1
Mightor and the Ice Trap JEF 1
Mightor and the Snow Men JEF 1
Mightor and the Tusk Men JEF 1
Mightor and the Vulture Men JEF 1
Mightor Against the Monster JEF 1

Moby Dick

Moby Dick Against the Electric Monster JEF 1
Moby Dick Against the Sea Monsters JEF 1
Moby Dick Under the Bottom of the Sea JEF 1

Motor Mouse and Autocat

Mini Messenger DFS 1, 4, 4s; PMF 1, 4, 4s
Soggy to Me DFS 1, 4, 4s; PMF 1, 4, 4s

What's the Motor with You? DFS 1, 4; PMF 1, 4
Wild Wheelin' Wheels DFS 1, 4; PMF 1, 4

Pixie and Dixie

Cousin Tex (1958, TV) FC 1; SFL 1
Jink's Mouse Device (1958, TV, copyright catalog has "Jink's *Mice* Device") FC
1; SFL 1
Judo Jack (1958, TV) FC 1; SFL 1
Kit Kat Kit (1958, TV) FC 1; SFL 1
Scaredy Cat Dog (1958, TV) FC 1; SFL 1

Quick Draw McGraw

Bad Guys Disguise FC 1; SFL 1
El Kabong FC 1; SFL 1
Lamb Chopped FC 1; SFL 1
Masking for Trouble FC 1; SFL 1

Scooby Doo

The Backstage Rage PMF 1
Bedlam in the Big Top PMF 1
Hassle in the Castle PMF 1
Haunted House Hang Up PMF 1
Mystery Mask Mix-Up PMF 1
That Snow Ghost PMF 1

Snagglepuss

Feud for Thought FC 1; SFL 1
Major Operations FC 1; SFL 1

The Three Musketeers

A Fair Day for Tooly DFS 1, 3, 4; JEF 1; PMF 1, 3, 4
The Haunted Castle DFS 1, 3, 4; JEF 1; PMF 1, 3, 4

Top Cat

The Grand Tour (1961, TV) SFL 1
Hawaii Here We Come (1961, TV) SFL 1
The Late Top Cat (1962) RFF 1
The $1,000,000 Derby (1961, TV) SFL 1
Sergeant Top Cat (1961, TV) SFL 1
Space Monkey (1961, TV) SFL 3
Top Cat Falls in Love (1961, TV) SFL 1
Top Cat Fights a Duel SFL 3
Top Cat Minds the Baby (1962) RFF 1

Yakky Doodle Duck

    Easter Duck FC 1; SFL 1
    Yakky Doodle Duck FC 1; SFL 1

Yogi Bear

    Bear on a Picnic (1958, TV) FC 1; SFL 1
    Big Bad Bully (1958, TV) FC 1; SFL 1
    Big Brave Bear (1958, TV) FC 1; SFL 1
    Home Sweet Jellystone FC 1; SFL 1
    Love Bugged Bear FC 1; SFL 1
    Nowhere Bear FC 1; SFL 1
    Pie Pirates (1958, TV) FC 1; SFL 1
    Slumber Party Smarty (1958, TV) FC 1; SFL 1
    Space Bear FC 1; SFL 1
    Touch and Go-Go-Go SFL 3
    Yogi Bear's Big Break (1958, TV) BHF 1; FC 1; SFL 1

UB IWERKS

Initially the chief animator for Disney prior to and during the early Mickey Mouse years, Iwerks left Disney in 1930 and operated his own studio for several years.

ComiColor Cartoons

    Aladdin and the Wonderful Lamp (1934) BHF 1
    Ali Baba (1932) BHF 1
    The Brave Tin Soldier (1934) BHF 1
    Happy Days (1936) BHF 1
    The Headless Horseman (1934) BHF 1
    Jack and the Beanstalk (1933) BHF 1
    Jack Frost (1934) BHF 1
    Little Black Sambo BMH 1; HFE 1; MWFS 1; NFP 1
    The Little Red Hen (1934) BHF 1
    Old Mother Hubbard (1934) TBF 1
    Pin-Cushion Man BMH 1; FC 1; HFE 1; RFF 1
    Simple Simon TBF 3, 4
    Sinbad the Sailor (1934) BHF 1; TBF 1, 2, 4
    Summertime (1934) BHF 1
    Tom Thumb BHF 2

Flip the Frog

    Bulloney (1933) BHF 2
    The Cuckoo Murder Case (1931) BHF 2
    Fiddlesticks (1930) BHF 1
    Funny Face (1933) BHF 2
    Jail Birds (1932) FFL 4

The New Car (1931) BHF 2
Nursemaid (1932) BHF 2
Pale-Face (1933) FFL 4
Puddle Pranks BHF 2
The Soda Squirt (1933) BHF 2
Spooks (1932) BHF 2
Techno-Cracked (1933) BHF 2

Willie Whopper

A Good Scout (1934) FFL 4
Rasslin' Around (1934) FFL 4

WALTER LANTZ

Walter Lantz produced a *Hot Dog* series in 1926-27, along with an "Unnatural History" series. These were released through Bray Productions. From 1930 to 1938 he produced *Oswald the Rabbit* cartoons, after Disney lost the rights to this character. From the 1930s on his "cartunes" have been released through Universal. Among his later "cartunes" was a *Swing Symphony* series.

Early Lantz Cartoons

Goodrich Dirt, Cowpuncher (1926, with Pete the Pup) GPS 4. *Note*: Thunderbird Films offers a cartoon with the exact same title, but identified as a Wallace Carlson film, 1919. This title is not listed in the copyright catalog.
Little Red Riding Hood (1926, a Dinky Doodle Cartoon with Pete the Pup) GPS 4
The Lunch Hound (1927, *Hot Dog* series) GPS 4
The Monkey's Tale (1926, *Unnatural History* series) GPS 4. *Note*: The copyright catalog lists this as "The Tail of the Monkey."
Pete the Pup (1926, *Hot Dog* series) GPS 4
Romeoing (ca. 1927, *Hot Dog* series, with Pete the Pup and Goodrich Dirt) GPS 4

Andy Panda

The Playful Pelican (1948) DMFS 1, 3, 4; RFF 1, 3, 4; SFL 4

Chilly Willy

The Big Snooze (1957) DMFS 1, 3; RFF 1, 3; SFL 2, 4
Clash and Carry (1961) BHF 1; DMFS 1, 3, 4; RFF 1, 3, 4; SFL 2
Fish Hooked (1960) DMFS 1, 3, 4; RFF 1, 3, 4; SFL 2
Polar Pests (1958) DMFS 1, 3; RFF 1, 3; SFL 2, 4
Room and Wrath (1956) DMFS 1, 3; RFF 1, 3; SFL 2, 4
Swiss Miss-Fit (1957) DMFS 1, 3; RFF 1, 3; SFL 2, 4
Yukon Have It (1959) DMFS 1, 3, 4; RFF 1, 3, 4; SFL 2

Dynamo Doc

Doc's Last Stand (1961) DMFS 1, 3, 4; RFF 1, 3, 4; SFL 4

Mouse Trapped (1959) DMFS 1, 3, 4; RFF 1, 3, 4; SFL 4
Pest of Show (1962) DMFS 1, 3, 4; RFF 1, 3, 4; SFL 4

Inspector Willoughby

Case of the Cold Storage Yegg (1963) DMFS 1, 3, 4; RFF 1, 3, 4; SFL 2
Case of the Red-Eyed Ruby (1961) BHF 1; DMFS 1, 3, 4; RFF 1, 3, 4; SFL 2
Hyde and Sneak (1962) DMFS 1, 3, 4; RFF 1, 3, 4; SFL 2, 4
Phoney Express (1962) DMFS 1, 3, 4; RFF 1, 3, 4; SFL 2
Rough and Tumbleweed (1961) DMFS 1, 3, 4; RFF 1, 3, 4; SFL 2

Pierre Bear

After the Ball (1956, copyright catalog calls this a "Woody Woodpecker" cartoon) DMFS 1, 3; RFF 1, 3; SFL 2
Calling All Cuckoos (1956, copyright catalog calls this a "Woody Woodpecker" cartoon) DMFS 1, 3; RFF 1, 3; SFL 2.
Hunger Strife (1960) DMFS 1, 3, 4; RFF 1, 3, 4; SFL 2
Salmon Yeggs (1958, with Windy and Breezy) DMFS 1, 3, 4; RFF 1, 3, 4; SFL 2, 4
Three Ring Fling (1958) DMFS 1, 3; RFF 1, 3; SFL 2

Woody Woodpecker

Bats in the Belfry (1960) BHF 2; BMH 1; DMFS 1, 2, 3, 4; RFF 1, 2, 3, 4
The Bird Who Came to Dinner (1961) BMH 1; DMFS 1, 3, 4; EPF 1; RFF 1, 3, 4; SFL 1, 2, 3, 4
Box Car Bandit (1956) BMH 1; DMFS 1, 3, 4; RFF 1, 3, 4; SFL 1, 2, 3, 4
Chief Charlie Horse (1956) BHF 2; BMH 1; DMFS 1, 2, 3, 4; RFF 1, 2, 3, 4
Convict Concerto (1954) BMH 1; DMFS 1, RFF 1
Fowled Up Falcon (1960) BMH 1; DMFS 1, 2, 3, 4; EPF 1; RFF 1, 2, 3, 4; SFL 1, 2, 3, 4
Frankenstymied (1961) BHF 2; BMH 1; DMFS 1, 2, 3, 4; RFF 1, 2, 3, 4
Gabby's Diner (1961) BMH 1; DMFS 1, 3, 4; EPF 1; RFF 1, 3, 4; SFL 2, 3
Hansel and Gretel (Woody's nephew and niece) DMFS 1, 3, 4; RFF 1, 3, 4; SFL 4
Knock Knock (1940, the first Woody cartoon, with Andy Panda) BMH 1; CE 1; DMFS 1; GSF 1; RFF 1; SFL 1, 2, 3, 4; MWFS 1
Log Jammed (1959 BMH 1; DMFS 1, 3, 4; RFF 1, 3, 4; SFL 1, 2, 3, 4
Misguided Missile (1957) BMH 1; DMFS 1, 2, 3, 4; RFF 1, 2, 3, 4; SFL 1, 2, 3, 4
Niagara Fools (1956) BMH 1; DMFS 1, 3, 4; RFF 1, 3, 4; SFL 1, 2, 3, 4
Private Eye Pooch (1955) BHF 1, 3, 4; BMH 1; DMFS 1, 3, 4; RFF 1, 3, 4; SFL 1, 2, 3, 4
Puny Express (1951) BMH 1; DMFS 1; RFF 1
Rocket Racket (1962) BMH 1; DMFS 1, 3, 4; EPF 1; RFF 1, 3, 4; SFL 1, 2, 3, 4
Round Trip to Mars (1957) BMH 1; DMFS 1, 3, 4; GSF 1; RFF 1, 3, 4; SFL 1, 2, 3, 4
Secret Agent F.O.B. BMH 1; DMFS 1, 3, 4; GSF 1; RFF 1, 3, 4; SFL 1, 2, 3, 4
Ski for Two (1944) BHF 2; DMFS 1; RFF 1, 2, 3, 4
Sleep Happy (1951) BMH 1; DMFS 1; RFF 1
Sling Shot 6-7/8 (1951) BMH 1; DMFS 1; RFF 1

Stowaway Woody (1963) BMH 1; DMFS 1, 3, 4; RFF 1, 3, 4; SFL 1, 2, 3, 4

Termites from Mars (1953) BMH 1; DMFS 1, 3, 4; GSF 1; RFF 1, 3, 4; SFL 1, 2, 3, 4

Three Little Woodpeckers BMH 1; DMFS 1, 3, 4; EPF 1; RFF 1, 3, 4; SFL 1, 2, 3, 4

Unbearable Salesman (1957) BMH 1; DMFS 1, 3, 4; RFF 1, 3, 4; SFL 1, 2, 3, 4

What's Sweepin' (1953) BMH 1; DMFS 1; RFF 1

Wild and Woody (1948) BMH 1; DMFS 1; RFF 1

Witch Crafty (1955) BMH 1; DMFS 1, 3, 4; GSF 1; RFF 1, 3, 4; SFL 1, 2, 3, 4

Woodpecker from Mars (1956) BMH 1; DMFS 1, 2, 3, 4; GSF 1; RFF 1, 3, 4; SFL 1, 2, 3, 4

Woody's Clip Joint BMH 1; DMFS 1, 2, 3, 4; EPF 1; RFF 1, 2, 3, 4; SFL 1, 2, 3, 4

The Best of Woody Woodpecker, Part 1 (400-foot reel). Excerpts from Bats in the Belfry, Chief Charlie Horse, Buccaneer Woodpecker (1953), Fowled up Falcon, Frankenstymied, Misguided Missile, Ski for Two, Unbearable Salesman CE 3; SFL 3.

The Best of Woody Woodpecker, Part 2 (400-foot reel). Excerpts from Box Car Bandit, Niagara Fools, Private Eye Pooch, Round Trip to Mars, Secret Agent F.O.B., Termites from Mars, Witch Crafty, Woodpecker from Mars CE 3; SFL 3.

Miscellaneous Lantz Cartoons

The Bandmaster (1947) DMFS 1

Barber of Seville (1944) BHF 1; DMFS 1; GSF 1; RFF 1, 1s, 2s; SFL 1, 2

The Big Bad Wolf SFL 2, 4

The Bongo Punch (1957, with Pepito Chickeeto) DMFS 1, 3; RFF 1, 3; SFL 4

Egg Cracker Suite (1943, a Swing Symphony with Oswald the Rabbit) DMFS 1; RFF 1, 1s, 2s; SFL 1, 2

Eggnappers (1961) DMFS 1, 3; RFF 1, 3, 4; SFL 4

Jack and the Beanstalk (1949, produced for the Coca-Cola Company) SFL 2, 4

Kiddie Koncert (1948) DMFS 1; RFF 1

The Mouse and the Lion (1953, Buck Mouse, "A Foolish Fable Cartune") DMFS 1, 3, 4; RFF 1, 3, 4; SFL 4

Musical Moments from Chopin (1947, a Musical Miniature) DMFS 1

Overture to William Tell (1947, Wally Walrus conducts) BHF 1; DMFS 1; RFF 1, 1s, 2s; SFL 1, 2

Papoose on the Loose (1961) DMFS 1, 3, 4; RFF 1, 3, 4; SFL 4

Poet and Peasant (1946, with Andy Panda) DMFS 1; GSF 1; RFF 1, 1s, 2s; SFL 1, 2

Scrub Me Mama, With a Boogie Beat (1941) BMH 2; HFE 2; TBF 2

Sinbad the Sailor SFL 2, 4

Swing Your Partner (1943, a Swing Symphony with Homer Pigeon) DMFS 1; RFF 1, 1s 2s; SFL 1, 2

MGM CARTOONS

Hugh Harman and Rudolph Ising produced a *Happy Harmonies* series for MGM in the 1930s. Tex Avery switched from Warners to MGM in 1942, directing a variety of cartoons until he left in 1955. Bill Hanna and Joe Barbera directed the *Tom and Jerry* series, which began in 1941. The MGM cartoon unit was closed in 1957.

Tom and Jerry

Casanova Cat (1950) BMH 1; CE 1, 4; DMFS 1; RAR 1; RFF 1
Cat Concerto DMFS 1; BMH 1
Cat Fishin' (1947) DFS 1, 3, 3s, 4, 4s; GSF 1; PFDL 1, 3; PMF 1, 3, 3s, 4, 4s
Cat Napping (1951) BMH 1; CE 1, 4; DMFS 1; RAR 1; RFF 1
Cruise Cat (1952) BMH 1; CE 1, 4; DMFS 1; GSF 1; RAR 1; RFF 1
Cue Ball Cat (1950) PFDL 1, 3; PMF 1, 3, 4
Designs on Jerry DMFS 1; BMH 1
Dr. Jekyll and Mr. Mouse (1947) DFS 1, 3, 3s, 4, 4s; PFDL 1, 3; PMF 1, 3, 3s, 4, 4s
His Mouse Friday (1951) DFS 1, 3, 3s, 4, 4s; GSF 1; PFDL 1, 2, 3; PMF 1, 3, 3s, 4, 4s
Jerry and Jumbo (1953) BMH 1; CE 1, 4
Jerry and the Goldfish (1951) DFS 1, 3, 3s, 4, 4s; GSF 1; PFDL 1, 3; PMF 1, 3, 3s, 4, 4s
Johann Mouse DMFS 1; BMH 1
Little Orphan DMFS 1; BMH 1
The Milky Waif (1946) DFS 1, 3, 3s, 4, 4s; GSF 1; PFDL 1, 3; PMF 1, 3, 3s, 4, 4s
The Million Dollar Cat (1944) BMH 1; CE 1, 4; RFF 1
The Mouse Comes to Dinner (1945) DFS 1, 3, 3s, 4, 4s; GSF 1; PFDL 1, 3; PMF 1, 3, 3s, 4 4s
Mouse Trouble DMFS 1; BMH 1
Night Before Christmas DMFS 1; BMH 1
Posse Cat (1953) DFS 1, 3, 3s, 4, 4s; GSF 1; PFDL 1, 2, 3; PMF 1, 3, 3s, 4, 4s
Professor Tom (1948) PFDL 1, 3; PMF 1, 3, 4
Quiet Please DMFS 1; BMH 1
Saturday Evening Puss (1949) BMH 1; CE 1, 4; DMFS 1; RAR 1; RFF 1
Solid Serenade (1946) PFDL 1, 3; PMF 1, 3, 4
Tee for Two (1945) BMH 1; CE 1, 4; DMFS 1; RAR 1; RFF 1
Tennis Chumps (1949) DFS 1, 3, 3s, 4, 4s; PFDL 1, 2, 3; PMF 1, 3, 3s, 4, 4s
Triplet Trouble (1952) PFDL 1, 3; PMF 1, 3, 4
The Truce Hurts (1947) DFS 1, 3, 3s, 4, 4s; GSF 1; PFDL 1, 2, 3; PMF 1, 3, 3s, 4, 4s
The Two Mouseketeers (1952) BMH 1; CE 1, 4; DMFS 1; RAR 1

Miscellaneous MGM Cartoons

Jerky Turkey (1945) BMH 1

WINSOR McCAY

The cartoonist of "Little Nemo" newspaper comic strip fame created ten animated films between 1911 and 1921.
Dreams of the Rarebit Fiend: Bug Vaudeville (1921) GPS 4
Dreams of the Rarebit Fiend: The Flying House (1921) GPS 4, 6
Dreams of the Rarebit Fiend: The Pet (1917) GPS 4
Gertie the Dinosaur (1914) BHF 4; GPS 4, 6; NFP 4, 6
Little Nemo (1911) GPS 4, 6
The Sinking of the Lusitania (1918) GPS 4, 6
The Story of a Mosquito (1912) GPS 4

GEORGE PAL PUPPETOONS

After beginning his career in Europe, Pal continued his puppet cartoons in the U.S., releasing them through Paramount.

A Date with Duke (1947) GPS 1
Hot Lips Jasper (1945) GPS 1
Jasper in a Jam (1942) GPS 1
John Henry and the Inky-Poo (1946) GPS 1
The Little Broadcast (1945) GPS 1
Phillips Broadcast of 1938 (1938, made for Phillips Radio in Europe) GPS 1
Rhapsody in Wood (1947) GPS 1
Ship of the Ether (1935, made for Phillips Radio in Europe) GPS 1
Tubby the Tuba (1947) GPS 1

SCREEN GEMS

Charles Mintz's "Screen Gems" studio operated from the 1930s on, with the cartoons being released through Columbia Pictures.

Fox and Crow

The Magic Fluke (1949) EPF 1; SFL 1. *Note*: This cartoon is printed on the box, and in all publicity and dealer catalogs as "The Magic *Flute*." "*Fluke*" is the spelling on the cartoon's title card.
Robin Hoodlum (1948, a Color Rhapsody) SFL 1

Krazy Kat (for earlier Krazy Kat cartoons, see the Miscellaneous listing)

Katnips of 1940 (1934) FC 1; SFL 1
Lone Mountie (1938) FC 1; MWFS 1; SFL 1
Lyin' Hunter (1937) FC 1; SFL 1

Miscellaneous Screen Gems Cartoons

Oompahs (1951, a Color Rhapsody) SFL 1

TERRYTOONS—PAUL TERRY

Paul Terry was animating cartoons in 1916. He worked on the *Aesop's Fables* series in the 1920s. Judging from the copyright records, he apparently left this series in 1929 to begin producing "Terry-Toons." Terrytoons, distributed by 20th Century-Fox, have continued to be made through the 1960s. In the middle 1950s, the studio became a division of CBS Films.

Early Cartoons of Paul Terry

The Ball Game (1929, an Aesop's Fable) TBF 2. *Note*: The copyright catalogue lists only a cartoon called "The Ball Park."
The Cat and the Monkey (1921) GPS 4. See also the Glenn Photo Misc. Compilation No. 2 in the Miscellaneous classification.
The Cat's Dilemma (a Jungle Jinks cartoon) TBF 2

Jail Breakers (1929, an Aesop's Fable) TBF 4
Lindy's Cat (1927, an Aesop's Fable) HFRP 2, 4
Prest-O-Change-O (1928, an Aesop's Fable) TBF 2

Farmer Al Falfa

Farmer Al Falfa's Wayward Pup (1917) GPS 4, 6
Fire! Fire! (1927) TBF 4
Rats in His Garrett (1927, an Aesop's Fable) (on the same reel: "Topics of the Day") GPS 4, 6

Astronut

Brother from Outer Space (1964) RFF 1
The Kisser Plant (1964) RFF 1
Oscar's Moving Day RFF 1

Deputy Dawg

The Astronut (1962, TV) DMFS 4, 4s, 6
Dagnabbit Rabbit (1962) FC 1
Dry Spell RFF 1
Honey Tree (1961, TV) EPF 1; RFF 1; SFL 1
Li'l Whooper (1960, TV) RFF 1; SFL 1
Low Man Lawman RFF 1; SFL 1
Orbit a Little Bit RFF 1
Safe an' Insane Fourth RFF 1
Shotgun Shambles (1960, TV) RFF 1
Seize You Later, Alligator (1961, TV) RFF 1
Space Varmint (1960, TV) RFF 1
Tents Moments (1961, TV) RFF 1; SFL 1
Terrific Traffic RFF 1
The Yoke's on You (1960, TV) RFF 1

Dinky Duck

The Beauty Shop (1950) RFF 1
Flat Foot Fledgling (1952) RFF 1; SFL 1
The Foolish Duckling (1952) DMFS 1, 3, 4, 4s, 6; FC 1; RFF 1; SFL 1
Life With Fido (1942) RFF 1
The Lucky Duck (1940) SFL 1s
Much Ado About Nothing RFF 1
Sink or Swim (1952) SFL 1s
Welcome Little Stranger (1941) RFF 1

Gandy Goose

Comic Book Land (1949) DMFS 4, 4s

Covered Pushcart (1949, *Note*: The copyright catalog calls this a "Sourpuss" cartoon) DMFS 4, 4s, 6

Doomsday (1938) DMFS 1, 3, 4; FC 1; RFF 1

Dream Walking (1950) RFF 1; SFL 1

The Frog and the Princess (1944) DMFS 1, 3, 4; FC 1

Ghost Town (1944) DMFS 1, 3, 4; FC 1

The Happy Gobblers (1952) FC 1. *Note*: This appears in the copyright catalog as "The Happy *Cobblers*"—unless there are two different cartoons.

It's All in the Stars (1946) RFF 1; SFL 1

Spring Fever (1951) RFF 1

Wide Open Spaces (1950) RFF 1

Hashimoto

Hashimoto-San (1959) RFF 1

Honorable Cat Story (1961) RFF 1

Honorable Family Problems (1962) RFF 1

Honorable House Cat (1961) RFF 1

House of Hashimoto (1960) RFF 1

Night Life in Tokyo (1960) RFF 1

So Sorry, Pussycat (1960) RFF 1

Son of Hashimoto (1961) RFF 1

Strange Companion (1961) RFF 1

Heckle and Jeckle

Bargain Daze (1953) SFL 1s

Bulldozing the Bull (1951) DMFS 1, 3, 4; FC 1; RFF 1; SFL 1

Cat Trouble (1947) NFP 1

Fishing by the Sea (1947) NFP 1

Flying South NFP 1

The Fox Hunt (1950) SFL 1s

Free Enterprise (1948) NFP 1; SFL 1s

Gooney Golfers (1948) DMFS 1, 3, 4; FC 1; NFP 1

Hair Cut-Ups (1952) RFF 1; SFL 1

Happy Go Lucky (1947) NFP 1

Happy Landing (1949) NFP 1

The Hitchhikers (1947) NFP 1; RFF 1

House Busters (1952) DMFS 1, 3, 4, 4s, 6; FC 1

The Intruders NFP 1

King Tut's Tomb (1950) BMH 1; DMFS 1, 3, 4; FC 1

The Lion Hunt (1949) DMFS 1, 3, 4, 4s; FC 1; NFP 1

Log Rollers (1953) DMFS 1, 3, 4, 4s; FC 1

McDougal's Rest Farm (1947) NFP 1

Magpie Madness (1948) NFP 1

A Merry Chase (1950) DMFS 1, 3, 4, 4s; FC 1

Movie Madness (1951) DMFS 1, 3, 4; FC 1

Out Again, In Again (1948) NFP 1

Pirate's Gold (1956) DMFS 1, 3, 4, 4s, 6; FC 1
The Power of Thought (1948) NFP 1
A Sleepless Night (1948) NFP 1
Steeple Jacks (1951) RFF 1; SFL 1
The Stowaways (1949) NFP 1
Stunt Men (1960) RFF 1; SFL 1
The Super Salesman (1947) NFP 1; RFF 1
The Talking Magpies GSF 1; NFP 1; RFF 1
Taming the Cat (1948) NFP 1
Ten Pin Terrors (1953) DMFS 1, 3, 4, 4s; FC 1
The Uninvited Pests (1946) NFP 1

Hector Heathcote

Daniel Boone, Jr. (1960) RFF 1
The Famous Ride (1960) RFF 1
High Flyer (1964, TV) RFF 1
The Minute and a Half Man (1958) RFF 1

James Hound

Dr. Ha Ha (1966) RFF 1
Frozen Sparklers (1967) RFF 1
Give Me Liberty (1967) RFF 1

Little Roquefort and Percy

Cat Happy (1950) SFL 1s
City Slicker (1951) GSF 1; RFF 1; SFL 1
Friday the 13th (1953) FC 1
The Haunted Cat (1951) FC 1
Mouse and Garden (1950) RFF 1; SFL 1
Mouse Meets Bird (1952) FC 1
Mouse Menace (1953) FC 1
Musical Madness (1951) FC 1; RFF 1
Pastry Panic (1951) FC 1; SFL 1s
Playful Puss (1953) RFF 1; SFL 1s
Seasick Sailors (1951) FC 1; RFF 1
Three is a Crowd (1950) RFF 1

Luno

King Rounder (1968) RFF 1
The Missing Genie (1963) RFF 1
The Prehistoric Inventor RFF 1

Mighty Heroes

The Monsterizer RFF 1; SFL 1

The Plastic Blaster RFF 1
The Shrinker RFF 1; SFL 1

Mighty Mouse

Aladdin's Lamp (1947) DMFS 1, 3, 4, 4s; FC 1
Anti-Cats (1949) RFF 1
At the Circus (1944) DMFS 1, 3, 4, 4s, 6; FC 1; NFP 1
The Catnip Gang (1949) RFF 1
A Cat's Tale (1951) SFL 1s
A Champion of Justice NFP 1
A Cold Romance (1949) RFF 1
Crackpot King (1946) DMFS 1, 3, 4; FC 1
Down With Cats (1943) NFP 1; RFF 1. *Note*: The copyright catalog calls this a
"Super Mouse" cartoon; apparently the name was switched to "Mighty Mouse"
after several cartoons had been made.
A Fight to the Finish (1947) DMFS 4, 4s, 6; FC 1
Frankenstein's Cat (1942) DMFS 4, 4s, 6; FC 1; NFP 1; RFF 1
Goons from the Moon (1951) BMH 1; DMFS 1, 3, 4; FC 1; SFL 1s
The Green Line (1944) NFP 1
The Gypsy Life (1945) DMFS 1, 3, 4; FC 1; NFP 1
Hansel and Gretel (1952) DMFS 1, 3, 4; EPF 1; FC 1; RFF 1; SFL 1
He Dood It Again (1943) NFP 1; RFF 1
Injin Trouble (1951) SFL 1s
Krakatoa (1945) NFP 1
Law and Order (1950) RFF 1; SFL 1
The Magician (1948) DMFS 1, 3, 4, 4s, 6; GSF 1; FC 1; SFL 1s
Mighty Mouse and the Kilkenny Cats (1945) NFP 1
Mighty Mouse and the Pirates (1945) NFP 1
Mighty Mouse and the Two Barbers (1944) NFP 1
Mighty Mouse Meets Bad Bill Bunion (1945) NFP 1
Mighty Mouse Meets Jekyll and Hyde Cat (1944) NFP 1
Mother Goose's Birthday Party (1950) DMFS 1, 3, 4, 4s, 6; FC 1
The Mouse of Tomorrow (1942) NFP 1; RFF 1
Outer Space Visitor (1959) DMFS 1, 3, 4, 4s, 6; FC 1
Pandora's Box (1943, a "Super Mouse" cartoon) NFP 1; RFF 1
The Perils of Pearl Pureheart (1949) RFF 1
The Port of Missing Mice (1945) NFP 1
Prehistoric Perils (1951) RFF 1; SFL 1
The Racket Buster (1948) RFF 1
Raiding the Raiders (1945) NFP 1
The Reformed Wolf (1954) RFF 1; SFL 1
The Silver Streak (1945) NFP 1
Stop, Look and Listen (1949) RFF 1
The Sultan's Birthday (1944) NFP 1
Sunny Italy (1950) DMFS 1, 3, 4; FC 1
Super Mouse Rides Again (1943, a "Super Mouse" cartoon) NFP 1
Svengali's Cat (1946) DMFS 1, 3, 4, 4s, 6; FC 1; NFP 1

A Swiss Miss (1951) RFF 1
The Wicked Wolf (1946) NFP 1; SFL 1s
Winning the West (1946) DMFS 1, 3, 4, 4s, 6; FC 1; SFL 1s
The Witch's Cat (1948) DMFS 1, 3, 4; FC 1
Wolf! Wolf! (1944) NFP 1
The Wreck of the Hesperus (1944) NFP 1

Possible Possum

Black and Blue Jay RFF 1
Hobo Hassle RFF 1

Sad Cat

All Teed Off (1968) RFF 1
Don't Spill the Beans (1965) SFL 1s
Dress Reversal (1965) SFL 1s
Grand Prix Winner (1968) RFF 1

Silly Sidney the Elephant

Banana Binge (1961) RFF 1; SFL 1
Meat, Drink and be Merry (1961) RFF 1
Really Big Act (1961) RFF 1
Sick, Sick Sidney (1958) RFF 1
Sidney's Family Tree (1958) RFF 1; SFL 1

Terry Bears

Baffling Bunnies (1955) DMFS 1, 3, 4, 4s; FC 1; NFP 1
Duck Fever (1955) NFP 1
Growing Pains (1953) NFP 1; SFL 1s
A Howling Success (1954) NFP 1
Little Anglers (1952) NFP 1
Little Problems (1951) NFP 1; RFF 1; SFL 1
Nice Doggy (1952) NFP 1; RFF 1; SFL 1
Open House (1953) NFP 1
Papa's Day of Rest (1951) NFP 1; RFF 1
Papa's Little Helpers (1951) NFP 1
Pet Problems (1954) NFP 1; SFL 1s
Picnic with Papa (1952) NFP 1
Plumber's Helpers (1953) DMFS 1, 3, 4, 4s, 6; FC 1; NFP 1
The Reluctant Pup (1953) NFP 1
Snappy Snapshots (1952) NFP 1
Tall Timber Tale (1951) DMFS 4, 4s; NFP 1; RFF 1

Miscellaneous Terrytoons

Beanstalk Jack (1946) RFF 1
Bird Symphony (1955) GSF 1

The Elephant Mouse (1951, with Half Pint) RFF 1
Good Deed Daly (1955) GSF 1

UPA (UNITED PRODUCTIONS OF AMERICA)

Organized in the mid-1940s, UPA pioneered with a new type of stylized and limited animation. Early UPA cartoons have the series title *Jolly Frolic*. The cartoons were released through Columbia Pictures; the 8mm versions are now distributed by the Columbia Home Movie Division.

Gerald McBoing Boing

Gerald McBoing Boing (1950) BMH 1; FC 1; SFL 1
Gerald McBoing Boing on the Planet Moo (1955) FC 1; SFL 1
Gerald McBoing Boing's Symphony (1952) EPF 1; FC 1; SFL 1
How Now McBoing Boing (1954) SFL 1

The Nearsighted Mr. Magoo

Bwana Magoo (1958) FC 1; SFL 1, 3
Destination Magoo (1954) FC 1; SFL 1, 3
Hotsy-Footsy (1952) FC 1; SFL 1
Love Comes to Magoo (1958) EPF 1; FC 1; MWFS 1; SFL 1
Madcap Magoo (1955) BHF 1; EPF 1; FC 1; MWFS 1; SFL 1
Magoo Beats the Heat (CinemaScope format) PMF 1
Magoo Goes Overboard (CinemaScope format) PMF 1
Magoo Meets Frankenstein (1960, TV) DMFS 4, 4s
Magoo Meets McBoing Boing (1960, TV) DMFS 4, 4s
Magoo's Moose Hunt (1957) FC 1; MWFS 1; SFL 1
Magoo's Private War (1957) FC 1; SFL 1
Magoo's Problem Child (1956) FC 1; MWFS 1; SFL 1
Magoo's Puddle Jumper (1956) FC 1; MWFS 1; SFL 1
Magoo's Three Point Landing (1958) FC 1; SFL 1
Magoo's Young Manhood (1957) FC 1; SFL 1
Matador Magoo (1957) EPF 1; FC 1; MWFS 1; SFL 1
Merry Minstrel Magoo (1958) EPF 1; FC 1; MWFS 1; SFL 1
Sloppy Jalopy (1951) FC 1; SFL 1
Trouble Indemnity (1950) FC 1; MWFS 1; SFL 1
When Magoo Flew (1954) FC 1; SFL 1, 3

Miscellaneous UPA Cartoons

The Emperor's New Clothes (1952, a Jolly Frolic) SFL 1
The Jay Walker (1955, a Jolly Frolic) SFL 1
Madeline (1952, a Jolly Frolic) EPF 1; SFL 1
Man on the Flying Trapeze (1954) SFL 1
The Miner's Daughter (1950, a Jolly Frolic) EPF 1; SFL 1
Rooty Toot Toot (1952, a Jolly Frolic) SFL 1
The Unicorn in the Garden (1953, a Jolly Frolic) EPF 1; SFL 1

VAN BEUREN

The Van Beuren studio operated in New York City in the 1930s; it was a reorganization of the Aesop's Fables studio, which Amedee Van Beuren had purchased. The studio produced a *Rainbow Parade* series.

Felix the Cat (for earlier Felix cartoons, see the Miscellaneous classification)

Bold King Cole (1926, a Rainbow Parade cartoon) BHF 1; BMH 1; RFF 1
Felix the Cat and the Goose that Laid the Golden Egg (1936, a Rainbow Parade cartoon) NFP 1, 2; RFF 1, 2; RI 1, TBF 1, 2, 4
Neptune's Nonsense (1936, a Rainbow Parade cartoon) BHF 1

Molly Moo-Cow

Molly Moo-Cow and the Butterflies (1935, a Rainbow Parade cartoon) BHF 1

Tom and Jerry (from 1931-33, Van Beuren made a series of Tom and Jerry cartoons featuring Mutt and Jeff-like characters, not a cat and mouse)

Happy Hobos (1933) HFRP 2, 4
Piano Tooners (1932) TBF 2
Red Skin Blues (1932) TBF 2

Toonerville Cartoons

Toonerville Picnic (1936, a Rainbow Parade cartoon) GPS 2; TBF 2; BHF 1
Toonerville Trolley (1936, a Rainbow Parade cartoon) BHF 1

Other Van Beuren Cartoons

Pals (1933) FFL 4
The Sunshine Makers (1935, produced by Borden Foods) HFE 1; BMH 1

WARNER BROTHERS

Looney Tunes began in 1930, and Merrie Melodies in 1931. The earliest series involved a character named Bosko, but when the original producers of the studio (Hugh Harman and Rudolph Ising) left in 1933, it was replaced with a *Buddy* series. At first, Looney Tunes were in black and white and featured series characters, while Merrie Melodies were in color and featured independent subjects. This distinction was abandoned by the late 1930s. The now famous group of Warner characters evolved in the late 1930s and early 1940s through the talents of Tex Avery, Chuck Jones, Bob Clampett, Frank Tashlin, Bob McKimson, Fritz Freleng, and others. For the following cartoons, the characters featured, if known, are given following the date, if known; and if identified by the title, they are not repeated.

All This and Rabbit Stew (1941, Bugs) BMH 1; EPF 1, 2; GSF 1; HFE 1; NFP 2; RFF 1, 2; SFL 1
Ant Pasted (1953, Elmer Fudd) FFL 1, 3; JEF 1
Back Alley Uproar (1947, Daffy) CBF 1; DMFS 1

Ballot Box Bunny (1952, Bugs) FFL 1, 3; JEF 1
Beep Beep (1952, Roadrunner) FFL 1, 3; JEF 1
Beep Prepared (1961, Roadrunner) FFL 1, 3; JEF 1; PFDL 1; PMF 1
A Bird in a Bonnet (1958, Tweety & Sylvester) FFL 1, 3; JEF 1
Boom! Boom! (1937, Porky Pig) HFE 2; HFRP 2, 4
Bosko at the Beach (1931) TBF 2
Buccaneer Bunny (1948, Bugs) FFL 1, 3; JEF 1; PFDL 1; PMF 1
Bugs Bunny Bond Rally (World War II patriotic cartoon) HFE 1
Bugs Bunny Gets the Boid (1942) FFL 1, 3; JEF 1; PFDL 1
Bugs Bunny Rides Again (1947) DMFS 4s; JEF 1
Bully for Bugs (1952) FFL 1, 3; JEF 1; PFDL 1; PMF 1
Cannery Woe (1960, Sylvester, Speedy Gonzales) FFL 1, 3; JEF 1; PFDL 1; PMF 1
Captain Hareblower (1954, Bugs, Yosemite Sam) FFL 1, 3; JEF 1; PFDL 1; PMF 1
The Case of the Missing Hare (Bugs) FC 1; GPS 2; HFE 1, 2; MWFS 1; RFF 1
Cat Tails for Two (Speedy Gonzales) FFL 1, 3; JEF 1; PMF 1
Cat's Paw (1958, Sylvester) FFL 1, 3; JEF 1; PFDL 1; PMF 1
China Jones (1959, Porky & Daffy) FFL 1, 3; JEF 1
Confusions of a Nutzy Spy (1943, Porky) HFE 2
Conrad the Sailor (1942, Daffy Duck) DMFS 4, 4s
Corny Concerto (1943, Bugs, Porky, Elmer) BMH 1; DMFS 1; EPF 1, 2; FC 1; HFE 1; MWFS 1; NFP 1, 2; RFF 1, 2; SFL 1; TBF 1
Daffy Duck and the Dinosaur (1939) BHF 1; BMH 1; EPF 1, 2; FC 1; HFE 1; NFP 1, 2; RFF 1, 2; SFL 1; TBF 1
Daffy-Duck-A-Roo GPS 2; HFE 2; MWFS 2
Daffy the Commando (early 1940s) BMH 1; GSF 1; HFE 1; MWFS 1; NFP 1; RFF 1
Daffy's Diner (1967) FFL 1, 3; JEF 1; PFDL 1; PMF 1
Daffy's Southern Exposure (1942) HFE 2
Deduce You Say! (1956, Porky & Daffy) FFL 1, 3; JEF 1; PFDL 1; PMF 1
Dig a Dog TBF 1
Dime to Retire (1954, Porky) FFL 1, 3; JEF 1
Ding Dong Daddy HFE 1; MWFS 1
Dixie Fryer (Foghorn Leghorn) JEF 1; PMF 1
Dr. Devil and Mr. Hare (1964, Bugs) FFL 1, 3; JEF 1; PFDL 1; PMF 1
Doggone People (1960, Elmer Fudd) FFL 1, 3; JEF 1
Don't Give Up the Sheep (1953, Sheepdog & Ralph Wolf) FFL 1, 3; JEF 1
Double or Mutton (1955, Sheepdog & Ralph Wolf) FFL 1, 3; JEF 1
The Dover Boys (early 1940s) HFE 1
Ducktators (late 1930s or early 1940s) HFE 2; MWFS 2
Dumb Patrol (1964, Bugs) FFL 1, 3; JEF 1
Easy Peckin's (1954, Foghorn Leghorn) JEF 1; PFDL 1; PMF 1
Eatin' on the Cuff (1942) CBF 2; FC 2; MWFS 2; RI 2
The Fair-Haired Hare (1951, Bugs) FFL 1, 3; JEF 1
Falling Hare (early 1940s, Bugs) BMH 1; HFE 1; MWFS 1; NFP 1; RFF 1
Fifth Column Mouse (early 1940s) BMH 1; HFE 1
Fin 'n Catty (1948, re-release) HFE 1

Flop Goes the Weasel (1949, re-release) HFE 1
Fourteen Carrot Rabbit (1952, Bugs & Yosemite Sam) FFL 1, 3; JEF 1; PFDL 1; PMF 1
Fox Pop (1941-42) HFE 1
Fresh Hare (Bugs, Elmer) BHF 1; BMH 1; HFE 1; MWFS 1; NFP 1; RFF 1
Gest Boyd (Bugs) PMF 1
Get Rich Quick Porky (1937) TBF 2
Gorilla My Dreams (1947, Bugs) FFL 1, 3; JEF 1; PFDL 1; PMF 1
A Gruesome Twosome (1945, Tweety & Sylvester) DMFS 4, 4s
Guided Muscle (1955, Roadrunner) FFL 1, 3; JEF 1
Hamateur Night (1938) EPF 1, 2; GSF 1; NFP 1, 2; RFF 1, 2; SFL 1
Hare Life (1951, Bugs) JEF 1; PFDL 1; PMF 1
Hawaiian Aye Aye (1963, Tweety & Sylvester) FFL 1, 3; JEF 1
Heaven Scent (1956, Pepe Le Pew) JEF 1; PFDL 1; PMF 1
The Henpecked Duck (1941) HFE 2
Here Today, Gone Tamale (1959, Speedy Gonzales) FFL 1, 3; JEF 1
Hiawatha's Rabbit Hunt (1941, Bugs) DMFS 4, 4s, 6
A Hick, a Slick, and a Chick (1947) NFP 1; TBF 1
Hold Anything (1940, Bosko) TBF 2
Hollywood Capers (1936) HFE 2
Hook, Line and Stinker (1958, Roadrunner) FFL 1, 3; JEF 1
Horse Hare (1960, Bugs) FFL 1, 3; JEF 1; PFDL 1; PMF 1
The Impatient Patient (1942, Daffy) BMH 1; NFP 1; SFL 1; DMFS 1
An Itch in Time (1948, re-release, Elmer Fudd) BMH 1; FC 1; RFF 1
Jet Cage (1962, Tweety & Sylvester) FFL 1, 3; JEF 1; PFDL 1; PMF 1
Jungle Jitters (1937) BMH 1; FFL 4; NFP 1, 2; RFF 1, 2; SFL 1
Knight Mare Hare (1955, Bugs) JEF 1; PFDL 1; PMF 1
Knighty Knight Bugs (1957) FFL 1, 3; JEF 1; PFDL 1; PMF 1
Lickety Splat (1961, Roadrunner) FFL 1, 3; JEF 1; PFDL 1; PMF 1
Meet John Doughboy (1941, Porky) HFE 2; MWFS 2
Mexicali Schmoes (1959, Speedy Gonzales) FFL 1, 3; JEF 1
Mexican Cat Dance (Speedy Gonzales) FFL 1, 3; JEF 1; PFDL 1; PMF 1
A Mutt in a Rut (1959, Elmer Fudd) FFL 1, 3; JEF 1
Notes to You (1941, Porky) BMH 1; NFP 1; RFF 1; SFL 1
Nothing But the Tooth (1947, Porky) DMFS 4s
Pagan Moon (1931) TBF 2
People are Bunny (1959, Daffy and Bugs) FFL 1, 3; JEF 1; PFDL 1; PMF 1
Pigs in a Polka (1949, re-release) HFE 1; DMFS 1
A Pizza Tweety Pie (1957) FFL 1, 3; JEF 1
Porky's Midnight Matinee (1941) HFE 2
Porky's Preview (1941) BHF 2; GPS 2; HFE 2
Porky's Railroad (1937) HFE 2
Presto-Change-O (1939) BMH 1; GSF 1; NFP 1, 2; RFF 1, 2; SFL 1; TBF 2
Puss and Booty HFE 2; MWFS 2
Rabbit Romeo (1957, Bugs) FFL 1, 3; JEF 1
Racketeer Rabbit (1946, Bugs) DMFS 4, 4s, 6

Ready, Woolen and Able (1959, Sheepdog & Ralph Wolf) FFL 1, 3; JEF 1
Robin Hood Makes Good (1939) HFE 1; DMFS 1
Saps in Chaps (1942) HFE 2
Scrap Happy Daffy (1940s) HFE 2; MWFS 2
Sheep Ahoy (1954, Sheepdog & Ralph Wolf) FFL 1, 3; JEF 1
A Sheep in the Deep (1962, Sheepdog & Wolf) FFL 1, 3; JEF 1
Sheepish Wolf (Sheepdog & Wolf) HFE 1
Smile, Darn Ya, Smile (1932) TBF 2
Sniffles Takes a Trip (1940) DMFS 4, 4s
A Squeak in the Deep (1966, Daffy, Speedy Gonzales) FFL 1, 3; JEF 1
Suppressed Duck (Daffy) FFL 1, 3; JEF 1
Swing Ding Amigo (1966, Daffy) FFL 1, 3; JEF 1
To Duck or Not to Duck (Daffy, Elmer) GSF 1; NFP 1; RFF 1; SFL 1
Tokio Jokio (1943) HFE 2
Trip for Tat (1960, Sylvester) FFL 1, 3; JEF 1; PFDL 1; PMF 1
Tweet and Lovely (1959, Tweety & Sylvester) FFL 1, 3; JEF 1; PFDL 1; PMF 1
Tweet Zoo (1956, Sylvester) FFL 1, 3; JEF 1; PFDL 1; PMF 1
Tweety and the Beanstalk (1956) FFL 1, 3; JEF 1
Tweetie Pie (1947) DMFS 4s
The Unruly Hare (1944, Bugs) DMFS 4, 4s, 6
Wabbit Who Came to Supper (Bugs, Elmer) BMH 1; GPS 2; HFE 1, 2; NFP 1
Wackiki Wabbit (Bugs) BMH 1; FC 1; NFP 1; RFF 1; SLF 1
Wacky Wabbit (Bugs) BMH 1; FC 1; HFE 1; NFP 1; RFF 1
Walky Talky Hawky (1944, Henery Hawk and Foghorn Leghorn) DMFS 4, 4s
West of the Pesos (1959, Sylvester & Speedy Gonzales) FFL 1, 3; JEF 1
What's Brewin' Bruin? (1947) DMFS 4s
What's My Lion (1961, Elmer) FFL 1, 3; JEF 1
Who's Who in the Zoo (1942, Porky) NFE 2
Wild About Hurry (1959, Roadrunner) FFL 1, 3; JEF 1; PFDL 1; PMF 1
A Wild Hare (1940, Bugs, Elmer) DMFS 4, 4s, 6
Yodeling Yokels (1931, Bosko, Looney Tunes No. 10) TBF 2
Zip and Snort (1961, Roadrunner) FFL 1, 3; JEF 1
Zipping Along (1952, Roadrunner) FFL 1, 3; JEF 1
Zoom and Bored (1957, Roadrunner) FFL 1, 3; JEF 1; PFDL 1; PMF 1

"Double Feature" Cartoon Reel: Bugs Bunny Rides Again (1947) and Nothing but the Tooth (1947) DMFS 4, 6. Abridged versions.

"Double Feature" Cartoon Reel: What's Brewin' Bruin? (1947) and Tweetie Pie (1947) DMFS 4, 6. Abridged versions.

MISCELLANEOUS

Aesop's Fables

Paul Terry seems to have been the guiding hand at this studio during the 1920s. Early in the 1930s the studio underwent a change of ownership and became the Van Beuren studio. The cartoons listed here are all from the 1929-31 period. Aesop's Fables identified as Terry's are listed under "Terrytoons."

A Close Call (1930) TBF 2
Foolish Follies (1930) HFRP 2, 4
King of Bugs (1930) TBF 2
The Night Club (1929) HFRP 2, 4
Play Ball (1931) TBF 2
A Romeo Robin (1930) TBF 2

Emergency Plus Four

Circus Story RFF 1, 3
Cry Wolf RFF 3
Danger at Fantasy Park RFF 3
Fire at Sea RFF 3
Million Dollar Ghost RFF 3
Winter Nightmare RFF 3

Felix the Cat

Felix apparently began his movie career in or about 1920. In the 1930s he was animated by the Van Beuren studio (refer to that classification for his later cartoons). The initial success of Felix was due to Otto Messmer who personally supervised and worked on the cartoons at the studio owned by Pat Sullivan, creator of the newspaper strip.

April Maze (1931) NFP 2; RFF 2; RI 2
The Big Rain GPS 4
Feline Follies (one part of a three-cartoon compilation in one of the *Paramount Magazine* series, 1920; reportedly the first Felix cartoon) TBF 2
Felix All Puzzled TBF 4
Felix Dines and Pines (1927) NFP 4, 6; TBF 4
Felix Dopes it Out GPS 4
Felix Gets the Can GPS 4
Felix Goes West (1925) TBF 4
Felix in Fairyland (1924) GPS 4, 6; NFP 4, 6
Felix in Hollywood (1923) GPS 4; TBF 4
Felix Strikes it Rich FFL 4
Felix Wins Out GPS 4
Felix Woos Whoopee GPS 4
Non-Stop Fright (1927) GPS 4
Pedigreedy (1927) GPS 4, 6
Skulls and Sculls GPS 4
Sure-Locked Homes (1928) GPS 4

Krazy Kat

Krazy Kat cartoons appeared initially around 1916, animated at the Hearst International Studios. A second series of *Krazy Kat* cartoons was released through Bray Productions around 1920. According to the copyright entries, Krazy wandered through several studios during the 1920s, finally settling down for a long run at Mintz's Screen Gems in the early 1930s. Refer to that classification for later cartoons.

The Great Cheese Robbery (ca. 1920) TBF 4

Glenn Photo Compilation No. 1: Krazy Kat and Ignatz Mouse at the Circus; Krazy Kat and Ignatz Mouse Discuss the Letter "G"; Krazy Kat and Ignatz Mouse in "He Made Me Love Him" (all 1916) GPS 4, 6

Glenn Photo Compilation No. 2: Krazy Kat and Ignatz in "A Tale That is Knot"; Krazy Kat and Ignatz in their 1-Act Tragedy, "The Tale of the Nude Tail"; Krazy Kat, Bugologist (all in 1916) GPS 4, 6

Glenn Photo Compilation No. 3: Krazy Kat Goes A-Wooing; Krazy Kat, Invalid; Krazy to the Rescue (all 1916) GPS 4, 6

Glenn Photo Compilation No. 4: Love's Labor Lost; A Chinese Honeymoon (both ca. 1920; Bray releases) GPS 4

The Lone Ranger and Tonto

Cult of the Black Widow BMH 1; RFF 1
El Conquistador BMH 1; RFF 1
Valley of the Dead BMH 1; RFF 1

Len Lye, Animator

Colour Box (1937, abstract art, made for the General Post Office) GPS 1
Rainbow Dance (1936, abstract art) GPS 1

Mutt and Jeff

In the 1915-25 era, many popular newspaper strip characters were featured in cartoons turned out by various New York animation studios. Raoul Barré supervised the studio for Bud Fisher, creator of the newspaper strip. The series was produced during the 1916-20 span, if not longer. The series was revived in the late 1920s for a short time by the Associated Animators Studio.

Accidents Won't Happen! GPS 4
The Big Swim GPS 4, 6
Cramps (1951) TBF 4
Dog Gone (1927) TBF 4, 6
Globetrotters GPS 4
Hell Froze Over GPS 4
The Magician GPS 4
The Outpost (1916) TBF 4
Playing With Fire GPS 4
Roman Scandals GPS 4

The New Three Stooges

A Fishy Tale (live-action and animation) TBF 1
Woodsman Bear That Tree (live-action and animation) TBF 1

Snuffy Smith and Barney Google

The Big Bear Hunt JEF 1
Farm of the Future JEF 1
Jughaid the Magician JEF 1

Snuffy Runs the Gamut JEF 1
Take Me to Your Gen'rul (1962) JEF 1
The Work Pill JEF 1

"Super Comic" Cartoons

Flukey Luke and the Diamonds JEF 1
The Grand Prix JEF 1
A Husband for Zolta JEF 1
The Mighty Mosquito JEF1
Super Chicken JEF 1

Super Heroes

Captain America vs. Zemo BMH 1; CE 1, 3, 4
Hulk: Power of Dr. Banner BMH 1; CE 1, 3, 4
Iron Man vs. Ultimo BMH 1; CE 1, 3, 4; GSF 1
Mighty Thor: To Kill a Thundergod BMH 1; CE 1, 3, 4
Origin of Spiderman BMH 1; CE 1, 3, 4
Spiderman: King Pinned BMH 1; CE 1, 3, 4
Spiderman: Sting of the Scorpion BMH 1; CE 1, 3, 4; GSF 1
Spiderman: Trick or Treachery BMH 1; CE 1, 3, 4
Submariner: Can My Power Save Me? BMH 1; CE 1, 3, 4

Raoul Barré

Cartoons on the Beach (1915, an "Animated Grouch Chaser," Edison Films) GPS 4, 6

Charles Bowers

A.W.O.L. (1918) GPS 4, 6

Bud and Susie

Down the Mississippi (Frank Moser; one part of a three-cartoon compilation in one of the *Paramount Magazine* series, 1920) TBF 2

Wallace A. Carlson

Dreamy Dud Learns to Smoke (1915, Essanay) TBF 4, 6. See the following entry.
Dreamy Dud Resolves Not to Smoke (1915, Essanay) GPS 4. This second "Dreamy Dud" title is the only one listed in the copyright catalog; the two cartoons may be the same.
Goodrich Dirt, Cowpuncher (1919) TBF 4. *Note:* Glenn Photo offers a cartoon with the exact same title, but identifies it as a Walter Lantz cartoon, 1926.

Col. Heeza Liar Series

Col. Heeza Liar at the Bat (ca. 1916, World War I theme) GPS 4
Forbidden Fruit (1923, Bray Pictures, directed by Vernon Stallings) GPS 4, 6

Hy Gage

Kartoono (ca. 1920, cutout animation) GPS 4

Glenn Photo Miscellaneous Compilations

No. 1: The Evils of Alcohol (early French cutout animation by Marius Rossilon, 1912); Swat the Fly (stop-motion clay modeling by Willie Hopkins); Morpheus Mike (animated figurines by Willis O'Brien, 1916) GPS 4, 6

No. 2: The Enchanted Drawing (J. Stuart Blackton, 1900, Edison Co.,); The Cat and the Monkey (Paul Terry, 1921); Luring Eyes (Bray Co., ca. 1922); Hey Diddle Diddle (magic Pen of Mother Goose, Terrytoons, 1935) GPS 4, 6

Jerry on the Job Series

Reel of two cartoons: A Tough Pull; Sufficiency (ca. 1921, Bray) GPS 4

Sid Marcus

Animated Hair Cartoon No. 1 GPS 4, 6
Animated Hair Cartoon No. 2 GPS 4
Animated Hair Cartoon No. 3 GPS 4

Earl Hurd, Animator

Before and After (1916) TBF 4
Bobby Bumps and his Goatmobile (1916, Bray) GPS 4
Bobby Bumps and the Stork (1916, Bray) GPS 4, 6
Bobby Bumps Puts a Beanery on the Bum (1916) TBF 4
Their Masters Voice (Bobby Bumps; one part of a three-cartoon compilation in one of the *Paramount Magazine* series, 1920) TBF 2

William Nolan

Indoor Sports (1919) GPS 4

Tom E. Powers

Glenn Photo Compilation No. 1: Parcel Post Pete's Nightmare; Phable of a Busted Romance; He (Mr. Nobody Holme) Buys a Jitney; Phable of a Phat Woman (all 1916) GPS 4

Glenn Photo Compilation No. 2: Cooks vs. Chefs; The Phable of Olaf and Louis; Feet is Feet; The Joys and Glooms Elope (copyright catalog: "The Joys Elope") (all 1916) GPS 4, 6

Glenn Photo Compilation No. 3: Never Again! (the story of a speed cop); A Newlywed Phable; Old Doc Gloom . . . He Orders Gentle Exercise (all 1916) GPS 4

Tony Sarg

Adam Raises Cain (1919, puppet silhouette animation) GPS 4, 6

Miscellaneous

A Coach for Cinderella (1937, produced by Chevrolet) TBF 1
The Great Foodini (late 1940s; Bunin puppets, from the "Lucky Pup" TV series) GPS 2
Hell Bent for Election (1944; Charles M. "Chuck" Jones, animator) BHF 1
Jack and the Beanstalk (ca. 1928, puppets, animator unknown) GPS 6
The Littlest Angel (1950, Coronet Films) BHF 4
The Wizard of Oz (1933, Eshbaugh, Carl Stalling score) HFRP 2, 4
The Wizard's Apprentice (1930, William Cameron Menzies) TBF 2
The Wrong Bedroom (1929, puppets) TBF 2

BRITISH CARTOONS

Animaland Cartoons/David Hand/Rank Organization

Bee Brother DFS 1, 4; JEF 1; PMF 1, 4
Forest Dragon DFS 1, 4; JEF 1; PMF 1, 4
Ginger Nutt's Christmas Circus DFS 1, 4; JEF 1; PMF 1, 4
The House Cat DFS 1, 4; JEF 1; PMF 1, 4
It's a Lovely Day DFS 1, 4; JEF 1; PMF 1, 4
The Lion DFS 1, 4; JEF 1; PMF 1, 4
Platypus DFS 1, 4; JEF 1; PMF 1, 4
Bonzo (ca. 1924, G. E. Studdy; first of the "Bonzo" series about a pup) GPS 4

Bubble and Squeak

Big City FFL 1, 2, 3, 4
Funfair FFL 1, 2, 3, 4
Old Manor House FFL 1, 2, 3, 4

Colonel Rat and Willie the Worm

Loch Ness Legend FFL 1, 2, 3, 4

Wombles (BBC-TV)

Bungo's Birthday Party PMF 1, 2, 6
Games in the Snow PMF 1, 2, 6
Marrow Pie PMF 1, 2, 6
What's Cooking? PMF 1, 2, 6
Wombles Circus PMF 1, 2, 6
Wombling Free PMF 1, 3

Miscellaneous British

Big Little Hero PMF 1
Bullies in a Toy Shop PMF 1
The Hold Up PMF 1
Noddy Goes to Toyland PMF 1, 3
Red Riding Hood PMF 1

Sooty's Olympics (puppet film, Harry H. Corbet, animator) PMF 1, 2
Who's Scared? PMF 1
The Yellow Submarine (1969, trailer [preview] for the animated feature with the Beatles on the soundtrack) BHF 1; BMH 1; GSF 1; NFP 2; RFF 1

Full-length Animated Features—British

Animal Farm (1955) HFE 1; RI 1

AUSTRALIAN CARTOONS

Bimbo's Auto (a Color Classic cartoon from the Eric Porter studios) BHF 1
Rabbit Stew BHF 1

OTHER FOREIGN CARTOONS

Emile Cohl

Drame Chez les Fantoches (1908, stick-figure animation) HFRP 4
The Hasher's Delirium (ca. 1910) GPS 4, 6
Glenn Photo Compilation: The Pumpkin Race; Joyeux Microbes; Le Peintre Neo-impressioniste GPS 4
Max und Moritz (ca. 1923, Germany, stop-motion technique; based on the strip by Wilhelm Busch) GPS 4
Willi's Nightmare (1920s, Germany, Paul Peroff) GPS 4, 6

Ladislas Starevitch

Starevitch animated his first film for the czar's children. His films involve animated puppets, not drawings. He emigrated to France in 1920 and continued his work there.
The Fox and the Bear (1939; this is a segment from a longer film) GPS 4
Frogland (1922) TBF 4
Two Cupids (1926) GPS 4, 6; TBF 4
The Town Rat and the Country Rat (1926) GPS 4, 6
The Voice of the Nightingale (1923) BHF 3

Zagreb Film, Yugoslavia

Piccolo (animator-director: Dusan Vukotic) MWFS 1

Selected and Annotated Trade Journal and Popular Press Reports in Animation, 1906-1979

INTRODUCTION

The materials described below are, in many cases, the only surviving records about the film and television industries, especially in the early years. Often breezy, occasionally superficial, and sometimes too speculative, these items are still valuable because they tell us what the industries were saying to themselves. They also give additional information about the range and depth of value about what was said. This documentation may be the basis for refreshing the memories of survivors, serving to bridge gaps in knowledge about trends and events, or it may help corroborate other evidence.

The selected reports in this chronological list are from the following journals, with the scope of the systematic canvass indicated:

New York Times (1906-1979)
Variety (1906-1950; 1974-1979)
Broadcasting (1950-1979)
Advertising Age (1960-1979)
Sponsor (1958-1968)
Motography (known as *Nickelodeon* in the early years; 1909-1918)

The criteria for selecting the citations were the many forms of animation defined in Chapter 1. These criteria also include the industrial setting in which animation was contemplated, produced, distributed, or exhibited along with other events which illuminate the past context or events. The *New York Times* articles are identified by their correct headlines, not the summary versions appearing in the *New York Times Index. Variety* citations, comprising the major portion of this list, were taken from a current indexing project started at Florida State University, College of Communication, in January 1974, by the author. Animation is one of several thousand categories embraced in the larger project which seeks to recover and organize film and broadcast material from *Variety, Billboard*, and *Moving Picture World*. Thus far, over two hundred student readers of these microfilms and other categorizers have worked on the project using a complex scheme for coding and review to safeguard the highest possible standards of validity and reliability. This project is still in search of funds to computerize the data. By mid-1981, about 152,000 citations were drawn from the microfilms; around seven hundred involved animation topics from the years 1905 to 1950 in *Variety*. These were organized with citations from the other journals identified above, resulting in an extremely long list.

A reassurance for those who may have misgivings or inexperience with the product of coding by students: the author and annotator of this list kept track of the coding and the error rate, assisted by Mitchell Shapiro for a generous portion of the coding. In this group of materials, there were five possible errors per card or 3500 potential mistakes in the animation topic. Upon final verification, twenty errors were discovered in this batch but none failed to locate a published report. All citations were retrieved and examined by the author before a selection was made.

Citations from *Broadcsting, Advertising Age*, and *Sponsor* were systematically sought for this list because of the new channel television provided for animation after 1950. *Motography* and a portion of *Variety* cards were initially pulled by Richard Nelson and I am grateful for his help as well as that of Mitchell Shapiro, Jim Gelwicks, Lee Berger, Paul Jamesson, Darlene Chenevert, Cheryl Farmer, Kathy Jones, Marlene McEwen, Wanda Pangrac, and Timothy Unger, and the hundreds of communication students at Florida State University who have participated in the larger indexing project since 1974.

Most film reviews, box office reports, TV reviews, obituaries, and traditional "firsts" have been omitted since these materials are retrievable through other finding aids.

Readers may recognize an abundance of Disney citations after 1930, but there is no surprise in this since *Variety* reported a great deal of Disney news and press releases. While others were not omitted, Disney was the most visible in the trade journals.

The first section of this appendix consists of the chronological listing of 409 annotated citations. A topic and personality index comprises the second section. A brief title index to the films mentioned or discussed in the citations concludes this appendix.

Searching for a uniform system of citation, particularly in newspapers and magazines across a seventy-four-year period of this systematic canvass clearly illustrates the old adage that ours is not a perfect world. Accordingly, a brief explanation of the citation systems used for the annotated citations may be helpful, since there is no uniformity among the cited sources. In item 001, "Winsor McCay Playing," the reader is directed to *Variety* 4:6:6:1 (20 October 1906). This means that the article is located in volume 4, issue 6, page 6, column 1 of the given date and title. Volume and issue numbers have been retained in this list until about 1973 because the microfilms are published with this data. *Motography* follows the same format. But after 1973 *Variety* citations were drawn from the national edition and follow the format of the serials *Broadcasting, Advertising Age,* or *Sponsor*. The newspaper *New York Times* has a slightly different format, as given in item 014. "Children's Films for Children," (20 June 1915), VI, 5:1 is available in section VI, page 5, column 1 of the given date in the microfilm edition, which later becomes the national or mail edition. Please be aware that the Roman numerals for volume numbers are not always used in the *New York Times*, as indicated by item 062. These numbers merely report the page number and column number on the microfilm edition. After 1973, the *Times* citations were drawn from the city edition, in which alphabetical section numbers were used, followed with a page number. *Broadcasting, Advertising Age,* and *Sponsor* citations are more uniform in this list, as indicated by item 326, which reports the date of the issue followed by the page number.

ANNOTATIONS

001   "Winsor McCay Playing." *Variety* 4:6:6:1 (20 October 1906). After a week's experience in vaudeville, McCay now plans to open to the public "new ideas" of *Little Nemo,* but he does not indicate what this will be.

002   "Trick Pictures." *Nickelodeon* 2:2:37:2 (August 1909). General article about pixilation and stop-action photography without any mention of titles or filmmakers. Discusses disadvantages of stop-action photography balanced with the P. T. Barnum perspective.

003   Gardett, L. "Some Tricks of the Moving Picture Maker." *Nickelodeon* 2:2:53:1 (August 1909). With some assistance from Albert E. Smith and J. Stuart Blacton (Vitagraph), Gardett explains the tricks, including stop-action techniques.

004   Gardett, L. "Teaching History By Motography." *Nickelodeon* 2:4:119:1 (October 1909). Describes stop-action techniques with objects and maps, as in illustrating progress of military campaigns or how battles were executed.

005   "The Kalem's Expanding." *Variety* 16:8:10:02 (30 October 1909). Following the pattern of French films, Kalem plans to add a second reel to their weekly releases, with a magic or trick film likely.

006   Pierce, Frank N. "Some Curious Uses of Motography." *Nickelodeon* 3:2:39:1 (15 January 1910). Numerous examples of scientific applications of cinematography discussed, including time-lapse techniques to show plant growth.

007   "Making Motion Pictures By Pencil." *Motography* 7:4:162:1 (4 April 1912). About the work of Winsor McCay. A quotation from McCay about his expectation of drawing prehistoric monsters in a film for the American Historical Society may indicate that his cartoon act with the animated "Gertie the Dinosaur" did not occur before April 1912. There are references to the "Nemo" and "Mosquito" films.

008   "Nankivel's Cartoons Immortalized." *Motography* 8:7:253:1 (28 September 1912). Live-action version of Fred Nankivel's comic in the *New York Herald* ("Uncle Mun") is in an Edison trick film with other actors identified in this piece. This appears to be an early example of a live-action adaptation of a comic strip.

009   "Novel Series of Animated Cartoons." *Motography* 9:13:481:1 (28 June 1913). Selig Polyscope Company announces a series of animations entitled "Seligettes, No. 1" to be released 8 July, featuring work of Sydney Smith and his comic-strip character "Old Doc Yak."

010   "Raoul Barré, Edison Cartoonist." *Motography* 13:12:452:2 (20 March 1915). Edison announces the release of *The Animated Grouch Chaser,* by French cartoonist Raoul Barré.

011   "Bray Cartoons in Pathe News." *Motography* 13:12:438:2 (29 March 1915). J. R. Bray takes a news topic and animates the sketch. Several years earlier,

Pathe had shown a newspaper cartoonist drawing a static comic of a news topic.

012   "Tad's Comic Series." *Variety*. 38:9:17:3 (30 April 1915). Pathe Co. signs *Evening Journal* cartoonist "Tad" to publish a series of comedy films based on his drawings.

013   "Bray's Method Patented." *Motography* 13:25:996:1 (19 June 1915). Comment about the outcome of litigations on patent infringements. "The impression seems to prevail that Mr. Bray's patents should not have been granted, since his methods of work had been previously used by other cartoonists."

014   "Children's Films For Children." *New York Times* (20 June 1915), VI, 5:1. A report that a few perceive that a public demand for children's films is becoming organized. Background of *Woman's Home Companion* research reported.

015   Editorial. "The Value of Cartoon Films." *Motography* 14:1:21:1 (3 July 1915). The cartoon is still attractive because of its motion. People like cartoon films, but the editorial advises that it would not be wise to give an exclusive program of them. They are good motographic vaudeville stunts.

016   "Arthur R. Momand Is to Make Cartoons for Gaumont." *Motography* 14:11:512:1 (9 November 1915). Harry Palmer will animate a Mutual film series, *Keeping Up With the Joneses*. In a separate item with the above headline, Arthur R. Momand, newspaper cartoonist, is planning to create cartoons for Gaumont.

017   "Bray Cartoons For Paramount." *Motography* 14:25:1284:1 (18 December 1915). Bray program to be seen exclusively through Paramount with first release in January 1916. Other animators and programs described. Bray also develops political animations for Paramount news pictures.

018   "The New Animated Sub-Title." *Motography* 14:26:1320:1 (25 December 1915). Subtitling with use of mirrors and distortions

019   "Hearst-Vitagraph Topical to Start Big." *Motography* 15:2:71:1 (8 January 1916). Newsreel will be released through Vitagraph-Lubin-Selig-Essanay on 4 January with two issues per week. Each reel will be about 1000 feet with 800 feet concentrating on national and international subjects and the remainder on regional subjects. Tom Powers's cartoons to be included.

020   "Powers Pens Film Fun." *Motography* 15:3:106:1 (15 January 1916). Tom Powers, newspaper cartoonist for the New York Hearst organization, contributes to the Hearst-Vitagraph News Pictorial. Comic strips to be seen in the newsreel are described along with his background.

021   "Bray-Gilbert Silhouette Pictures. An Odd Paramount Offering." *Motography* 15:4:163:1 (22 January 1916). C. Allan Gilbert, illustrator, teams with John Bray to produce live-action silhouettes, the first for release being "Sinbad the Sailor." Studio setup described.

022   "Bray Cartoons Now Ready." *Motography* 15:4:199:1 (22 January 1916). *Colonel Heeza Liar's Waterloo* is first of Bray's cartoon films to be released through Paramount.

023   "Teaches Psychology on Screens. Munsterberg Is Paramount Editor." *Motography* 15:9:465:1 (26 February 1916). First production of *Paramount Pictograph*, a screen magazine. Content described and future issues indicated.

024   "Gaumont Resumes Cartoon Series." *Motography* 15:11:582:1 (11 March

1916). Harry Palmer to devote full time to animated films "which are humorous reflections on the news of the day." Palmer claims Gaumont was first to animate the news of the day, claiming for himself the title "Father of Animated News of the Day."

025 "Mutt and Jeff." *Variety* 43:4:24:3 (24 March 1916). Review of the first offering in the cartoon series shown at the New York Strand with some perceptions of audience reaction to the cartoon.

026 "Pathe Signs Cartoonist Goldberg. Fun Films Coming Soon." *Motography* 15:13:685:1 (25 March 1916). Goldberg signed by Pathe with detailed information on his background.

027 "Fantasies Art Popular." *Motography* 15:11:736:1 (1 April 1916). Report of screening of silhouette films made by C. Allan Gilbert. Discussion of different animations.

028 "Pictographs Are Popular." *Motography* 15:15:806:1 (8 April 1916). Euphoric report about the success of Paramount pictographs which are "visualizing thought upon the screen." Despite opposition within the company, President William W. Hodkinson produced the series.

029 " 'The Boob Weekly' Shown." *Motography* 15:15:818:2 (8 April 1916). Press screens revealed a burlesque on news weeklies which apparently brought the press to laughter. Animation by R. L. Goldberg, to be released by Pathe.

030 "Grossman's Quick Progress." *Variety* 42:8:24:4 (21 April 1916). *Mutt and Jeff* films, in business six weeks, have set up eighteen cities and two countries.

031 "Hearst Plans Announced, Exchanges Organized." *Motography*. 15:16:861:1 (15 April 1916). According to Edward MacManus, general manager for Hearst, the entire staff of writers and artists is to become affiliated with the International Film Service. Detailed description of each exchange and personnel.

032 "Pictographs Teach Preparedness. Screen Magazine Full of Interesting 'Articles.' " *Motography* 15:18:975:1 (29 April 1916). Bray animated cartoons are a part of the *Pictograph* magazine. Earl Hurd quoted on his first experiences animating drawings.

033 "The Boob Weekly." *Variety* 42:11:19:1 (12 May 1916). First and exclusive showing of R. L. Goldberg's animated cartoons at the New York Strand. The review describes the material.

034 "Modern Publishing Extends to Films. Publicity the Feature of International Pictures." *Motography* 15:20:1079:1 (13 May 1916). W. R. Hearst claims that the film business is the modern extension of the publishing business. His film service is a publicity extension of other Hearst enterprises. Plans described.

035 Divine, E. C. "Programs for the Kiddies." *Motography* 15:23:1247:1 (3 June 1916). Mr. Divine is president of the Strand Theater, Chicago. He describes the producer's conception of what is suitable for children which does not match that of the exhibitor. He concludes that children always like the cartoon because they are familiar with the newspaper versions.

036 Rothapfel, S. L. "Model Program for Children." *Motography* 15:25:1365:1 (17 June 1916). Rothapfel considers the chief difficulty with so-called children's programs is that they are not what children want to see but rather what the adults want to see.

037 Barrett, B. F. "Mother's Ideas on Children's Programs." *Motography*

15:26:1423:1 (24 June 1916). Barrett opines that those programs from which children are barred are not as bad as those which children are permitted to see. Cartoons have manifested a high response from children, but many mothers condemn slapstick since they think this teaches kids to roughhouse.

038   "International Releases News Pictorial." *Motography* 15:26:1443:1 (24 June 1916). Hearst International News Pictorial is a new branch of the Hearst empire. Walter C. Hoban added to contributors; he originated "Jerry on the Job" strip in *New York Journal*.

039   "Advocate Children's Films." *Motography* 16:1:11:1 (1 July 1916). Recent convention of General Federation of Women's Clubs heard a number of critical speeches about films for children. John H. Freuler, president of Mutual Film Company, responded, indicating that local exhibitors were the key; patrons should tell them what product they want for their chidlren.

040   Mintz, M. J. "Mothers Hinder Children's Matinee." *Motography* 16:2:69:1 (8 July 1916). After mothers selected a matinee program for their children, the kids became bored and boisterous. Mintz also complained that parents put their children in the matinee and expect the exhibitor to baby-sit them.

041   Barrett, B. F. "What The Children Want In Pictures." *Motography* 16:4:191:1 (22 July 1916). Four hundred children from Chicago of unspecified age ranges were asked their choice in films. No background information given about how the survey was conducted but apparently children were asked to write out their reasons for choices. Animated films and dolls as actors ranked at the bottom of the list.

042   Reisman, J. B. "Children Want Real Heroes in Films." *Motography* 16:17:909:1 (21 October 1916). The manager of the Dale Theater in St. Paul, Minn., avoids Chaplin films because he thinks they are too rough for the kids who might emulate the stunts. Cartoons are very popular but for ages 3 to 6 the fairy story has no appeal. Twenty-one-year-old actors are best heroes for kids.

043   "Pathe News Scores Two Scoops." *Motography* 16:18:977:1 (28 October 1916). Cartoon Film Service (CFS) supplies political cartoons to Pathe. Watson D. Robinson recently elected president of CFS; John C. Terry, Secretary, and Henry D. Bailey, treasurer. Terry claims to have made animated cartoons as early as 1912.

044   "Pathe Gets Famous Cartoonists." *Motography* 17:6:311:1 (10 February 1917). Alternating weekly are Happy Hooligan" by F. Opper; "Bringing Up Father" by George McManus (Emile Cohl); "Jerry On the Job" by Walt Hoban; "Krazy Kat" by George Herriman; and "Joys and Glooms" by Tom Powers. Anecdotes about the personalities are included.

045   "Cartoonists, Too.," *Variety* 47:9:29:1 (27 July 1917). Vaudeville cartoonists deplore the high cost of drawing materials, including paper, dyes, chalk. Dye cutoff from Germany requires costly substitutes.

046   "Mutt and Jeff Enlist in Navy." *Motography* 18:7:346:2 (18 August 1917). The characters are used to promote enlistments.

047   "Trials of a Cartoonist." *Motography* 18:8:412:1 (25 August 1917). Bub Fisher reflects on content and form of the cartoon, cautioning against offending special audiences such as religious groups or blacks.

048 "Animated Sculpture Appears." *Motography* 18:11:546:346:2 (15 September 1917). S. S. Film Company of New York films Helena Smith Dayton's "cartoons in clay," released through Educational Film Corporation.

049 "Make New Animated Cartoons." *Motography* 18:24:1246:3 (15 December 1917). E. B. Hetrick, in charge of International Film Service animated-cartoon department, announces a series of cartoon comedies. International releases are usually a split-reel with an educational or travel film. Current series features the *Katzenjammer Kids* under the direction of Gregory LaCava.

050 "Government Uses Hy Mayer Cartoon." *Motography* 19:2:75:3 (12 January 1918). George Creel has selected one of Mayer's cartoons, which had appeared in Universal Current Events, for propaganda abroad.

051 "New Food Conservation Films Produced." *Motography*. 19:17:809:2 (27 April 1918). Details of John Bray film production and other activities of the U.S. food administration.

052 "Latest News of State's Rights Productions. Fox Makes Drive on Mutt and Jeff." *Motography* 19:17:814:3 (27 April 1918). Fox engaged in intensive campaign to book cartoon series in theaters; reactions given. Meanwhile, Fisher is a captain at the front.

053 "Mutt and Jeff Meet Theda." *Motography* 20:1:19:3 (6 July 1918). Calling this a first, Mutt and Jeff (animation) are joined in their cartoon by a live-action Theda Bara.

054 "The Inkwell Man." *New York Times* (22 February 1920), III, 11:2. *Out-of-Inkwell* praised for smooth, flowing movement in this background piece about Max Fleischer, an associate at the Bray studios. Fleischer draws the clown from a live model. His background of association with Bray is also discussed.

055 "Revolutionary Process Cuts Production Costs 80 Per Cent." *Variety* 58:12:38:1 (14 May 1920). Ferdinand Piney Earl's new process enables him to "paint any background or setting desired . . . [and to] . . . transfer the setting to film." Chief interest expressed in the article is on behalf of producers who foresee up to 80 percent savings in production.

056 "Tony Sarg's Invention." *Variety* 62:12:1:4 (13 May 1921). Magazine cartoonist Sarg, known for his marionettes, joins H. M. Dawley to produce animated pictures. Secret process to make animated soldiers lifelike.

057 "Screening Aesop." *Variety* 63:2:46:4 (3 June 1921). Pathe contracts with Fable Pictures to release the cartoons, drawn by Paul Terry.

058 "Bray to Make Wells' 'Outline of History.'" *Variety* 61:12:38:2 (12 May 1922). Bray, whose animations are distributed by Goldwyn, has obtained rights to produce the Wells book.

059 "Screen From the Front." *New York Times* (3 December 1922), VIII, 2:1. Report of a survey of exhibitors and others in the film industry conducted by L. C. Moon, Babson Statistic Organization, Dr. Towland Rogers, photoplay instructor at Columbia University, and William A. Johnston, president of *Motion Picture News*. Exhibitors say short subjects contribute "17 percent to the strength of a program." Popularity of program types listed.

060 "Relativity, Filmed, Is As Lucid As Ever." *New York Times* (4 February 1923), II, 1:4. Discussion of Hugh Riesenfeld's film at the Strand Theater, New York. Scenes in the film are described along with reactions to the film.

061   "Screen—Your Own Projector." *New York Times* (18 February 1923), 3:2.
       Einstein Theory of Relativity animated drawings credited to Max Fleischer,
       "it is understood." Film originally made in Germany including animations, but
       Fleischer purportedly replaced many of the earlier sections "done with less
       skill abroad."

062   Waller, Fred. "Models and Miniatures." *New York Times* (23 March 1924),
       5:2. Overview of three recent innovations in film technology that have enhanced
       storytelling on the screen. These are lamps with greater illumination, improved
       slow-motion film cameras, and uses of models and miniatures.

063   "Artigue's Suits." *Variety* 83:9:8:2 (16 June 1926). Pierre Artigue, asserting
       he invented the shadowgraph, sues several producers for $400,000 each and
       others for lesser amounts. Alleges that he patented his device on 16 April 1919;
       seeks injunctions and relief.

064   "Artists In Germany Take Heart As Business Brightens." *New York Times*
       12:2 (7 November 1926). A flattering account of Lotte Reiniger's *Prince
       Achmed*, an animated silhouette film using cutout figures" wired, il-
       luminated, made flexible, and finally photographed." Production took three
       years to complete.

065   "Cartoon News Reel." *Variety* 87:3:5:2 (4 May 1927). F.B.O. will produce
       "newslaffs" by Bill Noland. Noland, creator of *Krazy Kat* cartoons will use a
       new photographic process in this series.

066   "Aesop On The Screen." *New York Times* (3 June 1928), VIII, 3:2. Paul
       Terry discusses the making of the fables. Production in this series started in
       mid-1920. Remarks that audiences are studied in order to present a fable in
       tune with their preferences. The cartoons also draw from the news. Other
       facets of the series are discussed including the process for making the Aesop
       series.

067   "Disney's Portable." *Variety* 94:13:7:5 (10 April 1929). With six Mickey
       Mouse cartoons synchronized for states' rights distribution, Disney arranged
       for former DeForest men, William Garriety and George Loweree, to build
       Disney portable sound on film gear.

068   "Bray-Hurd Win Cartoon Suit." *Variety* 97:13:79:3 (8 January 1930). Follow-
       ing five years of litigation, consent decree obtained for alleged in-
       fringers, now requiring payment of royalties to Bray-Hurd. Details on the
       lawsuit and state of the sound cartoon.

069   "Technicolor Cartoon Short At 'King of Jazz' Opening." *Variety* 98:11:26:4
       (26 March 1930). Technicolor animated cartoon made by Walter Lantz, in-
       cluded in *The King of Jazz*.

070   "POVS Hot Over Cartoon Cycle." *Variety* 98:12:4:3 (12 April 1930). "Pover-
       ty boys" (small producers) plan to add cartoons to their output "and cash in
       while the cycle's hot."

071   "Trick Photography Proving Big Money Saver for Talkers; Cuts Out 'Loca-
       tion' Expense." *Variety* 99:1:4:1 (16 April 1930). Dunning process (early
       traveling matte) used mainly to reduce high costs of location work and to solve
       problems of exterior noises on sound tracks at various locations. Several pic-
       tures identified using the matte; producer reactions.

072   " 'Hot' Cartoon Drawers Must Watch Code." *Variety* 99:3:3:1 (30 April

1930). Some animations are accused of exceeding the prohibitions of the MP-PDA code, according to the Hays Office.

073 "Wholesale Demand for Cartoon Shorts—Nearly All Cos. Listening." *Variety* 99:7:13:1 (28 May 1930). Except for Warner Brothers, Fox, and United Artists, nearly every company in the business will include cartoons next season. Each company's plans are described.

074 " 'Looney Tunes' Delivery." *Variety* 99:7:33:1 (28 May 1930). Leon Schlesinger enroute to New York with prints of the first series of *Looney Tunes* and Milton Charles's musical shorts.

075 "How Funny 'Looney Tunes' Are Made." *Variety* 99:11:14:3 (25 June 1930). Brief overview of animation history, with some "first" landmarks. *Looney Tunes* are by Hugh Harman and Rudolph Ising, with music by Frank Marsales and animation by Isadore Freleng.

076 "Cartoon Acclaim." *Variety* 100:21:6:3 (3 December 1930). Introduction of American comic-strip characters, such as Mickey Mouse or Felix the Cat, popularly received to enhance book publication of the characters in Paris.

077 "Complicated Work of Making Film Cartoons." *New York Times* VII, 6:3 (28 December 1930). Work on character "Bimbo" by the Fleischer brothers for Paramount is described.

078 "Preserved By The Camera and the Microphone. A German Silhouette Production." *New York Times* (22 February 1931), VII, 6:6. University Film Foundation, Harvard University, sponsors showings of the Lotte Reiniger film, *The Adventures of Prince Achmed*. The production process is described by quotes from Mrs. Reiniger. Role of Walter Ruttman, as painter, is also discussed.

079 "Kids Respond to Cartoons Quickest." *Variety* 101:6:34:5 (21 June 1931). Midwest exhibitors turn to cartoons to draw children, especially to Saturday matinees.

080 "Mickey Mouse Convention." *Variety* 102:13:7:1 (9 June 1931). Fox-Midwesco Theaters promoted convention drawing more than thirty Wisconsin towns sending delegates. Concept of the Mickey Mouse Club is identified and described.

081 Tilkastone, Dorothy. "Constructing The Animated Cartoon." *New York Times* (6 December 1931), VII, 7:1. Reviews process of producing animated cartoons, which varies among Disney, Paul Terry, and Fleischer brothers. Stages of scenario, character development, music computations, drawing, photography, and postmusic recording are described.

082 "Popular Mickey." *Variety* 110:8:19:5 (2 May 1933). Reviews heavy merchandising activity for the Disney character including toys, pencil boxes, pennants, caps, banners, wash suits, robes, sweaters, bathing suits, silverware, and belts.

083 Hall, Mordaunt. " 'Another Language' In Film Form." *New York Times* (13 August 1933), IX, 3:3. Comment on Walt Disney's *Silly Symphonies* and the wide attention these are attracting. Examples given.

084 "Kids Go For Nabe Cartoon Mat Bills In Lieu of Old Westerns." *Variety* 112:11:29:5 (21 November 1933). In neighborhood theaters, cartoons appear to be taking the place of Westerns. Multiple "Mickeys" booked on same bill.

085 "Cartoonists Have Their NRA Squawk." *Variety* 112:12:5:1 (28 November

1933). Cartoon producers disagree with provisions in NRA code prohibiting business deals sixty days before expiration of current contracts.

086 "Walt Disney Turns Down 'Pig' Pie Series." *Variety* 112:12:5:1 (28 November 1933). Disney rejects proposals to develop a series of cartoons based on *Three Little Pigs* success.

087 Hall, Mordaunt. "Mr. Disney's Art." *New York Times* (31 December 1933), IX, 5:5. Hall discusses Disney's work.

088 "Boop Pix Nix in Eng." *Variety* 114:7:13:1 (1 May 1934). *Red Hot Mama*, a Boop cartoon, was rejected by all on the British Board of Censors.

089 "Cartoonist School Sponsored on WGN." *Variety* 114:7:35:5 (1 May 1934). Good Humor Ice Cream has purchased airtime to sponsor a WGN radio broadcast to attempt teaching animation over the air.

090 "Russian Mickey." *New York Times* (10 June 1934), IX, 4:5. "Yozh," a Russian cartoon character is credited to Disney influence. Recent issue of the *Moscow News* describes Russian adaptation of the conveyer system of animation production, patterned after the Fleischer procedures. Lucille Cramer, American technical consultant, advised against the Russian "handicraft system" in which one artist, with two to three assistants, completes an entire film.

091 "Wanted—5,000 Cartoonists; No Kiddin." *Variety* 115:2:1:2 (26 June 1934). Max Fleischer, advertising salaries of $100 to $300 per week, claims he would hire 5,000 animators tomorrow. Article reports state of the industry.

092 "Disney's $250,000 Cartoon Feature; A Year To Make." *Variety* 115:8:1:1 (7 August 1934). Disney going ahead with *Snow White* but does not predict conclusion of feature before end of 1935 or early 1936.

093 "America's 1st Cartoon Cinema; Paris Has One." *Variety* 116:4:2:5 (9 October 1934). In New York the Bijou plans to become an all-cartoon theater.

094 "Cartoon Spot's $725 Weekend." *Variety* 116:6:1:5 (23 October 1934). Bijou Theater in New York reports "above expectations" of audience response to all-cartoon programs.

095 Butcher, Harold. "An International Mouse. From Piccadilly to Darkest Manchouli, the Cosmic Cartoon Here Is Omnipresent." *New York Times* (28 October 1934), IX, 4:4. Butcher, returning from a 20,000-mile world trip reported that Mickey Mouse was readily available to him at most stops in Japan, England, and China.

096 "Mickey Mouse Falls Under Technicolor's Sway." *New York Times* (3 February 1935), VIII, 5:4. Historical background of the Kalmus Technicolor process, early contact with Walt Disney, and the first Mickey Mouse in Technicolor.

097 "Animated Cartoon Prod. Is Now The Big Coin for Sketch Artists." *Variety* 117:9:2:4 (12 February 1935). Salaries of animators are up and rising; details.

098 Nugent, Frank S. "Semi-Annual Report On The Cartoon Theatre." *New York Times* (7 April 1935), IX, 3:3. Report about the Bijou Theatre, New York, which shows cartoons exclusively. Established October 1934 and under new ownership, program policies are described. Notes that more children want spinach for dinner now. Birthday parties and baby-sitting functions account for continued life of the exhibition outlet.

099 "Mickey Mouse Mag With Film Exploit. Angles; Horne, Pub." *Variety* 118:8:6:2 (8 May 1935). Magazine featuring Disney character planned for May is described.

100 "Technicolor-Eastman Pool Color Patents." *Variety* 118:11:5:2 (29 May 1935). Eastman is primarily interested in development of Kodachrome for amateur market. Technicolor interests are in the 35mm theatrical field. Pooling some patents would benefit both companies where technology overlaps.

101 "By The Way, Mr. Disney—." *New York Times* (1 December 1935), XI, 9:2. Question-and-answer format in Mr. Disney's interview. He responds to various questions about features, his characters, and his role in the production of Disney animation. "I do not draw, write music or contribute most of the gags and ideas seen in our pictures today. My work is largely to supervise, to select and shape material."

102 Gerstein, Evelyn. "Ptushko, Puppet Master." *New York Times* (8 December 1935), X, 6:3. Profile of the animator responsible for *The New Gulliver*.

103 "Cartoons Flood Radio." *Variety* 121:1:33:3 (18 December 1935). Hearst and Scripps-Howard interests selling their syndicated comic features to radio. Details given of recent deals.

104 "Inventor of Animated Cartoons Now on Dole." *Variety* 121:7:1:5 (29 January 1936). Emile Cohl now lives on $7 monthly given him by public charity. Walt Disney mentioned this news in a recent speech given in Paris.

105 "Terry's New Set Up." *Variety* 121:13:6:3 (11 March 1936). Paul Terry elected president of Terrytoons, Inc., replacing retiring head, Frank Moser. Others described.

106 "Fleischer Explains His New 3D Dimension." *Variety* 122:6:2:4 (22 April 1936). In a demonstration, the process is explained; some secret aspects revealed. First film using the new process will be *Sinbad the Sailor*.

107 "MG's Own Cartoonics." *Variety* 126:6:25:2 (21 April 1937). Fred Quimby, MGM's shorts department head interviewing prospective animators on West Coast; Herb Morgan (shorts exploitator) interviewing on East Coast. Plans are for MGM unit to begin, summer 1937.

108 "Fleischer Prod. Halted, Says Union." *Variety* 126:9:3:1 (12 May 1937). Strike at Fleischer plant in New York by Commercial Artists and Designers Union. Strike began when fifteen organizers were dismissed, according to union. Fleischer employs 135 persons.

109 "Musicians Join Fleischer Strike." *Variety* 126:10:3:1 (19 May 1937). Music union, local 802, of which Dave Fleischer is a member, joins striking Commercial Artists and Designers.

110 "Fleischer Strike Still Dead Locked." *Variety* 126:12:2:5 (2 June 1937). Detailed report of strike activities and negotiations, with sharply conflicting versions of the strike reported.

111 " 'Snow White' Readying." *Variety* 126:13:3:2 (9 June 1937). Preparations continue for Disney's first theatrical multireel animated feature, which will stress human-drama aspects of the fairy tale.

112 "Fleischer Strike Still Deadlocked." *Variety* 127:1:2:3 (16 June 1937). Update on the continuing strike at the Fleisher studio in New York.

113 "IA Not Backing Fleischer Walkouts." *Variety* 127:3:6:3 (30 June 1937). In-

ternational Alliance of Theatrical and Stage Employees refuses to grant order to cease projection of Fleischer cartoons throughout U.S. Additional update given on the strike.

114   Churchill, Douglas W. "Hollywood Turns Back The Clock." *New York Times* (15 August 1937), X, 3:5. Fred Quimby and Jack Chartok, organizing an animation unit at MGM, are experiencing great difficulty getting qualified help for the production *The Captain and the Kids*.

115   "CADU-Fleischer In a Long Siege; Deny Boycotts." *Variety* 127:13:4:2 (8 September 1937). Strike of the Commercial Artists and Designers Union against Fleischer.

116   "Disney-Rinso Show May Be OK'd Today." *Variety* 128:1:38:2 (15 September 1937). Ad agency Ruthrauff and Ryan expect an approval for the program, to precede the Al Jolson show on CBS, Tuesday nights.

117   "Disney on Mickey Show." *Variety* 129:2:25:5 (22 December 1937). Ad agents Lord and Thomas produce the "Mickey Mouse Show" for Pepsodent to debut 2 January 1938. Only credits to be given are for Walt Disney and Felix Mills's music.

118   Chartier, Roy. "Unions in 1937 Advanced Under Wagner Law, C.I.O. Counter-Threat." *Variety* 129:4:44:2 (5 January 1938). As part of *Variety's* annual update on union activity, the CADU-Fleischer strike is reported in detail.

119   Roddy, Ralph. "Labor Picture In Hollywood." *Variety* 129:4:4:3 (5 January 1938). Annual review of labor activities.

120   "Disney's Big B.O. Kayoes Vauders." *Variety* 129:11:1:2 (23 February 1938). Suggested connection between success of Disney animated feature and demise of bookings for vaudeville acts.

121   "Cycle of Cartoon Features on The Way, Following 'Snow White's' Click." *Variety* 129:11:5:1 (23 February 1938). Detailed treatment of the reaction to *Snow White* feature with plans of other studios discussed.

122   "Par-Fleischer Set To Produce Cartoon Feature." *Variety* 129:12:4:3 (2 March 1938). Fleischer will begin the feature in New York and finish it in their Miami facility which is planned to open in August 1938. Charles ("Hasty") Hastings, former employee of Fleischer and Jam Handy (Detroit) plan to open New York animation school to meet anticipated demand for animators in U.S.

123   Churchill, Douglas W. "Disney's 'Philosophy.' His Creatures of the Screen, He Says, Are Simply Laughing At Our Human Weaknesses." *New York Times* (6 March 1938), VIII, 9. Summed up, the Disney credo is not to make great art but entertainment. The organization and operating style are described with long quotations from Disney.

124   "Elaborate Commercial Short." *Variety* 129:13:7:4 (9 March 1938). Walter Lantz directed *Boy Meets Dog*, one reel, Techicolor advertising film for Ipana account of Bristol-Meyers. Based on comic-strip character "Reg'lar Fellers."

125   Crowther, Bosley. "Pal of the Puppet Pictures." *New York Times* (13 March 1938), XI, 5:6. The work and personality of George Pal are described.

126   "Metro's Feature Cartoon." *Variety* 130:1:6:3 (16 March 1938). Harry Hershfield, syndicated comic-strip artist, anounced as new head of MGM cartoon unit.

127 "Snow White's: 12,000-15,000 Contracts Augurs a New Domestic Sales Record." *Variety* 130:7:26:5 (27 April 1938). Detailed report of the phenomenal audience attraction of this film, including speculations on repeat attenders and box office sales in small towns.

128 "Milt Gross Head MG Cartoons Dept., Hershfield Scrams." *Variety* 130:8:11:2 (4 May 1938). Hershfield ran into differences of opinion with studio executives; left with full pay.

129 "Patterson Short." *Variety* 130:9:5:2 (11 May 1938). Response to puppet films abroad is growing. Russell Patterson leaves Paramount to produce a series of puppet films similar to George Pal's *Puppet-toons* currently popular abroad.

130 "Mickey Out, Bob Hope In." *Variety* 130:10:28:5 (18 May 1938). "Mickey Mouse on the Air," running for twenty weeks, will end the series at the conclusion of the current season.

131 Churchill, Douglas W. "Peace Vs. Propaganda." *New York Times* (29 May 1938), X, 3:8. Brief reference to work of Russell Patterson and proposals to make animated doll films.

132 Woolf, S. J. "Walt Disney Tells Us What Makes Him Happy." *New York Times* (10 July 1938), VII, 5:1. Discussion of what is art, Disney's denial in defining it and his views about cartooning are presented.

133 " 'Snow White' Nixed for Kids Under 14 in Holland." *Variety* 132:12:11:3 (30 November 1938). Frightening scenes are perceived as unsuitable for children.

134 " 'Name' Voice Dubs for Fleischer's Cartoon." *Variety* 132:13:7:5 (7 December 1938). Lanny Ross and Jessica Dragonette signed to supply voices of Prince and Princess in the Fleischer feature *Gulliver's Travels* for Paramount.

135 Kaempffert, Waldemar. "The Week in Science. Mickey's Pants." *New York Times* (18 December 1938), II, 11:8. Report about the recording spectrophotometer used by Walt Disney Enterprises (hereafter cited as WDE) to measure various physical dimensions of colors in paint to ensure uniformity of color across thousands of cels.

136 Chartier, Roy. "The Unions." *Variety* 133:4:40:1 (4 January 1939). Annual wrap-up of union news, including animation.

137 Greene, Walter. "Films' Technical Advances." *Variety* 133:4:44:1 (4 January 1939). Review of technical achievements for 1938, including discussion of multiplane camera, mattes, and miniatures.

138 Nugent, Frank S. "Disney Is Now Art—But He Wonders." *New York Times* (26 February 1939), VII, 4. Superficial essay about the Disney reaction to a recent acquisition of Disney Productions artwork by the New York Metropolitan Museum of Art.

139 "Par Plans Extra Revenue From Cartoon Shorts." *Variety* 134:1:6:3 (15 March 1939). Lou Diamond, head of Paramount Shorts and Music Department, is organizing a new department to exploit commercial licensing of products based on cartoon characters developed by Max Fleischer.

140 "Walt Disney Is Now A Collector's Item." *Variety* 134:7:31:2 (26 April 1939). Disney original cels, according to Philadelphia dealer, have been selling from $5.00 to $75.00 each.

141 "Time's Parallel to Disney." *Variety* 135:5:6:7 (12 July 1939). Entry of "March of Time" series into feature production said to parallel Disney's. Disney shorts were becoming more costly to make, coupled with double-feature bills pushing out shorts. *The Old Mill* cost $72,000, about $20,000 above Disney average.

142 "4 Coast Cartoon Outfits To Vote Under NLRB Ruling." *Variety* 176:8:6:4 (1 November 1939). Elections among employees of four Hollywood animated film companies will be held to determine if they want representation by the Screen Cartoonists Guild. Lantz, Schlesinger, Ray Katz, and Loew's are the units involved.

143 "U. of Minn. 1st To Teach Animated Pic Cartooning." *Variety* 136:9:4:4 (8 November 1939). To be taught by Dr. Otto Radl and Karel Dodal of the Visual Education Department.

144 Stern, Herb. "Gulliver Reaches Hollywood." *New York Times* (12 November 1939), IX, 4:1. Director of the film, Dave Fleischer, currently in the West assembling *Gulliver's Travels*. Operation of the Fleischer's studio is described.

145 "Par Ties in Syndicates on 'Gulliver's Travels.' " *Variety* 136:13:8:5 (6 December 1939). *Gulliver* campaign is controlled and originated from New York.

146 "Cartoon Field Looks Lush to Metro, Will Turn Out Full-Length Fantasy." *Variety* 137:4:32:1 (3 January 1940). MGM's staff includes Hugh Harman and Rudolf Ising. Fred Quimby is head. Studio is still contemplating animating *Wizard of Oz*.

147 Roddy, Ralph. "Show Business' Hectic Labor Year." *Variety* 137:4:25:1 (3 January 1940). Annual wrap-up of labor activities involving entertainment business.

148 "The Unions." *Variety* 137:4:24:1 (3 January 1940). Detailed analysis of labor unions in entertainment industry; problems and controversies.

149 " 'Pinocchio' Pressbook Unusual for Novelties." *Variety* 137:13:10:2 (6 March 1940). There are more than 1500 gadgets licensed for this film; a record number for Disney. Fred Schaefer and Hal Green prepared the 76-page manual under supervision of RKO publicity advertising head S. Barret McCormick.

150 "Longer Pix Cut Shorts." *Variety* 138:6:5:3 (17 April 1940). Double features and longer A and B features are perceived as causes for decline in shorts production over last two seasons. Cartoons still sell well. Background of shorts production is described.

151 "How Shorts Shrunk Past Two Years." *Variety* 138:6:5:1 (17 April 1940). Table showing 1938-1939/1939-1940 season output versus the major studios.

152 "Schlesinger's 11th Year As Warners' Cartooner." *Variety* 138:7:28:4 (24 April 1940). New contract is for two years; calling for forty-two animated shorts in 1940-1941 season, comprising twenty-six *Merrie Melodies* and sixteen *Looney Tunes*. Longer shorts are perceived to be better money-makers, so two-reelers are being included.

153 "The Ascendency of Mr. Donald Duck." *New York Times* (23 June 1940), IX, 4:2. Humorous discussion of evolution of this Disney character.

154 "Par's Puppetoon's" *Variety*. 139:4:4:4 (3 July 1940). George Pal and

Stanley Neal will produce six one-reel novelty subjects using animated puppets instead of drawings.

155 Strauss, Theodore. "Mr. Terry and the Animal Kingdom." *New York Times* (7 July 1940), IX, 3:2. Twenty-fifth anniversary report of the Paul Terry organization based in New Rochelle, N.Y. Terry asserts Winsor McCay's "Gertie the Dinosaur" inspired Terry into animation. Produced fifty-two *Aesop Fables* a year with staff of nineteen. Process of Terry production described in detail.

156 "Disney's Own Distrib For 'Fantasia.' " *Variety* 139:11:6:2 (21 August 1940). For first time, Disney to become his own distributor. Technicians working to develop twelve sound units for the road-show sound tracks. Second reason for this distribution approach is the perception that the film is so different as to require a different sales approach.

157 "Swing May Spiel New War-Map Film Cartoon." *Variety* 139:11:2:4 (21 August 1940). Raymond Gram Swing may do commentary on new kind of animated war film, showing boundary changes, and other changes in European events. Swing is heard over WOR and Mutual network.

158 "First Par 'Superman' Short Ready By Xmas." *Variety* 139:13:7:2 (4 September 1940). Russell Holman, head of Paramount's Shorts Department, and Harry Donenfeld, president of Superman, Inc., announced deal for films to be made by the Miami-based Fleischer studios. Circulation of magazines, strip, and radio program described.

159 "Walt Disney's Self-Trailer, 'Dragon.' " *Variety* 140:4:2:3 (2 October 1940) *Reluctant Dragon* will include live-action and animation for first time in a Disney production. Feature will be sold as normally despite the fact that it is a plug for the Disney operation. Other details of the story given.

160 "R. G. Swing's 1st Cartoon Short for Release Nov. 5." *Variety* 140:7:6:2 (23 October 1940). Raymond Gram Swing signs with Cartoon Films for series of animated shorts to be distributed by Columbia. *Breakdown of World Peace* to be first. Other details of the series are described.

161 "One Way of Describing 'Fantasia.' " *New York Times* (27 October 1940), IX, 4:1. Description of how Disney artists approached the production of the film along with an overview of the major sequences.

162 " 'Fantasia's' Spot Between IATSE and IBEW Scrap." *Variety* 140:8:7:2 (31 October 1940). Union jurisdictional dispute puts Disney in middle with possible delay of *Fantasia* opening. Dispute surrounds the installation of new sound equipment. In another theater, similar dispute arose with a slugfest breaking out.

163 Robins, Sam. "Disney Again Tries Trailblazing." *New York Times Magazine* (3 November 1940), 6. Feature anticipating the release of *Fantasia* and description of the role of Deems Taylor, Disney, and Leopold Stokowski. Use of music in place of sound effects and other filmic techniques described.

164 "Labor's Truce; Co-op To Get 'Fantasia' B'way Premiere on Schedule." *Variety* 140:9:4:2 (6 November 1940). With apparent amity, IBEW and IATSE working side by side to finish installation at a 53rd Street theater in time for press premiere.

165 "Walt Disney Doubts 'Fantasia' Will Ever Show Him a Profit." *Variety*

140:10:4:3 (13 November 1940). In press interview, Disney candidly announced film cost $2.2 million with $200,000 going into the sound system. For exhibition, each sound unit costs $30,000, plus $2000 installation charge. The unconventionality of the film is expected to work in its favor, Disney said.

166   Crowther, Bosley. "Yes, But Is It Art?" *New York Times* (17 November 1940), IX, 4:1. Commentary on critical reaction to *Fantasia*, dismissing most of the criticism from the "flute and fiddle gentlemen" as being "not vital to us."

167   "U.S. Defense Demands Stall RCA-Disney on 'Fantasia' Equipment." *Variety*. 140:11:4:3 (20 November 1940). Government orders for radio apparatus have slowed RCA ability to fill Disney orders for Fantasound gear.

168   "Disney's Dumbo Gets Earlier Release Than Bambi; Cost Clipped." *Variety* 141:1:8:2 (11 December 1940). *Dumbo*, first feature to be produced entirely in the Burbank plant, is planned for release ahead of *Bambi*. *Dumbo* costs are about $1 million in contrast to other animated Disney features.

169   "H'wood Labor Relatively Peaceful During 1940." *Variety* 141:5:32:1 (8 January 1941). Annual wrap-up of labor relations across entertainment business in U.S. during 1940.

170   "Guilds Set Hollywood Pace." *Variety* 141:5:32:1 (8 January 1941). Actors, writers, and directors guilds' activities for 1940 detailed.

171   Brogdon, Bill. "Cartoon Improvements." *Variety* 141:5:49:4 (8 January 1941). Reviews technical and techniques improvements in animated films for 1940 including Fantasound, use of "de-dusting" procedures at Disney, and cycle sifters (which take static electricity from air). Fleischer's improved peg system, and nonphoto transfer to cel process also described.

172   "Films Technical Advances in '40: Highlight of Hollywood's Developments Was Improved Sound." *Variety* 141:5:36:2 (8 January 1941). Engineering wrap-up of technical achievements in 1940 described, including stereophonic recording (ATandT), Fantasound, Warner Brothers monaural improvements; improved raw stocks for optical recordings and other improvements.

173   "Fewer Shorts. Consent Decree's Tabu on Forcing 'Em — Cues Cut to 400 Briefies." *Variety* 141:5:38:4 (8 January 1941). Consent decree prohibited forcing shorts that exhibitors do not want. Warners cutting 1941-1942 shorts output to sixty, down from eighty. Other studios described. George Pal now contracted with Paramount. Cost problems of one- and two-reelers discussed.

174   "Drive on Walt Disney by Cartoonists Guild." *Variety* 141:6:16:1 (15 January 1941). Screen Cartoonists Guild filed petition with NLRB asking to be designated as collective-bargaining agent for the Disney artists. Moving Picture Painters Local has been willing to take lower hourly pay if guaranteed a sixty-hour week.

175   "Music to Suit Audience Mood for 'Fantasia.'" *Variety* 141:11:2:3 (19 February 1941). Varied music offerings at *Fantasia* nonroad shows recorded by Stokowski. Music is described along with film progress report.

176   "NLRB vs. Disney." *Variety* 142:6:21:3 (16 April 1941). Twenty affidavits filed with NLRB by Screen Cartoonists Guild and Society of Motion Picture Editors accuse Disney of sponsoring a company union.

177 "Shorts Loading Charged." *Variety* 142:6:6:3 (16 April 1941). At an exhibitors meeting, the method of selling shorts is attacked.

178 "Disney's Cartoons For OPM OK in D.C." *Variety* 142:8:5:2 (30 April 1941). First films Disney made for the U.S. government Office of Production Management delivered in D.C. for approval.

179 "Harman Will Produce Feature Inkers In Tint." *Variety* 142:9:27:1 (7 May 1941). Hugh Harman split from Rudolf Ising and MGM to make Technicolor feature-length cartoons under the banner Hugh Harman Productions, Inc. Distribution arrangement still to be negotiated.

180 "Disney-Cartoonists Settlement Imminent; Schlesinger's Lockout." *Variety* 142:11:20:1 (21 May 1941). Disney tentatively agreed to decree when informed that they did not have to admit they dominated the old Federation of Screen Cartoonists Union. But Schlesinger announced closure of his studio two days before his employees planned a walkout.

181 "Mickey Mouse Is Rated Among Better Envoys of Goodwill." *Variety* 142:12:13:3 (28 May 1941). Distribution of *Mouse* shorts to Latin America generated the headline's conclusion where Disney shorts drew well for years. Nazi houses in Germany presumably use Mouse cartoons to entice audiences to look at propaganda newsreels. Other details given of Disney South American plans.

182 "Disney Panned in Det. For Quick Return of 'Exclusive' Roadshowing." *Variety* 142:13:23:2 (6 June 1941). Detroit press complains that earlier roadshow advertised that film would not be shown in 150-mile radius, but Disney reversed this policy when road-show engagements did not measure up.

183 "Disney Calls In IATSE Exec To Mediate Strike." *Variety* 143:1:18:5 (11 June 1941). Details of the meetings to set up mediation explained.

184 "Studios Face Worst Labor Shortage in Film History." *Variety* 143:3:21:5 (26 June 1941). Shortage affects electricians, cameramen, soundmen.

185 "Sweeping Victory for Cartoonists In Strike Settlement with Disney." *Variety* 143:4:6:5 (2 July 1941). Four-week strike expected to end, following approval of contract by employees-Screen Cartoonist Guild members. Other terms of the agreement described.

186 "U.S. Labor Conciliator Steps In To Hasten Disney-Cartoon Peace." *Variety* 143:5:22:1 (9 July 1941). Discussion of two ads in *Daily Variety* explained in current controversy. U.S. government, because of productions at Disney, intervened in the Disney-Cartoonist Guild problems.

187 "Gov't Hold Off Action in Disney Strike; Studio Alone in Balking Arbitration." *Variety* 143:6:23:5 (16 July 1941). Disney refuses to submit dispute with Screen Cartoonists Guild to arbitration. Art Babbitt quoted; other developments at Technicolor relate to the strike at Walt Disney Productions (hereafter cited as WDP).

188 "RKO Draggin' Disney's 'Dragon' into N.Y. on Gumshoes and Picket Trailer." *Variety* 143:7:7:5 (23 July 1941). Strike news and *Reluctant Dragon* film seen by New York press as inconsistent; Disney publicists agree. Consequently, this is the least publicized of the Disney films in New York market. Labor unrest described at Disney.

189   "Cartoonists and Disney Settle." *Variety* 143:8:6:5 (30 July 1941). Striking employees returned to work. Terms described.

190   "Disney Strikers Win All Their Demands Including 100 Hours Back Wages." *Variety* 143:9:7:5 (6 August 1941). Terms of the agreement are discussed; arbitrators for Disney and strikers identified.

191   "Disney and Staff of 15 on South American Tour for Pickup Shots." *Variety* 143:10:31:2 (13 August 1941). Disney and others leave on two-month air tour of South America in preparation for films.

192   "Disney's Proposed Layoffs May Again Tie Up His Cartoon Plant." *Variety* 143:10:31:3 (13 August 1941). On same day that Disney departed for South America, Disney Enterprises announced layoff of 207 members of Screen Cartoonists Guild. Labor Department sending conciliation commission to negotiate. Controversy is described.

193   "Disney, MOT, Amateur Cameramen All Tie In For Pan-Am. Goodwilling." *Variety* 143:13:25:4 (3 September 1941). Announcement that Disney would make a film about South American tour for Rockefeller Committee on Inter-American Affairs. Extensive discussion of efforts by Twentieth Century-Fox producer on leave to government, Kenneth MacGowan.

194   "Woman Invents Animated Cartoons." *New York Times* (7 September 1941), II, 7:4. Mary L. Weiser, Los Angeles, patents a new procedure to give depth and texture to cels. Walt Disney Productions has acquired the procedure.

195   "Disney-Guild Peace Up to D.C." *Variety* 144:1:7:4 (10 September 1941). Mediation moves to Washington, D.C., if certain conditions are met.

196   "Disney Back From So. America Full of Gauchos, Sambas and Goodwill." *Variety* 144:7:6:1 (22 October 1941). Disney impressed with Samba music, gauchos, and other ideas. Details about disposition of 16mm color footage made by Disney and others in U.S. government films.

197   "Walt Disney in Radio Deal With Lou Cowan." *Variety* 144:10:3:3 (12 November 1941). Brief discussion on proposed radio series.

198   "Lantz Cartoon Scripters." *Variety* 144:13:4:3 (3 December 1941). Ben Hardaway, Charles Crouch, and Ford Baines, formerly at Walt Disney and Leon Schlesinger studios, join Walter Lantz story department.

199   "Cutting 45 Mins. From 'Fantasia' for Gen'l Release." *Variety* 144:13:5:2 (3 December 1941). Running time to drop from 125 minutes to about 80 minutes for general release. Test screenings of shortened version held in Pennsylvania and New York communities.

200   "Disney Turns Over Studio Bldg. To Army Detachment." *Variety* 145:2:3:1 (17 December 1941). Offer of the quarters to the army by Disney was accepted.

201   "Dumbo Contest Bally." *Variety* 145:2:15:5 (17 December 1941). Typical promotional story of contest and radio broadcast for public attention.

202   "U.S. Leases Large Portion of Disney's Cartoonery for Pan-Americanism." *Variety* 145:3:4:1 (24 December 1941). Treasury Department and Office of Inter-American Affairs to lease portion of Disney plant and staff, with Disney agreeing to devote one-half of his time to supervising government projects.

203   "Disney Cartoons As Tax Pain-Killer." *Variety* 145:8:2:2 (28 January 1942).

Disney plans cartoon to help ease the shock of tax payments by 15 March. Insignia also described; will be placed on export goods and foodstuffs given to U.S. needy.

204 "Fleischer Drops Cartoon Features After 'Mr. Bug.' " *Variety* 145:8:4:1 (28 January 1942). Change in plans necessitated by shortage of some materials used in *Bug*, increase in shorts production. Anticipate more shorts business aimed at war effort; do not expect any more features until war over.

205 "Instead of Getting $80,000, Disney Says He'll Lose 56G on U.S. Tax Short." *Variety* 145:10:19:4 (11 February 1942). Treasury Department offered film free to theaters; many exhibitors cancelled paid Disney shorts accordingly. *The New Spirit* finances explained in detail; also other Disney government film contracts.

206 "Much Ado About Disney's 80G; Got It Weeks Ago." *Variety* 145:11:4:2 (18 February 1942). Treasury Department paid Disney but House of Representatives deleted that amount from an appropriation bill two weeks earlier.

207 "Inkers Yield to Metro." *Variety* 145:13:24:3 (4 March 1942). Screen Cartoonists Guild agreed with some minor details on Metro's counterproposal on wages.

208 "SCG-Metro Pact." *Variety* 146:1:25:3 (11 March 1942). Screen Cartoonists Guild pact with Metro involves two-year contract for forty-hour week and new wages scales, retroactive to October 1941. Ceiling for animators, sketch, and story men is $95 per week.

209 "Cartoonists' Slow-Down." *Variety* 146:5:27:3 (8 April 1942). At Screen Gems, change in management resulted in release of news story that cartoonists were prohibited from striking, as a contract condition. Cartoonists went into a slowdown but Screen Cartoonists Guild ordered resumption of normal production.

210 "Schlesinger's WB Slate." *Variety* 146:6:5:2 (15 April 1942). Schlesinger starts his thirteenth year with Warner Brothers. Quota set at twenty-six *Merrie Melodies* and thirteen *Looney Tunes*; Technicolor to be used on six subjects.

211 " 'Fantasia' Bally Eyes Adult B.O., Foregoes Trys for Kids." *Variety* 146:7:15:4 (22 April 1942). Despite dropping large chunks featuring Stokowski, film is still a problem for Disney and distributor. Advertising now aimed only at adults and results appear to be better.

212 "Dave Fleischer Heads Col's Cartoon Unit." *Variety* 146:8:5:4 (29 April 1942). Columbia signs Fleischer to take control of cartoon unit, producing the *Rhapsodies* and *Phantasies* series in color.

213 "BMI Lands Score of Disney 'Bambi,' First Non-Berlin." *Variety* 146:9:43:1 (6 May 1942). Irving Berlin had previously published all of Disney's scores. Music will get six weeks plugging on radio networks before release in July.

214 "M-G Expands Cartoonery." *Variety* 147:7:14:5 (22 July 1942). New Metro cartoon unit headed by George Gordon. Webb Smith and Otto Englander, formerly with Disney, are Gordon's assistants. *Stork Takes a Holiday* is first production of the new unit.

215 "Cartoons Help Speed Up War Defense Work." *Variety* 147:13:60:3 (2 September 1942). About two-thirds of the Harman plant at MGM has been

turned over to the war effort. New unit added to produce more educational subjects related to the war effort.

216   "Short Subject Exec's Aver U.S. and Other Briefies Hog Screens." *Variety* 148:3:23:1 (23 September (1942). Short-subject dpartment heads complain to War Activities Committee that government and *Victory* shorts are crowding out regular subjects.

217   "WB's New Season Shorts and OWI's 'Salvage' Tip Strong '42-'43 Fare." *Variety* 148:4:20:1 (30 September 1942). In terms of numbers of one- and two-reelers, Warner Brothers is among stronger shorts leaders for the 1942-1943 season. Two cartoon described along with other shorts at the preview.

218   "Disney-SCG Make Peace." *Variety* 148:5:25:5 (7 October 1942). After thirty-six-hour negotiations, a record, Disney signs contract with Screen Cartoonists Guild. Labor-management clause included, requiring such a committee to undertake methods to increase production, eliminate bottlenecks, and improve labor-management relations. This is the first contract in the industry carrying such a clause.

219   "Schlesinger, SCG Sign Up." *Variety* 148:8:24:3 (28 October 1942). The new contract is similar to one Screen Cartoonists Guild signed with Disney but Schlesinger and the guild did not release details. Problems arose when twenty-seven assistant animators were not advanced; they walked out.

220   "NLRB's Curb on Disney and SCG." *Variety* 148:11:18:2 (189 November 1942). Arthur Babbit, active union organizer, was laid off 24 November 1941. He brought charges to the National Labor Relations Board. The board "recommendation" (which becomes an order in ten days if not complied with) tells WDP to cease discouraging employees from joining Screen Cartoonists Guild. Babbit was discriminated against, board concluded and Disney was ordered to rehire him with back pay.

221   Wear, Mike. "Outlook for Shorts: Stepchild Film's Future Depends on Governmental Edicts on Duals." *Variety* 149:4:47:3 (6 January 1943). Shorts' future tied to war and the double feature which shows no signs of lessening demand. War connection is controversial since some in trade consider film stock-shortage a myth.

222   Roddy, Rod. "Hollywood Unions. Crafts and Guilds Stabilized This Year in Light of the War Effort." *Variety* 149:4:52:1 (6 January 1943). Annual summary piece on labor-management relations in 1942 including Screen Cartoonists Guild fight with Disney. Detailed discussion on role of Herbert Sorrell and Pat Casey as labor bosses in Hollywood.

223   "Cutting of 'B' Pix and Shorts, But Increased Number of Government Briefies Noted." *Variety* 149:8:7:3 (3 February 1943). B features and shorts in a decline. Trend caused by cuts in raw stock by War Production Board. Exhibitors dismayed at large number of government shorts they are asked to play, though these are free.

224   "Disney Education Cartoons For Latins; In Spanish, Portuguese." *Variety* 149:12:6:1 (3 March 1943). First two of color teaching-cartoons under contract by Disney with Office of Inter-American Affairs to be released in six weeks. Films described.

225   "Disney Aero Film Will Help Fliers Whip Storms." *Variety* 150:1:22:4 (17

March 1943). *Aerology* is a film Disney is making for the U.S. Navy. Will illustrate how to maneuver airplane through lightening, rain, ice, and other storms.

226 "War Crimps Cartoonery." *Variety* 150:6:5:4 (21 April 1943). *Looney Tunes* and *Merrie Melody* productions cut about one-half because of material and manpower shortages.

227 "Disney Inkers Take Life for War Effort." *Variety* 150:6:29:3 (21 April 1943). Disney has five teams working in Brazil, and aircraft factories and navy training locations in U.S. for government-sponsored film projects.

228 "Disney Getting Back to His Own Pictures." *Variety* 151:1:5:2 (16 June 1943). About 92 percent of Disney plant devoted to making training films for government. "Bongo," a bear, planned as new character in new feature; other pending projects explained.

229 "Disney's Cartoon Mag For Ex-Employees In Service." *Variety* 151:2:20:2 (23 June 1943). Contents include stories about the former employees, addresses, pinups, and artwork drawn especially for the 36-page publication.

230 "Disney's Speed-up." *Variety* 151:3:20:3 (30 June 1943). Disney experimenting with technical equipment and production procedures to hasten production on animated features. *Alice in Wonderland* being contemplated. *Peter Pan* may go into early production.

231 "Disney Starts Work on Cartoon Pix Aimed at Post-War Global Education." *Variety* 151:9:3:1 (11 August 1943). Disney envisions vast postwar, world market for instructional films. For past six months, studio has hosted educator seminars. Outlines methods of how cartoons would increase literacy.

232 "Disney on Deal To Animate One World." *Variety* 151:9:3:2 (11 August 1943). With Twentieth Century-Fox, Disney is working on animated maps to fill in gaps in Wendell Willkie's *One World*.

233 " 'Superman' Pix-Radio Bally to Hypo Physical Fitness, Curb Vandalism." *Variety* 152:11:6:2 (24 November 1943). Spinning-out of the use of comic character "Hop Harrigan" to recruit air cadets. The U.S. government wants to use "Superman" to get kids off the street and into sports for physical fitness.

234 "Lantz's Voice Credits." *Variety* 153:2:8:2 (22 December 1943). For first time, Lantz is giving screen credits to voices in his cartoons.

235 Roddy, Ralph. "Coast Unions Delay Deals In Hope 15% Formula Will Be Out." *Variety* 153:4:50:1 (5 January 1944). Highlights of previous twelve months, including actions of Screen Cartoonists Guild, one of the most active in the industry for the year.

236 "Fleischer's New Tag." *Variety* 153:4:6:3 (5 January 1944). Animation, Inc., is name of Dave Fleischer's new production company.

237 Openheim, Beatrice. "Propaganda Puppets." *New York Times Magazine* (20 February 1944), VI, 43:2. All-marionette, color films made for the coordinator of Inter-American Affairs, by puppeteers Bill and Cora Baird described. Films are to be distributed throughout South America and consist of Latin-American music with Spanish and Portuguese dialogue. Content emphasizes diet and farming subjects. Sequences described.

238 "Make Sure of All Pix Credits-SAG." *Variety* 154:1:3:1 (15 March 1944). New

talent urged by Screen Actors Guild to get their screen credits following outcome of the Robert Cummings case.

239   "SCG's Video, Reissue and Other Demands." *Variety* 154:5:6:4 (12 April 1944). Screen Cartoonists Guild to sit in on negotiations for reissue and TV residuals with producers.

240   "Willkie's Withdrawal Influences Pix Plans on 'One World' Release." *Variety* 154:6:1:1 (19 April 1944). Status of film reported.

241   "Cartoonists' Tele Ideas." *Variety* 154:9:7:5 (10 May 1944). Screen Cartoonists Guild 20 percent demand was nixed by screen producers who do not want to pay anything for reissues and TV showings.

242   "SCG-Geo Pal N Ain't." *Variety* 154:10:6:2 (17 May 1944). Negotiations broken off concerning classification of job content. Talks deadlocked.

243   "U.S. To Judge Disney Inker Pact Dispute." *Variety* 154:12:3:2 (31 May 1944). Louis L. Livingstone, representative of conciliation division of Department of Labor, called conference to settle dispute.

244   "Disney Sees Postwar Boom in Eductional Pix; Rehabilitation." *Variety* 154:13:6:2 (7 June 1944). In statements to the press during his Eastern visit Disney stated that shortage of cellophane hampered production of theatricals. Gave more details on *Swing Street*.

245   "Cartoon Prods Set Demand For Rent Hike." *Variety* 155:3:13:5 (28 June 1944). Cartoon Producers Association calls for increase in rentals for their product. Walter Lantz, member of the board of directors, stated that costs have risen 40 percent since 1942.

246   "Gov't Pictures Seen Paving the Way for Comm'l Product: Offers to Disney." *Variety* 155:8:3:5 (2 August 1944). Roy Disney has been exploring postwar markets for industrial film. Several companies have offered contracts up to $1 million for industrial film production after the war.

247   "Vast Development on Non-Theatrical Pix After the War, Sez Arthur Mayer." *Variety* 156:3:28:5 (27 September 1944).

248   "SCG Sues Disney." *Variety* 156:3:11:2 (27 September 1944). Screen Cartoonists Guild seeks affirmation of $10,000 back-pay order to four hundred employees. Disney asserts that Treasury Department has not yet approved payment to forty employees whose income exceeded $5000 last year.

249   "Three-Way Tele Deal for Disney's Shorts." *Variety* 156:8:33:3 (1 November 1944). Among RCA, NBC, and Disney, Coordinator of Inter-American Affairs arranged for televising of Disney films in New York over WNBT.

250   "Tinted Film Hypoed 14-Fold in 10 Years." *Variety* 156:8:7:1 (1 November 1944). From the time Disney produced the Technicolor *Silly Symphony* in 1932, Techicolor output has increased to 125,000,000 feet in 1943.

251   "Rank's Cartoonery." *Variety* 156:12:10:4 (29 November 1944). J. Arthur Rank, Great Britain, is assembling staff of artists and animators to produce cartoons for worldwide distribution.

252   "Scramble For Color Film: High Priorities May Cue Trades." *Variety* 157:6:3:3 (17 January 1945). Detailed report about scarcity of color printing services and high demands for color prints. Producers may trade their position waiting in line for Technicolor service in exchange for story or star deals. U.S. armed forces films get highest priority.

253 "WLB Nixes SCG Gripe on Disney." *Variety* 157:7:7:4 (24 January 1945). Ten regional war labor boards disapproved the request of the Screen Cartoonists Guild for 20 percent of box office profits from reissues and TV showings.

254 "Inkers Won't Appeal Disney Pact Decish." *Variety* 157:8:6:1 (31 January 1945). Screen Cartoonists Guild announced they would not appeal matter dealing with reissues and TV runs.

255 "Film Comics, Educ'l Subjects For Kids." *Variety* 158:3:21:5 (28 March 1945). Steve Slesinger, publisher, has formed two production units for making comic and educational films.

256 "M-G Curtailing Shorts Due to Film Shortage." *Variety* 158:9:3:4 (9 May 1945). Raw-stock shortage necessitates curtailing shorts. They currently produce John Nesbit's *Passing Parade*, Pete Smith shorts, cartoons, and Fitz-Patrick *Traveltalks*.

257 "Harman Sues 20th." *Variety* 158:13:9:4 (6 June 1945). Hugh Harman, cartoon producer, filed breach-of-contract lawsuit against Twentieth Century-Fox for $1,072,900. Contends that he was asked to animate a 936-foot sequence combining actors and animation for Billy Rose's *Diamond Horseshoe*.

258 "Disney Protests Wage Hike Order by WLB." *Variety* 159:1:9:2 (13 June 1945). Disney declares it had boosted wages above the Little Steel Formula prior to the WLB action and now protests that order for a further boost.

259 "Paramount Telestation Signs NEA Comic Strips." *Variety* 159:5:37:3 (11 July 1945). First strips to be televised.

260 "Screen Cartoonists Consult WLB After 4 Dickers Collapse." *Variety* 159:5:9:3 (11 July 1945). Negotiations with Lantz, Metro, Warners, and Screen Gems broke down over 1945-1946 pact. Disney negotiations are stalled pending appeal to WLB in Washington.

261 "Bugs Bunny, Carrot Crunching Comic." *New York Times* (22 July 1945), II, 3:6. Exposition of "Bugs" creation with recollections by I. Freleng, Tedd Pierce, Michael Maltese, Mel Blanc, and Edward Selzer, chief of the Warner's cartoon unit. Wartime transformation of the character described.

262 "Disney Eases From War Pix to Entertainment." *Variety* 159:10:6:1 (15 August 1945). Anticipating the defeat of the Japanese, organization now has two features in production and six in various planning stages.

263 "Disney Mounts Tower of Babel; 1 Lingoes" *Variety* 159:11:9:5 (22 August 1945). Disney films now in ten languages.

264 "Latinos Kept Pic-Happy." *Variety* 160:10:16:3 (14 November 1945). Documentary films produced by Office of Inter-American Affairs have been exhibited to more than 200,000 persons in Latin America. Films are distributed through American embassies.

265 "Lantz Cartoons to Spot Live Talent." *Variety* 160:13:9:1 (5 December 1945). Lantz discussing featurettes (three-reels) with Universal that would include animation and live-action. Present plans include one featurette; thirteen regular cartoons for Universal in 1946. He is also producing four sponsored films backed by electric power companies, John Deere, National Carbon, and Shell Oil.

266 "Paul Terry's 30th Anniversary." *Variety* 161:4:15:2 (2 January 1946). Cocktail party held at hotel in New York.

267 "Par Cartoonists Agree To Union Contract, Up to Coast Wages." *Variety* 161:8:13:2 (30 January 1946). Famous Studios, New York, signed contract with Screen Cartoonists Guild following dispute before WLB a year earlier. Wage scales presented; key animation studios identified.

268 "Live Action-Cartoon Combo May Be M-G Series: Trial Pic Set." *Variety* 161:9:9:2 (6 February 1946). Fifty-minute feature with Margaret O'Brien incorporating live-action animation is to be a pilot to a possible series using the technique, based on successful eight-minute sequence from *Anchors Aweigh*. Data given on construction of this sequence for the film.

269 "Disney Signs Dali." *Variety* 161:10:3:2 (13 February 1946). Salvador Dali signed contract to contribute artwork to new cartoon *Destino*, a picture based on a Mexican love ballad by Armando Dominguez.

270 "Lamb Making Animated Muscial Cartoon Shorts." *Variety* 161:12:13:4 (27 February 1946). With *Three Blind Mice* as the lead-off offering, Herb Lamb begins production of musical cartoon shorts.

271 "M & S Quit Puppeting." *Variety* 162:8:25:5 (1 May 1946). Shortage of material and costs of miniature puppets were reasons for the Morey and Sutherland combo, formerly with Disney, to return to flat animation.

272 "Disney Rolls Lively Pic." *Variety* 162:11:11:5 (22 May 1946). *So Dear To My Heart* begins production; only three hundred feet anticipated for animation.

273 "Exhibs Catering to Sat. Mat Kids With Special Programs of Shorts." *Variety* 163:1:24:2 (12 June 1946). Report about reaction to revising Saturday exhibition schedules.

274 "Disney Letting Out 450 of 1,060 Personnel Following 25% SCG Tilt." *Variety* 163:8:8:5 (31 July 1946). John F. Reeder, vice-president and general manager of WDP, fired 450 personnel in an economy move. Screen Cartoonists Guild wage demands and continuing negotiations with craft guilds prevents long-range planning he said. WDP agreed to 25 percent pay boost for those who remained on payroll. Details of negotiations described.

275 "Disney, SCG Set Compromise Deal." *Variety* 163:9:26:2 (7 August 1946). Details of settlement not completely revealed but Disney will return 94 of 215 SCG members in larger group of 450 fired earlier. Names of negotiators of all guilds involved given; other details.

276 "M-G Cartoonists Set For Heaviest Schedule." *Variety* 164:1:7:5 (11 September 1946). "Heaviest production program in Metro's history" includes twenty Technicolor cartoons. Animators/directors Tex Avery, Michael Law, and Preston Blair involved.

277 "Heavier Costs May Force Disney to Drop Shorts." *Variety* 164:9:9:2 (6 November 1946). Single reelers now cost $55,000-$60,000, and this makes features far more profitable than the limited return for shorts. Spokesman for the financial interests reported that net for WDP would still be low due to government projects.

278 "Animated Shorts Too Costly, Geo. Pal Also Into Feature Prods." *Variety* 164:11:19:4 (20 November 1946). Predicting complete demise of short subjects, Pal announces he is discontinuing them for features. He says Disney, Columbia, and Lantz are dropping animated shorts.

279 "Walt Disney Back With Leprechaun Pic Ideas; Uncertain About Plans." *Variety* 165:2:15:5 (18 December 1946). Returning from Ireland, Walt Disney announces *The Little People* would begin production within a month with two- to three-year release date. Other pending projects discussed. Shorts production sharply curtailed.

280 "Disney Goes More to Live-Cartoon Feature Prods." *Variety* 165:12:18:2 (26 February 1947). Almost 50 percent of the four upcoming Disney features will be live-action. Loan-out of live talent can be timed more easily since cartoon aspect does not create schedule conflicts as other actors would. Other details of productions in process.

281 "Cartoon and Puppet Versions of 'Alice' Due via Disney and Bunin." *Variety* 166:10:3:1 (14 May 1947). Disney abandons live-action/cartoon combination for *Alice* in favor of all animation version. In France, Lou Bunin, an American, is doing a puppet version. Potential competition internationally discussed along with copyright aspect.

282 "Cartoon-Making Kicked Around." *Variety* 166:12:6:3 (28 May 1947). Paramount due to drop *Lulu* series early June; Columbia has discontinued *Screen Gems* and G. Pal is turning to features and commercials. Excessive costs in production of animation given as main reason for abandoning the form; cost increases detailed. Lantz switched from Universal to United Artists.

283 "Rank In Special Drive to Woo Kid Film Customers." *Variety* 166:13:10:3 (4 June 1947). *Bush Christmas* is especially designed marketed for children. Details of the Rank promotions.

284 "Cut Cartoon Output 45%." *Variety* 167:1:5:2 (11 June 1947). For the 1947-1948 season, Hollywood cartoon production will be down considerably, putting an estimated 60 percent of the employees out of work. Chief reason given is high cost of labor; 41 percent increase over 1946. Difficulty in getting Technicolor commitments is a second reason for downturn.

285 "Bilingual Cartoons From André Sarutt." *Variety* 167:13:15:4 (3 September 1947). André Sarutt, head of French cartoon studio Les Gemeaux, sees U.S. market as important one for cartoons, especially since dubbing requirements are minimal due to the emphasis on the visual.

286 Nugent, Frank. "That Million-Dollar Mouse." *New York Times Magazine* (21 September 1947), VI, 22. Reminiscences by Walt Disney on the creation of "Mortimer Mouse"; foreign names given. Changes in the Mickey character-drawings and different roles outlined. Artists working on character and Kay Kamen, Disney merchandiser, also featured.

287 "Cartoonists Shaving Costs." *Variety* 168:5:6:2 (8 October 1947). Cartoon Producers Association will hold meeting to determine ways of cutting production costs over loss of foreign markets.

288 "Disney Admits He Called Wrong Group 'Commies.'" *Variety* 168:10:4:1 (12 November 1947). Makes apology to League of Women Voters. Disney explains he meant to say "League of Women Shoppers" but became confused with the words when he testified before House Un-American Activities Committee, 24 October 1947.

289 "Par Ready to Debut Its New Polacolor." *Variety* 168:12:4:1 (26 November 1947). Major studios are working to evolve new color processes, but Para-

mount has teamed with Polaroid to develop new system to be demonstrated in new films.

290   "Lantz's 90-day Layoff." *Variety* 169:1:7:1 (10 December 1947). Under contract for twelve cartoons annually for United Artists, Lantz is curtailing production due to limited number he can get from Technicolor. United Artists' management problems described.

291   "Par's Two-Reel Shorts Exhib Economy Victims." *Variety* 169:12:7:2 (25 February 1948). Paramount decided to drop two-reelers from schedule; emphasis now appears to be on one-reel animated cartoons. Exhibitors have shunned two-reelers, attempting to cut back rental fees.

292   "More WB Cartoons." *Variety* 170:5:7:2 (7 April 1948). Increased by eight over 1947, Warner Brothers announced thirty-four cartoons to be released this year; twenty-six in Technicolor, eight in Cinecolor.

293   "Documentary Series of Travelogs for Disney." *Variety* 170:7:15:4 (21 April 1948). Animated maps will be the only animation in new travelog, *Story of Alaska* by Disney. Footage shot by Alfred and Alma Milotte. Disney got the idea for the featurette last August (1947) when he visited Alaska.

294   "Comic Strip Quartet." *Variety* 170:9:9:2 (5 May 1948). Describes upcoming films based on comic strips: "Jungle Jim," "Terry and the Pirates," "Prince Valiant," and "Barnaby."

295   "Cinecolor Readies Three-Color Process." *Variety* 170:9:15:2 (5 May 1948). Cinecolor has used a two-color process for live-action with occasional experiments with three-color in cartoons.

296   "$1,000,000 Loan on Book Royalties Enables Disney's Divvy Arrearages." *Variety* 170:10:9:5 (12 May 1948). Racine, Wisconsin, publishing company has all rights in publishing Disney characters in consideration of loan; Disney royalties to be charged against the balance over ten-year period. Disney has been getting $200,000 yearly, illustrating success of Disney publication efforts. Financial data.

297   "B. O., Foreign Lags Nip Disney Profits." *Variety* 171:1:4:4 (9 June 1948). Detailed financial announcement of first twenty-seven weeks of 1948 given by Roy Disney. He also hails U.S. Supreme Court ruling in antitrust case as opening the way to better playing times and rental fees, favoring the independents.

298   "Leffingwell's Puppet Plans." *Variety* 172:2:12:4 (15 September 1948). One-time employee Robert G. Leffingwell, now managing director of Signal Films, producers of puppet films in Technicolor, left London for U.S. to discuss distribution of his films in U.S. He recently assisted Les Gemeaux studios of Paris in the production of feature cartoon.

299   "Rank's Cartoons." *Variety* 172:5:11:4 (6 October 1948). Former Disney employee, David Hand, trained a team of animators for Rank. Press screenings of four films; all in Technicolor. Article reviews the films.

300   "Disney Donates 30-Min. Show to BBC Broadcast." *Variety* 173:2:13:4 (22 December 1948). BBC to celebrate twenty-first anniversary of "Mickey Mouse" and twenty-fifth anniversary of Disney's arrival in Hollywood. Details of the program described, including characters, recorded in Disney's studio and sent, via disc, to London.

301   "Disney's Net Loss of $39,038." *Variety* 173:5:9:3 (12 January 1949). Loss

reported for fiscal year ending September 1948, due primarily to less revenue from foreign business. Assets exceed liabilities, however. Blocked funds in foreign countries in Disney's name amount to nearly $1 million. Revenue from strips, publications, up about 3 percent. Other data furnished.

302 "WB Would Curb 'Bugs Bunny' Bits on Video." *Variety* 174:10:26:4 (18 May 1949). Warner Brothers warned puppeteer to stop using "Bugs Bunny" routine in his cafe act, giving rise to the rumor that the studio wants to preserve all TV rights.

303 "Getting No Big Pix, Reaction, Polacolor Shelving Its Process." *Variety* 174:10:5:1 (18 May 1949). Labor troubles and low print orders cited as main reasons for closing Cambridge plant.

304 "Disney Multi-Linguals For His Next Two Films." *Variety* 174:12:4:2 (1 June 1949). Disney anticipates foreign distribution will improve. Accordingly, *Alice* and *Cinderella* to be given wide distribution including ten foreign-language versions, making these two pictures the most widely disseminated of his films up to now. Plans outlined for making the foreign versions.

305 "Paris Hypoed as Disney Foreign Hqtrs. to Save on Expense, Sez Cutting." *Variety* 175:1:16:1 (15 June 1949). Paris established as center of Disney foreign production, said John W. Cutting, head of foreign operations. Disney can use blocked funds to finance the center.

306 "Inside Stuff-Pictures." *Variety* 175:4:20:4 (6 July 1949). Levinson-Flexer cartoons audience-tested by recording on tape where audiences laugh. Then films are recut, leaving in the best responses.

307 "U.S. Begging Playdates on Cartoon Health Short." *Variety* 175:4:25:3 (6 July 1949). Warner Brothers' cartoon short, produced for U.S. Public Health Service, will play WB theaters, but independent bookings also sought.

308 "Was a Time When Stoky and Disney Didn't Sell, Now It's Boffola B. O." *Variety* 175:4:4:5 (6 July 1949). *Fantasia* doing phenomenal business in locations that wouldn't even book the film nine years ago. Reasons and speculations offered in this detailed analysis of the film's history, cost, and revenues.

309 "Mel Blanc Doesn't Get Last Woodpecker Laugh." *Variety* 176:5:4:4 (12 October 1949). Judicial decision indicates that the laugh is public domain; not the property of its originator, Mel Blanc.

310 "Disney Personally to Carry on Kay Kamen's Licensing Bureau." *Variety* 176:9:3:5 (9 November 1949). Kay Kamen, for last eighteen years Disney's licensing agent, was killed in airplane crash. Disney plans to take over Kamen's staff.

311 "Disney To Operate Publishing Setup in Britain, France." *Variety* 176:9:35:2 (9 November 1949). Music-publishing firms established in each country.

312 "Shorts Producers Ask Reconsideration of One Oscar Award." *Variety* 176:10:14:3 (16 November 1949). Committee comprised of Lantz, Fred Quimby, Gordon Hollingshead, and George Bilson ask to split apart one- and two-reelers.

313 "Disney's Stress on Film Tunes." *Variety* 176:10:55:3 (16 November 1949). Fred Raphael heads new Disney music staff to exploit songs, even to point of developing shorts around music.

314 "Disney Dallying In Dali Ballet Pic Idea." *Variety* 177:2:9:1 (21 December

1949). Salvador Dali collaborates with Disney on ballet film.

315 "Goldwyn, Disney Bid for Jap Import Licenses to Test MPEA 'Monopoly.'" *Variety* 177:7:6:1 (25 January 1950). Disney and others in the Society of Independent Motion Picture Producers charge that the Motion Picture Export Association, operating under the aegis of the Department of State, has monopoly.

316 Crowther, Bosley. "McBoing, Boing, Magoo and Bosustow." *New York Times Magazine* (21 December 1952), 14.

317 Pryor, Thomas M. "Warners Order Halt In Cartoons." *New York Times* (17 June 1953), 32:1. Shutdown described as temporary. Company has forty cartoons awaiting release; others in laboratory stages.

318 Louchheim, Aline B. "Cartoons As Art. UPA Films Absorb an Important Function." *New York Times* (23 August 1953), II, 8:1. Positive critique of UPA style and descripton of recent animations. Director Robert Cannon discusses UPA art and idea.

319 Phillips, McCandlish. "Without Lisping Pigs. UPA Cartoons Penetrate TV's Culture Barrier with Esthetic Appeal." *New York Times* (23 August 1953), II, 8:1.

320 King, Vance. "From a 'Missing Link' To Tyrannosaurus Rex. Four Decades of 'Animation-In-Depth' Technique Marked By New Feature." *New York Times* (26 June 1955), II, 5:3. *Beast of Hollow Mountain* introduces the Regiscope process, developed by Dward Nassour, producer-director of the film. History of "depth animation" described. Regiscope uses predetermined movements recorded on tape, driving the models through electronic apparatus, ensuring consistent yet naturalistic movement.

321 "Lutheran Film Cartoon Set." *New York Times* (29 February 1956), 35:5. Described as the first, color, religious, animated film, Halas and Batchelor will produce the twenty-eight-minute subject for the Lutheran Church in America.

322 "Paramount Sells Shorts For Video." *New York Times* (4 June 1958), 40:1, 2. Description of the $1.7 million sale, the last of the Paramount animation library.

323 "'Painting on Light' For TV. Artist Andre Girard Readies CBS-TV Film." *Broadcasting* (23 March 1959), p. 101. The artist painted murallike scenes illustrating the New Testament text of the four gospels on one-hundred-foot strips of 70mm film in color. Religious specials identified.

324 "Do Tiny Cartoon Folks Sell?" *Broadcasting* (10 August 1959), p. 43. Institute for Advertising Research, affiliate of Chicago's Social Research, Inc., says cartoon characters are safe symbols. Summary of the report given. But there is some unpredictability of characters in animated commercials.

325 Bartnett, Edmond J. "Overseas Cartoons. Iron Curtain Films Shown on TV Here Are Screened Against Propaganda." *New York Times* (6 March 1960), II, 15:66. Cheaper European films appeal to TV programmers, including *Bozo the Clown*. Russian *Pixie* discussed by importer-distributor J. Jay Frankel and the reediting that is done on them.

326 "California Campaign Clash . . . Anti-Kennedy Cartoon Rhubarb: KPIX Rejects All 3; KRON-TV Uses 1." *Advertising Age* (7 November 1960), p. 3.

Sponsored by the Nixon-Lodge Committee of Northern California, three TV spots found offensive by some are described along with the reaction.

327 Thompson, Howard. "Animated Device for Films Show. Technamation Will Make Debut Here Next Month—Kramer Signs Lancaster." *New York Times* (30 November 1960), 41:3. Ten-minute theatrical short, *Wonderful World of Willie Doolittle*, illustrates process in a system using polarized light. Deal with Zagreb Films of Yugoslavia made to use the process which is claimed to reduce the number of cels by one-third.

328 Shepard, Richard F. "Factor for Television Funnies." *New York Times* (29 October 1961), II, 17:5. Description of process and personalities at CBS-owned Terrytoons, New Rochelle, New York. Director Tom Morrison, Vice-President Bill Weiss describe animation activities including theatrical series.

329 "TV Tape Animation Proves Economical, Quick." *Broadcasting* (19 November 1962), pp. 70-71. Aniform, Inc., a continuous-movement process and Ampex stop-frame animation process announced last week. Details of the process given.

330 "First Animated Video Tape Spot Debuts." *Sponsor* (4 February 1963), p. 48. Aniform process used; described briefly.

331 "Puppet Characters Open New Possibilities for Animation." *Sponsor* (4 March 1963), pp. 34-36. Advantages and disadvantages of the new videotape animation process called Aniform are described.

332 "Near-Sighted Magoo Was Far Sighted GE TV Buy." *Sponsor* 18:27 (6 July 1964), pp. 46-47. Brief history of the use of the Magoo character for General Electric bulb promotions, beginning in 1959-1960 TV season.

333 "Sponsors Hop Aboard ABC-TV's 'Beatles' Bandwagon." *Sponsor* 19:21 (14 June 1965), p. 26. Australian and British studios produced the animated version voiced by American actors. King Features produced the series. Songs will be the Beatles' actual voices.

334 Litwak, Leo E. "A Fantasy That Paid Off." *New York Times Magazine.* (27 June 1965), 22. Details about Audio-Animatronics, three-dimension animated figures that are synchronized to a slide and tape program. Abe Lincoln example discussed; others given.

335 "Hollywood Animators. Praising the Hue and Dye." *Sponsor* 19:23 (12 July 1965), pp. 35-41. Overview, as of 1965, for animation in 1965. Rise of color-TV set penetration important factor in rise of advertiser interest in color animation. Reasons for enhancing color in production given. One minute of color animation estimated as high as $12,000. Hanna-Barbera partially credit their animation programs for ouside commercial work.

336 "Animation Is Big Again at MGM." *Broadcasting* (3 January 1966), p. 126. Half-hour special is *How The Grinch Stole Christmas*, a thirty-minute film budgeted at $175,000. Other projects described.

337 "The Minute You Get Cultural, Nielsen-Wise You're in Trouble, Barbera Advises Admen." *Advertising Age* (9 May 1966), p. 3. Joseph R. Barbera says the current TV kids' show has the superhero as main appeal. Being educational-cultural is a potential disaster for ratings. Lists new Hanna-Barbera characters.

338   Wilford, John Noble. "Computers Turn To Movie-Making. Bell Shows Five
       Films That Machines Have Produced." *New York Times* (22 June 1966), 35:7.
       Kenneth C. Knowlton, A. Michael Noll, and F. W. Sinden worked on project.

339   " 'Super-Heroes' On the Way. New Animation Process Uses Actual Comic-
       Book Art to Depict Characters." *Broadcasting* (29 August 1966), p. 68. Using
       xerography, five characters from marvel Comic Group come to TV, via syn-
       dication. Process reproduces the comics to celluloid cels, but eliminates
       balloon speeches.

340   "Always on Saturday . . . (And Occasionally on Sunday)." *Sponsor* 21:2 (23
       January 1967), pp. 27-34. In this overview of the 1966-1967 TV season, car-
       toons are still better than ever in their ability to deliver kid audiences. ABC-TV
       is the leader in the sold position. Advertiser-owned programs are on the
       demise. Color and awareness of the audience has put old cartoon fare on the
       outs. Hanna-Barbera cartoons perceived as "hip."

341   Diehl, Digby. "On Saturdays, Super-Heroes and Talking Animals." *New
       York Times* (5 March 1967), II, 17:3. Critique of Saturday morning animated
       TV programming including issues of limited animation, violence, and story
       lines. Costs of animation described with specific program examples; other
       statistics.

342   "Animated Super-Heroes Conquer Kiddie's Saturday Block." *Broadcasting*
       (22 May 1967), p. 66. About Filmation Associates, Inc., and the product of
       the five-year-old company. Norman Prescott, once of Joe Levine's staff at
       Embassy Pictures; Lou Scheimer, one-time animator at Hanna-Barbera, now
       president at Filmation; and Hal Sutherland, former Walt Disney employee,
       now vice-president and supervising director at Filmation.

343   "The Screen. 'Man Called Flintstone' Opens in Showcases." *New York Times*
       (25 November 1967), 42:1. Review of the Columbia Pictures theatrical film of
       the *Flintstones*.

344   Adler, Renata. "Film: Tom and Jerry In the Real World." *New York Times*
       (20 January 1968), 21. About reduced animation used in this cartoon series.

345   "Last Flight for the Animated Horrors." *Sponsor* 22:5 (May 1968), pp. 36-41.
       Networks are making major shift away from violent programs to wholesome
       content. Plans of each network discussed in detail.

346   Windeler, Robert. "Violence in TV Cartoons Being Toned Down. Saturday
       Programs for Children Turn Toward Comedy." *New York Times* (20 July
       1968), 53:1. Comments from advocates and defenders on the issue of violence
       in children's cartoon programming given in this overview of the upcoming TV
       season, 1968-1969.

347   "Cartoons Sharpen The Point of WSB-TV's Editorials." *Television* 25:9
       (September 1968), p. 53. Bill Daniels, at WSB-TV, in-house cartoonist, films
       cartoons the same way a viewer would look at them, in parts. Techniques
       described here. Some history of editorial cartoons provided.

348   Baker, Stephen. "An Art Director's Viewpoint. Walt Disney Era Ends;
       Animation Comes of Age." *Advertising Age* (27 January 1969), p. 54. Baker
       concludes that art directors and writers are beginning to realize that animation
       is limitless. Commercials using animation employ tragicomedy, life vignettes,

and surrealism. Credits *Yellow Submarine* for acceptance of this trend. Considers what animation can do to expand technique of the illustrator.

349 "The Duo Responsible for Filling the Gap On Saturday Morning." *Broadcasting* (30 June 1969), p. 93. Feature profile about Bill Hanna and Joseph Barbera and their offerings for the 1969-1970 season. History of Hanna-Barbera.

350 Culhane, John. "The Men Behind Dastardly and Muttley." *New York Times Magazine* (23 November 1969), 50. Networks deal with Hanna-Barbera and Filmation because they have delivered hit shows for the networks. Hanna-Barbera also popular with networks because their costs are competitive. In the fall of 1969, ad revenue for kidvid about $90 million. $20 million realized as profit by networks. Process described. Pay schedules begin with $250 minimum, weekly, for journeyman-animator. Explains limited animation.

351 Jones, Stacy V. "Computer Aids in Cartoon Animation." *New York Times* (9 May 1970), 35:4. Von Haney, Xerox scientist, granted a patent for process using a live actor, wired with sensors at critical points for animated drawings, with the movement stored in computer memory.

352 Ammon, Robert. "Monday Memo. Computers Add a New Dimension to Commercial Animation." *Broadcasting* (2 November 1970), p. 2. Describes their work with Dolphin Productions, a division of Computer Image Corporation. Used Scanimate, involving conversion of artwork to Kodalith film, scanned by special camera, feeding signal into the computer, reemerging on a high-resolution screen.

353 Sutton, Howard. "How To Be Visible In the Clutter. TV Animation Isn't Just Cartoons." *Advertising Age* (31 January 1972), pp. 51-52. Advocates animation for "high visibility and a distinctive look." Includes moving graphics of any kind—drawings, symbols, line. Animation works well in compressed formats. Cost-effective when considering low talent fees, no location expense, no rental for sound stages. Implies that animated commercials are better remembered but has no empirical evidence for this.

354 "Children's Fare Stays Animated on Networks This Fall." *Broadcasting* (8 May 1972), p. 52. Preview of Saturday morning TV for 1972-1973 season on the networks. More reruns this upcoming season; networks also dropped one minute of their current twelve per hour.

355 "Coast Cartoon Shops Boomlet." *Variety* (1 August 1973), p. 271. Animators back into full employment; major studios' upcoming films listed.

356 Kasindorf, Martin. "Cartoon Vision and Brownsville Reality: A Kind of X-Rated Disney." *New York Times Magazine.* (14 October 1973), 40.

357 Thompson, Howard. " 'Fantastic Planet' Is Animated Feature." *New York Times* (19 December 1973), 54. Animated feature directed by Rene Laloux. A French-Czechoslovak coproduction in animation. Instead of drawing on acetate, artists have sketched on hinged and cutout paper.

358 Beaupre, Lee. "U.S. Cartoons, 1906 to 1973; Lewis Selznick's Scoffing Quip; New Trend to Adult (Sexy) Fare." *Variety* (9 January 1974), p. 76. Historical overview.

359 Segers, Frank. "New York As Animation Center; $475 For 38 Hours (If

Working)." *Variety* (9 January 1974), p. 76. News on the business of animation; wage scales in the New York area.

360 "Near-sighted Magoo was Far-sighted GE TV Buy." *Sponsor* 18:27 (6 July 1974), pp. 46-47. Recap of Magoo character as salesman for General Electric. Fall 1964 sales campaign would feature Magoo for president. Forty thousand votes cast for him in the 1964 elections, the article asserts.

361 Herzog, Arthur. "Science Fiction Movies Are Catching On." *New York Times* (25 August 1974). II, 2. Dr. Mark Chartrand, chairman of the Hayden Planetarium, states that science fiction has come out of the closet. *Planet of the Apes* (1968) to *2001* (1970), other films detailed.

362 O'Gara, Jim. "Animation Through Computer Offered as New Ad Technique." *Advertising Age* (17 March 1975), p. 58. Syntha Vision, using a computer, animates commercials. Explains cost savings of the process while describing examples of use at this time.

363 " 'Special Effects' Experts Fading." *Variety* (26 March 1975), p. 1. Albert Whitlock, who painted some of the *Earthquake* visuals, urges Hollywood to start training replacements for technicians in his line of work.

364 Harwood, Jim. "Animation Biz At Crossroads. Ascendancy of Live-Action Makes Sharp Inroads on Cartoonery Work." *Variety* (30 April 1975). p. 278. In upcoming 1976-1977 TV season, animation programs have less demand; some see animation as a troubled industry in danger of extinction. In heyday of IATSE Local 839 about 1300 were fully employed; now about 700 are fully employed.

365 Bellaire, Arthur. "TV: Getting Your Creative Money's Worth. Computer Animation Out of the Lab and onto the TV Screen." *Advertising Age* (2 June 1975), p. 34.

366 Farber, Stephen. "The Campaign to Suppress 'Coonskin.' " *New York Times* (20 July 1975), Leisure Section, p. 1.

367 Culhane, John. "What's New In Animated Films? Sex, Gluttony and Computers." *New York Times* (19 October 1975), Leisure Section, p. 1.

368 Bellaire, Arthur. "Breaking Through the 'Sameness' Barrier With More Creative Animation." *Advertising Age* (27 October 1975), p. 52. Bellaire concludes that animation should not be a substitute for tried and true live action. Thre is some concern that the creative possibilities of animation are not being used. Possibly the major problem is that art directors are afraid to take risks. Several animation applications given, with examples provided.

369 Murphy, A. D. "Credits Carelessly Omitted in Recall of 'Bugs Bunny.' " *Variety* (3 December 1975), p. 4. Critical review of ten Warner Brothers shorts resurrected from the past that also have Bob Clampett transitions inserted. Provides data on ownership of the cartoons. Others involved in their manufacture are mentioned.

370 " 'Tis the Season For Rankin/Bass To Be Jolly." *Broadcasting* (8 December 1975), pp. 69-70. Firm has almost cornered the market on prime-time Xmas specials. Ratings given. All of their work was done in Japan.

371 "50¢ Of Every Film Rental $ Adds To Disney Film Div. Profits." *Variety* (14 January 1976), p. 4. *Variety* publishes statistics for five-year period pointing

out that Disney caters to a specialized market, yet a profitable one for the film division. See figures in table.

372 "Animation Looks Like A Boom But Ink-and-Paint Hands Idle." *Variety* (5 May 1976), p. 39. While employment is up, animation union, IATSE, Local 839, says jobless rate is about 30 percent. Ink-and-paint and checkers are typically the last to go back to work.

373 "Film Forum Focuses Attention on Movie Animation, A Starved Art." *New York Times* (7 May 1976), C6:3. While animation is starving, the form survives on industrials, commercials on TV, and Saturday AM network TV. This piece describes offerings of the Film Forum expo on experimental animation.

374 "Hanna-Barbera Fight Animators Earnings Loss." *Variety* (16 June 1976), p. 9. Typical of gloom-and-doom talk about the demise of animation, Hanna-Barbera has embarked on a new schedule, making Saturday AM animations in the summer and theatrical films in the winter months. In 1957 Hanna-Barbera introduced limited animation to cut costs, but Hanna-Barbera points out that this has helped keep animators employed.

375 Culhane, John. "The Old Disney Magic." *New York Times Magazine* (1 August 1976), pp. 11. An update of Disney's new generation of animators with qualitative evaluations about goals and the future for Disney animation, quoted selectively from Culhane interviews and perceptions.

376 Culhane, John. "Can 'Raggedy Ann' Compete With Disney?" *New York Times* (20 March 1977), 8:3. Reviews Richard Williams's film and the key animators, Tisa David, Grim Natwick, Art Babbitt.

377 "Full Employment For Cartoonists Brings Charges of Overworking." *Variety* (25 May 1977), p. 61. International Alliance of Theatrical Stage Employees Local 839 allegation published in *Pegboard*, attacking Hanna-Barbera. Animation production is high with resulting increases in alleged work speedups. Three to four months earlier, Local 839 officials were complaining of unemployment.

378 McBridge, Joseph. " 'Star Wars' Speeds Scifi; George Pal 'Re-Discovered.' " *Variety* (13 July 1977), p. 21.

379 White, Hooper. "A Leading Animator Makes An Old Technique Look News." *Advertising Age* (18 July 1977), p. 50. Overview of animation on TV. Asserts there is nothing new in animation, citing friend Bob Kurtz of Kurtz and Friends, Hollywood, "master of metamorphic animation." Kurtz cites the rotoscoping of Levi-Strauss commercials to prove point. Other types of animation identified.

380 McMahan, Harry W. "Rating the Stars in TV Commercials: Bugs Bunny vs. Catherine Deneuve." *Advertising Age* (22 August 1977), pp. 37-38. Description of the Tell-Back popularity polling of stars in TV commercials and some examples. System does not explain fully the relationship between star and sponsor, or at least McMahan does not describe this part of the research.

381 Marty, Martin; Nyquist, Ewald B.; Zumwalt, Elmo R., Jr.; and Hollander, John. "The Incontrovertibly Enduring Impact of Mickey Mouse . . ." *New York Times* (3 December 1977), 23:3.

382 Christopher, Maurine. "Don't Touch That Dial. Saturday Morning Kiddie

TV Lineup—Mind-Deadening Prime Time Rejects." *Advertising Age* (10 February 1978), p. 50. Criticism of Saturday AM network TV and lack of learning offered in the 1978-1979 TV season.

383   Greene, Alexis. "The Coming Impact of Technology on the Arts—Computer Violins and the Electronic Palette." *New York Times* (26 February 1978), D2.

384   Brown, Les. "TV Cartoons Face Dim Future." *New York Times* (9 March 1978), 25.

385   Harmetz, Aljean. "Disney Incubating New Artists." *New York Times* (27 July 1978), p. C13.

386   Harmetz, Aljean. "Bakshi Journeys to Middle Earth to Animate 'Lord of the Rings.' " *New York Times* (8 November 1978), C17.

387   Tyler, Ralph. "R. O. Blechman Puts His Sly Mark On Christmas." *New York Times* (17 December 1978), D41. About the creator of *Simple Gifts: Six Episodes For Christmas* and contributing animators.

388   Harmetz, Aljean. "Disney Studio to Release PG Film It Didn't Make." *New York Times* (15 January 1979), C13.

389   Holsendolph, Ernest. "TV Cited on Stereotypes." *New York Times* (17 January 1979), p. C21.

390   Johnson, Sharon. "The Cartoon Creature As Salesman: Better Than Ever." *New York Times* (11 February 1979), F3. On merchandising cartoon characters.

391   Fantel, Hans. "Digital Recordings—Beautiful Music By the Numbers." *New York Times* (18 February 1979), D1.

392   Holsendolph, Ernest. "F.T.C. Opens Hearing On TV Ads Aimed At Children." *New York Times* (6 March 1979), C7.

393   Brown, Les. "Networks Try to Assuage Affiliates." *New York Times* (13 March 1979), C12. Refers to improved Saturday AM ratings with addition of certain new programs.

394   Hennessee, Judith. "Can Children's TV Workshop Recapture Its Youth?" *New York Times* (1 April 1979), D35.

395   Shepard, Richard R. "Television Networks Program More Educational Shows For Children." *New York Times* (14 April 1979), 40.

396   Schmeck, Harold M., Jr. "Mickey Sheds Light on Human Behavior." *New York Times* (16 May 1979), p. C3. Excerpts article by Stephen Jay Gould, Harvard biologist.

397   Ward, Alex. "Where Sid and All His Friends Live." *New York Times* (28 June 1979), C1. Former employees of Jim Henson, in puppet business.

398   Schaefer, Stephen. "The Studio That Mickey Built Boards the Sci-Fi Bandwagon." *New York Times* (22 July 1979), D1. $20 million *Black Hole* film. Visual effects by Peter Ellenshaw, British-born designer. Also did *Mary Poppins*. His career also to be highlighted in Museum of Modern Art retrospective.

399   Carmody, Deirdre. "Over 250 Comic Strips are Alive and Read in Most Papers." *New York Times* (29 July 1979), 20. Audience data on consumption of comics; and anecdotes.

400   Spiegel, Edith. "Yes, 'Sesame Street' Has Its Detractors." *New York Times* (5 August 1979), D23. Psychologist from Israel and teacher from India, along

with late Dorothy Cohen, criticize abrupt, fast-paced style of program.

401 "Strike Voted, Film-Industry Talks Set." *New York Times* (4 September 1979), C8. First possible strike since 1946. Unions seeking cost-of-living increases, higher wages, and more fringe benefits.

402 Harmetz, Aljean. "Disney's 'Sleeping Beauty' Is Awakening Again." *New York Times* (17 September 1979), C13. Disney spokesman says film was wrong for the 1970s. Values of true love were at lowest ebb in society in 1970; refers to market research demonstrating a return to these values. Discussion on film and techniques.

403 Harmetz, Aljean. "11 Animators Quit Disney, Form Studio." *New York Times* (20 September 1979), C14. Discussion of internal problems.

404 Ward, Alex. "Master Animator Chuck Jones: The Movement's the Thing." *New York Times* (7 October 1979), D17. Dovetailing around the *Bugs Bunny/Roadrunner Movie* review, Chuck Jones is interviewed about the film and his animation. What makes a character significant is not how he looks but how he moves, says Jones. Edward Bleier, vice-president at Warners, had the idea to create the feature.

405 McMahan, Harry Wayne. "Bring Back Old TV Commercials, They're Too Good to File Away." *Advertising Age* (22 October 1979), p. 67. Highlights some of the golden oldies such as use of Bill Baird puppets in a Cerebral Palsy spot.

406 "FCC Staff Gives Passing Grade to Kid Ad Reforms." *Advertising Age* (5 November 1979), p. 1. Releasing an 800-page report, FCC staff turned attention to children's programming instead of advertising. The report concluded that TV ads for kids promoted products harmful to children or were unfair. Little progress was made in increasing children's programming following the 1974 FCC program policy statement.

407 Beller, Miles. "Hollwood Is Banking On The Comics." *New York Times* (9 December 1979), sec. 2, 1-2. Nonanimated live-action films planned for 1980 including *Popeye, Flash Gordon, Terry and the Pirates.* Producers perceive wide appeal based on demand for comic-book heroes.

408 Fantel, Hans. "Stokowski—A Pioneer of Sonic Splendor." *New York Times* (9 December 1979), D25. Curiously, there is no mention of Stokowski's work with Disney and Fantasound, stereo process. The piece does establish that Stokowski was extremely motivated to utilize technology to make great music. By 1938 he was an expert in mike placement and other technical aspects of recording.

409 Culhane, John. " 'The Black Hole' Casts The Computer as Movie-Maker." *New York Times* (16 December 1979), D19. Use of the computer is discussed with John Dykstra and others. *Star Trek* animation is also described. Digital, computer-interpolation, and analog-image-synthesis methods are identified and discussed.

NAME AND SUBJECT INDEX

Numbers in this index refer to individual annotation entry numbers. Simply note the numbers following the topic or name and refer to the chronological and numbered listing for the complete citation and annotation of trade journal and popular press reports in animation.

TITLE INDEX

Numbers in this index refer to individual annotation entry numbers. Titles of produced and nonproduced films and TV programs are included when they were mentioned in the trade reports listed at the beginning of Appendix 6. Most of the reports are not reviews of the project but partial analysis, explanation, or criticism of the material.

Periodicals, Newsletters, and Irregular Serials in English of Animation Interest

INTRODUCTION

The literature of animation, as defined in this guide, comes from diverse sources. Many of these sources have published regularly for less than thirty years, perhaps reflecting a rapid rise in mass media specialties not accommodated in the older, traditional journals. In listing the publications, the wide range of titles and subject matter is apparent, yet the exploding technology in film and television will probably evoke new adaptations and syntheses, resulting in more specialized publications in the future. Hence, this list will not be frozen for long but will serve to point toward research and reading in several disciplines.

This list includes publications regularly or occasionally reporting business and industrial aspects of animation (*Advertising Age, Backstage, Variety,* for example), new technology in animation (*American Cinematographer, Computer Graphics, Engineering Graphics,* for example), history and criticism (*Sight and Sound, Moving Picture World, Film Quarterly, Cinefantastique,* for example), the how-to-do-it forms of animation and stop-action (*Super 8 Filmmaker, Cinemagic, Fantastic Films*), the buying and selling of animated films and videotapes (*Film Collector's World, The Big Reel, Classic Film/Video Images,* for example), reviews of new animated films and videotapes (*Film Library Quarterly, Sightlines, Media and Methods, Videophile,* for example), journals and fanzines almost exclusively devoted to animation (*Funnyworld, Animafilm, Animania,* for example), and materials about audience use of animated films and TV programs (*Educational Communication and Technology, Media Decisions, Radio-TV Age, Nielsen Television Index,* for example).

Unfortunately, few libraries outside of the Library of Congress are likely to have all of the publications listed below. The locating of even scattered runs requires diligence and long searching. And, when in hand, many of these volumes lack a systematic method or index for retrieving animation topics, resulting in a tedious page-by-page search. The periodicals most difficult to locate in libraries or research collections are the fanzines and some of the controlled circulation magazines, along with some film and TV industry trades. Interlibrary loan is the best solution to this problem, especially if requests are made to research libraries having one million or more volumes or to the Center for Research Libraries in Chicago. With regard to systematic access to the journals, the indexes indicated in *Ulrich's International Periodical Directory* for the current year, located under the title of the particular journal, will help provide access. Appendix 6 is a modest effort to provide a gateway to the most available trade journals on film and television and to the *New York Times*. Citations to articles in many of the journals listed below are also located in the bibliographies to the text chapters.

To exploit this list, readers are recommended to study carefully the finding aids described in Chapter 3.

BIBLIOGRAPHY

Advertising Age, 1929-. 740 North Rush Street, Chicago, Ill. 60611. Weekly. The business magazine of the advertising industry, which includes material about TV commercial production, computer animation, and broadcasting. Hooper White, Maurine Christopher, and Harry Wayne McMahon columns and articles are especially pertinent.

AFI Education Newsletter, 1978-. American Film Institute, John F. Kennedy Center for the Performing Arts, Washington, D.C. 20566. Bimonthly during the academic year. A newsletter that features announcements of new publications, special issues in film, festivals, symposia, job openings, course files (presenting detailed syllabi on various subjects including animation) and profiles of organizations that archive, program or display film related matter. A number of reports have been published on archives.

AFI Report, 1969-1975. The American Film Institute. Quarterly. No longer published, but one issue was devoted to animation (5:2, Summer 1974) with contributions by Judith O'Sullivan, Richard Huemer, Mike Barrier, Joe Adamson, Chuck Jones, Lee Mishkin and interviews with Robert Breer, Frank Mouris, Eliot Noyes, Jr., Mary Ellen Bute and Derek Lamb.

American Cinematographer, 1920-. Post Office Box 2230, Hollywood, Calif. Monthly. An authoritative cinematography journal published by the American Society of Cinematographers, an educational, cultural, and professional organization. The magazine has reported various types of animation devices, processes, and techniques over the years. Numerous articles have emphasized cinematography problems in particular features although full disclosure is frequently not given. Columns such as "Cinema Workshop" or "The Bookshelf" contain material of interest to scholars and professionals. As a consequence, this journal is preferred over the fanzines and amateur photography publications if your research involves contemporary film for theaters and TV.

American Classic Screen, 1976-. Traditions Press, 7800 Conser Place, Shawnee Mission, Kans. 66204. Quarterly. Claiming to be "the journal of America's Film Heritage," this publication contains only occasional articles on animation. Although some interviews are published, many of the articles are not documented. A few scholars contributing to the publication have helped maintain the generally high quality but occasional "fan articles" emphasizing the intangible and flashy aspects of the star system keep the publication close to the fanzine category. A national association connected with the journal attempts to provide contacts between the film collecting community and the film industry. The large amount of advertising from established film distributors selling

digests and the few features carried are in direct contrast to other, more inex-
pensively printed fanzines such as *Film Collectors World* or *The Big Reel,*
which report in great depth the various issues facing collectors and buffs.

American Educator, 1977-. American Federation of Teachers, AFL-CIO, 11 Dupont
Circle N.W., Washington, D.C. 20036. Quarterly. Contains a useful TV Supplement which frequently reviews upcoming animated and other programs with
special emphasis on how teachers might utilize the programs in the classroom.

American Film: Journal of the Film and Television Arts, 1975-. American Film
Institute, John F. Kennedy Center for the Performing Arts, Washington, D.C.
20566. Monthly. This journal, aimed at a broader audience than *AFI Report,*
embraces a large film and television spectrum, from historical to contemporary
films, filmmakers, and current issues. Occasional features on animation and
special effects by informed writers appear along with book reviews and AFI
editorials.

Animafilm, 1978-. Pol-ASIFA/Animafilm, Bank Handlowy S.A. 00-074 Warszawa,
Trebacka 3 (Warsaw, Poland). Quarterly. International review of animated
films published by the International Animated Film Association (ASIFA) and
the Polish Filmmakers' Association. ASIFA has regional organizations in the
United States. The publication includes detailed reviews and credits for current
animation films in many countries of the world. This resource is indispensable
for the serious scholar or animation buff.

Animania, formerly *Mindrot,* 1975-. David Mruz, 3112 Holmes Avenue, Minneapolis, Minn. 55408. Quarterly. Fanzine devoted to the animated film, featuring
contributions by buffs and animators such as Jim Korkis, Jeff Missinne, and
Mark Mayerson. Fanzines tend to cater to hobbyhorse opinions of writers and
this one is no exception, but the quarterly publication contains some intuitive
reporting along with valuable filmographies and in-depth articles about past
animation. One chief problem with publications of this type is that the contributors rarely give the sources of their information or other documentation except in the case of interviews.

Audio-Visual Communications, 1966-. United Business Publications, 475 Park
Avenue South, New York, N.Y. 10016. Monthly. Useful to producers and
managers looking for equipment sellers, (*Buyer's Guide* and *Who's Who*),
equipment descriptions, and materials on techniques including occasional
animation pieces. Also features brief notes on new publications including
resource volumes and production texts.

AV Guide: The Learning Media Magazine, 1922-. Trade Periodicals, 434 South
Wabash, Chicago, Ill. 60605. Monthly. Useful for media specialists and instructional personnel. Of particular interest is the long-running historical series on
the nontheatrical film by Arthur Edwin Krows, which began in September 1938
and continued to the mid-1940s. While undocumented, and sometimes containing errors or disputable assertions, these articles provide one of the earliest narratives in this long-neglected aspect of American film. With regard to animation, there are several references to little known producers and events in the
nontheatrical field, some of whom were users of the animated form. Those using the resources of the Factual Film Archive at Iowa State University, Ames,
Iowa (described in Appendix 2) would find this series useful despite the lack of

documentation. This journal was formerly titled *Educational Screen and Audio Visual Guide.*

Backstage, 1959-. 165 West 46th Street, New York, N.Y. 10036. Weekly. Emphasizing TV commercial production and to a lesser degree theater, and the talent business, this trade frequently contains animation material. The late August or early September issues have been almost exclusively devoted to animation.

The Big Reel, 1970-. Drawer B. Summerfield, N.C. 27358. Monthly. A film collecting fanzine of considerable importance, featuring advertising among traders and collectors, newspaper clips in film (including animation), and occasional columns and reviews of Super 8mm and videotape products commercially available. The publication also functions to air views affecting collectors, including copyright issues.

Broadcast Management Engineering, 1964-. Broadband Information Services, 295 Madison Avenue, New York, N.Y. 10017. Monthly. Controlled-circulation publication of interest to engineering managers and broadcasters. However, past issues have contained several technical articles about digital, aural, and video recordings which have possible application to computer-graphics and computer-animation. Annual buyer's guide is published.

Broadcasting, 1931-. 1735 DeSales Street, N.W., Washington, D.C. 20036. Weekly. Trade journal of the American broadcasting industry, containing timely news about TV animated programming, network plans, and the numerous regulatory and social-political issues in the industry. Distinctly reflecting a broadcast industry point of view, *Broadcasting* frequently publishes special reports about the new technologies, such as digital TV or computer-animation, and programming subjects, including annual guides to syndicators. An annual *Yearbook* published separately is an exhaustive compendium of radio and TV stations, advertising agencies, TV and film producers, equipment suppliers and many other industry service units. An index for recent years is available.

Cartoonews, 1975-. 561 Obispo Avenue, Orlando, Fla. 32807. Monthly. Occasional animation materials are published in this fanzine devoted almost exclusively to the cartoon (political or otherwise) and comic strip.

Cartoonist Profiles, 1969-. Editor, Jud Hurd. P.O. Box 325, Fairfield, Conn. 06430. Quarterly. While concentrating on print comic-strip artists and political cartoonists, this publication does feature a number of pieces on animators from time to time.

Christian Science Monitor, 1908-. P.O. Box 125, Astor Station, Boston, Mass. 02123. Five times a week. Important critical review sections for films and television in the United States.

Cinefantastique, 1970-. P.O. Box 270, Oak Park, Ill. 60303. Monthly. Probably the most prestigious and well-printed fanzine whose quality has steadily improved. Frequent articles on stop-action animation, important personalities in animation, and reviews of fantastic and animated films along with material on other facets of cinema and fantasy, including the horror genre.

Cinemagic, 1974-. P.O. Box 125, Perry Hall, Md. 21128. Quarterly. Fanzine for home moviemakers desiring to know trick photography and inexpensive special effects for amateur films. Several articles in past issues have emphasized miniatures, monster "techniques," double exposure, stop-action, glass shorts, and puppet animation.

Classic Film/Video Images, 1962-. P.O. Box 809, Muscatine, Iowa 52671. Bimonthly. Formerly *Classic Film Collector*, but still edited by Samuel K. Rubin. Regularly features reviews of public domain titles available in Super 8mm and 16mm and animation column; occasional reports on animation subjects. This journal would help update new additions to Super 8mm films available to collectors, educators, and archivists.

Computer (U.S.), 1966-. Institute of Electrical and Electronics Engineers, Inc., Computer Society, 5855 Naples Plaza, Suite 301, Long Beach, Calif. 90803. Monthly. Large circulation, technical journal containing part of the computer-graphic and computer-animation literature.

Computer Graphics, 1966-. Special Interest Group (SIG) in Computer Graphics (CG), Association for Computing Machinery, 1133 Avenue of the Americas, New York, N.Y. 10036. Quarterly. A primary professional journal in computer-graphics and computer-animation with coverage in standardization proposals, book reviews, and timely news in the expanding state of the art. Association membership is a very useful complement to anyone contemplating a career in computer-animation.

Computer Graphics and Image Processing, 1972-. Academic Press, 111 Fifth Avenue, New York, N.Y. 10003. Bimonthly. Publishes original research on the processing of pictorial information.

Computer Review, 1961-. GML Corporation, 594 Marrett Road, Lexington, Mass. 02173. Three times yearly. Looseleaf format. Another key abstract service that digests material from most of the technical computer journals in this list.

Computers and Graphics (GB) 1976-. Pergamon Press, Maxwell House, Fairview Park, Elmsford, N.Y. 10523. Quarterly. Publishes technical material on interactive computer-graphics, graphical models, data structures, picture manipulation algorithms (and related software), information systems, computer-aided education systems, computer-animation, graphic programming languages, integrated circuit design, and related topics.

Datamation, 1957-. Technical Publishing Company, 1801 South LaCienega Boulevard, Los Angeles, Calif. 90035. Monthly. Technical data-processing journal which features a number of reports on computer-graphics and computer-animation.

Educational and Industrial Television, 1968-. C. S. Tepfer Publishing Company, P.O. Box 565, Ridgefield, Conn. 06877. Monthly. Controlled-circulation magazine of primary interest to closed-circuit TV professionals and decision makers. Occasional pieces report animation techniques adapted to TV and videotape-media with additional reports on the state of digital technology and computer-animation and video programming sources.

Educational Communication and Technology, 1952-. Association for Educational Communication and Technology, 1126 Sixteenth Street, N.W., Washington, D.C. 20036. Quarterly. Formerly the *AV Communication Review*. Academic journal which occasionally reports research results involving animation and educational applications. Overall, this publication is the professional theory-and-research journal of the educational communications and technology field.

Emmy, 1980-. Academy of Television Arts and Sciences, 4605 Lankershim Boulevard, North Hollywood, Calif. 91602. Quarterly. Aimed at members of the TV industry and "intelligent consumers" (according to the editor's comments,

Winter 1980), *Emmy* joins several new 1980 periodicals about mass media, particularly TV. Thus far, little of direct interest to animation followers has been published, but industry viewpoints on programming and hardware have indirect value to animation.

Engineering Graphics, 1954-. St. Regis Publications, 6 East 43rd Street, New York, N.Y. 10017. Monthly. One of the oldest technical journals on this subject containing a considerable number of citations about computer-graphics and design, numerical control, and occasional reports on computer-animation.

Experimental Cinema, 1930-1934. Reprinted by Arno Press. Editors of this journal argued for the superiority of Soviet film due to theoretical and other orientations. Contains reviews and commentary on early experimental film in the United States and abroad, including those efforts using animation techniques.

Eye to Eye, 1950-1954. Bulletin of the Graphic History Society of America. Quarterly. An early attempt to systematically collect information on locations of photographic and graphic collections. Predecessor to *Picture Sources*, catalogue of Library of Congress iconographic collections, *Viewpoints*, and other recent publications. Has applications for filmmakers using collage and still-photo and/or kinestasis techniques.

Fanfare: The Magazine of Popular Culture and All the Arts, 1977-. 329 North Avenue 66, Los Angeles, Calif. 90042. Three times yearly. Fanzine was formerly titled *Graphic Story Magazine* but with issue Number 17, editorial policy included material "from the wildly popular to the obscurely esoteric." *Graphic Story* was devoted to the comic-book interests; *Fanfare* is more open-ended to include all aspects of "popular culture."

Fantastic Films, 1978-. Blake Publishing Corporation, 2701 Howard Street, Chicago, Ill. 60645. Bi-monthly. Fanzine focusing on special effects, animation, stunts, and cinematography as these relate to science-fiction or fantastic films, with more than occasional pieces on animation, defined broadly. Uses interviews occasionally.

Film Collector's World, 1976-. P.O. Box 248, Rapids City, Ill. 61278. Biweekly. Essentially an advertising medium for the film collecting market, including animation buffs. Similar to *The Big Reel* and others. Infrequent animation column by Mark Mayerson featured in past issues. Video column by Gary and Kay Anderson contains fan commentary on TV and film media. Later issues feature detailed reviews of Super 8mm product which can be very useful to collectors and educators contemplating Super 8mm prints and videotape purchases of animation.

Film Comment, 1962-. 140 West 65th Street, New York, N.Y. 10023. Monthly. Published by the Film Society of Lincoln Center. Features occasional articles on animation subjects, avant-garde or experimental film. Focuses on personalities rather than technical phases; also emphasizes techniques and aesthetics. Amos Vogel's columns frequently contain important updating material such as new journals and books in the field.

Film Culture, 1955-. G.P.O. Box 1499, New York, N.Y. 10001. Irregular. Earlier issues are scarce in many research libraries and book shops but reprints are available. This journal is important for the study of the expeimental film in the United States and abroad. Past issues have featured extensive interviews with experimental and animated filmmakers, profiles, reviews, and complete filmographies.

Film Fan Monthly, 1959-1973. 200 West 79th Street, New York, N.Y. 10024. Monthly. No longer published but still an important fanzine containing a number of articles on animation including filmographies. Al Kilgore's "The Disney Assault" (in Number 87) seems to appropriately balance Richard Schickel's *The Disney Version*. Editor Leonard Maltin in late 1980 was still selling back issues.

Film Library Quarterly, 1967-. Film Library Information Council, 17 West 60th Street, New York, N.Y. 10023. Quarterly. Valuable professional library journal of special interest to those in search of reviews of children's programs and similar content; frequently animated programs are discussed. Like *Sightlines*, this journal has featured interviews and profiles of animators.

Filmmakers Film and Video Monthly, 1967-. P.O. Box 115, Ward Hill, Mass. 01830. Monthly. This professionally oriented journal is among the better, more detailed, controlled-circulation publications aimed at the professional community. Howard Beckerman's regular animation column is important for animation practitioners and others who want to learn either what this is all about, or how-to-do-it. Frequent pieces on animation filmmakers and features. Very useful new books column and festival news.

Film News, 1940-. (incorporating *Learning Resources*). Film New Company, 250 West 57th Street, Suite 1527, New York, N.Y. 10019. Five times annually. By 1980 this journal had reached its forty-first year of reviewing shorts and features from the nontheatrical field, domestic and foreign sources. Frequent pieces on animated releases.

Film Quarterly, 1945-. University of California Press, Berkeley, California 94720. Quarterly. Reviews of contemporary film with analytical, theoretical, and descriptive pieces on experimental, animation, and narrative film throughout the world. About half of the current issues are devoted to reviews of contemporary films, including occasional animated films. The book review section and new periodical announcements are convenient updates.

Fleischer's Animated News, 1934-1937. Internal house organ for the Fleischer Studio, New York. Monthly. Extant issues at the New York Historical Society. Not complete. Microfilms are available. The survival of internal newsletters, memoranda, and other documentation from motion picture firms is extremely rare. Researchers are left with memorabilia collections selectively saved by the original participants in the business or interviews which present numerous reliability and validity problems. Trade press accounts, while breezy and sometimes superficial, can be used to raise questions or corroborate other findings, but these are still unindexed and not systematically organized. The *Fleischer Animated News* does provide some insight into the operation of some facets of the organization. A portion of the run is available at the New York City Historical Society.

The only work thus far that contains reproductions of Fleischer artwork and documentation is Leslie Carbarga's *The Fleischer Story*. However, this book does not fully attribute conclusions, commentary, or interpretation to documented sources or interviews. While the dustcover claims this is the "truth" about the organization, the reader is left with no resources to check conclusions, especially those dealing with the demise of the Fleischer organization in the early 1940s. Despite this, the book is valuable, especially when supplemented with the *Animated News.*

This collection is almost complete, starting with Volume 1, Number 1 in December 1934 and continuing through Volume 3, Number 5 (April 1937). There is a large amount of "office art" which depicts the Fleischer characters in various situations linked to interoffice activities and will probably bring a chuckle or two to the reader. Occasionally, policy statements concerning the organization are published. The most consistent feature is "Down Studio Lane" consisting of gossip and occasional assertions about organization activities. Also, a number of personality sketches are presented, sometimes with sophomoric criteria. Each sketch appears so similar as to indicate that a standard biographical form was used to elicit data. For example, we can now read of favorite foods, favorite drinks, personal appearance descriptions, heights and weights, youth history, birth data, pet peeves, and how each interviewee sleeps. Toward the end of the collection, the "interviews" seem to be more superficial but in most there are still the broad brushstrokes of professional background presented, especially for the animators.

Those individuals with biographies include: Max Fleischer (1:1), Dave Fleischer (1:1), Sam Buchwald (1:6), Nelly Sanborn (1:8), Lou Fleischer (1:10), Morris Fleischer (1:12), Bill Turner (2:2), Don Figlozzi (2:3), Erick Schenk (2:4), Eddie Nolan (2:5), Joe Oriolo (2:6), "Doc" Crandall (2:7), Edith Vernick (2:8), Jack Willis (2:8), Dave Tendlar (2:9), Joseph Edward Stultz (2:10), Joe Deneroff (2:11), and Hal Seeger (2:11).

In between the office sass and frolic are some valuable perspectives in the form of signed articles concerning the animation process, written by key personnel. These include: "Policy of the Animated News" (1:2), "Studio Relief Fund" (1:2), List of Long-term Employees (1:2), "Animation in the Good Old Days" (1:3), Fleischer Studio Compensation Plan (1:8), Lou Fleischer and the Music Department (1:9), "The Background Department" (1:10), "School Days" (1:11), "The Inbetweening Department" (1:11), "Planning" (1:12), "Inking;; (2:1), "The Relief Fund" (2:2), "Coloring" (2:2), "A Lesson in Photographing" (2:3), Service Certificates Explained (2:5), Radio Interview of Johnny Burk over WMCA, New York (2:8), "Looking Backward, 1931-1936" by Sydel Solomon (2:12), "The Art of Opaquing" (3:1), and "I Remember When" by Doc Crandall (3:5).

The first number refers to the volume and the second, the issue.

Funnyworld, 1966-. Funnyworld, Box 1633, New York, N.Y. 10001. Quarterly. Probably the most authoritative magazine devoted to comic and animation art. *Funnyworld* has elevated itself to a regular, high-quality publication featuring articles by Mike Barrier and several animators. Barrier is sometimes criticized for his heavy-handed reviews of animated films and TV programs but his publication does strive to provide balance with a lively Op-Ed section in most issues. In many articles, however, documentation for historical matters is often overlooked or omitted leaving the reader to wonder about the bases for the conclusions. There is some suggestion that *Funnyworld* will eventually recognize the future implications and role of computer-animation and the changing receptivity many audiences now exhibit to such forms. This is one journal worth its back runs and these are finally available from University Microfilms, 300 North Zeeb Road, Ann Arbor, Mich. 48106.

Hollywood Reporter, 1930-. 6715 Sunset Boulevard, Hollywood, Calif. 90028. Daily (5). Reports news of the U.S. West Coast TV and theatrical film interests featuring special issues in September and November. Animation reports made as the occasions arise. The publications most similar to *Hollywood Reporter* are the daily and weekly *Variety* but, of course, there are different editorial emphases among the three trades.

Home Video, 1980-. Home Video, 475 Park Avenue South, New York, N.Y. 10016. Bimonthly. A magazine for home video enthusiasts featuring data on home recorders (tape and disc playback units) and available programming, including animated products.

IBM Journal of Research and Development, 1957-. IBM, Armonk, N.Y. 10504. Bimonthly. Computer-graphics and computer-animation are among the numerous data-processing areas published.

Image, 1957-. International Museum of Photography at George Eastman House, Rochester, N.Y. 14607. Monthly. Has occasional literature reviews and critical-historical pieces on American film as well as descriptions of archival holdings.

Industrial Photography, 1951-. United Business Publications, 475 Park Avenue South, New York, N.Y. 10016. Monthly. A more technically oriented, controlled-circulation magazine for professionals and managers, featuring an occasional application of animation technology or technique. Several "advice" columns and technical features.

Information Display, 1962-. Society for Information Display, 654 North Sepulveda Boulevard, Los Angeles, Calif. 90049. Monthly. The journal contains some technical reports on computer-graphics and computer-animation.

Journal of Advertising Research, 1960-. Advertising Research Foundation, 3 East 54th Street, New York, N.Y. 10022. Bimonthly. Professional journal appealing to advertising research personnel that only occasionally publishes material related to animation. But the related areas are of considerable interest to animators since they involve children's advertising and programming questions along with occasional pieces about animation effectiveness.

Journal of the Society of Motion Picture and Television Engineers, 1916-. SMPTE Publications Office, 862 Scarsdale Avenue, Scarsdale, N.Y. 10583. Monthly. A most important journal in the technical aspects of filmmaking, including reports on developments in conventional and computer-animation. Abstracts of papers from other journals, book reviews, and brief technical reports are included.

Journal of the University Film Association, 1948-. Editor, Department of Photography-Cinema, Southern Illinois University, Carbonadale, Ill. 62901. Quarterly. The *Journal* has published numerous pieces on animation and experimental film. An annotated bibliography (1947-1979) was published in Volume 31, Number 4 (Fall 1979) which enables the user to tap the rich history of film and related media.

Kodak Professional Forum, 1978-. Eastman Kodak Company, Rochester, N.Y. 14650 (free publication). Irregular. Advertising brochure typically featuring profiles of filmmakers, animators, and TV producer-directors, who inevitably espouse some aspect of film or Kodak products. Aside from the subtle persuasion, the profiles sometimes provide interesting perspectives or leads.

Los Angeles Times, 1881-. Times Mirror Square, Los Angeles, Calif. 90053. Daily. Often overlooked and underestimated, this newspaper is indispensable for staying up-to-date with current developments in the film and TV business in a location where about 80 percent of what appears in American theaters and TV is manufactured. Reporting on the entertainment industry is more extensive and in greater depth than in any other U.S. mass audience newspaper including the *New York Times*.

Marketing and Media Decisions, 1965-. Decisions Publications, 342 Madison Avenue, New York, N.Y. 100178. Monthly. This is a professional publication for the advertising executive and broadcaster. Occasional pieces involve industry points of view on TV advertising and programming for children, marketing strategies involving several media, and incorporating animation as a device.

Media and Methods, 1965-. American Society of Educators, 1511 Walnut Street, Philadelphia, Penn. 19102. Nine issues per year. Features occasional how-to pieces in various types of animation and a defense of Disney by James Morrow (April 1978). Past issues have also contained useful lists of animation films of particular interest to scholars, artists, and buffs.

Media Asia, 1973-. Asian Mass Communication Research and Information Centre, 39 Newton Road, Singapore 1130, Republic of Singapore. Quarterly. Reports of personal observations and empirical studies about the use of film and TV, some involving animation, in Asia.

Millimeter, 1973-. 12 East 46th Street, New York, N.Y. 10017. Monthly. Another controlled-circulation magazine, but one which is extremely important to animation professionals or scholars. John Canemaker is a regular contributor. Other reports on special effects and up-to-date items about production houses are especially important for those planning to enter film and animation production professionally.

Motography, 1909-1918. Weekly. Originally titled *Nickelodeon*, this Chicago-based trade weekly became a very important source of detailed news of the film industry during the period of publication. In 1918 *Motography* merged with *Exhibitors Herald* to become *Exhibitors Herald and Motography*. Several detailed reports about animators in the early period of American film, published in *Motography*, are annotated in Appendix 6. This trade, like *Moving Picture World*, contains extensive columns reviewing the films of the day, including the content of newsreels, where many animators found access to theatrical screens. The journal is available on microfilm.

Moving Picture World, 1907-1927. Weekly. Probably the most valuable surviving resource for the silent film, this weekly trade reported detailed news about business practices and film content. Compared to *Variety* and *Billboard*, the style is less flashy and the information probably more reliable. For a useful overview of the early film magazines, see Tony Slide, *Aspects of American Film History Prior to 1920* (Metuchen, N.J.: Scarecrow Press, 1978), Chapter 11.

Volume 1 of *Moving Picture World* was indexed by Rita Horwitz and published by the American Film Institute in 1974. Film citations for this trade have been systematically collected in the College of Communication, Florida

State University, Tallahassee, Florida, since March 1977. The project is still in search of funds to complete the prototype and final computer phase.

New York Times, 1851-. 229 West 43rd Street, New York, N.Y. 10036. Daily. As indicated in Appendix 6, the *New York Times* today continues to cover key events along with reviews of new films and TV offerings. Access to the material is through their index which summarizes each report in a semiabstract style, but without specific headline identifications.

Nielsen Television Index, 1966-. Media Research Division, A. C. Nielsen Company, 1290 Avenue of the Americas, New York, N.Y. 10019. Biweekly. National audience ratings of network TV programming, are issued about twenty-two times a year, including hour-by-hour set-usage, audience comparisons by program types, rankings of programs in the two-week period reported, and program audience estimates.

Print, 1946-. R. C. Publications, 19 West 44th Street, New York, N.Y. 10036. Bimonthly. Past issues have contained overview pieces about animation status, computer graphics, and animation history. Volume 28, Number 2 (March-April 1974) is devoted to animation.

Sight and Sound, 1931-. British Film Institute. In the U.S., write Eastern News Distributors, 111 Eighth Avenue, New York, N.Y. 10011. Quarterly. Important international film publication which has published reviews and articles about animation subjects and personalities.

Sightlines, 1966-. Educational Film Library Association, 43 West 61st Street, New York, N.Y. 10023. Quarterly. Among the most worthwhile publications for film scholars and those with animation interest, this professional library journal contains detailed bibliographies and numerous articles on animation topics. Updating lists by Jim Limbacher describe what is available in 16mm and Super 8mm formats. There are detailed lists of new film publications each quarter. Articles on animators and other filmmakers typically describe their major works in detail and include exhaustive filmographies.

Starlog, 1977-. O'Quinn Studios, 475 Park Avenue South, 8th Floor Suite, New York, N.Y. 10016. Eight times yearly. Billing itself as "the magazine of the future" this fanzine frequently reviews special-effects films and animators.

Super 8 Filmmaker, 1972-. PMS Publishing Company, 3161 Fillmore Street, San Francisco, Calif. 94123. Eight times yearly. Designed for the amateur moviemaker market, provides up-to-date news of animation techniques and equipment.

Take One, 1972-1979. Irregular. This journal is no longer published. Occasional pieces on animation appeared in early issues.

Television Magazine, 1961-1968. Monthly. Taken over by Broadcasting Publications, in January 1961, this feature publication merged with *Broadcasting* in late 1968. Like *Sponsor* and *Broadcasting*, the magazine published several articles on production, including animation, that focused on business and advertising implications for mass communication markets.

Televison/Radio Age, 1953-. Television Editorial Corporation, 1270 Avenue of the Americas, New York, N.Y. 10020. Biweekly. This is an indispensable industry trade journal that typically reports on the children's TV programming issue, new animation technologies such as digital TV, and animation advertising techniques.

TV Guide, 1953-. Box 400, Radnor, Pa. 19088. Weekly. This longest running periodical reporting news about U.S. TV programming now has an index. Details are available from the publisher. Back runs are also available on microfilm.

University Film Study Center Newsletter, 1972-. Box 275, Cambridge, Mass. 02138. Monthly. Occasional reports and bibliographies on animation-related subjects. Updating of items on symposia and conferences in the New England area and elsewhere. Reviews of new reference guides, texts, and general film subjects.

Variety, 1905-. 154 West 46th Street, New York, N.Y. 10036. Weekly. Probably the most important trade journal in the entertainment business, with frequent material about the animation business in theatrical film and commercial TV. Extensive reviews of major TV special programs and theatrical releases. Selected and annotated citations for the period 1904-1950 are contained in Appendix 6. The trade is selectively indexed in *Music Index* (1948-) and *Topicator* (1965-). Film and broadcast citations of more than 4000 categories embracing the years 1905-1950 have been systematically collected in the College of Communication, Florida State University, Tallahassee, Florida, since January 1974. This indexing project, under the direction of the author, seeks funds for completing the prototype and computer phase.

Videodisc Newsletter, 1980-. Videodisc News, P.O. Box 6302, Arlington, Va. 22206. Monthly. An overpriced ($144 for twelve issues) monthly letter aimed at a specialized market of potential disc users.

Videography, 1975-. United Business Publications, 750 Third Avenue, New York, N.Y. 10017. Monthly. Controlled-circulation magazine targeted for the closed-circuit TV industry. Of interest to animation from the standpoint of electronic special effects and computer graphics.

Videophile, 1976-. 2003 Apalachee Parkway, Tallahassee, Fla. 32302. Bimonthly. Aimed at the home video enthusiast with numerous reviews of tapes and discs available for the home video market, including lots of advertising for cartoons and stop-action films. Considerable space is given to anecdotal evaluations of new video recorders which should help the new home video person become a better-informed consumer.

Videoplay, 1979-. C. S. Tepfer Publishing Company, 51 Sugar Hollow Road, Danbury, Conn. 06810. Bimonthly. Another video magazine catering to home video recording, emphasizing new technology and programming sources, including animation material.

World of Yesterday, 1974-. 13759 60th Street, Clearwater, Fla. 33520. Irregular. A nostalgia magazine which occasionally features subjects in film, animation, and other aspects of popular culture. Issue Number 18 contained a lengthy profile of Mel Blanc.

Zoetrope, 1978-. Larry Janiak, 655 West Irving Park Road, Chicago, Ill. 60613. Three times yearly. Calling itself the "publication of commercial and experimental concepts," *Zoetrope*'s past issues have had a large share of reports, interviews, and book reviews on animation subjects. Other emphases include video, computer animation, and Chicago business news in design and animation.

Index

This index organizes names and subjects embraced in the text and Appendix 1. Additional finding aids in this book should also be consulted, such as the section Personalities in Animation contained in Chapter 4, the organization explanation in the Introduction to Appendix 5, and the index to Appendix 6. While general topics relating to all appendixes are cited in this index, specific topics should be searched in Appendixes 2 through 7.

Music: computer-generated forms, 159; literature, 158-60

Muybridge, Eadweard, 9, 185-86; influence on Disney, 193; studies of movement, 16

Myerberg, Michael, *Hansel and Gretel*, 29

National Cartoonist Society (NCS), 167

National Center for Experiments in Television, 34

National Film Board of Canada: *City of Gold*, 210; formation, 202

Natwick, Grim, 197

New York Filmmaker's Cooperative, established, 215

Niepce, Joseph Nicéphore, 8, 229

1948 Consent Decree, as a factor influencing theatrical animation in the U.S., 25-26

Nolan, Bill: *King of Jazz*, 197; moving background system, 13, 15

Object animation, 4; *Empire Strikes Back*, 9; *Hansel and Gretel*, 29; of Ray Harryhausen, 22; *Jason and the Argonauts*, 34; *King Kong*, 22, 199; *Land of the Lost*, 221-22; of Willis O'Brien, 13, 22, 199; references, 95-99; titles by Saul Bass, 26. *See also* Dawley, Herbert W.; Vinton, Will

O'Brien, Willis: *Dinosaur and the Missing Link*, 13, 191; *King Kong*, 22, 199; *Lost World*, 15; research archives, 258

Oriolo, Joe, *Felix the Cat*, 212

Oxberry, John, 204; animation stand, 30, 208

Paganelli, Al, 194

Paik, Nam June, experimental video, 219

Pal, George: abandons puppetoons, 25, 205; association with Paramount, 201; *Destination Moon*, 29, 206; Puppetoons and Madcap Models,

202; research archives, 246; *War of the Worlds*, 207

Paramount: ceases animation production, 210; *Color Rhapsodies,* 200; Famous Studios, 203, 204; Famous Studios characters, 21; *Pictographs*, 192; research archives, 244. *See also* Fleischer, Max, and Dave Fleischer; Pal, George

Parker, Clair, and Alexandre Alexeieff, 199

PBC Associates, laser-light techniques, 223

Perpetual Motion Pictures, Mr. Hipp, 33, 223

Personalities in animation, references, 106-32

Pfenniger, Rudolf, 197

Photo. *See* Object animation; Stills-in-motion animation

Photomontage: Berlin exhibition, 197; influence on animation, 17; Man Ray, 195; Ben Rose, 215

Picabia, Francis, 17, 192

Picture sources, for stills-in-motion animation, 161-62

Piene, Otto, experimental video, 219

Pixilation, 9; use by Oscar B. Depue, 188. *See also* Fischinger, Oskar

Plateau, Joseph Antoine, Phenakisto-scope, 184

Pop art, influence on *Barbarella*, 218

Porter, Edwin S., 10; editorial innovations in *Life of an American Fireman*, 188; *Fun in a Bakery Shop*, 188; titles in stop-motion, 189; use of matte shots, 187

Prescott, Norman, established Filmation, 214

Production process, 90. *See also* Creating animation

Propaganda. *See* Social and political aspects

Pudovkin, V. I., on sound, 196

Pulitzer, Joseph, 186

Puppet animation, 22-23; changes in television forms, 32; combined with